Imperial London

Imperial Whitehall, with banners flying.

Imperial London

Civil Government Building in London 1850–1915

M.H. PORT

PUBLISHED FOR THE PAUL MELLON CENTRE
FOR STUDIES IN BRITISH ART BY
Yale University Press
NEW HAVEN & LONDON · 1995

The right of Michael H. Port to be identified as the author of
this work has been asserted by him in accordance with the
Copyright, Designs and Patents Act, 1988.

Designed by John Trevitt

Set in Baskerville by Best-set Typesetter Ltd., Hong Kong
Printed in Hong Kong through World Print Ltd

This book has been published with the aid of a grant from the
Marc Fitch Fund.

Library of Congress Cataloging-in-Publication Data
Port. M.H. (Michael Harry)
Imperial London : civil government building in London 1850–
1915 / M.H. Port.
    p.   cm.
Includes bibliographical references and index.
ISBN 0-300-05977-9
1. Public buildings—England—London.   2. Public
architecture—England—London.   3. Eclecticism in
architecture—England—London.   4. London (England)—
Buildings, structures, etc.   I. Title.
NA4287.L6P67   1995
725′.1′0942109034—dc20   94-10254   CIP

To
MARY,
HELEN,
and
ELISABETH

Contents

Note

Officers of the Office of Works (Secretary, Surveyor, etc.) have been distinguished by the initial letter in upper case.

Abbreviations in quotations have for the most part been silently expanded, but original spelling otherwise retained.

The form 1890/91, etc., refers to a financial year.

Preface

IN THE AFTERMATH of research on the *History of the King's Works* and the Houses of Parliament completed in the early 1970s, I had hoped to write a history of the major building work, commercial and financial as well as governmental, that contributed to make a London worthy of its role as metropolis of the nineteenth-century world's greatest empire. An increasing burden of administrative duties interrupted progress, and when liberated I realised that my original concept could not be achieved in a single book of acceptable dimensions. This book is therefore limited to examining the process of erecting the civil buildings of central government: the actual offices from which the empire was ruled, the courts in which its justice was administered, the museums and galleries in which its publicly-owned treasures were displayed for the instruction of its people.

Over the years I have incurred many obligations. While this book is in part a synthesis of specialist studies, it has also involved much primary research, and I first would acknowledge the generosity of those owners of manuscripts, goldmines of history, who have allowed me to work them.

First, I wish to thank her Majesty the Queen for access to and permission to quote from the Royal Archives. I am likewise grateful to his Grace the Duke of Rutland, the Marquess of Salisbury, the Marchioness of Aberdeen and Temair, the Earl of Wemyss, Viscount Esher, Mr Keith Adam of Blair Adam, the Trustees of the British Library, and those of the Victoria and Albert Museum, the Broadlands Papers and the Harcourt Papers, The National Trust, the Centre for Kentish Studies, the Royal Commissioners of the 1851 Exhibition and the Controller of H.M.S.O., for permission to quote from their papers.

The Twenty Seven Foundation (now the Scouloudi Trust) kindly contributed towards my travel costs.

The Editors of *Architectural History*, the *Historical Journal* and the *London Journal* have allowed me to draw on my articles published in those journals, and the Editor of the *Economic History Review* to reproduce a graph of building costs from Dr Maiwald's 1955 article.

To the Rt Hon. John Patten and Rt Hon. Sir George Younger I am most grateful for facilitating my visits to government buildings. Kate Crowe and Mr D. Brown (F.O.), Mr C.R. Cowell (Public Services Agency), Mr D.J. Lodge (Treasury), Mr J. Reynolds (Ministry of Defence) and Mr I. Cress and his staff (Admiralty building) were very helpful over the detail of such visits, and I am grateful to Derek Keene for coming with me on several occasions and contributing his impressions.

Acts of kindness by friends old and new have been many. I am deeply grateful to Francis Sheppard for reading an early, incomplete draft, and for encouragement at a vital moment of decision; and to Victor Belcher and Gordon Roberts CBE for commenting on sections of the text. David Cronin instructed me in computer lore and twice rescued lost chapters. Dr Andrew Saint and Professor Martin Daunton made available to me material they had collected; Hermione Hobhouse made me free of the files of the Survey of London, and John Greenacombe guided me therein.

For help in various ways I thank Lord Blake, Mr John Charlton LVO and Mrs Charlton, Mr H. Cobb CBE and Mr D. Johnson (House of Lords Record Office), Mr J. Cox (Highgate Literary & Scientific Institution), Mlle A. Croizat, Lord Dunluce, Mr Oliver Everett (Royal Librarian) and Lady de Bellaigue and her colleagues in the Royal Archives, Mr G.G. Harris, Dr J.E. Hoare, Mr F. Luke (Naval History Library), Professor N. McCord, Dr R. Mettam, Mr Bernard Nurse (Society of Antiquaries), Dr R. Olney (National Register of Archives), Mrs V. Phillips (1851 commission), Lord Plymouth, Lord Plunket, Mr C. Plunket, Miss Anne Riches, Mr Michael Roper CBE (late Keeper of the Public Records) and his staff at Kew (particularly in producing great quantities of drawings, and in disentangling the intricacies of Treasury papers), Mr J.R. Stephenson, Professor Paul Smith, Mr C. Sorensen, Mr J. Turner (Department of the Environment Conservation Unit Library), Mr R. Harcourt Williams, and Mr J.C. Woods (MoD Library). The staffs of the many libraries and record offices I have worked in have made their several contributions to forwarding the labours of research.

Miss Olwen Myhill (Centre for Metropolitan History), Dr F. Crompton-Roberts (Queen Mary & Westfield College), and my daughter Elisabeth designed the figures and tables on computer. Dr C. Giry-Deloison (Institut français) organised my visits to public buildings in Paris, where the offices of M. Jacques Chirac, Maire de Paris, and of the président de l'Etablissement Public Grand Louvre were most helpful, and Mme Françoise Dijeaux and Mlle Hélène Lefèvre were my obliging guides.

To such a book as this ample illustration is an essential. The prevailing ethos that services must be remunerative has persuaded a number of institutions, including some commonly regarded as public, to impose unreasonable fees for reproduction rights. The so-called 'academic' discount offered by some, even if 50 per cent, may still leave charges unbearably high, while it is ludicrous that the same illustration may be used in a print-run of tens or even hundreds of thousands at only double the fee. In consequence, I have been unable to include some illustrations that I wished to use, and have had, on occasion, to substitute less satisfactory ones.

I am therefore profoundly grateful to the Trustees of the Marc Fitch Foundation for their grant in aid of illustrations, as I am to Professor M. Kitson and the Mellon Centre for the Study of British Art for generous assistance in kind; and to those institutions and repositories which still pursue a traditional liberal policy towards the scholarship they were established to promote. Neil Clarke of Messrs Cecil Denny Highton Architects and Richard Eckersley (DoE Conservation Unit) have been generous in their help. To those private citizens who have given me the freedom of their collections I am deeply indebted: Ben Weinreb, Peter Jackson and Ralph Hyde especially. In technical asistance, the Media Services Department (T. Storey, R. Crundwell and D. Bacon) at Queen Mary & Westfield College has been indefatigable.

Over the course of two decades it is not always easy to keep full recollection of all the debts incurred, and should I by mischance have omitted anyone, I must beg their indulgence.

M.H. Port

LONDON NW5

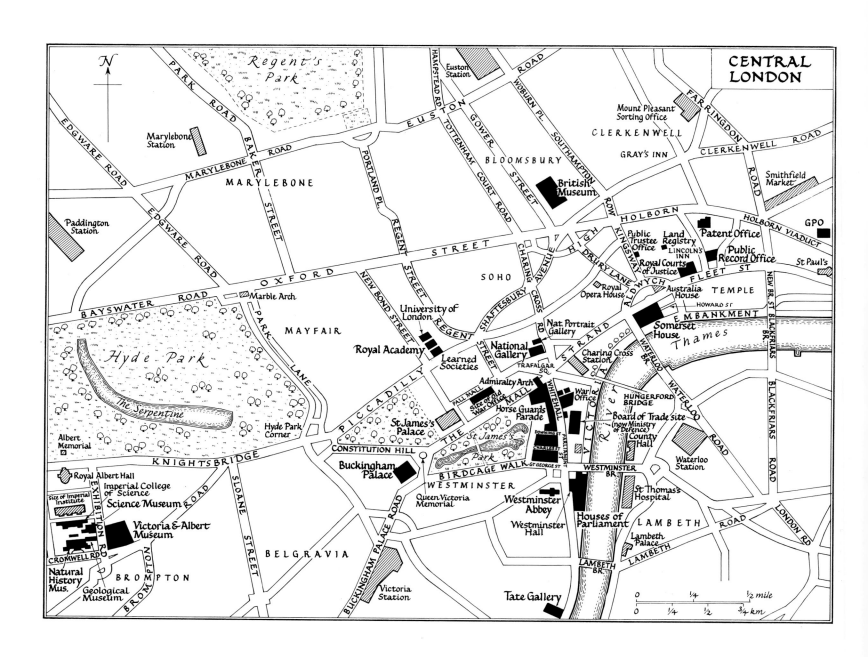

CENTRAL LONDON

1
Introduction

THIS is the story of civil governmental building in London in the period when London was being rebuilt to equip it for its role as the capital city of a world-wide empire. That rebuilding was in great measure a rebuilding of the financial and commercial districts.[1] It was also to be seen in terms of a metropolitan infrastructure without which the city could not function effectively: providing adequate sewerage; improving communications by cutting straighter and wider streets; and above-ground and underground local railway lines. While much has been written on transport and housing, and individual public buildings have been studied, there has been no overall study of government building (though the sum of the *Survey of London* provides a major contribution towards that): the provision of suitable accommodation for a government which was trying to carry out traditional functions more efficiently at the same time as it was taking on manifold new tasks at an increasing rate; the provision, too, of galleries and museums for elevating popular taste and instructing the people in design, and making available to them the realms of nature and invention.

Rather than produce a series of loosely-connected studies of particular buildings (some of which have already received exhaustive treatment in print), our aim has been to analyse the problems involved in constructing the various types of building provided by the late-nineteenth-century state. We begin by establishing the general metropolitan context in which this work went forward. We next elucidate the need for particular new buildings, and examine the mechanisms devised to execute them.

The provision of means was a problem even in authoritarian regimes like the Second Empire. In a parliamentary state costs were a subject of constant observation, chiefly 'within doors', but also in some measure out of parliament.

The location of such buildings in a city at once as congested and as extensive as London was a major problem that could give rise to prolonged public controversy in an age when an uncontrolled press was enjoying the benefits of the abolition, first of stamp duty and then of paper duty. The trade and professional press was able to take advantage of these benefits, looking not merely to a growing business readership but also to a wider public educated by controversy about architecture fostered by church-building and church restoration.

Thus the question, 'What style?' became crucial in an age which had available the whole gamut of historical – and indeed geographical – styles. (It is perhaps worthy of comment that although English architects in India in this period were developing an imperial style embracing elements of those of earlier rulers, there was no feeding-back of this work to London, despite the publications of James Fergusson in Indian architecture.) Had the building of the India Office been deferred twenty or thirty years, it would still in all likelihood have been a classical building.

Finally, when all these contentious matters had been settled, there were the problems that arose once the work was put in hand; problems of both cost and execution.

It is only when we have appreciated the complexities of these various strands woven into the final product that we can fairly evaluate what was achieved, despite the apparent 'almost unbelievable' parsimony of English governments and 'astonishing insularity' of Victorian architecture.[2]

A primary difficulty in creating the infrastructure of an imperial capital was the lack of any multifunctional metropolitan authority before the creation of the Metropolitan Board of Works in 1855. Before that time metropolitan improvement was a largely haphazard and impromptu affair financed by a variety of sources. The greatest improvement, the construction of Regent Street from 1816 onwards, was paid for by the Crown Estate, statutorily embodied as the Commission for the New Street, and with powers of borrowing, the loans to be repaid by the profits from the development. Other important improvements, from the construction of Blackfriars Bridge (1760–9) to the formation of new streets in the 1830s and 1840s (considered below), were paid for largely out of taxes on the import of coals into London, augmented, from 1782, by £11,500 a year from the revenues of the City of London and certain other fees levied by the City; some of these improvements being within, and others without the City limits.[3] Many minor improvements in the way of paving and lighting, however, were financed by rates levied on the inhabitants of the relevant districts by local commissions; and some new roads were the work of similarly-established turnpike trusts. All these bodies were established by private initiative which obtained statutory authority and local or private acts of Parliament.[4]

As a chart through the complex channels of the bogs and marshes of Victorian and Edwardian public building, the following summary history of the major projects may be helpful:

Admiralty. Extension proposed 1852. Committees recommended building adjacent to War Office in 1867 and 1877, and new building (with War Office) authorised by 1882 Act. Two-stage competition, 1883–4, won by Leeming Bros. of Halifax with well-planned and well-drawn but crude designs. Committee substituted 'economical' scheme for extending the old building, 1887. Extension built in four blocks, 1889–1914, at vastly greater expense than contemplated, to widely-contemned designs in red brick with stone trim.

British Museum. New museum constructed by Robert Smirke, 1823–48, inadequate for rapid growth of collections of natural history, antiquities, and books. New Reading Room, 1854–7. Debate over splitting collections in 1850s led to decision in 1863 to remove natural history. Additional galleries by Office of Works in 1880s. Northern extension by J.J. Burnet, 1905–14.

Burlington House. The Learned Societies. Old Burlington House was purchased by government in 1853, but the question of what to put on the site was not resolved for nearly twenty years. Finally the

Royal Academy was given the old house itself, the garden frontage allocated to London University, and the Piccadilly front to a number of Learned Societies (including the Royal Society and the Society of Antiquaries), most of which had had rooms at Somerset House now required for government offices. R.R. Banks and C. Barry jnr were given the commission, carried out in 1869–77.

Colonial Office. New building (with Home Office) by G.G. Scott, 1870–4, to replace decrepit houses in Downing Street.

Foreign Office. Rebuilding proposed, 1836: D. Burton provided plans, shelved because of financial stringencies. New proposals in 1854, with designs by J. Pennethorne, rejected by Commons in 1855. In 1856 Sir Benjamin Hall, First Commissioner of Works, decided on open competition for Foreign and War Offices in Downing Street in which French influence was pronounced, but Gothic entries did well. Results disapproved of by Commons as too palatial, so Palmerston revived Pennethorne's design; but Hall insisted on one of the competition winners. Change of ministry led to appointment of G.G. Scott (whose Gothic design had been placed third in competition) for Foreign Office only, 1858. Return of Palmerston to power produced 'Battle of the Styles', he insisting on a Palladian building. Scott surrendered. Palladian F.O., with India Office, built 1863–8.

Houses of Parliament. After the destruction of the old Houses by fire in 1834, a press campaign persuaded ministers to propose an open competition, for which Gothic or Elizabethan styles were specified, won by Charles Barry. His optimistic forecast that the building, to cost about three-quarters of a million pounds, would be completed in six years was falsified by problems with the foundation, serious dissension with the government-appointed ventilation expert, strikes, and alterations and additions required by the two Houses, which served to increase the cost to over two millions by Barry's death in 1860. Considerable internal works remained to be completed, together with exterior works in New Palace Yard, by his son Edward during the 1860s. A progressive programme of decorative works was halted by Ayrton as First Commissioner of Works in 1870, and Edward Barry summarily dismissed. Many MPs were dissatisfied with their accommodation, its Gothic character and in particular the ventilation. Charles Barry's proposal for a suite of rooms on the west side of Westminster Hall was abandoned in 1865. When the old law courts were removed in 1883, the much-damaged west side of the Hall was exposed, to be controversially restored by J.L. Pearson in 1886–90.

Home Office. Rebuilt in 1846 as north wing of 'Treasury Buildings' (Soane's Council Office and Board of Trade, 1823–8, remodelled by C. Barry, 1845). New building by Scott, 1870–5, next to C.O.

India Office. Transfer of government of India from East India Company to British government in 1858 created need for new offices, so India Office was substituted for War Office in juxtaposition to new Foreign Office. Exterior by Scott, but interior by M.D. Wyatt, architect to the East India Company, built 1863–8.

National Gallery. A purpose-designed gallery by Wilkins, 1832–8, in Trafalgar Square, was shared with the Royal Academy. From the late 1840s there was intense argument whether to remove the paintings to purer air (perhaps at Kensington Gore, as Prince Albert hoped), or remove the Academy and extend or rebuild Wilkins' unadmired gallery, though the scope for extension was limited by an adjoining barracks. A ministerial decision to move the pictures to the Burlington House site was rejected by the

Commons in 1860, so the Academy was eventually persuaded to move there instead. Alterations were made at Trafalgar Square by Pennethorne in 1860–1. In 1866–7 a limited competition for designs for building a new gallery or remodelling the old one proved inconclusive. A commission for rebuilding was, however, in 1868 awarded to E.M. Barry on the strength of his entry; but this was subsequently reduced to adding several galleries at the north-east of the site in 1871–6. Further additions and alterations were made by the Office of Works' architect, John Taylor, in 1885–8; and a western extension over part of the barracks-yard by another Works' architect, H.V. Hawkes, in 1907–12.

Natural History Museum. The natural-history collections formed the most popular part of the British Museum, and proposals in the 1850s and early 1860s for their removal elsewhere provoked great opposition. Nevertheless, overcrowding in Bloomsbury was such that division of the collections was inevitable, Gladstone supported removal, and the influential Librarian, Panizzi, wanted space for a world-class library. A decision in 1864 to place the collections at South Kensington led to a competition for designs won by Capt Fowke, R.E., who died in 1865. He was replaced by A. Waterhouse, who substituted his own quasi-Romanesque designs. In 1868–9 a strong attempt to transfer the site to the new Thames Embankment was made, but failed. Waterhouse's building was erected in 1872–86, amid considerable controversy about the use and cost of terracotta.

New Public Offices. The unceasing need for additional office space for government departments (increasing in number as well as size) led to the decision in 1897 to acquire the Great George Street site that had been recommended by a Treasury commission in 1867. The rapidly expanding Education and Local Government Boards were to be located there, together with the Board of Trade. J.M. Brydon, appointed architect in 1898, died in 1900, and his designs, somewhat modified, were executed by Henry Tanner of the Office of Works. The northern and eastern sectors were completed in 1908, but the existence of the Institution of Civil Engineers' building of 1896 in Great George Street hindered completion of Brydon's plan. The remaining quadrant was completed in 1914, but it had already been recognised that there was too little space for the Board of Trade (for which a special building was then projected). These offices are now occupied by the Treasury.

Royal Courts of Justice (New Law Courts). Soane had built new law courts immediately west of their ancient seat, Westminster Hall, in 1821–8, but these soon proved inadequate. Proposals to build in Lincoln's Inn Fields (including a design by Charles Barry) in the 1840s came to nothing. Reforms in the legal system (including the uniting of the systems of common law and equity) encouraged demands for a consolidation of the courts. After lengthy disputes about funding, a seven-acre site between Carey Street and the Strand was acquired in 1866–8, and a limited competition held inconclusively for designs, all of which were Gothic in style. This led ultimately to the appointment of G.E. Street as architect. Proposals to move the site to the new Thames Embankment caused delay in 1868–9, but they failed to win parliamentary approval. Street won a prolonged fight with the Office of Works over the cost of his revised design for the Carey Street site in 1870–2 when he secured cabinet backing, but his diffused Strand front was heavily criticised. The choice, through competitive tendering, of an under-capitalised contractor caused serious building problems.

South Kensington Museum. Established in 1856 under the auspices of the Department of Science & Art, encouraged by Prince Albert, in order to raise the standard of British manufactures by making examples of good (and for a time, also bad) design available to all. The Museum authorities, led by Henry Cole, employed military engineers instead of architects to design their buildings until the 1880s, when the Office of Works secured full control. Construction of a vast complex, stage by stage, was interrupted by Treasury hostility in 1872 for several years, and again in the 1880s by the attitude of the Works and the Treasury. In 1890 public pressure secured a limited competition for completion of the Museum (housing both art and science), but funds were not provided until 1899, when Aston Webb's winning design was begun, after extensive modification; it was completed in 1909. The 'Victoria and Albert Museum', however, as it was renamed, was a museum of the arts; provision for the science collections being then made (after loud demands by the scientific world) on the west of Exhibition Road.

University of London. This was an administrative and examining body for which government had provided temporary accommodation in the Burlington House forecourt. In 1867, it was allocated the northern part of the site, and Pennethorne was commissioned to design a building. Parliamentary criticism arrested his Italian Gothic elevations in execution, and he consequently built a High Renaissance structure in 1868–70.

War Office. The civilian departments of the British army were reorganised during the Crimean War under a new Secretaryship of State with offices in a range of old houses in Pall Mall. The minister demanded a new building there in 1856, for which Pennethorne provided designs that were rejected by Hall at the Office of Works. Hall instead included a new War Office in his competition for new government offices in Downing Street. The competition having been aborted (see *Foreign Office,* above), a new War Office was postponed. In 1867, a Treasury commission recommended a new War Office and Admiralty fronting Great George Street. Gladstone's ministry took up the question in 1870, but an intensive campaign by the commander-in-chief, the Queen's cousin, to retain his ostensible independence at the Horse Guards, together with factional opposition in the Commons, deferred a decision. Disraeli's ministry proposed to build on the Embankment, and a committee in 1877 urged immediate action; but a fiscal crisis in 1879 aborted that proposal. In 1882, a keen reformer, Shaw Lefevre, at the Works, secured cabinet and parliamentary approval for a new Admiralty and War Office on the old Admiralty site in Whitehall. A two-tier competition was held in 1883–4, won by an obscure Yorkshire practice. Their design was not well received, and an alliance between economists on both Front Benches put an end to it in 1887. Work on a new War Office, possibly to be sited on the east side of Whitehall, was to be postponed until the completion of an extension to the existing Admiralty. Not until 1896 was the new War Office scheme taken up again and the eastern site agreed upon, William Young being appointed architect in 1898. After his death in 1899, his designs were executed by his son with the assistance of Sir John Taylor of the Office of Works, and completed in 1906.

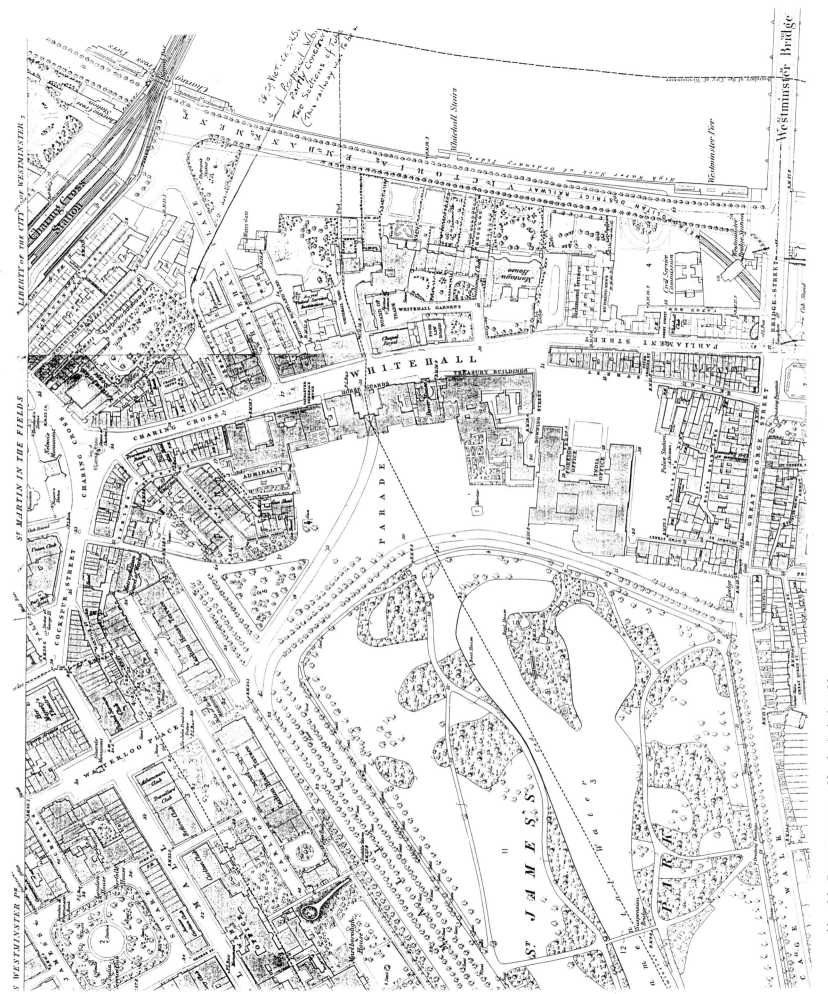

1. Map of the Government quarter of London in the late 1860s.

2
Imperial City

LONDON was the world's greatest city. From about the middle of the eighteenth century it had been the largest city in the western world, and throughout the nineteenth it was probably the most populous in the entire world. But it was not a planned city. Rome, for all its decay, possessed finer vistas. Vienna had more magnificent palaces. Paris, despite the departure of the kings to Versailles, developed a grandeur of scale lacking in London, and under Napoleon I became worthy of its role as an imperial capital.[1] St Petersburg, planned by its founder on spacious lines, determined under Alexander I to outshine the new Paris.[2] Berlin, already graced with fine Baroque buildings, was from 1815 given a noble centre by Schinkel.[3] Even the smaller capitals of Europe possessed or were developing notable monumental features: Turin, Naples, Stuttgart, Karlsruhe, Munich.[4]

London differed from all those cities in that it was ungoverned. 'London' was a geographical expression of indeterminate and ever-growing dimensions. There was the City of London, the ancient 'square mile' with its livery companies and corporation, a body kings had learned to respect, with rights granted or acknowledged by practically every sovereign since the Norman Conquest, with 'exceptionally extensive institutions of self-government'.[5] The concentration of political, commercial, industrial and financial strengths in London[6] encouraged a vast growth of population in the seventeenth and eighteenth centuries, spreading over an ever-lengthening distance from Guildhall. The land between the City and the seat of the national government in Westminster was built over in the seventeenth century; the well-to-do settled yet further west, even as far as Hyde Park; the main roads out of London were lined with houses for three or four miles, and extensive suburbs created from Hampstead to Clapham, and from Chelsea to Bow, by the end of the eighteenth century. Yet this huge urban area, far exceeding the 36 miles of circumference calculated by Defoe in the 1720s,[7] lacked any comprehensive government.

The corporation of the City, though claiming to exercise jurisdiction over profitable operations such as markets within a seven-mile radius, declined any responsibility for governing the districts beyond its ancient boundaries. The so-called City of Westminster possessed only a vestigial form of government. Local administration lay in the hands of the county magistrates and the parish vestries. The magistrates of highly-urbanised Middlesex, where there were few gentry residing on ancestral estates, were notoriously venal; the densely-inhabited inner suburbs beyond their control. The vestries were either tiny self-perpetuating and self-interested bodies, as in St Martin-in-the-Fields, or open meetings of the inhabitants at large, as in St Pancras. Neither form was capable of controlling building development or providing the desirable infrastructure. Sewerage, paving, lighting, the very construction and maintenance of highways often, were the charge of irresponsible bodies created largely by local or private acts.[8] No authority existed capable of taking a strategic view of London's needs. Although a series of building acts, notably those of 1707, 1709 and 1774, effectively controlled building construction within the inner area,[9] the only control over planning and land development lay in the hands of the landowners.[10] Defoe's comment was still valid at beginning of the next century: 'It is the disaster of London, as to the beauty of its figure, that it is thus stretched out in buildings, just at the pleasure of every builder, or undertaker of buildings, and as the convenience of the people directs, whether for trade, or otherwise; and this has spread the face of it in a most straggling, confus'd manner, out of all shape, uncompact, and unequal; neither long or broad, round or square.'[11]

As regent and king George IV did his best to make London as fine as Napoleonic Paris. His time was not wholly propitious: although Marylebone Park, a large area of some 540 acres on the northern edge of 'town', the prime residential area, reverted to the Crown in 1811, offering the opportunity of lucrative development for high-class housing, the years from 1811 to 1816 were dominated by the war against Napoleon and characterised by high deficit spending, a rise in interest rates, and the 'virtual cessation of private credit'.[12] But the man was at hand to rise above these difficulties. John Nash, architect to the Office of Woods and Forests, in 1811, following up an idea of his predecessor, John Fordyce,[13] submitted a plan for the development of Marylebone Park as a first-class residential area in the form of parkland peppered with villas, surrounded by terraces.[14]

To establish the economic viability of this development, Nash recognised not merely the need for a street to lead direct to the centre of 'town' – suggested by others before Nash – but the need for that street to follow the 'line of social cleavage' separating the 'Streets and Squares occupied by the Nobility and Gentry, and the narrow streets and meaner Houses occupied by mechanics and the trading part of the community'.[15] Such a street of 'magnificent dimensions', adorned with colonnades and balconies, and public buildings and monuments at key points, would encourage the upper classes in a northward migration. It would also be a relatively inexpensive proposition, as one-third of the line of the street belonged to the Crown, and the rest ran through the poorer districts. Parliament authorised construction of the new street under a government commission in 1813. Compulsory purchase of the requisite properties began the following year, but Nash's estimates were overturned by generous juries awarding excessively large sums to tradesmen in compensation for disturbance and loss of goodwill.[16] This characteristic of juries was to affect public works for much of the century, and brought the estimates of Nash and his successors into disrepute. Nash's own financial involvement in the 'New Street', although it proved essential for the comprehensive development of the great curved section known as the Quadrant, served in these circumstances to deepen both the speculative character of the business and the suspicion with which it was viewed by the House of Commons. When Nash was shown to have mishandled the rebuilding of Buckingham Palace [Pl. 2] for his royal patron, King George IV, and to have allowed costs to soar beyond esti-

3.   The Privy Council Office and Board of Trade, John Soane, 1822–7. The Privy Council in the corner pavilion was appropriately dignified with free-standing columns; the Board of Trade's offices lay to the right. Rebuilding of the Home Office, then in the Tudor building to the far right, was frustrated by parliamentary opposition.

2.   Buckingham Palace, East Front:
a. As originally built, John Nash, 1825–8, ostensibly in 'gusto greco', but much less pure than Smirke or Wilkins.
b. New block, closing quadrangle, E. Blore, 1846–9, widely criticised as 'mere street architecture.'

4.   The Law Courts: Court of King's Bench, 1823–5, John Soane. Soane's top-lighting enabled all the courts to be located in the restricted space between Westminster Hall and Margaret Street.

mates, no one was surprised, and the management of public building was brought further into disrepute.[17] In any case, the building trade was generally regarded as one designed to fleece the client; and architects were seen merely as adjuncts to the trade.

Nash was one of a triumvirate of government architects who from 1815 replaced the old monopoly of the Surveyor-General of the King's Works, an office discredited by the laziness of James Wyatt (revealed by an inquiry after his sudden death in 1813). Nash's colleagues, John Soane and Robert Smirke, were acknowledged leaders of the architectural profession, but Soane's designs were too idiosyncratic and Smirke's too dull to please generally. Although the return of prosperity after the Napoleonic Wars encouraged the government to embark on a programme of public buildings – a new Privy Council Office and Board of Trade [Pl. 3], new Law Courts [Pl. 4], extensions to the Houses of Parliament, a State Paper Office (all the work of Soane), a new Mint, GPO [Pl. 5], and British Museum [Pl. 7] (Smirke), State Mews (Nash), Parliamentary Mews and works in the Parks (Burton), and an extensive provision of new churches – their taste had been lashed by parliamentary critics and their efforts identified in the public mind with the fiasco and extravagance of Nash's work for the king.

Nonetheless, George IV, Nash, his professional colleagues at the Office of Works, and Lord Liverpool's administration, between them 'improved' London to a remarkable degree and enabled it to bear comparison with the continental capitals:[18]

5.   General Post Office, St Martin's-le-Grand, Robert Smirke, 1823–8. Smirke devised his Greek Revival design after a public competition failed to produce any designs applicable to the purpose. (This building was demolished in 1912.)

Augustus made it one of his proudest boasts, that he found Rome of brick, and left it of marble. The reign and regency of George the Fourth have scarcely done less, for the vast and increasing Metropolis of the British empire: by increasing its magnificence and comforts; by forming healthy streets and elegant buildings, instead of pestilential alleys and squalid hovels; by substituting rich and varied architecture and park-like scenery, for paltry cabins; by making solid roads and public ways, scarcely inferior to those of ancient Rome . . . and, by beginning, and continuing with a truly national perseverance, a series of desirable improvements, that bid fair to render LONDON, the ROME of modern history.[19]

A conscious emulation of Imperial Rome on the part of George IV (well known for the grandeur of his visions) and his classically-educated ministers is not improbable;[20] although Nash may well have been more conscious of Napoleonic Paris. In the flowering of prosperity in the early 1820s it was possible to advance from prospectively profitable development to the provision of new public and administrative buildings appropriate to a national capital.[21] But that was possible only in time of prosperity; and it was achieved only at the cost of popularity and parliamentary trust. The executive government initially had the courage to take decisions about commencing public works; but as trade and taxes declined and irresponsible *dilettanti* in and out of parliament heaped withering criticism on the new buildings, ministers abandoned large-scale views and looked instead for short-term economies. The change of regime in 1830, with the appointment of Whig ministers, intensified the tendency to retrenchment. The triumphant parliamentary reformers were looking for cheap government, and public building, associated as it was with jobbery and profiteering, was an obvious target. Nash's position did not survive his patron, George IV. Continued parliamentary enquiries discredited yet further both monarch and servant.[22]

One significant change the Whigs made in the public works regime on coming to power in 1830 was to abolish the triumvirate of Crown architects and amalgamate the Office of Works with that of Woods and Forests (Crown estate). This bid for economy was doomed to failure because it united a spending department (Works) with a revenue-producing department (Woods), so that within the combined office expenditures could be undertaken that escaped parliamentary control. It also deprived government of the services of a permanent staff of first-class architects. Henceforth, government had to buy architectural services in the open market.

During the 1830s, however, the spirit of metropolitan improvement was not extinguished, merely subdued. The concept was actually widened, to include the removal of slums.[23] Brougham had declared: 'The schoolmaster is abroad in the land'; and a new idea of popular education embraced the arts as a means of raising the levels of design and craftsmanship in English manufactures, where standards were felt to be inferior to those of other countries.[24] A National Gallery had been founded in 1824 in a house in Pall Mall; by 1828 it was, thanks to munificent bequests, already full.[25] After much pressure from the trustees, including Sir Robert Peel, opinion-maker in the Commons, the Whig government in 1832 accepted a proposal, first to extend the redundant King's Mews, and then to build a new gallery on the site, which should also accommodate the Royal Academy for the time being.[26] Wilkins' low Grecian-Revival building, with top-lighted galleries, was not completed until 1837 [Pl. 6]. It did nothing to redeem the bad reputation of public works: style and cost were savaged in parliament and in the press, where a number of new periodicals gave extensive scope to critics.[27] The Academy's right to occupy the west wing until such time as the space should be needed for the Gallery was to cause some irritation in later years.

6.   The National Gallery. Another Greek Revival Building, by William Wilkins, 1833–8. Columns from the portico of Carlton House were re-used in the side porticos.

7.   The British Museum, Robert Smirke, 1823–46. As in the GPO, Smirke drew on his study of remote Priene in Asia Minor for his columns.

In this public-works question, Whig and Tory governments behaved much alike: when the Houses of Parliament were burned down in October 1834, Lord Melbourne's administration handed the problem on to their successors, led by Peel. Peel was content to see the rebuilding entrusted to Smirke (who was also his personal architect). But a campaign in the press was powerful enough to upset that decision, and a competition of architects was invited, thus giving effect to earlier resolutions in the Commons that all designs for public building should be obtained by competition.[28] The Houses of Parliament competition of 1835 provided a basic model for subsequent competitions for public buildings.[29]

Meanwhile a much greater Grecian-Revival building than the National Gallery was rising in no-longer-fashionable Bloomsbury. Smirke's giant Ionic facade, designed about 1823, was revealed to an unsympathetic public only some twenty years later, when taste had changed.[30] But he equipped the British Museum [Pl. 7] with galleries worthy of their rich contents, increasingly drawn from many parts of the world.[31] Nash's idea for a road to link the Museum with Trafalgar Square was not carried out, so that an area of mean streets cut it off from the 'town'. Nevertheless, it was generally accessible and attracted large numbers of visitors of all classes. Moreover, its library, transformed by Panizzi into a world-class institution during the 1840s, brought growing numbers of readers.

Nor was the concept of new roads in the capital wholly lost sight of. The need for improved east-west communications was evident even to the 'ratepayer democracy' of the remodelled metropolitan vestries. In 1836 a select committee on metropolitan improvements investigated the need for practical improvements by way of new streets, particularly in the City, recommending that Oxford Street be continued eastwards, and better north-south communica-

tions created in the district to the west of the City. R.L. Jones, an important City figure, spoke of a growing public demand for such works: 'I hear it every day. It is the admiration of the public to see what improvements have been made in the City of London; and I hear them expressing hopes that there will be a great deal more done'.[32] William Routh, an iron-master, commented that the new roads would arrest the recent trend for his trade to leave the City; while the merchant and philanthropist William Cotton saw in a new highway linking Whitechapel to the City a means of social control – new inhabitants in the shape of respectable householders keeping the masses in check.[33]

A similar committee in the following session recommended the rebuilding of the Royal Exchange. R.L. Jones again gave evidence, urging that an enlarged exchange was essential because the railways would bring in merchants from 'Liverpool and other places', and it would become an emporium for 'persons resorting from the towns of Europe and America'.[34] The insistence that 'notwithstanding the very extensive interests connected with the transactions which are conducted in the Royal Exchange' the cost of improvements 'ought not to be cast upon the resources of the Nation at large, but should be defrayed by local taxes, or contributions derived from the Metropolis itself, and the districts immediately adjoining to it',[35] was one that articulated a major issue in the financing of metropolitan works. In 1838 a select committee looked at plans for improving east-west communications, and advocated opening up areas of dense working-class population unexposed to the moral influence of better-educated neighbours: the flow of 'public intercourse' would improve their moral condition, as the flow of air would extirpate their prevalent fevers.[36]

In the face of governmental inertia, a further select committee in 1839 recommended three specific projects: a new major west-east route via Coventry Street and Long Acre to relieve the Strand [Pl. 8], linked to a north-south route from Holborn to Waterloo Bridge; a more northerly west-east route, between Oxford Street and Holborn; and a north-south route through the Whitechapel slums to link Spitalfields with the docks.[37] These works would, the committee believed, encourage parliament and the public to develop similar improvements throughout the capital, so that it would 'be ultimately rendered in every respect worthy of its high station, as the largest, most opulent and most commodious metropolis in Europe'.[38] An act designed to implement these recommendations was nullified by financial difficulties: the general estimates on which the 1839 committee had proceeded proved 'considerably below the actual cost which such undertakings must necessarily entail'. The Works and Woods suggested that only one of the proposed plans should be carried out, the Treasury to determine which. There, a select committee in the 1840 session discovered, the matter rested.[39]

There was, at the same time, some recognition that such objects were more than mere local improvements; a sense that they benefited the nation at large. The 1840 committee therefore, while not daring to propose that national taxes should be used for metropolitan improvement, ventured to suggest that they 'partake so much of a national character', particularly in the improvement they would bring in health and the moral condition of the inhabitants, that the Treasury might provide cheap money for the works by issuing Exchequer Bills bearing no more than 3.5 per cent interest, repayable out of the coal dues revenue.[40] Not all members of the committee felt that 'questions of health and morals' fell within their scope, and this no doubt encouraged the financially hard-pressed Melbourne administration to ignore their reiterated recommendations for the construction of the commodious thoroughfares previously proposed: three roads that would unite improvements in health and morals with better communications, at a cost of £279,000.

Despite the general indifference they commonly evoked, London questions were now calling for a good deal of parliamentary consideration. In the same year, 1840, other select committees considered the supply of water to the metropolis, and the best means of effecting the embankment of the Thames.[41] The work of the latter committee, however, was brought to a premature close by the prorogation of parliament. A committee on metropolitan improvements became an annual feature, but that of 1841 (with much the same membership as in the previous year) was appointed too late in the session to complete its labours.[42]

A new administration came into power in 1841. Peel's Conservative ministry determined to remit the question of metropolitan improvements not to the political squabbling of annual Commons' committees, but to the expertise of a more permanent royal commission. Appointed on 23 November 1842, the commission's role was 'to inquire into and consider the most effectual means of improving the Metropolis, and of providing increased facilities of communication within the same'. The commission looked first at the role of a capital city: 'The point to which in every kingdom a native looks with pride, and a foreigner with curiousity, is undoubtedly its Metropolis. Other cities may be the especial depositaries of learning, of science, of the arts, of manufactures, or of commerce, but the foreigner expects to find all these more or less represented in the chief city of the kingdom; and no enlightened native considers his acquaintance with his country complete till he has visited her Capital.'[43] As well as being 'the seat of Government and Legislation of this vast empire', London was 'the central point of the commerce of the world'. It had come to contain interests 'municipal, commercial and professional . . . the magnitude and weight of which is without example in any other great city', which necessarily exercised 'an extensive influence on the public opinion'; an influence, however, 'various, and often conflicting', which presented great difficulties in the way of devising 'any one general and systematic scheme for the reconstruction' of imperfect parts of the capital. Improved communications – the 'most useful and the most difficult' of improvements – involved the invasion of private rights and private comforts, and also the outlay of public money; but experience showed that their advantages to the community far outweighed the private sacrifices entailed. Although the great extension of London had been achieved entirely by private resources, the improvement of the more ancient central districts was 'not of a character to be accomplished, upon any extensive scale, by private means, nor without the intervention of the State, and the authority of Parliament'. Since they would be 'for the advantage and gratification of every class of the community', they were 'in every sense proper subjects for public aid'. Accordingly, the commission had concentrated its attention chiefly on this aspect of improvement.

By this time (1844) a number of the proposals made by earlier select committees had been embarked upon: the linking of Oxford Street and High Holborn, and Coventry Street and Long Acre respectively; and the north-south routes, Long Acre to Great Russell Street and East Smithfield to Spitalfields. The major problem of crossing the Fleet valley was solved only on paper. The actual works carried out were relatively small in scale. No overarching municipal authority existed capable of undertaking such improvements; and the precedent of Regent Street – placing the works under the commissioners of Woods – did not recommend itself either to MPs suspicious of the scope for jobbery in governmental undertakings, or to ministries which could see no adequate source of funding short of general taxation, not regarded as applicable to local improvements.

Of the outstanding proposals, the commission decided that the Thames Embankment was the most valuable. It had in a sense been already begun, with the short stretches in front of the Houses of Parliament and Hungerford Market;[44] not only would it offer a greatly needed improved communication between Westminster and the City, but it would also improve the condition of the river, at this period still a major highway. The alterations of deeps and shoals that were frequently occurring, especially since the removal of the barrier formed by Old London Bridge, were a serious navigational hazard. The foreshore, exposing accumulations of evil-smelling mud and ordure, was a serious health risk.

Proposals for embanking the river had been discussed since Wren's concept of a 'Thames Quay' in the aftermath of the Great Fire. More recently the meddlesome (Sir) Frederick Trench (1775–1859), a member of the Duke of York's circle and a intimate of the architecturally-minded Duke and Duchess of Rutland, had promoted a scheme for the embankment of the Thames by a private company in 1824–5, and had published proposals in 1827 and again in 1841.[45] Such proposals constantly encountered the powerful opposition of the commercial interests that held wharfage rights on the river-front. Despite the development of the enclosed docks down river, the wharves between Westminster and the City remained valuable for the coal trade and other commodities. The opposition of vested interests was consistently an impediment to metropolitan improvement. Even if parliament authorised the compulsory purchase of properties, contention over compensation, and the reference of the question to arbitration, persistently resulted, as noted above, in unexpectedly high awards, pushing costs seriously above estimates and discrediting the whole concept of improvement.[46] Thus, when the City Corporation had sought to bring in a bill in 1840 to embank both banks between London and Vauxhall Bridges, the opposition of the wharfingers was sufficient to block the proposal. However, a general survey was undertaken in 1841, and reports and plans laid before the City's Common Council by a number of engineers and projectors. Of these, that by Thomas Page, C.E. (1803–77),[47] was favoured by the royal commission, which calculated that it could be financed by a 5d. or 6d. duty on coal (then yielding very nearly £11,000 for every penny).[48]

In its subsequent reports, the commission was concerned with striking the appropriate balance between public and private contributions to improvements. It pursued first the question of embankment, concentrating on the stretch between Vauxhall and Battersea Bridges, where three of the largest metropolitan sewers ran into the river, and whence three of the water companies drew their supplies. But much as embankment would have contributed to the health and convenience of the capital, the commission felt unable to recommend its execution entirely at the public expense in view of other proposals for opening 'low and densely crowded neighbourhoods in the heart of the Metropolis . . . where not only the health but the moral condition of the population would be advanced by their adoption'. They recommended executing the Chelsea embankment on the basis that individual riparian property owners would contribute a total of half the estimated cost of £94,000, the remainder coming from the surplus of the London Bridge Approaches Fund, derived from the coal dues.[49]

They then turned to the appalling slums of south Westminster. An act of 1840 had allocated £39,000 in aid of the building of a new street (Victoria Street) through the district, under the management of a company promoted by a radical barrister and developer, Rigby Wason. The commission recommended granting an additional £11,000 as 'an incitement to private enterprize' and a contribution to 'a great public improvement, to be paid for in great measure out of private resources'. It would 'supply an important defect in the existing thoroughfares' of west London, and promote the health, morals and social comforts of the inhabitants.[50] Much of the evidence on this question concerned the high cost of buying up poor-quality property. The government surveyor, James Pennethorne, declared that 'It is now an established principle . . . that you cannot, without great loss, buy up ground and houses in the heart of the town, to be converted only into building ground, with a large portion of it abandoned to form the thoroughfare.'[51]

Further away from the centre, however, a large recreational park could be provided at a small profit if part of the land obtained were developed for building. A park in Battersea Fields would, by means of the great highway of the river, be open to the 'vast and crowded masses of the metropolis'; a bridge to link it to the north bank might be financed by tolls.[52] Such opportunity of exercise and pleasure would put an end 'to scenes of demoralization which the existing almost lawless state of the locality presents daily, and chiefly on Sundays'.[53]

So by the start of the second half of the century there had been much discussion of the concept of metropolitan improvement, the establishment of financial guidelines respecting the means, the determination of certain ends, and the implementation of a small number of the contemplated projects. The new line of street from Oxford Street to High Holborn had been completed together with its buildings; Commercial Street, linking the London Docks with Spitalfields, had been opened in 1845, and its continuation northwards authorised the following year, when Battersea Park and the embankment of the Thames from Vauxhall Bridge to Chelsea Bridge had also been voted, although little had been constructed because of the failure of the riparian landowners to co-operate. Battersea Park made slow progress because of lack of funding from the Loan Commissioners.[54]

Such a state of affairs left considerable dissatisfaction about the condition of London. The Great Exhibition of 1851 had put London on top of the world: the subsequent realisation that London was not the most advanced, healthiest, most beautiful city of the world was a rude shock to the collective consciousness.

One of the problems about leaving metropolitan improvement to Londoners was that London, as we have observed, had no definition: there were a score of Londons. The corporation of the City of London, which had been for centuries past the overwhelmingly predominant local authority in the metropolis, had in the seventeenth century turned its back on the growth of London beyond its bounds and shrugged off responsibility for the new suburbs, many of which therefore developed in an unplanned and unco-ordinated manner. Yet at the same time the corporation insisted on its right to speak for London and manage its business. Such claims no government ventured to outface until the 1880s, and reports of royal commissions bent on reform lay gathering dust on the shelves to which they had been consigned.[55] Meanwhile the world's greatest city was emerging shaped by the hands of private landowners and developers driven by a capitalist ethos, unaided by governmental subsidy and unhampered by many legislative restrictions.

The City apart, there was no coherent local government for London: a mass of authorities with overlapping if not rival jurisdictions heaved and tossed among the primeval slime,[56] waiting for the word that would establish order. It was not until 1855 that that word was spoken.

In 1855 a select committee on metropolitan communications insisted on the need for more new roads to cope with existing, let alone prospective, traffic; but concluded: 'Until some authority is established in the metropolis sufficiently comprehensive to effect improvements on a scale adequate to the existing and prospective wants of the traffic, little can be done by the interposition of the Legislature'; yet the state of London made it 'impossible much longer to postpone' action. All the same, the committee insisted that public improvements be paid for by a metropolitan rate.[57]

A year earlier, a new prime minister, Palmerston, had appointed as President of the Board of Health (a ministerial post) a tough Radical, Sir Benjamin Hall, a Welsh landowner who had represented Marylebone since 1837. Hall's experience in office rapidly converted him from an advocate of local self-government at vestry level to an exponent of centralization, and it was Hall's resolution that saw the Metropolis Management Act[58] onto the statute book. Primarily it was a response, not to the congested streets, but to the filthy Thames, a huge open sewer where at low tide reeking sewage was exposed on the unembanked shores. A compromise between traditional defenders of community self-government and rationalist reformers, the new act created a two-tier administration for the built-up metropolitan area. The larger vestries and groups of smaller vestries (known as 'district boards') elected representatives to a Metropolitan Board of Works created specifically to carry out the main drainage of the capital and relieve

it of the intolerable stink that devastated dutiful legislators in Westminster's committee rooms by purifying the Thames – itself the chief source of water supply to the citizens (and hence frequently of infection likewise). The second function of the new board was to make new streets.

Once the Board was established, it was not long before further metropolitan functions were entrusted to it: as building the long-desired Thames Embankment, which provided at once a new road and a low-level intercepting sewer; and slum-clearance laws gave it the demolition-man's chain-and-ball in addition to the excavator's shovel. Although over the course of years it acquired not a few of the characteristics of a metropolitan government, the MBW lacked moral authority and financial muscle. It was, as stated, indirectly elected, the vestries themselves being elected on a narrow rate-payer franchise;[59] and it drew its principal funding from the rate, or local property tax, of so many pence in the pound on the assessed rateable value, on the strength of which it was able to raise loans for capital works. Furthermore, parliamentary authority was requisite for any major work.[60]

The rates fell unequally on the metropolitan parishes,[61] originating from inconsistent valuations[62] and bearing most heavily upon the poor East End parishes where maximum valuations were the practice. The richer west enjoyed lower valuations, so exacerbating the difference between rich areas, where the rate in the pound was low, and the poor areas, where it was high.[63] Attempts to equalise the burden between parishes and to rate the landowner rather than only the occupier met with little success, despite the recommendations of select committees in 1861, 1866 and 1867, the last of which recommended that there should be for the whole metropolis a municipal council able to make a uniform rating assessment.[64] In opposition, the Liberals were prepared to surrender the national house duty to municipalities (the advantage going chiefly to London which paid about half the total); but in government, all they provided was an act consolidating rate claims and providing for quinquennial reassessments.[65] Not until 1894 was there an effective move towards equalising rates throughout the metropolis.[66]

Thus the MBW was generally fighting with one if not both hands behind its back, as the vestries opposed expenditure that would not bring them immediate benefit, and parliamentary approval, both expensive and lengthy, was an uncertain quantity.

One other source of finance to which the MBW might look lay in the coal, corn and wine dues, a traditional source for funding metropolitan improvements.[67] The wine dues were of little significance; the corn dues, collected by the City Corporation, in 1868–70 amounted to an average £33,000 p.a.[68] The impost on coal imported into the port of London yielded an ever-richer harvest as a coal-burning metropolis spread its bounds.[69] 'It is difficult', commented the 1836 improvements committee, 'to suggest a duty upon which so large a sum of money can be raised by so small an amount of charge as the duty upon Coal, and at so little expense in the collection; its operation is scarcely felt, except by the very large consumers . . . while the poor are affected by it in a very trifling degree': on the two tons a year which would be a large average for family consumption, the duty would be but one shilling.[70]

Such an impost of long-standing charged on Londoners roused at this period little hostility in any quarter.[71] After the Great Fire it had financed the rebuilding of the City churches and of St Paul's cathedral; later, it had subsidised a range of improvements carried out by the City Corporation, culminating in the rebuilding of London Bridge and its approach streets in the 1820s and 1830s. An act of 1845 enacted that the duties should be levied within twenty miles from London; but the organisation of the coal retail trade entailed payment of these dues by the inhabitants of towns

9. Holborn Viaduct, (W. Heywood, 1863–9), crossing Farringdon Street. This obviated the steep descent into and climb out of the Fleet Valley, giving London a new east-west artery for heavy traffic.

even further afield.[72] This too, apart from a duty of 4d. per ton claimed by the City for improvements [Pl. 9], was the subject of parliamentary enactment, and such a grant of revenue might be resisted for a variety of reasons, among which we may enrol contention between the Board and the City. Lord Randolph Churchill's populist refusal to renew this resource in 1887 erected a major obstacle to further metropolitan embellishment.[73]

The work of the MBW was considerably facilitated by the innovatory Loans Act of 1869, which created a metropolitan consolidated stock, redeemable within 60 years out of a consolidated loans fund financed by a metropolitan consolidated rate (levied by the parochial authorities as hitherto) and other revenues and profits, including the coal dues. This simplified the collection of the Board's rates as well as enabling it to borrow on better terms, its stock indeed soon acquiring trustee status.[74]

Despite the growing wealth and power of the mid-century provincial centres, from Cardiff and Birmingham to Glasgow and Aberdeen, London remained the great focal point of the British Isles:[75] the administrative capital; the principal port; the country's largest concentration of industry;[76] its financial centre; and the focus of its artistic and intellectual life.[77] London remained the great market of the nation.[78] That the MBW's first major road-building project (Southwark Street, 1858–64) was a direct communication between the railway termini at London Bridge and that at Waterloo points to the important relationship between the metropolis and the railways which radiated from the capital; it was often quicker to travel between two provincial centres via London than by making the shorter cross-country journey.

London was also the centre of a world-embracing empire, a super-power that, if receding from its early-nineteenth-century dominance, played an active role in many parts of the world. From Whitehall were ruled India's millions, as well as the growing numbers of colonists in the Antipodes; the decisions made there and in 'Lombard Street' determined the trade alike of the Ottoman and Chinese empires and petty African chiefdoms. From London a network of imperial contacts mapped the world and gathered the data for systematising geology and zoology.[79] It was 'the supreme money market of the trading world'[80] in 1870 as in 1815; the 'clearing-house of the world'.[81]

Yet this world city had failed to achieve either monumentality or beauty. 'For most of its history London served as an expression of private values rather than of public exhortation', a perceptive historian has lately remarked.[82] Professor Olsen posits different principles governing Regency London, which he argues that Victorian London repudiated: but we see in the 1850s and 1860s the same greed for excessive compensation for compulsory property sales, the same festering of plague-spots, the same petty-mindedness of vestrydom, as had characterised George IV's day: or to look at it more positively, the same search for a noble architecture; the same seeking after the grand gesture – new palaces of legislature, administration, law, science and commerce;[83] the same desire to clean up the city (fostered by a growing awareness of the risks to the health of all classes engendered by dirt); the same desire to eliminate corruption. All such exercises are selective. We take a period, label it 'Regency' or 'Victorian' and ascribe to it the characteristics that our eye lights upon, no doubt in response to our predilections and prejudices.[84]

Thus the 'London' of which we write has many diverse, even opposed characteristics. Yet even in opposition there may be an underlying unity: the 'rents' of the East End that sustained some of the opulence of the West End: 'machines for manufacturing rent'.[85] Too large and too diverse ever to kindle a sense of civic identity, London was nevertheless an intricately-woven tapestry. A strategic authority was needed to ensure the continuity of its weft and warp. In practical terms, some body was necessary to ensure adequate sanitation and communications (though the Victorians were slow to realise that traffic grows to clog up the arteries created for it),[86] and tap the wealth of London for these purposes. Despite the succession of select committees on metropolitan improvements, parliament was unwilling to foot the bill: it would do no more than diagnose the problems and create the machinery for their solution. Nor were successive administrations keen to create a powerful metropolitan authority: the lesson of Paris in revolutionary times was rehearsed often enough.

Meanwhile private effort was remodelling the face of London to secure the maximum advantage for itself.[87] New railway lines penetrated the capital destroying swathes of poor dwellings and terminating in grand hotels.[88] Following the architectural fashion set by the gentlemen's clubs in the West End, insurance companies, merely checked by the financial crisis of 1858, continued to erect Italianate palazzi, themselves copied in the 1860s by the banks' 'temples of Mammon' in Lombard Street [Pl. 10].[89] Development companies raised extravagantly, even outlandishly, fronted offices; merchants, responsive to fashion in architecture as in goods, fancy Italian or Gothic warehouses.[90] 'Buildings of a costly and even an important character, some of them such as a few years ago would have been regarded with very general interest, are now begun, carried on, and quietly completed, on every side without calling forth anything more than a passing remark', noted one architectural critic in 1862. London was seen as a progressive city; less stately than Paris, but more various in its architecture, and 'in the end, perhaps equally picturesque'.[91]

Parliamentary reluctance to tackle London's problems was in large part a factor of the notorious under-representation of the metropolis in the House of Commons. It was true that many members, perhaps a hundred, had close links with the City of London and its corporation – so it was seldom difficult for the City to block proposals inimical to its interests.[92] But the Reform Act of 1832, leaving the unique City constituency in enjoyment of its four members, and Westminster and an enlarged Southwark continuing to elect two members each, created only five new two-member metropolitan constituencies.[93] Even if the two members for Middlesex are regarded as 'London' men, the metropolitan total was no more than 20 out of a House of 658. A contributory factor to the weak-

10.   'London Assurance'; the new dignity of City architecture: National Provincial Bank, Threadneedle Street, John Gibson (1817–92), 1864–5. Architectural monumentality and allegorical sculpture in the service of Finance.

ness of London's representation was the heavily popular character of the new constituencies and the unpopularity in the House of some of those elected.[94] Nor did the 1867 Conservative redistribution much mend matters, adding only four members to the overwhelmingly Liberal metropolitan constituency.[95] Between 1832 and 1885 there was a great mass of members from essentially rural constituencies (small boroughs as well as county divisions) who were consistently opposed to spending national taxation on London purposes. In this they were generally supported by members from the great provincial cities, who, refulgent with civic pride, felt that they should share in any benefits bestowed on London. A 'Looker-on' condemned attacks on the then First Commissioner, Sir Benjamin Hall, for his wide vision of public works, by members representing small constituencies, and remarked: 'When it is recollected that London and its environs comprise about one eighth of the whole population of England, and of course contribute in the same ratio to its expenditure, surely something like a generous sympathy from those not doomed to pass the whole year in its crowded neighbourhood might be expected, and something like a nobler feeling towards the individual anxious to carry out not only sanitary improvement but the long-required embellishment of the first city of the first country in the world.'[96] Attacked by country and provincial urban members, governments were reluctant to embark on large schemes because of the opposition they might arouse; the amount of that scarce commodity, parliamentary time, that they might occupy; and the damaging effects that inability rapidly to carry through its business would have on a ministry's standing generally.

Not until 1885 did London receive a representation in any way commensurate with its population and wealth, gaining an additional 42 members.[97] *The Times* rapidly grasped the significance of this shift in the balance of parliamentary representation. When in March 1886 a deputation from the Royal Institute of British Architects presented to the First Commissioner of Works costly proposals for widening Whitehall in the context of the designs for a new Admiralty and War Office, a leading article observed that it would be not unreasonable for the ratepayers to contribute – the cost might not fall short of a round million pounds. But it remarked

both the presence in the deputation of the chairman of the MBW, and also the fact that London now had 63 MPs.[98]

> It is scarcely too much to say that the architectural future of London is involved in the question raised by the Royal Institute of British Architects. . . . We are convinced, on the one hand, that every Englishman is proud of London, and that most Englishmen would be glad to have something more in London to be proud of. On the other hand, times are very hard, taxation is very heavy, the calls on the national purse are great and pressing, and money spent on the beauty of London is taken from the pockets of many who can ill afford it, and of still more who have little prospect of personally enjoying the results obtained. . . . Can the British taxpayer be asked to bear this burden contentedly in these difficult times? If so, the thing can be done, and certainly it is well worth the doing. The opportunity can never recur.

The decision rested with the House of Commons: 'DEMOS is king now, and he must decide how he will have his servants lodged, and whether he cares to have his capital beautified.'[99]

What distinction, then, might be drawn between purely 'London' purposes and 'national'? Clearly, the National Gallery or the British Museum served a national function. Their collections were for the delectation or instruction of the whole nation, and improving communications steadily made them more accessible to provincial folk. Government offices, too, were a national charge. But beyond the merely functional, they were an embellishment to London. If they involved widened streets, that was an advantage to Londoners. Thus there was an inherent 'Country Party' mistrust of proposals for fine public buildings in the capital, since they conferred a bonus on London at the cost of the country taxpayer, beyond what was strictly necessary for national uses. Although, for example, 'Parliament had always exercised a control over Westminster Bridge' and the government had taken the 'bridge estate', the income from which had kept the bridge in repair, when it came to rebuilding it at the public expense, several MPs expressed their opposition, and a Sheffield member objected to the principle of the whole country paying for 'improvements in London'.[100] The New Government Offices project of 1856 would seem to be clearly a national object; but many members were highly suspicious of the ideas of 'Magnificent Benjamin' Hall. His own chancellor of the Exchequer, Sir George Lewis, had confined its scope distinctly.[101] In Opposition two years later, Lewis exhorted the Conservative ministry to go ahead with a new Foreign Office, but expressed his hostility to a large scheme originating partly from those 'who wished to give a more imposing character to the Civil Service, and partly from others who wished to embellish the metropolis at the public expense'.[102]

From time to time, national spirit might be sufficiently roused to sweep away such objections: 'Clearly, in national works, the preliminary measure is to see what is wanted for convenience and use. The means can be found – with economy and return of interest – both for that, and for any amount of decoration which an architect may deem accordant with the purpose of the structure', declared the *Builder*.[103] 'I am one of those who think it desirable that any public building should be in good taste, and should be made worthy of a great country', boldly asserted William Cowper, newly appointed First Commissioner of Works, in 1860. 'I think that it is not desirable we should have our public buildings inferior in character to those of private individuals.'[104] Then the critics would reassert themselves, or a financial crisis would threaten, as in 1857, and parliament would veto what parliament had proposed. Cowper had to admit that these conditions had induced in ministers 'such unwillingness to propose large sums to Parliament for the erection of public offices that the subject has been continually postponed'.[105]

The Commons's 'strongest objection' to give anything to metropolitan improvement was remarked on again in 1861,[106] after opposition to spending any national revenue on a Thames Embankment had surfaced. In 1860 that noble project had been brought measurably closer by the opportunity of combining it with planned work on the main drainage of the metropolis (the primary function of the MBW).[107] A select committee heard evidence from the chairman of the MBW, who argued that while embankment should be executed by the Board the cost should be at least partly borne by the government.[108] The committee agreed that the MBW should act, recommending funding from the traditional source for major metropolitan improvements, the coal and wine dues.

All looked plain sailing until Cowper, fearing that the MBW would perpetrate a metropolitan 'job', upset the boat with the announcement of a royal commission to consider the plans for embankment, thereby implying a 'public work' at taxpayers' expense. The Tory member for West Norfolk, George W.P. Bentinck (1803–86), insisted that 'London ought to be at the expense of its own improvements'; London's ratepayers, not taxpayers, should pay. Cowper retorted that such remarks might 'encourage the desire of some hon. Gentlemen in this House to resuscitate the ancient country party, and in antagonism with the towns and the Metropolis'. Like the investigating committee, Cowper saw the Embankment as a solution to the perennial traffic problem: it would relieve the great east-west thoroughfares which were so blocked that it was quicker to go on foot than in a carriage.[109] But some London members saw it merely as a 'job', contrived by engineers and contractors for their own benefit. The Radical A.S. Ayrton (1816–86)[110] thought that the improvement of the direct routes into the City – the Strand and Holborn [Pl. 9] – was what London needed. The Thames Embankment concerned only a few Westminster residents, a 'very small portion of the ratepayers'; 'It

was . . . of the essence of local administration that it should have the initiation of such projects, and that they should not be driven against their will into the adoption of any fanciful project.' If the government was going to exercise its taste in embanking the Thames, then the government should pay for it.[111]

The royal commission duly deliberated and recommended a plan. Cowper introduced a bill enabling the MBW to carry out the plan, but the select committee to which the bill was referred resulted in delays. There were two groups of interested parties who opposed the embankment: commercial wharfingers whose interests had for so long blocked any embankment; and the aristocratic Crown leaseholders of Westminster, who, supported by Gore of the Woods and Forests (Crown estate), objected to a great new road in front of their riverine properties. A powerful speech by the prime minister swept aside these diversions, the bill was carried, and the Victoria Embankment duly built, at a net cost of £1,157,000.[112] But the critics were not silenced: the *Solicitors' Journal*, for instance, attacked it as nothing but a scheme to decorate London.[113]

Opened by the Prince of Wales on 13 July 1870, the noble hundred-foot-wide thoroughfare [Pl. 11], although at first relatively little used by traffic, for the first time dignified London's relationship with its river: it could vie anew with Imperial Paris. 'For the first time since the Great Fire', observed the First Commissioner, 'an opportunity presented itself of making London a metropolis worthy of this great Empire and of placing it, in regard to public edifices and to architectural improvements, on a footing with the other capitals of Europe. The Government had to decide upon the erection of a larger number of important buildings than had probably ever been raised in any capital at one time. . . . Here, then, was an opportunity . . . of placing on the Embankment a continuous line of great public buildings from the Temple to the Houses of Parliament, and thus opening one great highway through the metropolis, unequalled for its magnificence in any capital in the world.'[114]

Already, in mid-1868, the *Builder* had warned that the future

11. Thames Embankment (J.W. Bazalgette, 1863–70). The Victoria Embankment complemented Holborn Viaduct (Pl. 9) in relieving pressure on the Strand, hitherto the only feasible east-west route for heavy traffic.

12.   Paris: prototypes of ministerial offices:
a. Conseil d'Etat and Cour des Comptes, formerly Ministry of Interior, begun by J.-C. Bonnard, 1814; completed by J. Lacornée, 1821–35. (Destroyed by Communards, 1871). Note Lacornée's dexterous introduction of mezzanines, a solution to the problem imposed by the height of *salles de réception* that eluded Scott in Whitehall.
b. Foreign Ministry, Quai d'Orsay, Salon de la Rotonde in 1893. J. Lacornée, 1845–54. Foreign visitors were struck by the splendour.

13.   Paris: new Louvre, Aile Richelieu. Designed by Visconti (d. 1853) and completed by Lefuel in 1857 as government offices and ministerial suites.

architectural rank of London among European cities would depend primarily on the use to be made of the new Embankment. 'The stately magnificence of a capital city is one of the elements of national *prestige*, and therefore of national power and influence. The architectural beauty of Paris is not the least of the claims of the French nation to rank their capital as the metropolis of civilisation. . . . We have fresh and noble sites freely offered to the architect in the very centre of population.'[115] Similarly, the *Architect* (newly established and aiming at 'a first place among those journals which are quoted as authorities') reflected that 'London is not merely the city of the Londoner, it is the Metropolis of every Englishman. What affects London public works will have a direct or a reflex influence on every public work in England. . . . We win from the river a quay of the greatest beauty, and we bedizen the Embankment wall with piers and balustrades wanting in every propriety . . . if architecture had been as capriciously treated and taste as little cultivated in Paris as in London, that brilliant capital would not have possessed the attractions which it exerts so potently over all wanderers from home.'[116]

Comparison with Paris was a recurrent theme. The Orleans monarchy had completed a decaying Napoleonic project for a 'massive block of government offices dominating the left bank of the Seine' [Pl. 12],[117] complemented from 1845 by Jacques Lacornée's Foreign Ministry (Quai d'Orsay), sumptuously completed by the Second Empire in 1854; Palmerston commented on its magnificence.[118] Vast works linking the north side of the Louvre to the Tuileries, *l'aile Richelieu*, were nearing completion, to house ministerial offices including a suite of ostentatious apartments for the ministry of state [Pl. 13].[119]

Louis Napoleon, soon after his election as president, had drawn up his own proposals for street improvements, which were effected under Haussmann (1853–70). A general plan for new streets had been drawn up by a 'Commission des Artistes' established as long ago as 1793.[120] Haussmann decided to abandon projects for street widening in favour of driving new streets through the city, which facilitated slum clearance, relieved traffic congestion, and provided work.[121] His great programme was financed largely by loans raised by the municipality, Haussmann arguing that the debt would be covered by the growth of revenue brought about by the improvements; but there was a significant element of state subsidy also.[122] But to Hall's eyes at least it was the length and breadth of the new streets that gave them importance, their architecture appearing 'very bad'.[123]

Cheap excursion fares enabled even British workmen to visit the Exposition Universelle of 1855 in Paris, and the ruling classes went in considerable numbers – an exposure to imperial glories that aroused much dissatisfaction with a London that seemed dirty and insignificant in all save extent, dissatisfaction that had encouraged successive First Commissioners [Pl. 71], Sir William Molesworth and then Sir Benjamin Hall,[124] in their proposals for new government offices. Hall in 1856 consequently gained parliamentary support for an open competition for new government offices in Whitehall – but the palatial designs (and an unsympathetic chancellor) at a time of financial panic and threat of colonial wars struck down his grandiose schemes.[125]

The improvement of Trafalgar Square (termed by Peel 'the finest site in Europe') as a focal point in the imperial capital was another desideratum, to be achieved principally by rebuilding Wilkins' National Gallery, regarded as lacking height and dignity. Edward Barry's design for 'a striking and publicly conspicuous building on a grand scale' [Pl. 178] was regarded as 'the first step towards making Trafalgar-square more like what we all feel that it might be made'. But 'the old warning against putting your trust in princes may be equally applicable to less autocratic forms of Gov-

14. Vienna: new public buildings on the Ringstrasse. The demolition of Vienna's fortifications enabled a noble thoroughfare to be built round the old city, an impressive series of public buildings emerging in the 1880s.
a. The Parliament Building (T. Hansen, 1883), with, beyond, the spires of the Town Hall (F. von Schmidt, 1884).
b. The Justiz-palast, 1874–81. Alexander von Wielemans (1843–1911), unknown when he won the competition, echoed the pavilions of the New Louvre in the central block.

15. Berlin: Platz am Opernhaus, with Rauch's statue of Frederick II (1851), and Unter den Linden beyond. On the left, palace of William I (C.F. Langhans, 1834–6), Academy (1749) and University (1748–66) on the right.

ernment'. The National Gallery's front was to remain 'a discredit to a metropolis where search for more ambitious architectural scenery is devoted to the front of a railway hotel'.[126]

Another imperial capital, Vienna, was transformed from the 1860s onwards. In 1857, the Emperor Francis-Joseph, inspired perhaps by Hall's competition for a new Westminster, decreed the abolition of the old ring of fortifications, and the holding of a competition for a ground plan to incorporate certain specified features. Eighty-five plans were received and three prizes awarded, though the implemented plan was drawn up by the public works department. The magnificent public buildings of the Ringstrasse – 'a triumph of variegated space' – were financed by the sale of surplus land for speculative development [Pl. 14].[127] In 1893, the Vienna municipality launched another open competition for re-modelling the old centre, as well as for the systematic extension of the outer city.[128]

A smaller German state, Bavaria, resumed in the 1850s the noble town-planning works of the first kings in Munich, the Maximilienstrasse (1852–9) providing a setting for Bürklein's Government Offices (1856–64) and Riedel's Altes National–museum (1858–65), and leading to Bürklein's and Semper's Maximilianeum (1857–74).[129] Berlin [Pl. 15] had already been given a new and beautiful centre by Schinkel, ready to assume its imperial role when the new German empire rose on the ruins of the French.[130] Subsequent developments were facilitated by the government's right to take, for due compensation, land required for public purposes. The protracted, 'costly and uncertain' parliamentary campaign necessary in London before improvements were begun was unknown in Berlin.[131] Another new state, the kingdom of Italy, embellished its newly achieved capital, Rome, with grand national constructions [Pl. 16].

Given such developments on the Continent, increasingly well known to the English, it is not surprising that in the jingoistic years of 'Beaconsfieldism' there was a renewed demand for public offices at least to match the commercial and financial palaces of the City of London. Baillie-Cochrane (see app. 4) chaired a select committee on new public offices, and the publication of its report (1877)[132] stirred the *Builder* to remark: 'After many years of objectionable conservatism, we seem at last to be getting into the stage of public feeling in regard to metropolitan improvements which is exhibited in a general desire to have the subject, to use an established phrase, "thoroughly ventilated". It is rapidly becoming the topic of talkers and of newspapers, and seems likely, within the circle of metropolitan interests, to succeed the sewage question as "the question of the day".'[133]

Reviewing the history of the government offices over the past thirty or forty years from the *Builder*'s editorial chair, George Godwin impartially criticised on the one hand Baillie-Cochrane's chase after 'the grandiose, the expensive and the sublime', and the 'spirit of waste which pervades the practice of Public Works in this country – almost equal to what has long been tolerated in the

16. Rome: the Palace of Justice, G. Calderini (competition winner), 1886–1910. On the banks of the Tiber, this 600ft façade is placed axially in relation to the contemporary Umberto I Bridge.

Indian dependency'; and on the other, 'the letter of "rigorous economy", which is the theory of a Select Committee'. Such committees 'do over again what was done ten, twenty, and even thirty years ago; sometimes by men who were members also of the previous Committees. This, however, [Godwin concluded] is what we have to endure for the sake of the stability which is the distinguishing feature of the English Constitution. Paris was rebuilt in at least fifteen years less time than it has taken the English nation to build one block of four Public Offices. But the cost to Paris has been a catastrophe which no one believes could happen to London.'[134]

Unfortunately, although the English constitution might offer stability, the English party system offered the instability of the Penelope syndrome, one ministry unravelling the web woven by its predecessor. It was also possible for a single ministry to make a U-turn, as in 1878, when threatening colonial troubles wrecked expansive budget hopes and all immediate intention of new office-building was abandoned. In this story of 'pull devil, pull baker', public opinion played little part. Until the 1880s public opinion was (except perhaps in major international crises or when the country was swept by a wave of mass emotion) the opinion of the clubs, both formulating and formulated by the views of the dominant newspaper editors, *The Times* most dominant.[135] On rare occasions an agitation might be whipped up in the press presenting itself as the public voice with more or less success against some official proposal, such as Sunday bands, or the proposals for new roads in the Parks that will be discussed below. Public opinion was at its most effective in keeping in check any proposals for increasing taxation.

Throughout the second half of the century, the conventional line on public buildings was that governmental efficiency called for the concentration of offices, but that they should not be too palatial, and they should not be undertaken at times of fiscal stringency. As the influence of the popular constituency grew after the Third Reform Act (1884), and the rate of government intervention in national life increased, pressures mounted for increased expenditure on what may inclusively be termed public welfare. These demands on the Exchequer themselves discouraged expenditure on public buildings, particularly when W.H. Smith was Conservative first lord of the Treasury and Sir William Harcourt Liberal chancellor of the Exchequer. Because of the weakness of the English regime for public buildings, and its historic subordination to the Treasury, proposals for new buildings were among the first to be axed in times of financial stringency. Things could always go on as they were for a year or two longer: efficiency might suffer, but the political gain was seen as worth the administrative inconvenience. Fine public buildings were not necessary for the production of government documents.

A flourishing revenue however could provide, and a strong minister seize, an opportunity for a building programme, as happened in the late 1890s. By the twentieth century the inexorable extension of government activities made essential the provision of new offices. Scientists organised themselves to demand increased public provision for science – with museums to complement teaching establishments and laboratories. The national collections of paintings and artifacts grew by gift and purchase, and rising public revenues offered the opportunity to provide the additional museum and gallery space that educated opinion was demanding.

In 1896, contemplating the appointment of yet another select committee on public offices, Godwin's successor as editor of the *Builder*, H.H. Statham, observed that the history of the spasmodic and piecemeal efforts to complete the architectural housing of our government departments, without the slightest attempt at comprehensive treatment (he might more justly have said 'the determined opposition to comprehensive treatment'), was characteristic of 'the apathy and ignorance of the public and press of this country in regard to the whole subject of national and international architecture'. It had been a story of 'niggling and cheeseparing' ever since one of the finest opportunities ever afforded a nation for a 'grand and imposing group of national offices' had been thrown away in 1856–8. Statham lammed into an article in the widely-read *Daily Telegraph* which suggested that the public believed our national buildings were architectural triumphs: ' "No reasonable outlay of money [declared the *Telegraph*] will be grudged. The inhabitants of London, very properly, insist that their public buildings and their thoroughfares shall be worthy of the foremost city in the world, no matter what the cost" (!)' In truth, 'economic niggardliness and architectural blundering' had ensured a Home Office that was 'feeble and totally uninteresting'; a 'mean and commonplace' Admiralty that was 'simply a disgrace to the nation'.

There was little hope that individual buildings would be better, thought Statham, unless the constitution of select committees were radically amended. They were appointed on political grounds merely: 'people seem to think that Politics are a part of Art when the matter concerns a Government building, and that all that one could wish for is secured when, as we are told is the case with the present Committee, "every section of the House of Commons is adequately represented" '.[136]

Statham's ire had been roused previously, in 1884 by George Shaw Lefevre (1831–1928) as First Commissioner who had 'got round him' a 'party of mere nonentities (in this respect) . . . in order to carry out his silly scheme for making a sham-antique of Westminster Hall'.[137] When a committee was appointed in 1887 to determine whether or not to go ahead with a new palatial building for the defence ministries, Statham raged: 'The question whether some of the existing buildings of the Admiralty may with advantage be retained is of course purely one for the economists, architecture being generally regarded in the legislative assembly as a matter of pounds, shillings and pence, not of beauty or of national honour and glory.'[138] There was too much of 'the mercantile and Philistine spirit displayed and apparently gloried in by some honourable members'.[139] They did things better in Belgium: where that small kingdom had 'carried out its Palais de Justice . . . marked by the impress of genius and by the sumptuous liberality which disdains to carry out such work in a paltry and cheeseparing fashion' [Pl. 183];[140] or in France, where eminent artists and architects would serve as advisers on government building proposals.[141]

It has been argued that the economical spirit displayed by the British with regard to public buildings was 'part of a national philosophy'; the 'obverse side of supreme confidence in international competition in important affairs'.[142] 'The certainty of power and the assured confidence of success meant that there was no need to show off. Little Belgium might spend more than Great Britain on its metropolitan law courts, but the reality of power and religion of parsimony meant that the English regarded such petty one-upmanship with disdain or indifference.' This, once again, is to play the game of selective Victorianism. 'We are the richest nation in Europe; let us have the grandest art palace', retorts the *Fortnightly Review.*[143]

No doubt Statham scorched the paper as he wrote, but despite his above-cited condemnation of the 'apathy and ignorance of the public and press' with regard to architecture, there was a considerable public interest in the subject, as is indicated both by the increasing number of periodicals devoted to it, and the extensive coverage given to new buildings in such wide-circulation journals as the *Illustrated London News* and the *Graphic* as well as the 'heavy' quarterlies.[144] The exhibition in Westminster Hall of designs for the New Government Offices (1857), open for a month from

4 May, attracted 10,000 on the first day, and another 17,000 on the following two days [Pl. ••].[145]

Many Britons accepted uncritically the religion of national superiority, but thinking men were acutely aware of national weaknesses, as the appointment of the 1835 select committee on Arts and Manufactures had shown, and as the 1851 Great Exhibition and subsequent re-runs emphasised. One problem was the generally low standard of architectural achievement, a consequence of the lack of a system of training; another, and more serious one, was the English hostility to governmental activity in general: the reformers of 1832 believed that good government was cheap government, and that its sphere in the nation's life should be strictly circumscribed; though the discovery of intolerable abuses drove them to state action.[146] Consequently a parliamentary adversarial system required both parties to represent themselves as apostles of economy. To cut or defer capital expenditure on public buildings was one of the most effectively visible reductions for an incoming chancellor to make – and no doubt the easier because of deep-rooted dissatisfaction with the quality of public building design.

Victorian London may have been 'a statement against absolutism, a proud expression of the energies and values of a free people';[147] but some of those free people thought that grand public buildings, matching the financial and commercial palaces, would be no bad expression of English freedom.[148] Municipalities erected grand civic buildings without being charged with despotism [Pl. 18]: at Leeds, despite a struggle over adorning the town hall with a tower, those rejecting a purely utilitarian philosophy carried the day [Pl. 17], arguing for appropriateness, conduciveness to 'dignity and beauty', and an 'outward symbol' of 'public government'.[149] Nor were parliament and press without exponents of similar requirements in national buildings. It was impossible to adopt a policy of 'Haussmannisation' in London because of the power of the urban landlord (which was related to the huge value of inner urban property) and the lack of a governmental structure such as prevailed in Paris. London lacked any effective municipal government thanks to the vested interests of well-to-do ratepayers; and parliamentary tradition favoured a weak executive, which was to limit the ability of governments to engage in a public buildings programme. Summerson's condemnation of Victorian public building, which has cast such a blight on its reputation, has to be seen in the context of his position as an advocate of the Modern

18.   Manchester Town Hall, A. Waterhouse, won in open two-stage competition, 1867–8. 'A brilliant imaginative concept' (J.H.G. Archer).

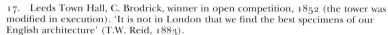

17.   Leeds Town Hall, C. Brodrick, winner in open competition, 1852 (the tower was modified in execution). 'It is not in London that we find the best specimens of our English architecture' (T.W. Reid, 1883).

Movement, to whom Victorian architecture as a whole (up to 1870) was a failure.[150]

What has to be admitted is the unsatisfactory character of the English public works regime, long a matter of critical comment by contemporaries. Statham's suggestion that architects and artists should be called in to advise on public works had a respectable ancestry.[151] Various modes had been tried successively: a professional head; an administrator supported by professional advisers; a politician with bureaucrat colleagues; and finally a politician with full ministerial control within the department.[152] All these models were subject to an unparalleled degree of Treasury control[153] – as the Earl of Morley, First Commissioner of Works, put it in 1886, 'I am not entirely independent'.[154]

The Office of Works ranked low in the hierarchy and its head was frequently moved.[155] The idea of a non-political commissioner with a degree of permanence therefore attracted many of those interested in the metropolitan landscape,[156] but this was to overlook the acute political sensitivity of votes of money for public buildings. The experiment of having a non-parliamentarian at the head of a spending department had failed disastrously with the

Poor Law Board: a permanent commissioner could not answer parliamentary questions. Equally, the idea of a permanent commissioner alongside a political one had been found to produce controversy when tried at the Woods and Works between 1832 and 1850.[157] To upgrade the commissioner to permanent cabinet status[158] might have liberated him from strict Treasury control, but would have done little to secure longer individual tenure (the average tenure of the high office of secretary of state for War between 1854 and 1905 was two and a quarter years).[159] As an alternative, an advisory council was from time to time proposed. Lord John Manners, a former Conservative Works minister opposing such a proposal in 1869, feared that an effective council would displace the minister; but he also wanted a clear demarcation between the minister's powers and those of the municipal authority. He put the 'country party' view that London affairs were best left to Londoners;[160] the Metropolitan Board of Works could vet building designs, including those for government buildings.[161]

However, although the MBW successfully carried out the Herculean task of the main drainage of London, and the successive embankments of the northern and southern shores of the Thames, it was never a popular body, or one to which government might defer. The solution to the problem of the annual uncertainty of parliamentary funding that the Conservatives adopted in 1897–8, when the revenue was flourishing, was to fund a whole building programme from the year's surplus revenue, instead of surrendering it to the National Debt Commissioners.[162]

For the most part, the MBW remained a local authority of limited powers labouring on relatively small-scale but nonetheless expensive schemes of road improvement[163] and slum clearance.[164] Of road improvements, the most important were the new 60 ft-wide, mile-and-a-half east-west route from Shoreditch to Oxford Street (Great Eastern Street, Old Street, Clerkenwell and Theobalds Roads), carried out in 1872–8 at a net cost of more than a million sterling; and similar north-south routes from Oxford Street to Piccadilly (Shaftesbury Avenue) and to Charing Cross (Charing Cross Road), that were the necessary sequel: a combined length of over a mile at a net cost of nearly £1,360,000 – work delayed for several years by impossibly stringent conditions imposed on the Board by Parliament as to rehousing the displaced poor.[165] The historian of the MBW has called its record 'impressive', but admits that, 'limited by its fear of ratepayer's revenge and its own uncertain taste, the Board failed, aside from the Embankment, to beautify the metropolis as it might have done. . . . No critic placed the Board's accomplishments on a level with Haussmann's rebuilding of Paris.'[166] We may add that Haussmann was subsidised by the national government, enjoyed prefectorial powers greater than those of the MBW, and left the municipal government with a crushing burden of debt and an unfinished programme of street improvements when dismissed in 1870.[167]

When the MBW was replaced in 1889 by the directly elected London County Council, there were hopes of a new era opening in London's history. The government still had the proposal for a new War Office on its agenda, and the widening of Parliament Street was linked to the possible erection there of new government offices. Government and council negotiated over new arrangements to relieve the traffic congestion at Hyde Park Corner. The long-contemplated new street from Holborn to the Strand, abandoned by the MBW in 1883 when the government refused to renew the coal dues, was taken up again hopefully – and without success. The council insisted that property-owners benefiting from the improvements should contribute to the costs: government hostility prevented legislation. But when the LCC acquired property from the Duke of Bedford for widening Southampton Row, as well as powers to deal with insanitary property around Clare Market, the question of the Strand link became inescapable.[168] Chaired by Lefevre, the LCC improvements committee agreed on a 100 ft-wide direct route from Holborn at the end of Southampton Row to the Strand, bifurcating into a crescent form at Stanhope Street; the western branch forming an approach to Waterloo Bridge, the eastern to the Strand at St Clement Danes church. The Strand also would be widened. Sufficient property was to be acquired – as in Haussmann's Paris[169] – to enable the council to benefit from the improved values, instead of leaving them to adjoining owners as hitherto. A contentious bill provided unusual powers to enable the council to avoid the disputatious progress of compensations under the Lands Clauses Acts, and to levy an improvement charge on certain areas. Although considerably modified during its passage, the bill was carried through in all its essentials in 1899. It authorised 'the largest scheme of town improvement that had ever been placed before Parliament', involving a site of 28 acres, and about three-quarters of a mile of new streets, mostly of the exceptional width of 100 feet [Pl. 19]. The total cost was estimated at £6,120,380, though £4,363,200 might be recouped by disposal of building land, leaving a net charge on London's ratepayers of £1,757,180. The whole of the road-building works, including a tram subway, executed by the council's works department, were completed with remarkable celerity by October 1905.[170] The metropolitan body was showing itself capable of thinking imperially in a way that Victorian governments had never – the Embankment apart – ventured to do.

This bold and extensive project had aroused keen interest among architects.[171] In a further bold but impulsive step, the LCC's Improvements Committee invited eight architects,[172] some nominated by the council, some by the RIBA, to submit designs for the elevations of the new crescent and the widened Strand, Norman Shaw and the council architect, W.E. Riley, acting as assessors.[173] Unfortunately, there was a gulf between the LCC's notions and the architects': each architect treated the Aldwych and Strand frontages as comprehensive designs, whereas the council wanted 'a kind of fund to draw upon for street frontages'. This was to say nothing of leaseholders' attitudes: the LCC lacked powers to carry out the building work itself, and prospective tenants were unwilling to be inconspicuous units in a general design. Thus nothing came of what could have been a magnificent opportunity: 'Taking the collection as a whole, it is a very fine one, and a credit to the English architects of today.'[174] Just as Nash had been unable to impose a uniform architecture on Regent Street in the 1820s, so the LCC nearly a century later found itself lacking in capacity to impose uniformity in Aldwych.

Continuing to think imperially, the LCC had in 1909 offered the eastern horn of the Strand-Aldwych segment to the government of the recently-created Commonwealth of Australia as a location for that 'worthy memorial of the Commonwealth in the metropolis of the empire' that it needed.[175] The Commonwealth government sought to combine its need for representational accommodation 'with symbolic statement of the strength and stability, the wealth and importance of Australia as an Imperial unit'. Australia House [Pl. 20] had to 'harmonise in respect of balance and weight' with the Gaiety Theatre (by Ernest Runtz, with modifications by Norman Shaw) at the segment's western horn. Gibbs's and Wren's neighbouring churches are also said to have given 'a note to the design' by A.M. and A.G.R. Mackenzie, founded 'in the Roman architectural style' – so striking a symbolically imperial note – 'modified by such of the qualities of the French work of the eighteenth century as were regarded suitable', a curious design to symbolise the new Commonwealth.[176] Save for Australia House,[177] work

19. a. Kingsway-Aldwych. Plan. A long-contemplated north-south highway, planned by the London County Council in 1892 and executed in 1900–5.
b. Excavations in Kingsway, c. 1905.

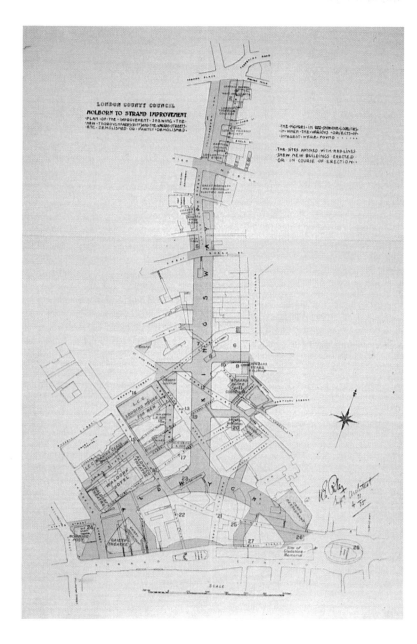

20. Australia House, Strand front, A.M. and A.G.R. Mackenzie, 1912–18. The embodiment of the new Commonwealth of Australia in the Empire's capital.

on Aldwych and Kingsway was interrupted by the First World War. The imperial note was maintained afterwards with Africa House (commercial premises, 1922) and India House (for the Indian High Commission, 1928–30), though finding its grandest expression in the office block of Bush House (1925–35) forming 'a fine point-de-vue' at the south end of Kingsway.[178]

'Thinking imperially' was necessary if London were to continue to hold up its head as a city worthy of its significance in the world. In the first place, London, although a relatively healthy city, showed little improvement in health between 1874 (when foreign cities were first included in the registrar-general's annual summaries) and 1890–1; whereas foreign capitals (no doubt starting from a higher death-rate) had markedly improved.[179] Secondly, traffic delays were notorious, and deaths and injuries from traffic accidents increasing.[180] Thirdly, in an age when international tourism was beginning its take-off into sustained growth, London needed new hotels, shopping streets and handsome public buildings. In Paris, the work of improvement had continued, if on a diminished scale, under the Third Republic, notably the Avénue de l'Opéra (1877) and the Boulevard Henri IV (1879); as well as the reconstruction, 1873–82, in a most opulent manner of the Hôtel de Ville [Pl. 21], ruined in 1871.[181]

21. Paris: Inauguration of the restored Hôtel de Ville (Théodore Ballu and Edouard Desperthes, 1873–82), reproducing the original sixteenth-century façade of the central block, but heightening the wings of 1837–46 and improving the internal planning, at a cost of more than 12,000,000 francs.

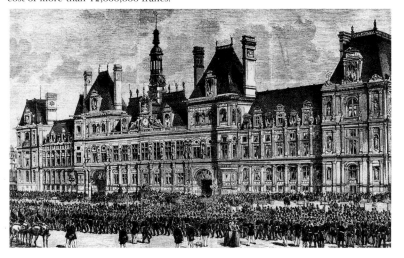

The resolution of the discord between the general vision of London in the final quarter of the nineteenth century as 'hideous' and completely wanting in 'rational human beauty'[182] and the desire to create a fitting imperial capital lay essentially, as the would-be town planner Arthur Cawston recognised, in funding. Cawston proposed graduated taxation in the form not only of an improvement rate but also of a death duty on land and buildings.[183] But death duties had just been seized upon by the Liberal chancellor Harcourt to raise national taxation, and a graduated local tax in addition to the rateable valuation, itself a sort of graduated tax, even if ineffectively so, was too daring an innovation. A milder solution, discussed by many municipal improvers, was a modification of the arrangements compensating property owners for the acquisition of their properties.

Generally speaking, the capital was left to fund its own road improvements. There were, however, two areas in which the government acknowledged a special responsibility: the Royal Parks and the approaches to the Houses of Parliament. The great chain of Royal Parks from Westminster to Kensington was proudly regarded as a metropolitan glory unrivalled in any other European capital. There were considerable pressures for relieving traffic congestion in western London by building roads across Hyde Park from north to south, and similarly across St James's Park. *The Times* pushed in 1856, printing variously-signed letters said all to have been written by the same man.[184] There was then no road from the Mall to Storey's Gate, and carriages were admitted only by special permission. Prince Albert, conscious of the increase in population both north and south of St James's Park, had realised that the public would require a route across it. He favoured 'the shortest route North and South' from Pall Mall running between St James's Palace and Marlborough House (the German Chapel, as Inigo Jones's chapel was then called, being removed) across St James's Park to Birdcage Walk.[185] Hall accordingly prepared plans which were submitted to a select committee in 1856. The *Daily News* and the *Sun* campaigned against the idea, *The Times* joining in with 'most offensive', 'perverted and incorrect' reports.[186]

Hall's proposals were mauled by the committee, that for the 'shortest route' being deflected along the Mall to the foot of Constitution Hill, and one for a road from Pall Mall to Storey's Gate on the line of the Duke of York's Steps being carried only by his casting vote[187] – and both were rejected decisively by the Commons.[188] The government then submitted much less expensive proposals, which the Commons accepted, for a footbridge across the ornamental water in St James's Park (despite the Tories making a party question of it, for fear that its evident utility would create a demand for a carriage road)[189] and a road through the palace garden, leaving the chapel untouched.[190] By November 1857 between twenty and thirty thousand persons were crossing the bridge daily.[191]

The pressure had then shifted to Hyde Park. Cowper as First Commissioner planned a new horse ride. Metropolitan MPs keen to win favour with popular constituencies seized upon it to attack a 'bloated aristocracy' making inroads on 'the solitude of thousands'.[192] Yet by 1862 he realised that the world was being invited to come to the International Exhibition at South Kensington without a road to get there: a route between Paddington station and the Exhibition site was essential. But exactly where it should cross Kensington Gardens or Hyde Park was an intransigent problem. Queen and Court took the view that the primary object of the Parks was 'to afford a place of exercise and recreation for the great body of the people'; even a temporary road from Victoria Gate to Queen's Gate would cut off Kensington Gardens from the whole of London by a stream of omnibuses and public carriages, and destroy Hyde Park as a pleasure park. The Queen sensibly proposed the use of the Broad Walk between Kensington Gardens and the palace. Feeling in and out of the Commons was very hot on the subject. A 'sentimental feeling about preserving inviolate' the 'quiet beauty and retirement' of the Gardens contributed to the general support for a road through Hyde Park, long contemplated by successive Works ministers, and advocated by the local authorities, the Society of Arts, and two leading articles in *The Times*.[193] What the ministry most dreaded was some metropolitan members' taking up the social argument (certain to be 'rife in penny papers'), against aristocratic privilege thrusting away the traffic 'to a place which is chiefly enjoyed by those who are too poor to ride or drive', in order to preserve unspoiled its own enjoyments in Rotten Row. 'There is no matter upon which the House of Commons is so difficult to deal with as Hyde Park and Kensington Gardens', declared Palmerston, 'because every man thinks he can form an opinion about them.' Assured that the ministry would be defeated on the alternative routes, the Queen gave way, informing Sir Charles Phipps, acting as her secretary, that he 'must tell Lord Palmerston that she reluctantly gives her consent but it must be made QUITE CLEAR that it is only temporary'.[194]

The Parks continued to exercise the minds of First Commissioners. In 1865 Cowper bemoaned his responsibility: 'The most opposite accusations may be expected such as that too much or too little money is spent on them – too much of the general taxation for the benefit of Londoners, or too little to render them places of beauty and enjoyment worthy of the Capital of the Empire. The latter accusation [he told the Queen's secretary] is the more frequent of the two particularly with people who have been to Paris and have been struck with the great pains that are taken to improve the Imperial Gardens and Parks.'[195] So impressed, indeed, was William Robinson, curator of the Royal Botanic Gardens at Kew, by the tree-lined boulevards and new parks of Haussmann's Paris that he published 'an admiring study . . . attempting to shame English authorities into action'.[196] Robinson looked for a central authority similar to Haussmann's that might make London 'the noblest city in the world'.[197]

Hyde Park Corner had become by 1874 one of the worst traffic blocks in the capital, and the MBW proposed a plan for realigning the roads. The Marquis of Westminster, a major property-owner in the district, put forward his own project, which involved taking part of the Park.[198] From 1862 the Victoria terminus of the London, Brighton & South Coast and the London, Chatham & Dover Railways provided a new focus for traffic and a main route to and from the Continent, which made Grosvenor Place and Park Lane an important north-south route. The Reform Riots of July 1866 demolished 1400 yards of the Park railings and immediately suggested to the new Conservative First Commissioner, Lord John Manners, the opportunity of widening Park Lane by taking in some 10 to 18 feet of the Park.[199] At the end of the first Gladstone administration, the Works minister, Adam, was considering the proposals of the MBW and the Marquis of Westminster. The cabinet decided that the time was unfavourable, because of serious arrears of public business and 'the inconvenience of proposing near the close of a Parliament a matter which is small and local yet not unlikely to excite many differences of opinion'; and also that the plan itself was inadequate.[200]

His Conservative successor, Lord Henry Lennox, lamented: 'The Want of a new road, to relieve the Traffic at the top of Grosvenor Place, has become very urgent, and the difficulty of planning one, is very great indeed.'[201] A major factor was the keeping Constitution Hill as a private road to Buckingham Palace. The Queen approved a scheme submitted by Lennox, involving a subway under Constitution Hill, and rejected the newly-created Duke of Westminster's alternative. A Vote of £5000 was made to start the works.

At this point 'insuperable objections' were found in the character of the embankment required, and Lennox substituted a cross-road on the level that could be closed from Constitution Hill by bars. He told a courtier, 'The clamour for a relief to the Block at Hyde Park Corner is so great that I dare not abandon, as I would willingly do, the idea of any infringement on the Park and I really think that the new scheme would be the one, which, would be the least inconvenient to Her Majesty.'[202] When the Queen expressed her dislike of a level crossing, Lennox offered to take the responsibility for doing nothing, as no other scheme could be managed. But opinion in the House, on both sides, demanded action, Gladstone adopted a threatening posture, and after discussion with the prime minister the Queen agreed to withdraw her objection. A Commons' debate was followed by a promise of immediate action from the chancellor of the Exchequer, but a comprehensive scheme had to be deferred in 1878 for want of funds. Noel, the then First Commissioner, took the plan to Lord Beaconsfield, who crushed it with a *bon mot*: 'Do away with the congestion of traffic at Hyde Park Corner? Why, my dear fellow, you would be destroying one of the sights of London!'[203]

The arrival of a new Liberal First Commissioner, Lefevre, in 1880, brought a new mind keen to secure a solution.[204] Lefevre believed that

> it is worth while, even with the merest utilitarian object, to do our best in our generation to render London as conspicuous as possible for the beauty and interest of its public buildings. It is the centre of our vast Empire; it is the point of contact for the whole of the Anglo-Saxon race. Its history and traditions are of unexampled interest. It has more buildings of the highest importance than any other city in the world, with the exception only of Rome.[205]

He determined to carry out the 'bold and sweeping' changes proposed by the Works some years previously [Pl. 22]. The 'very large expenditure' that had wrecked previous proposals continued to be a mountainous obstacle. Lefevre therefore looked elsewhere for funds. He hoped briefly to obtain help from a Pneumatic Railway Company, but its failure threw him back on the Treasury and the

23.   Burton's Arch, crowned by M.C. Wyatt's controversial equestrian statue of the Duke of Wellington, in its original position in line with the gates into Hyde Park.

22.   Hyde Park Corner. Plan of alterations proposed by the First Commissioner of Works, 1882, moving Decimus Burton's Arch from its position parallel to the Hyde Park Gate, so as to retain Constitution Hill as a royal route, while relieving traffic congestion by a new road for north-south traffic from Hamilton Place directly into Grosvenor Place.

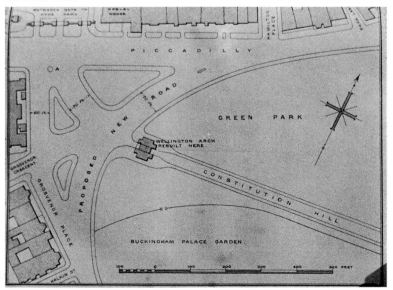

MBW, with some assistance from the Duke of Westminster.[206] Having secured the Queen's approval, and the support of the MBW and the prospect of a £20,000 subvention, Lefevre was then confronted by an intransigent Treasury, which refused any funding on the ground that the improvements were 'solely for the benefit of the metropolitan ratepayers'. This obstacle surmounted,[207] and cabinet approval obtained, Lefevre was urged by the premier 'in some way [to] get at the opinion of the public on the plan before it was finally decided upon'.[208] He had then to overcome not only rival proposals from the RIBA and Lord Elcho, but also opposition within the cabinet led by Gladstone – who had 'always desired a scheme on another basis'[209] – which caused the Queen temporarily to withdraw her sanction. In the autumn session Lefevre explained his proposals to the Commons, and won favourable comments from *The Times*.[210]

A crucial element was Decimus Burton's triumphal arch that stood at the top of Constitution Hill immediately opposite the Ionic Screen and gateway into Hyde Park [Pl. 23]. Since 1846 the arch had been surmounted by Matthew Wyatt's colossal and controversial equestrian statue of the Duke of Wellington.[211] The removal of the arch to a position further down Constitution Hill – essential for widening Grosvenor Place, where the worst traffic blocks occurred – inevitably required the removal of the statue, which took place in January–February 1883, the arch itself being taken down in March–April. A committee of experts recommended re-siting the statue opposite the Horse Guards, but public opinion was hostile when a wooden model was tried out, and it was ultimately given to the Army and re-erected at Aldershot. The new road was opened on 1 May 1883, the works having cost some £23,300.[212]

That, however, was not the end of the story. Favourable comment in the press there may have been,[213] but the traffic block was not annihilated, merely shifted to the debouchement of Hamilton Place on Piccadilly.[214] Lefevre was also criticised for his clumsy re-siting of Burton's arch, which necessitated one 'leg' longer than the other. But the immediate result seemed a success: 'What a pity that Mr Shaw Lefevre cannot be appointed to the much needed office of permanent aedile of this metropolis! . . . The reorganised Hyde-Park-corner – the Place Lefevre, as it might justly be called – is entirely due to him, and it would be well if it could be completed according to his recommendations', remarked one contemporary.[215]

Simultaneously Lefevre was planning the improvement of the second area in which the government was particularly concerned, the approaches to the Houses of Parliament. Under proposals drawn up by Lord John Manners's Treasury commission in 1866–8, which contemplated the eventual use of the block south of Scott's government offices bounded by Parliament Street and Great George Street, the government had gradually spent about £320,000 in buying up property there. Lefevre however was enacting a scheme for locating new offices to the north of the Scott block, so that the southern sector was disposable. As generation succeeded generation, the widening of Parliament Street remained an objective, and Lefevre now saw a means of achieving this metropolitan improvement through the local authority. He obtained Treasury authority to negotiate with the MBW for their purchasing the extensive government property in Parliament Street, 'upon the condition of their undertaking to widen the street and to secure the erection of suitable buildings along the new frontage'. The Treasury insisted that this 'highly desirable' project was not one on which public money should be spent 'either directly or indirectly or by selling Government property at less than its market value'. But it was too costly a project for the MBW, unless it could buy the government property at 'very much less than its cost price'. Impaled on this dilemma, Lefevre sought escape by dealing with the whole of the area westward of Parliament Street, mostly poor housing. Sir Henry Hunt, the government surveyor, thought that building new streets there could so improve the area that their frontages would recoup the cost of purchasing the whole

site at market value. This would involve extinguishing the ancient thoroughfare of King Street, already encroached on by Scott's Home Office [Pl. 124, 273].[216]

Here again, Lefevre collided with the prime minister's views. 'Your plan for the reconstruction in Parliament Street is what I may call the traditional one . . .', Gladstone told him. 'But I have long been in radical objection to the scheme of making one vast unit all along the Whitehall line, so that as the matter is now alive I have put my ideas roughly into form.' Gladstone identified three streams of traffic in Parliament Street: one going to the Houses of Parliament or along the river bank; a second seeking to cross to the Surrey bank; and that directed towards Victoria Street. The 'bridge' traffic he hoped might be siphoned off by a new bridge. For the Victoria Street traffic, King Street was the natural route, and should be improved, a far less expensive operation than Lefevre was proposing. An unaltered Parliament Street would then carry only traffic heading for Palace Yard [Pl. 24].[217]

Lefevre justifiably complained of the premier's technique of raising difficulties after the Treasury had given him the green light, he had negotiated successfully with the MBW, and the proposals had been published and 'most favourably commented upon by the Press'. He pointed out that it was the government's only possibility of realising the value of its investment in the district, 'now to a great extent lying idle'; and that relief of traffic was not the only consideration. 'It has been felt that since the widening of that part of [Parliament Street] in front of the Home Office its completion up to Parliament Square must almost necessarily follow; that thus widened the street would form a most noble approach to the Houses of Parliament and the Abbey, not surpassed in general effect in any city in Europe. Along the greater part of it the Abbey would be in full view.' He also condemned Gladstone's plan as financially unattractive, and impossible to carry through Parliament.[218]

The failure of government to resolve this question left the scene open for private enterprise. For some ten years any resolution was stultified by the legislative approval given to a private company to develop the area subject to its ability to raise the necessary finance.[219] In 1895, in order to take the land for new public offices that were urgently required, the government decided to oppose a bill renewing the company's powers, which was accordingly rejected (30 May 1895).[220] The Conservative administration that took over shortly afterwards developed its predecessor's ideas; a select committee that recommended a concentration of departments on the Parliament Street site[221] also heard evidence on traffic flows from a police superintendent.[222] The question of replanning Parliament Street was put off till the next session, although plans were appended shewing three choices for the layout [Pl. 137].

Duly re-appointed, the committee recommended in 1897 that Parliament Street be widened and King Street [Pl. 124] obliterated. But, 'in view of the great metropolitan improvement here to be carried out at the cost of the Government', the London County Council (which had by now replaced the MBW) should be invited to contribute to the cost. Herbert Gladstone battled for a version of his father's scheme to hive off the Westminster and Victoria traffic by dividing the street into two roadways, but won no support.[223] The committee's recommendation was promptly implemented by the government.

The RIBA took advantage of these proceedings to re-launch its own scheme for widening the north end of Whitehall originally proposed in connexion with Lefevre's new defence-ministries proposal. Their past president, John Macvicar Anderson, remarked that 'it seems a pity (to put it in the mildest form) to spend large sums of public money on public buildings and leave the principal

24. Parliament Square prior to the demolition of the old Law Courts in 1883. The octagonal tower of Soane's Courts on the extreme right flanks the railings and piers around Old Palace Yard, erected when Barry's proposal for a block of parliamentary offices was rejected about 1866.

approach to them in the miserable condition in which it now is'. He proposed to take 'an axial line from the centre of the National Gallery through the Nelson Monument, to move King Charles' Statue, and to align and widen [Whitehall] as far as the northern end of the Horse Guards'.[224] Although it would have been much cheaper to demolish the indifferent property on the east side of Whitehall than the expensive new banking houses on the west, Anderson insisted that 'you would lose the whole object', the aim being to 'make a wide central place straight down from Trafalgar-square, forming an access to the public offices of the country'. He was keen also to make the outlets from Trafalgar Square 'perfectly symmetrical', making an opening into the Mall from Charing Cross (the north end of Whitehall) balance Northumberland Avenue and 'get a vista from the Strand into the Mall'.[225] Expensive as this would be, Anderson declared that

> as a taxpayer, and I think that most taxpayers would take the same view, I would very much rather that public money should be spent upon what produces a worthy return than an unworthy one; . . . Trafalgar-square, is worthy of all the consideration that can be bestowed upon it. It is the finest site we have in London, and it is absolutely ruined just now by the egress from it to all our public buildings in Parliament-street. If what is proposed in our plan were carried out, I have no hesitation in saying it would be one of the finest things in London, or indeed in any principal city.[226]

Akers-Douglas, the Works minister, however, insisted that even if 'this is the sort of improvement which should be made by the nation rather upon Imperial grounds', it was also a metropolitan improvement, to which the capital's ratepayers ought to contribute.[227] Such a grand axial piece of town planning might be accomplished in a country nurtured on classical traditions – even in a small state like Bavaria – but it was beyond the imagination of the governors of the richest country in the world. The cost of rebuilding two private banks prohibited a noble scheme [Pl. 25].[228] Although it was not adopted, the RIBA plan is an interesting example of the reviving influence of classical concepts and 'Beaux-Arts' planning in British architecture of the end of the century, which was to find further expression in Brydon's design for new government offices in Parliament Street.[229]

Two royal jubilees contributed powerfully to the 'swelling act of

25.   Charing Cross. Drummond's Bank on the left, rebuilt in 1878, was a block to the development of the west side of Whitehall. Improvers wanted the heterogeneous buildings opposite cleared away, but that would not have straightened the street.

the imperial theme'. The very word 'Imperialism' was remarked upon in 1878 as having lately 'crept in amongst us'.[230] John Seeley's *The Expansion of England*, emphasising a consciousness of imperial unity, was published in 1883 and sold 80,000 copies within two years: a work that contemporaries saw as 'galvanising public opinion into a state of enthusiasm for imperial affairs'.[231] An Imperial Federation League was founded in 1884. Two years later, a Colonial and Indian Exhibition was held at South Kensington under the aegis of the Prince of Wales, who sought to give it permanent form, and initiated a scheme to perpetuate it to mark the forthcoming jubilee.[232] The fiftieth anniversary of Queen Victoria's accession, which fell in 1887, was celebrated under a Conservative government happy to exploit the new imperialistic enthusiasm evidenced among the people at large. The Queen was unusually visible to her people, driving, for example, into the East End to open the People's Palace. A great naval review at Spithead marked the apogee of Britain's power, and colonial premiers from three continents gathered in London. On Jubilee Day itself, the Queen drove in state to Westminster Abbey preceded by the world's envoys and a conspicuous cohort of Indian princes.[233]

As the principal memorial of her jubilee, Queen Victoria favoured the idea of a permanent imperial exhibition at South Kensington. The 1851 Commissioners were able to provide a site of nearly six acres lying across the centre of the Royal Horticultural Society's former garden [Pl. 26], thereby destroying any prospect (as the *Survey of London* points out) of 'developing any north-south scenic axis' between the Natural History Museum and the Albert Hall.[234] With money being raised by public subscription, a limited competition was held for an 'Imperial institute', though the instructions were somewhat vague as the precise functions of such a building had not finally been determined. The Institute's charter defined its functions essentially as educative, fostering the economic development and promoting the cohesion of the empire. Collcutt's highly picturesque and very grand structure [Pl. 189] proved to be not financially viable for its original purpose, and in 1899 part was made over to the University of London in place of its outgrown quarters in Burlington Gardens.[235]

In the decade between the jubilees, imperial sentiment deepened.[236] An increasing number of propagandist institutions was set up. Newspapers, from the *Pall Mall Gazette* to the mass-circulation *Daily Mail*, founded in 1896, preached the imperial theme. London's claims as an imperial city ranking with Rome and Paris were firmly asserted, and doubters trounced, despite complaints of official inadequacy.[237] The Diamond Jubilee of 1897 was celebrated with even greater pageantry. The Queen was persuaded to follow precedents dating back to Queen Anne, and drive in state to St Paul's, although she did not actually enter the cathedral [Pl. 27]. The crowds in London were 'indescribable', the cheering 'quite deafening'.[238] Reginald Brett, as Secretary of the Office of Works, was responsible for the organisation, and was enthusiastically praised by W.T. Stead, editor of the imperialistic *Pall Mall Gazette*: 'The Jubilee was a great success, an epoch-point marking in a manner known and understood of all men the coming into consciousness of our Royal and Imperial democracy'.[239] No fewer than eleven colonial premiers met in conference, though their doing so revealed how little support there was for any concept of Imperial federation.[240] Nevertheless, London was the capital of the world's greatest empire, one that many public men believed should 'lead the world in the arts of civilisation'.[241] That London's streets and public buildings should be worthy of this role was one aspect of this creed.

The structure of the late-Victorian press – the concentration of ownership, and the centralisation in London of production, particularly of periodicals – gave London a high profile in the increas-

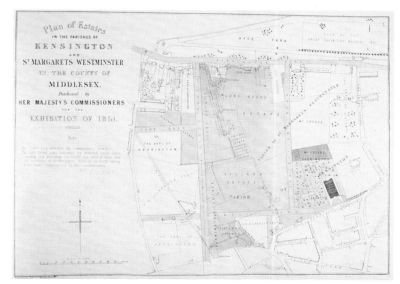

26. South Kensington. General plan of the estate bought by the Commissioners of the 1851 Exhibition out of their profits.

27. Centre of Empire: the Diamond Jubilee Service outside St Paul's, 1897.

ingly commercial atmosphere of the end of the century, when papers needed to deploy their resources frugally. Dr Garside has suggested that London's huge population, its high level of newspaper purchase, and its metropolitan character ensuring a continuous supply of newsworthy events and information 'would favour a rise in press coverage of London while depressing critical analysis of its role and function'.[242] In her study of *The Times*, *Telegraph*, and *Daily Chronicle* in 1873, 1889 and 1910, she found 'an absence of any promotion of the capital in terms of its local, national or international power or dominance. There is virtually no "boosterism", more a low key, affectionate even self-deprecating account.' 'Even the *Illustrated London News*, "the great illustrated news magazine of the time directed at an educated readership", treated the capital as simply one place among many.'[243]

No such physical memorial as the Imperial Institute was built in consequence of the Diamond Jubilee. But when Queen Victoria died on 22 January 1901 various ideas were immediately floated for a national memorial.[244] A committee was very quickly gathered,

which decided that the national memorial should be in London, of an architectural character, but not utilitarian, and should include an effigy of the Queen. Subscriptions would be invited from all quarters.[245] With remarkable celerity a small executive committee was appointed with Lord Esher, Secretary of the Works, as secretary, which adopted a plan drawn up by 'a young and talented draughtsman', Richard Allison of the Office of Works, for moving the carriageway in the Mall towards the south, forming a wide *place* in front of Buckingham Palace with a seated statue of the queen in the centre, and a triumphal arch at the eastern, Trafalgar Square end of the Mall. The King approved.[246] A public meeting at the Mansion House launched the scheme, and five architects were invited to prepare competition designs.

Thomas Brock was chosen to design the sculpture, which was approved three months later, along with Aston Webb's plan for the general treatment of the space in front of the palace [Pl. 28], the

28. Queen Victoria Memorial. Design for the architectural surroundings to Brock's Queen Victoria Memorial statue, and plan of the Mall modified as a grand processional route. Aston Webb, 1903. Perspective by T. Raffles Davison (1853–1937). (*Royal Academy*)

29. a. View from Trafalgar Square towards Spring Gardens, from which the Mall could be reached on foot. Drummond's Bank is the building behind the lamp-post.

29. b. View from the same angle after construction of the Admiralty Arch, showing processional route along the Mall to the Queen Victoria Memorial and Buckingham Palace.

rest of the programme being postponed until the outcome of the subscription was known.[247] The formal contract with Brock was concluded in June 1902, after the King had approved his model; and Webb began work in July 1903. Subscriptions totalled £323,609. Parliament had allocated £100,000 for additions to the Admiralty,[248] which were combined with the eastern triumphal archway, a means of achieving the long-desired opening into the Mall from Charing Cross [Pl. 29]. The necessary land purchases and road-works, defined as a metropolitan improvement, had already been funded by appropriating the invested surplus from the formation of Battersea Park, a neat escape from the persistent tension between ratepayer and taxpayer.[249]

In a report of its entire proceedings published in 1991, the Memorial Committee stated: 'An attempt has been made on a large scale to treat a public memorial in an architectonic spirit, and under the auspices and largely at the initiative of King Edward the Memorial and its surroundings may be said to be the first example

in recent times of Town Planning in the Metropolis.'[250] Together with what Esher called 'a galaxy of public offices stretching from . . . Parliament Street to St James' Park', the whole formed 'a far-reaching and magnificent series of London improvements'. At the western end of London's new great processional way, the surplus of the memorial fund was just enough to refront the decaying early-Victorian façade of Buckingham Palace in an appropriately palatial if somewhat uninspired *dixhuitième* design, again by Webb, a fine backcloth to the memorial statue.[251] Thus from the Palace to Charing Cross was achieved what Akers-Douglas called 'one of the finest additions ever made to the appearance of London':[252] the result of a new co-operation between government, municipality, and the private citizen, both at home and overseas, wholly appropriate, for, as the professional press often proclaimed: 'London is not the mere town of Londoners; it is the heart and soul of England, and the joy of all English-speaking peoples, and it ought to be so cherished'.[253]

3
The Case for Public Buildings

THE ARGUMENTS for new public buildings were both practical and aesthetic. Many departments were accommodated wholly or in part in rented houses built for family living in the normal vertical London manner: they were expensive to hire [Table 1, p. 31] and expensive to maintain, both structurally and in terms of house-keeping.[1] The Treasury, partly in a specially-designed building by William Kent[2] and partly in the surrounding congeries of old buildings, described in 1888 as 'a rambling rabbit warren', was typical [Pl. 30]:

> The ground floor contained a few really good rooms, including the famous Board Room . . . reserved for the heaven-born, but most of the staff lived in dens and holes, some in the basement, some in remote attics, some at the end of long passages or dark staircases. If a senior officer wished to see one of his juniors . . . the usual procedure was to put in a ferret in the shape of a messenger to find out if that particular rabbit was in his burrow and bolt him. If one young rabbit wished to commune with another young rabbit, he had to track him as best he could through the labyrinth.[3]

Somewhat untypically, this state of affairs survived into the mid twentieth century, thanks largely to the Treasury's 'wilful, and even conceited, addiction to false economies':[4] 'the lair of My Lords of the Treasury still [1937] remains the most inconvenient building for the dispatch of business that the wit of man could devise'.[5]

Working conditions were not quite as bad in the neighbouring Old Foreign Office, formerly two large and two smaller private houses [Pl. 31–2], where 'some of the rooms were comfortable enough in their way – far more so, indeed, than those in the new building – still, they were most inconveniently arranged. . . . The Secretary of State in going from his own room to the Cabinet Room

31. Downing Street, 1834, with the Colonial Office at the far end, and the Foreign Office on the left (drawn by John Buckler).

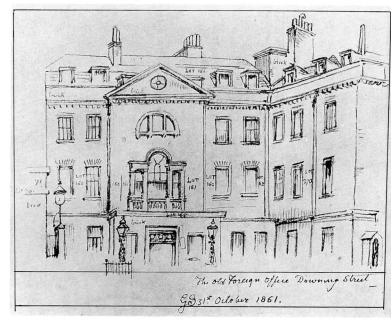

32. The Old Foreign Office, marked up for auction of building materials prior to demolition, October 1861. Drawing by George Scharf.

30. The Old Treasury Building, William Kent, 1733–6, stands between the backs of Barry's Home Office (1846) to the left, and no. 10 Downing Street. To the extreme left, Dover House (west front rebuilt by Holland, 1787). Stands erected for guests at the Trooping of the Colour emphasise the imperial significance of this area.

had to pass through two rooms occupied by other persons.'[6] Structurally, the building was in poor shape. In 1839 a select committee had judged it and the adjoining Colonial Office as 'inadequate to the present extent of public business, [and] in parts unsafe'.[7] Plans were in fact prepared for the rebuilding by Decimus Burton [Pl. 117], but the government's inadequate finances barred action. Palmerston, who had ruled in the Foreign Office from 1830 to 1834, 1835 to 1841 and 1846 to 1851, reported to the Commons in 1855 that: 'The floors were propped up, the houses really were in a very dangerous state, it was necessary to keep in the kitchens and cellars books which ought to be accessible in the upper rooms, and very great inconvenience was experienced every day in consequence of the dilapidated condition of the building.'[8] One of his successors, Lord Malmesbury, could confirm the truth of his statements, for a few days after his appointment, in February 1852, 'the ceiling came down upon the table' at which he wrote, just after he had left the room.[9]

Even more at risk was life in the War Office buildings in Pall Mall [Pl. 33]. Cumberland House (1760s) and adjoining houses (nos. 83–7, consec.) had been bought for the Ordnance Office in 1806–10 and enlarged by Pennethorne in 1850–1; close by, Soane's Buckingham House (no. 91) was acquired in 1855 for the seat of the newly-created secretary of state for War; and the intervening three houses, nos. 88–90 (consec.) added in 1859:[10] 'an Ordnance Department, a private house, shops, and all kinds of buildings pushed together into one', 'thrown together by the single process of making doors in the walls between them'; a maze of 'dark and mildewed passages' [Pl. 34]; 'a slow machine patched up in parts, worn out in others, creaking along to the best of its power on lines that have never been properly laid'.[11] The secretary of state, under-secretary, and assistant under-secretary all died within a few

months of each other in 1861–2, 'and there can be little doubt that a contributory cause, if not the chief cause was the awful sanitary condition of the War Office'.[12]

The courtier Sir Thomas Biddulph reported to the Queen in June 1875 that he had called at the War Office by request of the commander-in-chief, whose accommodation was 'most inadequate and unhealthy'; 170 officials were crammed into space sufficient only for a quarter of that number. Two military secretaries and two deputy adjutants-general had died 'perhaps not directly from the unhealthiness of the building, but probably being delicate men their health has been injured by the bad air. The Clerks and people of a lower grade constantly complain.' Despite being assured by Mr Secretary Hardy (1814–1906)[13] that 'the bad *smells* (which are said again *now* to be quite awful) were caused by new carpets!!' her Majesty insisted that Dr Jenner (her own physician) and another sanitary expert should inspect, and report to her.[14] The *Pall Mall Gazette* carried a report from the *Sanitary Record* that the Office was built on a 'system of undrained cesspools' from which sewage probably percolated through the brickwork; the greater part of the basement floor was impregnated. 'In one room all the clerks complain greatly of lassitude and inability to continue their work, and the former chief clerk in the room died some time ago of typhoid fever.'[15] Jenner[16] and a colleague, 'very high medical authorities', duly inspected and declared that its defects were inherent to the structure, and could not 'be so effectually remedied as to render possible the retention of the present War Office';[17] though Hardy and his under-secretary thought it no more unwholesome than even the new offices.[18]

'The experience which the past few years have afforded in the substitution of new and costly buildings for the old Public Offices has not been of a kind to produce the most complete confidence

33. The Old War Office, Pall Mall. The pedimented house nearest the camera is the surviving two-thirds of Schomberg House, 1698, taken for War Office use in 1859, with the two-bay house immediately to the left (east), erected in 1850; the adjoining three-bay building is Pennethorne's Ordnance Office, 1850–1. Further left are the lodges of Brettingham's Cumberland House, 1760–3 (built for Edward, Duke of York). Continuing eastwards, nos. 88–90 Pall Mall (the central house formerly the office of the Globe Insurance Co.) were taken over by the War Office in 1859; and finally Soane's Buckingham House, of seven bays (six visible on second floor), 1792–5 for the first Marquess of Buckingham, acquired for the War Office in 1855.

34.   The Old War Office, Pall Mall:
a. One of the maze of corridors.
b. Head of principal staircase, Buckingham House, Soane, 1792–5.

that a new building must necessarily afford improved Sanitary conditions and greater convenience for the transaction of public business', declared a Treasury minute initialled by W.H. Smith (1825–91), the financial (political) secretary, no doubt after a chat with Hardy. 'My Lords are therefore of opinion that the greatest possible care and deliberation will be required before it is finally determined to abandon the existing War Office.' Works about to be undertaken would, it was hoped, 'for some time to come afford sufficient and healthy accommodation for the staff'. Smith conceded that 'under any circumstances structural facilities for the conduct of public business' in Pall Mall could 'not be entirely satisfactory', and that it would be necessary 'to consider the propriety of erecting a new Office', for which the only sufficiently large site currently available was the 'Fife House' site. 'It will be for H.M. Government to determine whether the urgency of the case is so great as to require that that site shall be appropriated for the War Department.'[19]

Such complacency was followed by a severe outbreak of typhoid fever, justifying *The Times*'s comment that 'employment in the War Office, in consequence of the sickness and mortality attending it, should rank in point of danger at about the same level as an Ashantee campaign'.[20]

Although the principal offices were in Pall Mall, the War Department's business was carried on in eleven different places, 'having separate establishments of clerks and officers, amounting altogether to 498, and varying in number from two to 160 at the several establishments'. Twenty years earlier, it had seemed to Sir Charles Trevelyan (1807–86) of the Treasury the most pressing

case of all: 'The existing disintegration . . . is full of evil and trouble. . . . Other departments are cut in half, but this is broken into numerous fragments, and the head is at a distance from them all . . . a standing cause of inefficiency, of expense and of inferior work. It is impossible that the establishment can be reduced, or the proper arrangements can be made for the speedy transaction of the business, until the numerous separate offices . . . are consolidated.'[21] The doomed under-secretary, Sir Benjamin Hawes (1797–1862), graphically described the consequences to a select committee in 1858: 'papers are in confusion; we have messengers running about with papers every hour in the day. The Assistant Chief Examiner, for example, who is now at the Horse Guards, wishes to see me; he comes up; I am engaged; he waits; perhaps he goes away; I then send and say I am at leisure; he is down again at the Horse Guards; and thus very often a day is lost altogether.'[22] Twenty years later, little had changed: Mr Secretary Hardy, despite his complacency about health hazards, said he 'could not conceive a more inconvenient office, or one that put a Secretary of State to greater disadvantage'.[23] Another 15 years on, a senior Treasury man minuted: 'No argument is needed to prove that a new W.O. is required – the present one, a mere collection of old houses stitched together with several passages and stairs, is probably the worst Public Office in the world, and is very costly both in the way of casual repairs, and because of the vast number of messengers &c employed.'[24] In 1886–7, with no new buildings, the War Office employed 164 messengers out of a total staff of 958 officials.[25]

The other great defence department, the Admiralty, had suf-

35. The Horse Guards, W. Kent and J. Vardy, 1750–8, seen from the Parade. This side of the building was generally admired by the Victorians. Until 1872 the office of the commander-in-chief occupied part of the central block.

fered similarly from being housed principally in two widely-separated locations: the Admiralty building in Whitehall [Pl. 36] and the Navy Office at Somerset House. The Admiralty had been built as a group of private houses for the lords commissioners, with a splendid room for their meetings. Sir James Graham's reforms in 1832 made the junior lords each responsible for a department at Somerset House, so that they had to go from the Admiralty in a cab at least once a day 'to do business there for a short time, and then to come back to other business which had to be transacted at Whitehall'.[26] Of the conversion of the Admiralty houses into offices, when the Navy Office was brought to Whitehall in 1868, a sometime Chief Clerk of the Admiralty, Sir J.H. Briggs, remarked in 1892:

> I can bring my personal testimony to bear as to the ill effects it has upon the health of the Government *employés*, which is chiefly due to the want of those sanitary arrangements that cannot, from their construction, be expected in buildings erected for the use of private families. Nothing can be more fatal to health, efficiency, discipline, and comfort than the makeshift system pursued twenty-five years ago, and which exists, to some extent, to this very hour.[27]

The effect of these conditions on the health of employees is easily comprehended, but, as Briggs observed, efficiency suffered too. A royal commission examining the civil service criticised in 1887 the 'miserably inadequate accommodation, and the multiplicity of small rooms', contributing to the excessive numbers of higher-grade clerks employed in the War Office, with work 'being done under conditions which are unfavourable from any point of view, sanitary or otherwise, to its being well done'. 'These observations', the commissioners remarked, 'apply with equal force to the Admiralty buildings' – and, they might well have observed, to the Board of Trade [Pl. 37] and other important departments.[28]

It is clear enough, then, what the Victorians considered to be bad public offices. What did they want to substitute for these ill-adapted private houses [Pl. 38, 46] and worn-out structures? On the one hand were those who argued that government offices were merely factories for the production of documents for the most part ephemeral; any conditions that were not positively unhealthy might serve. On the other, were those who believed that government buildings performed a representational function, necessitating a degree of dignity – which touches on the aesthetic factor considered below.[29] But this involved the risk of civil servants getting above themselves.[30] Yet others might not look for imperial character, but nevertheless recognised that the growth of 'collectivism', as Gladstone and Dicey termed it, or the substitution of dynamic for static administration, as modern historians describe it,[31] required purpose-built accommodation which would enable

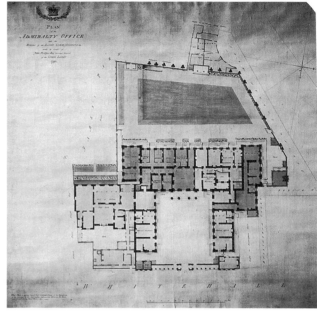

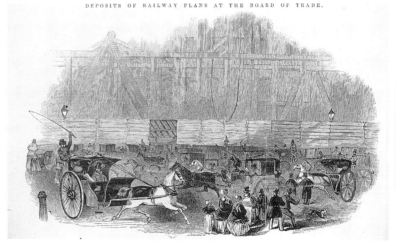

DEPOSITS OF RAILWAY PLANS AT THE BOARD OF TRADE.

37.   Pressure of business at the Board of Trade, Whitehall:
a (above). In Whitehall, 30 November 1845, the last day for the delivery of railway
bills for consideration by Parliament in the ensuing session.
b (below). The Railway Bill Office, November 1845.

36.   The Old Admiralty:
a (top left). From Whitehall, Thomas Ripley 1722–6. The proportions of Ripley's
building were commonly condemned, and Robert Adam's screen was built in 1759–61
to hide its demerits.
b (top right). The Old Admiralty: Plan, 1792. The Admiralty lords lived in the wings;
in the central block was the boardroom.
c. (above). A room in one of the former Admiralty residences, converted to an office.

bureaucrats to function more efficiently, i.e. with fewer numbers
and at less expense – increasingly so, as governments hired more
and more private houses, and rental values in convenient locations
were high, so that the argument for buying and building as against
leasing became a convincing one (Table 1). It is perhaps significant that it was two Radicals who, as successive Works' ministers in
the 1850s, pushed forward the building of new public offices,
representing greater efficiency and hence cheaper government:
Sir William Molesworth [Pl. 71] and Sir Benjamin Hall [Pl. 71].

From the instructions to a long series of architectural competitions, two key factors that emerge are light and air. The old riddle:
'Why are clerks in public offices like the fountains in Trafalgar
Square? – Because they play from ten till four', serves to remind us
of their dependence on good light – preferably natural light – in a
regime that largely consisted in reading hand-writing and then

38. a. Reception of a deputation in the President's room, Board of Trade offices, Whitehall, 1845.
38. b. Pembroke House, Privy Gardens, Whitehall, Sir W. Chambers, 1759–60: First floor state room used as office by the Board of Trade, c. 1929.

Table 1. *Rents*[1] *paid for public offices by the Office of Works, at three-year intervals*

Year	£
1852/3	6,713
1855/6	19,773
1858/9	22,587
1861/2	24,748
1864/5	25,238
1867/8	28,100
1870/1	36,946
1873/4	37,988
1876/7	40,977
1879/80	38,143[2]
1882/3	43,377
1885/6	43,791
1888/9	42,338
1891/2	45,767
1894/5	50,262
1897/8	53,292
1900/1	92,761
1903/4	124,949
1906/7	119,948
1909/10	89,230
1912/13	95,850

Notes: 1. 'Rents' include insurance and tithe charges.
2. From this time, caretakers' wages no longer charged under 'rents'. The charge in 1879/80 was £2018.
Source: PP, Appropriation Accounts.

copying it, or computing hand-written figures. Good candles were expensive; gas gave off too much heat and offensive smells; as late as 1884, a civil-service newspaper pondering plans for a new ministry was primarily concerned with good natural light, and secondly with adequate ventilation.[32] Square rooms lighted from the side were considered best [Pl. 63]. Corridors should have rooms on only one side, so as to have windows on the other:[33] an arrangement possible on a limited site only if either there were a number of inner courts, or the building were raised to five or six storeys – a feature inadmissible before the acceptance of lifts for human conveyance. The location of staircases was important, particularly for the great number of junior clerks and messengers who had to wait on their seniors: best at the corners of blocks, so as to give access to the corridors running at right angles.

Senior officials expected rooms to themselves; juniors seem to have preferred some company.[34] Less popular within the departments was the concept of the very large room where a dozen or twenty or even more copying clerks would labour away under a supervisor's eye: a plan much recommended by businessmen in parliament and reforming ministers. 'We strongly recommend', declared the commissioners inquiring into Civil Establishments (1887), 'that in building the new War Office ... arrangements should be made for an introduction of the system which prevails in Banks and other Mercantile houses of concentrating a number of clerks in large rooms. Supervision would thus be much better effected, and by fewer hands.'[35] The 'lady typewriter' appears only at the end of the nineteenth century,[36] the 'typing pool' still later, and the open-plan office was a concept imported from America that, with the rare exception, the civil service experienced only after the end of our period.[37] A board room, or room for the reception of deputations was considered necessary [Pl. 38], and waiting rooms; libraries and a cabinet room (in the Foreign and War offices); but the committee rooms demanded by the modern bureaucrat do not appear, save for a conference room in the Consular department (1856).[38] The space standards targeted were by modern calculations ample, even generous (Table 2), and a room 25 × 20 ft for a senior official might well then have sufficed even for a meeting of the small number of departmental heads of that time.

The question, however, was not merely one of replacing individual buildings. The argument that administrative efficiency demanded a concentration of the public offices – necessarily in purpose-built accommodation – was perhaps first put forward by Sir Charles Trevelyan [Pl. 39], assistant (i.e. permanent) secretary to the Treasury 1840–59. He conceived a vast new range of government offices, concentrating the work of administration close to the Houses of Parliament so that ministers and their officials could constantly be in close contact, and communication facilitated between the various departments: creating the necessary infrastructure for the reformed civil service recommended by him and Stafford Northcote in their famous *Report*.[39] His ideas probably grew out of the administrative hurly-burly experienced in the Crimean War.[40] Proposals to build a new range of government offices designed by the official architect, Pennethorne, starting with the Foreign Office, ran into parliamentary opposition in 1855 (see below, p. 117), but a new public works minister, Sir Benjamin Hall, exploited a promise of a select committee on the project to provide a platform for Trevelyan and bring forward an even more

39. Sir Charles Edward Trevelyan (1807–86), assistant secretary (i.e. permanent secretary) to the Treasury, 1840—59; reformer of the civil service, and strenuous advocate of the concentration of departments in purpose-built offices in Whitehall.

sensational scheme.[41] One of only two witnesses, Trevelyan declared that he had 'long formed a very decided opinion that, next to the appointment of proper officers, the thing most conducive to the public service will be to have proper offices'.

The high cost of renting old houses (Table 1) was itself a good reason for providing the state with its own purpose-built property. In 1854, Trevelyan and Northcote in their report on the Office of Works had pointed out that:

> The sum now paid for the rents of offices represents an annual interest of a capital of more than £500,000. We are induced to believe that a much less sum than this would be sufficient to provide for the erection of a range of offices capable of containing the whole of the departments now in want of accommodation. Such offices would be less expensive and troublesome to keep in order than the detached and unsuitable premises now in use. There would be no waste of room in them. They might be so contrived as to bring several departments which are in relation to one another into close neighbourhood, and so facilitate the transaction of business between them. They would prove advantageous to the public, who are frequently obliged to go from one department to another, at considerable inconvenience. They might be made to include a common library, common waiting-rooms, a common staff of office-keepers and housekeepers, and many other advantages, which, though apparently trivial in detail, would in gross be productive of a large saving.[42]

Table 2. *Standards of accommodation in public offices*

1867			1867		1968
Rooms for	Area in Ft	Sq Ft per head	Rank		Sq Ft per head
Officers sitting by themselves					
1 Officer	25 × 20	500			
2 Officers	22 × 20	440			
3 Officers	20 × 20	400			
4 Officers	18 × 16	288	Assistant Sec.		200–250
5 Officers	16 × 14	224	Principal		150–200
Clerks					
2 Clerks	18 × 18	162	Senior Executive		120–150
3 Clerks	20 × 18	120	Higher Executive		100–120
4 Clerks	24 × 18	108	Executive		75–90
Copying & Account Clks					
8 Clerks	27 × 20	66.6			
12 Clerks	40 × 20	66	Clerical Officers		55–65
20 Clerks	60 × 20	60	Typists		40–60

Sources: 1867: *PP* 1868 (281-I) LXVIII *Report of Sub-Committee of [Treasury] Commission for Concentration of the Public Offices*, p. 3.
1968: *The Civil Service. Vol. 4: Factual Statistical and Explanatory Papers: Evidence submitted to the Committee under the Chairmanship of Lord Fulton 1966–68* (1968), p. 650.

Trevelyan now, in 1856, estimated rents for public offices at nearer £30,000 a year than the earlier figure of £15,000 a year on which the capital sum of £500,000 had been calculated.[43]

In respect of inter- and intra-departmental efficiency, Trevelyan thought that concentration would mean that 'the business will not only be cheaper done, but it will be much better done'. The time of officials 'continually going . . . in hackneycabs' between one branch and another would be saved. The substitution of personal for written communication (often conducted between two or more branches of the same establishment) would familiarise departments with one another, create 'more of a common understanding', establish 'a better division of labour', and show that 'the same thing is done better in one place than another, and the better plan will be adopted'.[44] For the proper division of labour between his recommended intellectual and mechanical classes of work, the rooms must be apportioned accordingly: 'for the intellectual work separate rooms are necessary, so that a person who works with his head may not be interrupted; but for the more mechanical work, the working in concert of a number of clerks in the same room under proper superintendence, is the proper mode of meeting it'.[45] This would diminish the amount of space required and make both classes more efficient. 'The general scheme of accommodation required for an office is, that first of all there should be one or two central rooms, the floors of which should be well strengthened,

40. The Whitehall Quarter, c. 1855, redrawn from plans in *PP* 1854–55, VII; 1862, VII; and 1864, XXXII.

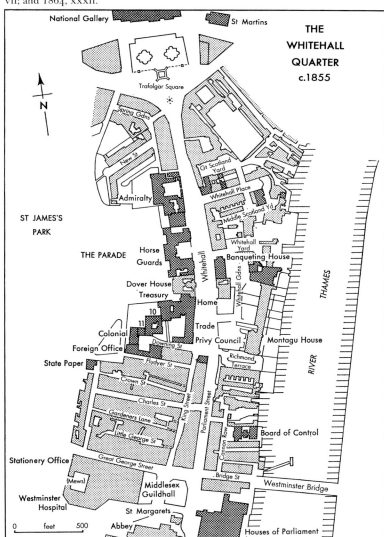

because great weights are placed in them, for the registry, and paper, and book department of the office; that is the heart of the office, through which the circulation takes place. Then there should be one or two large rooms for copyists; those also should be as central as possible', so that the copyists would be all brought together, as in the new arrangement at the Board of Trade, which was being repeated at the Treasury. The consolidation of departmental pay offices into that of the Paymaster-general had saved £40,000 a year in salaries alone.

First of all must come a new War Office. The War Department in 1856 was accommodated, as we have seen, in a congeries of buildings in Pall Mall, as well as in the Horse Guards, three houses in different streets south of Downing Street, five houses in streets east of Whitehall, a pair of houses lying north-west of the Admiralty, and two in other parts of Westminster, a total of 17 separate offices [Pl. 40].[46] Inigo Jones's 'original designs of Whitehall Palace' [Pl. 41] should, Trevelyan suggested, be made use of to build wings north and south of the Banqueting House from Whitehall to the river. The Admiralty might be rebuilt on its existing site and the adjoining Spring Gardens, while a vast block, 'a lofty and handsome range of buildings', running south from Downing Street to Great George Street, and west from King Street to the Park, would house the remainder, arranged in groups around their principal offices – Treasury, Home Office, Board of Trade, and so on. The demolition of the Horse Guards [Pl. 35], then occupied by the commander-in-chief (it being 'of great consequence that the military administration should be brought under the immediate view and control of the financial and civil administration'), would throw open the Banqueting House to the Park.[47]

Questioned whether there was any need to concentrate the revenue departments with the Treasury [Pl. 30], Trevelyan insisted on the advantages to be gained:

> You may see it stated daily in the *Times*, that Sir Thomas Fremantle, Mr John Wood, and other gentlemen have been wasting their time in going to and fro between the Custom House and Somerset House and the Treasury; and then there is the correspondence, a great part of which would be saved; the clerks who are now employed in carrying on that voluminous correspondence, giving full details of everything, might be reduced, or be employed on really useful business. The principle on which we proceed is, that everything comes up to us complete, fully stated, like a lawyer's brief. In the majority of cases, a few words, or at most ten minutes' conversation, would prevent all that; and then we should become familiarly acquainted with the business, and they would know what our wishes and intentions were. Above all, we should obtain such knowledge of the establishments superintended by us that we should be able to select the ablest of the officers possessed of practical experience of the different branches of the revenue to fill the permanent situations at the Treasury, without which the security for good administration which arises from efficient superintendence, cannot exist.[48]

Although there had been a great increase in the business of the public offices in late years, with a corresponding increase in the number of public servants, Trevelyan thought that proper attention to administrative details, of which concentration of departments was the most important, might counteract that growth, 'operations which, while they facilitate the transaction of business, tend also in a very great degree to diminish the number of persons required to perform it'. That this was not an idle hope was shown by the reduction of numbers in the Treasury as a result of 'getting rid of unnecessary business, and introducing simple and more expeditious modes of transacting that which remained'.[49]

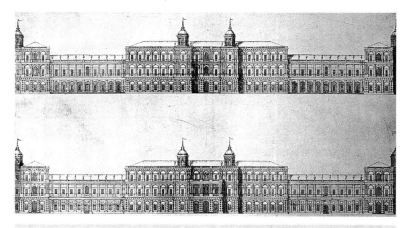

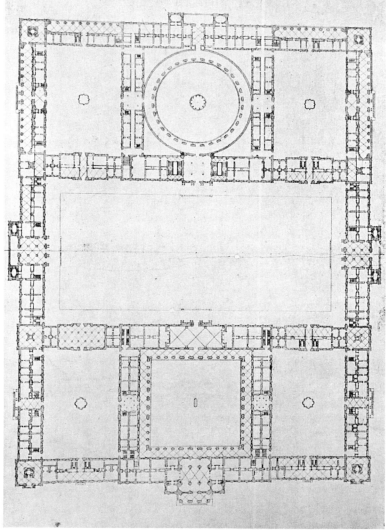

41. Whitehall Palace, Inigo Jones.
a. East and West elevations. These designs were highly regarded by the Victorians, and frequently recommended as the basis for new government offices.
b. One of a number of plans by Inigo Jones, incorporating the Banqueting House. J.M. Brydon borrowed the great circular court as the central feature of his New Public Offices, Great George Street, 1899, cp. Pl. 266.

42. 'Treasury Buildings', Whitehall, c. 1860. Charles Barry re-cast Soane's Privy Council and Board of Trade Offices in 1845–46, raising them a storey. At the same time, he rebuilt the adjoining Home Office to match. The whole works cost £45,000, but the increased accommodation saved £2250 p.a. in rents.

This was an appealing argument to Victorian politicians who had yet to come to terms with the inexorable growth of state activity and the steady increase in the number of public officers, so that the demand for accommodation was constantly outstripping the supply of purpose-built premises. Used to the administration of the country being carried on by small numbers, they objected to the great expansion in personnel between, say, 1840 and 1856; although it was of course the readiness of parliament to confer new duties on departments that was responsible for the increase. Thus, in 1830 the Education Department did not exist. In 1840 its business was done by an assistant secretary and a clerk, with the help of two clerks on the staff of the Council Office, of which the Educational Department formed a new limb. In 1856, in contrast, it consisted of 50 officers in London, some 10 or 15 temporary copyists, and 41 inspectors. The development of a national prisons system under the Home Office from 1846 saw a similar growth from the two officials dealing with convict hulks in 1840 to 18 in 1856. The Board of Trade [Pl. 42], responsible for overseeing the new railways among its multifarious functions [Pl. 37], had grown from 28 persons in 1840 to 82 in 1856, and its dependent departments, such as the Registry of Merchant Seamen, had likewise more than doubled, while new dependent offices, such as the Registry of Joint Stock Companies, had been created.[50]

Such increases were a part of the new government dynamic. As early as 1883 Goschen, who had headed the Poor Law Board and the Admiralty in Gladstone's first administration, had noticed the keenness of the new breed of civil servants (entering by competitive examination) 'for adding field after field to the regions in which they labour'. It was true, he remarked, that public demand for the action of central agencies had contributed to government's taking over much that previously had been left to local and private enterprise, but 'the stimulus came also from the departments'.[51] It is, however, difficult to calculate precise total numbers of civil servants, because of changes in the compilation of statistics: for example, post office staff are not always included.[52] Figures for headquarters offices are more comprehensible. Thus by 1904, the Board of Trade proper employed 148 civil servants, apart from messengers and office-keepers, the General Registry of Shipping 58, and the Commercial, Labour and Statistical Department no fewer than 310. By that date, too, the Local Government Board had developed out of a section of the Home Office into a fully-fledged ministerial office with 295 civil servants. Another late-nineteenth-century blossom (1889) was the Board of Agriculture and Fisheries, with a staff of 256 by 1904.[53] Salaries and wages for the ten principal civil ministries more than doubled in the period 1894/5–1912/14, a factor of increasing numbers rather than increased salaries (Table 3).

In all, government offices in 1856 occupied about one million square feet, apart from the Admiralty and Somerset House. Many departments were asking for up to three times their existing accommodation for current needs. The area bounded by Downing Street and Richmond Terrace to the north, the river to the east, Bridge Street and Great George Street to the south and the Park to the west contained about 825,000 square feet, of which about half would be required for roads and open space. The existing departments could be accommodated in a four-storey building covering 242,380 square feet, according to the computation of the government surveyor, Hunt, but the remaining 170,120 square feet would, he thought, soon be required by the departments. His estimate was that all of that site not already owned by the government could be acquired for about a million and a quarter sterling, though by surveyor's prestidigitation he reduced this alarming sum to half a million net.[54]

The chancellor of the Exchequer, however, was sceptical. A keen intellect and an experienced administrator, George Cornewall Lewis [Pl. 43] had cut his teeth as a Poor Law investigator. At a time of increased taxation and heavy borrowing to meet the costs of the Crimean War, he saw neither the need for nor the desirability of adding to the public burden two and a half millions in order to erect a great palace of administration in Westminster.[55] Unmoved by select committee reports or press comment, he assessed what was essential and what could be afforded.[56] 'Lord Palmerston's notions and Trevelyan's about public offices seem to me wild and extravagant in the extreme', he wrote to a Treasury colleague.[57] Accepting that the Foreign Office was structurally insecure, and the War Office inefficiently dispersed,[58] he authorised the First Commissioner to go ahead with a competition for those two offices only, to occupy a site on the south side of Downing Street (though Palmerston was thinking in terms of rebuilding the War Office in Pall Mall), the Foreign Office to include an official residence with reception rooms to accommodate 1500 visitors.[59]

43. Sir George Cornewall Lewis, Bt (1806–63). Chancellor of the Exchequer, 1855–8, and an opponent of public building on an imperial scale.

Table 3. *Salaries and Wages Bills*[1] *for Principal Civil Ministerial Offices, Classes I and IV, at three-yearly intervals, 1894/5–1912/13*

	1894/5 £	1897/8 £	1900/1 £	1903/4 £	1906/7 £	1909/10 £	1912/13 £	% inc
Treasury	50,400	51,300	50,600	50,700	53,500	53,700	55,100	9
Home Office	29,900	32,100	34,100	35,400	39,000	44,300	49,300	65
Foreign Office	43,300	44,600	49,000	50,900	52,300	57,600	60,600	40
Colonial Office	35,300	34,500	42,400	48,100	51,600	54,100	56,000	59
Privy Council Office	11,700	12,900	12,900	10,200	12,100	11,900	11,700	0
Board of Trade	51,300	53,300	53,700	56,500	58,200	58,700	127,000	148
Board of Agriculture	33,300	35,100	37,100	53,700	60,200	77,200	109,000	227
Local Government Board	75,200	80,800	93,200	99,500	103,600	114,400	132,400	76
Office of Works	49,500	50,400	51,900	62,300	71,600	89,800	126,700	156
Board of Education	68,300	69,700	117,700	146,900	159,400	189,600	192,800	182
	448,200	464,700	542,600	614,200	661,500	751,300	920,600	105

Note: 1. To nearest £100.

Source: PP, Appropriation Accounts: 1896 (17) LVI, 1899 (44) LVII, 1902 (35) LXIII, 1905 (37) L, 1908 (37) LXVII, 1911 (7) L, 1914 (55) LVI.

In addition to the practical arguments, there was the aesthetic argument, most controversial of all because the Commons possessed a perdurable knot of radical opinion opposed to state expenditure, capable of linking up with the 'Country Party' to oppose expenditure on public works in the capital. Utilitarian radicals might accept the arguments for efficiency, but factories for the manufacture of government documents could be as plain as those for the manufacture of any other product. Many Liberals shared their view that they required no architectural embellishment at the taxpayer's expense. Lewis Isaacs (1830–1908), for instance, himself an architect, urged the 1887 select committee on the Admiralty rebuilding to adopt the character of the utilitarian Railway Clearing House near Euston Square; or the 'sufficiently ornate' St Thomas's Hospital [Pl. 44].[60] Twenty years later there were still MPs who regularly protested against 'multiplying marble palaces for innumerable junior clerks'.[61]

On the other hand were those who declared that government buildings set forth the dignity of the state, represented it in the eyes of the nation and the world – and London's world roles guaranteed many eyes were focused thereon – and must therefore be built in a handsome if not magnificent manner. Here was 'the shuttle of the imperial loom. Here the wishes of an Imperial people are registered and enforced. From these buildings goes forth the motive force which moves armies and navies, and controls the destinies of millions in every part of the world. And it will be satisfactory to know that these high purposes are not wanting in grandeur and dignity.'[62]

For these buildings, Somerset House [Pl. 45], handsome but not over-elaborated, was often cited as an ideal. The architect P.C. Hardwick (1820–90) told the 1887 Admiralty committee that 'It would be a great misfortune . . . to the country if the existing [eighteenth-century] Admiralty building were to be taken as the datum of a large new building.' In a large building, an ornamental exterior added proportionately little to the cost.[63]

44 (above).   St Thomas's Hospital, Henry Currey, 1868–71:
a. Seen across New Westminster Bridge (1854–62, Thomas Page and Sir Charles Barry).
b. Detail. Lewis H. Isaacs, MP (an architect) put forward this as a suitable style for government offices in 1887.

45 (below).   The river front, Somerset House, Sir William Chambers, 1775–96. The first purpose-built government office block in London, and frequently recommended by Victorian MPs as an appropriately sober model for new government buildings.

Trevelyan had made the same point in 1856:

As it costs little more to build handsome public offices than
unsightly public offices, [Trevelyan thought it] very desirable on
general national grounds to take this opportunity of embellish-
ing the town. . . . I consider that we have a very important national duty to perform in this respect; this city is something
more than the mother of arts and eloquence; she is a mother of
nations; we are peopling two continents . . . and we are organising, christianising and civilising large portions of two ancient
continents, Africa and Asia; and it is not right that when the
inhabitants of those countries come to the metropolis, they
should see nothing worthy of its ancient renown. Now, I conceive that a plan of the kind that I have sketched . . . would give
the honour due to the focus of all our liberties, of that regulated
freedom which we hope will overspread the world.[64]

The respected connoisseur A.J.B. Beresford Hope (1820–87)
[Pl. 47], when the results of the competition for New Government
Offices were announced in 1857, told the Commons that they
'ought to be the most magnificent building of the age'.[65] A major

47. Alexander J.B. Beresford Hope, PC, MP, 1874. The leading amateur advocate of
the Gothic Revival in his day, Hope's wealth enabled him to play a leading role in
architectural affairs, and he was the last layman to be president of the Royal Institute
of British Architects. He was a major influence in the appointment of Scott to design
the new Foreign Office, 1858.

46. Upper hall, Dover House, Whitehall, James Paine, 1754–8. Built as a private
residence, it reverted to the Crown in 1885. When it was proposed for the prime
minister's official residence, Gladstone complained that it would oblige him to
entertain; instead it was used for the Scottish Office, though inconveniently planned
for such use, the principal floor consisting of rooms of parade.

DOVER HOUSE. HALL ON FIRST FLOOR

factor in the 'magnificence' of the submitted designs had been the
requirement to include an official residence for the Foreign secretary, with 'Five Reception Rooms, en suite . . . to accommodate
1500 Visitors', and a state dining room for 50, with adjacent 'Supper and Tea rooms, Library, Morning Room, &c', and 'All the
other requirements of a Nobleman's Town House'.[66] Gladstone,
however, warned that the master plan was 'astounding and incred-
ible' having 'regard to the real necessities of the public service';
and the chancellor, Cornewall Lewis, said the government had to
consider 'what reasonable amount of architectural decoration we
think ourselves justified in proposing'.[67] That remained the problem for successive governments; one that the mode of obtaining
designs by public competition made difficult of resolution.[68]

The acceptance of the concept that the state had a function in
forming collections of art and science, obviously involved provision
of due space in which to exhibit those collections; though there
might still be controversy about the extent of display, as happened
over the natural-history exhibits of the British Museum in the
1860s, or the extent of acquisition, as occurred with the South
Kensington Museum at several stages in its development, and in
the British Museum with its multifarious and often mutually warring departments throughout much of its history (see pp. 92ff. below). The basic problem here, however, was how much in the way

of public resources could be devoted to extending and housing the public collections.[69] There was a generally accepted view, in an age when artificial lighting involved a naked flame or the emission of fumes and much heat, that sky-lighting was the best form of lighting, not only for pictures, but also for artifacts and scientific displays; another strong influence on design was Durand's *Précis des leçons* (1802–9), a selection of monumental ideal projects devised by students of the Académie des Beaux Arts.

'South Kensington' was not a homogeneous entity: it was both an administrative office and an exhibition, and one in which the art and science sides did not have wholly common interests, particularly after Major-General John Donnelly, R.E., became secretary of the Department of Science and Art in 1884 and vigorously encouraged the expansion of scientific education. The department's offices fought for space with the collections, which included semi-independent entities such as the models of inventions from the Patent Office.[70] Donnelly claimed in 1882 (when assistant secretary) that the offices were 'so confined, crowded and insufficient as to be absolutely dangerous to the health of the staff', no unusual situation for a government office, as we have seen, while the entrances to the museum were unworthy and dangerous.[71] Late in 1884 a new lord president (the minister responsible for South Kensington), Lord Carlingford, renewed the struggle, Welby at the Treasury admitting that something must be done: the scientific collections should, he thought, be moved into new buildings to the west of Exhibition Road, leaving the eastern side for art. On reference to the Works, Lefevre, who had his eyes focused on his great target of rebuilding the Admiralty and War Office, and wanted nothing to deflect his aim, denied that there was any immediate urgency. Though 'an addition must be commenced before long in a style adequate to and in harmony with the existing structure . . . the ultimate cost of which will be great', it could be built 'by degrees as the requirements of the Museum increase'.[72]

Lord Cranbrook (formerly Gathorne Hardy), lord president in Salisbury's second ministry from August 1886, was able to secure a somewhat more sympathetic response. A Works official who inspected the premises in December reported: 'The rank and file of the staff are distinctly over-crowded, and the worst feature of the situation is that some 16 clerks are compelled, for want of room space, to sit about in the corridors. This is a state of things which, in my experience, is without a parallel in a government office.'[73] The new Works Secretary, Henry Primrose, suggested that the large collection of naval models should be shifted to Greenwich and two of the residences for officers be converted to offices, a solution unacceptable to Science and Art, which consequently had to endure its narrow circumstances for some years more.

At the National Gallery, purchases (77 paintings from the Peel Collection in 1871 alone) and bequests had filled the wall space gained by the Royal Academy's removal in 1869 – which had really only allowed the existing collection to be more satisfactorily displayed. Edward Barry's additional rooms (1872–6)[74] permitted the return of the British School from exile in South Kensington[75] – attracting an average of more than 7700 visitors a day. Thirty-seven purchases in 1882–3 contributed to a new crisis, the trustees demanding additional galleries that were authorised in 1884 and completed by John Taylor of the Office of Works in 1887[76] – 'but the Trustees, rich in bitter experience, gave the Treasury clearly to understand that this addition must not be regarded as more than a temporary alleviation of present difficulties . . . [but] Twenty years were to be haggled away before the extension required . . . was wrung from a dilatory and indifferent Treasury.'[77] Land immediately north of the Gallery offered a possibility for expansion, but the western portion was occupied by barracks long judged essential to the maintenance of order in the metropolis; so

that the eastern portion alone seemed available. The government's allocation of that site to the donor of a permanent home for the National Portrait Gallery in 1889 led the trustees to demand compensation in an extension westward over the barrack-yard, and the First Commissioner of Works told the Commons that 'in the event of a necessity arising for the enlargement of the National Gallery', the government would give that site.[78]

It proved, however, that the barracks would not be surrendered until new ones had been provided. Despite repeated urgings from the Gallery trustees, and warnings about the danger of fire, nothing happened until on 30 May 1900 a fire broke out in an adjoining shop. Public alarm then ensured the sweeping away of the barracks and shop, but it was not until 1906 that the Office of Works prepared plans for a western extension, built in 1907–11.[79]

The National Portrait Gallery referred to above had been established in 1856 on the initiative of Lord Stanhope and encouragement of Prince Albert, to collect portraits of 'the most Eminent Persons in British History'. It opened at no. 29 Great George Street, where it was soon overwhelmed by donations.[80] Accommodation was provided in 1869 in the Western Gallery of the Horticultural Society's gardens at South Kensington until a fire occurred nearby in 1885, when it was transferred to the Bethnal Green Museum. The trustees, led by Lord Hardinge, pressed strongly for a new building, and the Works produced designs for one in Delahay Street, close to Parliament Square; but the Treasury would not provide the means. Private philanthropy in the person of William Henry Alexander relieved the government of this problem, though Lord Lamington commented that it was 'not quite dignified on the part of a great country like this that it should be dependent for such a building on private generosity'.[81] The Treasury, however, supplemented Alexander's gift of some £80,000 with £12,000 to connect the new Gallery with the National Gallery by an eastern wing.[82]

Similarly, courts of justice (likewise needing offices and display space) suffered congestion: the inexorable growth of population, the development of commerce and industry, and the larger numbers of wealthy people promoted a vast increase in litigation, while at the same time the opportunities for crime multiplied: an exponential increase in legal business had to be crammed into the few small cabins that were the courts. An eminent Q.C.[83] described conditions in the Westminster courts in 1863 to a House many of whose members were familar with the scene, after a judge had been obliged to suspend his court because its state was dangerous to health: the courts were

utterly unworthy of the country and totally unfit for the purposes they had to serve. They combined all the defects which a Court could possibly exhibit, and were as objectionable on account of their want of space as on account of the absence of convenient arrangement. The Bar might, perhaps, become acclimatized to the bad atmosphere . . . but some consideration should be given to the suitors, witnesses, jurors, and the general public, who were occasional visitors. Of the six or seven courts of Westminster, only two, the Queen's Bench [Pl. 48] and Exchequer, were in the least suitable for the transaction of business. The Common Pleas, in which a full third of the important land business was conducted, was much too small, and extremely ill-ventilated. . . . The Bail Court and the Court of Exchequer Chamber, which were now used for purposes for which they were not originally intended, were utterly disgraceful. . . . There was but one entrance, and the greatest difficulty was experienced in transacting the business with common decorum and decency. . . . Neither at Westminster nor in the City were there

waiting-rooms or retiring-rooms for witnesses, many of whom were women; and all attending the courts had either to haunt the purlieus or to remain in neighbouring taverns until they were called.[84]

From the Lincoln's Inn side, Richard Malins (d. 1882)[85] declared that the defects of the courts of law 'sink into insignificance compared with those of the courts of equity'.[86] The lawyers and often their clients were articulate and well-placed; the need for new courts [cp. Pl. 48] was hardly denied; the problem merely how they were to be paid for. Since litigation was regarded as a voluntary option, there was doubt how far it should be facilitated by the public purse.[87]

About activities that yielded a revenue to the Exchequer one might have expected less controversy. Such profitable functions were discharged by the Post Office, along with the Inland Revenue one of the largest of government departments, and the Patents Office. An act of 1852 had established the commissioners of Patents for Inventions, whose staff were provided with ground-floor rooms in the offices of the lately-abolished Masters in Chancery in Southampton Buildings, Chancery Lane, near the heart of legal London. Under their entrepreneurial superintendent, Bennet Woodcroft (1803–79), models of inventions were assembled, and a library was established that by 1864 was 'perhaps the finest scientific library in Europe'. By that time, although the models had been removed to the South Kensington Museum in 1857,[88] the offices were 'totally wanting in the accommodation requisite', the public having to inspect specifications and drawings in a place little better than a 'dark passage, in which there is barely standing room'. A select committee in 1864 urged the provision of adequate buildings, pointing out that there was a surplus of some £210,000 already from the duty charged on registering patents[89] – repeating the call already made by the commissioners of Patents themselves.[90]

Similarly the Post Office expanded fast with the growth of wealth, increase in population and literacy, and expansion of commerce and industry.[91] The General Post Office designed by Smirke in St Martin's-le-Grand (opened in 1829) [Pl. 5, 50] proving too small to handle an immense traffic generated partly by the penny post of 1840, another large building [Pl. 78] was erected opposite in 1869–71,[92] of which the second floor was occupied by the telegraph service, taken over by the state in January 1870. Within ten years that too was inadequate, and the administrative staff had to be found additional offices in the neighbourhood. A depart-

48. Old Law Courts, Westminster. The Court of Queen's Bench in 1883. Soane's Law Courts had long ceased to be adequate for the vastly increased amount of legal business in Victorian England.

49. New Law Courts: G.E. Street, transverse section looking north, 1870.

mental committee in 1883 learned that rentals totalled £10,000 a year for 930 officers,[93] a number grown to 1020 two years later. Although a fourth storey added to GPO West[94] [Pl. 243] would serve the telegraph service for a few years, a new adjacent administrative building for the secretary's office (increased from 102 in 1868 to 357 in 1883) and the receiver and accountant-general's department (likewise increased from 61 men to 493 men and 210 women)[95] was 'most essential'. Obviously, the telegraphs could have been given a distinct building, but the 'extreme costliness and inconvenience of removing the telegraph plant and machinery . . . the very limited choice, to say the least, of other suitable sites of sufficient area; and generally the magnitude of the outlay involved' told against such an arrangement – the more so, because it was impossible to foresee 'the requirements of the Postal System of the British Empire'.[96] To this demand from an increasingly remunerative service, the government responded favourably, property to the north of GPO West being acquired and a building designed by the official architect Henry Tanner erected in 1896–7.[97] The government had been similarly responsive in 1887 to the demands created when the development of a parcels service[98] proved extremely popular.[99] Early in the twentieth century the continuing irresistible expansion of postal services necessitated acquiring the site of Christ's Hospital (contemplated as an option in 1884), near the GPO buildings in St Martin's-le-Grand, on which vast offices were erected by Tanner in 1905–11.[100]

By 1866, however, for reasons discussed below, all that had been achieved in the way of a concentration of government offices in Whitehall was the shell of the Foreign Office and an India Office [Pl. 64] – a consequence of the state's taking over responsibility for India from the East India Company after the Indian Mutiny: a public office that had the additional advantage of being paid for by the Indian government. A select committee on military organisation had, however, in 1859 recommended bringing the War Office (seat of the secretary of state) and the Horse Guards (that of the commander-in-chief) 'under the same roof': 'separation engenders the belief that they are two distinct departments. Public opinion confirms the error, and necessarily leads to divided action, if not to antagonism on the part of military men against the supremacy of the civil power.'[101] The Admiralty had in 1865 under-

50. The Inland Sorting Room at the General Post Office, 1841.

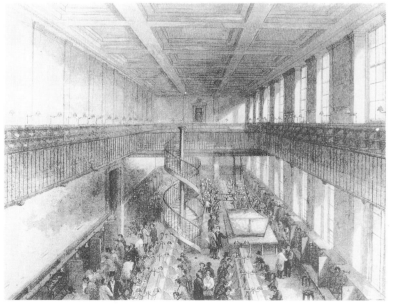

taken to bring together its Whitehall and Somerset House departments.[102] Trevelyan in 1866 also pressed for bringing the whole War Office and Admiralty together: 'Owing to our insular position, every service on which our army is employed is a conjoint naval and military operation. The War Office also provides armament for the Navy, and the Admiralty provides transport by sea for the Army. The intercourse between the two departments is constant even in time of peace.'[103]

To consider the next steps, Lord John Russell's ministry appointed a Treasury Commission by a Treasury Minute of 28 February 1866.

My Lords have had under their consideration the present arrangements for the accommodation of the Public Departments in Whitehall, Pall Mall, Somerset House, and their neighbourhood. It appears to them that with a view to the efficient conduct of the public business, and especially to economical arrangement, the present state of things is far from satisfactory; and for the following reasons:

1. It is desirable that the Departments should be as near together as may be practicable, and especially that (at the least) each Department should have all its branches under one roof. But this is not the case with respect to any of the principal Departments. For instance, the War Office is in Pall Mall, while the Horse Guards are in Whitehall, the Commissariat and Topographical Offices in Spring-gardens, the Fortification Office in Parliament-street, and the Judge Advocate and the Council of Military Education in Great George-street. The Board of Admiralty and the Comptroller's Office are in Whitehall. But the Coast Guard and Marine Offices are in Spring-gardens, those of the other five principal officers are at Somerset House, and the Solicitor's is in Lancaster-place. The Exchequer, the Pay Office, the Audit Office, and the Office of Examiners of Criminal Law Accounts are at inconvenient distances from the Treasury. The Colonial Office, the Home Office, and the Board of Trade have sub-departments in Parliament-street, Park-street, and in Richmond terrace.

2. It is important that so far as possible the public departments shall be in public buildings constructed for the purpose, and not in rented houses. It may be sufficient to refer to the inconvenient arrangements of the War Office or the Pay Office, and to observe that the rents now paid for the use of private houses (exclusive of the rents of land on which public buildings have been erected) amount to nearly £25,000 a year.

3. It is notorious that the accommodation in many of the offices is not only ill-arranged, but absolutely insufficient, even on sanitary grounds. My Lords would refer, as an example to the state of the Education Department, of the Board of Trade, of some of the branches of the Admiralty, and of the Inland Revenue. It appears to My Lords that a favourable opportunity is now afforded for initiating an inquiry into this question, with a view to the adoption of a general plan to be submitted for the consideration of Parliament, and to be carried out gradually in future years.

The commission then appointed did not complete its work before the change of government in June. A further Treasury Minute, 26 November 1866, substituted five Conservatives for three Liberals, with Lord John Manners [Pl. 51][104] as First Commissioner, and Lord Devon who chaired a sub-committee (Trevelyan and W.H. Stephenson of the Inland Revenue) to draw up a scale of accommodation. They checked the proposals against existing official rooms, the new Foreign Office and Inland Revenue offices at Somerset House, and 'several recently-constructed offices and suites of apartments in the City, which were supposed to furnish

All the Public Offices would be accessible to the public from one grand thoroughfare on their eastern side, while intercommunication between them all being secured without crossing any public street, they would on the western side face the park. It would thus be actual concentration, combining accessibility with quiet.[107]

The new Conservative ministers were however keen to display their credentials as guardians of the public purse. Although General Peel had in 1859 expressed himself strongly in favour of bringing together the defence departments, Henry Thomas Corry (1803–73), a once and future Admiralty minister, proved much cooler towards the concept: 'I think it is desirable, certainly; but I doubt whether it would be worth while to spend a large sum of money for it.'[108] Similarly, Sir John Pakington (1799–1880),[109] the Conservative War minister (previously First Lord of the Admiralty), had 'not in any serious respect found practical inconvenience' from the separation of the War Office and Horse Guards, though the diffusion of the departmental offices caused 'great inconvenience' and made 'an improved and extended' War Office a necessity: but the War Office and Horse Guards were better not under the same roof. He thought that General Peel's opinion reflected circumstances no longer existing, 'before the official relations between the Commander-in-Chief and the Secretary of State for War had become thoroughly arranged and understood'. As far as the relations between the defence departments were concerned, he favoured the Admiralty supplying its own guns, and the army its own transport. Anyway, their buildings were 'at this present moment in point of fact really very near' each other.[110] Another witness, 'perfectly satisfied as things are', was H.R.H. the Duke of Cambridge [Pl. 130], commander-in-chief: there was 'not the slightest' advantage in bringing War Office and Horse Guards [Pl. 52] closer.[111] For all Pakington's dismissing the issue as no longer pertinent, there remained a contentious constitutional consideration, and Cardwell as War Minister in 1869 insisted on the commander-in-chief's coming under his roof.

The Treasury commission's report was implemented only in its first stage: the completion of the Foreign Office block eastwards. A departmental committee (Trevelyan, Stephenson and James Fergusson, then architectural adviser to the First Commissioner)

51.   Lord John Manners (1818–1906), 7th Duke of Rutland from 1888. Conservative politician and three times First Commissioner of Works, he awarded a number of crucial commissions for the design of government buildings after inconclusive competitions. He tended to favour Gothic Revival architecture.

models of accommodation for banks and mercantile establishments'. Rooms for individual officers should measure from 16 × 14 ft to 25 × 20 ft; those for two clerks, 18 × 18 ft; for four clerks, 24 × 18 ft; for copying and account clerks, herded in larger groups, from rooms 27 × 20 ft for eight, up to rooms 60 × 20 ft for 20 clerks (see Table 2, p. 32).[105]

The requisite offices they divided into five groups: Home and Colonial and their dependencies, requiring some 46,000 sq. ft, which could be fitted on the eastern extension of the Foreign Office block with a little to spare; the much larger defence departments, requiring 125,400 sq. ft, which could go south of the new block, as far as Great George Street; the Treasury and its subordinate offices (including Works), 54,000 sq. ft, immediately north of Downing Street; and the new Civil Service Commission (10,000 sq. ft), Council Office and its branches (Health and Education), and Trade (some 40,000 sq. ft) which might go south of Great George Street or west of Parliament Street [Pl. 40].[106]

These proposals were rearranged by the full commission, which decided to retain the Horse Guards, establish the War Office on the adjacent site of Dover House and southwards as far as Downing Street (involving a reconstruction of the Soane-Barry block), and enlarge the Admiralty by adding the adjoining Pay Office, so providing 147,000 sq. ft for the defence departments' immediate need of 140,400, including official Admiralty residences. As 'a most convenient if not necessary consequence', the civil departments (Treasury, Trade, and smaller offices) could then be concentrated on the Parliament Street/Great George Street site [Pl. 126]. Thus

52.   The Horse Guards, from Whitehall, 1750–8, William Kent and John Vardy. The office of the commander-in-chief until 1872, as well as of the secretary at War until 1855. Sentimental admiration for the building blocked successive proposals for building new government offices on the site.

examined Scott's plans, modified them, and recommended that the Colonial and Home Offices be accommodated there, together with their dependencies.[112] A bill for the purchase of part of the Great George Street site for one office was abandoned by the Liberals in 1869; but subsequently, under pressure of 'a great deal of outside discussion',[113] Captain Galton of the Office of Works was called upon to report on the best plan.[114] The principal needs that Galton identified were those of the War Office, Admiralty, Council Office, Board of Trade and Offices of Works and Woods. He did not however analyse the demands of each department for space. Although enabling legislation was proposed in 1872 and again in 1873,[115] the ministry was not able to press it through, any more than it was able to proceed with its proposal to move the Mint to the Thames Embankment.[116]

The Liberals' electoral defeat in early 1874 returned the War Office problem to the Conservative cabinet.[117] Hardy, the new War Secretary, 'shocked and horrified' by conditions in Pall Mall, claiming 'the first right to the new buildings', was offered part of the new Scott offices [Pl. 53], but his officials reported: 'Let us stay where we are, because, bad as the old buildings are, and founded as they are upon a series of disused cesspools, we prefer them to the ghastly, ghostly, uncomfortable, dark, draughty, incommodious, inconvenient building which you have been good enough to build for us'.[118] Dissensions about the best site then deferred action.[119] A bill prepared for the 1876 session to complete the purchase of the Great George Street site was not proceeded with. Instead, a select committee was appointed in 1877, chaired by Baillie-Cochrane, to consider the problem of a comprehensive plan, when the inadequacy of private houses hired as public offices at a total annual rental of £33,878[120] was again rehearsed, some stress now being laid also on their sanitary condition.[121] The War Office by this time had eleven houses in Pall Mall and four other departments, as well as the old Horse Guards, and was just about to occupy Winchester

House in St James's Square. The Board of Trade, too, was housed principally in hired buildings.[122]

Stephenson of the Inland Revenue, a member of the 1866 Treasury commission, thought that much had been achieved: 'Upon the whole, I do not know that you require more concentration of the offices. . . . You have all the principal Secretaries of State's offices in a very convenient juxtaposition.'[123] He was reluctant to admit that even the War Office needed to be more concentrated, though acknowledging that as a group of converted houses it was 'in many parts . . . a very inconvenient place for a public office'. Similarly, though admitting the advantage of bringing together the various Admiralty departments, he could see no great advantage in bringing the two defence ministries together.[124] More detailed information about the War Office was obtained from the Chief Clerk, Ralph Thompson, who pointed out that not only did the office require additional space for its usual work, but the application of audit to the army accounts brought an additional demand. Business in connexion with the defence loan of the early 1860s was now coming to an end, but a large staff was now required to implement the Localisation of the Forces Act.[125]

At the Admiralty, as we have seen, the accommodation was 'insufficient in quantity and indifferent in quality'. It was true that the move of the civil administration from Somerset House in 1868 had resulted in considerable economies, because records had formerly to be kept in two separate places, so that work had been done in duplicate; union enabled the number of clerks to be very considerably reduced.[126] Nevertheless, working conditions were very cramped. About 250 clerks were in the old Whitehall building, and another 350 in Spring Gardens, besides 120 messengers and the like.[127] Since many of the rooms had been designed as servants' bedrooms, they were very low 'and very uncomfortable'. One room in which estimates were prepared by three clerks was only 12 × 8 ft, a former water-closet. The clerks' health suffered from such condi-

53. New Government Offices, Whitehall, George Gilbert Scott, 1868–78. The Colonial Office, adorned with allegories of the continents and busts of proconsuls and explorers, occupied the nearer portion; the Home Office, with allegories of industries, arts and sciences, and busts of appropriate practitioners, the central and further parts.

tions, as noticed above. Much of the Old Admiralty building was taken up by staircases, although some had now been converted into water-closets.[128] The accountant-general's department, with 246 clerks and some 50 messengers, was spread along one side of New Street, Spring Gardens, in 14 houses, 'all more or less separately located, and entered by six separate entrances'; in many of the houses, the floors were on different levels, 'not designed to be connected in any way'. A quarter of the men were in garrets, where 'the heat of the lead upon the top is so suffocating, that we have been obliged to try every species of ingenious invention for . . . getting some little air in the rooms. The rooms are left open, and the men are working without their coats and waistcoats', reported the accountant-general. The senior men were 'at a distance' from those they had to supervise; the conditions had induced nervous exhaustion in 'men of high position'. The reference books were scattered in diverse places; the library was 'spread about in the different offices in locked cases'; and the numerous committees had to meet outside, sometimes in the Westminster Palace Hotel.[129] The director of stores complained that the rooms were too small for his clerks because there was not enough room for their books: only one could be examined at a time; 'when one book is opened another has to be closed; whereas several of them ought to be referred to at the same time, to compare the stock at one place with the stock at another, and the past expenditure, and so on'.[130] The clerks were unable to refer to the patterns of stores, because they were kept in a different building. Accommodation in basements or attics that might be used for patterns was occupied by house- and office-keepers for the individual houses. Because there could be no provision for luncheon, men had to go out 'just at the busiest part of the day', whereas at the Foreign Office 'there are arrangements for luncheon in the office' [Cp. pl. 61].[131] Yet £25,000 had been spent in adapting these houses and £11,000 on buying up leases, and there was an annual rental of £5700.[132]

The 1877 Baillie-Cochrane committee was not only more concerned about working conditions than earlier committees had been; it also looked more closely into internal design. This was in part a consequence of Scott's new offices, now in operation, having been the subject of adverse criticism. As Scott himself said wryly, 'people do not complain in old buildings; they only complain in new ones'.[133] That this was not wholly true is shown by the evidence given above by civil servants about life in the Admiralty offices, though it might perhaps be argued that that reflected the change from their old habitat in Somerset House.

Somerset House [Pl. 45] was, as we have already noted, regarded as the *ne plus ultra* of a public office: MPs frequently recommended its exterior; civil servants praised its interior. 'That was my ideal of a public office', declared the accountant-general of the navy, who spent more than thirty years there. Nevertheless, when it was suggested that 'great complaints are made of the darkness of the passages', he admitted: 'Yes, that was always the case.'[134] Now dark passages were alleged to be one of the primary faults of Scott's New Government Offices, along with smells and excessively high rooms. Scott had followed the conventional plan for large offices of central corridors with rooms on either side, a compact plan occupying minimal ground area, and reducing the time taken in going about the building. As he pointed out, the consequence was that 'the passages must either be a little dark in parts, or you must waste a great deal of inside room expressly for the admission of light'. As it was, he had sacrificed rooms here and there for the direct admission of light to the corridor. His personal view was that there was no 'inconvenience from want of light', though 'some parts are a little obscure' [Pl. 54].[135] The government architect, Taylor, agreed that they were 'sufficiently lighted for day purposes', but thought 'It would be very much better to have the passages lighted directly,

54. New Foreign Office, G.G. Scott, 1853–68. Corridor, ground floor north. Largely lacking direct natural light, Scott's corridors placed between two lines of offices had to be lighted by gas, even during the summer, creating heat and unpleasant smells.

and ventilated directly, from the court.' Nonetheless, a Foreign Office clerk insisted that 'the passages are undoubtedly dark', and that the complaints of want of ventilation arose principally from the accumulation of gas from the lights.[136]

No doubt the gas lights were used when not actually necessary, though 'during the dark weather in the winter they have to burn gas continually in the corridor',[137] thus contributing to, if not causing, the smells that were constantly complained of in the Colonial and Home Offices, the Home secretary himself finding his office mephitic. The secretary of the Office of Works ascribed the source of these obnoxious smells to water-closets and urinals having been 'built in the heart of the building' and to soil-pipes being made of iron (instead of lead) and built into the walls. Scott however explained that the Home secretary's room had been affected by a blocked drain outside the building, a consequence of the local authority's having brought street drains into the system; and that other smells had resulted from a suggestion from Galton that drains in the sub-basement should not be buried, but left exposed where they could be got at. Little settlements cracking a

55 (following page). The State Stair at the Foreign Office. George Gilbert Scott, 1863–8. Murals by S. Goetze, 1914–19.

pipe or disturbing a joint had allowed soil to ooze out 'and create a nuisance in the room above'; but the defect could be immediately detected and rectified. This problem had arisen because the department insisted on occupying the building before Scott had certified it as finished. After the pipes were attended to, Scott averred that 'I spent a long time in crawling all through those sub-places, and smelling at them (and I am pretty quick in my smell), and I could find in no place any smell until I got to one particular part, where I at length perceived one. I smelt at every drain and every place that I could think of, and I could find nothing; but at last I opened a door, and I found that it came from a dust-bin which was crammed up with all sorts of filth.'[138]

A further persistent criticism of Scott's offices was the inconvenience of the great height of rooms. That was determined by two factors: the height required for the grand reception rooms on the first floor of the Foreign Office [Pl. 56, 59, 60], and Scott's attempt to meet the demands made in the press for a building to equal Jones's Banqueting House. 'Now', declared Scott, 'the beauty of that building arises from the enormous height of its architectural storeys; and having that building always thrown in my teeth, I tried to make my architectural storeys as high as I could, although they were seven feet or more lower than Inigo Jones's.' The result was that the rooms were 'higher than we require', and there were 'frequent complaints . . . that the men could not transact business there, because they could not hear themselves speak on account of the echo'. One Foreign Office official declared that in his 22 ft-high room 'I not only cannot hear what others say to me, but very often I cannot hear what I am saying myself'. Gathorne Hardy, who as War secretary had declined to move the War Office into Scott's new buildings, complained afterwards of 'offices with vast reservoirs for bad air above the windows'; and Taylor of the Works referred to the 'enormous waste of cubic content, owing to the extreme height of the rooms'.[139] However, the low attic rooms also were unsatisfactory because (for the sake of external architectural effect) the windows were at floor level and 'perfectly useless'; so that skylights had to be inserted. Skylights, however, were disliked 'because they make the rooms so hot in the summer and so cold in the winter'.[140]

Scott's rooms also tended to be too large generally.[141] One person might be found sitting in a room 25 ft square, nearly as large as a Commons committee room – unnecessarily large for even a first-class clerk, though convenient for the modern official's layout: desk; reception area with arm-chairs; table and chairs for small meetings. The resultant 'immense floor space' made the corridors longer than necessary, and 'the extreme ends of the building much further apart'. The secretary of state's vast room [Pl. 69] occupied one floor of the corner tower, with another such room below it for the permanent secretary; and (the proposed official residence having been renounced) the three great reception rooms, one intended for cabinet meetings, lay on two sides of an internal courtyard.[142]

In 1893 this did not matter; there was room for everybody. The main departments occupied only the ground floor and first floor; on the ground floor there was also a series of rooms for the Library, and on the first floor the three great reception rooms [Pl. 56, 59, 60]. Here the Foreign Office party was given by the Secretary of State on the King's Birthday, when the great double staircase [Pl. 55], with the guests ascending and filling the open corridors above, provided one of the most magnificent sights in London; never more magnificent, perhaps, than when Cardinal Vaughan in his scarlet robes, unintentionally no doubt, took his stand at the top of the staircase and held a miniature Court. The rooms near the top of the staircase

were turned into supper-rooms, and those below into royal dressing-rooms.[143]

Such a nostalgic view of the Foreign Office was not shared by the next generation of denizens of Scott's later and less magnificent Home and Colonial Offices. One senior official thought that there was 'a good deal to be said in favour of a landmine being dropped plumb on the Colonial Office . . . from the practical administrative point of view so inadequate a building, wasteful of space in construction and ill-adapted for modern offices, could well now [1947] be spared'. He admitted, however, that in 1909, when there were only 125 officials and 24 women typists, 'there was reasonable space for all. . . . In the largest rooms there would be not more than four of the junior administrative officers, second-class clerks as they were then called, now assistant principals. The whole of the typing was done in one room.'[144]

Even in 1909, the similar Home Office could evoke a hostile reaction from those who worked there:

No one but a real genius could have designed a great building which, from its main plan down to its smallest detail, is absolutely unsuited to the purpose for which it was intended. The 'grand staircase' ends at a half landing, from which another set of stairs leads to the principal floor. And a dark passage on that floor leads to the principal rooms. The Secretary of State's room was originally so ill-lighted that an important structural alteration was needed to make it habitable; and even when it was so altered, Sir William Harcourt [Home Secretary, 1880–6] fitly likened it to a railway station waiting-room. . . . The building, as viewed from the street, contains only three floors above the basement. But as in fact there are four, one window has to do duty on two floors. The result is that the second-floor rooms are like bear-pits, the windows being placed so high that no one can see the opposite houses from them much less the street. And in the upper rooms the windows reach but three feet from the floor. But as in an office light is wanted above the table and not under it, none of these rooms could be brought into use until, at considerable cost, a skylight had been inserted in the massive fire-proof roof. . . . The explanation current at Whitehall was that Sir Gilbert Scott deliberately set himself to spite the Government for rejecting his original plans.[145]

Taylor of the Works in 1877 thought the rooms in Soane's 'Treasury Buildings', as altered by Barry in 1845–6, were 'a very good specimen of what is required for public offices'.[146] On the other hand, there was a growing belief in the merits of having large rooms in which a sizable number of clerks might work together under a supervisor, a policy recommended, as we have seen, by Trevelyan in 1856.[147] Mitford, Secretary of the Works, formerly of the Foreign Office, thought it 'should be essential to any scheme for a new office' to have some large rooms in which to 'employ a number of men who are engaged in bookkeeping and in similar occupations under supervision'; though the head and second man of a division should have a room each, and the remaining four or five a room together. In the Foreign Office, however, because 'We have a great deal of work requiring that the men should not be disturbed when they are engaged upon it', small rooms were preferable.[148] Taylor advocated a number of 'very large rooms in which you might place a certain number of clerks who had one head over them'; and the former Liberal whip, William Adam, likewise suggested the advantage of having 'a great many clerks in one room', properly supervised.[149]

The leading advocate of the large room under supervision, or 'bank parlour system' [Pl. 58] as it was often termed,[150] was the great commercial entrepreneur W.H. Smith. Highly scep-

56 (previous page).   New Foreign Office: Larger Conference Room. The spandrels of the iron beams are decorated with various national coats of arms. (This and the other state apartments have recently been restored under the architectural direction of Messrs Cecil Denny Highton.)

tical about the merits of any recently-constructed government office,[151] sceptical too of the merits of concentration,[152] he was yet convinced of the advantages of bringing large numbers of clerks together under supervision, and successfully pressed his views on Lefevre, First Commissioner in 1880–5 – a receptive hearer who had already persuaded the War Secretary to plan a number of large rooms. 'The experience of business which I have', Smith told the 1887 committee, 'all goes in the direction of saying that a number of men, who are working at the same work, are much better brought together under supervision in one large room than when they are working in a number of small rooms by themselves and without adequate supervision.'[153] Lefevre had already persuaded the Admiralty and the War Office to reduce the number of rooms in their plans from 189 to 138, and from 260 to 170, respectively. He thought still more might be achieved, but recognised that 'the pressure is generally in the opposite direction'.[154] H.E. Childers, who had served at the Exchequer and been both War and Admiralty minister, agreed that 'in managing large bodies of men doing clerical work you ought to have large rooms'. Similarly, Sir Andrew Clarke, who had headed both ministries' works departments, declared: 'My own practical experience has been, and I fancy that of every merchant in England has been, that the larger the number of persons you can put into a room for one common object, the greater the turn out of work; and therefore you require fewer of them.'[155]

However, Taylor reported, 'there seemed . . . to be a great difference of opinion between the heads of Department on that point. Some were decidedly in favour of having a large number of clerks in one room; others wished to have them subdivided.' Were they to be grouped in tens or twenties, there would be a considerable saving of space in the Admiralty.[156] The Admiralty accountant-general, whose staff, in the First Lord's view, carried out work 'which would enable those who undertake it to be put together in

57. William Henry Smith (1825–91), MP for Westminster from 1868; secretary to the Treasury 1874–77; first lord of the Admiralty 1877–80; secretary of state for War 1885; leader of the House of Commons 1886–91. Utilitarian in his attitude towards new government buildings, in 1887 he overthrew Lefevre's scheme for a new Admiralty and War Office.

58. The 'Bank Parlour System', strongly advocated for government offices by W.H. Smith, G. Shaw Lefevre, and Sir C. Trevelyan. A large number of clerks worked together in a spacious office under the eye of a single superintendent. This office (Room 148 Quartermaster General's (Finance) department) was one of the largest in the New War Office, designed for 20 clerks (photographed in 1920).

59. New Foreign Office: Smaller Conference Room, or Dining Room.

large rooms', was one of the opponents: 'by no means an advocate for large numbers being employed in big rooms'; while 'quite prepared to group together a number whose duties are . . . in harmony and relationship to each other', he would 'be very sorry to put into one room the duties discharged in paying two and a half millions to public contractors who occasionally come asking all kinds of questions'.[157]

The result of these differing official views was that in the 1883–4 competition for designs for the new defence offices, architects were instructed to provide only five rooms for between 16 and 22 clerks each, and four for 12 or 13 clerks, on the basis of '300 [square] feet for the first official, and 20 feet for each one after'.[158] Several rooms about 40×75 or 80 ft, intended for up to 25 clerks, were provided in Leemings' winning plan, the War Office already concentrating some of its clerks.[159] For the Admiralty, no fewer than 46 rooms were to be provided for single individuals.[160] After all the bad smells experienced in the Home Office, much stress was also laid in the instructions on providing satisfactory sanitation, especial attention being directed in the finalists' competition to the 'number, position, and ventilation' of w.c.s.[161] The *Civilian* ('The Accredited Organ of the Civil Service') reprinted a letter in *The Times* from George Godwin of the *Builder* about the unhealthiness of the winning plan with its small courtyards, and commented: 'This must be enquired into. The health of the offic-

ials must be considered as well as the artistic effect, or even the cheapness of the buildings.'[162] In subsequent articles, devoting rare consideration to the topic of buildings, it praised the plan for its well-lighted corridors 'attached to a single set of rooms'; but criticised the deep narrow rooms ('a square room is the best'), and deeply recessed windows – a sacrifice to architectural effect: the lighting would be 'very defective . . . the Clerks who will have to work there will be crying in vain for those rays which by better management might have been given in abundance'.[163]

In the outcome, extensions to the Admiralty only were built from 1888 [Pl. 133], the building of a new War Office being again deferred, so that it was a principal item in the list for rehousing submitted to parliament in 1896. The other main contenders this time round were the Board of Trade, Education Department, Local Government Board, the newly created Board of Agriculture, and the Offices of Woods and Works, joined again in 1897 by the Admiralty. The naval armaments race that gave rise to the Naval Works Loans Act of 1896 required a considerable amount of extra accommodation, not purely clerical. The hydrographer in particular was 'very magnificent in his ideas'. The two departments of the director of Works and the Naval Works Loan Branch alone required as much space as Leemings had calculated on adding in 1887, 45,000 sq. ft, for 122 persons in 42 rooms and 65 persons in 30 rooms respectively.[164] Minor departments also in the queue

60 (right). New Foreign Office: Grand Reception Room, measuring 72×38ft; called by Scott 'The Cabinet Room', and so used by Lord Salisbury. The Treaty of Locarno was signed here in 1923. The ceiling was painted by Clayton and Bell.

were housed entirely in hired buildings, at an annual rental (excluding those on Crown property) of £5600. Rents paid to the Crown were about £7150 annually, and those for the War and Trade offices on government land about £8400 a year. The removal of the Local Government Board from Scott's block to a new building would enable the Home Office to expand.[165]

The War Office was still in 11 different houses (counting all the Pall Mall premises as one), with 1140 persons in 440 rooms. The urgency of its needs may be indicated by the personal appearance before the 1896 Commons committee reviewing the government's proposals of the War minister, Lord Lansdowne. He, like Hawes in 1858, complained of the loss of time in having to send for officials from outlying offices, and the inconvenience and unnecessary labour in the 'movement of papers from one branch of the office to another'. With some 900 officers and clerks to house, an increase of about 150 permanent staff since 1873, he wanted 256 rooms for officials and a further 133 for committees, storage of 'an immense mass of comparatively recent documents', and so forth. Since 1883, reductions in one class of clerk had been balanced by increases in another class, and the Military Intelligence Department was increasing. Military works under the 1895 Loans Act required 42 temporary clerks. There were also 198 messengers and 36 attendants employed. 'A really convenient building' would reduce the number of such personnel, and probably the number of clerks also. Lansdowne was happy with whichever site would involve the least delay, fearing that 'Parliament might change its mind . . . and we might still find ourselves in Pall Mall without any prospect of extrication'.[166]

When, however, the discussion reached the floor of the House of Commons, there was the usual tension apparent between those members who could see little or no need for new public offices, and those who felt that national pride required noble buildings. Sir John Leng remarked: 'When we see splendid edifices erected for Government offices in foreign countries [Pl. 182], we may hope that our own country will not be backward. In the provinces, the buildings are superior in recent years to those buildings which have been put up in London . . . an effort should be made, especially in the frontages to Parliament Street, to give them some dignity.' As a modern official put it: 'A building can be terribly important in setting the style of its inhabitants'; an appropriately Delphic remark.[167] Thomas Gibson Bowles (1843–1922),[168] on the other hand, was 'no admirer of those enormous buildings set up in Belgium, which are buildings far too large. My experience is, the larger and handsomer a building is, the less satisfactory is the work done in it.'[169] But the general radical suspicion of the military did not necessarily find expression in hostility to decent War Office buildings. However hostile to war fever, John Burns (1858–1943) [Pl. 134], one of a handful of Labour MPs and a member of recent select committees on public offices, declared that to support the proposal for a new War Office it was

> not necessary for any Member . . . to identify himself with the deification of Tommy Atkins and the military spirit prevalent in this country . . . if we want a substantial and permanent reform of the War Office, the most effective method . . . is by bringing the War Office officials into a decent building where they could be subjected to the public gaze, where we shall no longer find talent hidden and incompetence obscured, and that Members of Parliament should have an opportunity of going into a decent place when they require information instead of the present rabbit-warren in which Government officials hide their diminished heads. . . . where you have a large staff in detached buildings the amount of supervision and control is hardly worth the name, and the result is that the staff gets lax in its administration, and the only way out of it is to follow the example which

commercial concerns and banks adopt; that is, to mass our staff into one perfectly-equipped building and have perfect control and rigorous supervision.

The Board of Trade building Burns called 'a disgrace to any government'. The Education Department, 'sadly in need of better accommodation', needed to bring the bulk of its staff from South Kensington to Parliament Street. The 'extension of municipal life' demanded more room for the Local Government Board.[170] But no official should be allowed 'to quarter himself in very decent and palatial accommodation at the expense of the country', as had happened at the South Kensington Museum, where 102 rooms had lately been cleared from residential occupation – though the Museum, looking from the road 'like a cross between a tramway stable and a goods yard', needed to be completed. As an economist (i.e. one who sought economy) he believed 'that it is an economical thing to have the offices for the Government staff large and commodious, and the staff well housed in decent, healthy offices

61.   Kitchen in the New War Office of 1899–1906 (photographed in 1919). It was thought that all government departments should be provided with luncheon rooms so employees need not leave the office during the lunch hour.

62.   New War Office, W. Young, 1898–1906. Room 401 in 1920: a room in a corner tower, probably originally intended for two officials (carpets were provided only for senior men).

with every accommodation, if we want the government of this country well carried out'.[171] Thus the two great blocks of the Parliament Street buildings (for Education and Local Government Board – and originally Trade, by J.M. Brydon) and, at long last, the War Office in Whitehall (by W. Young) were approved [Pl. 61–3, 66].

As Burns's remark suggests, it was not government offices only that needed better accommodation. Conditions in the South Kensington Museum were a serious cause for concern to those responsible for the collections. A Treasury committee investigating the scientific collections (where the number of visitors had increased from 150,000 in 1884 to 260,000 in 1888) concluded that 90,000 sq.ft of new exhibition space was required without delay, itself sufficient for a creditable Science Museum.[172] Despite an architectural competition for completing the Museum, nothing was executed.[173]

63a.   New War Office, W. Young, 1898–1906. Room 15b: a larger room, to take eight clerks; squarish and lighted from the side (regarded as the ideal design). Ajustable electric lighting, however, removed the planning constraints previously imposed by need for natural light.

63b.   New War Office, W. Young, 1898–1906. Room 162 in 1920. The telephone had become a necessary adjunct, offering the possibility of reducing the amount of paper passed between departments. Officials still provided their own towels (and soap) for the lavatories.

By 1898, even the Irish Nationalist W. Redmond admitted: 'I believe it is a standing disgrace to any civilised country that the collection at South Kensington should be left neglected and so badly housed.'[174] Campaigns in parliament (led by Lord Balcarres) and in the Press (in which M.H. Spielmann, editor of the *Magazine of art*, played a lead) led to the appointment of a select committee in March 1897, which issued an interim report in May on the risk of fire. In the same month, distinguished artists presented memorials to the committee and to the lord president urging completion of the Museum. In their full report, the committee felt 'bound to express their sense of the importance of completing the building on the east side of Exhibition Road with a view to the safe deposit and satisfactory exhibition of the art collections'. They argued that the treasures (like the War Office clerks) were so massed together that they were in considerable danger. 'The collections are now so crowded that they cannot be seen by the ordinary visitor . . . a better exhibition of these articles will be a revelation to the public.' It was difficult even for students in numbers properly to examine 'these magnificent and delicate objects'.[175] Ernest Gray (1857–1932)[176] warned that if the proposal to house all the collections, both science and art, to the east of Exhibition Road, were implemented, 'the congestion which will exist there will be as serious as that which exists at the present moment, and consequently at a very early date it will be necessary to erect buildings upon the other side of the road'.[177] Although completion of the east site would free space to the west of Exhibition Road for the science collections, the chancellor of the Exchequer 'had scented the possibility of using Webb's new building to accommodate both science and art'. However, both the Science and Art Department and leading scientists opposed this idea, and after fruitless negotiations between the Department and the Works, it was decided in 1899 to confine the eastern site to the art collections, and provide a new building for science on the west.[178] The Science and Art Department was united with its sponsoring body, the Committee of Council for Education, in 1899 to form the Board of Education, freeing space at South Kensington as the bureaucrats moved to Whitehall.[179]

Nevertheless, the scientists had to endure some trauma before the Science Museum on the west side of Exhibition Road became a certain commitment. Pressure was applied by eminent 'establishment' scientists such as Sir Henry Roscoe, MP (1833–1915), and Sir N.J. Lockyer (1836–1920), the latter 'an active propagandist in 1907 in *Nature*' and as an 1851 commissioner.[180] By 1909 the case looked hopeful: a departmental committee was set up to examine the precise purposes that the Science and Geological[181] Museums 'can best serve in the National interests'; the lines on which the collections should be managed to fulfil those purposes; and the special characteristics required by the proposed new buildings for them at South Kensington.[182] Its preliminary report declared that the objects then exhibited were 'so much crowded that their due classification and utilisation are now impossible'; the cases so crowded and so close to one another that it was 'often extremely difficult for visitors to examine the objects in them'. Electrical engineering needed five or six times its present space; structural engineering and geography were scarcely represented; the scientific study of the sea had no adequate place. The Museum of Economic Geology collections in Jermyn Street should be melded with the palaeontological and mineralogical collections in the Natural History Museum and the world geological examples in the Science Museum. Science needed 300,000 sq.ft, Geology 60,000. Then it would be possible to 'afford illustration and exposition of the various branches of Science . . . and of their applications in the Arts and Industries'. The Museum should be 'a worthy and suitable house' for the presentation of important discoveries and inventions. The exhibits, 'accessible for close inspection by accredited

65. New Public Offices, J.M. Brydon and H. Tanner, 1898–1912.
a. From Parliament Square (Great George Street front). b. Parliament Street front (completed 1907).

64 (left). India Office: Matthew Digby Wyatt, the Secretary of State's room. Imperial grandeur as a setting for receiving Indian princes in Whitehall. The two doors are allegedly for receiving simultaneously two princes of equal rank.

visitors', should be 'so selected and exhibited as to arouse the interests' of casual visitors, so as to convey 'at least general ideas on the subjects which the Collections illustrate'.[183] Further reports followed,[184] the building was approved, and work began in the summer of 1914.[185]

When the government proposed in view of ever-mounting pressure for more accommodation for both museums and offices [Pl. 65], almost at the end of the 1903 session, to allocate another half million pounds for public buildings, discussion in the Commons had focused on the financial arrangements, and no case had to be made as to the need; though Gibson Bowles remarked, 'If they were going to put all their civil servants in vast palaces in Whitehall, and to buy up the whole of Westminster, they were committing a tremendous mistake.' The government merely stated that it had been found that additional land would be required for the new War Office, among other expenses, and that costs had risen sharply since 1898.[186]

Additional land had already been acquired for an expansion of the British Museum on its Bloomsbury site with the purchase of the perimeter from the Duke of Bedford in 1895 for £200,000. The insatiable demands of the library – in 1888, a million and a half printed books; by 1910, twice as many – the enormous growth of the British and Medieval Antiquities collection, and the steady enhancement of the other departments meant that space, once again, was at a premium. One recourse was to hive off the newspapers to a suburban site at Colindale, North London, a proposal that initially met a hostile reception.[187]

Newspapers, however, were one category growing almost at the rate of Jack's beanstalk: there were 1673 titles in 1882 and 3343 in 1896–7, filling a hundred yards of new shelf space every year.[188] In 1899 the trustees proposed a £150,000 extension, to be partly funded by a £50,000 bequest, but the Treasury insisted that the Museum must first dispose of ephemera. A bill was therefore drawn up to enable it to hand over its post-1837 newspapers to relevant local authorities (though retaining ownership and rights of inspection), and to destroy such ephemera as advertisements and Christmas cards. Introduced into the Lords on behalf of the trustees in the following session, in the Commons by 'all the signs that one may read in the Parliamentary sky', it was 'by no means likely to be an unopposed measure', but rather would 'give rise to a great deal of contention'. The government, the real sponsors, therefore declined to find time for the bill, instead striking a bargain with the

trustees that they would consider asking the House for £100,000 in the next session to extend the Museum.[189] Still unable to agree with the trustees' ideas, the Treasury delayed the scheme to build a newspaper depository at Hendon (Colindale) until 1902, when some MPs continued to object to the inconvenience it would cause them in checking speeches made in the country (reported only in provincial papers) by fellow-Members.[190] An authorisation for an extension of the Museum buildings to the north and west had to wait yet one session longer (it was included in the 1903 act).

Still the pressures on official space grew: a Liberal government pregnant with social reforms required more officials and more offices. Already-established departments demanded permanent and purposeful accommodation. Lane-Fox, a Yorkshire country gentleman, drew attention in 1908 on the Vote for supply, to the inadequacy of the offices rented for the Board of Agriculture, established in 1889, and since 1903 responsible for fisheries also; offices divided between several 'small holdings' [Pl. 67]:

> Everybody who went to the Board of Agriculture knew how difficult it was either to find the official required, or to transact business there. He had occasion to go to the Board for some information, and went to St James's Square, where he was informed that the official he desired to see was at Whitehall Place. He went to Whitehall and found the official, but was told that the information he required was at St James' Square and Delahay Street. He had either, therefore, to go back for the information or wait until a messenger could go to St James' Square and Delahay Street and bring it back, so that he might discuss the matter in company with the official he was dealing with. . . . Then there was the question of the typists. At the present time the typists of the Fisheries Department were compiling the records in Delahay Street, another set of typists were compiling other records in Whitehall Place, and it was quite impossible to interchange these typists, although in the Fisheries Department there might be great pressure whilst in other Departments the typists were doing nothing. . . . What was wanted was a central office in connection if possible with the Department of Woods and Forests.[191]

The First Commissioner, Lewis Harcourt [Pl. 89], responded that he was looking for a suitable site. The Public Offices Sites bill of 1908, which provided for the completion towards the Park of Brydon's Parliament and Great George Streets office block, offered

66.   Royal Courts of Justice: west extension, 1908–14, Sir Henry Tanner. North and South elevations. Street's great work soon was found too small; four more courts and offices were provided.

such a possibility. But primarily it was intended for the Board of Trade, then mainly accommodated in old houses in Whitehall Gardens,[192] but with many out-offices, a total of 21 buildings. Sir Frederick Banbury (1850–1936),[193] a persistent meddler in public buildings questions, opposed the bill as unnecessary:

It was a self-evident proposition that up to the present time they had got on very well without this building. He did not know that the efficiency of the public officers had, in any kind of way, been lessened on account of the inadequacy of the housing provision . . . there was a tendency to increase the public service with the erection of new buildings; and the bigger the buildings the more that tendency increased. New buildings had a direct tendency to create new posts and on that account he would rather see the present buildings somewhat congested.[194]

His obdurate criticism of the bill was supported by Bowles, who 'objected to the junior clerk being ensconced in marble palaces, and in his opinion the larger, the more beautiful and the more expensive the public offices became the less work was done in them'.[195]

A senior official subsequently criticised Brydon's building (of which the interior was largely the work of official architects) but for different reasons:

This building is fine, but in my opinion leaves much to be desired internally; the most spacious part being the well-lighted passages. The second floor, occupied by important technical officers, had a great defect, inasmuch as one cannot look out of the windows towards the road with any comfort. I think I can confidently say that no new Government office will ever be designed and erected on the lines of that building. The aim should be to have movable divisions so as to provide for large rooms for mass staffs, if required.[196]

To a user of Brydon's building after it had been taken over by the Treasury, it seemed, 'with its vast corridors, some of them describing impressive circles around courtyards, and vaulted in a slightly cloistral manner', to be 'a bit like an aquarium'; in contrast to Scott's Home Office which, with its show-case and book-lined, tesselated corridors, had an effect 'more that of a swimming-bath'.[197]

Even before the Extension Act of 1908 had passed, Works' officials were casting doubt on the likelihood of housing Trade in an extension that would not be completed until about 1915; by June 1909 they were resisting a proposal from the Board to acquire no. 5 Whitehall Gardens, on the grounds that it was 'in contemplation before many years have elapsed' to build a new Board of Trade.[198] Arrangements were however made to bring together the Commercial department and its branches, the Labour department and Statistical branch, in Gwydyr House, Whitehall which, the *Civil Service Gazette* commented, 'should enable the work of the Department to be carried on with greater efficiency and less loss of time, than was the case when papers had to be referred from one building to another . . . such a method of housing Government departments is obviously wasteful and we are glad to notice that steps are being taken to lessen and remove such evils. There is still plenty of room for reforms of this kind.'[199] We may note, incidentally, that such comment on buildings was curiously rare in the civil service press.[200]

A few months later, the Works recurred to the arrangements for allocating the new buildings, in view of 'the constant growth of the larger departments'. The Local Government Board and the Education Department as well as the Board of Trade were expanding fast (see Table 3); the LGB had already spread 6000 sq. ft outside its headquarters. Between 1909 and 1912, the salary bill for these

three establishment alone rose about 25 per cent.[201] The Works therefore proposed that the Brydon buildings be reserved for the two great departments of Local Government and Education, together with some smaller departments that could be removed if necessary, primarily the suffering Works itself, which had moved from Whitehall Place to hired premises in Storey's Gate. 'Immense delay and inconvenience are now occasioned by so many sections of this Department being dispersed in separate buildings . . . and the evil is likely to become more acute. Moreover, the present temporary premises being necessarily in expensive situations involve a heavy outlay for rent' amounting to about £9000.[202] Lionel Earle, taking over as Secretary in 1912, recalled 'several water-tight compartments' resulting from this physical division, 'bad from the administrative point of view and inelastic and inconvenient as regards staff'.[203]

For once, the Treasury was on the side of the expansionists. One official noted: 'there has for some years been a general and very rapid increase in the amount of new accommodation which different Departments are requiring. No abatement of this constant growth seems probable in the future' (see Table 3). Congestion in the Office of Works would become worse in 1911 when it would take over responsibility for telephone exchanges. Discussions between the Treasury and the Works produced a confidential print for cabinet consideration in April 1911: the southern extension of

67. No. 43 Parliament Street. Despite the large amount of new building in the early twentieth century, the growth of government business resulting from pre-war social legislation and wartime controls perpetuated the tradition of hiring private houses.

the Brydon building would contain about 165,000 sq. ft, on which Education and Local Government had first claim, amounting to about 30,000 sq. ft; Trade already occupied as large an area as the extension. If the Works, occupying 62,000 sq. ft at a rental of £10,400, were allocated 85,000 sq. ft, there would still be enough in the extension for the Charity Commission, the Exchequer and Audit Office, and occasional royal commissions. The growth of the Inland Revenue demanded more space at Somerset House, so the Registrar-General might be moved to Westminster. The Admiralty might need the 26,000 sq. ft still vacant at Charing Cross, 'and it is difficult to assign limits to the future requirements of the Public Service arising from prospective legislation and increase of population'.[204] Following a cabinet committee's decision to rebuild Trade in Whitehall Gardens, the Works again hammered home this last point: 'it is difficult to set bounds to the demands likely to be made in the future for office accommodation; but considering the continuous growth of population, and of the legislation on labour, state insurance, and other social subjects, those demands are certain to be heavy'.[205]

68. Whitehall: Ministry of Defence. Vincent Harris's winning design for the Board of Trade, 1915, (cp. pl. 201a) was ultimately realised in the 1950s, incorporating eighteenth-century 'fine rooms' from Pembroke and Malmesbury Houses formerly on the site.

These official lucubrations emerged into the parliamentary daylight as the Public Offices (Sites) Bill was hurried through the Commons late in the 1912 session, on the grounds that the offices were urgently required,[206] the government resisting any amendment whatever in order to avoid a report stage.[207] It was ironic in the extreme (but typical of this whole story) that the principal site, that in Whitehall Gardens for the new Board of Trade, was not built on until the 1950s. A competition for the new building was held in 1914–15, but because of the war work was not begun. Although a huge office to house seven thousand civil servants was proposed in 1929–31, the economic crisis of 1931 compelled the First Commissioner, George Lansbury (1859–1940), to abandon his bill.[208] When the economy picked up in the mid 1930s, the project was resumed, but arguments between architect and client developed,[209] and nothing was begun before the Second World War. No major government building was undertaken in central London between the two world wars. When building was resumed, it was a modified version of Vincent Harris's winning design of 1915 [Pl. 201] that was erected in the 1950s [Pl. 68].

A study group appointed by the Treasury during the Second World War to consider civil service working conditions concluded scathingly in 1944 that:

So far as this country is concerned, the end of the 1914–18 war is usually regarded as somewhat of a landmark in office building. Before then, large offices – especially public offices – were either built primarily as architectural creations or were very much like large private houses. They may possibly have been in some cases designed to meet the immediate requirements of the original tenants, but they provided no facilities for expansion or for re-arrangement of working spaces. They show few signs of consideration being given to efficient work or to the comfort of the inhabitants. In general, apart from any special halls or ceremonial rooms, the working parts of the buildings were made up of comparatively small rooms. In government headquarters offices the convenience and healthiness of the interior were often sacrificed to exterior architectural features, such amenities as good natural lighting and ventilation taking second place in the scheme. . . . After 1918 new ideas, largely imported from America, began to materialise.[210]

There can be a great deal of beauty to be seen in and satisfaction to be derived from a building whose structure has frankly been dictated by the use for which it is intended. . . . [it is] difficult not to fall amongst several stools in any attempt to create a building which shall be a modern office, a piece of monumental architecture designed to typify the solidity and permanence of the Nation and the authority of the Government, conform to an inconvenient site contour, and harmonise externally with Georgian and Victorian buildings of the same class – which is the problem in Whitehall.[211]

Given these views, it is not surprising that officials determined to pull down Scott's block, and replace it by something to suit modern needs. Sir Cosmo Parkinson, permanent secretary of the Colonial Office, writing in 1947 before the 'winds of change' had begun to blow very fiercely, looked for

a building worthy of British colonial administration! It should, of course, be an up-to-date and well-appointed building: there would be grand scope for the architect in the interior decoration with some of the lovely woods from colonies. . . . But at last we could have so much that is wanted besides the ordinary office rooms: for instance, conference and committee rooms; proper accommodation for the hard-pressed typing and shorthand staff and rest-rooms for their use; congenial waiting-rooms for visitors; a dignified Chancery, long overdue, for the Most Distinguished Order of St Michael and St George, and a suitable room for the use of the Corona Club. It should be a general colonial centre, not just an administrative headquarters; and into the picture would fit the dream of the Library Committee for an expanded and reorganized library serving both the Colonial Office and the public in ways not possible under present conditions.[212]

69.   The Secretary of State's Room, The Foreign Office (G.G. Scott, 1863–8): nerve centre of ganglia circling the globe 'from China to Peru'.

4
The Office of Works, 1851–1873

To create a splendid modern city, worthy to rank among great capitals, London needed new administrative machinery. The setting up in 1855 of the Metropolitan Board of Works (MBW), with the limited purposes of draining London's sewers and making better roads, has been referred to above. Its history is told elsewhere.[1] Between the MBW's activities and those of the Office of Works there was little direct connexion; central government held aloof, as its parliamentary watchdogs desired, from any question of mere 'metropolitan improvement'. The royal commission of 1853 which had recommended the creation of the MBW thought it should be 'entrusted with the management of public works in which all parts of the metropolis had a common interest'.[2] Although the 1855 Metropolitan Building Act transferred to the new authority the functions of the Metropolitan Buildings Office,[3] and the MBW created an Architect's Branch which gradually acquired an extensive range of functions,[4] these were essentially municipal in character. Only occasionally was there any kind of partnership between the central government and the MBW. Financed by rates charged upon Londoners, composed of men elected by the metropolitan vestries, the lowest tier of local government authorities in the capital, the MBW was incapable of taking a generous view of metropolitan improvement; although during the Board's existence from 1855 to 1889 it spent some thirteen million pounds on street improvements (of which more than four millions were recouped by sales of surplus lands),[5] the end result was merely to keep pace with 'the wants of an ever-increasing population, and the needs of a traffic which has grown relatively even more than the population'.[6] The new or widened streets scarcely compared with Haussmann's *grands boulevards*. Once a street had been laid out, private enterprise had a free hand erecting the buildings that flanked it. The lack of any control, such even as Nash had exercised over Regent Street, left the standard of design generally low.

What then of central government's new building? The separation in 1851 of the Office of Works from that of Land Revenues[7] was designed to create a ministry of public building which in the first place should be under the control of the Treasury, so that no grandiose schemes should be promoted that had not been scrutinised (and cut down) by that department, which saw its role primarily as one of restraining expenditure; and secondly should be entirely dependent for funding on parliamentary votes. This system ensured that any project for a major public building would be, if not strangled at birth, exposed to the utmost rigours of an uncongenial climate and likely to mature as but a puny caricature of the original concept.

In such a climate it was improbable that this ministry of public building would be equipped with a staff capable of initiating and conducting major public works, such as France enjoyed in the *Bâtiments Civils* and parallel services.[8] The crucial personnel in the Office of Works were the First Commissioner, the Secretary, and the Architect. The First Commissioner was so entitled because the 1851 Act[9] retained the notion of a 'Board of Works', composed of the secretaries of state, and the president and vice-president of the Board of Trade. On only one occasion, however, did the Board as such exercise any function,[10] although the term was constantly employed in formal correspondence, and it came to be understood as meaning 'for the practical purposes of the daily work of the Office' the First Commissioner, the Secretary and the Assistant Secretary, a usage that appears as early as 1867.[11]

In reality, the First Commissioner was Minister of Public Works. But he was bound by Act of Parliament 'to act in conformity to the views and wishes of the Treasury, who, moreover, have the entire control of the estimates and are thus able most effectually to govern the policy and action of his Department'.[12] This subordination to the Treasury was to be the despair of innovative and enterprising First Commissioners. The minister, however, was not chosen for his interest in architecture or the arts, in contrast to contemporary France; the office was 'always one of political convenience', as Lord Wemyss remarked in 1889: 'Looking back for well on 50 years, I do not know of any single holder of that office whom any noble Lord in private life, if he were building a house of his own, would have consulted as to what he ought to do – except one.'[13] Lord Rosebery, himself briefly First Commissioner in 1885 (between February 1885 and August 1886, there were five changes)[14] explained that 'The ordinary First Commissioner is supposed to be a man of business, not unversed in public affairs,[15] who will take a common-sense view of the situation, and get the opinion of experts as far as he can.'[16] Lord Fortescue commented that the consequence was that 'naturally they were under the practical ascendancy of some permanent officials whose zeal is more remarkable than their taste or practical skill'.[17] This situation led to calls for a permanent Minister of Works, or a permanent advisory council, such as the French possessed in the *Conseil de Bâtiments Civils*.[18]

Thus Lord Llanover (as Sir Benjamin Hall, First Commissioner 1855–8) told a committee in 1860: 'I think that one of the greatest absurdities existing in the State now is, that the First Commissioner of Works should be a political officer. . . . The duty of the First Commissioner is to carry out those works which are sanctioned by Parliament and he ought to be a man who has some knowledge of works . . . that would enable him to go into the matters of architecture and building and surveying with those with whom he is brought into contact.' He had 'a strong feeling upon the subject that these works ought to be carried out under a permanent head', whom he would put on the same footing as the Master of the Rolls (a judge), independent of party and government. Exclusion from the Commons would give him time to work during the session, something that Llanover had found a problem. One of the junior Treasury lords could answer parliamentary questions.[19]

This was like today's oft-heard cry, 'Let's take education out of politics.' It was simplistic to argue that 'the Office of Works is a mere department for structural works, to carry out the works which have been sanctioned by Parliament'.[20] As had been seen in

1855–9, public building questions could become extraordinarily contentious, and it was necessary to have someone in parliament who could answer for them. A junior, such as the Treasury lord suggested by Hall, would not have carried the necessary weight. And the First Commissioner, for all that he was little more than 'the chief clerk of the Treasury',[21] was able to take decisions (such as dismissing Edward Barry from his position as architect for the Houses of Parliament) which reverberated in Parliament.[22] Llanover's view ignored the circumstance that many of his ministerial decisions affected directly or indirectly the common man, who was all too likely to have strongly-held (if erroneous) opinions on them; and that such issues are of the very matter of politics, though not necessarily party politics. The position of the New Law Courts, or the site of the National Gallery were among the most contentious issues of their day.

Nevertheless, the idea of a permanent First Commissioner or 'Ædile', or two permanent commissioners alongside a political one (as recommended by the Office Surveyor),[23] or a council of experts to advise the minister on artistic questions, and the possibility of transforming the Works into a powerful Ministry of Fine Arts were canvassed in the press from time to time,[24] and were further discussed by a select committee chaired by Lord Elcho (later Wemyss) in 1869. Elcho himself, supported by Cowper and Layard with their experience as First Commissioners, and the eminent architectural amateur A.J. Beresford Hope, PPRIBA, was keen to extend the authority of the First Commissioner over all major building works in the metropolis, and proposed an advisory council to support him;[25] but Lord John Manners, another ex-Commissioner, was opposed: either the council would 'exercise all real power', as in France; or it would be merely advisory, not a function that would attract men of eminence.[26] The current Secretary, George Russell, favoured enhancing the standing of the First Commissioner, but thought that what was needed was not permanence, but continuity – to be supplied by the permanent officials. In the event, Elcho was unable to carry recommendations for strengthening the position of First Commissioner.[27] The architectural press continued to debate the question from time to time, but the political realities ensured that no action was taken. It was impossible, as the experience of the Poor Law Commissioners had shown in the 1830s and '40s, for controversial questions of public expenditure to be 'taken out of politics', as members of the Miscellaneous Expenditure committee of 1860 clearly appreciated;[28] and in view of that difficulty it was at that period thought essential for the First Commissioner to be a member of the Commons.[29]

Given the ephemeral lifespan of the average First Commissioner, it is clear that the role of the Secretary was of crucial importance. The first holder of that post, the able and industrious Trenham Walshman Philipps (1795–1855), who had held a similar position under the previous combined Office,[30] died in 1855 from his unremitting devotion to duty. He was succeeded by Alfred Austin, from the Poor Law Board, who was a capable administrator. On his retirement in 1868, the aristocratic Assistant Secretary George Russell[31] was promoted. Layard pointed out that 'the office of both Assistant Secretary and Secretary to this department requires peculiar qualifications and especially tact, firmness and a knowledge of the world in dealing with the various persons, some placed in the highest position, with whom the Office of Works is constantly brought into relations'.[32] Thereafter, it was accepted that high social standing was a prerequisite for this post closely connected with the royal Court. But it was not until the arrival of Russell's successor, Bertram Mitford, a diplomatist, that the Secretary appears to have played a major role in what may be termed the technical department, the more purely planning and architectural side of the department's work. That was partly because the earlier

70. James Pennethorne (1801–71), kt 1870. Government architect and surveyor, 1845–70, responsible for street planning, new parks, and a notable series of public buildings. Pennethorne worked towards a synthesis of antique and modern architecture such as leading contemporary critics were calling for, but relatively few of his major designs were executed, Sir Benjamin Hall preventing his being employed for new government offices in 1856–8.

Secretaries were trained administrators, but largely because of the standing of the third significant figure, the architectural adviser. By the loss of such a character, Mitford, as Secretary in the 1880s, despite his lack of architectural knowledge, 'was left apparently master of the situation.'[33]

Since 1845 James Pennethorne (1801–71)[34] [Pl. 70], sometime assistant to John Nash, had been sole Architect and Surveyor to the Board, continuing to serve both Works and Woods & Forests after 1851. Standing well in his profession, he was responsible for metropolitan improvements, conducted under the Office of Works until the responsibility was transferred to the new Metropolitan Board of Works in 1855; and he designed such public buildings 'as he could undertake with his other duties'[35] between 1848 and 1856, executing most of the architectural work under the Office. Sir William Molesworth (1810–55) [Pl. 71], First Commissioner of Works 1852–5, called on him for plans for new public offices around Downing street [Pl. 118]. Sir Benjamin Hall (1802–67)[36] [Pl. 71] as First Commissioner re-introduced the marketplace principle of open competition for government commissions in 1856, and Pennethorne was marginalised, though a departmental committee redefined his role in 1859, and he did not retire until 1870. Hall brought in as his adviser Henry Hunt, probably the leading surveyor of his day (who had, as was not unusual at that time, himself designed buildings). Hunt continued to exercise a powerful influence until his retirement in 1886, a role examined in greater detail below. When Austen Henry Layard (1817–94)[37] [Pl. 72] became First Commissioner in 1868, he appreciated the need for an adviser specifically on design questions. After the collapse of Layard's high hopes in 1869, that adviser was, as we shall see,

71.   a. Sir William Molesworth, Bt (1810–55), Radical politician. First Commissioner of Works Jan. 1853–July 1855. He took up the question of building new government offices, and commissioned plans.
b. Sir Benjamin Hall, Bt (1802–67), Radical MP for Marylebone 1837–59, cr. Lord Llanover 1859. First Commissioner of Works, 1855–58. Hall carried out major reforms in the Office of Works, and revived the practice of open competition for choosing architects for public buildings.

72.   Austen Henry Layard (1817–94), Radical MP for Southwark 1860–69, G.C.B. 1878. First Commissioner of Works 1868–69; trustee of National Gallery from 1866. Layard excavated Nimrûd (which he believed to be Nineveh) in 1845–7, from which important antiquities were sent to the British Museum. A connoisseur and collector of Italian art, he took a keen interest in architecture. His efforts to transform the Office of Works into a means of making London the finest of European capitals having been thwarted in 1869, he accepted a post in the Diplomatic Service.

replaced by a Royal Engineer officer, as Director of Works.[38] The precise demarcation of function between Director of Works and Surveyor was hazy, and neither was an authority on design. In a period when the Office bought architectural designs in the open market, this was less crucial than when Office employees were largely preferred, as from the later 1880s; but it was nonetheless a serious weakness in the British public works organisation, the more so as British architects had little schooling in design of large public buildings.[39]

With the huge growth in the activities of the Office of Works in the later nineteenth century the capabilities of the second-tier professional men, the salaried 'surveyors' – not conceded the title of 'architect' until this century – became of much greater importance, an issue that will be discussed below. During Mitford's secretaryship (1874–86) they lacked the professional standing that would have enabled them to oppose him effectively: salaried architects were regarded with some contempt in a profession which most practitioners still regarded as a gentlemanly art, to be remunerated by fees – a profession in which the potential rewards were vastly greater than the miserable salaries paid by the state.[40]

The role of the Office of Works in the 1850s was, to draw an analogy from the building trade, essentially that of a jobbing builder, not a contractor. It was organised for the maintenance of the royal palaces and government buildings, with an official in charge of each major building or group of buildings who had to refer to Whitehall Place for authority to carry out any but works of the most crucial urgency. The staff in Whitehall Place were engaged on correspondence, the examination of accounts of work executed, or the preparation of the annual estimates to lay before Parliament. Average annual Works expenditure under parliamentary votes between 1851 and 1861 was some £528,000.[41] Much of its labour (though only a small portion of expenditure) was devoted to matters of 'housekeeping' for departments – supplying coal, wood, oil, candles, soap, etc.[42] The supply of furniture was another, more costly, burden.

Apologists of this system argued that it was unnecessary to salary or retain a leading architect (as had been done between 1815 and 1832),[43] because whenever Parliament should approve a major building operation, it should promptly be entrusted to the market. Competition would produce a design better than could be expected from any salaried architect; and the responsibility for executing it soundly and within the agreed estimate would lie fairly and squarely on the architect thrown up by competition. Unfortunately, this state of beatitude was seldom realised. MPs all too often tended not to like the designs thrown up by competition (it was not always clear whose designs had been thrown up, anyway): they were too grand or too insignificant, too eccentric, too trivial, too lacking in true taste. When they were costed they invariably proved to be more expensive than the Treasury had contemplated, and the reduced designs were likely to meet with further objection. When a revised design was ultimately settled upon and put to the test of the market, i.e. competitive tendering, the lowest tender often turned out higher than expected, so that further revisions of design would be called for. When the work was being executed, strikes, or difficulties in obtaining requisite building materials, or changing needs, resulted in delays that provoked parliamentary criticism which the minister would shrug off on the architect, whom it was difficult to hold to account as he was an independent man with intrinsic resources beyond the work he was doing for the public. Thus successive ministers of Works came to appreciate the need for public officers capable of vetting the designs thrown up by competition, and capable of keeping an eye, such as any private client might do, on building operations once they were under way.

The first critical comments came from the enquiry into public offices conducted by Sir Charles Trevelyan, Secretary to the Treasury, and Sir Stafford Northcote, formerly Gladstone's private secretary, in 1853. They looked to the setting up of an organisation that should be responsible for government building operations as a whole, the Works taking over building for the Post Office and the Boards of Customs and Inland Revenue.[44] But the existing Office lacked adequate strength, and was badly housed. Arrangements had been settled

> with too exclusive a reference to immediate pecuniary considerations, and with too little appreciation of the importance of securing the services of duly qualified persons to succeed to its more responsible situations . . . the invariable tendency of builders and others engaged upon extensive works to outrun their estimates renders it very important that a strict watch should be kept upon their proceedings; and the eminence of the professional architects, engineers, and contractors, who are employed upon the chief public edifices, is such as to make it necessary that the controlling Department should have at its command the services of men of high and well recognized ability.[45]

Regarding the Professional Branch, they remarked:

> The greatest care should at all times be taken in supplying the important position of Surveyor of Works by the appointment of gentlemen of sufficient eminence as architects to be able to maintain a proper degree of authority in acting on behalf of the Board of Works in cases where it is brought into communication with the leading professional men of the day.

(The then Surveyor, William Southcote Inman (1798–1879), a survivor from the 1840s, did not satisfy that criterion.)[46] The First Commissioner's proposal to make special reference from time to time to 'eminent practising architects and engineers' might advantageously be adopted, but would not obviate the need for 'strengthening the permanent appointment of Surveyor of Works and Buildings as much as possible', and the government must be prepared to pay an appropriate salary – which was, indeed, a general theme of the report. Thus, the 'examiners' were not mere clerks, but really auditors, and should be paid accordingly:

> they do not confine themselves to a mere computation of the correctness of the figures in the accounts, but they also exercise a critical check over the details, such as none but professional persons can apply; thus, if in an account for mason's work it appears that the quantities of materials charged for are out of proportion to the time occupied in the work and charged for in the labour account, the Professional Examiners detect and call attention to the discrepancy.

Similarly, in the General Branch (Secretariat), 'Economy is dearly purchased by the sacrifice of efficiency; indeed it cannot be said to be so purchased at all.'

The Treasury responded by approving the addition of an Assistant Secretary; but within a year the long-serving Secretary, Philipps, fell ill, did not attend the Office for eleven months and, 'really worn out in the public service', died in November 1855. The new Assistant Secretary, Thornborrow, was 'seized with a malady which affected his head', and retired. The Surveyor of Works, Inman, 'acted, in point of fact, [merely] as one of the principal clerks in the office'; while the Assistant Surveyor told the minister in 1855 that 'he had nothing to do at that time particularly' – whereupon he was sent on indefinite leave before being retired, along with his chief. The way was then clear for the new First Commissioner, Sir Benjamin Hall, appointed in July 1855, to re-model the office

organisation.[47] Administratively one of the most effective First Commissioners,[48] Hall created the framework of the mid- and late-Victorian Office of Works. As mentioned above, he persuaded Alfred Austin (1805–84)[49] to exchange a Poor Law inspectorate for the Secretaryship, and secured George Russell (1830–1911) from the Treasury as Assistant Secretary. This still left the question of to whom he was to turn for advice on architectural questions.

Hall appears to have viewed Pennethorne as part of the worn-out furniture of the Office. He had formed this unfavourable impression because 'scarcely any metropolitan improvement had been carried out by this department [the Office of Works] for the amount at which it had been estimated'; Pennethorne's reports on the current improvements that he was conducting – particularly the formation of Battersea Park[50] – Hall regarded as 'not . . . at all satisfactory'. Austin described him as an executive officer, executing the directions of the Board (i.e. the First Commissioner and Secretary); what Hall required was the advice of an experienced professional man, a surveyor to 'know every new mode that there was of carrying out buildings, of combining the different materials that are used in building, iron, and wood, and stone, and seeing how they were worked up'.[51] Given the salary he could pay, a full-time top-rank surveyor was beyond his grasp. He therefore proposed part-time employment to the eminent surveyor Henry Hunt,[52] who was unanimously recommended by the principal London architects. Engaged for one day a week at a salary of £1000 a year, Hunt in the event was to give up about half his time to the work of the office.[53] He advised on 'all matters which require the advice of a professional gentleman of his experience . . . every question of the slightest importance . . . as to which we want correct and judicious advice'.[54] He drew up the specifications for the Government Offices competition of 1856–7, having 'sat down' with the permanent under-secretaries at the Foreign and War Offices.[55] He then ensured that the drawings and specifications for the actual building were 'properly matured, and the subject thoroughly investigated and understood' before putting them out to tender, so that he could be 'quite sure that the lowest tender will not be exceeded when a building is completed'.[56] Hall was convinced that this system was 'one of the most perfect arrangements which can possibly be conceived, for a public department', with the one drawback, that the head was a political officer.[57] He believed, as we have seen, that he should be permanent.

In order to achieve the perfection of his organisation, Hall needed Treasury approval for an increase in staff; only minor improvements had been made following the Northcote-Trevelyan report. In 1857 a departmental committee consisting of Trevelyan, Lord Duncan (a lord of the Treasury) and G.A. Arbuthnot, auditor of the civil list, was appointed. 'After 1853 the committee of inquiry . . . became the Treasury's most important and effective instrument for controlling establishments', remarks the historian of Treasury control of the civil service in this period. In 1854–66, such committees investigated more than forty departments or sub-departments. 'At the same time they epitomized the willingness of the Treasury to seek agreement with the departments, the desire to cooperate with them, which is apparent in the day to day control.'[58] They consisted usually of two Treasury representatives, and one from the department, but departments subordinate to the Treasury rarely appointed a member. The Treasury representatives were generally selected from a small group: Trevelyan, Hamilton, Arbuthnot, Anderson, Stephenson; which thus acquired valuable expertise. 'With a continuous growth in the area and volume of government activity, they provided an efficient, informal, prompt, and cheap method of making changes in the machinery of administration.'[59]

The committee of 1857 reported little improvement since 1853;

the staff of the Works were too few and their salaries still often insufficient. Expenditure controlled by the Office had risen from nearly £600,000 in 1851–2 to £900,000 in 1855–6. It was 'expenditure of a kind peculiarly susceptible of being influenced both as to its amount and as to its proper application, by the employment of suitable professional agency and the exercise of a vigilant supervision'. Accordingly they recommended strengthening the staff.[60] This, however, still left undefined the position of Pennethorne, who had been effectively marginalised by Hall's decision that all the business of the Office properly pertaining to a surveyor should be executed by Hunt, at the same time as he rejected Pennethorne's designs for new government offices as 'objectionable' and such as 'would never be accepted'. He determined that such major works should be open to public competition.

Pennethorne ultimately declined to compete for the new government offices on the grounds that he was anyway entitled to the work, and that the knowledge he had acquired during the preliminary work would given him an unfair advantage over his competitors.[61] He was thus left with only works of a minor description, such as 'the repairs of two small houses for the Post-office',[62] whereas previously he had since 1851 been earning an average £6500 p.a. for his services to the two Offices of Works and Woods.[63] Pennethorne appealed to the Treasury, which supported Hall's actions, offering Pennethorne the anodyne reassurance that 'as regards your position as architect and surveyor, that you should not lightly be deprived of such business as has heretofore been entrusted to you in the valuation of property previous to sales or the grant of leases, or any arrangements connected with improvements'.[64]

A change of ministry in 1858 led to yet another departmental enquiry, to define the terms of Pennethorne's employment.[65] These were embodied in two Treasury minutes of 13 and 29 June 1859. Pennethorne, an able and original architect, though not to the taste of contemporary fashion, had a genuine grievance in that he had given up all private practice since 1845; if he were now reduced to Office odd-job man, he had little hope of resurrecting a profitable private practice. The Arbuthnot committee's decision offered a reasonable compromise: in return for a fixed salary of £1500 p.a. plus £850 for his office establishment, he was required to 'advise the Board on such questions generally as might be referred to him relating to works and public buildings'; he was to receive a commission on the public buildings on which he was still engaged (Public Record Office and London University), and the ban on private practice was rescinded: but in future he was not to accept commissions (public or private) without the consent of the First Commissioner.[66] He was, of course, also still surveyor to the Office of Woods (the Crown estate).

By 1860 Gladstone, back at the Treasury for his second stint as chancellor, had become sufficiently concerned about the system to call the prime minister's attention to the problem: 'The present system is very unsatisfactory', his financial secretary reported; '. . . There is no efficient check on the vast expenditure for public works and buildings either in the first design or in the erection – The first design is often the result of a parliamentary scramble, or of a public competition for plans where every motive operates for architectural display and against utility and economy. The erection is not properly controlled because changes of officer bring changes of views and weaken responsibility.' What was needed was a permanent head of the Office of Works under Treasury control. 'We could then plan all our Foreign offices and build them without throwing the whole matter loose for parliamentary committees and competing architects to gratify their tastes and build up their

reputations at the public expence, and without the same risk of Gothic extravaganzas whenever fortune gave us a medieval First Commissioner.'[67]

Gladstone himself denounced 'the lamentable and deplorable state of our whole arrangement with regard to the management of our public works' in a typical outburst in the Commons later that year. 'Vacillation, uncertainty, costliness, extravagance, meanness, and all the conflicting vices that could be enumerated were united in our present system.' But it was not the Office of Works that the chancellor was condemning. 'When anything was to be done they had to go from department to department – from the Executive to the House of Commons, from the House of Commons to a Committee, from a Committee to a Commission, and from a Commission back to a Committee – so that years passed away, the public were disappointed, and the money of the country was wasted. He believed such were the evils of the system, that nothing short of a revolutionary reform would ever be sufficient to rectify it.'[68] In other words, it was the defects of the nineteenth-century parliamentary system, with its annual votes of supply, which really invited the Protean Commons to interpose in questions of public works.[69] Gladstone, at this very period fighting the premier's proposals for long-term funding of defence expenditure,[70] had no solution, but his attack chimes with his determination to reassert executive control of policy.[71]

It was in such an atmosphere during the summer of 1860 that the select committee on miscellaneous expenditure investigated the Office of Works.[72] Members questioned the two senior officials, Austin and Hunt, the new First Commissioner William Cowper (1811–88)[73] [Pl. 73], and his predecessor Hall, now Lord Llanover. The latter naturally took the opportunity to defend the regime he had introduced, depicting in the blackest colours the one that he had superseded. He explained that he had 'wished all responsibility to centre in myself' (q.1436); his real difficulty had been to find the time for his duties while parliament was sitting (q.1381). The committee, as we have seen, investigated his views on having a permanent first commissioner. Austin explained the workings of the current system, while Cowper, still learning the ropes (he had been in post for only three months), discussed the constitution of his office, and his relationship with the Treasury. He described the Works as the initiating, the Treasury as the deciding department in the ordinary course of business (q.853); at any stage which required discretion, it was necessary to obtain Treasury sanction (q.772). He explained that the arrangement by which the Office of Works was under the control of a single head, himself under the control of the Treasury, gave in a more satisfactory manner that balance of power aimed at previously by constituting a board (q.855). This relationship between the Office of Works and the Treasury was to become a crucial issue.

The 1860s were a period of intense activity for the Office, and we must ask how successful Hall's machine was in withstanding such pressure. Questioned by a select committee shortly after coming to the Office, Cowper declared that he had found it 'in very good order. I found no arrears.'[74] Cowper himself stood very much in his step-father Palmerston's shade, and at first possessed little standing in the House. Indeed, one squire noted that he was 'often turned down as a sort of bag fox for the evening's sport'.[75] But he grew into the job, and the routine work of the Office was carried on efficiently. Austin brought its 'housekeeping' functions to a high pitch of economy. The departmental committee of 1867 found that two First Class clerks were quite enough for the more important work of the Secretariat and the Examiner's Branch, most of the business transacted by the clerks, while extensive, being intellectually undemanding.[76] A system of limited competition confined to contractors 'of known character and probity' ensured the successful working of the policy of accepting the lowest tender for new buildings.[77] The near collapse of the office in 1869–70 was not a fault of the design structure, but rather of the size of the Technical Branch, not adequate for the enormous new burdens heaped progressively on it, notably responsibility for crown post offices (from 1858) and county courts throughout the country. Consequently the Treasury was obliged to approve an increase in Office staff.[78]

The major weakness in Hall's structure was the lack of an architectural adviser, i.e., one competent to discuss the aesthetic merits of a design. Hall's enthusiasm for obtaining designs by competition perhaps led him to overlook this need. Although an architect might be selected through the competitive mechanism, it invariably proved that he had to remodel his design very extensively before it was executed: the Office of Works was expected to intervene at that stage to advise the Treasury on the merits of the modified design before it was submitted to Parliament and the people. Hall clearly had his own ideas about architectural style, though he confessedly was no expert. He was in frequent communication with the Prince Consort's secretary, who clearly transmitted his master's views.[79] He may have relied on Hunt for such advice as he felt he needed. Hunt's distinction was as a surveyor; although he had designed and executed building works on a large scale, and was 'always ready to give his chief the advantage of his extensive experience and varied knowledge',[80] he was not a professed architect, avowedly possessed of the *arcana* of design and the power of aesthetic judgment. Nevertheless he was always consulted on planning.[81] He himself recommended the appointment of a non-professional permanent commissioner to advise the parliamentary commissioner.[82]

Cowper initiated great projects and like Hall sought to purchase design in the marketplace; it fell to his Conservative successor, Lord John Manners[83] [Pl. 51], a supporter of the Gothic Revival, to appoint the architects; but their designs were still in embryo when Henry Layard took up the reins of office in November 1869. Layard was known politically as a Radical and an administrative reformer, attitudes associated with a zest for economy in public expenditure: it was doubtless this aspect of the man which induced Gladstone to appoint him to the Office of Works.[84] But Gladstone's intricate mind probably conceived a double coup, for Layard was a notable aesthete, a connoisseur of painting, who had himself sketched a new National Gallery and was full of ideas for building an imperial London: a pre-eminent candidate for Minister for the Arts.

Layard, zealous both for 'real economy' and for better architecture, immediately identified the need for an architectural adviser. With an unparalleled government building programme, 'I thought it absolutely necessary . . . that there should be some officer attached to the Board who could revise the plans and elevations of Architects, advise the First Commissioner with respect to them, and control the expenditure connected with them.'[85] 'No such control as was necessary to economy existed. The wasteful and unnecessary expenditure on the new Foreign Office, the manner in which space has been thrown away in providing for the different scientific societies in the new buildings on the Burlington House Site, and several other instances might be mentioned in proof of the necessity of this control.' His predecessor Lord John Manners had been aware of the lack of an officer to keep watch over the execution of major public buildings.[86] Hunt could not fulfil this role; he was 'in every sense a consulting surveyor, and not in any sense an executive officer. It was no part of his duty as surveyor to examine plans with reference to their architectural merits or defects'.[87] Pennethorne, for his part, was not an adequate adviser: he was a practising

73.   William Francis Cowper (1811–88), cr. Lord Mount-Temple 1880. First Commissioner of Works 1860–6. Ostensibly son of the 5th Earl Cowper (d. 1837), his real father was commonly thought to be Lord Palmerston, who married his widowed mother in 1839, and to whose estates Cowper ultimately succeeded. As Works minister, he sustained the principle of competition for designs.

architect; 'and being a member of the profession declined to give opinions upon the plans, elevations, and estimates of other architects'.[88] Furthermore his entire time was taken up in handling negotiations for government property and the Crown estate.

Pennethorne's role might advantageously be filled by an officer of the Royal Engineers, such as were employed by the Department of Science and Art. The requisite adviser was not to be a consultant architect but an officer of the Board of Works. It needed 'someone sufficiently well acquainted with architecture, carrying with him a certain weight with the Public, and with the Architectural profession, and of business like habits'.[89]

Therefore with Treasury approval Layard appointed a 'Secretary for Works and Buildings' to superintend works and buildings undertaken by the department, 'the supervision of Architects Plans and Estimates, and a general control over the expenditure connected with public edifices under the charge of the Office of Works'.[90] 'Not exercising the profession of an architect, nor necessarily an architect, [he] might advise and assist the First Commissioner in all questions connected with public buildings and monuments' and, apparently, divide the administration with the Secretary.[91] His choice was his friend, the eminent critic and historian of architecture, James Fergusson (1808–86)[92] [Pl. 74–5].

The administrative reformer in Layard seized on a plan for greatly lightening the burden of routine in the Office, which would

THE LATE MR. JAMES FERGUSSON, F.R.S.,
ARCHITECT AND ARCHÆOLOGIST.

at the same time finance this new appointment. As the average annual expenditure of each government department on ordinary furniture and housekeeping was, thanks to Austin's scrutiny, accurately known, an annual sum might be allocated to each department which would henceforth conduct its own house-keeping, so relieving the Works of an immense routine labour of checking departmental expenditures on candles, coals and the like. The post of assistant secretary could then be abolished and more than one clerk dispensed with. The suggestion was regarded favourably by the economically-minded chancellor of the Exchequer, Robert Lowe, who appointed a departmental committee of Stephenson and G.A. Hamilton, permanent secretary of the Treasury,[93] with Austin, the retiring Secretary of the Works.

They realised that the division of responsibility would have led to confusion, but recognised that the weakness of Hall's machinery was the lack of an 'adviser in some of the most important parts of his [the First Commissioner's] functions, namely, the forming a judgment upon the designs of public buildings and controlling their execution, whether in the construction of new buildings or the alteration of old ones'.[94] It rested, as we have seen, neither with Pennethorne nor with Hunt to supply the defect in the Office structure. Layard's appointment of Fergusson was therefore justified. Fergusson had supposed that he would be devoting his mind 'principally to architectural questions, and larger questions'; and that he would be inspecting public buildings and monuments 'in all parts of the country'.[95] But under a Treasury minute of 14 January 1869 laying out his duties, he found himself burdened with a multitude of secretariat duties, for the Treasury had refused to redistribute the house-keeping functions of the Office to departments. The new Secretary, too, George Russell, found similarly that he was carrying out his former duties as Assistant Secretary, as well as those of his new post. The committee pointed out that the duties of the secretariat were 'very various and extensive, and they are increasing from year to year', involving scrupulous attention to

74. James Fergusson (1808–86). Architectural historian and advocate of a modern architecture that would reflect the age. A friend of Layard, who appointed him Assistant Secretary, Office of Works, 1868–9, charged with advising on the merits of architectural designs.

75. Competition design for New Government Offices, 1857, by James Fergusson: an attempt to create a contemporary style of architecture.

detail 'and an amount of correspondence greater than might appear to be in proportion to the total expenditure'. To transfer some of the secretarial functions to Fergusson 'would entail confusion of duties and embarrassment in the transaction of the business of the Office'.[96] Fergusson's office should therefore be re-designated 'Inspector of Public Buildings and Monuments', not only to examine 'the designs of large public buildings or proposals for extensive alterations', but also 'that their proper execution should also come under his observation'. There was also the likelihood that 'public monuments and historical buildings generally' might be placed in the First Commissioner's care, some already being in his charge. A reduction in Fergusson's salary to £750 p.a. would go towards the re-instatement of an Assistant Secretary.

In accepting these recommendations, Layard insisted that Fergusson's appointment was not that of a consulting architect; it was a post that 'need not necessarily be filled by an architect'. His duty should be 'to advise the First Commissioner on all matters connected with public buildings and monuments, and on the plans, elevations and estimates of architects, and to exercise a control over the expenditure arising out of the erection of public buildings'. He should be free from routine business, and not even obliged to attend the Office at fixed hours.[97] He followed up this with a proposal that Pennethorne's post as Consulting Architect be abolished within six months.[98]

Unfortunately the new arrangement was given little opportunity of success. Layard was bitterly disappointed by his subordination to the Treasury. 'I find that the Office [of First Commissioner] is little better than that of a clerk in the Treasury. . . . I am responsible to Parliament and the country without having any independent action of my own', he told the premier.[99] 'Of late', it seemed to him, 'the Treasury has attempted to control the whole Government. Gradually the Office of Works, the Post Office, the Mint etc have been reduced to mere subordinate sections of that department.'[100] This was no new thing, so far as the Works was concerned: the act of 1851 made its subordination to the Treasury quite explicit. William Cowper had stated in 1860: 'Complete authority is given to the Treasury. . . . I look upon the First Commissioner now, as in point of fact he is, like an officer of the Treasury.'[101]

Disillusioned and subjected to malign attack in parliament, Layard was replaced as First Commissioner in October 1869 by the very man he regarded as his chief enemy, Acton Smee Ayrton (1816–86),[102] Financial Secretary at the Treasury [Pl. 76], where he had quarrelled with the Chancellor, Robert Lowe. Although both men sought economy keenly, their personal hostility ensured that the course of business did not flow smoothly. Ayrton's narrow conception of his new role ensured that Fergusson would not find his place congenial, and he resigned at the end of 1869. Hunt summed it up: 'It was soon discovered . . . that Mr Fergusson applied himself chiefly to matters of taste, his previous habits not having fitted him for the technical investigation that was needed.'[103] But that was a surveyor's view, and a rival's.

Ironically enough, arch-economist and contemner of architects as he was, Ayrton had no sooner cleared the Office of his predecessor's intimates than he began, in his turn, to urge upon the Treasury the need for an architectural adviser. In doing so he could not resist criticising Layard's arrangements to the extent of distorting the truth.[104] He referred to the lack of that 'Superior Officer or Chief Architect and Surveyor, with whom the First Commissioner could advise in superintending the duties of these executive officers', postulated by the Treasury minute of 25 June 1859. A 'number of important questions connected with Public Buildings in course of erection and with others which are in contemplation' required the advice of 'a competent Architect possessed of practical experience, and acquainted with all the modes in which the

76. Acton Smee Ayrton (1816–86), Radical MP for Tower Hamlets 1857–74. Secretary to the Treasury 1868–9; First Commissioner of Works 1869–73. Ayrton boasted of his ignorance of art, sneered at critics, sought to employ government employees to design public buildings in an economical style, and was ruthless in cutting down estimates for new buildings. He recreated, in effect, a government architectural service.

technical business of an Architect and Surveyor is carried on, devoting himself exclusively to the Public Service'. Ayrton paid lip service to Hunt's 'valuable services' which would continue 'on his present footing', but suggested that when he retired he should be replaced by an additional technical assistant. He blamed the weakness of the department on the arrangement that the Architect's salary was 'deemed a remuneration for . . . general supervision and advice relating to existing buildings' while services relating to new buildings were paid by commission. 'By this arrangement the Architect was placed in a false relation to the head of the Department and the practice had grown up of not employing [him] to the extent originally intended for the general and special business of the Department, but of remitting all important matters either to him as an Architect on Commission, or of calling in other Architects independently of him to execute works on commission.'

While it is highly improbable that the framers of the 1859 Treasury Minute had any such intention as Ayrton ascribed to them, it was true that the large sums expended for professional services were 'withdrawn from the notice of the Treasury' by being paid out of the parliamentary Votes for the various new buildings, to the extent of nearly £24,000 in 1866–9. A competent crown architect and surveyor would 'require a considerable salary and an establishment to use his services efficiently'. Ayrton doubted whether their time would be fully occupied by their Works duties, and suggested that they should, like Pennethorne, service the Woods and Forests also, that department meeting half the cost. A net increase of £1150 would probably be saved by 'putting an end to the practice of employing in future, Architects and others on commission for technical services'. The Treasury might then consider how far the employment of special architects might be dispensed with.[105] Ayrton was thus proposing in effect a reversion to eighteenth-century practice. In this he stood little chance of success, partly because neither he nor the Treasury was prepared to pay a salary

77. Douglas Galton (1822–99): 1862–9 assistant under-sec. for War; 1869–75 director of Works and Public Buildings; 1895 president, British Association. Perhaps the most eminent Royal Engineer of the century, he served on many commissions investigating sanitary matters.

that would attract an architect of the necessary distinction,[106] partly because it is inconceivable that the House of Commons would have tolerated a crown monopolist. Ayrton was forced to shift his ground and campaign against the concept of paying architects by commission on outlay, a principle which many MPs and laymen found repugnant as it gave the architect no incentive to restrain the costs of a building.

Even an advisory architect was to be denied Ayrton. Lowe had indeed made up his mind before Ayrton's letter, for the two men had had a previous conversation in which Lowe had made clear his objection to appointing an architect and his preference for an engineer officer, as Layard had suggested as a replacement for Pennethorne.[107] The use of Royal Engineers was an enthusiasm of the Science and Art Department, under the influence of Henry Cole, who developed the buildings at South Kensington with the aid of Captain Francis Fowke (d.1865) and Colonel Henry Scott. In evidence to Lord Elcho's select committee of 1869, Cole had urged the value of employing Royal Engineers (available like tap water) to prepare preliminary plans for public buildings and watch over the execution of 'the artistic completion' for which an architect would be employed if possible on a full-time engagement.[108]

The need to provide for an influential but lately-displaced civil servant may, however, have been the explanation of Lowe's stand. Captain Douglas Strutt Galton, R.E., C.B., F.R.S. (1822–99) [Pl. 77], a cousin of a Liberal politician, Lord Belper,[109] and ally of Florence Nightingale, had a high reputation as a sanitary engineer. From 1862 to 1869 he had been permanent assistant under-secretary at the War Office, in charge of army finance. His office was then abolished, under Cardwell's reforms. He had already, under Gladstone's Exchequer rules, been obliged to relinquish his military rank. He had therefore to be re-employed, or compensated. To Lowe, an old friend, he seemed the ideal person to instal at the Works: an administrator of proven efficiency, and a man familiar

with building design and works (he had designed the Herbert Military Hospital at Woolwich, sat on the Thames Embankment royal commission and was deeply versed in railway engineering).[110] Lowe had powerful justification for his action, in that it met the recommendation of Hunt – seen by Gladstone as 'adviser of the Government, and not merely of the 1st Commissioner' – who, aware that a suitable architect could not be obtained for £1500 a year, counselled the Treasury to appoint a Royal Engineer officer.[111] Gladstone found the argument conclusive, and Galton was appointed Director of Works and Buildings. At the same time, the appointment of an assistant surveyor was authorised.[112]

At first, Ayrton's resentment was palpable: he drew up instructions by which the new Director was to prepare not only estimates but also plans – driving Galton to protest – effectively – to the Treasury.[113] Then, no advantage, Ayrton insisted, could come from Scott's government offices designs being examined by Galton, 'who is not an architect . . . attempting to supersede the responsible functions of so skilful an architect as Mr Scott'. It required Lowe's reiterated instructions to bring the plans under Galton's scrutiny.[114] But Ayrton came to appreciate Galton's abilities. He drew up revised instructions by which he was to take instructions from the First Commissioner, 'give directions for the preparation of all plans, elevations, and estimates of new works, &c'; 'superintend the preparation of contracts with the assistance of the solicitor'; 'give instructions as to the mode of executing works'; and generally run the technical department.[115] Thus he advised not only on ways of reducing estimates for the new Home and Colonial Offices, but also recommended modifications in the plans for the new Law Courts, Natural History Museum and additions to the National Gallery. He kept a watchful eye upon buildings in progress, 'in the way that a person who is building a house looks in on behalf of his own interest, to see how the work is going on'; though careful not to diminish in any way the architect's responsibility.[116]

Part of Galton's work was to build up the Technical Branch, which had started with two Assistant Surveyors under the 1857 establishment, posts now held by John Taylor[117] for London, and William Starie, Country. In February 1871 an assistant, Henry Tanner, had been appointed after examination. When two more assistants were required in June 1873, Galton played his cards cleverly to obtain the man he wanted. He insisted that the examination must be more extensive for the superior post (£210–£300),[118] which led the Treasury to assert that examination would be inappropriate; the post should be filled by promotion, 'because there is no test like trial'. Galton responded that there were no juniors to promote, and an Order in Council of 1873 prohibited the permanent appointment of temporary employees commencing their duties after June 1870. In fact there was a suitable temporary assistant, and after Ayrton took up the cudgels on his behalf, the Treasury acquiesced in his appointment.

The Treasury very much disliked the employment of 'temporary' staff, paid weekly, continuously over long periods. Some of the Works' draughtsmen had been so employed for more than six years in 1872. Galton pointed out that their circumstances were quite different from those of clerks; they were taken on for a job because of their special qualifications, and if not required a permanent employee would be an incubus. At one time it might be a specialist in drainage that was needed; at another, one in decorative work. The use of temporary men gave the necessary flexibility. Nevertheless a core of permanent draughtsmen would be an advantage, and he suggested appointing one first-class (£200 × £15 − £300) and one second-class (£100 × £10 − £200) draughtsman for each of the four Assistant Surveyors (two were handling Post Office business). The Treasury sanctioned the establishment, but was less happy about making temporary men permanent: only their service antecedent to June 1870 secured their position.[119] But these men provided the pool from which were promoted the Assistant Surveyors of the future.

Resentment of the control imposed on him by the Treasury was somewhat ironically – given that he was 'perfectly sound on finance'[120] – to be Ayrton's downfall. In 1873 he clashed fiercely with the Treasury over the sum that Street might be allowed for his New Law Courts design, his recalcitrance eventually requiring the intervention of the cabinet. 'There is something thoroughly "mulish" about him', commented a colleague. 'He seems to resist for the pleasure of resistance.'[121] He then compounded his sins by disassociating himself at the earliest opportunity from responsibility for decisions imposed on him by the Treasury, in an official speech in the Commons[122] – behaviour which called forth a rebuke from *The Times*, and from Gladstone an assertion of the doctrine of ministerial responsibility.[123] His removal from the Office followed in the recess.

Ayrton had some justification in that Lowe at the Exchequer tended 'to undertake . . . to perform the functions which would seem to belong to this Board'.[124] Ayrton had, in a manner habitual with him, called attention to the problem by transgressing the customary mores of parliamentary behaviour; but it remained a problem, and was inquired into by the Childers committee on Civil Service Estimates during 1873. R.E. Welby, the permanent secretary of the Treasury, when asked whether his department did not sometimes decide on public works expenditure 'over the head, so to speak, of the First Commissioner, and without having his necessary concurrence?' argued that 'The Treasury is very often the common organ of the Government, and . . . expresses its views in a Minute which only appears to come from the [Treasury] Board, but which comes really from the Government, and is the organ of the Cabinet.'[125] There was 'nothing in the system' to prevent the Treasury acting 'without any control of an independent department'. Welby, asserting that 'I scarcely look upon the Board of Works as an independent department', nonetheless drew a distinction between the Treasury's financial control and the First Commissioner's 'executory' control; if the Treasury on rare occasions overstepped, as a matter of necessity, the bounds of financial control, it was from the need to see whether a proposed expenditure was justified.[126] Nevertheless, the notorious mutual hostility between Lowe and Ayrton[127] had encouraged 'executory' action by the Treasury, as, for example, over an abortive scheme to rebuild the Mint on the Embankment.

Despite Ayrton's somewhat ignominious removal from the Works – he was transferred to the minor post of Judge-Advocate-General – he is one of the most important First Commissioners. 'As First Commissioner [he] effected useful improvements in the administration of H.M.'s Works and Public Buildings which have been of permanent benefit';[128] or, as the secretary of the RIBA put it succinctly: 'Mr Ayrton, in an ungenial fashion, did much good.'[129] In his excessive zeal for economy, accompanied by public expressions of scorn for architects and artists as leeches that had fastened on to the Exchequer, he made many enemies; and he had no intention of building imperially. His ideal of the public office was James Williams's new General Post Office on the west side of St Martins-le-Grand [Pl. 78].[130] 'The fact is', wrote Layard (still burning with resentment against Ayrton) to his friend William Gregory (1817–92), 'that this is an instance of Office of Works architecture. The designs were completed and everything ready when I came into office. . . . Fergusson, very justly, did not approve of them and we made all the alterations which we could make without interfering with the estimate, to improve them. You know what patching up a design is – you can never make a really good thing of it. When Ayrton thought that he could gain credit for economy he claimed the merit of having had the designs made in the Office.'[131]

The large sums that had recently been paid in commission to outside architects were one of Ayrton's first targets on taking office. He urged the Treasury to put 'an end to the practice of employing, in future, Architects and others on commission for technical services under this Department, reserving any special cases to be dealt with as they arise, when it may be thought desirable to pay a certain sum for a particular report or design'.[132] In accord with this policy, he terminated Edward Barry's employment at the Houses of Parlia-

78. General Post Office West, James Williams, 1869–71. Williams, an Office of Works surveyor, was appointed by Lord John Manners to design the major new Post Office building in the City; his work was acclaimed by Ayrton as ideal public architecture. Smirke's original GPO may be seen on the left.

ment, subsequent works being executed by Office architects.[133] Those outside architects engaged on major new buildings – Street, Waterhouse, Edward Barry – were bound to a contract, being obliged to sign a memorandum defining terms of employment and payment.

Instead of the controversial commission on outlay, they were to be paid a pre-determined fixed sum. The architect's designs were to have 'a strict regard to the proposed cost', and if the 'most approved tender' exceeded that cost, he was to revise them accordingly. He was to 'perform, or cause to be performed, all other services necessarily or ordinarily rendered by an Architect or his assistants, with reference to the works, to their final completion';[134] but was to have a clerk of works, paid by the government. Ownership of all plans, drawings and specifications – another disputed point – was to lie in the government. Finally, 'No rules of the Royal Institute of British Architects or any other society shall be held binding upon the Commissioners in reference to the works or matters herein referred to.'[135]

Ayrton also pressed for bringing all public civil buildings under the Works, as the post offices had been in 1866. In consequence, the hitherto independent operations of the Science and Art Department at South Kensington[136] were so transferred early in 1870, to that department's considerable annoyance.[137] To the Works was transferred also control of the buildings of the British Museum, and the county law courts throughout the country.[138]

Ayrton's immediate demand to meet the increased workload was for another Assistant Surveyor (£500 × £20 − £700), 'thoroughly

trained up to the business of erecting and repairing substantially and ornamentally well constructed houses and buildings of a similar nature and largely experienced in all practical details. Very serious injury would result to the Public Service from any deficiency on his part in those respects', for Ayrton planned a reorganisation in the interests of 'efficiency and economy', dividing England into two districts (in addition to London), with an Assistant Surveyor in charge of all works in his district.[139] He also secured four additional draughtsmen for the London District Assistant Surveyor, and additional help in Examiners' Branch, at three guineas a week. To reduce the amount of mere copying required, the ink-flimsy copy-letter technique was introduced in August 1870. The number of men employed in the Office altogether rose from 85 in 1870/1 to 131 in 1872/3, though the appointment of urgently required assistants was delayed by the selection processes imposed by the Order in Council of 4 June 1870 which introduced the principle of open competition for entry to the Civil Service and was immediately applied to the Treasury and its subordinate departments: 'My Lords' declared roundly that they would not agree to any other system of recruiting except open competition followed by probation.[140] This increase in turn demanded additional accommodation: the bulk of the staff were in three adjoining houses in Whitehall Place, with overflows in Mid Scotland Yard and further south in Parliament Street.[141] As in other departments, the situation steadily deteriorated, and relief was still only prospective at the end of our period.

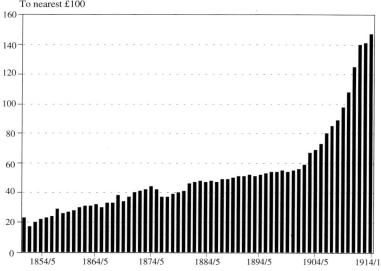

Fig. 1.   Total salary expenditure: Office of Works, 1851/2–1914/15.
Source: PP, Appropriation Accounts.

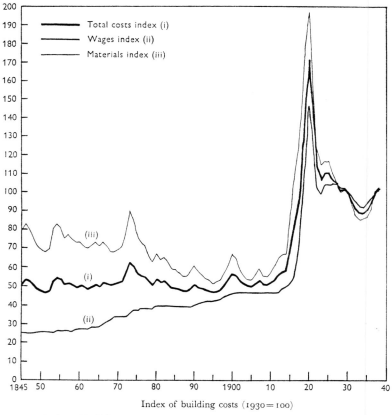

Fig. 2.   Index of building costs.
Source: K. Maiwald, 'An Index of Building Costs in the United Kingdom, 1845–1938', *Economic History Review*, 2nd ser., VII (1954–55), 195.

5
The Office of Works, 1873–1915

So LONG as Ayrton kept a tight control over the Office of Works, Galton's appointment proved advantageous for the public buildings regime. But personal jealousies were boiling up. Galton was used to an independent command, and found it increasingly irksome to have a younger man, a society 'swell' with no technical training in overall charge: George Russell (1830–1911), promoted on Layard's recommendation from Assistant Secretary to Secretary. Even during Ayrton's rule, Galton reacted fiercely to any entrenching on what he regarded as his prerogative sphere.[1] Under the looser rein of the largely absentee William Patrick Adam (1823–81) [Pl. 79],[2] who succeeded Ayrton in August 1873, relations between the two officials rapidly deteriorated, and Russell became more and more frenzied as Galton defied his authority.[3] Hunt, too, the Surveyor, had developed suspicions of Galton's 'desire for power', and in December 1872 had already been threatening an 'explosion' with him.[4] Galton offended him by issuing instructions to the Assistant Surveyors (as Ayrton's instructions empowered him to do) and asserting views on professional questions 'peculiarly Mr Hunt's, his opinions being probably the best in England, while Mr Galton is evidently ignorant of many points of practice'.[5] Hunt clearly resented the incomer's influence with Ayrton, complaining that Galton appeared 'to be desirous of making subordinate to himself the Superior Officers of the Board, and of assuming the control of Business with which it was never intended that he should be charged'.[6]

The situation in the Office came to a crisis in February 1874 with the simultaneous eruption of several volcanoes. Adam had been desperately attempting to keep his work-horses running in tandem, supporting, for example, Russell's demands that all papers to whomever directed must come to him on delivery for registration,

80. Algernon Bertram Mitford (afterwards Freeman-Mitford) (1837–1916), cr. Lord Redesdale 1902. Secretary of the Office of Works 1874–86. He preferred 'the ornamental and the antiquarian' aspects of his duty to the administrative (*DNB*); but was a dominant influence in the Works.

but telling Galton that this was merely an administrative procedure that did not 'imply any special subordination of the Works Branch to the Secretary's Branch of the Office'.[7] But Adam's authority was evaporating: the ministry had been in difficulty for some months, and Gladstone had announced on 24 January the general election that was to see the Liberals' defeat. He resigned on 17 February.

Galton, refusing to accept instructions from Russell, now absented himself from the Office. Russell was himself overwhelmed by a personal crisis. Moving in the Prince of Wales's circle, he had obviously been maintaining an aristocratic life style for which his official salary of £1200 a year was inadequate.[8] In late February he was expelled from the elite Turf Club 'over some card transaction'.[9] He too absented himself from the Office. Although he denied any impropriety, and did not resign until April,[10] his post was immediately regarded as a plum ripe for picking by supporters of the newly elected Conservative ministry; by 25 February 'half the Carlton' Club were reported to be 'showering in applications for his post'.[11]

Disraeli had appointed as First Commissioner Lord Henry Lennox (younger brother of the Duke of Richmond, Conservative leader in the Lords), an old friend about whose abilities, however, he had little illusion – a modern historian has called him 'an intellectual flibbertigibbet'.[12] Lennox had expected cabinet rank, regarded the Works as a slight, and 'took very little interest in the business of the office'[13] according to the man whom Disraeli appointed as Russell's successor,[14] Bertram Mitford (1837–1916) [Pl. 80].[15] Overriding Lennox's strong recommendation of the 'energetic' Assistant Secretary, Callender,[16] the prime minister told this unemployed diplomatist and friend of the Prince of Wales[17] that 'the place was an Augean stable and must be swept out'. 'I was to

79. William Patrick Adam (1823–81). A descendant of the family of great Scottish architects, he was Liberal chief whip 1874–80. First Commissioner of Works 1873–4 and 1880.

evolve kosmos out of chaos', Mitford recalled, 'and chaos it certainly was. I was at once opposed tooth and nail by Lord Henry Lennox backed by the solicitor to the department and the director of works, an engineer officer.'[18]

Captain Galton had returned to the Office on Russell's resignation, but the Treasury determined that the crisis and a near doubling of Office personnel since 1870 called for yet another departmental inquiry into the organisation of the Works, despite a protest from Lennox.[19] This time the committee was unusually political in membership: the former Conservative and Liberal First Commissioners, Lord John Manners and W.P. Adam, and W.H. Smith, parliamentary secretary to the Treasury, were joined by the former Secretary, Austin. They agreed unanimously that the Secretary must be the head of the permanent staff, but Adam would not join in the explicit declaration that the Director of Works was subordinate to him.[20] Lennox, who was determined to uphold Galton's independent position, and resented Treasury interference with the patronage of his office,[21] refused to co-operate with the committee. In August, Mitford was formally appointed Secretary and the Treasury called on Lennox to establish him as the permanent head of the Office. Lennox sought to upset this by private intrigues, but eventually was compelled to respond officially; he complained that Manners and Austin had not comprehended the great changes that had taken place since their day, and the necessary changes in organisation; they had taken no oral evidence, had failed to ask Galton to explain his conduct and had ignored Ayrton's instructions to the Director of Works (approved by the Treasury) which nowhere subordinated him to the Secretary. Lennox's persistent resistance to Treasury interference and his sustained refusal to give effect to the committee's findings led Mitford to submit his resignation.[22]

If Mitford found Lennox difficult to work with, Lennox reciprocated: 'If you only knew what I have endured at the hands of the Secretary you would be astounded at my powers of endurance', he told Disraeli.[23] Disraeli might have made the same comment about Lennox. 'He is an eel', he told Lady Bradford, 'but I do not think he will escape my grasp, which can be firm.'[24] To Lady Chesterfield, he compared him to the tale-spinner of the Arabian Nights; 'I have still a regard for him, although he worries and mortifies me', he confessed. A cabinet session had to be devoted to his 'most extraordinary' conduct, where he was reported to have been 'most offensive' to Mitford.[25]

After Lennox had appealed to the ex-officio members of the Board of Works,[26] the whole question was referred to a cabinet committee, which upheld the Secretary.[27] Although, complaining that his health had been broken by the anxiety of his office, he threatened resignation, Lennox finally accepted the cabinet's ruling, and drew up a minute establishing the primacy of the Secretary in the Office.[28] Galton resigned in consequence, despite Lennox's attempt to keep him; the Treasury insisted on a reorganisation, and Galton's post was abolished in September 1875.[29] In October 1875 the prime minister reported Lennox to be at last 'starved out' and to have shaken hands with Mitford.[30]

Clearly the Office of Works was in little shape to produce an effective policy for public works at this period. His 'nervous system . . . greatly shattered by 12 months of deep anxiety' (as he told the prime minister's secretary in February 1875), Lennox was a frequent absentee from the office, sometimes for prolonged periods.[31] The sustained battle of wills between him and Galton on the one hand, and Mitford on the other can only have inhibited the smooth running of existing mechanisms, and gave no opportunity for devising better ones. Even after Galton's retirement, Lennox clearly maintained his grudge against Mitford, and whether a symbolic handshake contributed to a real dispersal of

the clouds may be doubted. Indeed, Galton's removal reduced such measure of control as the Office had been exercising over the great public erections of the day, for he had been accustomed to visit the building sites, much as a private client might have done, and pass on his resultant observations to the architect.[32]

In March and April 1876 Lennox withdrew to Bognor with an ankle injury so severe that he doubted his ability to return to Westminster to move his departmental estimates. Finally, in the following July the cabinet was forced to demand his resignation in face of judicial aspersions cast on the conduct of the directors of the Lisbon Steam Tramways, of whom he had been one.[33] *The Times*, judging merely from externals, regretted the departure of one who had 'always been ready to add to the amiability of the world, and . . . eager to use all his powers to make London more pleasant to those who live in it'.[34]

Great public buildings, however, were not the only ones to concern the Office of Works at this time. It had been loaded with so many new responsibilities by successive recent governments that it was creaking under the strain. Lennox's irresponsibility only exacerbated matters,[35] and the Office welcomed his tactful and assiduous successor Gerard Noel (1823–1911).[36] A revision of the establishment was the more necessary in the wake of the Playfair Commission's report on the Civil Service,[37] which stressed the need to separate intellectual and mechanical labour. Another departmental committee[38] revised the salary scales and reorganised the Clerical Department before turning to the technical side.[39]

There, Henry Hunt's position was their chief problem. As we have seen, that eminent surveyor had taken over from Pennethorne the valuation of properties intimately connected with the planning of the government's building programme, but on a part-time basis. His duties had 'never been formally defined, but they may be said [asserted the committee] to consist in advising the Board upon any matter submitted to him. Those references have not been confined to merely technical matters, such as advising on architects' estimates and contracts for buildings determined upon. They have also included such matters of policy as the comparative merits of schemes for the erection of new public offices and buildings, and the selection of the most suitable sites.' On his appointment in 1860 Hunt had made it a rule not to take on government work in his private practice, or accept private work that would bring him into antagonism with government. In 1869, however, the Treasury, when cutting his salary to £750, had sanctioned his employment in his professional capacity, though all the government's business brought him little more than £250 p.a. But towards the end of 1875 he was employed by the Works on land-purchase negotiations in the Parliament Street area expected to net him £20,000. The committee condemned this union of the functions of advising, and of conducting consequent negotiations, as 'wrong in principle'.[40] The surveyor should be a man eminent in his profession and in private practice, but debarred from executing what he recommended. His title should be changed to 'consulting surveyor' and his salary doubled to £1500.

The situation of the full-time members of the Technical Branch was also reviewed. The Office surveyors should be awarded increased salaries to reflect their function. The Assistant Surveyor of Works for London, John Taylor (1883–1912), performed a 'very responsible character' of duties. 'Besides the structural charge of all the [official] buildings in London, he is constantly called upon to design and carry out new works of considerable magnitude.' The designation 'assistant' should be dropped, and his salary scale rise to a maximum of £1000 p.a. The First Itinerant Assistant Surveyor, James Williams, designed most of the public buildings (i.e. county courts and post offices) required in northern England, and had also been responsible for the new General Post Office building in

St Martins-le-Grand.[41] However, they should not be provided with a clerical staff of their own, which led to duplication of work.[42]

Even with these rectifications, the Office still suffered from the lack of an architectural adviser to the First Commissioner. Appointed as a 'man of business', often, as mentioned above, a party whip entering the ministerial ranks for the first time, like William Adam in 1873 and Gerard Noel in 1876, the First Commissioner rarely possessed much knowledge of art or architecture. To critics in the architectural press, it seemed that to be a country gentleman was thought sufficient qualification.[43]

When the Liberals were re-elected in 1880, Adam returned only briefly to the Works as a spring-board to the governorship of Madras. George Shaw Lefevre [Pl. 81],[44] who succeeded him, 'a man of ability and industry' with experience of several departments as a junior minister, was said to be 'obviously marked for promotion'.[45] Though keen to improve the face of London and the quality of our public buildings, as well as ambitious,[46] he disarmingly admitted his lack of architectural discernment. He was nonetheless deeply interested in the work, and used the press to put over his policy. His obituary noted that 'For all subjects connected with art he had a natural taste, which was cultivated by assiduous study.'[47] Much, too, might have been expected of his successor (for Lefevre duly obtained his promotion in 1885), the young Lord Rosebery, but Gladstone's ministry fell after a few months.

The two succeeding administrations were short-lived, but stability returned with David Plunket (1838–1919) [Pl. 82] in Salisbury's 1886–92 government. Of a distinguished Anglo-Irish family, Plunket was a much-liked barrister noted for his pungent wit.[48] As First Commissioner, his administration had, in Gladstone's view, 'the merit of being modest',[49] though his colleague Balfour was franker in discussing ministerial promotions with the prime minister: 'He already has the pleasantest place in the Govt for an idle man; and he is both idle and unambitious.'[50]

Discussing the lack of an architectural adviser before the select committee on public offices in 1877, Mitford criticised the inconvenience of the buildings erected within the previous 20 years, and remarked:[51]

81. George John Shaw Lefevre (1831–1928), cr. Lord Eversley 1906. First Commissioner of Works 1880–3 and (with a Cabinet seat) 1892–4. On the Radical wing of the Liberal Party, as Works minister he was particularly keen to build the long-deferred new Admiralty and War Office, and to end the traditional traffic jams at Hyde Park Corner. He began, in his second term, to plan further building, more comprehensively carried out by the Conservatives.

82. Hon. David Plunket, Q.C. (1838–1919), cr. Lord Rathmore 1895. A tactful First Commissioner of Works in Salisbury's administrations, 1885–6 and 1886–92, he 'did nothing in particular, and did it very well'.

I think that one of the reasons which has caused the badness of the new offices has been that during the time of their construction under the architect the Office of Works have had no power of supervision at all. The architect appoints his own clerk of the works, and although the clerk of the works is supposed to represent and to protect the Government, still, in practice, it is often found that the duty is neglected.

He pointed out that 'a surveyor of the Office of Works had no locus standi' during the erection of the new Foreign Office.[52] Similarly, although Edward Barry's extension to the National Gallery had been carried out under the nominal control of the Office, 'it was carried out by an architect and his clerk of the works. We had no footing in the matter until it was handed over to us.'[53] There had been very little consultation with the architect during the progress of the building, 'excepting as to variations from the existing plans with regard to decoration and things of that sort'.[54] 'When once a building has been put in the hands of an architect, the architect and his clerk of the works are responsible to the Government for the execution of that building. . . . They are alone responsible' and the government 'employs no overseer', Mitford told his interlocutors. If the Office superintended the work, 'there might be a divided responsibility, and nobody would know whose the responsibility was',[55] as one MP summed it up.

Members clearly found this an unsatisfactory state of affairs.[56] Mitford straightly declared that he thought the system wrong;[57] but he chose completely to ignore the role that Galton had played from 1870 to 1875, which met precisely one of Mitford's major criticisms: that the Office of Works was not 'in the same position as a private employer', who could 'go round and point out to the architect, This is not being done as I wish.' Even more, he suggested that such an officer as Galton would be useless: if the First Commissioner were to send such an officer, the architect need not recognise him, or might 'say that the responsibility was taken out of his hands'. Yet Mitford admitted that the need was there, because his impression was that the architect was often careless 'in carrying out the details of the building'.[58]

Sir Gilbert Scott, on the other hand, told the same committee that he would have welcomed 'being placed in official communication, without diminishing my own responsibility, with any competent officer appointed by the Office of Works'. There would be, he thought, no 'obstacles on the point of professional etiquette or artistic pride'; though he saw little prospect of the Office paying sufficient to retain a first-rate architect on its staff.[59] Of late years communication between architect and department had grown, but it had never been 'so much so as I could have wished'. When the Home Office had been occupied, before Scott actually certified its completion, he found that the government clerk of the works refused to communicate with his own man, it being 'the rule of the office to communicate only with itself'.[60]

The changes Mitford desired, however, were far-reaching. He, like Ayrton, disliked the practice of employing architects from the market-place:

I believe that if you were building a new War Office or a new Admiralty, it would be infinitely better built and more satisfactory in every way if it were built in the department, and if our own surveyors were to draw the plans. There are no men in England so thoroughly cognisant of all the requirements of public departments. They are practically architects, and the only additional expense involved would be the hiring of a few temporary draughtsmen, and you would have a thoroughly satisfactory building.

This was to go back to the system prevailing before 1813; and it was a 'building carried out in the style of Somerset House' [Pl. 83]

that was Mitford's *beau idéal* of a public office.[61] He suggested that the Office was quite capable of producing work in whatever style might be designated by a committee of taste – 'Members of the House of Commons and others'. Should the Office not have 'very clever architects' when there was call for a major building, 'which would court comment or criticism, not only in this country, but from abroad,' then outside talent would have to be brought in. But it would not be by competition, limited or unlimited – 'a mischief altogether'– that he would select that talent: 'architects are known by their works; and you could pick an architect; you would get the most talented architect of the day'.[62] The unasked question, of course, was whether Parliament would allow the Office to get away with such an exercise of patronage.

It was in fact John Taylor, responsible for the London District since 1865, who designed the new court and police station at Bow Street (1879), added a storey to Marlborough House for the Prince of Wales in 1886 and undertook great state occasions and the enlargement of the National Gallery in 1887.[63] His salary-scale maximum of £1000 p.a. represented 'considerable worldly success',[64] though it was by no means equal to the rewards possible in private practice. By the 1890s he was extensively employed as the government architect:[65] the Bankruptcy Buildings in Carey Street (1890–2), extensions to the Public Record Office, including the Chancery Lane front (1892–1902) [Pl. 84], and the Patent Office Library (from 1891).[66] Although these were large buildings, they were not at the focus of public interest. A major government office in or about Whitehall required, ministers felt, the skill of an accredited architect. Indeed, the same view was held powerfully in the Office itself. A new Secretary, referring in 1886 to the completion of the South Kensington Museum, took a line distinctly less self-assured than Mitford's:

for a building intended as a temple of art, and therefore peculiarly exposed to artistic criticism, occupying moreover so conspicuous a position, it would be wiser to employ an architect

83. Somerset House, Sir William Chambers 1775–96: the Strand Front. Based on Antoine's Hôtel des Monnaies (1771–7), Chambers's design was often regarded in the later nineteenth century as an appropriate model for new government buildings, and evidently influenced J.M. Brydon's design for New Public Offices (1898) – cp. Pl. 198.

84.   Public Record Office, Chancery Lane, John Taylor, 1895–1902. Taylor, the Office of Works principal architect, who spent his whole career in government service, added a western block in the same general character to Pennethorne's PRO of the 1850s.

of acknowledged standing, rather than proceed on designs prepared by men who, however capable, are not professed architects [i.e., Taylor, and Henry Scott of the Science and Art Department], and whose work would have to be discussed and settled, and then the sanction of the Treasury and of Parliament would have to be obtained.[67]

Mitford and Lefevre, another economy-seeking First Commissioner, produced a plan in 1883 for at once reducing staff costs and improving the efficiency, 'and more especially the directing power' of the Office. The post of Assistant Secretary, held since 1869 by Callender 'with zeal fidelity and ability', was abolished, as redundant: the First Commissioner and Secretary were quite enough of a directing staff. (Had Callender – Lennox's candidate for the Secretaryship – shown too much zeal, or crossed swords with Mitford, one wonders?) The two senior clerks, on whom considerable responsibility must always necessarily devolve, argued Lefevre, were promoted to principal clerks, the senior taking over also the responsibilities of the chief examiner of accounts, whose post was abolished. So each branch would be run by a principal, relieving from routine business the Secretary, who remained responsible for the overall administration.[68] Mitford continued in that important office until June 1886, when, after the death of his cousin Lord Redesdale, he resigned to manage the family estates.[69] He was succeeded by Henry Primrose (1846–1923),[70] an old Treasury man and Gladstone's private secretary, who as cousin to Lord Rosebery enjoyed the necessary social cachet. Subsequent Secretaries were similarly drawn from the elite aristocratic group of principal private secretaries.

In 1884 the organisation of the permanent draughtsmen or 'assistants', as they were now termed, was modified in the interests of greater flexibility, and the minimum age for a Third-class assistant reduced from 24 to 21 years, with only four years of qualifying service under an architect. Mitford commented that this would 'ensure our getting a higher class of young men than that which wd be tempted by our present system', as the salary scale of £100 × £10 − £200 would 'hardly tempt good men over 24 years of age to compete'.[71]

At about the same time as Mitford, Sir Henry Hunt also retired, being succeeded by Robert Ritchie, an experienced property valuer,[72] who himself retired from ill health three years later. The First Commissioner thought his services insufficient to warrant a salary of £1100 p.a., so no successor was appointed. Instead, it was decided to resort to outside advice when needed in way of general criticism; an appropriate expert could be employed when necessary, whose entirely independent advice would carry more weight with Parliament and the public. Such advisers were not expected to 'check quantities or do similar detail work' as the Surveyor had done.[73] The saving enabled a better career structure to be established in the Technical Branch, which good men had been quitting, and where the prospects were not enough to attract men 'competent to become in time first class surveyors . . . expected to act as architects of important new buildings'.[74]

During this period the Office was indeed steadily being strengthened, not by the appointment of distinguished experts with high-sounding titles, but by recruitment to the Technical Branch, which had already, as Mitford claimed, several 'surveyors' of considerable skill, with as much architectural experience as most Victorian architects: but Ayrton refused a request to adopt the new term on the grounds that the office of 'Surveyor of Works', vested in the First Commissioner, was 'the style which has been in use for centuries . . . the Officers will always be esteemed according to their works and not their names of Office', a rather doubtful assumption.[75] Clearly they were of different mettle from their pred-

ecessors. John Taylor was joined by Henry Tanner (1849–1935):[76] men able to undertake tasks of the sort that Mitford and Ayrton had envisaged.

Further re-arrangements of the organisation were made in 1889 and 1893 in consequence of the ever-mounting burden of provincial work, above all for the Post Office.[77] The Assistant Surveyors were engaged in administration quite as much as in design work: James Williams, in charge of Country and Post Office work, permitted 'a very loose system of adjusting accounts' on the completion of a contract, that 'renders valueless the whole system of accounts and checks which have been laid down for the security of the public expenditure' – doubtless because he and his colleague 'had too much on their hands'; but he knowingly allowed contractors to charge in their maintenance bills sums disallowed as extras in their contract accounts. Obliged in consequence to resign aged 58 without pension, he was replaced by two Second class Surveyors. Henry Tanner, who was to design many of the major provincial post offices, took over his work.[78] Certainly, by 1902 the Secretary could comment on the high salaries in the Architects' and Surveyors' Division compared with municipal posts – noting also their unusual degree of independence for a salaried architect, and their need for 'much tact and professional knowledge'.[79]

An immediate effect of the abolition of the Consulting Surveyorship, however, was discovered in 1892, when Leemings presented a revised estimate for the Admiralty extensions in November 1892 that was about £100,000 more than their original, 1888, figure of £192,600. Treasury reaction was to criticise the Works for inefficient control of the outside architects:

> It becomes, therefore, important to enquire whether, in the large expenditure for public buildings for which the Office of Works is responsible to Parliament, the Department is adequately supplied with competent professional advisers by whose assistance it might check the original Estimates of Architects and revise them from time to time in accordance with circumstances which ought to be within its cognizance. It seems to Their Lordships that this matter should be carefully considered, and that some steps should be taken to enable the Office of Works to exercise this necessary control before any further public works of importance are undertaken.[80]

One would have expected a consequential proposal to add an experienced surveyor to the establishment. But the political attitude, unchanged by this gruesome experience, remained: buy in expert advice when necessary.[81]

The whole business of the Admiralty extensions shows how effectively parliamentary interference could undermine such authority as the Office of Works exercised over outside architects. On the instructions essentially of W.H. Smith, Conservative leader in the Commons and arch-opponent of Lefevre's great defence ministries scheme, John Taylor had in 1885 prepared a block plan to shew how much land the Admiralty would require for an L-shaped extension of the same height as the old building.[82] Leemings, as winning architects for the big scheme, submitted a sketch to the last public meeting of an investigatory committee, which was then adopted as illustrating what the committee recommended. Taylor was not again consulted; nor, it would seem, was Ritchie. Plunket enthusiastically recommended Leemings, whom he regarded, in view of their earlier work, as being in 'a position of exceptional advantage for elaborating a detailed scheme of the kind required'.[83] Leemings produced modified plans that were 'approved generally' by Plunket, adopted by the Admiralty and laid before parliament in 1888, obtaining the seal of approval by the vote of funds.[84]

When Taylor, having examined the working drawings, renewed

his earlier criticism of the 'want of height' in the upper floors,[85] Lefevre, back in office, used that as a lever to try to overthrow a scheme he intensely disliked.[86] The Treasury blamed Taylor, who had effectively taken over the Surveyor's functions, for not having secured alterations beforehand.[87] It had not been Hunt's practice or Ritchie's to check any revision in estimates made necessary by a rise in wages or difficulty with foundations, and so Leemings had not submitted their revised estimate to Taylor's scrutiny; though he had 'been constantly in communication with Messrs Leeming and has cut down the details of their plans in many directions involving an expenditure of many thousands of pounds' – exercising 'a control over the expenditure on the Admiralty extension greater than has been the case, I believe', declared Lefevre, 'in regard to any public building erected by Architects outside the Department in recent years'. In future works undertaken by outside architects, revised as well as original estimates were to be submitted to Taylor for criticism.[88]

As this episode illustrates, Taylor was to an extent dependent on the views or the energy of the minister – and despite his 'extraordinary industry', even Lefevre, lacking magnetism and too self-absorbed to win sympathy,[89] was thought to 'want strength' in cabinet.[90] It is clear that the true responsibility was not even Plunket's or Lefevre's: it was the Treasury's. The persistent demand for trifling economies time and again resulted in large sums being expended on unsatisfactory works. It was the tradition of Gladstone – and even more of Lowe: a tradition manfully upheld by Sir William Harcourt, godfather, with W.H. Smith, of the Admiralty extensions. But Treasury memoranda suggest that Treasury ranks were not entirely solid.[91]

As an old Treasury man, Primrose was *persona grata* with the Treasury principals, and he remarked on the harmonious relationship the Office had enjoyed with them during his tenure of office, doubtless facilitated by two at least of his ministers, the easy-going Plunket, 1886–92, and Gladstone's son Herbert, 1894–5 [Pl. 85], himself a former junior Treasury lord.[92] When in May 1895 Rosebery promoted him chairman of the Inland Revenue Board, Lewis Harcourt, the chancellor's son, intrigued to secure the Secretaryship for their common friend Reginald Brett (1852–1930) [Pl. 86], son of the Master of the Rolls, Lord Esher.[93] The chief

85. Herbert John Gladstone (1854–1930), cr. Viscount Gladstone 1910. First Commissioner of Works in Rosebery's ministry 1894–5. Youngest son of the former prime minister, he worked to implement the large projects envisaged by his predecessor, Lefevre.

86. Reginald Baliol Brett (1852–1930), suc. as 2nd Viscount Esher 1899. Secretary of the Office of Works, 1895–1902. Committee-man, courtier and adviser 'behind the curtain'.

whip called the new appointment '*execrable*', remarking, 'It will be looked upon as Whiggery with a vengeance.'[94] The original suggestion seems, however, to have come from Sir George Murray, the Treasury permanent secretary, who warned: 'From some points of view it is almost the most interesting place in the public service. But in the matter of administration and particularly of finance there is a good deal of work of a rather sombre sort.'[95] Brett, who after a brief period as an MP had been looking for a public appointment, told a close friend, 'It is not a post I have contemplated holding, but it has charm of a certain sort. It is a *permanent* office, worth from £1200 to £1500 a year. So it is not to be despised. It has always been my wish to have . . . definite service under the Crown apart from politics.'[96]

Brett – former private secretary to the Liberal Unionist leader Lord Hartington, and known to the Queen through his wife, daughter of a former Belgian envoy who retired to live in England – was not dissimilar in his social standing to Mitford, though lacking his established aristocratic origins. In character the two men were markedly different.[97] Brett was a mole, shunning the daylight of a political role, but ever burrowing assiduously in public affairs and courting royalty.[98] The Office of Works' Secretaryship was an ideal position for him. Despite the rapid departure from office of his Liberal friends, Brett (who succeeded his father as Viscount Esher in 1899)[99] worked effectively with their Conservative successors. When, not relishing the thought of 'a new master' (changes in the ministry were imminent), Esher resigned in June 1902 in order to make money with Sir Ernest Cassel, Mitford wrote to him: 'I can't tell you how much I regret your departure from the O. of W. Nobody ever did the work so well; or so amicably.'[100]

Almost as soon as he took up the reins, Brett set about improving the organisation of the Technical Branch, to achieve a lightening of the load on the senior men, and a clear chain of command.[101] (He seems also to have introduced the typewriter.) This was taken further in 1897–8 in view of Taylor's imminent retirement; there would be no additional promotion, but Henry Tanner, already a Principal Surveyor, would take over the whole responsibility for England, with the work organised in five departments, each pre-

87.   Aretas Akers-Douglas (1851–1926), cr. Viscount Chilston 1911. First Commissioner of Works 1895–1902; Home secretary 1902–5. An industrious and decisive Works minister.

sided over by a Second-class Surveyor (to be re-titled 'Surveyor') responsible to him. Tanner was to supervise every branch, 'and the primary responsibility for all works and maintenance, and for all new works will be his'. He was to delegate as far as seemed desirable, but the Surveyors were not to carry out any new work without special authority.[102] In 1899 Brett emphasised and clarified Tanner's instructions: the First Commissioner

> expects you to be very careful to impress upon the Surveyors the necessity of their submitting to you for your approval *in pencil* and in *their initial stages* all plans and drawings of buildings of any importance with the erection of which they are entrusted. Yours will be the responsibility for the final approval of plans and drawings, before they are agreed to by the Board.... The FC looks to the Principal Surveyor as his adviser upon all questions of Architecture, and must beg of him to exercise effective control over the original work of the Officers of the Branch.[103]

Another clarification occurred in 1901, when Brett changed the title 'Surveyor' to 'Architect and Surveyor', 'as indicating more correctly the functions of those officers'. The old title had become 'misleading and an anachronism'. He told the Treasury, 'It is of importance also to emphasize the facts that the work of the Department requires the possession of Architectural knowledge and that the Board's "Surveyors" possess it', a more realistic attitude than Ayrton's antiquarianism.[104]

Financial control over the execution of building contracts was now exercised by means of Examiners from the Financial Division periodically measuring variations as work proceeded. The outside architects engaged on the War Office and at South Kensington were at first allowed to employ their own quantity surveyors for this purpose, but the arrangement proved unsatisfactory, so that the Examining Branch had to be afforced in 1901.[105]

Despite the rigours of Treasury control, 'for the administrator who enjoyed firm political support, the Treasury held few ter-

rors'.[106] Under Lord Salisbury's third administration, Aretas Akers-Douglas (1851–1926) [Pl. 87], 'the best type of English country gentleman', was a First Commissioner with political clout. Formerly Conservative chief whip, he was a 'shrewd judge of character' and a 'charming chief'.[107] When Akers-Douglas in 1897 urged on the Treasury the need to retain the services of the once-maligned but lately knighted Taylor,[108] who was due to retire, 'My Lords' avowed 'their high appreciation of his long and valuable services.'[109] The minister stated the importance of securing Taylor's help 'if only during the initial stages of the vast building operations about to begin' – the new War Office and Parliament Street offices. He

> would become primarily responsible for the internal planning of the buildings in question, and would act as chief technical adviser to the First Commissioner upon all architectural and other details which will have to be settled in respect of them. He would undertake the onerous and highly responsible duty of watching and checking the work of the contractors in the interests of their Department; and he would have to deal from time to time with the inevitable changes of plan, and the varying demands of the public departments whom it is proposed to house. He would in short continue to exercise a control in connection with the new Admiralty, the Record Office and the Post Office, which he exercises at the present time, and extend it to such other buildings as are in contemplation.[110]

If the Treasury would not agree to keep Taylor for three years at a salary of £500 in addition to full pension, it would be necessary, threatened Akers-Douglas, to hire 'an eminent architect of tried capacity', who would not only be expensive but also lack 'the special training and experience which from the point of view of the Government make the continued service of Sir John Taylor so invaluable'. The Treasury quibbled about the amount of pension, but finally gave way.[111]

When the architect of the new War Office, Young, died in 1900, Akers-Douglas proposed that Taylor should assist his son, a relatively inexperienced architect, in the construction of the building, his salary to be deducted from the total commission that Young was to have received, rather than pay off Young junior and engage another architect. Mowatt of the Treasury minuted: 'The true advantage of the arrangement ... is to be found in the exceptional ability, moderation, tact and energy of the man, rather than in the economy.'[112] But Taylor was 68 in 1900; when the Lord Chamberlain's department was desperate to move the new sovereigns into Buckingham Palace at the end of 1901, an official complained: 'Dear old Taylor would make an excellent monthly nurse but he hasn't the physical *push* in him to get things forward.'[113]

Brydon dying a few months after Young, his principal assistant was engaged at four guineas a week, although he had left 'complete working drawings'. Taylor was made formally responsible, but Tanner (little known to MPs) took over the work, assisted by an additional First-class Assistant Surveyor. 'There is no reason to suppose that at the end of five years, or of such further time as the erection of the Public Offices may take,' reported the Secretary, 'the services of the new Assistant will be superfluous; in fact the normal growth of the Office work foreshadows that his services will be permanently required.'[114] The extent of Tanner's labours here proved considerable: he

> decided that drastic economies in construction etc., could be effected some of which might be anticipated by amending the Bills of Quantities already prepared ... in carrying out the work it became evident that the contract drawings practically without exception, could not be used except as a guide to indicate Mr Brydon's intention as regards architectural treatment if proper

economy was to be observed. The work was, therefore executed from entirely fresh drawings prepared in the Department, heavy savings in the quantities of brick, stone, steelwork, etc., resulting in reconsideration of the construction but without interference with the architectural scheme . . . although an additional storey was provided over large areas of the building. . . .

The total economy effected . . . was very substantial but it is impossible to state a definite figure. . . . it is reasonable to assume that the numerous subsidiary contracts were dealt with more economically than . . . had the original Architect survived to carry out the work to completion.

In dealing with the Western Section . . . similar economical methods were followed and the opportunity was also taken to introduce more modern and less costly forms of construction than had been decided upon in . . . the Eastern Section and the new War Office.[115]

By 1906 Taylor was keen to retire completely to his suburban golf course. The Works organisation was growing rapidly in size. The senior personnel of the Office, too, was changing. Esher had been succeeded as Secretary[116] in 1902 by Sir Schomberg McDonnell (1861–1915), a younger son of the fifth Earl of Antrim and previously private secretary to Lord Salisbury as prime minister.[117] A change of government in December 1905 had brought in a new First Commissioner. Despite the wish of Asquith and his intimates to see John Burns at the Works, Campbell-Bannerman appointed Lewis Harcourt, son of the former Liberal chancellor of the Exchequer. He promptly wrote to thank his friend Esher: 'I am "Works". I am very happy and *most* grateful to you. I consider myself your nominee. . . .'[118]

Despite some increase in staff and salaries conceded in 1902 to the clerical departments after Esher had insisted on having some appointments of First-class clerks, the Office remained 'so short-handed that we cannot do what we ought to do', declared the Permanent Secretary, McDonnell, who saw his compeer at the Treasury, Sir George Murray, as out to 'discredit Tanner and the Department generally'.[119] McDonnell introduced changes in the Architects' and Surveyors' Division designed to lighten the burden on the Principal Architect and more precisely define his duties and relationship with his staff. He was 'not to be burdened with the task of designing buildings himself, nor with the execution of them unless the Board specially request it'; but was to advise and supervise.[120]

In 1904/05, the Office accounted for an expenditure of £2,061,000, of which administration accounted for 3.5 per cent. The number of papers registered had increased from 11,918 in 1900 to 16,510 in 1904. The Architects' and Surveyors' Division now contained 6 Architects, 13 First-class assistant architects and 19 Second-class.[121] A large number of draughtsmen were still employed on a so-called temporary basis, and from their ranks the Assistant Architects were selected by competition; in fact, they often remained in Works' employ for many years.[122] Since 1898, when the pay scales had been fixed, there had been built 110 post offices, 75 Inland Revenue offices, and about a hundred other public buildings; the additional posts of one Architect and two First class Assistants sanctioned the previous February being required for dealing chiefly with country post offices. 'Each Architect is now practically responsible for a sum amounting to over £150,000 annually [which in private practice would have earned £7500 in commission], and such an amount of work presses unduly on them . . . they are working to the full limit of their physical and mental powers.' The work could be got through only by a staff motivated by esprit de corps, prepared to sacrifice leave.[123] The First Commissioner, Lord Windsor, therefore, shortly before the Balfour cabinet's resignation, submitted an extensive scheme of reorganisation, promptly rejected by the Treasury on the inaccurate ground of the 'comprehensive character' of the 1902 review, which had excluded the technical divisions.[124]

The late nineteenth century had seen more rigorous standards set for entrants to the architectural profession. In 1889 the RIBA established 'a formal relationship with other architectural societies', and imposed a 'much higher standard than heretofore' in its examinations, which became obligatory for the associateship.[125] The high standards now demanded for government architects' posts were spelled out to the Royal Commissioners on the Civil Service by McDonnell in 1912. They generally entered the office as draughtsmen (as Taylor and Tanner had done), usually straight from architectural school, on the nomination of one of the Works Architects, when 'we see very quickly what they are worth'. The architects were asked to pick out the able men, who would be nominated for competitive examination; there were usually ten or twelve for three vacancies.

McDonnell was not willing to admit the drawbacks of this system of nominating competitors from a group of men who had already been selected by nomination. It was not merely that the field was unduly narrow. More significantly, the successful candidate for a post as Assistant Architect, having for years been employed exclusively on drawing, now found himself engaged primarily in administration: 'before appointment he is trained most in the work of which he may ultimately have to perform least, and not trained at all in that class of work on which he will be mainly engaged'.[126] The design of new works was a comparatively small part of the laborious duties of the Architect at the head of a section,[127] and in the view of architects in private practice his design skills were likely to atrophy without constant use.[128]

McDonnell was asked: 'What steps does your department take to see that in the case of important work, your architect has the benefit of the very best professional advice, so that your public buildings are as dignified in an architectural sense as you can possibly make them? Do you keep your department abreast of the best artistic architectural feeling of the day?' He replied: 'I should say that is generally done by the communication which goes on between our architects and others. . . . naturally they are in touch with all the great architectural buildings and papers, and they attend the institute and hear papers read there. It is an instruction by the Board that they shall keep themselves in touch in that respect.'[129] Nevertheless, the Works Architects found themselves bogged down in routine administration, writing official files, answering references and questions from other divisions, keeping close watch on details and expenditure of buildings under their charge, and controlling large maintenance staffs whose reports and returns they reviewed personally.[130]

There was justification for the frequent complaints about the large amount of new building allocated to official architects and its unexciting quality, made not only by aggrieved outside architects or parliamentary 'free traders', but also by departments, such as the Post Office, for which the Works was supplying designs.[131] Nevertheless, the continuing relative cheapness of the system was acknowledged by the select committee on Estimates of 1912, which calculated that the work of the Architects' Branch cost 4.01 per cent, as against the 5 per cent paid to outside architects, and also included 'a variety of services' for which architects were entitled to charge additional fees, to say nothing of maintenance work.[132]

Although by the end of the nineteenth century England had achieved a public works organisation that offered a career structure for its employees, it was one in marked contrast to the French system. There, the *Ecole des Beaux Arts* offered a five-year training at government expense, followed for the most able by a similar term at the French Academy in Rome, imparting an historical consciousness and a tradition of controlled design and planning; with thereafter the opportunity of a career in the *Bâtiments Civils*, or parallel services, or in local government. Like the Office of Works, the *Bâtiments Civils* was responsible for both maintenance and construction of major government buildings, but these were distinct services, the former organised territorially, the latter building by building, each under an *architecte-en-chef* with a supporting staff of executant architects, clerks of works, and draughtsmen and clerks. Each new building had to undergo scrutiny by an advisory board of architects that exercised real power, reviewing highly detailed estimates and functional and aesthetic aspects of the designs.[133]

In England, ministers' fears and doctrines of parliamentary sovereignty blocked the introduction of a powerful advisory body for many years;[134] and enthusiasm for the competitive system and the problem of the outside architect prevented the building up of a permanent staff largely devoted to the scrutiny of proposals for new buildings. Parliamentary demands for economy, registered in the Treasury on tablets of stone, ensured that such government architectural service as had developed here rarely attracted talent of the first quality.

A Treasury clerk explained the process of control to the 1912 Estimates committee: the Works sent in draft estimates to the Treasury in January; they were examined by the principal clerks, and discussed by the financial secretary, the chancellor's political assistant. A conference with the First Commissioner and the Secretary of Works then took place, at which the items were reviewed seriatim and reduced. The estimates were then formally re-submitted in response to a specific form, and then formally approved for submission to parliament. He stressed that it was the Treasury's 'especial duty to watch the interests of economy'.[135]

'The parsimony of the Treasury ends in expenditure', McDonnell argued; 'I maintain that the only way we can prevent this kind of mistake [excess expenditure on building works] is by proper supervision by a trained expert of our own staff: and unless and until we have money given to us to provide that expert we have no security that our estimates will not be exceeded.'[136] The influence of the new Liberal First Commissioner, Lewis Harcourt, secured the appointment of a strong committee of inquiry (including the president of the RIBA) to examine the technical departments of the Office, resulting in what McDonnell termed 'simple justice' in the augmentation of the Works establishment, 'a notable victory'.[137] Between June 1903 and February 1906, the department's work had increased by about thirty per cent. The six 'Architects and Surveyors' were now allowed one additional First-class and one Second-class assistant, as well as general improvements in salaries.[138] Almost immediately the government's decision to set up a system of labour exchanges throughout the country involved the Works in a massive new building programme, of which the dimensions had not been foreseen.

Between the Conservatives' last financial year, 1905/06, and 1909/10, Works expenditure increased by over 50 per cent; and the Office salary bill rose sharply from £63,000 to £90,000 [Fig. 1]. The 1911 National Insurance Act required local offices built nation-wide. In January 1912 the telephone system, with its buildings, would become part of the Post Office.[139] Such items might be regarded as routine; but, furthermore, 'At no time in the history of the Department have there been so many large public buildings in contemplation', complained McDonnell to the Treasury: 'and only those who have had practical experience can form any idea of the numerous and complicated processes involved in housing large Public Departments, from the commencement of the negotiations for the acquisition of a site until the Department is satisfactorily settled in the completely furnished building, with its modern sani-

tation and ventilation in full working order.'[140] Harcourt emphasised his belief in the advantages of having the Office of Works as 'the sole authority for the provision and maintenance of accommodation for Government Departments', ensuring as it did continuity and uniformity of policy (surely said tongue-in-cheek), standardisation of requirements, avoidance of duplicating technical and clerical staffs, and power to obtain the best terms from contractors. To function effectively, the Office had become a complex mechanism of departments: Secretariat, Finance, Architects', Supplies and Engineering.[141] Subsequently a Contracts Branch was formed to take over work previously done in the Secretariat, thereby saving thousands of pounds.[142] But dispersed in half-a-dozen and more separate buildings, the Works could not function efficiently as the national public buildings organisation.

In the expansive days of Lloyd George's 'New Liberalism', in order to cope with this great increase of responsibilities, the Office of Works was able to obtain remarkable increases in its technical staffing, the average annual salary bill for the division rising from £15,358 in 1907/08–1909/10 to £19,554 in 1910/11–1912/13, an increase of 27 per cent.[143] The largely increased expenditure on the division did not escape notice by the 1912 select committee on Estimates which, lacking the time for inquiry, called the Treasury's attention to the question, so leading to the appointment in 1913 of a Treasury committee under Sir George Holmes, whose conclusions are considered below.[144]

The system as it existed in England in 1913 consisted of Tanner as Principal Architect, with eleven 'Architects & Surveyors' immediately under him. One 'Architect & Surveyor' served as deputy to Tanner, and the other ten divided the work by services, each in charge of a particular class of building, e.g. Labour exchanges and Insurance buildings. The Post Office sector, however, was so large that it was sub-divided territorially into four sections.[145] Each Architect had his own staff of Assistant Architects, Architectural Assistants, and 'temporary' draughtsmen and technical assistants, as well as clerks, attempting to reproduce the pattern of an architect's office in private practice. Each Architect organised his section as he chose. This arrangement was found to be 'extravagant in cost and objectionable in other respects', encouraging notions of independence in the Architect, making control difficult, and creating friction between clerical and technical staff.[146]

By 1910, in fact, with seven major buildings in contemplation,[147] the Principal Architect, Tanner (knighted in 1904), aged 62, was 'as nearly as possible breaking down' under his responsibilities, although supported by an Architect, an Assistant Architect First class, and an Architectural Assistant on his personal staff – he himself dealt with the new public offices 'specially assigned to him by the Board', *ab ovo*. 'The amount of paper work has grown so immeasurably within the last few years and lately in particular that I find myself quite unable to cope with it properly while it occupies time which should be devoted to other matters', he complained. He suggested that the limit for new buildings dealt with by the Architects without referring the papers to him should be raised from £500 to £5000.[148] He pressed first for additional assistance, and then for the appointment of a deputy who would carry out the buildings he had in hand,[149] leaving him free 'to devote himself to the proper function of a Principal Architect, viz. supervision and criticism,' except that he should continue to carry out the new buildings on Great George Street with which he had been intimately connected. 'Loulou' Harcourt as First Commissioner supported this proposal very strongly, discounting the possibility of appointing Tanner consulting architect. Such an arrangement with Taylor had apparently not worked well, perhaps obscuring the clear responsibility of the Principal Architect.[150]

The Holmes committee's inquiry into the Technical Division was searching and far-reaching.[151] Appointed in February 1913, it did not report until October. Sir George Holmes (1848–1926)[152] was supported by the Works' Assistant Secretary, W.A. Robinson, and E.W.H. Millar, a Treasury First class clerk. They concluded that the physical dispersion of staff in London prevented the implementation of a comprehensive policy: concentration was urgently necessary.[153] The organisation by which each Architect was responsible for a particular service (or, for Post Office work, part of a service), tended to narrow the experience of their staff and promote a feeling of independence in the mind of the Architect in charge; as if conducting a private practice. All the Architectural Assistants, draughtsmen and technical assistants should be brought together, with a central drawing office under one head. Their clerks should be attached to the Secretariat, and all typing done by a central staff of male typists.[154] The Architects should be relieved of the routine duties of administration that were overwhelming them. More delegation was essential, notably in respect of the 'buff estimates', forms introduced some years previously as a means of exercising tight control over expenditure on new works, but unnecessarily petty while simultaneously failing to record actual expenditure.[155] As things were, design and supervision of new buildings occupied 'a comparatively subordinate place in the work of the Board's Architects', whereas 'undoubtedly the work of designing ought to be the most important function of the higher rank'.

The controversial question of whether to employ outside architects also exercised the committee, which took evidence from Aston Webb and Reginald Blomfield, PRIBA, who argued that under the pressure of administration the designing skills of official architects must atrophy. Although the committee did not agree that 'even from the purely artistic point of view, the State cannot obtain good results from the employment of an official architectural staff'; indeed, rather that 'the experience of official Architects must often enable them to produce more suitable and cheaper buildings' from their intimate knowledge of the requirements of government departments; yet they admitted that there was 'a certain class of buildings with regard to which the artistic point of view must obviously predominate'. For buildings of the first class in the national capitals it was 'rightly demanded by public opinion that the best talent of the whole architectural profession should be at the disposal of Government'. Even so, they concluded that it was 'desirable that the official Architects should be allowed to do some work of the highest class, if they are considered to be capable of it, because we fear that their total exclusion . . . would discourage them from keeping abreast with current ideas, and so re-act unfavourably on the general work of the Department'.[156]

Sir Henry Tanner's career provides a commentary upon this section of the Holmes Report: for several decades in charge of new building for the Post Office, he was responsible for the design and execution of major buildings in a considerable number of provincial cities, acquiring a deep knowledge of economical modern constructional techniques. Taking over the Great George Street public offices after Brydon's death in 1901, he introduced major economies in construction, saving more than a thousand tons of steelwork, and in the western section, from 1908, introduced 'more modern and less costly forms of construction'. In the new General Post Office Buildings, from 1906, he introduced the first large-scale use of reinforced concrete construction in the metropolis, and he subsequently chaired an RIBA committee on that subject.[157] But the quality of his design work was often criticised.

On the other hand, when J.J. Burnet was employed on the northern extension of the British Museum, from 1904 (actually in preference to Tanner), the nation got a first-class design, but at considerable cost: 'Although the design was substantially adhered to the variations in detail made by the Architect . . . were so extensive that the remeasurement of practically the entire building was involved in the settlement of the contractors' accounts.' Defective workmanship, departures from the specification, and faulty construction methods were later discovered.[158]

Two issues the Holmes committee was unable to resolve satisfactorily. Tanner was about to retire. The Board thought it would be difficult to find a suitable internal successor. Because his importance depended 'at least as much upon his experience and ability as an Administrator as upon his qualifications as an Architect' (so ruling out an outsider), the Architect's Division in England should revert *pro tempore*, as the Board proposed, to the pre-1898 system, under three Principal Architects. The other problem was how best to ensure the control of the Board (i.e. First Commissioner, Secretary and Assistant Secretary) over the Technical Branches. Holmes considered that the Board's lack of technical knowledge left it in the hands of the Principal Architect, who as responsible to it for the work of his division was forced to defend whatever happened. The Board had to follow his recommendations as to promotions and organisation of the Architects. It needed to be strengthened by the addition of a member with technical knowledge.[159] In other words, although the Office of Works now had the technical adviser, the lack of whom First Commissioners had so bemoaned in the Gladstonian era, so large had the technical arm become that it had acquired a life of its own. Once again the First Commissioner needed the independent technical advice that Layard had looked to Fergusson to provide.

This view, Holmes' colleagues did not share. As the Board was itself responsible to the Treasury, and to Parliament, the final control was exercised by non-technical persons. 'The basis of the arrangement is that in the last resort the decision depends on the application of ordinary principles of administration and policy to technical questions, and that application is most conveniently made when a proposal comes before the Board.' It would be impossible, they argued, to define the functions of lay and technical Assistant Secretaries: the result would be confusion within the Board, which would spread down through the Office[160] – an argument which, again, might have been validated by reference to the Fergusson-Russell imbroglio in 1868–9, and the subsequent Russell-Galton clashes.[161]

The reorganisation on Tanner's retirement accordingly provided for three Principal Architects, one dealing principally with post offices, a second with art and science buildings, labour exchanges and oversea properties, and a third with royal palaces and public buildings.[162] Under them served 9 Architects, 20 First-class Assistant Architects (£350 × £15 − £450), six of whom were ARIBA and four FSI, and 26 Second-class Assistants (£200 × £10 − £300) of whom eleven were ARIBA. Most of these had been recruited as temporary draughtsman. They were assisted by 39 clerks of varying grades, 33 Architectural Assistants First and Second class, two lady typists and a shorthand-writer, three sanitary assistants, one building inspector and 29 clerks of the works (in charge of specific buildings). There were also 200 'temporary' draughtsmen, and 74 clerks of works employed on building sites.[163]

The Secretariat was similarly divided into three sections, each under a Principal Clerk, supported by four First class clerks (£350 × £25 − £650, eight Second class (£200 × £20 − £500), and 18 Second Division clerks, £70 × £7.10s − £130, × £10 − £300), along with staff clerks, registry officials, 18 lady typists and three shorthand writer typists. There were also measuring surveyors, attached to the Finance Division, to measure up variations in contract works; but the quantity surveyors who took out quantities of materials and labour for a building before tenders were invited were not Office employees, because the amount of work varied too

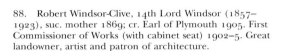

88.   Robert Windsor-Clive, 14th Lord Windsor (1857–1923), suc. mother 1869; cr. Earl of Plymouth 1905. First Commissioner of Works (with cabinet seat) 1902–5. Great landowner, artist and patron of architecture.

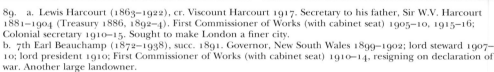

89.   a. Lewis Harcourt (1863–1922), cr. Viscount Harcourt 1917. Secretary to his father, Sir W.V. Harcourt 1881–1904 (Treasury 1886, 1892–4). First Commissioner of Works (with cabinet seat) 1905–10, 1915–16; Colonial secretary 1910–15. Sought to make London a finer city.
b.   7th Earl Beauchamp (1872–1938), succ. 1891. Governor, New South Wales 1899–1902; lord steward 1907–10; lord president 1910; First Commissioner of Works (with cabinet seat) 1910–14, resigning on declaration of war. Another large landowner.

much for a regular staff to be efficient, and furthermore contractors were unwilling to take figures from a public department.[164] Finally a building inspector was charged with making surprise visits to building sites to check on compliance with the terms of contract, and the quality of materials and workmanship – visits such as Galton had made in the early 1870s, and Mitford had in the following decade regretted were impracticable.[165] It is interesting to notice the appreciably higher salaries attainable by the First Division clerks compared with the Assistant Architects, despite the professional qualifications obtained in examination by many of the latter.[166]

In its first four twentieth-century First Commissioners, the Office of Works was unusually lucky. They were men of political weight, smooth administrators, and well-versed, or at least deeply interested, in architectural questions. Aretas Akers-Douglas has already been considered. When Balfour succeeded Salisbury as prime minister in July 1902, Akers-Douglas became Home Secretary. He was succeeded by Lord Windsor (1857–1923),[167] [Pl. 88] with a seat in the cabinet. A mining magnate with great estates in Glamorgan and on the Welsh border, he was greatly interested in painting and architecture, 'a friendly referee in matters of taste to many societies and individuals', a notable but unostentatious contributor to national culture.[168] An 'artist of no mean ability' and author of a book on Constable, he had also indulged himself in building magnificent country and town houses.[169] He carried through the replanning of the Mall initiated by Esher and Akers-Douglas.[170]

With the change of ministry in December 1905, Windsor was replaced by Lewis Harcourt (1863–1922) [Pl. 89], commonly known as 'Loulou', another connoisseur, son of the Victorian Liberal politician Sir William Harcourt, and for many years his private secretary.[171] As we have already seen, he was an active minister much concerned to promote both the efficiency of his office and the improvement of the capital, described as 'witty and amusing, ever ready in the House to defend his Department if attacked'.[172] Tall, fair, rich, 'he had "a genius for organisation and a super-

genius for making things run smoothly"'.[173] Just after Harcourt's first year at the Works, McDonnell wrote to him: 'Last night H.M. and I held an impromptu service at which we sang a duet of thanks to Providence, and to the Prime Minister, for having bestowed upon us the ideal First Commissioner.'[174] A cabinet colleague thought him 'a hard worker, and a good office chief'.[175] As early as 1896, he had taken the opportunity of a visit to Paris to study 'the French Office of Works'.[176] As First Commissioner he used every opportunity of making 'public generosity supplement official parsimony',[177] as he and his father had earlier done in securing Tate's gift of a gallery for British Art.[178] Promoted to the cabinet in March 1907, he continued to hold the First Commissionership until appointed Colonial Secretary in November 1910. Asquith then appointed Earl Beauchamp (1872–1938) [Pl. 88], another large landowner with 'a very considerable artistic sense',[179] already a cabinet minister.[180] They presided over the renewed wave of government office building from 1908. 'Sweetheart' Beauchamp,[181] a Free Trader, reverted to the old policy of competition for major buildings, though continuing to allocate large works in somewhat less import-ant parts of London to his own staff.[182] Opposed to the declaration of war, he was one of four ministers who resigned in August 1914, but was persuaded by Asquith to stay on, though in another post. He was succeeded by a Lancashire cotton-spinner, Lord Emmott (1858–1926), 'the genius of commonsense', 'cautious, efficient, public-spirited and hard-working', who had been Chairman of Committees throughout the parliamentary battles over the 1909 People's Budget and subsequent Parliament Bill.[183]

Until 1912 these successive ministers had been able to rely on the skilful administration of Sir Schomberg McDonnell. When he retired in that year, he was succeeded by the last of the aristocratic Secretaries of the Works, Lionel Earle (1866–1948).[184] Nephew of Lord Lytton, Earle had, like McDonnell, previously served chiefly as a private secretary – from 1907 with Lord Crewe, and from 1910 with his successor as Colonial Secretary, his cousin Loulou Harcourt.[185] He found a rapidly-expanded department that had had to overflow into a number of buildings, 'creating several water-tight compartments, bad from the administrative point of view and inelastic and uneconomical as regards staff'.[186] If efficiency and economy were to be secured, it was essential to concentrate the whole of the staff in one building: only so could a comprehensive scheme of organisation for the Technical Branches be achieved.[187]

Nevertheless, the government now possessed a public works department that was large and active enough to offer a structure to young men interested in an architectural career that offered greater security than private practice and, though less than the financial rewards of success in the private sector, a share in the decorations that had become a feature of advancement in the civil service. Taylor and Tanner, themselves distinguished men, had attracted others of very considerable ability such as (Sir) Richard J. Allison (1869–1958)[188] and (Sir) Frank Baines (1877–1933).[189] It offered opportunities, also, to design and superintend works of extent and importance, if not those of the very first class. If still excessively bureaucratic in its functioning, it was, on the eve of the First World War, at least competent in discharging the very important, if somewhat limited, functions allowed it by a public opinion that insisted on private sector participation in public works design. Despite some professional, press and parliamentary pressure for open competition,[190] the use of staff architects was economical, as the select committee on Estimates of 1912 noted.[191] A later Permanent Secretary summed it up:

> There are occasions when the Minister, on the advice of the Director General of Works [who replaced the Chief Architect], appoints an eminent private architect to design and supervise the erection of an important building. . . . The Ministry takes the view that it is in the public interest to engage outside architects for some of the larger and more important schemes. At the same time it is equally important that the professional staff of the Ministry should be given full scope for exercising and developing their own skill in important and architecturally interesting projects; without such opportunities it would be difficult to attract and retain officers of the right calibre, and the Ministry is jealous of its reputation for good building.[192]

The Office of Works remained, however, as much a handmaid of the Treasury as it had been since 1851: 'The First Commissioner operates and is by the statute under practically complete Treasury control, unless in any case he has express liberty to act by statute, which cases are most rare.'[193] The Office might not 'initiate a new work costing more than £100 without Treasury sanction'; nor begin a work for which a Vote had been passed without obtaining 'definite Treasury authority'.[194] Rising costs had compelled an increase in discretionary limits: for works estimated at more than £6000 the Office was now allowed to exceed estimates by up to five per cent without Treasury sanction; but the total for each sub-head must not be exceeded without previous sanction, and works provided for in the annual Votes must not be postponed to release funds for other works.[195] It is true that, at this period, care and control had done much to eliminate the chronic tendency to overrun estimates; such excesses as now occurred were generally the consequence of late changes of mind on the part of the commissioning department, often themselves in consequence of enlarged responsibilities emerging in the long period imposed by the parliamentary system between departmental approval of designs and their execution. Nevertheless, as a Treasury clerk put it: 'If the Treasury do not watch the interests of economy it is not probable that anybody else will. The Office of Works are themselves, of course, economically minded, but it is our especial duty to watch the interests of economy subject always to the general interests of the Public Service.'[196]

6
Art and Science

'IS THIS the region, this the place, the clime?' The choice of site was a fundamental element in the building process, parliamentary and professional critics alike insisting on the need for harmony between a proposed building and its surroundings which might therefore dictate its form. It affected the character and development of a whole neighbourhood, which the new work might well dominate. Site was an important component of cost – quite out of the usual order – because of the prime locations and the lengthy process of purchase, often involving arbitration and juries (considered in ch. 9), it could be fifty per cent of the total cost of a building. For our investigations we can divide public buildings into two main classes: those primarily designed for public access and those not primarily so intended.

Into the former category fall the museums and galleries; into the latter, most government offices – though some, like the military and naval departments, had a large clientele of occasional visitors. Courts of law may be regarded as a sub-group of the first class, in that, although designed for those employed therein and their limited number of clients – and so, seemingly, more akin to government offices – yet public access was a fundamental consideration, English law being administered, for the most part, publicly. In the same sub-group of buildings open to clients we may include the Land Registry and the Patent Office, both closely connected to the legal system.

While there was considerable debate over the precise location of specific government offices, there was a general acceptance of the desirability of concentrating them in the vicinity of Parliament; and their demands for space were containable. The galleries and museums presented another problem. Victorian concern with establishing facilities for rational recreation for the mass of the population; the ongoing concern about the inferiority of English industrial design and the consequent need to foster appreciation of good design among craftsmen; these required the location of museums where they were readily accessible to the widest possible public. As in our own time, public access was sometimes seen as at odds with the need to conserve the nation's collections. Paintings were vulnerable in Trafalgar Square to the smoke generated by neighbouring chimneys; should they, then, be moved away from the smoke, which meant, necessarily, to a less populous region – one where the businessman could no longer drop in for half an hour, one that cost of transport might rule out for the working man and his family – ? To some extent, technical progress and developments in public transport offered a solution, so that what seemed a right decision in 1850 might seem wrong twenty years later.

Museums

Another pressure affecting museums more than public offices was the ever-increasing demand for space. The civil service grew slowly; collections grew rapidly both by purchase (despite the tightfistedness of the Treasury) and by gift. Turner's bequest of his studio – including more than three hundred paintings – created a demand for hanging space not satisfactorily resolved for over a century. Munificent gifts such as Turner's were indeed often conditional on space being provided to display them adequately. Museums and galleries having been established in the old city, extension, if even possible, was expensive, and the attraction of green-field sites enhanced. As the chancellor of the Exchequer, Cornewall Lewis, told the 1857 royal commission on the National Gallery, 'if we have to go to Parliament to ask them to vote not only the expense of a large building but also the expense of the purchase of a site to the extent of £150,000 or £200,000, the difficulty of obtaining the consent of the House of Commons is greatly increased'.[1] Developments in science brought yet further demands for space; a random exhibition of entertaining or exotic stuffed animals no longer satisfied the savants, who called for comprehensive typological collections.

By mid century, the principal national collections were contained in two institutions: the British Museum, founded in 1753 [Pl. 90–1], and the National Gallery, founded in 1824. The Museum had been located in a former aristocratic mansion, Montagu House, in Bloomsbury, then on the edge of 'town', but subsequently engulfed in an on-rolling tide of housing; not even the benevolent despotism of the Bedford estate could prevent deterioration. The gift of George III's library in 1823 had crystallised proposals for rebuilding, and Smirke's neo-Grecian pile had gradually emerged from the scaffolding over the next three decades.[2] But the Museum was the seat of warring baronies: books, antiquities and natural history fought vigorously for space within the enlarged but still confined building (even overflowing into the colonnade),[3] which was wholly surrounded by the valuable estate of the Duke of Bedford.

The National Gallery had obtained its purpose-built structure on

90. British Museum: arrival of Layard's winged lion from Nimrûd, February, 1852.

91. British Museum Library: the Reading Room, 1841. Even in the 1840s it was difficult to find a seat, but the circular Reading Room was not opened until 1857.

St George's Barracks, an essential military base for the control of Westminster in any public tumult, and by the parish workhouse and baths. Raising the Gallery a storey, though regarded by many as aesthetically desirable, was inhibited by the accepted need of skylighting for the proper display of large paintings. The removal of the Royal Academy was the most obvious option, but that body was powerful, and whither to remove it a serious problem. In 1854 a possible solution appeared when the government purchased Burlington House in Piccadilly.

A fledgling that was to make a complex situation even more complex appeared in the shape of the Government School of Design, founded in the Royal Academy's old rooms at Somerset House in 1837, and removed, together with its art collections, to Marlborough House in 1852. This establishment grew into the Department of Practical Art, directed by Henry Cole under the Board of Trade, supervising art education nationally and developing a Museum of Manufactures containing examples of both good and bad.[5] To this was added a wide range of works of art, notably from the Bernal sale in 1855. By that time the department had outgrown its strictly temporary quarters, destined as the home of the Prince of Wales when he should attain his majority. Prince Albert had since 1851 been contemplating using the profits of the Great Exhibition as a means for establishing a cultural centre at Kensington, where ample ground was still available;[6] and Cole and his colleague Richard Redgrave (1804–88) put forward in 1854 a departmental proposal for a huge museum there that could be erected in parts progressively.[7] This was discussed with Prince Albert, who asked Gottfried Semper to prepare plans on the basis of his own suggestion for galleries, a proposal which (despite the inclusion of shops and residences) was rejected as financially impracticable.[8]

Trafalgar Square during the 1830s [Pl. 6, 92], but half the building had been allocated on a *pro tempore* basis to the Royal Academy, removed at the government's wish from the rooms at Somerset House given to it by George III. The Gallery had been set back from the square in order to preserve a frontal view of St Martin's church (to the annoyance of its architect, who declared that he had wasted many years of study if he could not produce something finer than Gibbs's portico);[4] extension northward was blocked by

92. National Gallery, Trafalgar Square. Site plan, shewing potential extensions, with plans of the major Continental picture galleries, to the same scale, 1850.

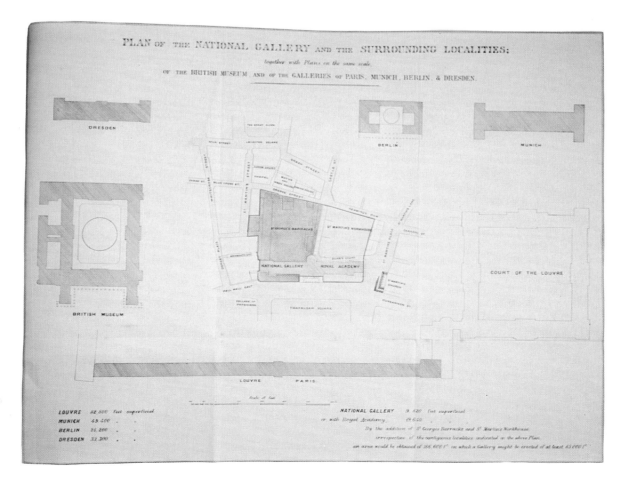

The eastern salient of the estate purchased by the Commissioners of the 1851 Exhibition[9] [Pl. 26], formed by Brompton Park House, was extraneous to the comprehensive but undetermined schemes for the use of the estate, and there in 1855 the Prince decided to establish the department, renamed in 1856 the Department of Science and Art. In June the Commissioners applied to the Treasury to erect an iron structure to house the department's collections; but in late July, as the parliamentary session was drawing to an end, they found it was blocked by the hostility of James Wilson[10] and Trevelyan, the Treasury secretaries, political and permanent. The Prince made a direct appeal to Palmerston to frustrate his subordinates' 'departmental jealousy', and secured MPs' support for a vote of £15,000.[11] The existing buildings there were adapted and extended, and the schools as well as the museum moved there in 1856–7, under the supervision of the Committee of the Privy Council for Education and the direction of Cole, who became secretary and virtual ruler of the department. Thus a step was taken towards the realisation of Prince Albert's great scheme, but under an establishment that lacked popularity with the ruling classes.[12]

Other national collections included the Museum of Economic Geology, housed in a purpose-built structure of 1847–8 in Jermyn Street, Piccadilly;[13] the Public Record Office, originally intended for legal records only and therefore built on the estate of the master of the Rolls in Chancery Lane in 1851–8;[14] and the Patent Office, also sited in the legal quarter, having taken over the quarters of the Chancery master formerly dealing with patent applications.[15] There were also the learned societies. In addition to the Royal Academy, the Royal Society, Society of Antiquaries and Astronomical and Geological Societies had also been given rooms at Somerset House, premises wanted by the 1850s for the expansion of the Revenue departments.

The question of siting the national collections thus proved to be highly complex and contentious. Essentially there were four major sites in play: Bloomsbury; Trafalgar Square; Burlington House; and South Kensington. The land surrounding the British Museum, entirely owned by the Duke of Bedford, had been developed in the late eighteenth century as a superior residential estate, though it had ceased to be fashionable.[16] The National Gallery could only be extended or rebuilt in Trafalgar Square at great expense, and the military at least seemed irremovable. Burlington House offered some three and a half acres in central London, but connoisseurs regarded the house as itself an important work of architectural art.[17] The estate at Kensington Gore and Brompton acquired by the Commissioners of the 1851 Exhibition was spacious but distant from the mass of population.[18] The National Gallery problem was minutely examined and turned upside down and inside out, conclusions were formulated and reversed, decisions made and countermanded: the years rolled on, 'resolution sicklied o'er with the pale cast of thought', losing the name of action.

The fate of the National Gallery was intricately entangled with the controversial problem of the Royal Academy – governed by members not necessarily of one mind, a private body yet under royal patronage and housed at the public expense – which for three months of the year needed spacious rooms and easy public access for its annual exhibition of new paintings. It was a bone of contention between those who believed that the arts should be supported by public money (themselves split into advocates of maximum – especially working-class – access and those who gave priority to preserving the paintings), and those who saw painting as a trade that should be treated like any other, or a national gallery as an improper public provision for court hangers-on inefficient in their business. It was also a battleground between on one hand xenophobes and keen-nosed sniffers-out of jobbery and court influence, and on the other, serious-minded advocates of public improvement clustered around the Queen's German husband, with his own master-plan for bringing together a range of institutions that would 'extend the influence of Science and Art upon Productive Industry'.[19] These issues were fought out in private manoeuverings and public contention, not only in the Commons which could vote or withhold the necessary state funds, but also in a press which was attaining new strengths: *The Times* remained the dominant daily, generally attuned to public opinion as expressed in the clubs – but a periodical press also exerted pressure, whether trade and professional periodicals such as *Builder* and *Building News*, or politico-literary quarterlies and monthlies such as the *Quarterly Review* and *Athenaeum*.

As early as 1848, only ten years after its opening in Trafalgar Square, the National Gallery's needs were the subject of parliamentary enquiry. The previous year the Gallery's trustees had requested plans for extending it by constructing a large picture gallery over the existing entrance hall. Academicians had objected, because the effect would have been to put their sculpture gallery in a basement, so a compromise design was prepared by Pennethorne, the official architect. A select committee to consider the best means of providing additional room for the nation's works of art, chaired by Lord Morpeth, First Commissioner of Works, asked Barry for his ideas, and recommended 'an enlarged and improved National Gallery . . . constructed on the site of the present Gallery' [Pl. 94].[20] The commanding position of the site; its accessibility and nearness to the chief thoroughfares and centres of business; uncovered ground to the rear that might be available; and the economy inherent in a position that called for only one ornamental front were determining factors.

The condition of the pictures, however, was giving rise to concern: there were complaints that many of them were covered with a thick film of dirt. A Treasury commission was appointed in 1849, consisting of (Sir) Charles Eastlake (1793–1865), keeper of the Gallery 1843–7 and president of the Royal Academy from 1850, Michael Faraday (1791–1867), the scientist, and the trustee William Russell. They sat poised between the needs of conservation and access. The Gallery was exposed to smoke from the parish baths, the steam engine driving the Trafalgar Square fountains, the great club-houses, and the Thames steam-boats, to say nothing of the noxious factories and workshops of Lambeth. But it lay on gravelly soil, giving good drainage, and the open space fore and aft offered a purer atmosphere than was often obtainable in city centres. Yet its central position attracted not only large crowds of viewers, but also those sheltering from the rain, those wanting a picnic spot or a children's play-park, and numerous idlers who followed the military band to the barracks; people whose 'effluvia' caused further deleterious deposits on the paintings, and whose habits disturbed those who came to study the pictures.[21] This report left unresolved several questions that were giving rise to public concern: should the cleaning of national pictures be encouraged; where should new bequests be located; should the Royal Academy be removed from Trafalgar Square?

While the commission was deliberating, letters in *The Times* in March 1850 urged the removal of the Academy;[22] parliamentary questions elicited the prime minister's support: the problem was where to put it. Russell promised a bill; but then in view of the commission's report proposed a new select committee to determine where to put the national pictures.[23] Chaired by Lord Seymour (1804–85),[24] First Commissioner of Woods & Works, the indecisive report of the new committee (dominated by the fear of the continuing deterioration of pictures in Trafalgar Square) failed to advance matters:

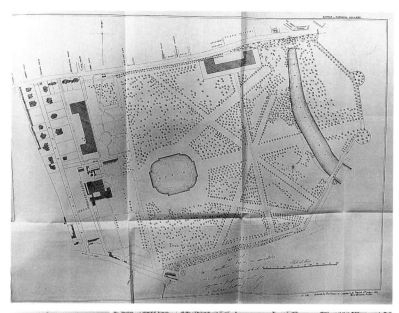

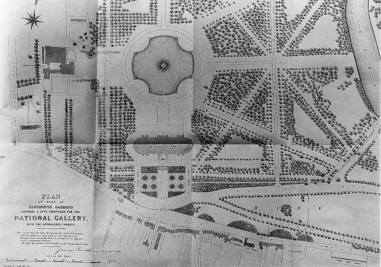

93. Alternative sites for a new National Gallery:
a. On the Bayswater Road, Kensington Gardens. The site preferred by the 1851 commission. Note the MS comment by the chairman, Lord Seymour, referring to 'a preferable site'.
b. The site, south-east of Kensington Palace, preferred by the Mure committee, but admitted to be probably unobtainable.

94. Design for rebuilding the National Gallery in Trafalgar Square, Charles Barry, c. 1845. Wilkins' National Gallery was widely considered to lack elevation, and proposals for improving it were a popular architectural exercise.

If the present site were in all respects suited for the accommodation of the national pictures, Your Committee would at once recommend that the portion of the building now occupied by the Royal Academy should be added to the National Gallery. It appears, however, that the present site, although well adapted for a public edifice, is considered by most of the witnesses whom your Committee have examined as unfavourable for the preservation of the pictures.

The committee declined to recommend incurring any expenditure 'for the purpose of increasing the accommodation of a National Gallery upon the existing site'. In other words, the government should not foot the bill for removing the Academy.

On the other hand, they were unwilling to recommend removing the Gallery:

Your Committee are not prepared to state that the preservation of the pictures and convenient access for the purpose of study and the improvement of taste would not be better served in a Gallery further removed from the smoke and dust of London; but being in ignorance of the situation that might be selected, the soil on which it might stand, and the expense which might be incurred, they cannot positively recommend its removal elsewhere.

All they called for, therefore, was increased attention to the regulations and ventilation of the Gallery; in particular, 'while they feel that one of the great objects of all public Institutions is, if possible, to form the public taste, and gratify the public eye', they thought the exclusion of very young children to be desirable. (Lord Liverpool, in establishing the Gallery, had realised that many of the poor could not attend unless they could bring their children.) Finally they suggested that 'a building, large enough for the present national collection, and constructed in a style admitting of successive additions in future years, would induce patriotic and generous men' to donate further paintings.[25]

The upshot of this uncertainty was the appointment of a second Treasury commission, specifically to consider the question of a site for a new National Gallery. Its membership represented the interested parties: government, Gallery, Academy, Commons and Lords: Lord Seymour, Eastlake, the sculptor Richard Westmacott (1799–1872), William Ewart (1798–1869) MP, ceaseless campaigner for public access to the arts, and a connoisseur, Lord Colborne (1779–1854).[26] They spelled out the indispensable conditions for a new site:

An insulated position, where the Gallery may be secured from the obstructions to light and air occasioned by neighbouring buildings, and where additional space may hereafter be provided for the increase of the collections, or for other Departments of Art which it may be deemed desirable to unite with a National Gallery.

A Situation which may be easily accessible to Visitors resorting thither on foot, and in public conveyances.

. . . it is obvious that the choice is limited.[27]

Their conclusion was that 15 or 20 acres might be obtained at a reasonable price in the neighbourhood of Kensington Gardens, but if such outlay were deemed inexpedient, as they clearly judged it would be to a government in chronic difficulty with its budgets, then the best site were the part of Kensington Gardens on the Bayswater Road, between Porchester Terrace and the Serpentine. They admitted that taking part of the Gardens might be unpopular, but argued that the position would increase the attractiveness of the gallery, the beauty of the approaches counteracting 'the distance from the more crowded districts of the Metropolis'. An alternative site immediately north of Kensington Palace, though

95.   Hon. Francis Charteris (1818–1914), styled Lord Elcho 1853–83, from 1883 Earl of Wemyss. Ruskin's 'ideal Scotsman' (*Praeterita*) was a notable individualist. Keen to achieve a higher standard of public building, a skilful amateur artist, a judicious collector of Old Masters, and above all a promoter of the Volunteer Movement of the 1860s, he sat uneasily in a House of Commons classified by Party.

not part of the Gardens, would, they thought, cause even more interference [Pl. 93]. The commissioners appear to have taken no evidence themselves, merely perusing that of the Seymour committee and the report of the 1849 commission.[28]

The government for once veered towards buying land rather than incur the unpopularity of abstracting part of Kensington Gardens, which probably also met with opposition from Prince Albert. At all events, it was the 1851 Exhibition Commissioners, chaired by the Prince, who came to the rescue when the government dropped its project in January 1852. As explained above, Prince Albert was keen to found a cultural centre at Kensington; the National Gallery would provide an invaluable magnet. A minority Conservative administration in which Disraeli, an active member of the Seymour committee, was at the Exchequer, agreed to provide the commissioners with a large grant-in-aid for the purchase of land at Kensington Gore that would accommodate a new National Gallery, as well as museums of raw materials, machinery and manufactures, thereby affording to the people 'a complete industrial education', as Disraeli put it, 'which will raise our productions in the scale of invention, and which will . . . tend to pro-

mote the improvement of the humbler classes'.[29] In the face of criticism, Disraeli played down the National Gallery element in his proposals, and the grant was voted just before the ministry's demise in December 1852.[30] This enabled the 1851 Commissioners to add, in partnership with the government, 48 acres to the 21.5 acres they had already bought.[31] Growing public interest in the site question is indicated by a report that pledges to vote for retaining the Gallery in Trafalgar Square for its ease of access had been exacted from candidates in the 1852 general election at a borough 'within a hundred miles of London'. In an article in the *Art Journal*, however, the influential German art-critic Dr G.F. Waagen strongly advocated the royal commission's proposal.[32]

When Parliament reassembled with a new coalition ministry in office, William Mure (1799–1860) of Caldwell, a scholarly Scottish laird (and Kensington resident), inspired by persistent doubts about alleged over-cleaning of some paintings,[33] moved for a committee on the Gallery. It examined the whole extent of National Gallery issues with unparalleled thoroughness. Its members included men intensely interested in the arts: the connoisseur William Stirling,[34] Leicester Vernon[35] (nephew of the collector), Ewart, Monckton Milnes[36] and Francis Charteris, later Lord Elcho [Pl. 95].[37] The four principal issues that it addressed were the constitution of the Gallery, the cleaning of the pictures, the site problem, and the desirability of uniting with the collections of fine art from the British Museum. It examined witnesses on 26 occasions between April and July 1853, and spent eight sessions on compiling its final report.[38] A great deal of the committee's time was devoted to the highly contentious issue of the extent to which the pictures should be cleaned, but the problem of access *v.* conservation was very fully argued. Eastlake was primarily concerned for the preservation of the paintings, and therefore wanted them to leave Trafalgar Square.[39] William Dyce R.A. (1806–64) agreed: smoke, bad ventilation, the bad effect of crowds were all reasons for removal. So too that 'indefatigable collector of pictures', Richard Ford, than whom 'in all matters of connoisseurship there was no higher authority'.[40] Another conservation-minded collector was Wellington's nephew, the Rev. Henry Wellesley (1791–1866), who thought the nation's paintings had deteriorated since they were in Trafalgar Square.[41]

In the other camp were a number of artists, who asked what the Gallery's prime object should be. 'I imagine that the object of a National Gallery is to improve the public taste, and to afford a more refined description of enjoyment to the mass of the people', asserted Fred Hurlstone (1800–69), president of the Society of British Artists;[42] the present site was the most convenient for all classes, including artists using the Gallery for reference. Similarly, George Foggo (1793–1869), another historical painter who in 1844 had published the first annotated catalogue of the national collection, argued that a National Gallery 'should be for the instruction and improvement of the intellect and the moral condition of the people'. He pointed out that the large numbers of the working classes who lived in east and south London could easily come to the centre (Monday was a half-holiday for many), but to go on to Kensington added to their fatigue and expense, making it impossible for working men to take their families. Morris Moore, a picture-dealer, thought that removal 'would, to a great extent, neutralize the very object for which the institution was established, to elevate public taste'; 'the increased facilities for contemplating works of excellence, which a central site would afford, must so improve the taste of the people, and, thence, both the style and commercial value of our manufactures, as to amply repay . . . even a very considerable pecuniary sacrifice'. The architectural critic James Fergusson also claimed that Kensington was too far, and advocated the greater economy of a new building on Trafalgar

Square, requiring only one architectural façade; a green-field site would require four.[43]

Influenced by the conclusions of the 1850 commission and committee on the dangers it presented for the pictures, the committee accepted that 'the site of the present National Gallery is not well adapted for the construction of a new Gallery', and commented that its enlargement would be 'attended with unusual expense and difficulty'. Of five western alternatives, while it preferred a site recommended by Pennethorne at the end of Kensington Gardens, difficulties attending its acquisition made the committee recommend the Kensington Gore site.[44] Mure's draft report had remarked on several witnesses' support for a spot roughly in the centre of Hyde Park-Kensington Gardens. Monckton Milnes successfully proposed Kensington Gore. Only Baring Wall favoured the existing site. Only Elcho and Lord William Graham supported Mure's idea for referring the site question to a royal commission; but Vernon, Stirling and Graham shared his dislike of Kensington Gore, and succeeded in watering down Milnes's clear recommendation.[45] [Cp. Pl. 93]

So far as the site question was concerned, the Mure committee's report was regarded as disappointing. The *Art Journal*, keen to see the pictures removed from the harmful atmosphere of Trafalgar Square, declared, 'The result of all is that we have come to no definite intention, and must expect years to slip pass, while discussing what should be done.'[46] But it was the outbreak of the Crimean War that caused 'years to slip by' before a Treasury minute, 25 April 1856, approved the Kensington Gore site. The government, convinced that the existing gallery was irremediably too small and so a block to further bequests,[47] brought forward a bill for enabling it to build a National Gallery on a part of the 86-acre Kensington Gore estate. Lord Elcho, a member of the Seymour and Mure committees, thwarted its intentions. 'I hear that the Bill for the site of the National Gallery is to be violently contested, and that Lord Elcho hopes to gather a sufficient number of votes for his *Times* proposal to take Kensington Palace from the Crown for the purpose and to throw away the site that we have acquired', wrote Prince Albert to his fellow-1851 commissioner, Lord John Russell, seeking his 'powerful aid when the debate comes on'.[48] But Elcho, once an advocate of a Kensington Gardens site, came round to making the best of a central site 'when [he] found that the public insisted on having it'.[49] With a convert's enthusiasm, he was determined that the Commons should reconsider the issue,[50] and he enjoyed the support of *The Times* (now consistently pro-Trafalgar Square), which argued that the country was 'drifting down upon a wrong site': attention had been concentrated on foreign affairs for three years past, and time was wanted for considering the site question; what the paper, exploiting fashionable hostility to the Prince, called 'Prince Albert's plan' combined 'every conceivable disadvantage'.[51] When the government agreed to postpone the bill, the Queen boiled over with indignation: 'Really nothing worthy of this country can ever be produced if the repeated decisions of Royal Commissions & Committees of the House of Commons, Govts &c &c are thus to be everlastingly set aside. . . .'[52]

Letters in *The Times* kept the issue before the public, and, though the Queen had urged the prime minister, Lord Palmerston, to whip in his followers, Elcho carried by nine votes (154: 145) a motion, 27 June 1856, calling for a royal commission.[53] Despite powerful speeches by Cornewall Lewis, chancellor of the Exchequer, and Palmerston for the government, ably supported by the Opposition leader, Disraeli, all taking the commonsensical view that the question had already been thoroughly examined, the existing gallery too small, its site deleterious to the pictures, and the suggested alternatives (St James's Palace, Kensington Palace, sites in the Royal Parks) illusory, Elcho's arguments – and fears of

expensive buildings – found sufficient support among a cross-section of the Commons to carry the day.[54] The *Art Journal* regarded Elcho's success as 'unaccountable', an 'idle pastime of replacing the ninepins that have been bowled down, for the express pleasure of bowling them down all over again'. There were only two questions: 'Can the National Gallery remain where it is? If not, whither is it to go?' The danger to the pictures and the lack of space for proper arrangement and classification, let alone the need to bring together all the arts of design, pronounced a clear negative to the first; the process of exhaustion would inevitably lead a commission to answer 'Kensington Gore' to the second. The objection of distance applied to any alternative; it was a great mistake to suppose that the working population made 'habitual use of the Gallery, in the short daily intervals at their disposal'. Rather, they liked an excursion; art was more intelligible to them 'amid the flow of waters, and the song of birds, and the scent of flowers'.[55] The *Observer*, however, arguing that Kensington would benefit only the upper classes, urged that the site of Burlington House (currently allotted to the learned societies, which, it suggested, would benefit from the quiet of Kensington) was the best and most economical.[56]

This proposal was to exercise a powerful influence over the deliberations of the next decade. Burlington House was the property of a cadet of the ducal Devonshire family, who offered it for sale early in 1854. The government agreed to buy it in view of the shortage of official accommodation. A decision to bring the Excise Department together with the Inland Revenue at Somerset House made it highly desirable for the government to obtain the rooms there originally allocated to the Royal and other learned societies. There was also a 'growing demand [for accommodation] from the multiplication of all the public departments'. Nearly three and a half acres in Piccadilly was 'an opportunity that might not readily recur', as Gladstone remarked, 'while the necessity was pressing'. In recommending the purchase to the Commons, Gladstone explicitly excluded the questions of the National Gallery (raised by one Radical MP) and the 'great State offices' from the discussion: the Piccadilly site was intended for royal commissions, the learned institutions and the various objects which must in a few years be cleared from Marlborough House, destined for the young Prince of Wales.[57]

The government's subsequent handling of the site was uncertain. Some of the learned societies were persuaded to move there from Somerset House, under the impression that they were being given permanent premises; but the Treasury regarded it as a merely temporary arrangement. London University (then an examining, not a teaching, body) was also accommodated there.[58] Gladstone had contemplated demolishing the old house, but the architectural cognoscenti rallied in its defence. The *Building News* attacked the learned societies as 'drags upon our intellectual progress' that should not be given state assistance. In June 1857, the financial secretary to the Treasury admitted that 'no decision had been come to . . . as to the permanent occupation of Burlington House'; and it remained a factor in play in the sites game for a decade or so.[59]

It proved very difficult to mount a National Gallery royal commission, which called for men of metal. The Treasury's first list consisted of Lord Wrottesley P.R.S.,[60] Thomas Baring (a collector),[61] the sculptor Sir Richard Westmacott and Michael Faraday the scientist (both of whom had served on previous commissions), and Sir J. Watson Gordon,[62] President of the Scottish Academy.[63] Some prominent politicians were also considered necessary. Palmerston vetoed a volunteer, the Radical archaeologist Henry Layard, though Lewis thought Layard's views 'as to the necessity of provision for antiques on a large scale would doubtless lead him to look favourably on a spacious site, and his somewhat noisy independence might give weight to his judgment'.[64] Even so, he clearly did not regard the possibles as a strong team: 'We must rely on the arguments rather than on the authority of the Commissioners for producing public conviction.'[65] At one point he was almost in despair, and suggested that they would have to pay commissioners to get any to serve.[66] A few days later, he was more hopeful: as chairman they might have the Dean of St Paul's, Henry Hart Milman, a poet and historian, whose 'acquaintance with polite literature is a sufficient connexion with the subject'; a man of business who 'knows everybody'.[67] He could be supported by an enlarged commission of perhaps eight, making up in number what it wanted in 'weight of metal' – possibilities included Dickens, Maclise, Marochetti and Lord Robert Cecil.[68] Palmerston failing to enthuse, Lewis recalled the difficulties they had had: 'My notion is that what we want is a full, impartial, & clear statement of the case. This would carry conviction to all unprejudiced minds, & the names which I have suggested would I think produce such a Report.'[69] Rationalist that he was, Lewis failed to appreciate the strength of prejudice in such questions. One element was Prince Albert's unpopularity, which caused his friend the Duke of Newcastle to decline the chairmanship. At length a chairman was found in the elderly Lord Broughton, perhaps better known as John Cam Hobhouse (1786–1869). He was supported by Milman, Faraday, the architect C.R. Cockerell (1788–1863) R.A., and the artist George Richmond (1809–96), very much a 'South Kensington' man.[70]

Meanwhile Sir Benjamin Hall at the Office of Works was introducing complications, suggesting the purchase of Devonshire House, Piccadilly, for the National Gallery (though the government already had Burlington House).[71] An alternative idea of building the new Gallery in the gardens of Burlington House was withered by Palmerston's scorn. 'We are then driven', he declared, 'by the Method of Exhaustion . . . to the Ground which we have at Kensington Gore and so far from that being in the Country there is a New Town fast rising on Three Sides of it.'[72] The ground at Kensington Gore was in fact already being developed for picture galleries. John Sheepshanks offered his collection of modern British paintings to the nation on condition that a suitable gallery was erected at South Kensington within twelve months, a condition that Cole surely engineered.[73]

From the questions the commissioners put to witnesses it appears that Broughton, Milman and Cockerell had already made up their minds in favour of the existing site.[74] Richmond alone favoured Kensington Gore. Faraday spelled out the problem with scientific clarity: preservation and access were 'highly antagonistic'; but the majority voted down his resolution, preferring to declare that: 'The evidence hitherto adduced, considered collectively, does not lead to any decisive conclusion against placing the new National Gallery within the metropolis.' Feeling that 'general opposition' would greet any encroachment on the Royal Parks (and the use of St James's or Kensington Palaces would also involve encroachment), they concluded, as ministers had argued, that the choice was limited to Trafalgar Square or Kensington Gore; the former was 'incontestably, more accessible'; its 'surpassing merits' had been set out by the 1848 select committee, which was aware of the impediments to enlargement; better care, an improved building, legislative controls on smoke emission, and the glazing of pictures would secure their preservation; and 'the substitution of a building worthy of the British people for the present edifice would command universal admiration, and do honour to the age'. Faraday abstained, 'his mind equally balanced between the two sites'. Prince Albert, seeing his Kensington complex of arts and sciences fading into the smoke, stigmatised the report as 'hardly honest'.[75] On the question of removing drawings from the British Museum collections to the Gallery, the majority was again for the status quo.[76]

The report showed how little faith was to be placed in Lewis's belief that the facts must convince: 'If the evidence here printed be right', declared the *Art Journal*, 'the Report *must* be wrong.'[77] The preservation of the pictures should outweigh other considerations. However, this view was not universal: Mr Justice Coleridge[78] wrote to the commissioners as a representative of a numerous class very much occupied in business who had an occasional half hour's leisure which they could spend in Trafalgar Square, but would be unable to travel to Kensington. 'The existence of the pictures is not the end of the collection', he asserted, 'but a means only to give the people an ennobling enjoyment . . . and wean them from polluting and debasing habits. If while so employed a great picture "perished in the using" . . . it could not be said that the picture had not fulfilled the best purpose of its purchase . . .'.[79] Invincibly hostile to Kensington, the *Building News* declared: 'the honest and straightforward report of the Royal Commission has scattered to the winds the hollow and insubstantial objections against the site in Trafalgar square'. Even the friendly *Builder* admitted, 'Kensington Gore as a site for the National Gallery is not popular.' People were not willing to go out of their way for art.[80] The commissioners did undertake some market research to evaluate the argument about access, circularising 75 major employers in the capital to ask their employees how many visits they had each made to public institutions in 1856. Thirty-five made a return, showing that the principal locations visited were, in the main, the British Museum, the National Gallery, Kew Gardens and Crystal Palace, Sydenham, information providing no clear guidance as to the best location.[81]

There matters rested for a time. Palmerston's administration was planning a select committee to examine how space might be provided at Trafalgar Square, but the Conservative ministry under Lord Derby that unexpectedly replaced him in February 1858 decided to determine the matter for itself. In July 1858 Elcho, asserting that the commission's finding in favour of Trafalgar Square 'had been ratified generally by the public out of doors' – certainly by *The Times*, 'who always manages to indicate the current of public opinion'[82] but had also been a consistent advocate of the accessible Trafalgar Square site[83] – urged that the Academy be given notice to quit; expenditure on a new building would thereby become unnecessary, for some time to come.[84] The Conservatives decided to move the Academy to 'part of the ground round Burlington House', and build additional galleries at Trafalgar Square, with an overflow collection of modern British art in a temporary gallery at Kensington Gore made urgently necessary by the need to hand over Marlborough House, hitherto used for that purpose, to the Prince of Wales.[85] The Piccadilly frontage of Burlington House was allocated to the Academy in a general plan for the entire site drawn up by Banks & Barry.[86]

The Derby government also agreed to the request of the 1851 Commissioners to dissolve their partnership in the land at Kensington. Henry Cole had pointed out in 1856 that the Commons' vote in favour of a royal commission showed that the House would not be favourable to the Kensington plan, unless guided by public opinion. Such funding as had been obtained had been voted 'almost by accident. . . . Even the Treasury has been almost hostile since the first vote. . . .'[87] One cause of hostility was, he thought, the 'unlucky Iron Shed', the famous 'Brompton Boilers' [Pl. 96a] – a denigratory term invented by the *Builder* which did much harm – then erecting to house cheaply the collections of the Science and Art Department; another, the popularity with the public of the Crystal Palace, now set up as a rival attraction at Sydenham. There was also the belief, disseminated vigorously by the *Building News*, that Prince Albert was personally engaged in land speculation at Kensington, for which the National Gallery scheme was simply a promotion.[88] Discussions between the commissioners and ministers eventuated in the repayment of £120,000 of the 1852 grant-in-aid, so that the commissioners acquired full control over the estate, though some twelve acres to the east of Exhibition Road were left in the possession of the Science and Art Department.[89] The Queen, at least, did not give up hope of seeing the National Gallery at South Kensington; and Cole's success in establishing the Sheepshanks Gift there was followed in December 1858 by an agreement to move the Turner and Vernon collections, housed temporarily at Marlborough House because of lack of room in Trafalgar Square, to new galleries adjacent to Sheepshanks. These were constructed with amazing rapidity in order to forestall any change of mind.[90]

The Liberal government, again headed by Palmerston, which took office in June 1859 did not implement its predecessor's decision, ostensibly in consequence of the British Museum trustees' vote

97.   Burlington House, Piccadilly front: building for the Learned Societies, Banks & Barry, 1868. After prolonged tergiversations, the government finally decided to erect buildings here for the Learned Societies (formerly in Somerset House), and gave the commission to Messrs R.R. Banks & Charles Barry, jun., in effect as compensation for losing the new Foreign Office commission to Scott (they having come second, and Scott only third in the competition of 1857).

to remove their natural history collections to another site – so that Burlington House had to lie fallow for the various contenders, and the plans just commissioned from Banks and Barry were abandoned. As there was no immediate likelihood of a decision, the Liberal government abandoned Captain Fowke's 'very good' but expensive plans for re-fronting the National Gallery [Pl. 98] in favour of a much cheaper reconstruction of the central hall at Trafalgar Square:[91] a new room was created by continuing the floor of the upper galleries across the central hall, and the ground floor re-ordered to create a sculpture gallery for the Academy, an arrangement reconcilable with any subsequent enlargement of the building to the rear. In a thin House, Palmerston concluded the discussion on a vote of the necessary funds by reiterating that

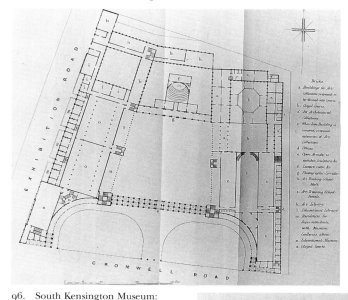

96.   South Kensington Museum:
a. Proposed layout of buildings on the Brompton site, 1860.
b. Plan, sections and elevation of the original iron building, nicknamed the 'Brompton Boilers'.

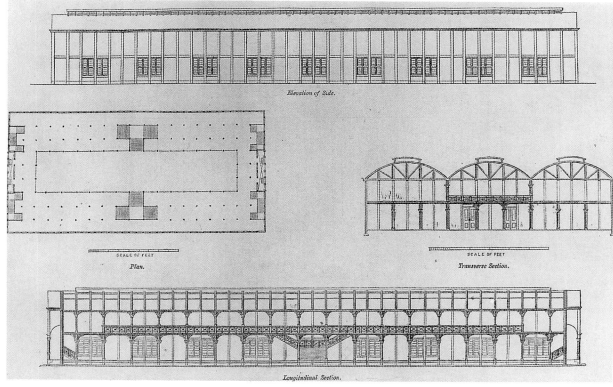

98.   Proposal for improving the National Gallery, Captain Francis Fowke, R.E., 1859. Fowke wanted to simplify the façade, making it more massive; raise the floor of the central hall to gallery level; create a central tribune, top-lighted; and thereby increase the hanging space by more than one half: all without disturbing the Royal Academy. Although publicised in the new *Cornhill Magazine* (then publishing Trollope's *Framley Parsonage*), nothing came of Fowke's proposal.

the purpose of the proposal was 'to make the present building more suitable . . . for the permanent reception of the national collection'.[92]

The First Commissioner, William Cowper, in fact proposed in a lengthy memorandum to the prime minister that the Academy should be invited to build themselves a new gallery on the Piccadilly frontage of the Burlington House site, as under the plan of 1859; and that a plain brick wing supported on iron columns be built at the rear of the National Gallery on one side of the barrack yard. Subsequently a balancing wing might be built over part of the workhouse site, and the two connected by a lateral gallery. The first stage, costed by Pennethorne at £22,000, would (by taking in the Academy's rooms) enlarge the Gallery from 9295 to 22,290 sq.ft. The entire scheme would provide 41,464 sq.ft of top-lighted space at a total cost of £197,000. Although a larger scheme might be adopted if the Gallery moved to Burlington House – 'an upper storey of picture galleries may be combined with a lower storey occupied by the learned societies . . . arranged according to the suggestions of Messrs Banks and Barry with two inner quadrangles' to provide 68,900 sq.ft –. Cowper thought 'the enlargement of the building in Trafalgar Square' seemed preferable to building a new Gallery elsewhere.[93]

Arrangements that might benefit the Royal Academy were not to every one's taste.[94] It was seen as a private body intent on gaining financial advantages for its self-elected membership, yet at the same time a state-supported, exclusive body, contrary to contemporary views in favour of free trade in art, as in other commodities. The prime minister had to declare that its ultimate removal was a

settled question.[95] Even so, a royal commission (moved for by Lord Elcho)[96] investigated it, establishing that the Academy had a moral, though no legal, claim 'to apartments at the public expense'.[97] The commissioners could hardly avoid the issue of buildings: they pointed out that even if the Academy gave up its present rooms, they would only temporarily alleviate the Gallery's inadequacy. The government should construct a new Gallery, either on the present site, or at Burlington House; if they decided to move the Gallery, the old building would very nicely meet the Academy's future needs, the government imposing whatever conditions, such as building a new façade, as they might think fit. Academicians had been willing to move to Burlington Gardens, but Trafalgar Square was more convenient for their purposes.[98] Elcho's personal view was that the Commons were determined that the Academy should be separated from the Gallery, but whether they would favour altering the present or building a new Gallery he was 'wholly unable to form any opinion'.[99]

The Keeper of the National Gallery, R.N. Wornum (1812–77), seized the chance of appearing before the select committee on Public Institutions, early in 1860, to urge that the Gallery be kept in central London, and that the Academy be removed – though admitting that would not in itself provide sufficient space for the nation's pictures. He attacked Fowke's plan as both expensive and inadequate, pointing out the need to provide residences (for himself and others), stores, rooms for cleaning and repair and framing, as well as for Turner's great bequest, which he was keen to see in its entirety at Trafalgar Square.[100]

Determination of the Gallery question had in fact been made the more urgent by a legal opinion that unless Turner's paintings (exhibited temporarily first in Marlborough House and then in a specially constructed gallery at South Kensington) were hung in the National Gallery in accordance with his will, the bequest would be lost.[101] A House of Lords committee favoured a limited addition to the existing Gallery unless there were a reasonable prospect of a new one 'erected on a comprehensive plan on the present or any other site'. Pennethorne, who declared he could construct a Turner Gallery there in nine months, asserted that 'the public generally have thought the present National Gallery the best site'. This alarmed Eastlake, who as its president was keen to see the Academy stay in Trafalgar Square: the erection of such a gallery would 'virtually decide the question as to the future site of the National Gallery' – which he obviously regarded as still an open question – and certainly would be of no use to the Academy were it to remain.[102]

Despite the assurances that Palmerston had given in 1860 and his original scorn for the Burlington House National Gallery notion, 'subsequent considerations' induced him 'to alter that view'. Burlington House, it seemed, would provide the requisite additional picture space at the least expense, whereas 'to make the [existing] gallery answer . . . you would be led into an enormous expenditure'.[103] The government therefore decided to adopt the Stanhope commission's recommendation to build a new National Gallery at Burlington House. 'The general opinion about the National Gallery I take to be', wrote Palmerston to Gladstone in June 1863, 'that the best general arrangement would be to erect an unpretentious Building [for the Gallery] in Burlington Garden between the present House and Savile Row, with no ornament except towards Savile Row, and lighted from the Roof, while the Building in Trafalgar Square might be sold to the Royal Academy . . . who I believe could give us £70,000 for it which Sum would go a long way towards the Cost of a suitable Building in Burlington Garden.'[104] They accordingly invited plans from Banks & Barry.[105] On 5 May 1864 the First Commissioner of Works, William Cowper, informed the Commons of the government's

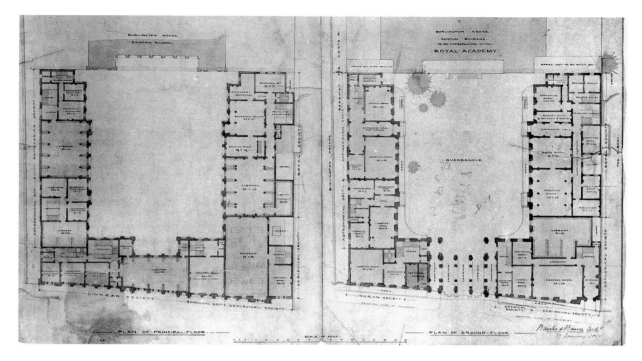

99. Burlington House Forecourt: buildings for the Learned Societies, Banks & Barry.
a. Plan of ground and principal floors, 1868.
b. Drawing for the second contract (upper storeys, 1869) for the Great Archway and central bays of Piccadilly front, in the same 'Roman' style as their Foreign Office design, which, they said, was little seen in the streets of London.
The financial collapse in 1871 of the contractors, Mansfield & Price, halted the works, which were resumed by Perry & Co. and completed in 1873.

intention.[106] On 4 June he moved for £10,000 to start work on the gardens of Burlington House; the site offered (were the option of later extending the Gallery over the forecourt exercised) a space as large as any obtainable on Trafalgar Square, 'larger than the Galleries of Berlin or Munich ["the only models for imitation"], and more floor space than the Louvre'. The House, however, was not convinced by ministers' change of mind, and decisively rejected the proposal (174: 122), preferring Lord John Manners's 'clear and conclusive speech' (as Ayrton termed it) to Elcho's earnest appeal for 'the real interest of art'. After all, the air had been purified (by Palmerston's Smoke Prohibition Act), the Thames purified also, and the railway brought to Charing Cross; was 'the finest site in Europe', 'convenient to the great masses of the people', 'in the highest degree popular', to be handed over to a private body that charged for admission?[107]

Almost immediately, ministers were pressed to secure possession of the Academy's rooms at Trafalgar Square and take steps to acquire land at the rear. There was no difficulty about removing the Academy, which was prepared to spend about £80,000 of its capital in adapting Burlington House. But Cowper was still somewhat equivocal about rebuilding the Gallery in Trafalgar Square: 'to make such a gallery as that House and the country ought to be satisfied with' would take all the space to the rear and cost not less than £300,000.[108] As a start, negotiations were opened with the parish authorities and the military, occupants of the adjacent land.[109] Pennethorne was instructed on 11 August 1865 to prepare a location plan and book of reference for a bill to purchase the parochial interests during the 1866 session.[110] St Martin's parish required the government to cover the cost of reconstructing the auxiliary parish workhouse and schools and Archbishop Tenison's School on new sites, agreed in January 1866 at £82,758.[111] The necessary bill 'slipped through the House during the small hours of the morning'.[112] The next three months saw the organisation of an architectural competition which, unsuccessful though it was, led to the appointment of Edward Barry as architect and the construction by him of additional galleries on the former parish land in 1871–4. Further extensions by official architects followed in 1884–7 and (after a fire in an adjacent building led to its demolition and the clearance at long last of the barracks in 1901) in 1907–11.[113]

The Royal Academy was not as ready, however, as Cowper had thought to take up the site offered in the forecourt of Burlington House, fronting on Piccadilly, once Sydney Smirke had shown them that it would cost £135,000 to build suitably. Lord Derby, as president of the 1851 Commissioners, had offered them (to the Queen's satisfaction) a free site at South Kensington, where a plain structure would cost about £80,000, an arrangement the academicians preferred, though as Grant, their president, remarked, 'the public generally . . . have certainly expressed themselves averse to the distance of Kensington'. This gave for hesitancy, as its annual exhibition was the Academy's major source of income.

Nor was everyone satisfied with the fundamental decision to keep the Gallery in Trafalgar Square. Beresford Hope, a doughty fighter for lost causes, who had been out of the 1859–65 parliament, battled manfully in the summer of 1866 – after the bill to buy the St Martin's workhouse was in the Lords – to change the Commons' mind. Moved apparently by fear that Burlington House would be demolished, and sarcastic about the Academy's rumoured enthusiasm for Brompton, he moved for correspondence on the subject. The First Commissioner explained that there was none, because the Academy was still undecided; though, in consequence of the reforms instigated by Elcho's commission, that body, 'fired by the noble ambition of enlarging the sphere of their action', was considering a larger site. Elcho seized the opportunity to sing the advantages of Burlington House for the National Gallery, with Henry Layard, William Gregory,[114] and Bentinck[115] and several other Conservatives in supporting chorus.[116] Lord Henry Lennox's motion that Burlington House was the most eligible site for the National Gallery, set down for 19 June, was anticipated by the defeat of the government's reform bill in the early hours.[117]

A few weeks after the consequent change of ministry, Beresford Hope moved formally that a new National Gallery be erected on the site of Burlington House. He argued that it would provide more elbow-room at a lower cost, and 'be just so much more retired as to avoid the umbrella and nursery-maid element, of which those who go to Trafalgar Square to study the pictures so frequently complain'. The decision to put London University in Burlington House Garden could easily be rescinded: it could go to the Embankment or the St Martin's workhouse site. Layard and Thomas Baring declared the Gallery trustees' preference for Piccadilly. Cowper admitted that the decision of 1864 was a mistake, but thought it would be a worse mistake now to reverse it. Manners, now again First Commissioner, rightly declared that 'there was nothing new to be said on the subject', and that 'the question could not well be re-opened', the site purchase bill having passed both Houses; adding that the government was committed to London University and the Learned Societies [Pl. 97, 99], so that their accommodation elsewhere would add greatly to the cost. For all their fine speeches, the connoisseurs were able to muster only seventeen votes.[118]

Lord John Manners's known friendliness towards the Academy encouraged Grant to hope for a more desirable portion of the Burlington House site, obviating any need to take up their controversial South Kensington option. Discussions resulted in the government's offering the Academy old Burlington House itself, with some ground immediately to the north, as suggested by Sydney Smirke. He estimated the total cost of alterations and additions at £40–45,000, which would leave the Academy sufficient capital to develop its 'extended views of education' as a national college of art. The central location and enlarged space would encourage an increase of visitors to the annual exhibition. The lease was formally granted on 7 March 1867, and the development of the site was carried through by the Academy's architect, Smirke, at its own expense.[119] The Academy left Trafalgar Square in February 1869, after some twenty years of contention.[120]

The British Museum

Meanwhile, in parallel, controversy had raged over the British Museum, founded in 1753 by an act of Parliament that united the wide-ranging collection of Sir Hans Sloane (1660–1753) with the Cottonian and Harleian libraries of manuscripts into 'one General Repository' – 'all arts and sciences' having 'a connection with each other' – 'for publick Use to all Posterity'. The trustees (representatives of the families of the founders, holders of high office in Church and State, and those whom they co-opted) decided to buy Montagu House, a great mansion in Bloomsbury from which the tide of fashion had receded and was consequently going cheap.[121] The early nineteenth century saw important additions, several collections such as the Towneley Marbles (Greek and Roman), the Lansdowne manuscripts, the Greville minerals, and the Elgin and Phigaleian Marbles, acquired through parliamentary grant; others, including the Payne Knight (coins, antiquities, and drawings) and Banks (herbarium and library) collections, by bequest. Stuffed giraffes and brilliant birds contended for space with antique statues and shelves of folios.

Thus by 1826, the British Museum was 'a strange "Mismach" of works of art, natural curiosities, books and models, preserved in a miserable building'.[122] As early as 1802, the royal gift of antiquities captured from Napoleon's Egyptian expedition sparked off a scheme for enlargement to the north, which was implemented merely in building the Towneley Gallery. The Elgin marbles were given temporary housing. Another royal 'gift', that of George III's library in 1823, made it essential to undertake a programme sketched out by Robert Smirke, the Crown architect, at the trustees' request in 1821. The government agreed to an entire rebuilding around three sides of a quadrangle, the old mansion being demolished piecemeal as its contents could be transferred to the new. Smirke's design [Pl. 7], regarded by Antonio Panizzi (1797–1879),[123] a great power in the Museum, as sacrificing internal uses for external form, was carried out over the next thirty years [Pl. 100].[124]

In that time, the growth of the collections continued apace. Layard's colossal winged lions arrived from Nimrûd [Pl. 90]. Above all, Panizzi as Keeper of Printed Books established the library as a world leader. By securing a large annual parliamentary subvention and by enforcing the Copyright Act that required a copy of all books published in the kingdom to be deposited at the Museum, Panizzi ensured the expansion of the library from 125,000 printed volumes in 1823 to 435,000 by 1850. Ever ready, as Macaulay remarked, to 'give three mammoths for an Aldus', Panizzi exhibited a ruthless single-mindedness in making the library the dominant force in the Museum: a policy that ultimately entailed the separation of the collections. By 1848, Smirke's designs hardly realised, he was already pressing for additional buildings for his books: Forshall (the influential secretary of the Museum) and Smirke had misled the select committee that sat in 1837 by reporting that expansion would be at the rate of 8000 volumes a year – in fact, it was 12,000. For lack of space the annual parliamentary purchase grant could not be used in full. In December 1846 and again in March 1848 the trustees warned the government of the forthcoming need for more space for the library [Pl. 91], and recommended buying adjoining houses.[125] A royal commission, appointed in 1847 to enquire how the museum might be 'made most effective for the advancement of Literature, Science and the Arts', reporting in March 1850, 'showed an anxiety about the inadequate buildings'; Smirke's they regarded as 'a warning rather than a model to the architect of any additional structure'.[126]

So fortified, from December 1850 to July 1851 Panizzi wrote eight times to the trustees urging the absolute necessity of enlarging the library. Colleagues in other departments, asked for their views, all stressed the inadequacy of their own accommodation, Hawkins of Antiquities roundly stating that: 'No prospective arrangement appears to have been originally thought of, so that, although the building is not yet finished, scarcely a room remains as it was originally constructed, great alterations have been found necessary in almost all; the building is surrounded by inconvenient and unsightly excrescences, and it may be asserted with truth, that Europe cannot show any building so ill adapted for its purpose as the British Museum.'[127] The trustees then urged the Treasury to fund an immediate enlargement: they proposed buying 12 houses in Montague Street and 6 in Russell Square, to the east of the existing structure; Sydney Smirke (Robert's younger brother and successor) planned a new reading room, new manuscript department, administration and Antiquities, estimated at £67,600 in addition to site costs.[128]

A sum totalling perhaps £300,000 was too much for the insecure, financially-incompetent Whig ministry to contemplate. Nor did a change of government evoke a more fruitful response. In June 1852, therefore, the trustees proposed a plan drawn up by Panizzi and Smirke for building a new reading room and book store in concentric galleries within the inner quadrangle, at a cost of only £56,000. The minority Conservative ministry however refused to act 'during the present Session'.[129]

The Panizzi-Smirke scheme for building in the inner quadrangle was not a new idea, for the use of that space had been proposed as far back as 1837. Since then, several different solutions had been suggested; indeed, as Panizzi was to remark, 'schemes for covering over, or building in the quadrangle were numberless'.[130] While contents piled up – all book purchases had to be stopped in March 1853 – controversy raged between the advocates of eastward expansion and those of rival schemes for the inner quadrangle. The *Quarterly Review* suggested glazing over the whole court for sculpture and housing printed books in the galleries thereby vacated,[131] an idea developed by Sir Charles Barry, who wanted to remove the natural history collections to South Kensington and the National Gallery to Bloomsbury, housed in a new third storey. The coalition ministry of 1852 decided, towards the end of its first year, not to entertain any plan involving land purchases for the Museum until it had decided how far its Kensington site, purchased in partnership with the 1851 Commission, might enable it to dispense with purchases elsewhere. Subject to this, it was willing to consider increasing accommodation at Bloomsbury.[132]

Panizzi meanwhile was pushing hard with Aberdeen and his First Commissioner, Molesworth. He had presented the trustees with a detailed criticism of the Barry scheme in November 1853, declaring that they must decide now 'whether it is of greater public advantage to postpone providing room for readers and for books until after a general and comprehensive scheme has been adopted for the rest of the Museum', or to proceed at once with a new reading room.[133] The Office of Works had reported on various plans for increasing accommodation at the Museum in mid-1853; in January the Treasury approved a revised Panizzi-Smirke plan for a domed, circular reading room surrounded by book stacks filling in the quadrangle. Work began in May and was completed in three years [Pl. 101].

But if the needs of the library had been satisfied for some decades at least, that was not true of the Museum's other departments.[134] A decade of fruitful archaeological excavations had filled Antiquities to overflowing, so that valuable sculptures were stored under the portico: in June 1857 no fewer than 197 cases were arriving from Bodrum and 27 from Halicarnassus.[135] The keeper of the zoological collections reported to the trustees in 1851 that these were at least ten times as numerous as in 1836; in 1854 he complained that many important specimens would be destroyed by the dampness of the vaults in which they were stored.[136] In 1847 the

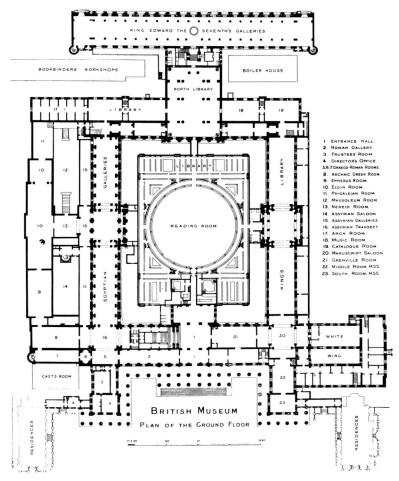

100. British Museum: Plan, *c.* 1915, shewing Sydney Smirke's Reading Room in the quadrangle of Robert Smirke's building of 1823–48; with Taylor's wing ('White wing') of the 1880s to the east, and Burnet's Edward VII Gallery to the north.

Museum possessed 1766 mammalian osteological specimens (mostly skulls or parts of skeletons); in 1861, it had 4255. Between 1860 and 1862, 33,000 specimens of fossils were added. Over 35,000 palaeontological specimens were added in the five years 1857–61. Some 15,000 minerological specimens were exhibited in 1857; in 1859 a collection of 9000 was purchased, and by 1862 the collection totalled upwards of 50,000 specimens.[137]

In evidence to the 1836 committee, and again before the Mure (National Gallery) committee in 1853, Panizzi had shewn his dislike of the scientists at the museum, preferring to see the scientific collections removed elsewhere; an option already considered by Peel in 1846.[138] In his report to the trustees, 10 November 1857, Panizzi urged that the scientific, ethnographical, prehistoric and post-classical collections should all go.[139] The idea that the museum should be broken up into its constituent parts had been forcibly expressed by the architectural critic James Fergusson in his *Observations on the British Museum* of 1849, and the issue became one of the great footballs of Victorian architectural politics. Edmund Oldfield of the Antiquities Department, who had for years been complaining of cramped quarters, proposed an independent 'Museum of Ancient Art', to be erected to the west of the existing museum, so leaving space for natural history.[140] Palmerston, as prime minister an *ex officio* trustee, was for once undecided:

On the one Hand the Collection of the Works of Nature Birds Beasts Minerological & Geological Specimens can be more easily distinguished as a separate Class & can be more easily removed to another Place & the works of Mans art such as Carved

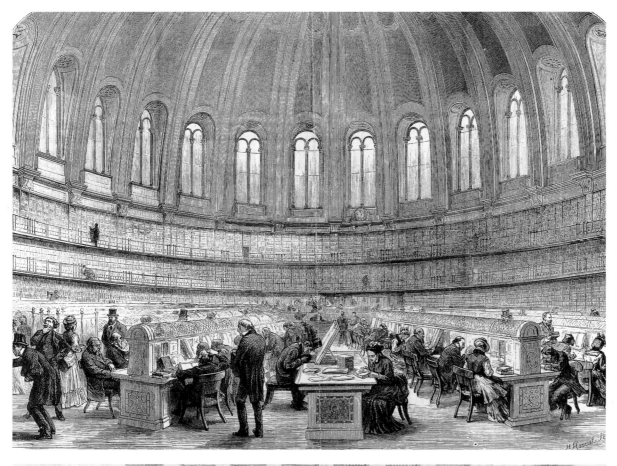

101.   British Museum:
a. The circular Reading Room (Sydney Smirke), with seats for three hundred readers, completed 1857.
b. The Egyptian Gallery, seen in the 1850s.

Marbles, Coins Vases, antient ornament, form a Class by themselves clearly distinguishable as an Order, to use a Botanical Phrase, & not easily subdivided & moreover this great Class of Things have much more connection with Books & Manuscripts & the Two great Classes have reference to & explain & throw Light upon Each other. These are Considerations which lead to the Removal of the Natural History Collection to some other Place. On the other Hand it is to be considered that the British Museum as a Place in which Things are to be looked at is as much removed from the Part of Town in which those Persons live who from Education Habits & Pursuits would take an Interest in works of Mans art, as would be Kensington Gore or any other Place to which any Collection now in the Museum would be transferred; while on the other Hand the Multitudes who live within walking Reach of the Museum & who flock weekly to see its Contents, take a very slight Interest in Marbles & Coins the value of which they little understand & chiefly devote their Time to looking at simpler objects of the animal Creation or works and ornaments of savage Tribes, which they can more easily grasp by their Mental Faculties so that by leaving the Works of Art in the Museum & removing the Natural Collections to a Distance we should place both very much out of the way of the Majority of those Persons who would most like to see them. I give no opinion but state doubts a la Gladstone.[141]

Richard Owen (1808–92),[142] world authority on osteology, appointed superintendent of the natural history departments in the re-organisation of 1856, 'whose voice can probably be heard in the [scientists'] memorial of 1858'[143] against their removal from Bloomsbury,[144] was a sturdy fighter who played a leading role in publicising the issue, which became acute in 1856 with the purchase of part of the Zoological Society's museum. Sydney Smirke suggested extending the Museum on three sides, or alternatively, like Barry, raising it a storey.[145] In order to meet the aim of the scientific memorialists, the trustees decided to build an additional gallery, but the government, inclining to removal, rejected the idea.[146] Lord Elcho felt the need to take a hand, suggesting to the Commons that the various national collections needed 'methodizing . . . bringing them into order'; the natural-history collections should be dispersed between the Museum of Economic Geology, Kew Gardens and the Zoological or Linnaean Societies, a policy that Disraeli, then in office at the Exchequer seemed to favour and that won general support in the House.[147] That provoked the famous memorial of 114 savants against dispersal; but failing to shift the government, one of its promoters, Owen, decided it would be unwise to persist in advocating a futile course. To show how inadequate the trustees' proposal would in any case have been, he presented them early in 1859 with a report, 'giving on one plane' (i.e. a single storey) the extent of the galleries required – some ten or eleven acres. He then established relations with Gladstone, then chancellor of the Exchequer. Owen's explicitly God-centred view of the natural world chimed well with Gladstone's, a view that did not fit altogether comfortably with concepts now set out in Darwin's *Origin of Species* (1859).[148]

Influenced by Owen, William Gregory raised the matter in the Commons on 17 March 1859. He proposed a select committee 'to inquire into the reorganization of the British Museum', but was persuaded to limit this vast subject to the questions of finding 'increased space for the extension and arrangement' of the collections, and 'rendering them available for the promotion of science and art'.[149] Gregory argued that as 'the collections of natural history were the most popular of all the collections in the British Museum', the question of their removal should be fully investigated. Such a decision was not, as Disraeli was inclined to suggest,

one purely for the executive government; it was a scientific question, and therefore no tribunal was more capable of advising the government than a select committee, which, 'accessible to the public and to the press' was infinitely to be preferred to the irresponsible body of trustees. Elcho, whose National Gallery commission had reported against removing the archaeological and fine art collections from the Museum, thought that probably the natural history collections must be removed, if room could not be found on the existing site: 'A butterfly might be removed without difficulty, but not a marble plinth.'[150]

Since pressure of business had prevented the government from taking a decision about the Museum such as it had taken about the National Gallery, Disraeli acquiesced in the call for a committee, which 'was often very useful in reconciling opinions, and in preparing the public mind for a solution of questions of this nature'.[151] However, the defeat of the government and a consequent dissolution killed the proposed committee. The former Home Secretary, Spencer Walpole, when as Junior Trustee he moved the Museum's vote for 1859–60, urged the new government to decide the question without further committees.[152]

Persuaded by Owen's arguments and the logic of the situation, the Liberal ministry proposed purchasing some five acres at South Kensington for a new Natural History Museum, the former partnership with the 1851 Commission having been dissolved by their predecessors.[153] But this was again to raise, perhaps yet more acutely, the issues that, as we have seen, were being fought out over the location of the National Gallery. Notice had indeed been given in the discussions in 1859 that while removal to a central location (perhaps a separate scientific establishment in Bloomsbury) seemed desirable, a move to Brompton would be opposed.[154]

Crucial, however, in this decision was a prior one, the extent of the new museum. As Owen remarked: 'Very different opinions of the aims or appliances of a National Natural History Museum have been propounded, and its extent estimated accordingly.'[155] A museum intended only for 'the amusement or amazement of the general public' could be limited to the spectacular; but a national museum should 'subserve the instruction of a people', for which a small exemplificatory collection would suffice. A further necessary function was 'to serve as an instrument in the progress' of various branches of science. Owen thought that the national museum should be, as the *Survey of London* has summed it up, 'a proportionate microcosm of nature itself'; giving, in Owen's own words, 'a comprehensive, philosophic, and connected view of the classes of animals, plants, or minerals'.[156] Even more than this, the public would expect to find there special information on relevant subjects: 'the intelligent wageman, tradesman, or professional man . . . comes in the confidence of seeing the series of exhibited specimens so complete, and so displayed, as to enable him to identify his own specimen with one there ticketed with its proper name and locality'.[157] Such a museum would, Owen believed, show forth the truth 'as it is in organic Nature', to be instrumental in removing current distortions of 'the rays of divine and eternal truth which have been transmitted from Above'.[158]

Owen, however, was in a minority of one among the scientists, who preferred Huxley's concept of 'typical arrangement': 'an arrangement for making a full and ample exhibition arranged in such a way as to be instructive to the public, and keeping a great mass of specimens which are of no use or intelligibility to the public in a compact form, for the use of men of science'. By careful organisation 'there would be ample room to arrange the collections in a most admirable manner' at Bloomsbury. Huxley and his friends now urged that organisation was more important than location, feeling that 'it was useless to argue the question of site any further, because the Government had made up its mind that the collections were to go to South Kensington'.[159]

Urgent representations from Museum officers on the want of space induced the trustees in November 1859 to press the Treasury for action. At the request of three members of the government who were trustees *ex-officio*, a special meeting appointed a committee to consider the cost of purchasing a site. Their report was considered by the trustees (again including ministers) on 21 January 1860, when by a single vote they resolved in favour of removing the natural history collections.[160] Yet once again the Commons interfered. William Gregory obtained a select committee that, despite the efforts of ministerial members and Lord Elcho, recommended obtaining space in Bloomsbury contiguous to the existing site.[161] Scientific witnesses displayed an impressively unanimous hostility to removing to Kensington, Professor Owen excepted. The report showed the preponderant popularity of Natural History over all the other departments – 'the objects exhibited, especially the birds, from the beauty of plumage, are calculated to attract and amuse the spectators', while 'works of nature [in contrast to artistic works] may be studied with interest and instruction by all persons of ordinary intelligence' – and asserted that their removal from their central position to one less accessible would 'excite much dissatisfaction, not merely among a large portion of the inhabitants of the metropolis, but among the numerous inhabitants of the country, who from time to time visit London by railway'.[162] Sir Roderick Murchison (1792–1871),[163] on behalf of 'the great body of the Cultivators of Science', sought to win Elcho's influential support for an additional building at Bloomsbury, sharing the library. However, Elcho, convinced of the need to take a long-term view of the problem and clear that the heterogeneous collections in Bloomsbury must be separated, thought that Natural History should go to Burlington House, both central and near the Economic Geology Museum in Jermyn Street.[164]

Thus, from 'the great popularity of stuffed birds and beasts with the mob', the enormous cost of a five-acre museum, and the opposition of the scientific world, it seemed certain that Kensington was unattainable. The trustees, after consideration of the Gregory committee's report, asked the government to make up its mind, 'particularly with respect to the removal or non-removal of some of the collections'.[165] Edmund Oldfield, assistant keeper of Antiquities, 'morally certain that Parliament could never be brought to remove Natural History from the Brit. Museum', had offered the committee an economical plan for separate development at Bloomsbury, involving new galleries for Antiquities on ground to the west fronting Charlotte Street (now Bloomsbury Way), a plan commended by Gregory in his draft report.[166] Oldfield complained bitterly to Elcho of an 'official party' which was determined to limit the Museum to its existing site, maintaining the 'confusion' of the existing arrangements.[167]

The trustees however persistently urged action on the government between October 1860 and November 1861, when a Treasury minute, redolent of Gladstone's ideas, asserted the duty of the executive government to decide the contentious issue:

> use and convenience impose certain limits upon the local extension [of museums; the real question was] whether reason and convenience recommend or permit the continued union of the collections for an indefinite time. . . . It seems difficult to find reasons for the opinion that in a city of 3,000,000, rapidly increasing and stretching outwards from year to year, it can be for the convenience of the population that all the extended and multifarious collections represented in the main by the three names of, the Library, the Natural History, and the Antiquities, should continue without limit of time to be concentrated and combined on a single spot.

102.   William Henry Gregory (1817–92), K.C.M.G. 1876. Peelite and then Liberal MP. Trustee of National Gallery from 1867. Prominent in parliamentary discussions on artistic and architectural questions, he chaired the select committee of 1860 on the British Museum.

Communications were being developed following the lines of through traffic; and spots on such leading lines might be more accessible generally than even the Museum itself.[168] The government's preference for a new natural history museum at Kensington was the solution adopted by the trustees after further consideration in February 1862. The all-powerful Panizzi, voracious for library space, wanted to be rid of Natural History; while Gladstone's friendship with Owen was another factor influencing the ministry's policy.[169]

Events then began to gather pace. The trustees recommended obtaining five and a half acres. The Treasury, although quibbling over the last half-acre, negotiated with the 1851 Commissioners, who offered various alternatives at the low price of £10,000 an acre and some works to the Horticultural Society's arcades. Unable to agree with the trustees about the architectural effect to be aimed for, the Treasury postponed negotiations with the commissioners,[170] but Gladstone nonetheless introduced a bill for the purchase of five acres at South Kensington. Its second reading[171] was decisively defeated on 19 May 1862, to the extreme annoyance of the lately bereaved Queen, guardian of Albert's projects.[172] But Thomas Huxley assured the objectors that they had 'earned the gratitude of men of science'.[173]

William Gregory (1817–92) [Pl. 102], a Liberal-Conservative, and one of the Commons' principal authorities on artistic questions, had led the opposition to the bill because it would make the natural history collections less accessible to the lower and middle classes, with whom they were extremely popular; even Owen, he claimed, said 'Not that I love Bloomsbury less, but that I love space more' – and ridiculed his concept of 'galleries 850 feet in length for the exhibition of whales'. The opposition of the Liberal Henry Seymour (1820–77)[174] was perhaps more significant: the ministry could not rely on its regular troops.[175]

103.   Building for the International Exhibition of 1862, South Kensington, Captain Francis Fowke, R.E. (perspective by T.S. Boys). Fowke's largely temporary building was almost universally condemned as ugly beyond comparison. Gladstone's proposal to clad it and use it for a Natural History Museum provoked a parliamentary storm.

The Times blamed the government's defeat on 'political jealousy' of the Museum's trustees, 'a hybrid trust, neither private nor yet public'.[176] But as well as the hostility to Court influence displayed by a faction, the injudicious behaviour of Gladstone as chancellor of the Exchequer clearly contributed to the government's defeat. Gladstone had consistently opposed the prime minister's expensive defence programme, and told him he was 'feeding . . . the spirit of expenditure'; declared in his Budget speech that there were no funds to spare; and in April 1862 in a speech at Manchester had asserted that 'the nation at large' had forced parliament and the government into a 'high amount of expenditure': yet he was now proposing a vast scheme of uncertain cost.[177] MPs clearly resented his criticisms, and now paid off the score by rejecting his own pet proposal – despite *The Times*'s warning that it was England's imperial duty to preserve the natural history collections because all animals were threatened by man. 'We have the best chance of all nations, for we boast to rule the waves, and to bask in the sunshine always in some part or other of our vast circumference. There is no variety of clime or of soil, of forest, plain, swamp, or sand, that we do not possess . . . the most preposterous estimate does not exceed the cost of two "Warriors".'[178] Clearly, the battle was to be continued.

Hostility to 'Albertopolis' found further expression during the following parliamentary session, culminating in a rowdy scene in the Commons when the government had a second bite at the cherry. It was Gladstone who was 'hot for buying the exhibition building',[179] but the prime minister himself took care to introduce the ministry's proposal to buy the site of the 1862 International Exhibition, rather more than 17 acres, for £67,000, a notable bargain.[180] This would accommodate a Patent Museum, the Natural History Museum, a National Portrait Gallery, and enlargement of the South Kensington Museum, as well as leaving ample space for further development. It lay immediately to the south of the area leased in 1859 to the Horticultural Society, another of Prince Albert's schemes, as a garden around which the landlords, the 1851 Commissioners, built Italianate arcades and galleries.[181]

Considerable opposition from several interested parties was ex-

pected to the purchase of the exhibition site.[182] 'I think it would help us through', the prime minister told Gladstone, 'that I should say that we have no intention of sending thither the learned Bodies nor the old Pictures in the National Gallery – this would disarm some objectors.'[183] Although Palmerston (on the advice of the Conservative front-bencher and 1851 Commissioner Stafford Northcote)[184] proposed to the Commons merely the purchase of the site and some minor buildings, he made it all too clear that the government intended also to buy and adapt the Exhibition building [Pl. 103], ornamenting it in stucco, as by far the cheapest way of proceeding. As it had, apart from its picture gallery, been designed as a temporary structure, it would require extensive works, though their extent was fiercely disputed, particularly between Gladstone and William Gregory, chairman of the 1860 committee on the Museum. Backed by an engineer's opinion, Gregory savaged the official estimate for reconditioning the exhibition building. He also denounced the project as 'a preparation for drawing into one focus all the different institutions of the country', attacking 'that craving meddling, flattering, toadying self-seeking clique that had established itself at Kensington'; 'parasites', 'hunters after honours or Court favour, or small clerks, who have promoted themselves into commissioners. . . .'[185]

Such 'gross and virulent personal abuse', as Gladstone termed it, served to defeat its object, though Bowring, the 1851 Commissioners' secretary, commented that he had never seen the House in such excitement, every attack on the building or the 'S. Kensington clique' being greeted with deafening cheers. Yet, thanks to effective whipping, MPs' anxiety for dinner and, possibly, to court influence, the ministry obtained a majority of 132 (including about a hundred Conservatives) for the land purchase.[186] Thus the principle of removal of the natural history collections to Kensington was implicitly conceded. The argument about non-accessibility had been undermined by the evidence given to the committee on Public Institutions in 1860, which showed that nearly 1,200,000 persons (of whom a high proportion were workmen or clerks) had visited the South Kensington Museum in two and a half years;[187] moreover, as Gladstone pointed out, the construction of the underground railway was making 'a fundamental change . . . in the facility of communication between one point of London and another'.[188] But some two weeks later, on 2 July, a vote to purchase the exhibition building itself was rejected.

By then the House was much more combative, 'very boisterous and resolved',[189] 'determined from the first to throw it out', according to one member,[190] and exacerbated by Gladstone's aggressive manner, clever and sarcastic, in introducing the proposal. Lord Henry Lennox, writing during the debate, commented that nothing could be 'more clumsy or *fatal*'.[191] The unpopularity of the 1862 Exhibition building, designed by Captain Francis Fowke, R.E., was notorious. Gladstone 'electrified' an incredulous House with the news that there was no covenant with the contractors to remove it; this 'was taken as a menace to force them [the House] to buy the building' or face a lawsuit with the contractors. Despite the attractive cost figures Gladstone offered, the House 'thought it had been entrapped' and carried overwhelmingly Lord Elcho's motion for rejecting its purchase.[192] Elcho had changed sides in face of the great hostility to the building; his powerful and effective speech called up the RIBA (which petitioned against the proposal as 'a grave discredit to the artistic reputation of England'), the *Spectator* ('Let us not have the shrine of art set up in the Temple of Ugliness. The building stands condemned by the taste of cultivated Europe . . .'), the royal commission on the National Gallery site, the *Daily News* advertisement columns, John Ruskin ('Do not rough-cast [your walls] with falsehood'), Lord Westminster, Professor Kerr and Prosper Mérimée ('preserve it if you wish to warn posterity of the faults to be avoided in the erection of a great public building') to support his onslaught.[193] His language, however, was temperate in comparison with that of others on his side.[194] Members returned from dinner to raise 'a din quite demoniac'. Despite the reasonable tone adopted by the First Commissioner of Works, William Cowper, and Disraeli's vain efforts as Opposition leader 'to stem the tide and stay the storm', Northcote's proposal for a committee was hooted down. The House 'rose *en masse*, and, after a scene of the utmost confusion and excitement, defeated the Government by more than two to one'.[195] 'I do not recollect having ever witnessed in the HC so disorderly a scene', noted Lord Stanley, a member since 1848.[196]

Thus died Gladstone's idea for a cheap multi-purpose museum, leaving him permanently scarred. Palmerston attributed Gladstone's ill-judged line to 'his extreme eagerness . . . his intire conviction of the advantageous nature of the proposed arrangement'; he told the Queen that the House was 'like an army that has taken a town by storm; they have broken loose from all control, and the only thing to do is what a prudent General in such a case does with his troops, try to lead them away out of it'.[197] In the next session the government could propose a well-considered measure for new buildings.

The victorious opposition, however, was a coalition of diverse interests. The prime minister identified popular prejudice against the Exhibition building, jealousy of Cole's circle managing the exhibition, 'narrow-minded' MPs 'who take a pride in opposing what is recommended from quarters above them', and artists and architects excluded from the planning of the exhibition, who looked for employment on new buildings that would take its place.[198] Undoubtedly, 'jealousy of Court dictation' and dislike of Cole's South Kensington clique were powerful factors.[199] Stanley thought also that the sight of the two front benches united aroused mistrust; while the cost of converting an unpopular building provided a rational basis for widespread opposition.[200] Elcho, wanting to separate himself from the self-interested, wrote to Palmerston on 23 July of his anxiety 'to say a few words to show that those who

were opposed to the keeping up of the Exhibition building are not simply destructive but are anxious to see a suitable and creditable building erected on that site for the Natural History Collection . . . and for such cognate subjects as can legitimately and advantageously be established there'.[201]

The 1851 Commissioners' secretary, Bowring, shared Palmerston's expectation that the war had not been lost. The exhibition building would have been at best a makeshift. A new building could be erected without loss of time.[202] But Gladstone retired from the fray, nursing his wounded *amour-propre*, and from then onwards it was Cowper at the Office of Works who pressed forward the issue of a new Natural History Museum. Having arranged with the contractors, Kelk and Lucas, for the removal of the Exhibition building 'with the utmost despatch', he told Gladstone in early December of his intention to invite a competition for designs.[203] Owen 'tried to short circuit matters by getting in touch directly with the Office of Works . . . and was reprimanded by the Trustees for his pains'.[204] The contract for the purchase of the 16 acres was not signed by the government until 14 September 1864.[205]

The subsequent competition of 1864 for a Natural History Museum and other museums at South Kensington [Pl. 104] having been won, ironically enough, by Captain Fowke,[206] architect of the loathed 1862 Exhibition building, he was commissioned to modify his designs in consultation with the British Museum trustees. On Fowke's death in December 1865, Alfred Waterhouse (1830–1905)[207] was appointed to carry out his plans, but proceedings were delayed by the change of ministry in June 1866. Although Waterhouse then submitted his own revision, Lord John Manners wanted economies and alterations, so that Gladstone's first ministry took office (December 1868) before any funds had been voted. Layard as First Commissioner, enthusiastic for lining the new Victoria Embankment with great public buildings, won much support for including the Natural History Museum among them. He claimed that 'in public opinion', the museum 'requires a central position'.

> In thinking over the different sites which might be appropriated . . . , it struck me that the site between Waterloo-bridge and Hungerford-bridge would be an excellent spot. . . . Various sites have been suggested . . . amongst others a site connected with the South Kensington Museum. Great objection has been taken to that site by various scientific men, upon different grounds, and considerable opposition has been raised to the transfer. . . . I communicated with a great many of the leading scientific men of this country, and they all accepted the idea as the one best calculated to solve the difficulties with regard to the removal of that Museum. . . . They admitted at once that it would be the most appropriate, as being central, very accessible from the south of London, from whence access to a museum is much required, as being immediately in connection with the British museum, as being removed altogether from South Kensington, South Kensington having been considered objectionable by scientific men on different grounds, and as having plenty of light and air, from having the river in front.

Unfortunately, the MBW was about to construct a road and viaduct linking the Embankment and Wellington Street which would have destroyed the possibility. A select committee was therefore appointed under Lord Elcho's chairmanship, to examine the problem: in May 1869 it recommended the erection of a natural history museum on the Embankment [Pl. 105].[208]

One difficulty was that the Embankment Act required that the reclaimed land proposed to be taken must 'be used for the

104. Competition designs for Museums at South Kensington, 1864, to provide for Natural History, Patents and Ship Models. This competition was held in consequence of the Commons' rejection of Gladstone's proposal to buy the 1862 Exhibition Building.
a. First prize: Captain Francis Fowke, R.E., architect of the contemned 1862 Exhibition Building.
b. Second prize: Robert Kerr. This design was preferred by the British Museum authorities, but the First Commissioner insisted on upholding the judges' award to Fowke, who died before he could revise his design.

105. Designs for Natural History Museum, Alfred Waterhouse.
a. At South Kensington. Waterhouse was brought in to execute Fowke's design, but eventually substituted one of his own. The site, however, was not acceptable to many scientists.
b. Layard in 1869 proposed building the Natural History Museum on the Thames Embankment, and accordingly Waterhouse made a more grandiose design suited to the more conspicuous position. But the government then reverted to South Kensington.

purposes of public recreation'. Layard suggested that 'nothing could tend more to public recreation and enjoyment than a great Natural History Museum on that spot, laid out with appropriate gardens in a way which would attract the public, which would lead the working classes to go to the Embankment, and from the Embankment to the museum; in every respect, I think, such a building would be eminently calculated for public recreation; therefore the words of the Act would be met by erecting a building of that kind on this site.'[209] He stressed the advantages that the Embankment site possessed for public access: 'It would give the south of London easy access to a great museum; by the bridges, and by the ferry steamers, people might cross the river in a very few minutes. On the other hand, by the Metropolitan Railway, you would have access to the museum from all parts of London, and all parts of England. For excursion people coming up from the country, and for the best class of working men, I think such a site would be of the greatest possible advantage.'[210] When it was suggested that the higher ground behind the reclaimed land would provide a better architectural effect, he pointed out that bringing the building forward would serve to screen 'that hideous construction', the train shed at Charing Cross Station; but in any case, the cost of buying land in the neighbourhood would rule out throwing back the building line.[211] Even Cole of South Kensington supported Layard's proposal, thinking it 'much more logical, in the way of arrangement, that the Natural History Museum should be on the Embankment than that it should be mixed up with industrial sciences and arts at Kensington'. Owen similarly had no doubt that the Embankment from its 'very central position' would be more convenient than Kensington, and Murchison and Huxley added their support, though the latter expressed the continuing preference of naturalists for Bloomsbury.[212]

Despite the committee's recommendation, the failure of Layard's agnate proposals for siting the New Law Courts also upon the Embankment entailed the failure of his whole Embankment concept. Although after a comparative costing his successor Ayrton recommended the more expensive Embankment site on grounds of easier public access,[213] in May 1870 the government decided to ask the Commons to rescind its ban on moving any part of the British Museum to South Kensington.[214] In July Lowe told the House that though the Embankment scheme was excellent, it could not be carried out without taking land dedicated by statute for gardens, and paying an enormous price for it.[215] South Kensington it was to be.

The Tate Gallery

Problems continued to beset the national picture collections. Many hoped to see paintings and drawings united in a National Gallery, but the British Museum even now continues to hold and extend its magnificent Drawings Collection. Lack of space in Trafalgar Square exiled the modern British school to the western galleries at South Kensington, where in 1883 Mitford of the Office of Works proposed to create a 'British Luxembourg', to house the Old Master drawings from the Museum and the Raphael Cartoons from Hampton Court, along with the Sheepshanks collection of British paintings permanently kept at South Kensington,[216] the germ of a 'National Gallery of British Art'.[217]

Sir Henry Tate (1819–99),[218] who had made a fortune out of selling cube sugar to the public, was an avid collector of contemporary British art. Desirous of bequeathing his collection to posterity, in October 1889 he offered it to the National Gallery on condition that rooms exclusively devoted to it were erected or provided within three years. The Treasury, somewhat concerned at the extent of buildings expenditure to which it was already commit-

ted,[219] replied that there was no room in Trafalgar Square (where a National Portrait Gallery had just secured a site previously earmarked for extending the National Gallery), and suggested South Kensington as an alternative. Tate then approached the chancellor of the Exchequer, Goschen,[220] with an offer himself to build a gallery for modern British art if the government would provide a site. A number of intermediaries were involved in the negotiations, including Humphry Ward[221] and Lord Carlisle.[222] Carlisle, an artist of considerable talent, as well as a trustee of the National Gallery, proposed joining the east and west 1862 Exhibition galleries [Pl. 190] at South Kensington with a cross-gallery north of the Imperial Institute, a very extensive space in which to gather the existing national collections of British art. A 'really representative collection of the British School oil and water' might have been assembled there from the South Kensington pictures, the Chantrey Bequest[223] purchases and those from the National Gallery, in addition to Tate's.[224] Negotiations continued through 1890, Sir Frederic Leighton P.R.A. and the official art world supporting Carlisle's proposal, and Tate was understood to agree.

The Treasury therefore in December 1890 authorised leasing the galleries at £3500 p.a., together with the upper floor of a cross-gallery to be constructed by the Imperial Institute council, at a further £1000 p.a. But Tate, according to Carlisle, 'could not bear the idea of his collection having to be taken up a few steps'.[225] Ward, however, doubtless expressing Tate's views, commented that the idea had 'not been regarded with unmixed satisfaction by the public'; the galleries were inconvenient in shape, wanting in compactness, and 'without any external attractiveness whatsoever'.[226]

Instigated by Sir J.C. Robinson (1824–1913), Surveyor of the Queen's Pictures and an enemy of 'South Kensington' (where he had once played an important role in building up the Museum), *The Times* had been running down Carlisle's proposal, advocating instead a new gallery adjoining Kensington Palace, and a public subscription. The great picture dealer Agnew[227] offered £10,000 if £100,000 could be raised. Humphry Ward told Goschen privately that an anonymous donor would give £80,000 if the government would give the Kensington Palace site. The anonymous donor was Tate; but when it proved impossible to obtain the necessary consent, he suggested the corner lying between land recently purchased by government in Imperial Institute Road for the Royal College of Science and that on the west of Exhibition Road proposed for the South Kensington Museum's scientific collections [Pl. 190].[228] Ministers agreed in principle, planning to use the scorned galleries for the science collections, despite opposition by the influential scientist Sir Lyon Playfair (1818–98),[229] who wanted the corner site for science laboratories. On 21 March *The Times* published an exchange of letters between Ward and Goschen, which Tate regarded as acceptance of his offer.

At a private interview on 16 April 1891 Goschen arranged that Tate's architect, Sidney R.J. Smith (1858–1913), should prepare plans for submission to the Works and a distinguished advisory committee.[230] Thereupon the whole official scientific world erupted in anger. A few days later, Lord Rayleigh, F.R.S., presented a memorial to the prime minister, signed by almost every scientist of any significance in the country, protesting that the art gallery would trench on the science buildings for which the site was destined, and would cut off the science schools from the museum – an opposition regarded by the Treasury as factious and inspired by other reasons, but nonetheless too powerful to resist.

An available site on the Embankment, to the east of the Temple, belonging to the City Corporation was warmly supported by the scientists and the advisory committee. The Treasury was prepared to offer a moderate ground rent. But the City, with its customary blindness to the national interest, and resentful at the government's abolition of the traditional City revenue of the coal dues,[231] just effective, refused to let the site go for less than its full value, estimated at £180,000, a proposal quite unacceptable to Goschen. In early 1892 Tate consequently threatened to withdraw his offer unless he could have the South Kensington site, at which the scientists renewed their protests. The art world seemed strangely little concerned: doubts were cast on the value of Tate's paintings; and his offer was seen as designed to boost trade for dealers amateur and professional. Having fruitlessly attempted to win over the scientists, Goschen therefore reverted to Carlisle's idea, offering Tate the three galleries, or a site of 180 × 150 ft previously proposed for the School of Needlework. Tate retorted that he had offered a new gallery expressly 'to save British Art from the humiliation of being housed in those tunnel-like edifices', and the Art Needlework school site was totally inadequate. So he withdrew his offer.

Although Robert Farquharson, MP (1837–1918), a physician who had been one of the leaders of the original scientific opposition, urged a resumption of the negotiations,[232] and the vestry of St Saviour's Southwark offered to mediate if the government would buy the Embankment site, Treasury official advice was against the idea. The importance of a 'National Gallery of British Art' had been diminished by the Law Officers' opinion against moving the Sheepshanks' collection; Tate showed himself indisposed to allow the government to settle questions of building and management (according to Lewis Harcourt the real reason for the breakdown of negotiations);[233] the persistent silence of the art world 'seemed to prove that his proposals in their present form were not generally acceptable'; and the government, owning several suitable sites already, was not justified in imposing a heavy cost on public funds.

So matters stood when a general election led in August 1892 to a Liberal government. Lewis Harcourt, son of the new chancellor of the Exchequer, and Humphry Ward acted as go-betweens in renewed negotiations. The Treasury now opened discussions with the City Corporation's rival, the Liberal-controlled London County Council (LCC), with the 24-acre site of the old Millbank Prison, closed in 1890, as a lure. The government would provide the site, and Tate the building, which the LCC would then maintain. Sir William Harcourt saw the scheme as a prototype for localised museums to be established in connection with the county council. Tate was favourable to the site, but was 'very anxious that the *nation* only should control what is intended for a national object'.[234] Keen to secure the main object, Harcourt proved willing to drop the LCC element, and at last met Tate, whose final proposal was to find £80,000 for the gallery if the government would provide for its maintenance and administration. His own collection would provide a nucleus of paintings, and the Chantrey trustees might make their home there. He showed Harcourt 'rather a nice elevation somewhat after the fashion and dimensions of the Fitzwilliam [Museum] at Cambridge'; he was quite willing that the government's surveyor supervise execution. But he wanted an early decision: he was 73 years old; he had 'been bandied about for two years from pillar to post'.[235]

Sir William Harcourt forthwith consulted his friend Lord Carlisle on views of the National Gallery trustees, and Sir Frederic Leighton, who as PRA chaired the Chantrey Bequest trustees. Questions of finance and management had to be decided, but by the end of 1892 arrangements had been made for the 'National Gallery British Art section', for the collection of British art of all epochs, to be built under a contract in which the government was associated, though Tate or his executors would be responsible for its accomplishment. Work began at Millbank on the new gallery in July 1893 [Pl. 193].[236]

7
Courts of Justice

FIERCE as were the struggles about the natural history collections, they yield by a long margin to those about the siting of the new Courts of Justice. Justice in England had been administered in Westminster Hall since 'time whereof the memory of man runneth not to the contrary' – at any rate, since the thirteenth century. By 1820 there was sad need of additional court accommodation, and the clearing of the Hall for the coronation of George IV acted as a catalyst. Soane was instructed to design new courts, which he arranged cleverly in the limited space immediately to the west, a remarkable range of mostly top-lighted courts [Pl. 4, 48], completed by about 1827.[1] But already by 1830 solicitors were petitioning Parliament about the unsatisfactory conditions. The increase in legal business is indicated by the growth of the legal profession, from 673 barristers in 1800 to 1664 in 1839, and from 4564 to 9421 attorneys.[2] In 1834, the need for additional courts was such that a storeroom in an older adjacent building had to be requisitioned as a bankruptcy court; the burning of the cast-out tally-sticks (disused since 1826) in the House of Lords furnaces caused the great fire of 1834 leading to the rebuilding of the Houses of Parliament. The Courts escaped the conflagration, but much of Chancery's work was carried on in Lincoln's Inn, on the border of the City, close to the ancient estate of the Master of the Rolls in Chancery Lane where the offices of the Chancery masters and clerks were to be found.[3]

The Inns of Court and Chancery, sometimes described as England's legal university, had developed in the thirteenth century to provide a legal education, especially in the common law not taught at the universities. They reached their apogee in the Elizabethan and Jacobean periods, when they attracted students from the gentry as well as those intending to profess the law. Powerful corporations controlling admission to advocacy in the courts, their property also provided accommodation, for solicitors and attorneys as well as barristers. Their eastward location was not the most obviously convenient for Westminster Hall, but the students were probably regarded as an element undesirable in the immediate vicinity of the royal seat; on the edge of the City, they were free from its regulations but well placed to enjoy its conveniences. The Inns of Court played a significant part in the Victorian disputes about the location of new courts. Lincoln's Inn traditionally had a special relationship with Chancery: under acts of 1774 and 1775 Chancery offices had been built in its garden; it had provided a court for the newly-created vice-chancellor in 1816; the chancellor sat there out of term; in 1841 a utilitarian brick court was erected at the Inn's expense for two new vice-chancellors; and in 1853 the Old Hall was divided in two to provide courts for the chancellor and the newly appointed lords justices.[4]

Barristers as a body were perhaps too conservative and remote from the public to press for change; but the solicitors, more numerous and in direct contact with clients, were only just institutionalising their profession. The Incorporated Law Society, founded in 1825 for the benefit of attorneys (practising on the Common Law

side) and solicitors (for the Equity courts), in 1831 established its premises in Chancery Lane, between the Temple and Lincoln's Inn. In 1835 it appointed a committee to consider the question of new courts, and in 1840 resolved to petition Parliament for the construction of courts of both law and equity in Lincoln's Inn Fields (first suggested by Joseph Hume in 1836), asking Charles Barry to prepare designs.[5] Pamphlets circulated for and against the proposal.[6] It won the support of Sir Thomas Wilde, the solicitor-general, who in April 1841 moved for and chaired a select committee on the need for new courts.[7] The solicitors argued strongly for siting new courts in Lincoln's Inn Fields (where many had offices), as did the barrister witnesses, but some of the judges preferred their traditional proximity to Parliament, acclaiming the benefits to barristers of the exercise of walking from their chambers to the courts. The trustees of the Fields, one of London's lungs, also objected to the proposal. A recommendation of the Rolls Estate in Chancery Lane by Lord Langdale, M.R., was rejected as too small. A better alternative, 'which might be a means of improving a portion of the metropolis', was put forward by the Radical MP and barrister Matthew Davenport Hill (1792–1872): the district of slums lying south of the Fields, between Carey Street and the Strand. When Charles Barry presented his proposal for courts in the Fields [Pl. 107] to the resumed committee in the 1842 session, he suggested what for brevity was called the Carey Street site as an alternative. The differences of opinion were evidently too strong for the committee to resolve, the evidence being reported without recommendations.[8]

The lawyers kept up the pressure with a petition to the Lords in 1843, when Lord Campbell, L.C.J. (1779–1861) iterated that the walk from their chambers to Westminster provided lawyers with

106. The Law Courts, Westminster, John Soane, 1822–5. The North front, as altered to meet the requirements of a House of Commons' committee, 1824.

107. Proposed New Law Courts in Lincoln's Inn Fields: design by Charles Barry, 1842.

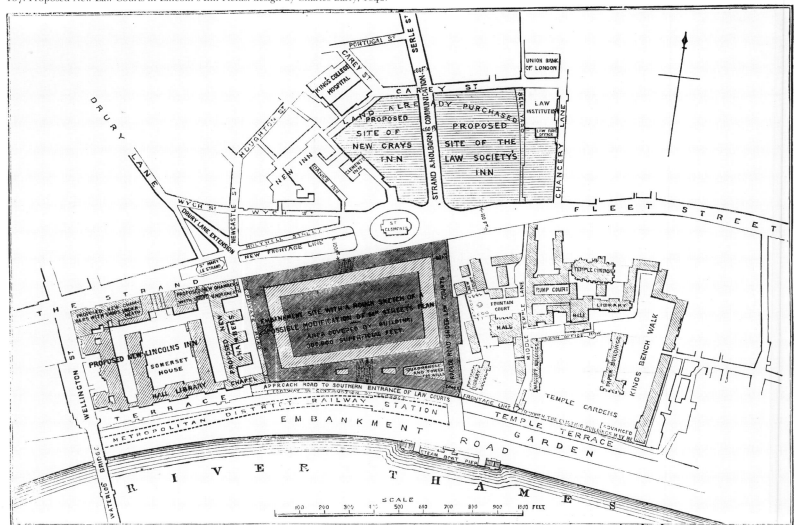

108.   The New Law Courts: rival sites, 1869. That between the Strand and Carey Street had already been purchased for the New Law Courts. Layard and others proposed instead a site on the Embankment, and Sir Charles Trevelyan elaborated the scheme, as seen here, moving Lincoln's Inn to Somerset House.

essential recreation: were the courts adjacent to chambers, they would over-work.[9] The Law Society in 1845 secured a second select committee, an opportunity for promoting the Carey Street site, about 700ft east-west between Bell Yard and Clements Inn, and 480ft north-south, some $7\frac{3}{4}$ acres [Pl. 108]. Barry, who again appeared as witness for the Law Society, suggested that the estimated cost, £675,000, could be reduced effectively by flanking the

courts with chambers for profitable letting; and there would be savings from vacating existing sites. He linked the proposal with the current 'health of towns' agitation, describing clearance as 'one of the greatest public improvements that I know of'.[10] The society petitioned the Commons again in 1852 and 1853.[11]

The Lincoln's Inn interest, however, was not yet out of the running. Law Society interviews with the prime minister and the

First Commissioner in January 1854 elicited support for Carey Street, but the Fields' trustees then, drawn on by hopes of profit, offered three acres for courts.[12] Molesworth was not impressed, but the Crimean War postponed a decision. Lincoln's Inn itself, after the war, offered to build handsome equity courts, and actually commissioned a design from George Gilbert Scott.[13] This idea was attractive to a minority Conservative administration anxious to prove its financial rectitude, but the Law Society attacked it as 'a practical decision against that blending of Law and Equity, which most thoughtful people consider desirable'.[14] The society issued another pamphlet, and the law reformers persuaded Lord Derby to appoint a royal commission to consider the whole question of concentrating all the superior courts.[15]

Chaired by Mr Justice Coleridge (1790–1876),[16] the commission, which reported in mid-1860, considered three sites: Westminster, Lincoln's Inn Fields and Carey Street.[17] At Westminster, lawyers were separated from their chambers and offices (though it was most convenient for barrister MPs or the few specialising in private-bill work). Soane's courts, 'an unsightly excrescence, marring the beauty and disturbing the uniformity of the magnificent structure of which they form a part', must soon be removed. The Fields, where four acres were now offered for courts if the government would pay £360,000 for improving the road approaches, afforded too little space: at least five acres were required for all the courts, their offices, and a will depository. Carey Street however was large enough, generally convenient (though separated from the Temple), with a good frontage to the Strand, and affording slum clearance.

Effective was the powerful advocacy of the attorney-general, Sir Richard Bethell (1800–73),[18] for the past five years a campaigner for Carey Street, 'a spot, which . . . appears to have been created, and left, as it were, on purpose for this great improvement'; together with that of Edward Wilkins Field (1804–71),[19] an 'energetic and accomplished' solicitor who had led the campaign for legal reforms and had in 1856 originated a scheme for financing new courts.[20] Bethell stigmatised the Lincoln's Inn proposal as self-interested. The equity courts had proved enormously profitable to the Inn, but were inconvenient for barristers, like himself, from the Temple. In any case, the Fields were too small, as was Westminster.

The clearance of Carey Street, however, would not only enable the superior courts to be concentrated on one spot – the more necessary in view of recent legislation drawing together the systems of common law and equity – but also sweep away a source of physical and spiritual contagion, a sink of fever and prostitution, and ventilate the metropolis (an important factor given the general belief in a 'miasmic' theory of disease propagation).[21] Of the 343 houses on the site, occupied by 4175 persons, half were occupied by 'tradesmen and other parties, who rent the whole house'; the other half by the labouring class (three-quarters of the inhabitants) among whom, the parish valuer reported, 'I do not think there really is an artizan or workman in regular work'. Many of them were prostitutes or thieves. 'Newcastle court [14 houses] consisted wholly of brothels until they were indicted; and now they are inhabited by costermongers and these black-faced fellows, and a very low class of persons.' They lived in closed courts often only ten or twelve feet wide, where typhoid fever was endemic and gin became a substitute for fresh air. Several houses each accommodated between 30 and 115 nightly lodgers at 4d. a head. The parish overseer reported that between December and March there would be a third more inhabitants than usual, attracted by the Christmas charities. There were also about sixty warehouses, stables and printing-offices. 'I have known most of the bad properties in London', reported Pennethorne, the government surveyor, 'and I do not know that I have met with any worse than some parts of this.'[22] The

109.   Bell Yard by E.H. Dixon: One of the doomed streets on the New Law Courts 'Carey Street' site. Planning blight affected the district while the decision about sites was pending, 'bad characters of nearly every description' moving in, and many of the houses 'being stripped of their valuable materials', according to the Office of Works Surveyor, 16 Nov. 1868 (PRO, Work 12/40/1).

purchase cost was estimated at the £675,000 that Barry had calculated for a slightly larger area in 1845, with an equal sum for buildings, and £150,000 for contingencies, a total of £1,500,000.[23] This figure was to become definitive and govern future proceedings.

The Treasury authorised a site survey and the preparation of the books of reference requisite for legislation, but warned that they did so only to enable the government to consider the Commission's recommendation 'with a perfectly unfettered judgment'.[24] However, two bills were introduced in 1861 to embody the commission's recommendations, one relating to the site, the other to finance. The site bill, pushed forward by Bethell, now lord chancellor Westbury, and supported by the prime minister, providing for an area slightly extended westwards, estimated to cost £678,000 (H.R. Abraham) or £700,000–£750,000 (Hunt), passed the Commons and received a second reading in the Lords before calculations on the shortfall of funds, and above all the approaching end of the session, halted the money bill.[25] When the bills were reintroduced in the 1862 session, the Treasury again made clear its lack of enthusiasm.[26] Meanwhile, the Fields' trustees withdrew their offer of a site, though Lincoln's Inn continued to struggle for its own interests, and raised a powerful opposition.[27] Once again, the fight concentrated on the funding, and the money bill was defeated by two votes (83: 81) in a fairly small House.[28]

'There are such difficulties in the way of a complete concentration of Courts of Justice that nothing further will be done about it at present', the First Commissioner told an MP on 25 October 1862.[29] He hoped to introduce a bill in June 1863, but the financial obstacles remained too great. Plans for legislation in the 1864 session were deposited in November 1863, as required by standing orders.[30] The report of the royal commission on chancery funds, February 1864, improved the prospects of a solution of the funding issue, which Sir Roundell Palmer, the attorney-general, indeed outlined to the Commons in June.[31] But the money bill was not ready, and by mid-July it was clear that there would be no move during that session.[32] At least the way was now clear for successful legislation in 1865, the site bill based on a new valuation by Pennethorne, calculated at £703,000.[33] Extensive lobbying was employed to secure the success of the new bills, and the indefati-

110.   George Edmund Street, R.A. (1824–81). Celebrated as a Gothic church architect, Street, having been placed in the New Government Offices competition of 1857, was nominated for both the limited competitions of 1866–7: the National Gallery and the New Law Courts. Awarded the first prize for the latter jointly with E.M. Barry, he was given the commission by the First Commissioner in 1868.

THE NEW LAW COURTS

gable Field spent most of his time from the summer of 1864 in 'looking after the measure', as he put it.[34] Introduced by Palmer at the start of the session, the bills went through, though not without obstruction.

One issue was a new alternative site, the Thames Embankment (then under construction), suggested in 1864 by Charles Selwyn, a bencher of Lincoln's Inn and steady opponent of Carey Street.[35] Selwyn was in fact spokesman for the Lincoln's Inn interest, and wanted to maintain the distinctiveness of the Common Law and Equity jurisdictions, the union of which was the aim of the law reformers.[36] The new proposal was taken up in both houses, Frederick Lygon unsuccessfully moving for a select comittee.[37] Further objections were excited by the census of working-class inhabitants (required under the Lords' standing orders), which showed a working-class population of some 3082 in 172 houses, an occupational density of 18 per house, out of a total of 4175 in 343 houses. Sir Francis Goldsmid (1808–78), a Lincoln's Inn Q.C., was supported by the philanthropic aristocrat, Hon. Arthur Kinnaird (1814–87), in urging that provision be made for those turned out. Palmer asked them to 'take a practical and not merely a sentimental view', and under Palmerston's guidance that question was dropped.[38] The bills received the royal assent in June 1865, setting up a Courts of Justice Commission to oversee the concentration of the courts at the 1860 calculation of a total expense of £1,500,000.

Powered by enthusiastic law reformers, such as Palmer and Field, the new commission planned the concentration of more than sixty departments, and recommended additional land purchases to improve access and permit full use of the site, which suffered from the lack of any adequate north-south route, the only existing road, Chancery Lane, being a bottleneck. The First Commissioner, William Cowper, had as early as 1862 looked for an architectural competition; in 1866–7 he organised one.[39] The commission itself demanded some 683,000 sq. ft of accommodation, rather than the 437,000 of the parliamentary scheme, and the invited architects asked for the site, which they found inconveniently narrow north-south, to be enlarged to 510 ft, including 15 ft of the Carey Street roadway for an area for lighting the basement.[40] The whole was purchased by July 1868 for a total of £785,000. The commission recommended yet further purchases costing £668,000 to provide adequate space for the chosen plan and improve access to, and round off, the site.[41]

Although these proposals infringed the statutes of 1865 (as a later First Commissioner was persistently to argue), they were permitted under an amending act of 1866, and the Treasury authorised the drafting of a new land-purchase bill.[42] When after some confusion as to the result of the competition[43] George Edmund Street (1824–81) [Pl. 110] was appointed architect, he endeavoured to meet the commission's requirements in designs still incomplete when the Gladstone administration came into office. Layard, the new First Commissioner, aesthete but also economical radical,[44] took up with enthusiasm the defeated idea of building the new courts on the just completed Thames Embankment, and stopped the bill for additional land purchases near Carey Street.[45]

Rumours had been circulating in May 1868 that the lord chancellor and the late premier, Lord Derby, preferred a different site to Carey Street, and Baillie Cochrane (the 'Buckhurst' of Disraeli's *Coningsby*, now nicknamed 'the apostle of the Thames Embankment') asserted that 'it was very generally felt that the proper site was the Thames Embankment . . . a most beautiful site. . . . It was not yet too late to change the plan.' A little later, he unsuccessfully introduced a motion in favour of the Thames-side site,[46] which however was taken up by *The Times* in the context of Lord John Manners's proposals for concentrating the public offices in Whitehall. A leading article argued that these afforded new reason for reconsidering the site: the advantages of the Embankment threw alternatives into the shade. *The Times* saw only three objections: that of Lincoln's Inn (where the Old and New Squares would soon need rebuilding); the financial (the new site would probably cost a million, but then Carey Street might be used 'remuneratively' for lawyers' chambers); and the 'settled and done with objection', to which the answer was that the Coleridge Commission had not considered a non-existent Embankment, for which the claims, 'most cursorily and imperfectly discussed', had in 1865 been rejected for fear of postponing the scheme indefinitely. 'A national work like this', thundered the leader, 'should be done in the best manner, or not done at all.'[47]

Meanwhile, William Tite, PRIBA, was advocating an ingenious scheme which would not only be more economical, but also reconcile the dispute between Street and Edward Barry (who had a very strong claim to the Law Courts commission),[48] and advantage the MBW – of which Tite was a leading member. He proposed to divide the new courts, locating chancery courts (to be built by Street) in Carey Street, convenient for Lincoln's Inn, while putting the common-law courts (to be given to Edward Barry) on an Embankment site belonging to the MBW,[49] which would be handy for the Temple barristers.

Layard, a prominent figure in the London artistic world, had as early as the summer of 1868 discussed with Street his preference for placing the new Law Courts on the riverside.[50] The architect had responded tactfully 'very much in favor of a façade for the Courts of Law on the Thames Embankment'; but foresaw two great difficulties – the inadequacy of the riverine site, and opposition from Lincoln's Inn lawyers.[51] Hunt, the Works' surveyor, who shared Layard's view, drew up for him a memorandum (14 December 1868) criticising the Carey Street site, where the rise in ground level from the Strand northwards would require about a hundred steps to give access to the public galleries, and 70–80 steps to the courts. The proximity to the poor buildings of Clare Market would be bad for ventilation, and King's College Hospital was inconveniently near. Additional land was required, because the architects found the original site too restricted. The Thames Embankment, on the other hand, was 'extremely eligible'. There was sufficient land between the Strand and the Embankment in the area between Somerset House and Essex Street. The courts could be level with the Strand, and a carriage approach could rise with easy gradient from the Embankment roadway. The existing approaches were adequate, and there would be abundant fresh air from the river. The cost would be no greater than for Carey Street, which could be sold for perhaps half a million.[52] This memorandum was probably a briefing for Layard's interview the same day with Street.[53]

Street's initial reaction was adverse: he clearly feared the consequences of delay. He stressed the disadvantages of the lower site,[54] and in a report to the Courts of Justice Commission proposed that work should begin at Carey Street immediately. Layard directed him to suspend work on his plans, but then discovered that not even the Treasury had 'power to controul Mr Street' until the Commission had made its final report.[55] But the Treasury and the Works were for once in accord. The new chancellor, Robert Lowe (1811–92), was an economy-minded zealot, and wrote to Layard, 'It is to me very plain that the Courts of Law will be placed on the embankment near Somerset House.' Somerset House [Pl. 45] was at that time generally regarded as the perfection of style for government offices, and the influence that the *genius loci* would exercise was one factor in Lowe's attitude, though Layard, who looked for a magnificent though economical building, warned him, 'Do not commit yourself to a Classic building on the Embankment or to any particular style until I have had an opportunity of talking the matter over with you.'[56]

Street proved pliable, ready to fall in with his client's decisions; on reflection, he had decided that the Embankment would be satisfactory, and he willingly suspended work, remarking that 'the details of arrangements of the various Courts and Departments' could no doubt 'be transferred to the other plans which I shall have to make'. What did give him anxiety was the extent to which 'we may project beyond the present frontage towards the Embankment': a projection that, as we shall see, important critics were to find unacceptable. Later, he even remarked that 'he did not know whether, if both sites had been open to him, he should not, on architectural grounds, have selected the Embankment'.[57]

The public debate began with a letter to *The Times* (5 January 1869) from Sir Charles Trevelyan, in favour of the Embankment site.[58] Lowe thought it 'very good', but the extravagant scope of Trevelyan's designs made him a risky ally. As with his plans for new government offices,[59] Trevelyan's ideas for reorganising the legal quarter were on the grandest scale. The Embankment between Somerset House and the Temple [Pl. 108] he believed to be 'the finest site in Europe – perhaps, all circumstances considered, in the world', and served by road, underground railway and river. The site could be enlarged by taking over King's College, which could be transferred to Lincoln's Inn, that society migrating to Somerset House, emptied by the construction of new public offices near Whitehall. Chambers on the Carey Street site would provide for the lawyers from the vicinity of Gray's Inn, which might be demolished for workingmen's dwellings. *The Times* immediately followed this letter with a leader hoping that Layard's appointment might produce a reconsideration of the new Law Courts site.[60] It appeared that the Carey Street site would require another two millions. Admittedly such a national undertaking should be done 'thoroughly and well, once and for all', but the increased cost gave the public the right to consider its own convenience, and it was the duty of those entrusted with the decision to ensure that the new Courts would do the greatest possible credit to the nation. The *Daily News*, however, opposed a reconsideration: 'the time for controversy has passed, and the time for action arrived'; further discussion would transform the expression 'when the New Law Courts are built' into an equivalent for 'the Greek Kalends'.[61]

Undeterred, Trevelyan, indefatigably energetic, then mounted a barristers' petition (sent to *The Times*) and sought to organise others and to influence opinion through powerful friends. So successful was his initial campaign that by the end of the month many regarded the change of site as a foregone conclusion – Trevelyan himself believed that 'as for numbers and popularity, they are entirely on our side'.[62]

The imminence of the change roused interested passions. Field used a meeting of the commission to alert the world to the new ministry's hostility to the great plan for Carey Street.[63] Lincoln's Inn and the Law Society shrilled their indignation at the threat to their established interests, the *Solicitors' Journal*, their principal mouthpiece, and petitions, pamphlets and deputations being pressed into service.[64] A passionate debate developed. The *Law Times* switched sides to support Carey Street, though 'the relatively unimportant *Law Journal* warmed from neutrality to faithful support of the Embankment'.[65] The other interested professionals joined in, with *Athenaeum*, *Architect* and *Builder* favouring the riverside; and *Saturday Review* and *Building News* in the rival camp. *The Times*'s correspondence columns provided a forum for debate. The Society of Arts debated the issue over three days, in a committee organised by Henry Cole and chaired by Lord Elcho, whose Commons select committee was about to hear evidence about siting public buildings on the Embankment. Street, seeing the question as yet undecided, argued for Carey Street. But although the positions were fully set out, members could not agree, though resolving that 'public and quasi-public buildings only should be erected' on the Embankment.[66]

The Law Society organised the earliest campaign of mass-produced letter-writing to influence MPs: a lithographic circular to all members of the profession asserted that 'The concentration of the Courts and Offices will fail to effect the objects in view unless that concentration be carried out in immediate proximity with the Chambers of Counsel and Solicitors. By the enclosed Statement and plan it will be seen that this proximity is secured by the Carey St Site, but would be lost on the Embankment.' They were therefore offering 'a determined opposition' to the change, which they believed 'most injurious both to the public interest and that of the profession.' The efforts of the profession should be directed to removing the misconception that still prevailed in many MPs' minds, so a lithographed letter was enclosed that might be sent to 'all those members of the House of Commons with whom you have personal influence'.[67] A printed 'Estimate of comparative cost of the competing sites' purported to show that the southern site would cost half a million more than the northern.[68] The Law Society also circulated a petition form claiming, *inter alia*, with typical lawyer's arrogance, that the petitioners, strongly in favour of Carey Street, were identified in interest with the suitors, their clients, and had the best opportunity of judging how clients' business were best conducted, 'most expeditiously, most economically, and most efficiently'. These solicitors, when their personal interests were at stake, were reacting just as the architects reacted to lay judgment of designs, claiming that they alone possessed essential *arcana* to which even the most intelligent layman was incapable of gaining access.[69] Yet another Law Society leaflet, *Reasons in favour of retaining the Carey Street site*, was alleged greatly to exaggerate the numbers of solicitors located close to Carey Street.[70] An estimate formed by the eminent surveyor George Pownall for the society was published as the battle hotted up, showing a loss of nearly half a million pounds on the purchase of the Embankment site and resale of Carey Street, and also condemning the proposed projection beyond the frontage of Somerset House.[71]

Neighbouring Lincoln's Inn, with its keen financial interest in the outcome, valiantly supported the Law Society's fight. Its own

petition attacked the principle of complete concentration as producing 'overcrowding and confusion'; but if insisted upon, then Carey Street were best. If the site were changed, concentration should be abandoned, and Equity remain in Lincoln's Inn. Similarly, the secretary of the Metropolitan and Provincial Law Association (25 Chancery Lane) insisted that suitors had 'no possible advocates in the matter' other than the lawyers. He asked his members to press its case on 'every member of the Legislature, whom from local causes or otherwise you have a claim to address'; and with some effrontery suggested that the proposed change was largely the work of those with a pecuniary interest in the new site.[72]

Meanwhile, what was the government doing? The chancellor of the Exchequer had promptly refused his assent – 'the first thing I did when I came into Office' – to the Courts of Justice Commission's proposal to spend £668,000 on additional land purchases for Carey Street. He then commissioned his friend the engineer F.W. Sheilds to report on the alternative sites: a not entirely satisfactory operation, as Sheilds calculated that the change to an equal area on the Embankment would cost an additional three-quarters of a million, but the necessary improvements to the communications of the northern site would cost £1,600,000 (partly borne by the Metropolitan authority), and a new underground railway to the Bank along the line of Piccadilly and his new road from Long Acre to St Paul's would cost rather more [Pl. 111].[73] It was probably this disconcerting report that led Layard to put forward a proposal that Lowe took up and ultimately presented to the Commons.

Layard's memorandum was dated 27 February 1869, ten days after Sheilds' report, and is of sufficient significance to reproduce at length:

I have examined, with much care, the several schemes which have been proposed for the erection of the consolidated Law Courts and Offices – those which have the principal claim to consideration are the following –

1st That proposed by the Royal Commission, which includes what is termed 'the Carey Street site' already purchased at a cost including preliminary expenses of £875,434.16.6 and an additional piece of land adjoining to it, for the acquisition of

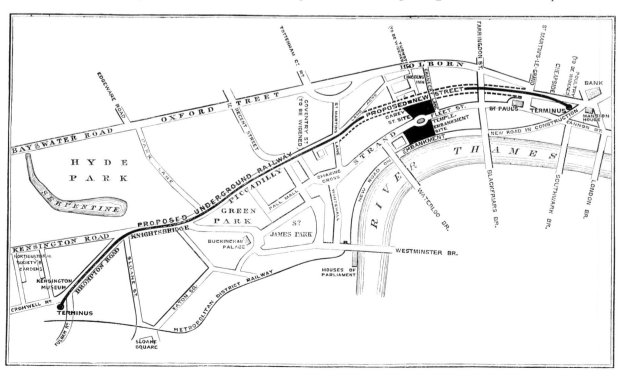

111. Alternative sites for the New Law Courts: Sheilds' proposal. The chancellor of the Exchequer referred the sites' question to an engineer, F. Sheilds, who suggested unhelpfully that the answer lay in an expensive new street and underground railway.

which a Bill was to have been introduced into Parliament this session, and which would probably cost little less than £800,000 – making a total expenditure for site of about £1,650,000. The buildings to be erected upon it would include 21 Courts, all the dependent Offices and a number of offices connected with the administration of the Law, but not actually dependent upon the Courts. This scheme has the support of the large majority of the Chancery bar and of the occupiers of Lincoln's Inn. Moreover it is supported by the Law Institution and by a large number of Attorneys and Solicitors residing in Grays' Inn, and the other Inns contiguous to Lincoln's Inn Fields. The great objection to it was the position of the proposed building in the midst of a crowded and ill ventilated quarter of the town, the absence of proper means of access except by the Strand, and the want of convenience to the judges, the legal profession at large, and the public owing to the necessary height of the Courts from the basement. But the cost of the site and building together must be the strongest objection on the part of the Government to this scheme. It would scarcely be less than £3,300,000, unless considerable modifications were made to the building and the value of a portion of the land to be acquired but not to be used, were deducted from the total cost: in this case the total cost might, according to Mr Fergusson's view, be reduced to £2,800,000 or £2,900,000. On the other hand it must be remembered that, sooner or later, communications must be opened with Holborn – which would require a considerable expenditure.

2nd The next scheme is that put forward by Sir Charles Trevelyan. It comprises the erection of all the Law Courts and Offices included in the plan of the Royal Commission upon a site bounded by the Strand, the Thames Embankment, Kings College and the Temple. The cost of carrying out this scheme, including the purchase of the site and the erection of the buildings, but excluding the loss upon the resale of the land already acquired on the Carey Street site, would not be less than £3,250,000. The sum might, however, be reduced to some extent by the modifications in Mr Street's plan proposed by Mr Fergusson. This scheme has received the support of the great majority of the Common Law bar, of the Common Law judges, of the inhabitants of the Temple, of the Attorneys and Solicitors who inhabit the West end and other parts of the Metropolis, except those connected with Grays Inn and the other such Inns in the neighbourhood of Carey Street, of the greater part of the press, and, as far as I can judge, of the public. It is strongly opposed by a large majority of the Chancery bar and Judges, and by an influential body of Solicitors. The great cost of carrying it out will probably lead the Government to reject it.

3. A third scheme has been submited by Mr Tite to the Metropolitan Board of Works, and to the House of Commons. It consists of dividing the Courts of Law from the Offices not immediately dependent upon them, and placing the Courts on the Carey Street site, and the Offices on a strip of land to be acquired on the embankment. The converse plan of placing the Courts on the Embankment and the Offices on a part of the Carey Street site facing the Strand may also be mentioned. As far as I have been able to ascertain the cost of both these schemes would be about the same, and would amount to £2,600,000. As these schemes have not been much discussed in the press or by the public, it cannot be satisfactorily ascertained who would support and who would oppose them. They offer this advantage, that the desire of the public to utilise the embankment, and to embellish the Metropolis by erecting a fine public building upon it could be met, and, at the same time, a grand edifice could be placed on the Embankment or on the Carey Street site, by bringing in a Bill to give powers for the purchase of all the land between the Thames Embankment and Howard Street, on the north, and between King's College, and the Temple on the West and East (leaving the Strand frontage) and then referring the question of the site of the Law Courts to a Commission, composed of representatives of the Common Law and Chancery bars, and of individual members to represent the public. If it were decided that the Courts should be built on the Carey Street site, only a small portion of the land on the Thames Embankment would be required for the Offices. If the decision were in the opposite direction the Courts of Law and the offices immediately dependent upon them could be erected upon the site between the Embankment and Howard Street, and only the Strand frontage of Carey Street would be required for the Offices. But to these two schemes the Government would probably also object on account of the cost.

4. There is still a fourth scheme – which I shall call the First Commissioner's scheme, as it is the one which I should venture to recommend to the serious consideration of the Government, and which might be adopted at a far less expense than either of the preceeding, and which ought to satisfy all the parts of the legal profession and of the public. There is a conviction in the minds of a large number of persons well able to form an opinion upon the subject, that not only is it not necessary to erect all the offices connected with the law in direct contiguity with the Courts, but that it is very desirable that they should be separated. Moreover many of the offices proposed to be erected with the Law Courts by the Royal Commission are already conveniently situated and afford ample accommodation. I propose, therefore, that only such offices as are absolutely dependent upon the Law Courts and which must be in close proximity to them, should be erected with the Law Courts. Ample space could then be found for such offices and for all the Courts between the Thames Embankment on the South, Howard Street on the North, the Temple on the East, and Kings College on the West. According to an estimate made by Mr Hunt this site could be obtained for £600,000 and the building would probably cost an additional £1,000,000 – or the whole would come to but little more than the original estimate for the Courts and building on the Carey Street site. There would, of course, be the loss on the resale of the Carey Street site. What the loss might be it is impossible to calculate – as it would depend upon many circumstances. It might perhaps be reduced to a small amount under skilful management. Moreover a part of that site might be used for public buildings, and for the construction of a line of communication between the Strand and Holborn, which has become absolutely necessary. There are no doubt several objections to this scheme, such as the difference of level between the proposed site and the Thames Embankment, the difficulty of access to the Strand &c, but there are none which a skilful Architect or Engineer might not get over. On the other hand a magnificent building might be fully met at a moderate cost, whilst all the necessary accommodation could be given to the legal profession and the public. Moreover the buildings might hereafter be extended to the Strand if it were ever found necessary to do so.

In order to place this fourth scheme fully before the government I annex reports which have been made to me on the subject by Mr Fergusson and Mr Hunt. I would particularly draw attention to Mr Hunt's suggestions for meeting the objection to loss of time which has been put forward against any change from the Carey Street site.[74]

Layard did nothing to discourage Trevelyan's tireless promotion of his own scheme, regularly reported to him, no doubt on the assumption that it would show the weaknesses of Carey Street and make his own smaller scheme the more acceptable.[75] Pressure of the government's programme – primarily the highly contentious bill for disestablishing the Church of Ireland – deferred bringing the proposal to the Commons.[76] The opportunity came when Layard's friend and fellow-aesthete William Henry Gregory proposed that the question of Carey Street as the site be reconsidered, inasmuch as the Embankment offered many advantages, a motion that, postponed from 3 March 1869, was debated on 20 April.[77]

The lengthy debate was characterised by the proposer's Hibernian wit and Sir Roundell Palmer's passionate opposition; but the dramatic success of the evening came with the chancellor's speech, delayed until the House had filled again after dinner. Lowe, a celebrated parliamentary performer, poked fun at Palmer's prejudiced lawyer's view of the problem – 'for, of course, in that view all mankind are made for the benefit of the legal gentlemen – the inconvenience of the public will be a matter of but small consequence so long as they themselves can walk, almost at a hop, from their chambers to the Courts' – declaring that jurors, witnesses, litigants and 'those persons whom curiosity or interest may induce to become spectators of a trial' had also to be considered; that 'it is impossible for a Court of Justice to properly discharge the province for which it is intended unless we provide good access to it' – adequate streets and not too many steps – and that such access could only be secured at Carey Street at a cost of millions. He 'put the question as a question of economy'. The Commission's scheme had grown from the £1,500,000 authorised by the 1865 acts to £3,385,000, out of a desire 'for concentrating the Courts, and everything connected with them, however slight the connection may be, in the same building'. Seized with 'a sort of frenzy of concentration . . . we have set ourselves to work to build a sort of Tower of Babel, which will be the centre of noise, tumult,

and confusion. . . . It cannot facilitate the administration of justice to form a sort of gigantic Vanity Fair, in which everything is to be collected and piled up one on top of another.' He warned members that 'if they launch into the headlong expenditure which has been proposed, they will be embarrassing the finances of the country for years'. As for the idea that most of the expense would be borne by a tax on suitors, new arrangements were about to transfer the Chancery Fee Fund to the public revenue, which in future would bear all charges connected with the courts. The expenditure of the courts exceeded their funds by £53,000 a year. The truth was, the money came from the general revenue of the country. He therefore proposed to determine the commission, and return power of decision to the Treasury.

What then should the government do? 'It is assumed by some that there are only two alternatives before us; and that if we do not ruin ourselves on the north side of the Strand we must do so on the south side. I do not acquiesce in that. . . . I can imagine no more melancholy spectacle than the British tax-payer walking along the Strand, with the knowledge that north and south frontages have been bought by Parliament for a building which can only be on one side.' Trevelyan's proposal was unacceptably extravagant. But they could do 'all we reasonably want to do, and yet not very far exceed what we originally intended'. Having raised the House to the peak of anticipation, he revealed his hand: 'There is a street called Howard Street': between it and the Embankment lay a site that could be purchased for £600,000, on which 'all the Courts with their auxiliary offices and other offices besides' could be erected for a million [Pl. 112]. Only on the river front would it need an ornamental façade, and for that, Inigo Jones's design for the Whitehall Palace river front lay to hand [Pl. 41]. But rather than 'go back to a career of extravagance', they 'should do without a new building altogether'.

112.   The Embankment or 'Howard Street' Site proposed for the New Law Courts by the chancellor of the Exchequer, 1869, between King's College London and the Temple, on land reclaimed from the river.

In a stupefied House the debate was formally adjourned. 'The Govt will now have to prepare a scheme', wrote Layard the following morning; 'the one sketched out by Chr of the Exchr last night offers many very important advantages.'[78] In response to a doubtless arranged question from Gregory on 27 April, Layard announced the government's decision formally to propose the Howard Street site. On 10 May his introduction of the requisite bill met unusual acrimony.[79] Putting economy in the forefront, he declared that Lowe had come to the same result on the financial question as he himself had done on the architectural one: that it

was impossible to sanction such an enormous expenditure as that proposed by the commission. What were the alternatives? Tite's was an expensive separation at £2,710,000. Trevelyan's views were correct, though regarded by some as visionary, but larger than his own scheme, 'and had indisposed many persons to it'. The Law Institution's latest proposal, made that morning, still involved new approaches which could cost up to a million, and their tendentious plan was wholly unreliable. The scheme he had suggested to the chancellor had met much adverse criticism, but Street now approved it, and his new plan [Pl. 113] was on a 'much better prin-

113. New Law Courts, Howard Street site, Thames Embankment, G.E. Street, 1869:
a. Plan: Street shifted his protective circuit of offices to an east quadrangle, but otherwise retained the principles of his Carey Street plan.
b. Detail of elevation, Embankment front, west wing, from the judges' entrance to the centre.

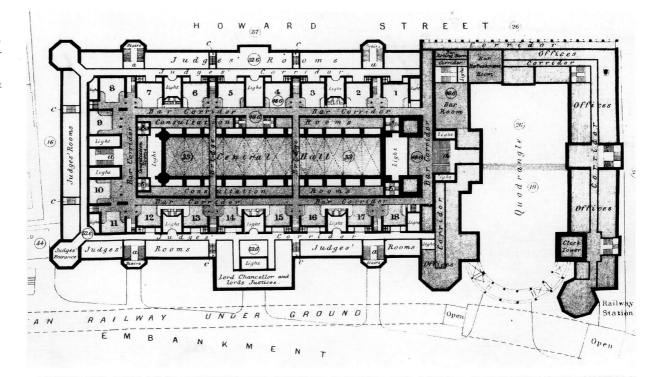

ciple' than that of a quadrangle of offices around the courts; it offered economy in design, construction and situation. Indeed, the sketch plans might be cut down further. Secular Gothic was a good style, superfluous ornamentation being unnecessary, so that one could have inexpensively 'an ornament to the metropolis and the country'. Building on Carey Street – for which there were already offers – could not be started any sooner.

A furious Roundell Palmer 'stamped on the ground and clenched his fist', conducting himself, 'to the amusement of the House, like an old woman in a passion'.[80] He declared: 'no worse scheme was ever proposed, or one more calculated to interfere with and mar a most useful project of reform'. It had taken him six minutes to get from Lincoln's Inn gate to the nearest point on the Embankment (Street did it in three). The proposed Courts would be no decoration at all to the metropolis, for it was hidden down in a hole. Lowe, riding down the 'whirlwind' of Palmer's eloquence, warned that the 1866 act had given the commission unlimited powers, and they unjustifiably proposed a 'large and extravagant expenditure'.[81]

The Carey Street men were not to be frightened. Layard wrote next day to his supporter the lord chief baron of the Exchequer Court: 'Every effort is being made by a party interested in the Carey St site, to make the House believe that the Judges, the bar, & the Solicitors are almost unanimously in favour of that site. It is of great importance to shew that such is not the case.'[82] Gregory, who hoped to secure 'a good deal of the Irish vote', wrote from Dublin of his horror that Layard should have introduced his bill in his absence: 'I am rather nervous about the upshot unless Gladstone comes out strong.'[83] Layard reassured him, admitting that they would have a heavy fight, 'but I think that we shall carry it'. Elcho had shown the plans to Disraeli, who had seemed favourable, and a good number of Conservatives could be relied on. The chief opposition came from Liberals led by Palmer. But 'The Attorneys of the Law Institution will move heaven and earth against us. . . . Unfortunately they have great influence in the Press. You see that the "Times" is gone round.'[84]

In this last assessment at least Layard was right. With Lowe's promulgation of the Howard Street site, press support began to slip away from him. *The Times*, long an advocate of the Embankment, had consistently argued that the work should be a noble one: if the Embankment scheme were to be a truncated version, then the merits of Carey Street shone the brighter.

The vital support of the prime minister was ambivalent: his concern was to cut down to size the Commission's great scheme. His doubts of the financial viability of Westbury's schemes will be seen below. On reading Layard's memorandum, he had observed that there would be a loss of 'say £35,000 a year' on Carey Street while it remained vacant; that the great scheme provided for savings by vacating rented property; that the reductions contemplated for Howard Street should be applied to Carey Street also; and that whereas Howard Street would require an immediate outlay for approaches wholly in connexion with the courts, enlargement of the Strand would be a metropolitan improvement (i.e. borne by the MBW). The cheapest plan would probably be a reduced building on Carey Street, where shop-fronts along the Strand front would reduce the cost; but the Embankment offered some great advantages. 'Some vigorous effort', he concluded, 'is needed to arrest the plan of the Commission as it stands, and give a new direction to the general scheme. We are much obliged to Mr Lowe for having given us breathing time.'[85] The Howard Street proposal had achieved all he wanted, having 'so far made a decided impression on opinion out-of-doors and within-doors [i.e. in the Commons] that it was generally admitted, both by friends and opponents of the Carey Street site, that it might be advisable to

think of a great contraction of the plan . . . the great scheme in Carey Street . . . has practically disappeared'. The plan for a reduced edifice on Carey Street was 'a new plan for all practical purposes like the plan of the Chancellor of the Exchequer and the First Commissioner of Works upon the Thames Embankment'. It was so late in the session, and there was such pressure of other business, and the government being aware that 'these are not subjects upon which the House of Commons is to be led merely by authority, and that there is no way of obtaining its assent except by carrying conviction to its mind', that he proposed to give up the bill for that session, and refer the question to a select committee.[86]

The Law Society intensified its campaign, the president issuing a circular stating: 'The concentration of the Courts and Offices will fail to effect the objects in view unless that concentration be carried out in immediate proximity with the chambers of Counsel and Solicitors. . . . The Council of the Incorporated Law Society feel it therefore necessary to offer a determined opposition to the proposed change.' Once again, members were urged to press all MPs 'with whom you have personal influence' to support Palmer in his opposition. Yet another lithographed letter set out the advantages of the northern, and disadvantages of the southern site.[87]

Sir Thomas Fowell Buxton (1837–1915) denounced the 'pertinacity *and unscrupulousness* of these Lincoln's Inn Fields Solicitors' as 'unparalleled'. 'These lithographed Letters are prepared by the Law Institution to be addressed by individual Solicitors to individual Members of Parliament over whom they are supposed to have personal influence under the pretence that the contents are the unprompted suggestions of the writer', he snorted indignantly.[88] They also circulated a map which Street described as 'rather a scandalous fabrication'.[89] As against Gregory's Irish influence, the secretary of the Society of the Attorneys and Solicitors of Ireland was circularising members in support of Carey Street.[90]

The rival party, too, rolled up its sleeves. Lowe guided Layard's tactics, warning him not to waste effort on winning over 'insignificant' judges:

> The real thing is what you are doing shewing how impossible it is to put the requisite buildings on the Carey Street site. It is very hard to fight with the lawyers. My opinion is that their influence will overbear all considerations of taste or of public convenience and that the only chance of beating them is to shew that they are involving us in a great expense, in other words that the buildings and strictly necessary approaches on the Carey Street Site cannot be made for anything like the £1,500,000 authorized by Parliament.[91]

His judgement that the comparative costs could prove a decisive factor was to be borne out. Layard issued a statement that the Office of Works' bill was in response to public pressure, and circulated all MPs with a lithograph of Street's new plans.[92]

Layard had at any rate won over the architect. Street had rapidly produced a 'rough plan' for the new site, but declared that much depended on the possibility of moving the proposed Metropolitan Railway station to the foot of Essex Street.[93] He now became enthusiastic about his latest offspring [Pl. 113], telling Layard:

> I am really delighted with the way in which my plan is working out, & hope now that it may live through the threatened opposition – I hear that the Law Society are straining every nerve to obtain votes against you. But if the question is between your site and the North side of the Strand *without additional purchases* of land I cannot doubt that your's is the best. The other site is so very awkwardly shaped, & surrounded on all sides by such wretched houses that it seems to me to be essential that more land should be taken in order to make it reasonable to put a public building there. This, of course, the scheme of the Com-

mission provided, & the absolute necessity for such a provision seems to me to be one of your strongest arguments.[94]

Trevelyan enthused about the new design,[95] which should, he thought, be lithographed and laid before parliament. 'It will be worth many and weighty arguments, for it fills the imagination and takes possession of the man.'[96] Although Chief Baron Fitz-Roy Kelly had obtained the support of a great many of the judges, most of them were unwilling to make it public before they had seen the plans, and Trevelyan urged that they be sent Street's report and plans, to obtain a '*collective opinion*'.[97]

Thornton Hunt of the *Daily Telegraph*, warning Layard 'how much the *want of information* is working against your splendid plan', offered to publish letters 'vindicatory of the Government plan', but his offer really came too late, as Gladstone had already determined to refer the matter to a select committee; one that Lowe thought should be made up of 'impartial men, with one man on each side to conduct the case'. Moved by reason himself (like his predecessor Cornewall Lewis) and fervent advocate of the economy he believed the public wanted, he made too little allowance for the other factors that might influence members. He seemed to think that if the financial position were made clear, the result would be plain.[98] He may also have expected that with four Inner Temple barristers on the committee against one Lincoln's Inn man, even with avowed Carey Street partisans in the persons of William Cowper and Lord John Manners (balanced by Tite and the official element), his rationality would prevail.[99]

The Works' surveyor, Henry Hunt, warned Layard of 'misapprehension about the comparative capabilities of the two sites'; it was being said that if the extent of the new courts was to be reduced, why not use Carey Street? – a point already made by Gladstone. Street should prepare a sketch showing how the reduced plan could be fitted on the northern site, so that a fair comparison could be made.[100] (Burnet, the commission's architectural clerk, had the same idea, for the opposite purpose, and prepared an unauthorised version of Street's reduced plan that called forth the architect's ire.[101]) Hunt laboured assiduously to establish the financial advantages of Howard Street.[102] Street urged Layard to rally his friends on the commission in order to carry a motion favouring the Embankment; 'it would strengthen your hands enormously: whereas to have any opinion from the Commission against you would go for nothing – For it is everywhere assumed that it is hostile.'[103]

As usual, Trevelyan was tireless with suggestions for witnesses to appear before the committee.[104] His efforts however were in vain. Although Hunt argued powerfully that Carey Street would cost a million more than Howard Street,[105] the government's reduction of concentration told, as he had feared, against his argument; and Street's advocacy of Howard Street was doubtless undermined by his earlier preference for Carey Street, publicly proclaimed before the Society of Arts' committee, while his very design was denounced by expert witnesses for its projection beyond the line of Somerset House.[106] Evidence about the difficulty of reselling Carey Street also made a stronger impression than Hunt's assertion of buyers waiting in the wings: the experienced architect P.C. Hardwick (1820–90) supported the view of George Pownall, who had been employed in the purchase of the Carey Street site, that there would be a loss on re-sale.[107]

When Lowe presented a draft report strongly setting out the merits of Howard Street and disadvantages of Carey Street, despite Lord Stanley's 'capital summing up of the evidence – so conclusive in favor of the embankment', the Conservatives Mowbray and Ward Hunt surprised Layard by following Lord John Manners in voting against it (even though this was in accord with the convention that front-benchers followed their principal).[108] Lowe's draft was accordingly rejected by 8 to 5 (three other barristers abstaining), in favour of one drawn up by the Conservative Gabriel Goldney (1813–1900).[109] But Goldney's clauses expressing a preference for the architectural effect of the northern site were both deleted by the chairman's casting vote. The decision for Carey Street was ultimately governed by considerations of convenience and cost, the convenience of the legal profession being identified with that of the public.[110] The solicitors' campaign had borne fruit, and they won the day [Pl. 114].

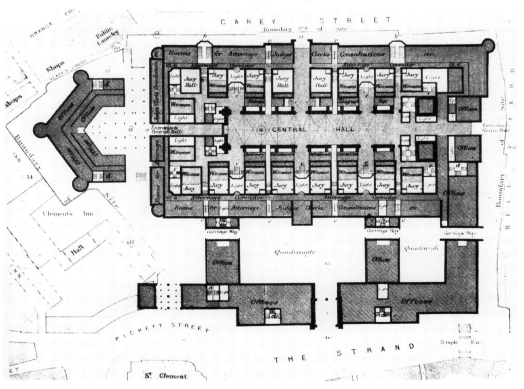

114. New Law Courts: plan for the Carey Street site, G.E. Street, 1869. *Parliament preferring the Carey Street site, Street again revised his plan to fit the available land, shifting his main office block to front the noisy Strand. Ultimately he was to place it to the east of the courts, rotating the central hall to run north-south.*

8
Government Offices

ALTHOUGH the options for sites for government offices were narrower than for buildings requiring public access, the decisions were not much less controversial. Officials could not agree whether juxtaposition and intercommunication of public offices were necessary or even desirable quantities; but the contention was chiefly over the siting of a new War Office: vested interests and penurious politicians postponed a solution until the end of the century. There was general agreement that ministers' offices ought to be near the Houses of Parliament. It was convenient, too, if they were near Clubland. And senior civil servants tended to live, like leading politicians, in postal districts West or South-West.

The royal palace of Whitehall had attracted a nucleus of government offices which had spread after the fire of 1698 destroyed the palace as a royal residence. In 1732 Walpole, as Minister, found George II's offer of houses in Downing Street too convenient to refuse, attaching them to the senior lordships of the Treasury. Kent's adjoining Treasury building remained uncompleted, but a little to the north the Horse Guards, seat of the army's administration, was rebuilt in mid-century to his admired designs [Pl. 52].[1] When in the Revolutionary Wars government departments expanded rapidly it was logical to accommodate them in the large, often old houses in the immediate vicinity, though a number of mansions – such as Pembroke House [Pl. 38], Gwydyr House and York (later Melbourne and then Dover) House [Pl. 46] – remained for a time in aristocratic occupation.[2] The creation of Trafalgar Square [Pl. 6] in the 1830s transformed the congested district just

north of Charing Cross, itself the northern continuation of Whitehall [see Pl. 25]. 'Whitehall', indeed, was often used loosely to refer to the north-south line of streets between Trafalgar Square and the open space in front of St Margaret's church: a formation crudely similar to a human body, narrow Charing Cross the neck, Whitehall the wider trunk, and ancient King Street [Pl. 124, 128] and the more recent Parliament Street the unequal legs, standing on a base line formed by Bridge Street running west from Westminster Bridge into Great George Street [Pl. 142] extending to St James's Park. These valuable frontages immediately south of Whitehall proper (which ended at Downing Street) accommodated surveyors, lawyers, parliamentary agents, men often closely involved in the mass of private bill-making that formed a major part of parliament's work.[3] Masked by this professional prosperity, an army of poor inhabited the back streets and yards, the revolting slums behind the Abbey in Tothill Fields the worst of all.

The opulent days of George IV had seen the reconstruction of the Whitehall-Downing Street corner site by Soane, but his projects for extending the range of offices [Pl. 115], whether to north or south, were brought to an end by the slump of the later 1820s.[4] The Crown estate on the eastern side of Whitehall had been improved by the erection of large houses in Whitehall Place, Whitehall Gardens and Richmond Terrace. In 1834 an economically-minded ministry was obliged by the burning down of the Houses of Parliament to contemplate undertaking what proved to be the largest and most expensive building of its age [Pl. 116]. But

115. Government Offices, Whitehall. In his *Designs for public and private buildings* (1828), John Soane published designs for completing his Board of Trade and Council Offices with a northern wing, and linking them by a triumphal arch across Downing Street to a similar block stretching southwards.

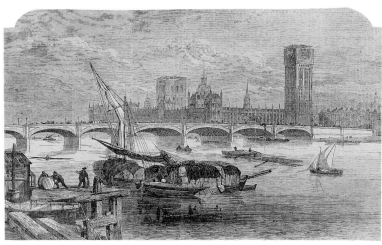

116. The New Palace at Westminster, Sir Charles Barry, 1840–60, and New Westminster Bridge, Thomas Page, engineer, and Sir Charles Barry, 1854–62. Barry's determination to carry out his design for the Houses of Parliament in its entirety proved a lengthy, costly operation that roused the ire of many parliamentarians. He had a hand also in the design of Page's new iron bridge, of much lower profile than Labelye's earlier one (1738–50), and of exceptional width 84ft between the parapets, almost twice that of Labelye's. The government, having taken over the Bridge Estates, paid for the work.

117. Plan of government offices in Whitehall, with flier shewing one of Decimus Burton's designs for new government offices, Downing Street, 1839. Financial stringency caused Burton's plans to be shelved.

the decision to rebuild the Palace of Westminster *in situ* was of fundamental importance for the future of the Whitehall quarter. It fixed the seat of ministerial government permanently in that area.

Thus, when the proponents of concentrating the government offices made themselves heard effectively in the 1850s there was no question of the general location of new offices: the argument as to site was a matter of detail: in what part of Whitehall they should be placed, whether to the north or the south, or in the middle; or on the east side or the west side. Nevertheless such questions proved extraordinarily contentious, even if passions did not reach the heights of those roused by the problem of where to build the new National Gallery or New Law Courts.

As early as 1836 Decimus Burton (1800–81) had been instructed to prepare plans,[5] and in 1839 a Commons' select committee had approved his project for 'reforming the public buildings in the neighbourhood of Downing Street' [Pl. 117],[6] which necesitated the purchase of Fludyer Street to the south. But a subsequent bill was abandoned because of the ministry's financial straits. Peel's ministry in the mid 1840s did no more than enlarge the offices on Whitehall.[7] By 1853 the deteriorating structure of the Foreign and Colonial Offices in Downing Street and the steadily enlarging activities of those departments convinced Sir William Molesworth, then First Commissioner of Works, of the need to rebuild them.[8] Molesworth was a Radical. Among Radical schemes at this time 'administrative reform' was much bruited. Essentially an attack on aristocratic monopoly of the executive, it included the concentration of government departments in purpose-built offices.[9] Such a proposal had, as we have seen, been made by Sir Charles Trevelyan, secretary of the Treasury, in his report on the

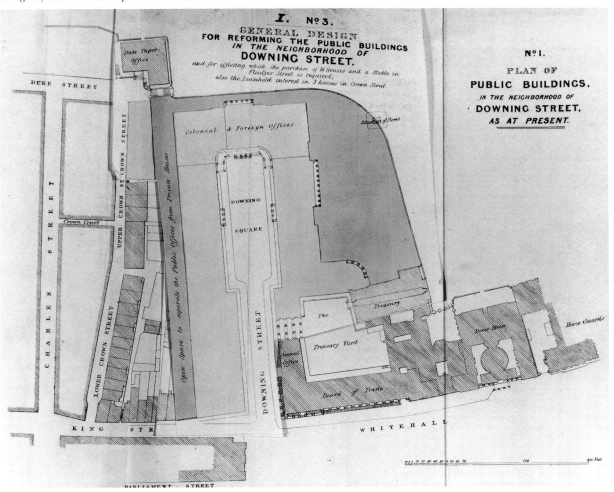

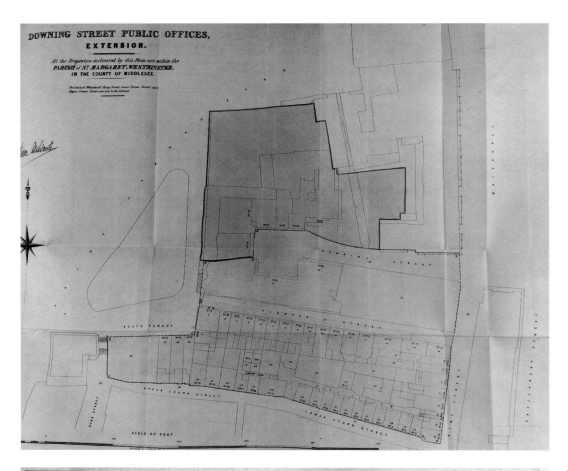

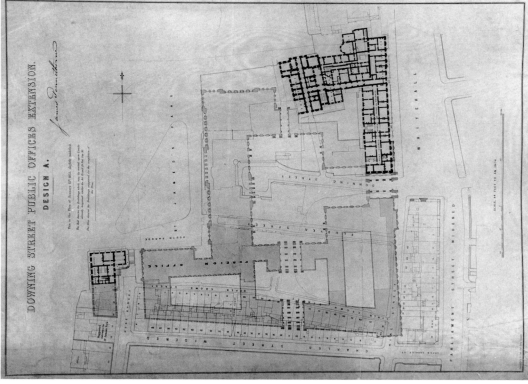

118. Plans for new government offices, 1855:
a. Area recommended by 1855 select committee. The northern (Downing Street) part was already in Crown possession; that further south had to be purchased, but the enabling bill was abandoned in face of parliamentary criticism.
b. James Pennethorne's plan, 1855. Adapting Soane's idea of making Downing Street the centre of a range of government buildings along Whitehall, Pennethorne provided new Foreign and Colonial Offices, hitherto in decaying houses in Downing Street, as well as a new War Office, together with a suite of ministerial reception rooms looking over St James's Park. In this plan, Soane's State Paper Office (1829), on the south-west corner, would have been retained (cp. pl. 121).

Office of Works in January 1854.[10] Molesworth shortly afterwards commissioned new plans for all the Downing Street departments from Pennethorne. These involved the purchase of land south of Fludyer Street.[11] Molesworth, arming himself with a report from his surveyors on the deplorable condition of the Foreign and Colonial Offices,[12] persuaded Gladstone at the Exchequer of the real

economy of this policy. In November 1854 the Treasury sanctioned the preliminary steps for the requisite bill.[13]

As the cabinet objected to opening the cul-de-sac of Downing Street into the Park, Pennethorne revised his plans during the winter, creating a Downing Square extending southwards, measuring 250 by 155 ft, with the centre of the west side immediately

119.   Perspective of new government offices, James Pennethorne, 1855, seen from the Park. Soane's State Paper Office, on the extreme right, stands next to the proposed Foreign Office, returned along the west front. The adjoining central block was given over to ministerial reception rooms, with the War Office to the left. Kent's Old Treasury and Paine's Dover House may be seen on the extreme left. (Collection Centre Canadien d'Architecture/Canadian Centre for Architecture, Montréal.)

opposite the approach from Whitehall [Pl. 118].[14] The total cost was estimated at £585,000, including £150,000 for land and leases.[15] Molesworth put the plan to the Treasury, suggesting a progressive development, starting with a new Foreign Office, estimated at £30,000 for land and £60,000 for buildings. The Treasury approved these proposals on 2 May 1855, and the empowering bill received its second reading on 10 May.[16] As a hybrid bill, involving both private and public interests, it was referred to a select committee, hanging fire for the next two months, but was approved by the committee on 10 July.[17] In the meantime, Lord Redesdale had been urging in the Lords the urgent need to build public offices, and recommending the early purchase of all the land south of Downing Street as far as Great George Street.[18] When the money vote was proposed to the Commons on 31 July 1855 a squall of criticism blew up, and Palmerston withdrew the proposal for the new building.[19] The site, however, was secured, as described above in chapter 3.

Thus much for the Foreign Office. The War Department was in an even worse state, as described above in chapter 2. During the Crimean War, the functions of the Secretary of State for War and Colonies had been split, and the new War Secretary had taken up his quarters in Pall Mall, seat of the former Ordnance Office and Secretary at War. These miscellaneous buildings were a rabbit-warren of dark passages and unsuitable rooms. Moreover, many sections of the War Department were scattered over the neighbourhood. Lord Panmure, the secretary of state, wanted a new building urgently. Pennethorne prepared designs [Pl. 166]; Panmure approved them.[20]

Progress, however, was impeded by another aspect of the system. The new War Office would be built under the administration of the Office of Works. The new First Commissioner of Works, Sir Benjamin Hall, appointed in July 1855, had long advocated open competition for public architecture. At first he planned to substitute a limited competition for War Office designs; then to embrace the War Office together with the Foreign Office in an open competition for the Downing Street site,[21] now confined to the area between Downing and Charles Streets. The Pall Mall buildings would be sold. When in 1857 Hall's celebrated competition encountered problems, the War Office element was discarded: the

site for a new War Office remained an explosive issue for the next forty years.

Hall had to surmount the adverse vote of July 1855 in order to realise his concept of a grand palatial administrative area. His first parliamentary move had been the appointment of a select committee. It had heard only two witnesses: Henry Hunt, probably the leading surveyor of the day, and Sir Charles Trevelyan of the Treasury.[22] Hunt suggested taking the whole area from Downing Street south to Great George Street, and from the Park eastward to the river, save Richmond Terrace and Montague House, some 825,000 sq.ft. For what he saw as 'a great architectural affair', he thought one-half at least should be allowed for open spaces and roads; the ground available 'would very soon be required' by the 'increasing business of the country'. If the Admiralty were to be brought there, even more ground would be wanted, such as the block between Great George Street and the Abbey.[23] The whole, he advised, should be bought at once: 'otherwise you will have to pay a much larger price for it when you want it, because if you only buy the freeholds as you pull down, of course you raise the value of that which you leave'. He calculated the cost at a million and a half.[24]

Trevelyan endorsed Hunt's views. Asserting that 'it is clearly according to the constitution of this country necessary that the public offices should be in the immediate vicinity of the Houses of Parliament', he proposed two great blocks: one from Downing Street to Great George Street, the other pivoted on the Banqueting House, with wings at right angles, facing north towards Charing Cross and south towards the Houses of Parliament. A third block for all the naval departments he would place on the site of the existing Admiralty and Spring Gardens. This would free Somerset House for sale or for law offices.[25]

After the committee's first meeting, Hall wrote for the eye of Prince Albert, '*I hope* I may be authorized to give notices for [buying] all the ground between the Thames and Parliament Street as well as the ground West of that street. I shall also try hard to get the South side of Great George Street so as to have a Grand Street from Storey's Gate to Westminster Bridge.'[26] The committee obligingly reported that 'it is most desirable for the public service, both as regards economy and efficiency in the transaction of public business, that there should be a concentration of the public offices, and that such concentration should be effected in the immediate vicinity of Whitehall and the Houses of Parliament'.[27] Taking Hunt's calculation, the area from the back of Richmond Terrace and from Downing Street south to New Palace Yard and Great George Street, and west from the Thames as far as the Park, measured some 825,000 sq.ft, of which 70,000 would be required for the approaches to the rebuilt Westminster Bridge; the remainder would cost about £1,250,000. Without additional expense, it would be possible to make 'a great opening from Whitehall to Westminster Abbey by erecting the new buildings on each side of such thoroughfare'.[28] [Pl. 118a]

Thus the parliamentary inhibition of July 1855 was deftly side-stepped: the promised select committee had sat and had pronounced. The project was on again. A competition was held for a general block plan, a Foreign Office and residence for the secretary of State next the Park and a War Office fronting Whitehall.[29] But the concept of laying out the whole block from the river to the Park was a non-starter. It was not so much the defects of the competition that resulted in the block-plan element being ignored, as the clear unwillingness of the Commons to contemplate such a far-seeing proposal. Relatively few MPs had woken up to the implications of the Victorian 'revolution in government', or were even aware of the substitution of a dynamic principle of government for a static one.[30] Furthermore, 1857 was a year of financial crisis, and Asian wars threatened to unbalance the budget. The Treasury ministers shared back-benchers' hostility to grandiose schemes, and in July 1857 put a stop to all Hall's land-purchase proposals.[31]

The Downing Street-Charles Street development proved independent of the larger scheme. Even the abandonment of the palatial competition designs in August 1857 [Pl. 120–1] did not kill it. Palmerston, prime minister for most of the ensuing eight years, was determined to have a new Foreign Office; and he got what he wanted. The change of control in India following the 1857 Mutiny necessitated a new secretaryship of state and a new ministerial building: one built at the expense of the Indian government; and one that could be combined with the new Foreign Office (with a reception suite instead of a residence) in lieu of the War Office, ever unpopular with many Liberals. The position of these two offices was turned through 90 degrees, so that both shared the Park front [Pl. 122c]. The building of two further offices to occupy the Whitehall frontage followed logically in the 1870s: the Colonial Office from its cramped and crumbling Downing Street abode, and the Home Office from Barry's 1840s replacement of Tudor buildings further north in Whitehall.[32] [Pl. 122d]

Meanwhile the Fludyer Street-Charles Street strip had yet to be obtained. A bill similar to that of 1855 was discussed in 1857, but not passed until 1859. A measure in 1861 added a small piece between Duke Street and the Park, another in 1862 squared off the actual building site, suggesting that surveyors or architect had blundered [Pl. 122].[33] The construction of the four offices of the secretaries of State took two decades; years largely taken up, so far as other public building went, with the problems of the national recreational institutions, as we have seen. Committed to huge expenditures for those purposes, governments, especially Gladstonian ones, were reluctant to go beyond what was immediately essential in rehousing and concentrating their own personnel. The consequence was lost opportunities and increased costs when the matter could no longer be shirked.

With the new Foreign Office due for completion on 1 September 1866, the Office of Works began planning for the next stage in August 1865, seeking Treasury sanction for preparing a bill for the compulsory purchase of houses in Parliament and King Streets

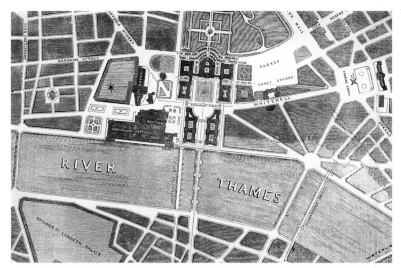

120.   Government Offices Competition, 1857. First prize for block plan, no. 12, 'A.C.': A.N. Crépinet (1826–92). This Beaux-Arts layout from one of the architectural team working on the New Louvre stood little chance of adoption in mid nineteenth-century London.

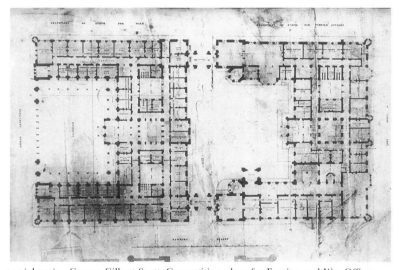

121 (above).   George Gilbert Scott, Competition plans for Foreign and War Offices, Whitehall, 1857. The judges placed competitors for only one office each, Scott coming third for the Foreign Office.

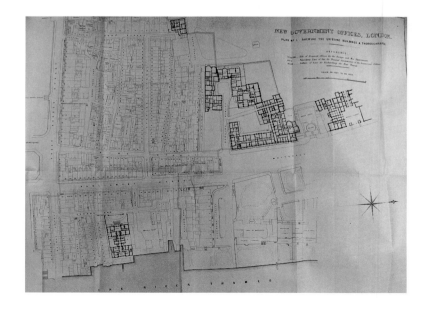

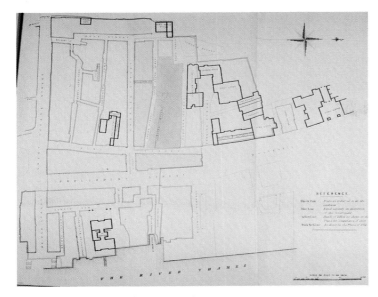

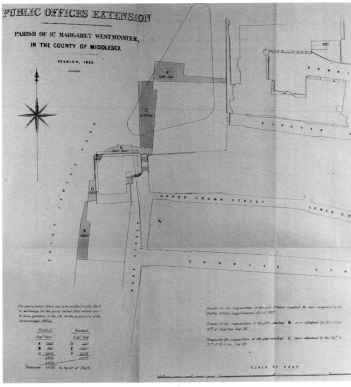

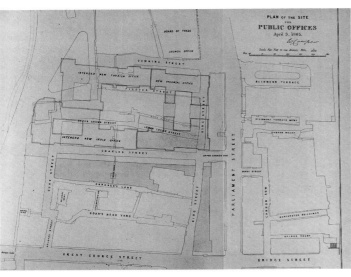

122. New Government Offices: plans of site:
a. (p. 118, bottom) An Act of 1855 authorised (but did not fund) the purchase of the strip between Fludyer and Upper and Lower Crown Streets, from King Street to Duke Street.
b (top). The Competition of 1856–7 invited block plans for laying out the area within the red line, but stipulated that the War and Foreign Offices were to be built on the area within the yellow line — the purchase of which was authorised by Hall's bill, abandoned in 1857. The 1858 committee on Foreign Office reconstruction recommended acquiring the areas coloured pink lying between Duke and Parliament Streets at an estimated cost of £260,000, but an Act in 1859 authorised the purchase of only the strip between Crown and Charles Streets, with the corner of the Park.
c (centre). The India Office having been promised a front to the Park, an Act of 1861 added the area immediately south of the State Paper Office to the authorised site. The site was further adjusted to meet the building plan by an Act of 1862 exchanging small strips.
d (bottom). An Act in 1865 extended the site over King Street. The consequence was the great widening of Parliament Street.

necessary to square off the site [Pl. 123–4].[34] This block of houses had been involved in most of the proposals for new government offices ever since Soane's in 1822, and was shown on a parliamentary paper of April 1865.[35] Pennethorne estimated their cost at £42,680; their value, as Hunt had warned, was rising rapidly in consequence of the government's building operations. The Foreign Office, however, was not completed until 1868, and meanwhile the government had set up a Treasury commission, remodelled by their minority Conservative successors of 1866–68, 'to inquire into the question of Accommodation of Public Departments'.[36]

Chaired by Lord John Manners, the commission appointed a sub-committee, consisting of Lord Devon, chancellor of the Duchy of Lancaster, Sir Charles Trevelyan, former Treasury Secretary, and W.H. Stephenson, chairman of the Board of Inland Revenue and former Treasury clerk,[37] to consider the standard of accommodation for different classes of civil servants, comparing departmental requirements with existing official rooms and with contemporary City offices. They recommended a scale,[38] on which basis they proposed five groups of four-storey offices: some 50,000 sq.ft between the new India and Foreign Offices and Parliament Street would provide principally for the needs of the Colonial, Home and Privy Seal Offices; all the naval and military offices could be accommodated immediately to the south of the first block; the Civil

123. The Parliament Street–Great George Street site: property purchased by government,

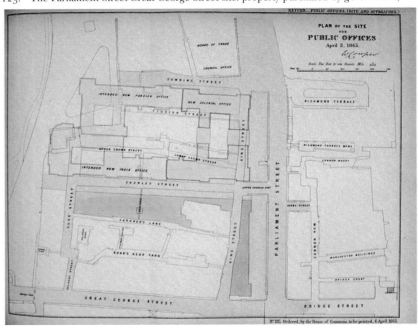

Service Commission might be placed south of Great George Street, and the Council Office (with its dependents, Health and Education) on the river side of Parliament Street. The Treasury Offices could be accommodated on the north side of Downing Street; while the removal of the Navy and Audit Offices from Somerset House would provide for the growing Inland Revenue and standing commissions.

The Devon sub-committee's proposals were not, however, entirely endorsed by the commission itself. The opposition of the Duke of Cambridge, the Queen's cousin and army commander-in-chief, to removing his Horse Guards office, either physically or conceptually, led Manners to suggest moving the War Office to the Admiralty site [Pl. 126]. Although Cambridge's view was contrary to that of the 1860 Graham committee on military organisation, he was supported by the new War secretary, Sir John Pakington, who argued that the relations of the two officials had now become thoroughly understood, the supremacy of the civil power acknowledged, and the need for bringing them together under a single roof had ceased.[39] Given the similarity of opinion of both the civil and the military heads of the War Department, Manners could hardly have persisted with the Devon proposal.

The First Lord of the Admiralty, H.T.L. Corry, was similarly doubtful of the need even to concentrate all the naval departments in one building, so long as they were all 'within easy reach of each other'; the Admiralty and Somerset House (Navy Office) communicated by telegram. It was more important, he thought, to ensure that residences were provided on the spot for the civil and naval

heads.[40] Manners accordingly recommended that the Horse Guards be retained on its site, but that the War Department should occupy the adjoining site of Dover House and the Soane-Barry block southwards to Downing Street. As for the Admiralty, which ought to be close to the military department, his commission preferred the existing site to that extending from Parliament Street to the river. There would be a surplus of nearly seven thousand sq.ft over present requirements to allow for expansion [Pl. 126a].

'Should this recommendation be adopted,' Manners reported, 'it would seem to follow as a most convenient if not necessary consequence, that the Civil Departments should all be concentrated in a line with the Military and Naval Departments', on the area bounded by Downing Street, the Park, Great George Street and Parliament Street widened by the incorporation of King Street. Thus, 'All the Public Offices would be accessible to the public from one grand thoroughfare on their eastern side, while intercommunication between them all being secured without crossing any public street, they would on the western side face the park. It would thus be actual concentration, combining accessibility with quiet.'

Except the Horse Guards and perhaps Kent's Treasury Building, none of the existing 'inconvenient and badly arranged' offices should be allowed to remain. The Home and Colonial Offices, to be erected without delay, should complete the Secretaries of State block; and the Treasury with its dependants, Trade, and the Council Office with its adjuncts would be housed on the Great George Street site. A widened Parliament Street would have a central reservation, so creating two two-way tracks separating the Victoria traffic

124.   Parliament Square looking north, *c.* 1880. Parliament Street (cut through a maze of courts and alleys in the 1740s) debouches right of centre. King Street, left of centre, runs up to Scott's New Government Offices; Great George Street to the left; Bridge Street to the right. In the foreground is a statue of Sir Robert Peel, the former prime minister, erected in 1876.

125. New Public Offices, 1867. Model of project by Col. Andrew Clarke (1824–1902), Director of Works at the Admiralty, for a linked range of offices on the west of Whitehall from Trafalgar Square to Parliament Square. Clarke designed economical buildings with little ornament making maximum use of the built area.

from the Westminster Bridge or Embankment traffic. The weakness of this proposal was that although it dealt with the west side of Parliament Street, it left the east side untouched. George Gilbert Scott in evidence to the commission doubted whether private occupiers would improve the street, 'except by chance' as in the case of the Whitehall Club: yet this was a site more important even than Trafalgar Square, 'of the utmost importance, architecturally speaking'.[41]

This difficulty was solved in a plan put to the commission by Sir Charles Trevelyan [Pl. 126], which placed the Admiralty and War Office in a huge building on the river side of Parliament Street, the Park front of the old Admiralty site being appropriated to first-class residences and the rest to business purposes.[42] But this provided 55,000 sq.ft more for the defence departments than Manners' plan – almost the equivalent of an additional Admiralty – and also demolished the Horse Guards to open an entrance to the Park from the river. The police and military were to be housed in the area immediately north of Downing Street, where they could command the park gates and the principal approach to Parliament, while the public offices would be concentrated in a square block immediately to the south, flanked by the river and the Park (which gave easy access to the barracks in Birdcage Walk and Knightsbridge), militarily more secure than a long line of offices flanked on one side by private houses. Undoubtedly Trevelyan's would have provided the finest architectural effect of the various proposals, as Scott admitted.[43] They were also expensive.

The commission examined several other ideas. One was a plan suggested by Henry Hunt, the government surveyor, 'for laying out the communications between Whitehall and Westminster', which entailed creating one wide street that would have taken some of the

site allocated for the Home and Colonial Offices [Pl. 131]. Gilbert Scott proffered his own variation, retaining two streets, that approximating to King Street being so designed as to give a 'very fine view' of the north transept of Westminster Abbey.[44] A plan for concentrating the public offices had been drawn up by Colonel Andrew Clarke (1824–1902),[45] Admiralty director of works, in 1865–6, involving the rebuilding of the entire west side of Whitehall and Parliament Street [Pl. 125]. The defence departments and residences would have been built on the Admiralty site extended north to Charing Cross, the Horse Guards demolished, the Treasury and state reception rooms built immediately north of Downing Street on the Whitehall front, and the other departments, complete with barracks, accommodated on the Great George Street site.[46] Clarke argued that his plan gave more to the public at a lower cost than any alternative; it could be carried out gradually without material disturbance of the departments; it left good sites free for parliamentary agents and other professional men involved in private bills; and provided ample accommodation for the police and the military, thus enabling Knightsbridge Barracks and St George's Barracks (at the rear of the National Gallery) to be dispensed with. He proposed that it should be managed by a statutory commission, to prevent 'arbitrary interference during its execution'.[47] Clarke's plan appears to have been the basis for a proposal by George Ward Hunt (1825–77),[48] Financial Secretary to the Treasury and a member of the commission; however, Ward Hunt (like Trevelyan) placed the Admiralty between the Embankment and Parliament Street, so affording handsome façades on either side of Parliament Street, though at the cost of losing the Great George Street and Park elevations of the southern block.[49]

The majority of the commission decided on a compromise

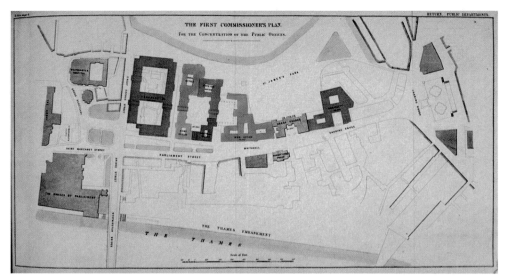

126.   New Public Offices. Proposals put before the Treasury Commission, 1867:

a (left).   Lord John Manners's plan, concentrating public offices on the west side of Whitehall, from a rebuilt Admiralty at Charing Cross to a new block fronting Great George Street on the south, the Park affording ease of access to troops in the event of disturbances.

b (right).   Sir Charles Trevelyan's scheme, placing the defence ministries on the east side of Parliament Street to create a magnificent approach to the Palace of Westminster.

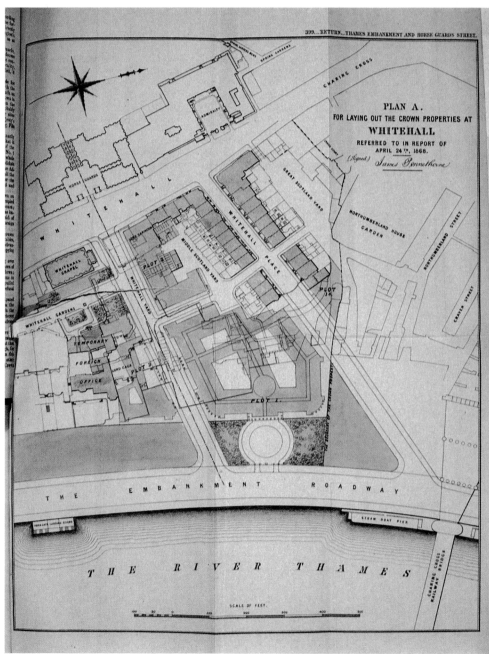

127.   New Public Offices, 1868. Alternative proposals by Pennethorne for the Embankment or Fife House site:

a (left).   Sites for ministries on either side of a new street from Horse Guards to the Thames.

b (right).   Sites for ministries above the Embankment.

These formed the basis for government proposals for a new War Office in 1870–1, and others in 1877 (cp. Pl. 131).

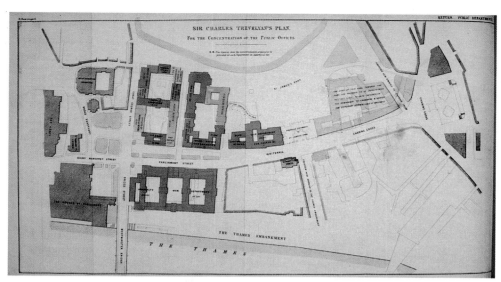

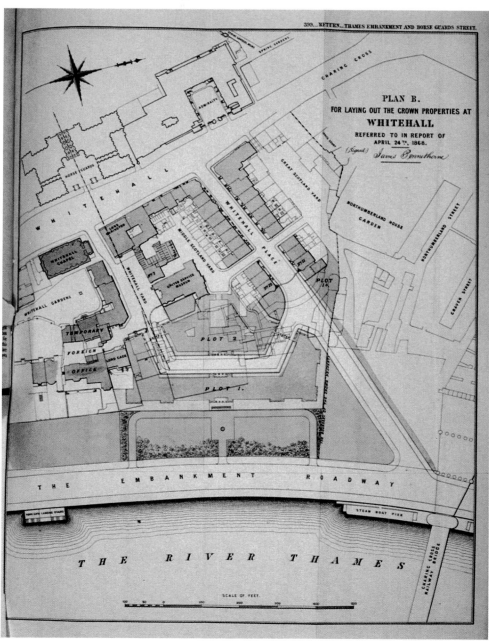

128.   Parliament Street shortly before demolition of west side in 1898. On the extreme right stands the Home Office, built across the northern end of King Street in the 1860s. The end of the remainder of King Street is visible behind the lamp-post. The block of eighteenth-century houses lying between the ancient King Street and Parliament Street (1741–50) was occupied at this time largely by solicitors and surveyors, whose leases proved costly to buy out.

arrangement that would offend as few powerful interests as possible: the Horse Guards was to be retained in its pivotal position, the Admiralty rebuilt to the north and the War Office in place of the Treasury buildings and Dover House to the south; the Treasury and agnate departments on the Great George Street site. Thus site costs would be kept to a minimum, though the building process was likely to be a protracted one, the rehousing of the Treasury being a necessary antecedent to the concentration of the War Department. Manners's proposals were approved by the cabinet on 23 May 1868.[50] Plans for taking the whole Great George Street site

129.   Home and Colonial Offices, Whitehall, plan. Completing the Foreign and India Offices in 1868 within his estimate, Scott was commissioned to continue the block towards Whitehall. His first proposals involved a carriage entrance from Whitehall, but Layard in 1869 insisted on more office-space. Scott's revision projected the block across the end of King Street, and created two small internal courts. It was thus possible to provide corridors with natural light, meeting a criticism of the Foreign Office plan.

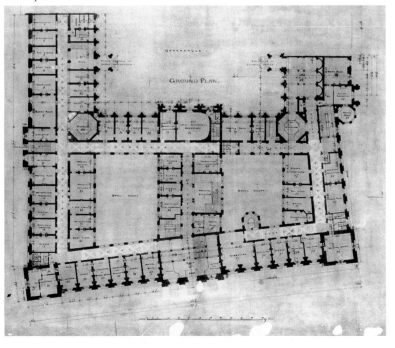

were accordingly deposited in Parliament to permit legislation in the coming session.[51]

This decision clearly turned on the argument that public offices were more secure on one side of the great thoroughfare of Whitehall and Parliament Street than if placed on both sides, even if linked by subways. The Reform Bill riots of 1866 were fresh in men's minds, and Chartist processions in Whitehall were still vivid in their memory.[52] There were many still alive who could remember the scenes in 1821 when the mob seized control of the streets to divert Queen Caroline's funeral procession. This factor seems to have determined the decision against Ward Hunt's scheme.

In preparing his plans for completion of the Foreign Office block eastward, Scott explained in March 1868 that: 'The decisions of the Commission for the concentration of the Government offices . . . seem in part to answer that portion of Lord Redesdale's question[53] which relates to the occupation of the land in Parliament Street and King Street, inasmuch as they recommend . . . the throwing of the site of the intermediate row of houses [between those streets] into the width of the street; subject to a readjustment of the western side of the street so widened; and I am studying out my design in conformity with this supposed determination.'[54]

The change of ministry, however, in November 1868, led to a reappraisal of governmental building projects; their already considerable extent imposed a moratorium on new schemes until expenditure should have fallen to a much lower level.[55] Layard, the Liberal First Commissioner, an acknowledged authority on aesthetic matters, was, as we have seen, enthusiastic for adorning London, and particularly the newly-completed Thames Embankment, with magnificent public buildings; but the Treasury ministers Lowe and Ayrton were keen retrenchers. The Conservatives had already appointed Scott to undertake the Home and Colonial Offices between the Foreign and India Offices and King Street, a tender for foundations having been accepted in August 1868. But a new departmental committee recommended including nearly a score of small departments within the new offices. Scott accordingly revised his plans, extending eastwards over King Street [Pl. 128] and aligning the front with Barry's Treasury [Pl. 129], to the delay of building operations.[56]

The question of the defence departments still remained on the cabinet's agenda;[57] but a malign influence was setting to work. H.R.H. the Duke of Cambridge [Pl. 130], commander-in-chief, wrote to his cousin Queen Victoria as early as 28 February 1869, asking her to warn Cardwell, the new War Secretary, against committing himself to a War Office (i.e. both minister and commander-in-chief) under one roof: 'The building of a new War Office is one thing, the removal of the Horse Guards and placing it in the War Office is another. The latter would be *most objectionable*, the former would with a little management be accomplished without much mischief perhaps.'[58] The gravamen of his objection Cambridge was to express in a subsequent letter to Cardwell:

. . . the removal of the Commander-in-Chief to the office at Pall Mall, deprived as he must be, moreover, of all his military surroundings, would place him in a position of subordination which would virtually deprive him of all his specific attributes, and would in fact place him more or less on an equality with . . . any one of the Under-Secretaries of State. . . . the Secretary of State . . . cannot, as such, take any active part in the command of the Queen's forces, and these duties are consequently delegated to the Commander-in-Chief appointed by the Crown . . . whilst the policy of the Government rests exclusively with the Secretary of State, the exercise of that authority in actual command devolves upon the Commander-in-Chief. Such being the case, it is clearly essential that the Commander-in-

Chief should have a certain independent status; this he must lose if he is brought to the War Office at Pall Mall, though he need not lose it if a new War Office be built next to the Horse Guards.[59]

In a memorandum to Cardwell clearly instigated by Cambridge's letter, the Queen expressed her concern about a tendency, even among subordinate members of the government, to run down the commander-in-chief and military authorities as obstacles to improvements in military administration. She trusted that nothing would be done to lower the commander-in-chief's position in the eyes of the public; in particular, to commit himself to 'what the Queen would feel herself bound to resist . . . the removal of the Military Departments of the Army from the Horse Guards to Pall Mall [the War Office]. Such a step cannot fail to damage the position of the Commander in Chief – though it might be desirable to build a new Office for the Secretary of State on the site of Dover House, & in communication with the Horse Guards.'[60] This attitude has to be seen in the context of the ongoing struggles between politicians and military men to reform the army, a struggle begun in the Crimean War, which reached a new climax with the report of Lord Northbrook's committee on army re-organisation in 1870, and Cardwell's wide-ranging reforms.[61]

Cardwell proved adamant on the need to bring the military authorities under the same roof as himself. A cabinet committee appointed on 24 April met twice at the Office of Works to consider plans for the uniting of the defence departments under one roof. After their first meeting, Cambridge discussed the matter with General Grey, the Queen's private secretary, and wrote to him expressing his very decided opinion 'that it would be far better to leave the Horse Guards as it is, the building being a very remarkable one to look at & sufficient for our wants, and to build a new War Office on the site of Dover House'. If a larger plan were decided upon, he wanted the Queen to see 'a beautiful model prepared by Colonel Clarke . . . a portion of which might at all events be taken up if not the whole as too expensive' [Pl. 125].[62]

Another courtier, Sir Thomas Biddulph, promptly wrote to Cardwell, referring to a conversation on the subject in the Commons:

the Queen desires to express the very strong feeling H.M. has in favour of preserving the present structure called the Horse Guards, in which feeling the Q believes a very large portion of the public participate, not only on account of its Architectural merits, but on account of the associations attached to it, as having been for so many years the military headquarters of London. The Q hopes that . . . you will bear in mind the importance H.M. attaches to the preservation of the present structure as the Head Quarters of the Commander in Chief.[63]

In thus citing the associational aesthetic philosophy so powerful in her youth, Queen Victoria presented her ministers with a means of escape from their dilemma: acceding to her 'very strong feeling' for preservation of the building as 'the military headquarters of London', they could insist on the more substantial issue of bringing the commander-in-chief under the civil authority's roof.

Layard's recently appointed architectural adviser, James Fergusson, prepared two plans for the cabinet committee. One, influenced perhaps by Manners's plan, occupied the site along Whitehall from Dover House northwards: the War Office and new 'Horse Guards' to the south, the Admiralty to the north. The alternative retained the Horse Guards building, and located the new offices on Crown land, reclaimed from the river in the process of forming the Embankment [Pl. 11, cp. Pl. 127]. A third plan, presented by Childers, first lord of the Admiralty, was in fact Colonel Clarke's scheme; although it appears to have been modified to

130.   H.R.H.George, Duke of Cambridge (1819–1904), cousin of Queen Victoria; commander-in-chief of the British army 1856–95. Cambridge's opposition to moving his office from the Horse Guards to the War Office – a sign of subjection of the army to civilian control – deferred the building of a new War Office for many years.

retain the Horse Guards, it would have destroyed its architectural effect by placing it between much loftier buildings; the necessary rebuilding of the Treasury offices would also have involved much delay.[64] The committee reported to the cabinet in August, as Biddulph had expected, in favour of the Embankment location. The Horse Guards building would be preserved to be used for the commander-in-chief's levées, 'and will still be considered as the Military Head Quarters of London'.[65]

The First Commissioner commented enthusiastically that:

the whole space on both sides of Whitehall between the present Admiralty buildings [and] the Houses of Parliament, with a considerable portion of the frontage towards the Thames Embankment, would then, with trifling exceptions, be either entirely in the possession of the Government or under the control of the government for building purposes, and would become, as it were, the official quarter of the Metropolis . . . a range of public buildings possessing unrivalled architectural features might gradually be erected between Trafalgar Square and the Houses of Parliament.[66]

Gladstone did not share this vision; he commented to Cardwell: 'I should be glad if Horse Guards or rather if Army and Navy Offices could be kept in their historic sites upon the Park end'; but he was prepared to ensure that the Queen's views did not 'operate as an obstruction' if there were serious difficulties, or if the responsible ministers and the cabinet took a different view.[67]

In February 1870, following the publication of the third part of the Northbrook Report on military organisation, Gladstone informed the Queen of the cabinet's decision:

> the Cabinet today heard a statement from Mr Cardwell with reference to the Buildings necessary to be erected for the purposes of Military Administration. Mr Cardwell read a letter from General Grey[68] conveying Your Majesty's desire that the present building of the Horse Guards should be preserved.
>
> The Cabinet determined accordingly; and an Estimate will be prepared for the erection of a War Office on the Thames Embankment, while the present Horse Guards will not be disturbed. The plan . . . contempletes the removal of the Admiralty within a very short time to the same site.[69]

Although Cambridge had written to Cardwell at the end of December: 'Nobody feels more strongly than I do the necessity for a combined office, but it must be a new one, where our respective positions can be fully maintained',[70] he now reacted sharply. Under strong pressure, he had agreed to 'go alone' to Pall Mall as a temporary measure, 'leaving all my chief work and offices' intact at Horse Guards, though the 'most instantaneous communication' by means of the telegraph made it, in his view, unnecessary.[71] His great fear was of losing status in the eyes of the army and the public. 'All that you require and that could be wanted, would be attained by the small inconvenience of a head of a department under me walking down to see me here from Pall Mall, or my walking up . . . Even a personal visit is not necessary on every subject. The heads of departments would in most cases have to act upon Minute Papers', sent in boxes between the two offices. Gladstone's proposal for a combined office on the Embankment was the last straw.[72]

Cambridge now declared that the wool had been pulled over the Queen's eyes. '. . . the time has decidedly arrived for Her Majesty to say She wishes to have the combined building at the Horse Gds, the old buildings there to stand & to be extended to the right and left. . . . This would be by far the best plan. I do not think they intend to pull down the Horse Guards but they mean to leave it for military purposes, but moving me out of it. . . . No moment is to be lost believe me. . . .'[73] Pressed by the Queen for fuller details, Cardwell admitted that 'the office of the Commander in Chief, it was thought by the Cabinet, with the War Office and the Admiralty had best be placed on the Embankment where there is Crown land now available and already cleared. This is a position, fronting to the new Embankment, near to the River, and accessible by water, by road, and by railway. The three buildings united would bring together all the naval and military administration.' Work might be begun at once, and 'completed in the shortest time possible'. The old Horse Guards, which could not have been kept with new buildings of much greater elevation on either side, could be used for the Guards and the general commanding the London district.[74] The Queen agreed 'there is a great deal to be said in favour of the plan proposed'; and General Grey told Cambridge that 'H.M. feels also that by giving in on this question, she will be better able to make an effective stand on the more important point of the changes proposed in the organization of the two Departments'.[75]

The apple cart was then overturned from an unexpected direction. The Conservative MP for Westminster, W.H. Smith, carried an address to the Queen praying that no public offices be erected on Crown land reclaimed from the Thames in the course of building the Embankment – work done at the expense of the metropoli-

tan ratepayers.[76] The hostility displayed by the 'country party' against expenditure on metropolitan improvements was for once retorted against them, although there was fierce contention. Lowe and Gladstone argued that the ground belonged to the Crown as absolutely 'as any Gentleman in that House held his estate'; W.H. Smith and his supporters, that 'The ratepayers of the metropolis had paid, and would continue during a considerable period to pay, for the cost of reclaiming this land.' Comparisons were drawn with the government's Irish land policy, 'giving compensation to persons who had reclaimed land and had the use of it', whereas Londoners were to receive no compensation for the loss of the open-space amenity. Despite objections from the ministers and from provincial representatives, Smith carried his address by 156 to 106, partly because Lord John Manners and his supporters objected to the modification of that close concentration of offices prescribed by his commission.[77]

This defeat halted the defence ministries project. Layard's plans for putting the Natural History Museum on the Embankment had been abandoned only a few days before, and it looked as if all hope of public buildings there were lost. Nevertheless, Layard's successor, Ayrton, himself a metropolitan MP, came up with an ingenious arrangement (submitted to the cabinet on 17 December 1870) to restore the apple cart to motility: 'though not literally complying with the Resolution of the House of Commons, [it] does . . . substantially comply with it'. That was, to set back the building 'from the embankment roadway to the limit of the ancient waterfront of the Palace ground with a slight diversion so as to bring the new building into the line of the embankment by which an agreeable garden space will be provided without touching on the just requirements of the Public Service'.[78]

The question was now urgent: an order in council in June 1870 had defined the position of the commander-in-chief vis-à-vis the secretary of State, necessitating his move to the War Office.[79] Cardwell reported that Cambridge was 'quite satisfied with the proposed arrangement' for the Embankment site; but the duke's own letter to the Queen's new secretary, Henry Ponsonby,[80] remarked that though he was prepared to trust Cardwell more than halfway, he still thought that 'by far the best arrangement' was to bring the War Office down to the Horse Guards.[81] Nevertheless, Ayrton assured the Queen that if she approved and Parliament voted the funds, work on the War Office section would begin at once. The Queen expressed approval, and her pleasure that a separate entrance was provided for the commander-in-chief, but asked to see the plans when prepared.[82]

Such fragile accord could not last. Gladstone himself derailed the plan. Pressed by Cardwell to settle the question of union under one roof, under discussion since 1860, and now crucial in consequence of military reforms, the prime minister saw Cambridge on 21 January 1871, and told him that to prevent 'an angry and jealous controversy', the question must be concluded 'at once'. The new building on the Embankment was 'too remote'. As an immediate temporary solution Cambridge must move to Pall Mall. The duke realised that, since there would be a delay in building a new office, there might yet be a chance of building on either side of the Horse Guards, a policy that would, he urged, remove 'all his difficulties'. The idea 'seemed to please [Gladstone's] fancy'. It was, the prime minister reminded Cardwell, 'a plan . . . I had earnestly desired, & of the great impracticability of which I have never been convinced'. He revived it now 'because it may be that this would help the matter with the Queen'. Cardwell agreed that the site was 'far better . . . than the Embankment', adding, 'but difficulties of which time was one, induced the Cabinet to adopt the Embankment Plan'. Now however reductions in staff at Pall Mall made it possible to accommodate the commander-in-chief and his staff there, while the union of the regular and reserve forces made it imperative to bring civil and military authorities together. The Queen agree, subject to guard's for the duke's status.[83]

Cambridge kicked desperately against the goad. He thought it would 'materially lower the status of the Commander in Chief and the ill-natured public would imagine at once & so would the Army, that the Military element was to be entirely swallowed in the Civil Department'.[84] His alternative was to remove the two branches 'simultaneously into a *new* building' or, '. . . better still, [if] the present Horse Guards were to be enlarged and extended on both flanks'.[85] He urged the Queen to press on ministers the need for an early start to alterations in Whitehall as soon as he moved to Pall Mall (where the accommodation was '*abominable*'). On the advice of Biddulph and Cambridge, the Queen insisted on a definite plan for remodelling the Horse Guards before the commander-in-chief moved to Pall Mall. Gladstone responded that instructions had been given for preparing a plan at once. Cardwell struck a warning note: 'There is also a difficulty from the Queen's desire that the present building should not be removed – and it will not be easy, I am afraid, to reconcile it with the high buildings which will be required on both sides.' But in Gladstone's view it was 'at best only a choice between serious & much more [serious] inconveniencies'.[86] However, within two months several plans were prepared, submitted to the cabinet and then to the Queen, who expressed approval of one in particular;[87] but all fell short of Gladstone's fancy.[88]

The ensuing months saw turmoil in the Commons. Lowe's match tax proposal had to be abandoned; the use of a royal warrant to abolish the purchase of army commissions after the Lords' rejection of a bill for that purpose roused a storm; and worst of all the ministry's Licensing Bill had to be abandoned in face of bitter opposition.[89] After the close of the 1871 session, the Collier and Ewelme Rectory cases brought Gladstone himself into troubled waters.[90] There was little leisure to consider schemes for rehousing the War Department.

Constantly harried by Cambridge, the Queen made known her anxiety that the commander-in-chief should again enjoy the prestige of occupying the Horse Guards, and referred to 'the extravagance of building a new Office'. Gladstone reminded her of 'the difficulties and delays, and sometimes disappointments which attach to the execution of public works in this country', and the need for 'much time' to prepare proper plans for a 'building of magnitude'. But Goschen, the new head of the Admiralty, was also complaining of the want of accommodation for his clerks. A bill for a new Admiralty, War Office and Horse Guards was introduced in the 1872 session.[91] In July it was withdrawn. Leading Conservatives were planning to join in a strong opposition preparing against it. Cambridge believed it was a plot by Ayrton, the First Commissioner of Works, because he did not like the Whitehall site.[92]

The truth was that Cambridge's obsession with his status as commander-in-chief had postponed for twenty years the erection of a new War Office. Gladstone's government had, by the end of the 1872 session, effectively lost control of the parliamentary timetable. When the Queen pressed for an early start on the new buildings, Gladstone replied: 'The Cabinet arrived with regret at the conclusion that they could not safely undertake to proceed during the present Session [1873] with the Admiralty and War Offices Rebuilding Bill; on account of the facilities it would present for adverse combinations, which would be certain to take effect under present circumstances, and would remove almost all hope of successfully carrying the Bill.' 'Members of some importance on both sides of the House' were hostile: the ministry would be beaten.[93] Cardwell explained to Ponsonby in greater detail: 'Lord John Manners objects on the ground that he prefers a site between the public offices now in course of erection and Great George Street but probably the most dangerous ground of opposition is

that of Mr Vernon Harcourt,[94] who moves to postpone new expenditure for such an object, until that now going on shall have come to an end.'[95] The defeat of the present bill would, the cabinet feared, prejudice the Whitehall site; so, in the expectation that the Home and Colonial Offices would be completed in the ensuing spring, the cabinet decided to postpone the bill until then. Manners, a close friend of the Conservative leader, naturally preferred the plan he had formulated in 1867. Vernon Harcourt, for his part, was a powerful Liberal critic of the government and of public expenditure, who had already earlier in the session pushed Gladstone into appointing a select committee on civil expenditure: clearly a man whose views could not safely be ignored, and one who was to make much trouble in the future.[96]

In preparation for the 1874 session, the Director of Works and Public Buildings, Captain Galton, drew up a memorandum in response to a series of questions from the Treasury about the extent of additional accommodation required for the public departments, how far it could be supplied by adaptation of existing buildings, and what new buildings were needed. Galton offered three choices: first, to build a new Admiralty on the site of Spring Gardens (as proposed in the 1873 bill),[97] and a War Office on the existing Admiralty and Pay Office site, with the Board of Trade either on the Fife House site or immediately south of the Houses of Parliament (where Millbank Gardens now stand); second, the Board of Trade might be built in Downing Street, the Treasury departments on the site of Dover House, a new First Lord's house facing the Parade; third (preferred by the First Commissioner), to widen Parliament Street for its full length, and build the Board of Trade and other minor offices over King Street, the Admiralty (possibly extended to the south and over its garden) remaining at the other end of Whitehall, and a War Office built on the Dover House site, with new Treasury offices and houses in Downing Street. This would permit the most rapid rate of completion, the whole within five years.[98]

During the recess, discussions between the Treasury and the defence departments produced a decision once again to defer action. Cardwell's position had been eased by acquiring yet another house in Pall Mall.[99] In any case, before the start of the 1874 session, Gladstone obtained a dissolution and was soundly trounced in the general election. The Conservatives were traditionally more sympathetic to the demands of the defence departments than were the Liberals. Disraeli and his War Secretary, Hardy, made early demands on the new First Commissioner, Lord Henry Lennox, to provide 'improved and increased' accommodation for the War Department. The necessity was now 'very pressing', the health of some of the clerks having suffered from 'the close atmosphere in which they were compelled to work; and by the very impure smells, to which they are exposed'. No cosmetic improvements could rectify the overcrowded and insanitary Pall Mall buildings. The evil demanded an immediate solution, so Lennox suggested that the War Department should move into the nearly completed Scott offices in Parliament Street, an idea eagerly seized upon by Hardy, but 'vehemently opposed' by the Colonial secretary, and 'less vehemently' by the Home secretary and others. Disraeli failed to support Hardy. A small committee was appointed to look into the whole question of official accommodation, but Hardy had no success with them, and the cabinet expressed 'a general approbation' of Manners's scheme of 1868.[100] The Queen continued to press for new buildings next to the Horse Guards, and Hardy agreed that that site was 'sufficient for the purpose', acknowledging that 'the traditions of the place naturally influence the views of H.M. as they do those of the Army generally'.[101]

The committee of ministers and officials[102] had been too much the field for contending personalities to produce an irresistible decision. Colonel Charles Pasley (1824–90),[103] recently-appointed

Admiralty director of works, recommended building the defence departments on the Embankment site, 'with a view of being able to begin immediately'; Sir William Jervois (1821–97)[104] of the War Office preferred building a War Office opposite Horse Guards, adjoining the Banqueting Hall. The committee was merely 'inclined to be in favour of the Great George-street site' for the defence offices, the old Admiralty site being thus freed for Trade and Works. Hunt, the Surveyor, drafted a plan[105] accordingly,[106] adopted by the cabinet in 1875 (driven, doubtless, by a highly critical report on the sanitary state of the War Office).[107] The Treasury, instructing Lennox to prepare the statutory notices for legislation to acquire the Great George Street site, invited his views on the merits of a War Office on the southern site, with an extension of the Treasury north to Downing Street, compared with Manners's 1867 plan.[108] Cambridge, informed by Lennox, hastened to alert the Queen of the threat to his pet scheme.[109] Although the statutory notices were served, once again it was decided not to proceed with the bill in the 1876 session.[110] Meanwhile Trollopes had offered their Parliament Street and King Street freeholds, bought by the government for £29,000. Other properties were similarly bought up as available.[111]

By 1877 sanitary conditions at the War Office were the subject of reports in the press, and a medical committee was appointed to investigate.[112] Queen Victoria, having 'rather ridiculed excessive sanitary precautions' to the War minister, '& said people never used to talk of smell when we were young',[113] now expressed her indignation with characteristic vehemence,[114] and the prime minister promised to bring the War Office problem before the cabinet forthwith. Ministers, told by the War Secretary that 'concentration under one roof is essential to the efficient working of the [War] Department and it is a matter of urgency to bring this about', fell back on the Embankment (sometimes called 'Fife House') site.[115] As it was immediately available,[116] construction could be completed in three years, and for that reason Hardy, the War secretary, preferred it to 'the immediate neighbourhood of the Horse Guards'.[117] Even Cambridge, driven by his present discomforts, grudgingly acquiesced: 'I should prefer that site which would get us *soonest* out of our present horrible and most objectionable buildings.' At his suggestion, the Queen intimated her continued preference for the Horse Guards site, but if it would take longer and the government would 'engage to commence operations at once on the other side and to state some definite time when they expect to finish', she would consent to the Fife House site.[118]

Despite all the pressures for rapid action, the government moved cautiously. A bill in the 1876 session for the purchase of the block of land down to Great George Street met strong opposition from the inhabitants, and it became clear that very heavy expenditure would be incurred. Although the government determined to buy any sites coming on the market, the big scheme was put off as not yet essential.[119] Instead, it referred the problem of accommodation for the public departments generally to a select committee, chaired by Disraeli's erstwhile friend, the back-bencher Alexander Baillie-Cochrane, presenting it as a move to diminish annual expenditure – some £20,000 a year being spent on renting houses in the government district.[120] The disadvantage of this approach was that it was so late in the 1877 session that the committee had too little time for deliberation,[121] and merely recorded that three plans for concentrating the government offices had been presented to it, though pressing the government to act at once.[122]

There was, of course, little that was new about the proposals. By this time, the possibility of using the area between the river and Parliament Street had evaporated because it was already being used to build an opera house and other costly buildings. The plans put forward by Arthur Cates, surveyor of the Office of Woods (responsible for Crown lands), were versions of Ayrton's 'Fife

House' scheme for placing the defence departments near the Embankment [Pl. 131a]. An area of Crown land of nearly seven acres, bounded by Whitehall on the west, Whitehall Place on the north, Embankment Gardens on the east and Whitehall Gardens on the south, was available for immediate building, offering a frontage to the Embankment gardens of nearly 800 ft for the defence departments, with buildings for the Board of Trade and the Council Office or Office of Works on Whitehall.[123]

Mitford, Secretary of the Office of Works, suggested a re-hash of the plans considered by the Manners committee a decade earlier, placing all the departments on the west side of Whitehall and Parliament Street, but not taking the whole depth of the Great George Street site to the Park, though including Spring Gardens and New Street and widening Charing Cross at the northern end of Whitehall, an expensive element [Pl. 131b]. He placed the Admiralty at the southern end of Parliament Street, and the War Office on the old Admiralty site; thus the Admiralty would be begun at once, and when it was completed the old Admiralty would be immediately demolished and the War Office commenced.[124] Although this plan left the two defence departments at either end of the range of public offices, Childers, the Liberal former First Lord, had stated that the department with which the Admiralty principally transacted business was the Foreign, though the Colonial and War Offices were also closely involved. Childers preferred associating the defence departments at the north end, but his strongest wish was to keep all the offices on the west of Whitehall.[125]

The third plan was that previously drawn up in November 1875 by the Office Surveyor Hunt, by the government's direction [Pl. 131c].[126] Hunt, now Sir Henry, maintained the views he had expressed in 1856 in favour of obtaining the Great George Street site in its entirety (costed at £1,300,000); on this he proposed to place the defence departments and the Council Office. New houses for the Treasury ministers would be built on the Park front and the old ones in Downing Street demolished; the Board of Trade would replace Dover House; and the Offices of Woods and Works would be placed north of the retained Horse Guards. Within a period of some seven years the old Admiralty site would be available for development, like the War Office site in Pall Mall: in all, sites worth a million. Thus all the major public offices would be concentrated on the west of Whitehall, but with considerable variations from Manners's plan of 1867.[127]

On the committee, the influential man of taste Beresford Hope was keen to see 'a grand uniform block of buildings, that would continue the Parliament-street and Parliament-square conception up to Storey's Gate, and then lock into the existing Foreign and India Offices, so as to have one great block of administrative offices . . . correlative to, and corresponding with, the great block of legislative offices furnished by the Houses of Parliament' – again, a return to an idea he had expressed in 1856.[128] He attempted at length but in vain to secure Cates's support for this proposal. The ministerial interest, represented by W.H. Smith and the First Commissioner, took a back seat; and the committee's lack of direction is a measure of the government's uncertainty how best to proceed. What the committee did elucidate was the deplorable working conditions in the old public offices.[129]

The powerful and notoriously parsimonious permanent secretary of the Treasury, Ralph Lingen,[130] 'vigilant guardian of the public purse' (*DNB*), declared in a highly significant minute to the chancellor[131] that of the choices he liked Mitford's plan least, and explained why:

I am very decidedly against mixing up (further than be helpful) the question of new public offices, and general metropolitan improvements. The latter is not our object; all we have to do is, to bear these improvements in mind, and do nothing unnecess-

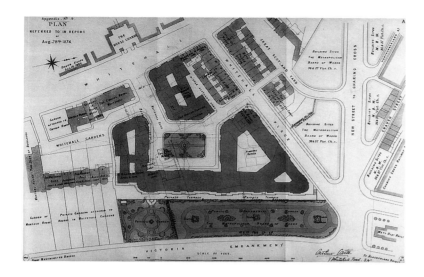

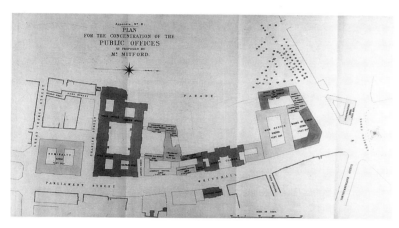

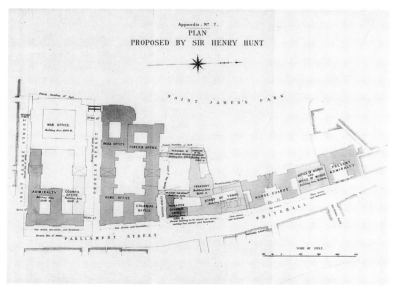

131. New Public Offices: proposals for sites presented to the 1877 Commons'
committee on public offices:
a. One of several plans for new offices on the east of Whitehall, with the defence
ministries above the Embankment, prepared in 1874 by Arthur Cates, surveyor to the
Crown Estate.
b. Plan submitted by A.B.Mitford, Secretary of the Office of Works. All the offices
would be on the west side of Whitehall, giving easy communication from Great George
Street to Charing Cross, demolishing the Horse Guards and Dover House, and
extending the Mall into a widened Charing Cross.
c. Plan of Sir Henry Hunt, Surveyor to the Office of Works: placing the defence
ministries between Parliament Street and the Park, demolishing Dover House and
those in Downing Street, and freeing the Old Admiralty site for sale.

arily to prejudice them; they are the business of the Metropolitan B. of Works. I am not disposed to give up permanently any
land, such as the Admiralty site, now belonging to the Government. I am not in favour of acquiring Dover House. The necessity of keeping up the establishment of the present Pay Office has
been long in question. If the Council Office were moved out of
the old H.O. all Treasury and Pay Office needs of the future
would be met, and possibly the present Pay Office might be
devoted to some other Department.

I incline to reject Sir H. Hunt's plan, and to utilize the Fife
House site. I should consider it an additional argument in favour of this plan if the South side of Whitehall Place be materially cheaper to acquire than the north side of Great George St.
Sooner or later, we should, I think, want the block.

'Concentration', in the sense of one roof, being an impossibility, distances within $\frac{1}{4}$ of a mile between offices are not very
material. . . .

Whether in view of the future, it might not be well to acquire
the fee simple of the Gt George St site, and then decide whether
to build at once there, or on the Embankment, may well be a
question; in the meantime, granting building leases with clauses
of resumption on certain terms, if the site [be] not immediately
used.

I think central land should everywhere be secured, at least
prospectively, where a good chance offers, by the state. Central
administration is a young giant in our time.

So powerful a voice speaking thus in the innermost councils of
the Treasury, it is hardly surprising to find that it instructed the
Office of Works to prepare a bill for acquiring the Great George
Street site in the 1878 session.[132] But the downturn in the economy,
with trade union unemployment rising sharply (and then nearly
doubling in 1878–9) and commercial disasters, headed by the
failure of the City of Glasgow Bank, together with mounting
troubles oversea made distant the prospect of building activity in
Whitehall. Yet the return of Gladstone to power in 1880 brought to
the Office of Works, after a brief interlude under William Adam, a
minister keen to leave his mark on London.[133] Shaw Lefevre, an
'ambitious and courageous' politician of 'extraordinary industry',[134] decided that a new War Office and Admiralty must be built.
With the Home and Colonial Offices in their new block, the Law
Courts nearly complete and the Natural History Museum well under way, capital expenditure on public buildings was falling rapidly, and difficulties with the 'economists' in the governing party
proportionately diminished. Lefevre first proposed a new War Office on the Great George Street-Parliament Street site, but this
being rejected by the cabinet as too costly,[135] he then suggested
combining both defence departments on an enlarged Admiralty
site, a variation on Mitford's 1877 plan. Approved by the departments, the plan [Pl. 132a] received approval from the cabinet (in
which William Harcourt was now Home secretary) on 20 August
1881, and Lefevre was authorised to give the necessary notices for
a land purchase bill.[136] In his cabinet memorandum, Lefevre
pointed out that practically the whole of the northern site already
belonged to the Crown, so that its purchase would be 'merely a
book transaction', and he held out the possibility of selling the
southern site to the MBW.

A question in the Lords in March 1882 from the newly-elevated
Baillie Cochrane, now Lord Lamington, elicited an announcement
of the government's decision, when Lord Redesdale lamented the
failure to secure the southern site.[137] During the site bill's passage,
the RIBA produced what Lefevere called 'a very obvious plan for
prolonging the Mall into Charing Cross by a street of the same
width' [Pl. 135], which would involve the purchase of houses to a
value of £150,000. The RIBA fought long and loudly, leading the

opposition against the government's proposal [Pl. 132].[138] While not inconsistent with the government's scheme, the plan was too expensive, in Lefevre's view, for 'either the present Government or any future Government'.[139] Lefevre was accused of pressing on his bill 'so fast', but he ensured its passage in the 1882 session – about the fifth attempt to pass a bill to deal with this vexed question. The select committee on the bill was chiefly concerned with the financial benefit of the northern over the southern site, and whether alternative plans, squaring off the building, would be advantageous; the conclusion was that they would not, given the moral impossibility of acquiring the site of Drummond's Bank at the Mall entrance to Charing Cross [Pl. 132] (for the government had ignored an inquiry from Drummonds in 1877 whether they needed the site, so that Drummonds had rebuilt at great expense – as also had the more southerly Cocks & Biddulph's Bank). The problem of building plan was left for a subsequent session, when funds would be voted.[140]

For once, most parliamentary discussion of the bill occurred in the Lords. Lord Stratheden and Campbell, whose brother had married Beresford Hope's daughter, objected to the annihilation of Spring Gardens, home of several distinguished men, an echo, perhaps, of the hostility said to have met the first Gladstone ministry's proposals of 1872 and 1873. 'It was an accepted principle that we should preserve as far as possible domiciles with which the names of distinguished men were associated.' Lord Lamington spoke in favour of the Great George Street plan, and complained that Lefevre's would deface the Parks. Lord Carnarvon doubted sagely whether the northern site afforded enough space. In committee stage, Redesdale argued on the lines of the RIBA objection that it offered inadequate frontage to Charing Cross and was not as convenient as Great George Street; 'public opinion', he asserted, 'was being so strongly pronounced against it'. The former Conservative War Minister, Hardy, now Lord Cranbrook, swept away these cavillings: he did not altogether approve the site, but it was better far to adopt some site than waste further time; though he regretted the failure to take in the banks and entire site to Charing Cross. As the government spokesman, Lord Sudeley, put it: during thirty years they had had 'select committee after select committee, plan upon plan, suggestion after suggestion, and nearly every First Commissioner of Works has had his own particular view of the question. Yet, still, we have the enormous inconvenience . . . of the War Office and the Admiralty being scattered over a number of different houses.'[141]

Even with the necessary legislation passed, the money had still to be found. Although Lefevre told the Commons in April 1883 that he proposed 'very shortly' to invite a competition for designs, still at the end of the session no action had been taken; the government spokesman in the Lords informing Stratheden (persisting in his opposition) that a vote for funds would be taken in 1884. The Great George Street site would be used for widening Parliament Street, to be 'exclusively devoted to the erection of such buildings as banks and clubs and insurance companies' offices, and other noble buildings of that kind', to be approved by the Office of Works.[142]

The competition, duly held in 1884, was won by the little-known provincial practice of Leeming Bros of Halifax. Their design [Pl. 186, 246] came in for considerable criticism,[143] and Lefevre required certain modifications before a supply vote was obtained and work on clearing the site authorised in April 1885.[144] The defeat of the Liberal ministry that occurred in June, giving rise to a general election in December and the return of Gladstone determined on introducing an Irish Home Rule bill, delayed further progress. Lefevre, who had been promoted to the cabinet as postmaster-

general in 1883, was unseated in the 1885 election, though returned in 1886. In February and March 1886 opposition to Leemings' plans became more evident, the RIBA circulated new proposals,[145] and Beresford Hope sought to re-open the site question.[146] When the Conservative leader, W.H. Smith (who had been accused of obstructing the new building), proposed a select committee 'to reconsider the whole question of the provision for a new Admiralty and War Office' (1 April 1886), the Liberal chancellor, Sir William Vernon Harcourt, keen for economy, was swift to support him: indeed, Lefevre alleged that he had put Smith up to it.[147]

The appointment of this select committee ensured that nothing further would be done until it had reported.[148] The defeat of the Home Rule Bill on 8 June brought another change of government

132.   New Admiralty and War Office, site plans 1882:
a. Office of Works' proposal, for building on Crown property. An awkwardly-shaped site excluded expensive property at Charing Cross.
b. Plan prepared by desire of the Commons' committee on the Site Bill, including Biddulph's Bank and adjoining property, which Gladstone's government refused to buy.

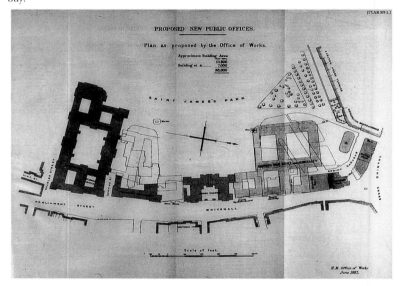

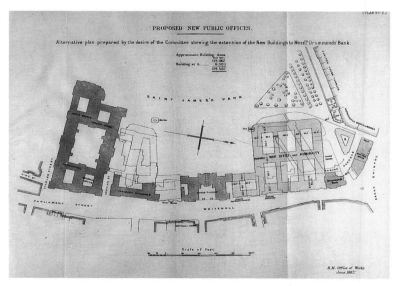

and another general election, in which Gladstone was defeated. It was consequently not till 4 March 1887 that the select committee was reappointed, dominated by such opponents of the 1884 design as Harcourt and Lord George Hamilton (now first lord of the Admiralty).[149] When it reported in June its conclusion was that 'the scheme should be abandoned'. Additions to the Admiralty [Pl. 133] would meet all that department's requirements at a moderate cost within two 'or at most three years'; a 'very large reduction of expense would thus be secured'; and a new War Office should subsequently be erected 'at no great distance'.[150] Thus the intrigue between the Conservative first lord of the Treasury and the Liberal chancellor of the Exchequer destroyed the scheme of 1884 and was to put back the realisation of new defence-department buildings for another twenty years.

The additions to the Admiralty then put in hand to the north-west of the Old Admiralty, thereby forming three sides of a quadrangle,[151] were not the end of the site question so far as the Admiralty was concerned, for the accommodation provided proved insufficient for a department constantly expanding in consequence of the international naval armaments race. In 1897, as work was beginning on Block II of the extension, the Admiralty served notice that it needed another 75,000 sq. ft. (The extension proposed in 1887 had been some 45,000 sq. ft.) Taylor of the Works had prepared a plan for building across the arms of the open square, forming a façade to the Parade, but the Admiralty wanted to expand over Buckingham Court northward along Whitehall. The Works alternative would 'very materially diminish the light and air which are considered indispensable for the health of the large number of men employed at the Admiralty' and replace the garden by a court of 200 × 100 ft. Cost and time of completion of his scheme, retorted Taylor, would be less; its effect on light and air 'practically imperceptible'; the accommodation greater, and architectural effect finer. The argument went to a cabinet committee, but was ultimately referred back to the departments. Finally in December 1900 the chancellor, Hicks Beach, decided that parliament could not be asked to increase the £150,000 allocated by the Public Buildings Expenses Act of 1897, which was effectively to decide in favour of Taylor's proposal.[152]

Thus when Lefevre returned to the Office of Works on the appointment of Gladstone's fourth ministry in 1892, he found that the rapid-and-cheap select committee project for additions to the Old Admiralty had run into the quicksands. Despite the cogent arguments he and his allies had put forward not merely in the select committee, but also in 1888 in the committee of Supply,[153] the Conservative ministry had decided to delay work on the War Office until completion of the Admiralty works, themselves delayed by difficulties with both planning and foundations, which had to be taken to a great depth. A group of speculators nominally headed by one Easton now brought the issue of the War Office site to a head by seeking renewed parliamentary powers to develop the Great George Street site. Lefevre pointed out that it would be suitable for the War Office if the price were right. Pall Mall was not big enough, though the Conservatives had contemplated rebuilding there; further houses might be bought in Carlton Gardens, but would 'interfere very materially' with the amenities of both the Carlton Club and Marlborough House: 'very great opposition may therefore be expected'. Furthermore, rebuilding would have to be a bit-by-bit job that could take twelve years; and then, too, the Pall Mall site was very valuable, worth £420,000.[154] The choice had to be made between Great George Street and the site of Carrington House, on the east of Whitehall. The latter offered 80,000 sq. ft, a little beyond what was required; the former, with 98,000 sq. ft offered space also for minor departments, but at a high cost, more than £600,000; whereas Carrington House would cost only £435,000,

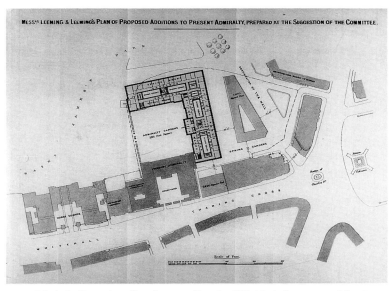

133. Admiralty Extension. Plan for extending the Old Admiralty, prepared for the 1887 Commons' committee. W.H. Smith and Sir William Harcourt (Conservative and Liberal leaders) insisted that extension would be cheaper and quicker than rebuilding.

the Crown was the owner, the site partly cleared, and the leasehold interests neither numerous nor long-term.[155]

On reflection, however, Lefevre saw an even more economical solution. It would be eight years before a War Office could be completed on the Carrington House site, at a total cost of £800,000. He therefore suggested to the Treasury that the case for combining the Admiralty with the War Department in a single building should be reconsidered: the Admiralty extension could be raised a storey, a fourth side built on Horse Guards Parade, and the Old Admiralty building removed. Ample space would thus be provided for both offices. Alternatively, if the existing elevation were retained, space could be found by using the surplus land in Spring Gardens. The whole might be completed in seven or eight years, at a saving of at least £260,000.[156] Harcourt, now at the Exchequer, was not prepared to consider this solution, to which he had always been inimical. In any case, he said, there could be no new War Office at present, because the engagements on public buildings were 'already sufficiently large'.[157] 'The Treasury do not deign (or dare) to argue the question', noted the Secretary of the Office of Works.[158]

Truth to tell, opinion at the Treasury was not monolithic. Pushed by Lefevre to decide their attitude to the Parliament Street site in the light of Easton's application for renewing the Parliament Street Improvement Act (a private speculation), Treasury officials were pondering the problem in November 1892. Hibbert, the financial (i.e., political) secretary, agreed with the 'peppery' principal clerk F.A'C. Bergne and Lefevre that for government offices the site was too dear, but put in a caveat respecting the cheaper area adjoining Delahay Street. 'Looking at the various Depts, which in the future will require offices', he thought it might be wise to purchase enough land there 'for the less important Depts, like the Bd of Agriculture and Civil Service Comm &c.'[159]

Lefevre was nothing if not persistent. Although Rosebery on becoming prime minister moved him to the Local Government Board, he maintained his interest in Works questions. By 1895, the promoters of the Parliament Street speculation were once again seeking parliamentary extension of the period of their powers, and the government had to decide on its attitude.[160] Lefevre's successor, Herbert Gladstone, pointed out that in ten years the syndicate had been unable to raise the requisite funds, and suggested that the government should acquire the rest of the site for one large block of offices to house a number of smaller departments.[161]

Against this Harcourt at first set his face: 'What I shd rather look to', he declared, 'wd be to combine the Parlmt St improvement with a new War O. site, at the same time selling Government land in Whitehall & the premises at present occupied by the War Office.'[162] Herbert Gladstone produced two versions of a plan to meet Harcourt's wishes, declaring that if they were too expensive, it would be better to postpone the development, rather than by endorsing a private syndicate 'to lose permanently so good an opportunity for effecting a very noble improvement in what should be the finest part of London, possibly at a profit to themselves, certainly at a great inconvenience to the general public'. He also produced calculations to show that the net cost of a War Office at Carrington House would be nearly £100,000 cheaper than in Great George Street.[163] Harcourt however was 'very well satisfied' by a financial exposition presented by Sir Edward Hamilton of the Treasury in favour of the southern site for War and other small Offices.[164] In view of the delays in obtaining designs, and approval of them from the Commons, he suggested a bill in the 1895 session for the sale of Carrington House and applying the proceeds to acquiring all the Parliament Street site. Pressed by the syndicate for a decision on their bill, Harcourt circulated a paper to the cabinet in May 1895 embodying such a plan.[165] Lefevre responded with his counter-proposal again recommending utilising the Admiralty site for a War Office also. Seven of his colleagues agreed,[166] but the cabinet apparently backed Harcourt, who told Herbert Gladstone to take action 'at once'.[167] The syndicate's bill was killed, the First Commissioner promising a bill 'at a very early date' to take a great part of the Parliament Street site for 'adding to existing [official] accommodation'.[168] In early June Treasury and Works officials met to draft the promised bill.[169] A few weeks later the ministry fell.

The new Works minister, Aretas Akers-Douglas [Pl. 87], had been Tory chief whip, and continued to play a significant role in party affairs. The Conservative and Unionist coalition won a large majority in the 1895 general election, and the government could look forward to a long term of effective power, perhaps six or even nearly seven years. Akers-Douglas was in a strong position to promote Office of Works' proposals, and he rapidly proceeded in the post-election session with the bill allocating £450,000 to enable the site to be purchased.[170] Four properties were thus soon obtained at a cost of £50,000.[171] Early in 1896 Akers-Douglas was actively forwarding plans for new government offices, but he decided 'to ask for a Committee . . . to locate the offices to be built on this particular site'. Meanwhile, he piloted another bill, containing the 'lands clauses' provisions to enable the property to be acquired compulsorily if necessary. Opposed by the young David Lloyd George, he remarked on 'the habit of people, when they knew that land was to be bought out of public funds, to put a few bricks on it and then ask the country to pay the cost'.[172]

The next step was a select committee on the appropriation of sites, which sat during July 1896.[173] Akers-Douglas used it to survey the whole problem of accommodation in hired premises; incurring a rental of about £61,500 p.a. They required an area of rather more than 200,000 sq. ft net of building site. The Office of Works proposed to provide this on four sites: Carrington House (for the War Office) an area of 110,000 sq.ft; Great George Street (Board of Trade, Local Government Board, Education Department), 133,000 sq.ft; Downing Street (Board of Agriculture, Irish Office, Parliamentary Counsel, First Lord, etc.), 27,000 sq.ft; and Spring Gardens (Boards of Woods and Works, Civil Service Commission), 21,000 sq.ft. Taylor of the Office of Works put the value of the sites at £1,360,000; they would release sites valued at £716,000 and rents of £16,564 p.a. which, capitalised at 25 years' purchase,

amounted to a further £414,000.[174] Taylor pointed out that the cost of acquiring the remainder of the Great George Street site, on which £293,000 had already been spent, had increased from £400,000 to £500,000. About these matters there was little contention in the committee.[175]

The problem of Parliament Street, however, proved more disputatious. King Street was the ancient north-south route between the Abbey and Whitehall; Parliament Street had been driven through in the eighteenth century as a continuation of Whitehall to the Houses of Parliament. Between the two lay a long, narrow triangular strip with its acute angle at the junction of the two streets near the mouth of Downing Street [Pl. 128]. The new offices would obliterate King Street,[176] but provide an opportunity for widening Parliament Street. Lefevre and Gladstone had tussled over the way to carry this out; Herbert Gladstone had prepared a plan which, as a member of the committee, he now sought to promote. Here impinged architectural, aesthetic and traffic problems. King Street had taken the Victoria traffic amounting to some 300 vehicles an hour; these would be thrown into a flow of an average of 950 vehicles an hour in Parliament Street. Herbert Gladstone wanted to see the latter widened to a trumpet-mouth at its southern end, facilitating the separation of the Victoria traffic, and extending northwards the point from which the Abbey could be viewed (an arrangement that, as John Burns pointed out, bore some resemblance to Lord John Manners's plan of 1867). The consequent obtuse angle on the corner of Great George Street would have created problems for the design of the new government offices [Pl. 137]. Herbert Gladstone forced Taylor to admit that his plan was superior so far as traffic and the view of the Abbey was concerned, but Taylor disliked the architectural effect.[177]

It seemed as if Akers-Douglas had killed the idea by further questioning to elicit that Gladstone's scheme would afford much less good accommodation for the offices, as well proving more costly; while Coningsby Disraeli, sustaining an hereditary hostility, pointed out that the view of the Abbey was blocked by trees and St Margaret's church.[178] But Gladstone, supported by John Burns [Pl. 134],[179] hammered away at the advantages of the trumpet-mouth, and Taylor reconsidered his offices plan so as to provide adequately for everything needed on the reduced area – by double-sided corridors instead of single, and smaller areas.[180] He also further considered the feasibility of John Burns's plan to put the War Office in Downing Street, which could have been accomplished by demolishing no. 10 and the Old Treasury and Dover House.[181] However, Burns was unable to persuade Taylor that this plan could be achieved within less than five years of the Carrington House alternative.[182]

This consideration was decisive. There appears to have been no opposition to Akers-Douglas's proposal for a bill in the next session to acquire all the interests on the Carrington House site, so that a War Office might be proceeded with.[183] The report was, however, really an interim report; the committee recommending its reappointment the following session to give more mature consideration to the details respecting the other sites.

Thus in March 1897 the committee was reappointed.[184] Akers-Douglas used it to bring forward a number of leading architects who endorsed Taylor's (now Sir John Taylor) preference for making the front of the new building in Parliament Street parallel with the opposite side of the street. Macvicar Anderson, PPRIBA, Waterhouse, RA, PPRIBA, and Aitchison, ARA, PRIBA, were wheeled in from the Institute and proclaimed the need to 'keep the Great George-street buildings absolutely rectangular'; a view supported by Oldrid Scott, FSA (George Gilbert's son and successor), and Colonel Edis, FSA, FRIBA; as well as by Freeman-Mitford, the former Secretary of the Office of Works.[185] Indeed, it appears that the minister had rehearsed the evidence with witnesses;[186] and the minutes of evidence also convey that impression.[187] Macvicar Anderson and his Institute colleagues also argued for the Institute's own plan [Pl. 135], based on that of Heathcote Statham, editor of the *Builder*, which essentially concentrated the new offices on the Great George Street site, extended to the Park, and the Carrington House site; Downing Street being tidied up architecturally, and the Spring Gardens triangle left as open space. The War Office site should be extended over Whitehall Place, the proposed opening from the Mall into Charing Cross improved, and Charing Cross widened on its west side to create an axial vista focussed on the National Gallery.[188] Herbert Gladstone's struggle for an obtuse-angled Parliament Street/Great George Street corner was borne down by weight of expert evidence, the committee recommending that new offices should be square-cornered – not even rounded as in the Works' original proposal [Pl. 136]. Cost however proved a decisive factor against the grandiose schemes for the creation of a *place* at the Charing Cross end of Whitehall. The committee accepted the general expert view that, while the old houses in Downing Street (save no. 10) should be removed, no new offices should be built there, and that it was preferable to provide whatever other accommodation might be required by extending the Great George Street site westwards towards the Park.[189]

Slow as the method of proceeding by select committee was, it had, under Akers-Douglas's skilful steersmanship, secured the

134. John Elliot Burns (1858–1943), trade unionist; Independent Labour MP for Battersea 1892–1918 (as Liberal from 1910); president of the Local Government Board 1905–14. Keen to embellish London, Burns was active in the 1890s parliamentary discussions on sites for new public offices.

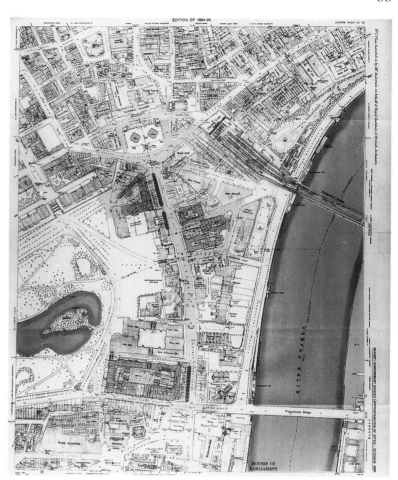

135. The RIBA pressed for opening the Mall into Trafalgar Square, widening Charing Cross by setting back the Admiralty on the west side of Whitehall, and building over roads to create a symmetrical War Office on the east.

136. New Public Offices. Plan submitted by Office of Works to Commons' committee of 1896, and approved in general by committee of 1897, with a rider that the south-eastern corner of the Great George Street block should be square, Parliament Street not divided, and the Mall be opened into Charing Cross north of Drummond's Bank.

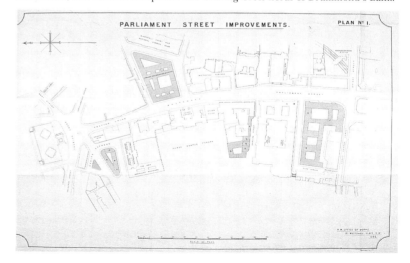

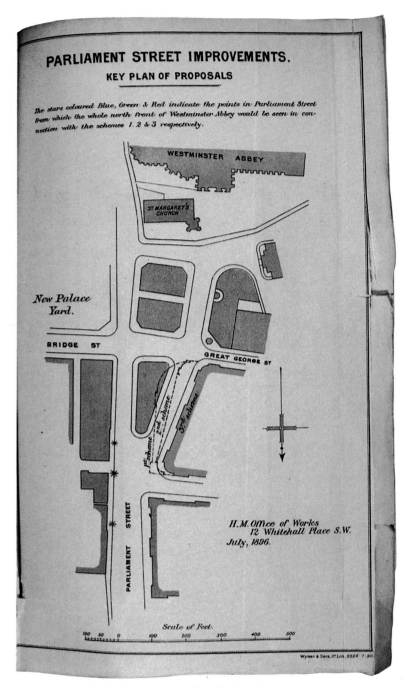

PARLIAMENT STREET IMPROVEMENTS.

KEY PLAN OF PROPOSALS

The stars coloured Blue, Green & Red indicate the points in Parliament Street from which the whole north front of Westminster Abbey would be seen in connection with the schemes 1, 2 & 3 respectively.

WESTMINSTER ABBEY

ST MARGARET'S CHURCH

New Palace Yard.

BRIDGE ST

GREAT GEORGE ST

1st scheme
2nd scheme
3rd scheme

PARLIAMENT STREET

H.M. Office of Works
12 Whitehall Place S.W.
July, 1896.

Scale of Feet

100 50   0   100   200   300   400   500

Wyman & Sons, Lth.Lith. 9535. 7-96.

137.   Proposals for Parliament Street, 1895. Herbert Gladstone argued that traffic for Victoria should be diverted into a substitute for the demolished King Street, requiring the new public offices on the corner of Parliament and Great George Streets to be set back, which would improve the view of the Abbey. There was consequent argument about the aesthetic merits of square or rounded corners for buildings. The advocates of square corners and short views won – in fact, trees and St Margaret's church blocked a view of the Abbey from higher up Parliament Street.

adoption of the Office of Works' plan to concentrate the principal new offices in two buildings of imperial capacity. Burns's scheme for a War Office immediately north of Downing Street would have involved the obliteration of several historic buildings.[190] Cheered by several years of financial abundance, the Treasury and Parliament offered no further obstacle, the necessary legislation passed – with very little comment on the location of the War Office[191] – and the recommended sites were duly acquired, architects chosen and designs approved.

One of the complexities of acquiring these sites lay in the distinction between the property of the Crown and that of the government. Crown lands, conventionally made over to the state at the beginning of each reign, were administered by the 'Woods and Forests' since 1851. Under Prince Albert's stimulus, that office took care to ensure that Crown land acquired by the state was properly paid for. Since the revenues of Crown lands were paid to the Treasury, however, the 'purchase' of Crown land by the state was merely a book-keeping operation. Nevertheless, it appeared to augment the cost of acquiring land for government offices, and some MPs objected to paying for Crown land. What was a real expense was buying out the leasehold interests in such land. On occasion the existence of an independent Crown lands entity could prove useful, as in 1898, when the Treasury agreed that the Woods should buy any freeholds in Great George Street and Delahay Street that might come in to the market, avoiding the need for immediate capital expenditure by the Treasury, and also enabling property to be bought more cheaply than if the government had announced its intention to purchase lands and taken powers of compulsion through legislation.[192] Hicks Beach, the Conservative chancellor, was reluctant to take further compulsory powers: though recognising that the government offices would eventually have to extend to the Park, 'he desired that this should be pressed upon him by public opinion and not that he should put it forward as a suggestion originating with the Government. He has no objection to be ravished', reported Mowatt of the Treasury, 'but he does not wish to be had up for "accosting gentlemen".'[193] So when Brydon's plans for new offices, extending in accordance with cabinet instructions over the whole site from Parliament Street to the Park, were exhibited in the tea-room of the Commons (March 1899), Akers-Douglas announced that 'having regard to the heavy extra outlay which the extension of the scheme would involve . . . [the government had] not felt themselves in a position to apply for the additional funds'; they would only carry out so much as would cover the area already acquired.[194]

Governments had, since 1897, gradually acquired most of the site; but a few patches remained for which compulsory powers were needed, and likewise power to close Delahay Street. The most serious problem, however, concerned the Institution of Civil Engineers, which stood in Great George Street barring the westward advance of the government offices. The Institution had rebuilt its premises in 1896 in a distinguished classical building [Pl. 138], and the costs of acquiring it and replacing it were regarded as inhibitory.[195] Macvicar Anderson, in 1897, had thought it possible to leave it standing, working it in 'as part of the façade of the new buildings'. That too was Taylor's preferred proposal. But Brydon's grand design [Pl. 139] postulated an archway flanked by towers just at that point of the Great George Street façade.[196] By 1903 the Office of Works was suggesting rehousing the Institution on the old Stationery Office site between Great George Street and Broad Sanctuary; and legislation that year provided funds for the purchase of the outstanding part of Great George Street.[197] By 1908 the idea of including the Stationery Office in the redevelopment had been abandoned. The first two-thirds of the Great George Street Offices had been completed; the remaining third should accommodate Trade and Works: but the inexorable growth of government services meant that by the time the whole block was completed the Local Government Board and the Education Office would probably take up much of the slack. Essential as it was to build the south-west third, along Great George Street down to the Park, it was doubtful whether it would be enough. 'The whole matter is in short so difficult to forecast that no definite allocation of the accommodation can possibly be made now.'[198]

Before the Great George Street front could be completed, the problem of the Civil Engineers Institution had to be solved. They

138.   The Institution of Civil Engineers, Great George Street. Government shilly-shallying about whether to buy the land down to Great George Street had allowed the Institution to build splendid premises designed by Charles Barry jun. in 1896. This prevented the realisation of J.M. Brydon's Public Offices plan, and the Civils had to be bought out expensively under the 1908 Act. They were accommodated with a site on the opposite side of the street.

139.   New Public Offices: plan by J.M. Brydon, 1899, for the Great George Street – Parliament Street site, distinguishing the part to be built immediately. Among other factors, the Institution of Civil Engineers at the centre of the proposed Great George Street front prevented carrying out the whole at once. Brydon's plan was influenced by that of Inigo Jones for Whitehall Palace, cp. pl. 41.

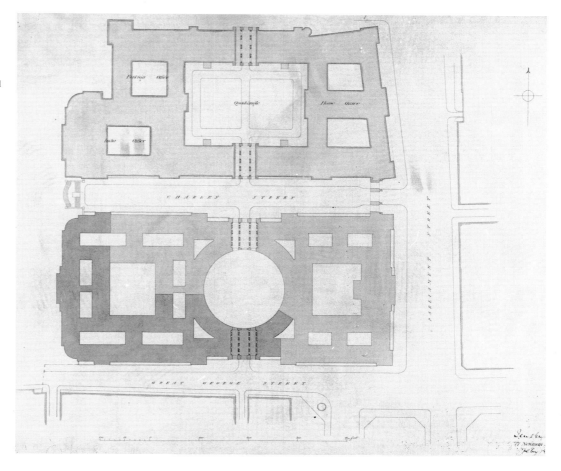

had to be provided with an alternative site before they would sell their building. The Liberal First Commissioner, 'Loulou' Harcourt, in 1907–8 negotiated an agreement to move them to a site to be provided by government on the opposite side of the road. But there was opposition to using compulsory purchase powers for the benefit of a third party, and the Lords inserted a clause in the 1908 Act which prevented the Works using such powers to acquire the agreed site for the engineers. Instead, the occupants had to be bought out at their own price.[199]

In 1909 the Office of Works suggested locating Trade on the Stationery Office site. This proved not only too small, but also subject to a ten-year delay, a new Stationery Office having to be built first.[200] It therefore became necessary to find another site for Trade, now, thanks to legislation of 1909, responsible for labour exchanges. The location chosen was partly that already occupied by Trade (in several old houses) in Whitehall Gardens, partly an extension over 1–6 Whitehall Gardens, ground running down to the Embankment. This would permit building in two stages, so avoiding a double removal of staff.[201] A cabinet committee agreed that Whitehall Gardens should be utilised primarily for the Board of Trade, and that a bill should be presented in the 1912 session for acquiring the full site.[202]

Lord Alexander Thynne (1873–1918) led an attack on the cost of this site, some £650,000, and the encroachment on open ground. He was unsuccessful in his attempt to persuade the government to 'put some of these fine public buildings on [the south] side of the Thames'; but with the help of the LCC (of which he had been a sometime member) he and others in the select committee on the bill did persuade the Office of Works to accept the line of Whitehall Court and the National Liberal Club as the building line, a concession of nearly 10,000 sq. ft of ground at a cost of some £40,000.[203]

The case argued by Thynne for locating government buildings in less expensive parts of London than Whitehall or Parliament Street was too obvious to have been overlooked by the Works and the Treasury. When a new Post Office Savings Bank was required to replace the inadequate building in Queen Victoria Street, it was decided to move out of the City to a cheaper site in the distant western suburb of Hammersmith, as early as 1898: the huge building, erected in 1899–1903, was designed (by Tanner) to accommodate four thousand employees, with capability of extension for three thousand more, to handle the accounts of investors in Gladstone's invention, the Post Office Savings Bank.[204]

Similarly, when it was necessary to replace the Stationery Office, lying immediately north of the Westminster Hospital between Great George Street and Broad Sanctuary, as early as 1903, removal to Millbank was proposed. When both that and a subsequent proposal for Vincent Square foundered, the controller in 1909 suggested a much cheaper, larger site in Stamford Street, near Waterloo Station, which was leased for 200 years from the Duchy of Cornwall.[205] New duties imposed by the 1911 National Insurance Act made its erection a matter of urgency.[206]

Other non-ministerial departments, rebuilt from the 1890s, remained in traditional locations. The Patent Office[207] premises in Southampton Buildings, Chancery Lane, site of the original office of the Chancery master charged with registration of patents, had,

140. Public Trustee Office, Kingsway, A.J. Pitcher and H.A. Collins of the Office of Works, 1912–16. Steel-framed construction. Conveniently near the legal district, such a second-rank office could be entrusted to Works personnel without widespread criticism.

after proposals to move to Burlington House gardens or Fife House proved abortive, been enlarged by Pennethorne in 1866–7. Despite this, and the incorporation of adjacent offices freed by the completion of the New Law Courts in 1882, the Office again became 'manifestly inadequate' in the 1890s. Its central position in Legal London, highly convenient for its principal clients, was a significant factor in the decision to extend to the south. Taylor directed additions in 1891–3 on the north side of Took's Court, to the east in 1894–5, and a rebuilding of the original office and extension westwards in 1898–1901. As the ever-increasing demand for patents out-soared Taylor's buildings, the government decided to purchase adjoining properties in order to extend the office, and successive extensions were opened in 1907, 1911 and 1912.[208]

Tanner's Land Registry, even more a handmaid of the legal profession than was the Patent Office, was erected in two stages from 1901–7 and 1911–14[209] in Lincoln's Inn Fields on the site of Soane's Insolvent Debtors' Court, which it had occupied after the Bankruptcy Courts were completed in Carey Street. A new legal facility, the Office of the Public Trustee, was established in the same district, on the LCC's new Kingsway, in 1914 [Pl. 140].

Nonetheless, for ministerial departments Whitehall remained the key location. 'We should be defeating the object we had in view to concentrate our public services if we dispersed the buildings', declared the Works' spokesman in 1912.[210] When at last the Office

of Woods, Forests, and Land Revenues (responsible for administering the hereditary estates of the Crown) was rebuilt in 1910 it was naturally rebuilt on its Crown site in Whitehall, north of the new War Office between Whitehall Place and a widened Great Scotland Yard [Pl. 203]. To the east in Whitehall Place, on a comparatively restricted site about 150 × 100ft formerly occupied by the Office of Works, were built premises [Pl. 204] for the long-promised Board of Agriculture, a department that grew very rapidly after in foundation in 1889, and took over responsibility for fisheries in 1903. Most important of overflowing offices, however, was the Board of Trade, which, as mentioned above, it was decided should be rebuilt on an enlargement of its Whitehall Gardens site (again, a Crown property) [Pl. 141].

Thus the pattern on the eve of the First World War was one of concentration of the parliamentary departments in and near Whitehall, while other official departments were spreading over London. Many of these were connected with lawyers' activities and were relatively conveniently situated in or near the legal quarter. Tacitly, a dual system of concentration and dispersal seems to have been determined upon; carried a further stage with the huge block of government buildings for the Ministry of Pensions in Bromyard Avenue, Acton, begun shortly before the First World War and not finished until 1922. But dispersal to Cardiff, Bradford or Newcastle-on-Tyne was still undreamed of.

141.   Plan of Whitehall Gardens site for new Board of Trade Offices, 1914, showing position of 'fine rooms' from Pembroke House, to be incorporated in the new building.

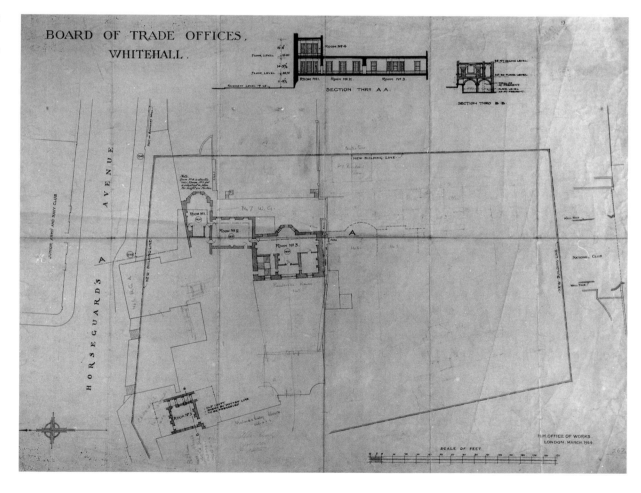

9
The Costs of Building

EXAMINING possible sites for the War Office in 1887, Lord George Hamilton remarked: 'cost enters a great deal into consideration of this question'.[1] The cost of public buildings was naturally a major factor when proposals were under consideration. Cost may be considered under four headings: site costs; building costs; fittings and furnishings; and architect's fees. Fittings and furnishings were often ignored in preparing calculations for Parliament (and proved an unpalatable seasoning to an already costly dish), while at other times they are embraced in the general estimate; we do not, therefore, intend to consider them in detail.[2] Architect's fees were traditionally five per cent, but whether on estimate or outlay was disputatious, and we shall see how the Office of Works sought to bind architects contractually to the former. Official changes of mind, or the need to cut down expensive designs, might well lead to an architect's demanding additional payments to which government was often obliged to accede to some extent; but the crucial element was the accuracy of the estimate. It was the failure of architects to deliver reliable estimates that brought public works into parliamentary disrepute – but the same trouble arose in private practice. Why was this weakness so extensive? Two elements will be examined in this chapter, but first one must consider how estimates were formulated. Nash had tossed off his on the basis of a price for the 'square' (100 square feet), or 'cubing' (so much per cubic foot), and this practice remained very general, and even acceptable to contractors:[3] it was, indeed, the only feasible way without an itemised costing made from working drawings – a costly process that could be undertaken only after a plan had been accepted, a point that parliamentary critics failed to take into consideration. But cubing could be done with more or less discrimination; as the *Building News* pointed out in 1887, 'The two most perilous rocks upon which the cuber comes to grief are those of taking a figure without verification of expense, and not making any allowance for internal elaboration of plan and decoration.'[4]

How were these various costs to be paid for? That the cost of public buildings should be met out of general taxation may seem platitudinous, but that has not always been so (nor may always be the case). We need therefore to examine the different methods of funding that were employed at various periods. This chapter will examine costs; the next, funding.

Site costs

Much of the property in or around Whitehall belonged to the Crown; that at South Kensington, to the Commissioners of the 1851 Exhibition. George III had surrendered the hereditary Crown lands in return for a parliamentary income, a procedure followed by his successors to the present day. Since it is always theoretically possible for a monarch to decide to retain the estates and forgo the Civil List, governments must treat the Crown estate as an independent entity, although the income goes into the Exchequer. During the period when the Office of Woods, responsible for administering the Crown estate, was united with the Office of Works, responsible for government building (1832–51) there was a tendency to treat Crown property as government property; and it was among Prince Albert's reforms to put the Crown estate on an efficient footing. Charles Gore (1811–97) as Commissioner of Woods and Forests from 1851 rigorously insisted on full compensation for any Crown land taken for government purposes, either by exchange or by financial compensation. Nevertheless, as the income accrued to the government's purse, the transaction might be looked upon as purely technical book-keeping. To some MPs the matter was too arcane: in 1897 an Irish member, J.P. Farrell, remarked that 'So far as he could understand the land to be appropriated . . . was the property of Her Majesty, and it seemed to him an extraordinary thing that the State should pay Her Majesty half a million of money for this purpose.'[5]

Such land, of course, like that of any private landlord, was not *tabula rasa*. For it to achieve productivity it was let. A block of land might thus be held by a variety of tenants with head leases terminating at varying dates. Doubtless, too, the actual occupants would include a number of sub-lease holders. While in the poorer quarters of the Whitehall area, west of King Street they might well be weekly tenants,[6] on the main street frontages – King Street itself, say, or Great George Street [Pl. 142] – the occupants were likely to be professional men, solicitors or surveyors, parliamentary agents, with lucrative businesses, whose leases were expensive to buy out, especially if they were unwilling to go, and the compulsory clauses of the enabling legislation had to be brought into play. In 1877, vacant land on the east side of Parliament Street was let at 7s. 2d. per sq.ft, 'with the obligation to erect an ornamental stone front'.[7] Compulsory purchase generally carried a ten per cent premium; and if the case went to a jury, the award was often even higher.[8]

An example of the number of interests in a single house is afforded by no. 22 Great George Street, part of a freehold property including no. 21, and no. 1 King Street, round the corner (see pl. 124) – the whole bought in 1897 for £50,000 and costs (the freeholder having claimed £65,000), subject to the leasehold interests.[9] The principal lease, held by Messrs Rawlence & Squarey, land agents, at a rent of £900 p.a., due to expire in 1907, was bought in 1897 for £2050, subject to the tenancies. These consisted of five yearly tenancies with a total rental of £202.4s.; parliamentary agents Baker, Lees and Postlethwaite's lease for seven years at £435 p.a. from 1894, terminable after five years on twelve months' notice, with a room on three months' notice at £15 p.a.; the Land Loan and Enfranchisement Company (paid £250 for removal and disturbance in December 1897); and the Royal Meteorological Society's £200 p.a. lease expiring in 1905 – where the parties could not agree, so that resort was had to a special jury that awarded £800 and costs.[10] No. 32 Parliament Street and 17b Great George Street formed a wholly contentious property: the freeholder demanded £31,640 11s. 3d., subject to his lease to the Aërated Bread Company for 7, 14 and 21 years from Christmas 1886 at £700 p.a. – the

142. Great George Street, looking to Bridge Street, *c.* 1898. By this time, most of the Great George Street houses were offices of professional men with parliamentary business.

case went to a special jury which awarded £26,000 and costs; while the ABC for the surrender of their leasehold demanded £19,000, the jury awarding £9490. Such proceedings took up to a year to complete.[11] Lord Brassey held no. 4 Great George Street in 1908 on a lease expiring in 1917, at an annual rent of £375, occupying the first floor himself, and sub-letting the rest: two rooms on the ground floor on a quarterly tenancy at £190 p.a.; two on the second and third floors on a lease of $17\frac{3}{4}$ years from 1897 at £110 p.a.; and two rooms on the second and two on the third floor on a similar lease at £140 p.a. He claimed £2454 for surrendering his lease, but accepted £1854 after negotiation.[12]

The Liberals who returned to office in 1892 thought that the Parliament Street site at not less than £600,000 was too expensive for the new War Office – more than the estimate for the building – which could be built on Crown land at Carrington House, nearly opposite the Horse Guards. Land in the back streets, however, was cheaper, and enough might be bought for lesser departments' needs.[13] But such needs were increasing almost in geometrical progression, and by the time the Conservatives returned to power in 1895, the whole Parliament Street site was clearly indispensable.

Another aspect of site costs, sometimes concealed, but one with which critics increasingly made play, was the loss to the country of ground that was actually *tabula rasa*, left unproductive for years while the controversies about where to locate a given office were resolved, or the government plucked up the courage to propose the necessary building expenditure. The ground adjacent to the old Foreign Office in Downing Street was vacant [Pl. 143] for more than thirty years – in 1853 the *Builder* referred to it as 'that receptacle for everything that is vile and refuse'[14] –, the Carrington House site [see Pl. 144] to the east of Whitehall nearly as long, at

143. Downing Street: the southern side between Whitehall and the Foreign Office, purchased under an Act of 1827, lay vacant for more than thirty years.

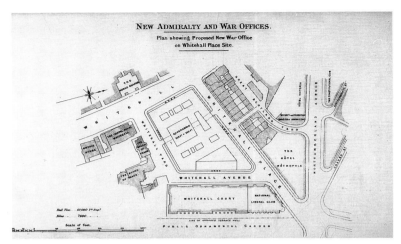

NEW ADMIRALTY AND WAR OFFICES.

Plan showing Proposed New War Office
on Whitehall Place Site.

144. New War Office: the 'Carrington House' site east of Whitehall considered by the Commons' committee of 1887, and ultimately adopted by the committee of 1897. Critics complained that no Continental power would build a ministry on such an awkwardly-shaped site.

an annual loss of perhaps £10,000,[15] 'a scandalous waste of income', Lefevre termed it.[16] Land in Charles Street, acquired in 1866 and valued at £130,000, stood vacant for more than thirty years. Meanwhile the country was paying £16,000 a year for temporary office accommodation.[17]

The cost of a given site was therefore an uncertain factor, however able the surveyor employed by government; and if it became known that government was intending to buy up a certain area, the parties involved often granted fresh leases or sub-leases and made 'improvements' or built anew in order to rack the highest possible sums from the purchaser.[18]

The great attraction of South Kensington [Pl. 26] initially for the space-hungry museums and galleries was its cheapness. The royal commissioners for the 1851 Exhibition were able to buy some 90 acres. They had hoped to secure the Gore House estate (21.5 acres) for about £2300 an acre, but the pressures of speculative developers were already forcing prices up, and they had to pay about £2790 an acre in 1852. The following year they obtained, after lengthy negotiations, the 48-acre Villars estate for some £3200 an acre. A portion of Lord Harrington's estate cost them, in 1858, £3218 an acre for the freehold, plus £468 an acre for the leasehold interest.[19] Their purchases were assisted by grants of £177,500 from the Treasury, in return for which the government was to have use of half the land, but the partnership was dissolved in 1859 and the grant repaid. Nevertheless, the commissioners remained willing to assist the government on very easy terms. They sold some 16 acres for the purposes of science and art in 1864 at 'just under half the supposed market value of about £15,000 per acre'. In 1890 they sold a further four and a half acres for a science museum: the estimated value had risen to £45,000 an acre, but the commissioners asked approximately one-third of valuation.[20]

These prices were much cheaper than those obtaining in the Whitehall district. Henry Hunt, the Works Surveyor, stated the cost of the site of the Foreign and India Offices about 1860 at £470,000, exclusive of the Old Foreign Office and the neighbouring empty ground in Downing Street which his predecessor Pennethorne had valued at £54,000 in 1855.[21] In 1856 Hunt had assessed the entire rectangle bounded by the river, Bridge and Great George Streets, the Park, and Downing Street and Richmond Terrace, a matter of 825,000 sq.ft, at £1,500,000. The Treasury in 1858 approved the purchase of the narrow slice bounded by King Street, Charles Street, Duke Street and Crown Street (immediately required for the New Government Offices) on an estimate of

£100,000, while refusing permission for that of the wedge between King and Parliament Streets [Pl. 128], estimated at £160,000, which was not immediately needed.[22] Hunt's estimate in 1877, for the shrunken portion between the new Offices (i.e. Charles Street) and Great George Street, west of Parliament Street, not one-third of the larger area, was £1,300,000.[23] In 1896, another committee was told that 133,000 sq.ft between the new Offices and Great George Street would cost £793,000 (for a building estimated at £722,000); 110,000 sq.ft on the east of Whitehall immediately north of the Banqueting Hall (Carrington House) £432,000 (of which £146,000 was for leasehold interests), for a War Office to cost £475,000; and 21,000 sq.ft in Spring Gardens, £135,000, for a £100,000 extension to the Admiralty.[24] The Carrington House site was valued at £4 16s. per sq.ft in 1887, roughly the same as in 1896; but rising values in 1894–6 had pushed up the Great George Street valuation by £100,000.[25] Seven houses in Great George Street and one round the corner in Delahay Street were valued at £157,500 in 1903, and a provisional arrangement was made to buy 19 Delahay Street from the Society for the Propagation of the Gospel for £27,500.[26]

Such high costs for sites near Whitehall led the government to look for cheaper ones for non-ministerial offices. The proposal to rebuild the Stationery Office near Great George Street was accordingly abandoned, and a site acquired on the south side of the Thames, near Waterloo. Thus Lord Alexander Thynne was to some extent beating on an already-open door when in 1912 he urged 'taking a rather wider range in which to build the public offices, instead of concentrating them on what is undoubtedly one of the most expensive sites in London'. But as noted above, that policy could only be pursued to a limited degree, or the object in view, the concentrating of public services, would be lost.[27]

Building costs

Given the problems of valuation and arbitration, the calculation of land purchase costs was open to a considerable margin of uncertainty. Additional costs raised parliamentary hackles. Even more true was this of building. As Nash used to insist, the only reliable estimate of a building's cost was a builder's tender, guaranteed by lump-sum contract, for prices of materials could vary sharply in a relatively short time, and labour costs, too, were not invariable (Fig. 3). In 1860 the Works' Surveyor spoke of building costs 'increasing very much' because of the uncertainty of the labour market and the great demand for materials for railway works and the gigantic metropolitan main drainage.[28] External events, too, could shake markets: the Franco-Prussian War of 1870–1 distorted demand (particularly for iron and steel) and in its aftermath sent prices up. Street complained of sharp increases of 15 per cent, occurring 'beyond all probability', in 1870–2; Waterhouse warned that tenders for the Natural History Museum in the summer of 1872 would be 10–20 per cent higher than his estimates of two years earlier; Scott put the increases at 'quite ten per cent'.[29] Labour disturbances at home had a similar effect: a First Commissioner pointed out that labour costs had increased unexpectedly by ten per cent in 1888–90.[30]

Yet even the lump-sum contract was not foolproof.[31] The final bill was susceptible to additions to and omissions from the contract, as with the Natural History Museum and the New Law Courts. And in Westminster, foundations – often contracted for separately – were particularly hazardous because of the presence of springs and quicksands. The Admiralty extensions of the 1890s were plagued by this problem, exceptionally deep excavations proving necessary before a firm stratum was reached. In consequence, a double basement had to be constructed at a greatly increased cost.[32] Similarly, on the Great George Street site, at the same period, there was between 14 ft and 18 ft 6 ins. of made ground, with a variety of strata below; water was reached in some places at 27 ft, while the London clay was not reached until between 34 ft and 43 ft below datum.[33] At the new War Office, excavated to 27 ft 6 ins. below datum, flooding and back-flow of sewage occurred in 1903–6, requiring the construction of storm chambers.[34]

Parliament, then, was intensely suspicious of architects' estimates, the fruit of long and bitter experience. Nash's rebuilding of Buckingham Palace for George IV was a notorious example of the worthlessness of an architect's estimate, an instance very much in the public eye, and etched on the parliamentary memory by the well-publicised investigations of two select committees.[35]

Commons and ministry alike thought they had taken precautions against a similar history when it came to rebuilding the Houses of Parliament after the fire of 1834, but once again the initial calculation proved false, and the great building – still far from finished in 1850 [Pl. 145–6] – was to MPs a constant reminder of the unreliability of architects: though in truth it should rather have warned them of the perils of parliamentary interference in building matters. But the perceived truth was the prevailing factor, so that we find one MP after another insisting that estimates were not worth a straw. Henry Drummond declared in 1854 that he had never yet seen 'a Government building erected which could not have been built under the supervision of a private gentleman at a considerably reduced cost'.[36] Sir Francis Baring objected to the proposal for new government offices in 1855:

'They were asked for 500,000l., but he suspected it would be nearer 1,000,000l. before they were done with it.'[37] Adam Black, sometime lord provost of Edinburgh and son of a builder, declared that 'every gentleman engaged in building knew that the cost was likely to exceed the original estimate; and this was more likely to happen with a public building than a private one'.[38] Bernal Osborne, contemplating plans for a new Foreign Office, 'advised the House to be on its guard and remember always that the estimate for the Houses of Parliament was £750,000 and the actual cost £2,500,000'; and a year later, on the bill to separate the collections of the British Museum, referred to the chancellor of the Exchequer's 'conjectural estimate of £650,000, which would involve an expenditure of a million and a half'.[39] 'Taste', as Palmerston remarked, 'is a very dear enjoyment.'[40]

Invited in 1885 to vote £7000 for preliminary works on a new War Office and Admiralty to cost £700,000, Sir Robert Peel (the younger) declared that estimates submitted to the Commons 'were always largely exceeded . . . [they knew] that the Estimate would not cover one-half of the expenditure that would be ultimately incurred'.[41] Discussing arrangements for building the new Gallery of British Art with Henry Tate in 1893, Sir William Harcourt 'warned him from our own experience of public buildings how widely the actual cost differed from the estimate'.[42] Harcourt came fresh from the bitter experience of the Admiralty extension, which he had worked to substitute for the new building that Peel had objected to. Originally costed at nearly £200,000 in 1888, by 1893 it was costing another £100,000; causing the Treasury to 'observe

145. The Houses of Parliament and the builder's wharf at Millbank, 'sketched on the spot' by J.W. Carmichael, c. 1856. With the costs of the new building exceeding two millions, many MPs were anxious to curb Sir Charles Barry's proceedings, and Sir Benjamin Hall as First Commissioner endeavoured to bridle him, with limited success.

that the heedlessness of the profession in this respect is well known, and that the untrustworthiness of their estimates is notorious'.[43] On the Public Offices Sites (Extension) Bill second reading debate, 13 May 1908, the Opposition spokesman, Lord Balcarres, remarked, 'As a rule I know the estimates are exceeded', but blamed the Treasury for 'cutting down those estimates to the minimum figure' when 'the scale of operations is so enormous, and the period necessary for their completion is so long, that it is difficult and in many cases impossible for the contractor correctly to estimate'.[44] Sir Frederick Banbury, when chairman of the Estimates Committee, complained that where the Office of Works vote provided for new work, 'There is nearly always a revised estimate that in almost every case exceeds the original total estimate.' The Estimates Committee suggested that the Office of Works should 'go to a contractor and obtain specifications, and ask that contractor to put in a tender for those works'.[45] Wedgwood Benn, replying for the Works, pointed out that such a programme effectively undermined economy, efficiency and parliamentary control.

First of all, as to economy. If you ask persons to prepare bills of quantities and get out specifications, they must be put before the Office of Works and examined and approved in the autumn. Then there is delay while the estimates are being considered by the Treasury. There is further delay through the estimates having to be laid before Parliament before they are taken in Committee, and then there is a further delay before building actually commences. If a contractor is giving prices for a building he will not be asked to begin for a whole year, he will obviously quote the highest prices to which the materials may rise in the course of the year, and base his estimate on those prices in order to guard himself against any possible rise. I do not think it is fair to assume that, if you ask a man to give a price in June, 1912, for a building he would not be asked to commence until June, 1913, you will get a better price than if you ask him to give a price in the spring of the ensuing year.[46]

Wedgwood Benn's opinion had a firm basis in the price increases for the Home Office and New Law Courts experienced in 1870–2, considered below.

Another reason for the increase in building costs over the estimate was changes of mind by the client. For public buildings, we may regard both parliament and ministry as client. The Office of Works handled building operations on behalf of the department for which new offices were being provided, subject to the Treasury's decision about the total sum to be allowed. It was more than an executive agent, however: it might initiate proposals, modify them, interpret them as seemed to it best; it was the Treasury's adviser on applications from departments and on designs from outside architects; and it was a watch-dog to see that designs were kept within budget. Increased costs would be a consequence of changes of mind on the part of the commissioning department, but often proved difficult for the Treasury to resist.

An example of a double change of mind on the client's part may be cited from the progress of the Natural History Museum. Waterhouse's towers in the centre of the main front [Pl. 287] had fallen victim to Ayrton's insistence on keeping the cost down to £330,000. Like Procrustes, Ayrton believed in cropping the over-tall (as on Scott's Whitehall façade). But Captain Shaw of the London Fire Brigade advised that they were needed to store water for fire fighting. Waterhouse then modified his design again, to meet the First Commissioner's taste. Such tergiversations proved expensive. The saving by truncation had been £8674; for reinstatement Bakers demanded £15,000, eventually agreeing to accept £13,778, though on the basis of their schedule £11,000 should have covered both entrance towers and the reinstated ventilation tower.[47]

The history of the Admiralty extension determined on by a select committee [Pl. 147] in 1887 in place of a new War Office and Admiralty building affords another good example of such costly changes of mind.[48] While the committee was sitting, and W.H. Smith urging the merits of grouping large numbers of clerks together on the 'bank parlour' system, the Admiralty seemed to favour such a policy.[49] The Works then checked that grouping staff together in greater numbers and fewer rooms would be acceptable.[50] In February 1888 new plans, approved generally by the First Commissioner and the First Lord, were exhibited in the Commons.[51] An estimate of £187,500 was sanctioned by the Treasury in

147. a. Members of Parliament in a lobby of the House of Commons in the 1850s. The fate of public building proposals was often decided in such conversations as these.

b. A Commons' select committee in session.

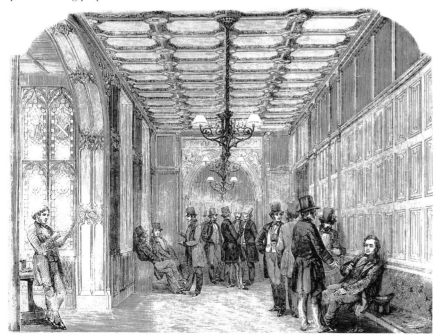

146 (left). Houses of Parliament: the Central Hall. Layard allowed mosaic work to be commenced here without prior parliamentary authorisation. The resultant storm of criticism was a major factor in his resignation in 1869.

June.[52] The Admiralty then changed its mind: having asserted that the 'leading officials were abundantly satisfied with their present official rooms [in the old building] . . . no sooner was the scheme for the extension determined on', with 'very large and plainly fitted rooms' than the Admiralty, examining the plans in detail, 'found that such rooms would not be suitable for any purpose to which the Department could apply them'. Instead, they decided 'to occupy the new block with the principal officials', entailing smaller rooms with 'a more elaborate and expensive stile of finishing', adding about £12,000 to the cost;[53] 'and in no part of the new building does it appear that the system of large rooms for clerks . . . has been adopted'.[54] Furthermore, the Admiralty decided it needed more accommodation, so that the new wing had to be extended 31 ft to the west.[55]

Administrative needs, site conditions, the weather, and labour disputes were all factors that might affect any building's progress under any regime, and all four hit the Admiralty extension, adding to the cost. Two blocks had to be built successively, in order to avoid the double removal of 240 clerks in buildings on part of the site: at least eighteen months added to building time. Then the unexpectedly rotten state of the ground required much deeper foundations: six months more. A labour strike which, it was thought, would prevent contractors from tendering, added another six-month delay. In the winter of 1892–3 frost seriously interfered with progress. The chancellor had ensured the loss of a whole year by refusing to provide means in the 1889–90 estimates for starting work.[56] And the Treasury was easily able to quash unwelcome initiatives from the Office of Works, as when Lefevre in returning to office in 1892 proposed modifications to the Admiralty extension (not such as that department itself demanded) in the interests of greater efficiency.[57]

In the early nineteenth century the concept of the 'contract in gross' or lump-sum contract had been devised as a solution to the problem of how much a given building was going to cost, and was widely used, being particularly successful in large works of a simple character such as warehouses.[58] On the basis of the matured plans and working drawings, quantity surveyors calculated the amounts of materials required, to which the great firms of public works contractors were invited to put their own prices. The lowest tender (given that the firm were reputable) formed the basis of a lump-sum contract for the building, so that the client knew beforehand precisely what his financial commitment was. But the beautiful simplicity of the device was often delusory. A great public building could never be constructed without various revisions of plan, which gave the contractor an opportunity to disturb the contract, even if omissions and extras (authorised by the architect) were to be costed at those prices that formed the basis of the tender.[59] Then unexpected obstacles, such as bad ground, or delays in securing complete possession of a site, or in the supply of stone, or strikes, or increases – over the several years of such a contract – in prices of material or labour; all these were grounds for varying the contract that a parliamentary government found it difficult to resist.[60] The lump-sum contract was also said to produce inferior quality of materials and workmanship in order to secure the contractor's profit.[61] Nevertheless, the system of competitive tendering and contracts in gross was generally prevalent in public building works in the second half of the century, the increasing professionalism of the architect's office, efficiency of the quantity surveyor, and proficiency of the Office of Works staff and clerks of works, as well as quality control of building materials, tending to ensure more satisfactory results.[62] In 1891 the government accepted the desirability of inserting a 'fair wages' clause in contracts, so confining competition to 'fair employers'.[63]

The care needed in preparing for a lump-sum contract is well illustrated by Street, explaining the problem of the New Law Courts to Ayrton:

I believe there were upwards of a thousand rooms to be provided and arranged, and that probably no one building has ever been planned which involved more difficulties or labour in arrangement. What now remains to be done is work which requires comparatively easy and agreable work (accompanied it is true by long labour) in my own Rooms, on the Elevations and details of the building, and comparatively little distraction in the way of constant conferences. . . . It appears to me that if a real endeavour is to be made to confine the Expenditure within the amount of an Estimate or Contract, the only chance of sucess lies in giving me time to work out the whole of my plans in so complete a manner that there may be no serious discrepancy anywhere between the work as first designed and contracted for, and the work as it is afterwards executed.[64]

Street therefore laboured on the contract drawings, making 'such complete and careful drawings that every portion of the building is shown in detail'. This, he explained, increased the labour and responsibility of the quantity surveyor, large portions of the work commonly being 'in the nature of provisions [i.e. in general terms, at a rate of prices][65] instead of being measured'. He spent 'day after day in answering questions, and making explanatory drawings for the Surveyors, and all these answers and explanations are incorporated from time to time in a specification book from which finally I propose to form the complete specification for the work. . . . In order to give no room for misunderstanding as to the character of the work you will find that my drawings are unusually full and complete.'[66] Hunt minuted that the First Commissioner must be assured that the drawings and specifications were 'so clear and explicit that a contract [might] safely be made within the sum' of £710,000.

George Gilbert Scott's block of government offices between Downing Street and Charles Street was one of the first great successes of the lump-sum contract for public buildings. First Commissioner Cowper, challenged in the Commons 'to name a sum beyond which they would not go in accepting tenders for the erection of the new offices', observed that 'there was no security for a definite expenditure so good as a contract . . . he intended, having procured plans and specifications to put them out to tender, and then to enter into a contract providing for their construction for a gross sum. Such a contract would be superseded only in the event of a departure from the original plans, which could only take place on the responsibility of the person holding the office which he occupied.' Although the estimate of £200,000 he submitted, founded on Kelk's two-year-old winning tender (actually £232,024) for Scott's rejected Gothic design, may have seemed impudent, it was based on a calculation by Scott that allowed for the omission of the proposed State residence (estimated at £30,000) and on a comparison of the cubical contents of the two designs. But he warned that it was not an estimate to which he could bind the government, as the result must depend on the builders' tenders.[67]

Scott and M.D. Wyatt (the India Office architect) agreed that it was desirable that the foundations of both offices should be executed jointly. On the basis of his 1859 tender Kelk was awarded the work for the foundations, contracts for both offices being eventually signed in May 1862,[68] considerable delay having been caused by the need for an act, passed in 1861, to acquire a small portion of land immediately south of the State Paper Office.[69] Instructed to prepare new working drawings and specifications, Scott then discovered that his regular Palladian design would not fit on the irregular site put together by successive acts.[70] Yet another act was required, for the exchange of small parcels of acquired land for other parcels taken in from the Park, which received the royal assent on 7 August 1862.[71] Work on the foundations, however, had already been begun, on 19 May. Although the buildings were 'erected on so unfavourable a foundation that the entire surface . . . [had] to be excavated to a very great depth and a continuous stratum of concrete laid to a thickness . . . of about twelve feet', so that 'it took the whole of a building season to prepare the foundations for the Foreign Office', the time, Scott claimed with characteristic self-exculpation, was not wasted, 'being devoted to the preparation of the plans and working drawings and the obtaining Contracts for the superstructure, so that *a whole year* may be said to have been saved by this double use of time'.[72]

The Office of Works invited prospective contractors for the superstructure to meet Scott on 12 August 1862, but the obtaining of competitive tenders was beset by obstacles.[73] Kelk finished the India Office foundations by 14 March 1863, when Scott's quantity surveyor was still preparing the bill of quantities for tenders; it looked as if progress would be interrupted. Wyatt recommended an interim contract with Kelk for a further three months' work on the India Office, based on prices his quantity surveyor had negoti-

148.   Work in progress on the Home Office, Charles Street, *c.* 1872: a contemporary photograph.

ated. With work under way, Wyatt reported in May that Kelk had retired and that the contract should be awarded to Smith & Taylor, to whom Kelk had made over his business and who had in fact executed the foundations. Meanwhile Cowper was still waiting (despite Scott's asseverations quoted above) for the 'Drawings, Specification and Conditions of Contract for the New Foreign Office'. Those submitted on 29 May were regarded by the Works as likely to exceed the estimate of £200,000, and it was not until 15 July that the requisite data were supplied, after Cowper had warned Scott that 'the First Commr cannot allow any deviation from the strictest regularity of proceeding even for the sake of hastening the commencement of the work'.[74] Tenders were obtained from eleven contractors;[75] but the firm already engaged on the site was able to underbid its competitors (as had been found at the Houses of Parliament) at £195,573.

Thus it might have been feared that the new government offices would prove one of the unhappy examples of the contract in gross. Such, indeed, was alleged by trade unionists appearing before the Royal Commission on Trades Unions of 1867. Smith & Taylor subcontracted some of the work to Messrs Wilkinson and Bone. Edwin Coulson, secretary of the Operative Bricklayers, claimed that work was given out ostensibly as piece work, but really to get more out of the workmen: 'Inexperienced young men are put in by the foreman . . . and they pay them at what you might call reduced wages . . . and then put in at the end of the week the whole money', so that 'the Government pays the full price', as Lord Elcho put it, 'but gets an inferior article'. Smith controverted Coulson's charges, stating that alterations made a few weeks previously showed that the walls were 'all perfectly solid'. A few walls, built on iron girders for a fireproof construction had been built hollow to lessen the weight.[76] Robert Applegarth, the general secretary of the Amalgamated Carpenters' union, who went through the India Office 'from the basement to the very attics', seeing the work 'in every stage of progress', declared that it was 'as good work as could possibly be produced by the hands of man'. His members working 'at the Foreign Offices' told him that 'there has been no hurrying or scamping'.[77] The contract protected the government from a 15 per cent rise in wages between 1863 and 1867, 'a great deal more', according to Smith, 'than the profits'.[78] The total cost of the New Foreign Office was £285,473, including painting and decorating the interior (£11,845), lifts, bells and fittings (£14,003), paving (£6990), alterations (£3398) and commission (£12,570).[79]

Similarly, the contract for the eastward extension of the Foreign and India Offices to house the Home [Pl. 148] and Colonial Offices, 1871–5, protected the government from a rise in costs put at more than 30 per cent by the contractors Jackson & Shaw.[80] Layard regarded Scott's original estimate of £407,272 as too high for what it offered, so that he had him recast the design to incorporate more departments for a little more expense, £436,468;[81] but Lowe at the Treasury demanded further economies, including a less palatial finish and omitting the towers proposed for the Parliament Street front. Ayrton, Layard's successor, told Scott to set 'boldly and unflinchingly to work' to reduce the total by about £100,000. Galton, the Director of Works, minuted: 'We cannot tell what Mr Scotts *real* reduction is until the tenders are received.'[82] The tenders were in the comparatively tight range of £242,000–280,000; and Jackson & Shaw, who took the work at £242,323, complained that they were losing 'very heavily'. Ayrton however, on official advice, refused them any increase, even for agreed extras included after the rise in prices had occurred.[83]

Horror stories about contracts in gross found, however, some support in the less happy history of the New Law Courts. The Office surveyor, Henry Hunt, thought it generally inexpedient to proceed with foundations until contracts were concluded for a

149. New Law Courts: design for a Common Law Court, G.E. Street, 1867, from his competition entry. Street's not having provided specifications for every court when the contract was put to tender was exploited as a grievance by the appointed contractors, Bull & Sons of Southampton, who had miscalculated in costing this item.

whole structure, despite the precedent of the New Government Offices, but, admitting that the New Law Courts were 'exceptional', agreed to separate contracts provided Street prepared full plans and specifications for the foundations.[84] The successful tender for foundations (the range of more than £30,000 astonishing the *Builder*), by the ecclesiastical specialists Dove Bros, proved somewhat lower than Street's own best estimate;[85] though faced with an operation beyond their usual capacity they over-ran their time by 15 weeks.[86] However, it was with the superstructure contract that the serious financial problems emerged.

The final list of tenderers for this huge contract contained 22 names, including four provincial contractors as was current practice, the Office of Works seeking to break the monopoly of the London builders.[87] By far the lowest tender was by Joseph Bull and Sons of Southampton, a firm of some consideration in Hampshire.[88] But it exceeded Street's estimate by some £79,000, if the cheaper Chilmark stone were employed, with deal fittings in the courts [Pl. 149] rather than oak and omitting £14,000 for contingencies. Portland stone, oak, and contingencies would bring the excess to £108,316. Street declared that the cost of both labour and materials had risen considerably (labour about 14 per cent, bricks 15, timber 30, glass 70 per cent) in the two and a half years

since his estimate had been framed, very much of it in the year since his plans were finished.[89]

This exceeding was grist to the mill of Ayrton's animosity towards Street's design. There was prolonged wrangling between the First Commissioner, Street and the Treasury, with 'noises off' from Bull and Sons. Ayrton wanted to accept Bulls' tender subject to alterations to reduce it to £658,816 (i.e. within the statutory limit of £710,000, including foundations and architect's commission). Bulls welcomed the opportunity to deliver a priced bill of quantities as basis for readjusting their tender. Street however urged rapid acceptance of the original tender before Bulls became frightened; the reductions could be made after signing the contract. But Ayrton instructed Street first to make major alterations, principally the omission of the central hall and clock tower, to save about £100,000, an issue examined in more detail below. The architect, having vainly urged Ayrton to compromise on his own reductions of about half that amount – which would leave 'no opening for the re-measurement of the work, no uncertainty as to its real cost, no more delay in its execution' – then negotiated direct with a more sympathetic Treasury which allowed (as described in chapter 16) an additional £54,000 (half the excess of tender over estimate) in view of increased costs. Approving the reductions Street recommended, priced by Bulls at £53,915, the Treasury instructed the First Commissioner to accept Bulls' tender thus modified.[90]

Labour costs having continued to rise while the parties argued, Bull and Sons began (as Street had feared) to repent their rash bid. They raised one point after another in order to reduce their expenses. Not until 7 February 1874 was the contract, for £693,429, actually signed.[91] Bulls' inadequacies then soon became patent, as we shall see in chapter 16. Their lack of adequate working capital was indicated by a series of requests, for a reduction from 15 to ten per cent in the sum reserved until completion, and for advances in respect of plant and machinery – a breach of faith with their competitors, asking the government to provide some £60,000 or £70,000 of capital. Their seeking a right to resort to arbitration if they disputed the architect's monthly certificates for payment was yet another such indication.[92]

When the New Law Courts were opened by the Queen in December 1882, Bulls were 121 weeks behind schedule, and went into liquidation soon after.[93] To bolster them, the government had paid them about £20,000 more than they were entitled to. Street's son claimed, after his father's death, that 'It was owing to his unremitting and constant care that the building was ever got through at so low a cost and with a contractor of such limited means'.[94] Thus the advantages of a lump-sum contract, unless the contractor had a sound capital base, were shewn to be very much at risk.

Problems with a lump-sum contract also reared up over the Natural History Museum [Pl. 151]. Much of the exterior was to be clad in terra-cotta [Pl. 150], and Waterhouse declared that there were only four or five satisfactory manufacturers. He suggested dividing the work among two or three firms, who should be asked to submit samples according to his plaster models along with their tenders. Advising against a separate competition for terracotta, Hunt of the Works claimed that 'great inconvenience' had arisen from such arrangements. The terracotta was therefore included in the general building contract, though obviously the builders would have to sub-contract with the manufacturers.[95] As with the New Law Courts (for these two great buildings were proceeding simultaneously), the architect warned that by mid-1872 tenders were likely to be 10–20 per cent higher than his estimate of 1870.[96]

The immediate official reaction was to require reductions in the architectural decorations and finishings so as to bring the cost down to £330,000. Waterhouse proposed that the specifications

150. Natural History Museum: terracotta detail. Waterhouse had expected that the use of terracotta for the exterior would be an economy, but the lack of large-scale manufacturers and the architect's changes in the specification resulted in its proving an expensive operation.

remain intact until after the tenders had been opened; it would then be easy to see how far reductions were necessary, and only one firm would be required to make the alteration, rather like Street with Bull and Sons. But Hunt insisted that this would be 'greatly inconvenient' (as he had found with amending the lowest tender for E.M. Barry's National Gallery works). The bills of quantities for the Museum had been prepared with such care that Waterhouse

should have little difficulty in coming to a very close approximation to the probable amount of the lowest tender (a notion only conceivable in a system of invited tenders such as the Works then operated but later discarded), and making the necessary reductions immediately.[97]

Waterhouse himself was not an enthusiast for competitive tendering, remarking that, 'having had experience of many of them [on the list of invited contractors], I am persuaded that the majority are not on a par with the rest, and that it might be the truest economy to accept the tender of one of the best even though it might be somewhat higher than the lowest'. However, he agreed to make certain reductions.[98]

Nonetheless, when the tenders were opened on 16 September 1872, Waterhouse's expectations were realised: the lowest, that of the experienced public works contractors Baker and Son, showed an excess of £83,000 over his estimate. He blamed a combination among the terracotta manufacturers, pointing out that Gibbs & Canning had quoted £88,000 to the builders, whereas the previous March they had given him a figure of only £57,000. Galton at the Office of Works suggested economies.[99] The Treasury, conscious that two years' Votes had not been touched, supported the British Museum trustees in urging a start on the foundations. Waterhouse reported that no more favourable terms could be secured than Baker's revised estimate of £352,000 (still more than £40,000 higher than Waterhouse's original figure), and Galton commented that the exceptionally high price of iron (£90,000 of the total)[100] and the small number of terracotta manufacturers (£76,000) caused the increase. The Treasury then authorised acceptance of Bakers' revised tender, the contractor requiring that the terracotta be paid for monthly on delivery, and an additional six months be allowed for completing the pavilions.[101]

The inadequate supply of terracotta caused serious delay in the progress of the Museum, and changes Waterhouse made in its design and required in its fixing led to large claims from the contractor, amounting to some £26,100 for changes in the building, and another £21,115 for extra expenses of sorting and setting the terracotta. Waterhouse's own calculation priced additions to the terracotta at £22,182 and omissions at £14,133. That this was only part of a larger problem is indicated by the surveyors' figures: Trollope (for Baker & Son) claimed £147,412 additions and £121,315 omissions; while Rickman (for Waterhouse) put them at £122,998 and £125,161 respectively – sums that indicate a very considerable reworking of a contract of £352,000 in all.[102]

Some of the trouble might have been avoided had the Works listened to Waterhouse's request to have his additions and omissions measured and accurately valued as work proceeded. He refused to undertake it himself as it did not fall within the duties 'ordinarily rendered by an Architect' to which he was contractually bound; but the Office's usual unwillingness to foot the relatively small bill for the measuring surveyor caused Rickman to drag his feet until his pay was secured, and the contractors, too, had shown 'such disinclination to go into the question of extras and deductions as to preclude these necessary investigations being made during the greater part of the progress of the building'.[103]

As with Bull & Sons at the Law Courts, so with Baker & Son at the Natural History Museum: the government in order to avoid the collapse of the contractor had been obliged to advance money beyond what was contractually due. Although Bakers were a London firm that had been much engaged in major public works for many years,[104] nevertheless the Natural History Museum contract proved a disaster for them, and they collapsed into bankruptcy in 1880–1. That the unreliability of the lump-sum contract was not peculiar to that period is shewn by the history of the Admiralty extensions of the 1890s, examined in chapter 16. It was a perennial problem, made acute by labour unrest, sharply fluctuating prices, and unexpected site problems.

We have referred to fittings as another unpalatable source of increased costs, difficult to calculate; and this emerged clearly in making the Natural History Museum ready for exhibition. Waterhouse designed wall-cases and fittings for the displays as well as those for the offices [Pl. 286]. The enormous cost of this specialised furniture invited scrutiny by a cash-strapped Treasury in 1879. Completion was deferred, and some fittings were designed by the Office Surveyor, John Taylor, though in the end little saving was achieved on the architect's original estimate of £177,000.[105]

151. Natural History Museum. Waterhouse's grand Central Hall provided space for large exhibits, but the single staircase hampered easy communications between the floors in the wings.

Architects' charges

A prolific source of dispute was the charges made by architects. The traditional charge was a commission of five per cent upon the outlay for executed work, with two and a half per cent on the estimate for full drawings if the work were abandoned. This gave the architect no incentive (save reputation) to keep down the cost of a work, and was heavily criticised in Parliament. Between 1815 and 1832, the Crown architects were paid an annual retainer of £500, plus a three per cent commission on new buildings; though at the same time they were relieved of measuring works and making up accounts, then normally regarded as part of an architect's duties.[106] After the disasters of the 1820s, the Office of Works came to favour the payment of an arranged fee in place of a commission; £25,000 was offered to Charles Barry for the Houses of Parliament. Although the government would never explain the basis of its calculation, it appears to have been on the same scale as the earlier Crown architects: viz., £500 p.a. for the seven years that Barry expected the work to take plus three per cent on estimate, rounded up to the nearest thousand. This would have been not inequitable had the Works continued the measuring and making up the accounts that they had performed for the Crown architects; but Barry was required to pay all expenses himself. His ambiguous reply left the impression that he accepted the situation. Years of wrangling followed, until in 1856 he was obliged to accept three per cent on outlay plus one per cent on measured work.[107] Barry was scurvily treated, considering that Pennethorne was simultaneously receiving five per cent on outlay for his new public buildings; but Barry was under the close scrutiny of Parliament, and Parliament tended to regard public building as 'a job', i.e. corrupt.

At the same time as the Treasury was imposing its will on Barry, Hall, at the Office of Works, was complaining that he feared he was bound to Pennethorne for enlarging the National Gallery: 'an exemplification of the many inconveniences which result from the Treasury (in former years) having unfortunately appointed an architect who is to be paid by a *per centage*'.[108] Ayrton while still Secretary of the Treasury took up the issue, writing to the First Commissioner, 'pointing out that the mode of paying an Architect a Commission on an indeterminate amount affords no guarantee for economy, but is a distinct premium on expense'; preliminary plans 'should be contracted for with a due regard to the possibility of the building not being completed'.[109] When he arrived at the Office of Works himself, Ayrton's solution was, as we have seen, to oblige the architect to accept a pre-determined fee, though one based on the traditional five per cent – but on his estimate, rather than outlay.[110]

Yet even so there remained room for controversy. Street in particular had cause for resentment. Appointed on 30 May 1868 as architect for the New Courts of Justice, he was then 'engaged constantly with a staff of Clerks for more than 12 months in preparing various plans required first by the Courts of Justice Commission and then by the Government' at an estimated cost of £1,523,000. He was then instructed to redesign the Courts for a new site on the Thames Embankment. Parliament rejected the site. On 31 December 1869 the new First Commissioner, Ayrton, instructed him to prepare plans for a smaller building on the original Carey Street site, necessitating, he claimed, 'an entirely fresh plan in every particular': it was true that he was familiar with the requirements of the various departments, 'But the obligation to reduce all these requirements necessitates fresh arrangements of every room in the building. . . . The plans which I have made have been of altogether exceptional complexity: . . . owing to the necessity of pleasing not only the Courts of Justice Commission, but also all the Heads of Departments . . . I have had to alter and redraw my plans repeat-edly, with an amount of trouble which I never remember to have seen paralleled.' Commission at 15s. per cent on the great plan would have given him £11,422. He put his own time and his office expenses, on a low estimate, at £3000.[111] Ayrton dismissed this as absurd: the instructions to the competing architects had stated that Parliament had allocated £750,000 for the project; 'I think it would be sufficient if he were allowed the £800 which he received as premium for his larger [competition] design as a sufficient compensation for the trouble it has occasioned.' For the Embankment scheme, the £750 he asked for was proper. The Treasury took an even more cautious line: until the plans and cost were finally settled, any payment to Street was to be treated as an advance only; there was to be no settlement of his claims.

At this point, a disagreement between the two advisers of the Office of Works emerged. Hunt, the Surveyor, thought Street was 'fairly entitled' to payment for the Courts of Justice Commission's great scheme, as the Treasury had known all about it, and had not stopped it; he proposed £2100. But Galton, Director of Works, insisted that £800 was enough, as Street 'must have known' that the expenditure was limited to £750,000, and the information he had collected was necessary for maturing his final plan.[112] 'The excellence of the plan cannot however be made a ground for extra remuneration; indeed such excellence', he remarked cynically, 'indirectly benefits the Architect by increasing his reputation and obtaining for him additional employment.'[113] The matter dragged on. Street received sizable payments on account (under the erroneous impression that his request for Hunt to arbitrate had been agreed to by Ayrton, who refused to let him see Hunt's report), until in September 1873, with a new First Commissioner, the tactful William Adam, taking office, he asked for arbitration on his claim for the great plan, on the question of payment of measurers' fees, and on whether his commission for the final scheme was payable on the contract sum and agreed extras (as laid down by the competition conditions), or only on the £710,000 determined by Ayrton on the basis of the statute.

The First Commissioner called for a joint report from Hunt and Galton, but on the first claim they stuck to their original differing opinions. The measurer's-fee issue they considered was governed by the agreement with the architect (23 September 1870): he was bound to provide all necessary assistants, clerks of works, etc. Therefore he had no claim. If allowed, it might lead to a re-measurement of the whole building, 'for he would have a great inducement so to alter his design as to render that course absolutely necessary', and the fees would be £25,000 – and this about a man who had made alterations in Dove Bros' contract for the foundations to save two or three thousand pounds, alterations which gave rise to this claim for a miserable £109 for the architect's share of the measurer's fee. As to the third claim, the principle of the agreement with the architect was a fixed fee. Increases in the cost of labour and materials had increased the cost of the building without any extra work for the architect. 'The soundness of that mode [i.e. agreed fee] of remunerating an Architect is proved by the result in this case.' The second and third claims might go to arbitration, but the first might fall under the responsibility of the Courts of Justice Commission, to be adjudicated by the attorney-general.[114]

Adam had hoped to discuss the question with Gladstone, but a sudden general election resulted in a change of ministry, in February 1874. The new Treasury authorised the payment of £2100 in lieu of the £800 previously offered, in full satisfaction of all Street's claims. Street accepted, with the proviso that the arbitrator in Dove Bros.' claim for their surveyor's fees having also awarded the architect his surveyor's fees, the question of principle had been settled. But the Office jibbed at admitting this. Street then insisted that either they accept the award, or submit all his claims to arbitration: 'Architects who take out their own quantities always make a charge for this work and speaking generally it is felt by the higher class of Architects that those who do so are wrong in undertaking work which is likely to be better done by men who confine themselves to it.' This question had become the more important as Waterhouse too was claiming for measurers' fees at the Natural History Museum. Hunt's determination to resist rested on his fear that it would admit the right of the architect to make alterations without authority so long as there was no increase in the cost. At the same time he was anxious to 'avoid further contention with these eminent architects'. A number of conferences between the architects and Hunt during 1875 resulted at length in the Office paying the £2100 authorised 16 months previously, and agreeing to pay surveyor's fees resulting from alterations sanctioned officially. Street for his part undertook to ask official authority for any proposed alterations. He would give up any claim to further commission if the First Commissioner concurred, as he did, in Hunt's view that the 1870 agreement was intended 'to make payment for the work by a fix'd Sum and not by way of a percentage upon the Cost'.[115]

This prolonged episode, essentially a struggle between client and architect about whether traditional practices (the method of paying architects, their precise functions, their power to order alterations) should be superseded, illustrates the poor opinion that bureaucrats had of professional men. It also reflects on the unsatisfactory conditions in the Works at this time; the delays in communicating with Street are not surprising in an office loaded with work beyond its capacity; riven, as we have seen, by quarrels between Russell (as Secretary the permanent head) and Galton (head of the technical branch), with an independent, long-established and intrinsically important professional adviser in the person of Hunt able to challenge the latter's authority; and sinking in morale under the administration of the widely-criticised Ayrton and the resentful Lennox.[116]

In resisting architects' claims, the Treasury was commonly more stringent than the Office of Works with its close relationship to Scott, Street and their colleagues. This was true even under the arch-economist Ayrton's administration. He, for instance, accepted Scott's case that he should be paid for revising plans for the Home and Colonial Offices. In February 1870 he had directed Scott to make major reductions in his plans, and in July the Treasury had ordered further reductions. For the drawings rendered useless Scott claimed £2212; the Works recommended £1530; the Treasury refused anything: 'No architect is entitled to more than his commission on the actual cost, unless his employer virtually abandons his original intention and give [*sic*] him a fresh order. . . . When plans are merely reduced in cost, the commission on the lowest sum covers any charge.' Scott pointed out that the client had changed his mind: for Lord John Manners he had prepared a complete set of working drawings; then, under Layard, 'a wholly new scheme was struck out greatly exceeding the other both in extent and cost'; but he had 'relinquished all extra charge' as the new scheme was larger. He had been ordered to prepare working drawings for tenders, but after most of the quantities had been taken out, the Treasury decided on '*most extensive* reductions[117] . . . of a sweeping character rendering useless many of the drawings before made . . . a work of *radical change* in many portions of the building, removing what before existed and substituting new work . . . a work of much labour and study.' By custom he would be entitled to two and a half per cent on the estimate; but he was willing to abide by the Works' decision as to the amount. Ultimately, however, in view of Ayrton's persistence, the Treasury conceded the case.[118]

10
Financing the Costs

ONCE the case for a great public work had been accepted, the over-riding consideration was how to pay for it. The normal means was by annual Vote creating a charge on the national purse, the Consolidated Fund. Because of the hazards of asking the Commons for annual Votes, an alternative method of long-term funding was occasionally sought in the form of loan finance. Whether by annual Vote or by loan, the cost still ultimately fell on the Consolidated Fund, which is to say on the taxpayer. As in the 1980s, the question sometimes arose whether the burden should fall on the taxpayer as such at all. While pride was often expressed in London as capital of the world's greatest empire, and there was a view extensively held that the capital should be worthy of the empire, nevertheless when it came to paying for worthy buildings, too often the feeling prevailed that national taxes should not be spent for what were often regarded as local objects. The state needed offices; but offices need only be utilitarian [Pl. 152]: 'Allow not nature more than nature needs.' Architecture, in the widely-held Ruskinian view, is the art which impresses on the form of a building 'certain characters venerable or beautiful, but otherwise unnecessary'.[1] If it was desired to add architecture to offices to make London look more splendid, some MPs thought Londoners should pay for it. Certainly, if roads were widened in the course of such works, that was 'metropolitan improvement' for which the charge should not fall on the national Exchequer.

The distinction between 'public works' and 'metropolitan im-

provements' had to be carefully weighed by ministers contemplating new works. It was commonly resolved by treating road works as metropolitan improvements, while buildings, their ornament pared down as far as possible, were regarded as public works. Thus the case for alternative sites for the New Law Courts could be made out by treating certain necessary or desirable ancillary works as metropolitan improvements to be excluded from calculations of cost. The clarity of this distinction was blurred, as we have pointed out, at two sites in particular: the redevelopment of Parliament Street, and Hyde Park Corner.

The persistent serious under-representation of the metropolis in the Commons until 1885 allowed criticism of the embellishment of London at the public expense to drown London's voice. Metropolitan improvement had therefore to be paid for by the Londoner. To achieve this there were two principal means: the local property taxes or 'rates' which varied according to the local authority; and the coal, wine and corn dues dues discussed in the opening chapter. The passion that these questions might excite was displayed when W.H. Smith, MP for Westminster, moved an address to the Crown in order to preserve as open space land reclaimed from the Thames in the course of embankment.[2] With rumours flying that the government proposed to use for a new War Office the two and a half acres near Charing Cross allocated to the Crown in consequence of its claimed foreshore rights, metropolitan members demanded that it be left as public gardens. The chancellor of the Exchequer claimed that that was to confiscate national property, because it took away 'all possibility of making any use of it'. Gladstone pointed out that 'in former times' the Commons had voted money for metropolitan improvements, but that it had also levied sums in taxation from the metropolis. The last of these, the hackney-cab duty, had been given up the year before. He did not intend to be any party to re-opening the system of 'making virtual grants to the metropolis from the purse of the nation'.[3] Although defeated on this particular occasion, governments throughout the rest of the century maintained this principle, as the debate on the Post Office Sites bill of 1889, already referred to, makes explicit.[4]

There were of course other options for securing metropolitan improvements that were less susceptible to parliamentary pressures. Limited companies from time to time proposed building offices that government might hire, but never succeeded in raising the necessary funds. Another means was private benefaction – which provided a home for the National Portrait Gallery in 1889 when the government refused to finance it (as we have seen in ch. 3), and shortly afterwards supplied a National Gallery of British Art, lengthy negotiations with Henry Tate being successfully concluded (as seen in ch. 6) through Lewis Harcourt, who as First Commissioner exploited this means, thereby securing, for example, the Duveen extension to the Tate Gallery.

152. Government Offices: Col. Andrew Clarke, R.E., when director of works at the Admiralty, proposed a vast range of public offices on an economical plan, with six floors plus basement and attics instead of the conventional three floors of the 1860s.

Londoners may be regarded as one class of interested parties obliged to contribute to desirable public improvements. Users of certain buildings constitute a second class. In the years of discussion that preceded the building of the New Law Courts the view was consistently expressed that those who used the courts should contribute to their cost. The existence of funds under the control of the courts, and above all the Court of Chancery [Pl. 153], was an irresistible attraction. Chancery was proverbial for the slowness of its procedures.[5] Estates that had 'fallen into Chancery' tended to stay there for a long time. Eventually they might be eaten up by lawyers' fees, but meanwhile they produced an income; and ultimately there might be no one entitled to claim that income. A large fund had accumulated by 1850, the income from which went towards paying the expenses of the court. There was also a suitors' fee fund. The government was anxious to cover as much as possible of the cost of new courts out of these funds. Unfortunately the common-law courts were not as richly endowed. There was considerable resentment among Chancery lawyers that their resources should be raided for the benefit of their common-law brethren. Thus the former lord chancellor Lord St Leonards[6] expressed his disgust at the way things fell out: he had laboured in vain to prevent the misappropriation of the suitors' fund in the erection of Common Law courts, and that battle lost, took no interest in the Law Courts question.[7]

The Coleridge Commission that examined the problem of concentrating the courts of law and equity[8] had been composed of five lawyers and Sir George Cornewall Lewis, late chancellor of the Exchequer. They examined the previously-bruited idea of using court funds, and concluded it was legitimate to use them for common-law purposes as well as Equity. A Fund, A, had been formed by legislation for the surplus funds of Chancery; the interest from it was appropriated to Fund B. On several previous occasions large sums arising from the surplus income had been used for specific purposes, and also to cover payments of staff or pensions. In 1852 the surplus income was ordered to be carried to the Suitors' Fee Fund, C, established by the 1834 Chancery Regulation Act; the surplus from which went to form Fund D. The commissioners (Page Wood[9] dissenting) proposed that Funds B (£1,291,629) and D (£201,028), together with the Common Law courts surplus fee fund E (£88,254), should be applied to the concentration of the courts. Suitors would benefit more from such concentration than they would from abolition of the small fees then being charged.[10]

As chancellor of the Exchequer, Gladstone looked into these proposals, and drew a very different picture from the same data.[11] He warned the cabinet that there was likely to be a deficiency of over a million pounds. In a typically ambivalent memorandum, he advised his colleagues that it 'would not be desirable to withhold from the Profession and the Suitors the benefit of the proposed measure'; yet 'on the other hand, adverting to the charges now existing under the head of Law and Justice, it is very doubtful whether we should be justified in submitting to Parliament proposals virtually involving an estimated expenditure of a million with a view to the concentration of the Law Courts'. His conclusion was that savings expected from a reform of Chancery funds then under consideration should be applied in the first instance 'in reimbursement of the public charge incurred' in funding the courts, and if these savings were 'manifestly inadequate' a charge might be imposed on suitors.[12]

The Coleridge Commissioners had stated that: 'The providing suitable courts and offices for the due and convenient administration of justice is an object of supreme national importance . . . it is, in fact, one of the primary and paramount duties of the State, and that even if its fulfilment involved even a large and permanent

153.   Court of Chancery, Westminster; John Soane, 1822–5. 'The law's delays' were proverbial, and the Court of Chancery the most notorious focus of delay. Reformers sought a unified legal system properly equipped in terms of 'plant'. Many thought that litigants should contribute directly to the cost of new buildings.

addition to the public burdens, the State could not with propriety shrink from the obligation.'[13] This was a view which Gladstone evidently did not share: he argued that the state should merely provide loan finance.

Gladstone's revised statement of facts was set forth in a Treasury minute 16 July 1861, i.e. while the necessary money bill was before the House: the capital value of the funds had been over-estimated by about £100,000. The interest on Funds B and D, nearly £45,000, was applicable to officials' salaries and pensions, and general court charges; in 1858–9 the surplus was only about £3000, so if the capital were used, a large annual deficiency would have to be provided for (though gradually decreasing as former officials died). Against reduced rents for old buildings must be set maintenance charges for the new. Fund E's income was payable to the Exchequer under an act of 1853.[14] Although the Commons still resolved in favour of meeting any loss of court income out of the Consolidated Fund (i.e. taxation), the money bill was given up, allegedly because of the approaching end of the session. The Law Society, however, blamed the Treasury, which had long had the figures, but only after the commission had reported did it issue a minute which, if well-founded, 'stultifies the report by a Royal Commission, and utterly defeats a Government measure professing to be founded thereon'. The Treasury figures themselves were conjectural, founded partly on the current value of stock that well might rise.[15]

Early in the following session, Gladstone told the lord chancellor that he was 'perfectly satisfied' if his plan remained on the basis of the previous year's bill, 'provided only that the House of Commons by its Committee on the Bill . . . be moved by the Government to form its own judgment on the question of the probable cost as well as on the rest of the plan'. Given the uncertainty of any committee's reaction, this was a major proviso, despite his assurance that he would 'do all that depends on me to expedite the proceedings'.[16] When a bill was introduced in June, providing for the sale of stock up to £1,500,000 from Funds B and D to replace moneys voted by parliament for new courts, the Chancery and Lincoln's Inn interest (which wished to retain its remunerative Chancery courts) attacked the measure furiously, arguing along Gladstonian lines that the funds were not free and disposable, the money was not really there, and the estimates were illusory. At a time when expenditure on public works was looming alarmingly – museums, galleries, public offices – such arguments told powerfully: the second reading was defeated by two votes.[17]

'There are such difficulties in the way of a complete concentration of Courts of Justice', reported the First Commissioner in October 1862, 'that nothing further will be done about it at present.'[18] Law reformers criticised the failure to act in 1863 or even in 1864.[19] Sir Roundell Palmer, the attorney-general, remarking that it was effectively too late in the session to carry a bill, thought it useful to explain to the Commons the plan 'upon which the Government had at last determined'. They were very anxious that the pecuniary arrangements should be satisfactory, and had therefore had the estimates checked. Only part of the Chancery funds would be taken, the retained funds meeting officials' salaries, and the difference being made up by the value of sites and buildings freed, and a small charge on clients of non-Chancery courts.[20]

In fact, only a few days earlier a Treasury minute had embodied a cabinet decision on a scheme proposed by the lord chancellor and the First Commissioner: Chancery would provide a million only from its surplus unappropriated funds, the other courts providing a share by means of a stamp duty levied on proceedings. The Treasury would control expenditure, approving plans and estimates. Payments would be made out of moneys voted by parliament, to be repaid from the courts and a contribution from the Consolidated Fund to the extent of property currently occupied by the courts and offices and of the estimated relief by the cessation of rents.[21] It was very much the pattern sketched by Gladstone in 1861. 'Law and Finance', he now declared, 'are two beautiful damsels. How charming to see them hand in hand.'[22]

If the funding of a public building were to be met from the Consolidated Fund by means of annual Votes in the conventional manner, it would be exposed to as many perils as Odysseus in his return home from Troy. The parliamentary process was inherently slow. Once a building had been determined upon and an architect appointed, delay might be caused by further discussions between the Works and the architect and the department involved, either to secure a design likely to be more acceptable to the Commons or to meet departmental criticisms (which might of course occur under any regime). When the architect produced his estimate, it would be considered by the Office of Works, and perhaps cut down before transmission to the Treasury, where it would be further considered and again, perhaps, cut down, before being submitted to Parliament in June or July. In the six months or more this process would have taken, prices might have risen, sometimes (notably as with iron) swiftly and sharply. By the time the work was put to tender, conditions in the trade might be, as Street found, considerably different from those prevailing when the architect made his calculations. Whether the Treasury would allow an increase was a moot point; but parliamentary critics were unsympathetic to such explanations for increased costs, laid before them the following year. The Treasury might indeed decide that no funds could be allocated for that year, and postpone consideration for twelve months – an immediate saving of a large capital sum for any hard-pressed chancellor. In March 1879 the junior Treasury minister, Sir Henry Selwin-Ibbetson, wrote: 'The depression of trade at home and complications abroad and in the colonies have so seriously affected the national revenue, and the charges which have to be imposed upon it, that My Lords feel it incumbent upon them to restrain the public expenditure within the narrowest possible limits.'[23] Again, in 1889, when demands for increased defence spending were very strong, a minister stated that 'it is useless to put a scheme before the Treasury which is not one which is immediately and imperatively required. I quote the words "immediately"

and "imperatively" from a Circular from the Treasury; and this is a rule strictly laid down by the Department.'[24] And both these were Conservative ministries, sometimes thought laxer financially than Liberal governments.

Once the estimate was before the Commons, delays in voting funds might be such that most if not all of a building season might be lost, so that of £20,000 voted for works in a given year, only £3000 might be spent. Tenders could be rendered unrealistic. Before 1866 moneys voted for a particular service might be retained, so that annual Votes often bear no relationship to the sums expended on given works. The auditor-general then required that unexpended balances had to be surrendered annually and, if necessary, re-voted. Parliamentary critics demanded the reason why funds had not been spent. The Treasury was, in consequence, very reluctant to approve estimates unless there was every probability of using up the Vote, as the sum granted was termed, during the year. At the outset of a work, this attitude was often fully justified – for two years, the Vote for starting the Natural History Museum was untouched – but once a work was fairly under way, Treasury paring of estimates was itself a cause of delay.

Delays, temporary sojourn in some bewitched isle, were the least of the dangers of the annual round. Scylla or Charybdis, radicals or aesthetes, might wreak destruction, particularly in the 1850s or 60s.[25] As we have already seen, government plans for new public offices foundered, those for a new National Gallery were set at nought, the proposal to buy the 1862 Exhibition building negated, and as late as 1869 the official recommendation of an Embankment site for the New Law Courts rejected. The history of the Admiralty and War Office project of the 1880s provides a notable example of the perils inherent in this system. Shaw Lefevre, determined to build a new Admiralty and War Office, carried his proposals successfully through cabinet and Parliament in 1882, held his competition in 1883–4 [Pl. 154, 184–6], and even obtained a grant of funds in 1885 for beginning the foundations, a Vote that he reasonably regarded as parliamentary acceptance of the design by Leeming Bros. The project then ran into a series of political storms: unexpected ministerial defections brought down Gladstone's second ministry over the budget in June 1885; a minority Conservative administration followed, their candidates thrashed by the newly-enfranchised agricultural workers in the ensuing general election; Gladstone returned to power intent on an Irish Home Rule bill which split his party.

The design by Leeming Brothers [Pl. 186] had been much criticised in the press,[26] and the Conservative leader W.H. Smith (a former Admiralty and War minister), who had never liked Lefevre's scheme despite having been a judge of the competition, was, as we have seen, keen to exploit any dissatisfaction. Henry Broadhurst (1840–1911),[27] the ex-mason MP, had charged him with 'obstruction' of the necessary Supply Vote in 1885.[28] The following year, a few days before the Home Rule bill was introduced, Smith asked whether the government would consent to a select committee to 'reconsider the whole question of the provision for a new Admiralty and War Office'. The chancellor, Harcourt (who, according to Lefevre, had put Smith up to it),[29] expressed his support for the idea of retaining the existing Admiralty and meeting the department's needs at less cost.[30] But the Home Rule bill absorbed the attention of legislators between its introduction on 13 April and its rejection on 8 June, a second general election in June made the Conservatives the largest party, and Lord Salisbury became premier for the second time, governing with Liberal Unionist support.

Consequently it was not until 4 March 1887 that a renewed committee[31] on the defence ministries project was nominated.[32] In April and May it examined witnesses from the Office of Works; the

154.   New War Office and Admiralty Competition, 1884: design for principal Admiralty stair, Aston Webb & Ingress Bell. After completion of the Home and Colonial Offices in 1874, attention was focused on the plight of the War Office and lack of room at the Admiralty. The entry of Webb & Bell in a two-tier competition was the most widely admired, but thought to be too palatial.

RIBA (critical of the planning of the site); the Admiralty director of Works, with a proposal for a plain extension 'running round two sides of the garden' to cost only £120,000; an architect MP in favour of economy; and the architect himself, ready with ideas for meeting the committee's wishes. Lefevre gave lengthy evidence in support of his own project[33] and called in two experienced supporters, Hugh Childers,[34] who had presided over both War Office and Admiralty, as well as the Exchequer, and Sir Andrew Clarke,[35] former Admiralty director of Works and himself author of a plan, mentioned above, for concentrating the government offices. But the dominant witness was W.H. Smith himself, now first lord of the Treasury, whose 'strong opinion' it was that the Old Admiralty should be retained and additional buildings be constructed alongside. Postponement of a War Office would ensure that the Admiralty would get its accommodation 'very much sooner', saving 'a great many years' and leaving 'a very large surplus' over Lefevre's scheme, to provide for a new War Office.[36]

The committee ignored Childers's weighty plea to 'view with suspicion any partial stopgap plan', and his belief that even the then Commons would listen to 'a great and complete and well-considered plan, to be spread over a large number of years'; far more economical than 'doing these things bit by bit'.[37] Smith's great personal weight and cool demeanour, coupled with Sir William Harcourt's effective interrogations as a member of the committee, ensured victory for the economical party and short-term views.

In order to take 'the sense of the House' on the committee's report and clear the way for fresh proposals, the First Commissioner insisted on a supplementary Vote (a feature normally disliked by the Treasury as disturbing the original Supply calculations) for paying Leemings for their discarded plans.[38] The House duly obliged, and planning went ahead on the basis of the committee's proposal [Pl. 155], the consequences of which we consider

155.   Design for extending the old Admiralty building, Leeming Bros, 1887. A Commons' committee engineered by the economy-minded Conservative and Liberal leaders. W.H. Smith and Sir William Harcourt, overthrew the design for a combined new Admiralty and War Office, replacing it with a two-block Admiralty extension. It took much longer to build than had been expected, and proved inadequate, so that a third block was built, closing the courtyard.

elsewhere.[39] But we may note here that progress did not prove rapid. 'Owing to the difficulties which have arisen in finally settling the plans', reported the Works in January 1889, 'it will be impossible to expend any of the vote [for the extension] for the current year.'[40] But the contract for foundations would be made shortly, and a figure of £30,000 was submitted for 1889–90, only to be cut by the Treasury to a mere £5000. The ultimate cost of the extension blocks designed by Leemings round three sides of the Admiralty garden, with alterations to the old building, amounted to over £400,000, and building them took 18 years.[41]

Another difficulty in seeking Supply was MPs' hankering for more details than ministers were able to supply. Thus when asked for funds for buying a site, members might demand plans, worked-up plans, that is (which there was little point in preparing until the site was available), or architects' estimates for the projected buildings, which might not be commenced for another two sessions, and would therefore have been highly unreliable even if the detailed plans could have been made ready in time. Young David Lloyd George complained in 1896 during the discussion on the resolution to authorise the money clauses in the bill for the purchase of the remainder of the Great George Street site that 'the Government ought to state what they intended to do with the money they were now asking for. . . . If the site itself was going to cost £450,000, he should like to know how much the buildings that were going to be erected upon it would cost.' He opposed the resolution, 'because it was perfectly clear that the Government not only did not know what money they intended to spend upon the site, but did not want the Committee to know either'.[42] On the second reading of the 1897 bill for acquiring the Carrington House site for the new War Office, Mr Lough 'desired to have further information about the scheme, and particularly as to what offices were to be built upon the site, what was to be the total cost, and whether it was intended to provide for the Board of Trade. . . . The House ought to know what was the whole programme of the Government in this matter.'[43]

Underlying the Commons' suspicion of government proposals for public works was, as noted above, members' experience of the building of Charles Barry's New Palace at Westminster, the royal palace which provided their own House [Pl. 145]. A cautious select committee had in 1836 insisted on the preparation of working drawings and estimates; and the government surveyors employed seven assistants on calculating the costs. In 1837, architect and government agreed on a figure of £707,104 (less £14,000 receipts from sales of old materials). This was the approved estimate, impressed on members' recollection, but it omitted the architect's fee (originally fixed at £25,000), and costs of land purchases (£70,000), ventilating and warming, and fittings and furnishings, as well as the necessary works of embankment in the Thames, which in all were calculated initially at about £150,000 more.[44] The failure to put these figures before the House was a fundamental blunder, probably due to sheer carelessness on the part of the Works, cut down by Whig economies to a point of doubtful efficiency,[45] and marginalised in the building process by the new 'market place' principle.[46]

This error was compounded by three major factors: demands over many years by the Lords as well as the Commons for improvements in their accommodation, the full financial consequences of which were not explored; the appointment by government of an independent (and quirky, pugnacious and inadequately-experienced) expert to arrange the heating and ventilation of the palace; and the continuation of the works beyond the first lump-sum contract (limited to the river front) by the original contractor on a schedule of prices.[47] By August 1848 Barry's estimate, including site costs, had risen to over £2,000,000.[48] A serious rift between

156. Charles Barry, R.A. (1795–1860), kt 1852, by John Linnell. As architect of the Houses of Parliament, the largest permanent building of its age, Barry was continually under pressure to hasten its completion and keep down its costs – but Parliament's own interventions altered the plans and increased the cost.

architect and ventilator led to prolonged building delays. This in turn exposed the work to rising prices in the 1850s. Confusion was further confounded by the long-running dispute between Barry and the government over his remuneration already referred to, which delayed the measuring necessitated by the contracts 'being let on a schedule of prices'.[49] A yet further complication was introduced by the appointment of a royal commission to organise the decoration of the palace with works of art, including sculptures, frescoes and stained-glass windows often integral to the design – a commission of which Barry was not a member, and for the expenses of which he was not accountable.[50] By 1850, the estimated cost had more than doubled; by mid-1854 it had trebled – though that included between £300,000 and £400,000 for additional works that were never commissioned, such as raising the roof of Westminster Hall and building a range of offices around New Palace Yard [Pl. 157].[51] In 1854–7 alone, the Commons voted some £245,000 for the palace; the estimate for 1857/8 was £68,000 (making an excess of £36,000 over the total estimated in 1854), and Barry warned that increased prices added yet another £50,000 to that figure. Many MPs were angered by the ever-mounting costs;[52] irritated by the failure to complete the palace rapidly;[53] squeezed by overcrowding;[54] infuriated by not being able to hear;[55] chilled or overheated by the unsatisfactory system of ventilation, heating and gas-lighting;[56] and alienated by the Gothic character of the palace.[57] All was blamed on Barry, who was said to exceed 'in his ingenuity in devising extra charges, every other member of his

157.   Design for completing the New Palace at Westminster, C. Barry. Aware of the need for new law courts, Barry anticipated the time when the west flank of Westminster Hall would be exposed. He was keen to conceal its difference from the Houses of Parliament by enclosing it and New Palace Yard with a block of offices and a ceremonial gateway to the House of Commons. The cost of the essential parts of the original design dissuaded governments from embarking on this extension, though in recent years the facilities it would have offered have had to be provided north of Bridge Street.

profession'.[58] Even the redoubtable Sir Benjamin Hall was unable to bring him to book.[59]

Death itself failed to end the saga: Edward Barry [Pl. 158] assumed his father's mantle in 1860, and continued, with elaboration, the work of decorating the interior, at annual sums approximating to those voted for major new works.[60] Crowded debates on the 1866 and 1867 Reform Bills, and an increase in the practice of questioning ministers, resulted in a select committee in 1868–9 proposing building a larger House in an adjoining courtyard [Pl. 159].[61] Henry Layard, as First Commissioner, enthusiastically promoted young Barry's scheme for enriching the gloomy stonework, particularly of the dark Central Hall and the Royal Staircase, with mosaic, lately revived with Layard's encouragement by Salviati of Venice.[62] A watchful retrencher promptly moved a reduction in the Office Vote.[63] Defeated in committee, his friends returned at report stage to attack more vigorously this example 'of the wasteful expenditure which was going on . . . in every Department of Government' – Gladstone's first government! [Pl. 160] Layard was forced himself to propose a reduction in the Vote (omitting the mosaic work), and only avoided defeat through a weighty intervention by the prime minister (who had been prepared to abandon the Vote altogether) setting up a principle by which continuation works (previously approved by the Commons) might be undertaken in anticipation of a Vote, but new ones must not be.[64] Layard's resignation in October 1869 was largely a consequence of

158.   Edward Middleton Barry (1830–80), younger son of Sir Charles Barry, succeeded him as architect at the Houses of Parliament in 1860, but was unceremoniously dismissed by First Commissioner Ayrton in 1870 as an unnecessary source of expense. He was also invited to compete in the National Gallery and New Law Courts Competitions of 1866–7, gaining a first place in both; but was commissioned only to enlarge the Gallery.

159. Proposal for building a larger House of Commons, E.M. Barry, 1868. Crowded debates on the 1866–7 Reform Bills led to demands for a larger House of Commons. E.M. Barry proposed building in the adjoining courtyard, converting the existing chamber into a lobby (top right). Top left: the new House; below left, the new division lobby; below right: the new reading room. (Gladstone's influence secured the rejection of the idea altogether.)

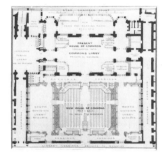

160. Gladstone's Cabinet in session at Downing Street, 1869. Gladstone himself was interested in architectural questions, and powerfully influenced decisions on public works as chancellor of the Exchequer 1859–66 and as prime minister 1868–74, 1880–5, 1886, and 1892–4. Robert Lowe (1811–92), at the Exchequer 1868–73, and Hugh Childers (1827–96), at the Admiralty 1868–71, War Office 1880–2, and Exchequer 1882–5, also acted in public works' matters.

A CABINET COUNCIL IN DOWNING STREET

this incident and the subsequent unjustified attack on his integrity as a sometime shareholder in Salviati's concern.[65]

However, this determination to halt what must have seemed a never-ending expenditure on an unpopular building in which MPs were working, and hence experiencing all its defects, many of them incurable in the then state of the art (if indeed the diverse wishes of multifarious members as to ventilation could ever be satisfied), has itself to be seen against the background of a public-works programme greater than any in living memory: the Home and Colonial Offices, the Natural History Museum, the New Law Courts, a new National Gallery, a new War Office and an additional General Post Office building being only major items under construction or planning or in immediate expectation – quite apart from numerous provincial post offices and county courts. The reactions of government to this unparalleled burden are examined below.

When the Office of Works in the mid-1890s embarked on another programme of comparable dimensions, it had before it the example of the fate of what may be called the 'Manners agenda' just referred to. First Commissioner Akers-Douglas's arrangements for financing his vast programme are not its least interesting feature. Experience had shown the difficulties of financing public works by annual Votes of the House of Commons. There were at least two major hurdles to surmount: the Treasury's assessment of what could be put forward, which was the most difficult to jump; and the Commons' appraisal, the more troublesome, as, while the money was seldom refused, much adverse criticism might be expected, stimulating public hostility and increasing ministers' reluctance to embark on public works: the hurdler might get over, but was hardly in a condition to continue the race.

As early as 1850 the *Builder* had discussed the problem of defraying the cost of public works by annual parliamentary Votes, and looked to the creation of a special fund. 'Watchman' recalled that with regard to Buckingham Palace and the National Gallery 'all elevation of sentiment and feeling suitable to the occasion was lost in the consideration of reducing the sum voted to the lowest possible amount, in order to meet the views of the economists and political partizans of the day'. Now a new era had dawned, of which the palace of the legislature was but the first fruit. Such buildings were not merely for the present generation, so why should posterity not contribute, by creating a fund of which the interest and sinking fund should be paid annually?[66] But in a subsequent leading article Godwin was less sanguine: 'No sooner is it proposed to rear an edifice for the accommodation of the public, the convenience of the state, or the dignity and comfort of the sovereign, than a thousand querulous pens are instantly called into requisition to thwart and hinder its accomplishment. . . . First comes the wrangling over the estimates; which generally ends . . . in their being cut down to such an extent as to preclude all adequate grandeur of thought and conception relative to the purpose intended.' It became not a matter of how much was necessary but how much the minister could contrive to persuade the majority to vote. If, as with the Houses of Parliament, a generally approved design was obtained, then there was quarrelling over the necessary adjuncts. A bad year for the national finances brought a cry for curtailment of expenses; 'some of the chief characteristics and features of the original design are altogether omitted, or so altered, as to destroy the general effect of the whole. By and by, after years of delay, the costly structure is at length finished; but the circumstances which led to its defect or deformity are either unknown or wholly forgotten; and the thoughtless or ignorant portion of the public, seeing only the result, abuse the architect, and growl and grumble over their bad buildings, as well they may.' So other nations, less wealthy and less free, 'contrive immeasurably to surpass us'.[67]

Palmerston, faced with a similar problem of securing funding for his fortifications programme in 1860, had contrived a solution. The need appeared urgent; the cost enormous. 'To spread their Completion over 20 or 30 years would be Folly.' To raise the whole sum by additional taxation over three or four years was, though doubtless the method 'best in Principle and the cheapest', probably electoral suicide, and open to the risk 'that after the First year the Desire for financial Relief might prevail over a provident sense of Danger, and the annual Grants would dwindle down to their present insufficiency'. The alternative was to raise 'a Loan for the whole amount payable in Three or Four annual Instalments, and repayable in annual Instalments with Interest in Twenty or Thirty Years' – 'financially as light or nearly so, as the present system', while gaining the advantage of early completion.[68] To the prime minister's proposals, Gladstone at the Exchequer put up a determined resistance.[69] In consequence the sum sought was much reduced, but the principle of raising it by borrowing in the form of terminable annuities was accepted.[70] However, it was seen as strictly limited to defence purposes. As prime minister himself, Gladstone warned his chancellor, 'I could not accede to the doctrine that we are likely to be borrowers in the market, rather than buyers of stock: more especially if you base it in any degree upon the supposition that democracy is to cause us to borrow money in time of peace for the purpose of civil government. *That* I hope at any rate will not happen in the residue of my time.'[71]

Nonetheless, it was this Palmerstonian idea that was resurrected in the 1880s. In the course of debate on the Vote to cover preliminary expenses on the new Admiralty and War Office, 9 April 1885, General Sir George Balfour suggested that the building should be financed by means of annuities, 'and thus save the necessity of applying to Parliament for annual votes'; the work might then be completed in three or four years, rather than the ten that it might take on the footing of annual parliamentary Votes. However, Hibbert, as Financial Secretary of the Treasury, set his face against so un-Gladstonian a proceeding: he 'did not think they had quite come to the position of undertaking the erection of their public buildings by means of Annuity; indeed, he thought it was better to postpone their erection than to adopt such a principle'.[72] The wisdom of General Balfour's suggestion was shown when the subsequent change of mind of the Commons resulted in the abandonment of the large scheme for united defence ministries, and the substitution merely of additions to the Old Admiralty.

When the question of a new War Office came forward again in the early 1890s, official calculations suggested that about £750,000 would be needed, of which £350,000 would be required almost at once to complete the purchase of the proposed Great George Street site, while the building would take four annual instalments of say £100,000. Sir Edward Hamilton of the Treasury advised the chancellor that the money might be borrowed from the National Debt Commissioners, to be repaid over 30 years by three per cent annuities charged on the Office of Works vote. 'As a whole', Hamilton remarked, 'I consider the scheme to be sound financially. It is legitimate to borrow for works of a really permanent nature: and, so long as there is kept up a large Sinking Fund which is pegging away at the discharge of perpetual debt, it is more than legitimate to borrow for permanent works by means of raising terminable debt.'[73] Sir William Harcourt, the Liberal chancellor, was 'very well satisfied' with the financial aspect presented in Hamilton's 'clear and able minute'.[74]

Although the change of ministry shortly afterwards delayed proceedings, the loan principle was maintained for the land purchases,[75] as for the preceding Naval Works Loans Act of 1895. The Treasury was empowered to borrow £450,000, and repay it by terminable annuities (i.e. payable for a fixed term, usually 30 years) charged on the annual departmental Vote.[76] Bolstered by a flourishing revenue, the Conservative ministry adopted the principle for a series of measures. The Naval Works Loans Act of 1896, however, was the first to annex the surplus revenue of the year, which would otherwise have gone to the reduction of the national debt.[77] The act to acquire the interests in the Carrington House site in Whitehall for the War Office for half a million followed the earlier pattern;[78] but the keystone of this public buildings legislation, the Public Buildings Expenses Act, 1898, introduced a revolutionary feature.[79] Instead of the funds (here derived, as for the 1896 Naval Works Act, from the surplus revenues of the year, i.e. 1897/8) being paid into the Exchequer, the sums not immediately required were to be invested in interest-bearing government stock ('Consols'), and the interest applied to the purposes of the act.

'The advantage of proceeding by Bill to take a lump sum out of the Consolidated Fund is apparent', Akers-Douglas told the Commons in proposing the 1898 bill.

> It is obvious in all matters connected with building that it is unwise and uneconomical to proceed haphazard. A recognised scheme must be settled, and the work steadily proceeded with. This course is exceedingly difficult under the system of annual Estimates. Money available one year may not be forthcoming the next. A prolonged frost or bad weather may stop the works, and the money voted for the year is not nearly all spent, the balance has to be returned to the Exchequer, and the money has to be re-voted in a following Session. Our method also settles definitely the adoption of the scheme, and removes them from risks of changes of policy which have been so fatal in the past.

He therefore asked for a total of £2,550,000 for the War Office (£475,000), Parliament Street Offices (£700,000), South Kensington Museum (£800,000), Admiralty extension (£275,000), and Post Office (£300,000 for acquiring Queen Victoria Street P.O. Savings bank for GPO use, and building a new P.O.S.B. in West Kensington), thus meeting 'all the pressing needs of the service'.[80]

The proposal to invest the surplus revenue met with some criticism as 'an entirely new method of finance', and one 'which mystifies the public and makes the expenditure of next year appear very different from what it really is'.[81] Nor did the principle itself go unchallenged. A government supporter, L.H. Courtney,[82] sometime professor of Political Economy at University College London, pointed out that the appropriation of the surplus revenue (which otherwise would have gone to reducing debt) meant 'an increase in the National Debt, and practically we are making this expenditure by the outlay of capital for the repayment of which there is no provision whatever'. Provision should be made for raising an equivalent sum in a limited period. From the Opposition benches, T.C.T. Warner[83] similarly remarked: 'I do not like the system of payment out of surplus, because it is a wrong system. An amount of money ought to be paid year by year as it is expended. The sums ought to go into a yearly account and not be confused in this way by paying expenditure out of capital.'[84]

Unfortunately, this operation did not work out profitably. Consols were standing at a peak in 1898, and the government bought at an average price of $109^1/_2$, but thanks to the shocks of the South African War they fell thereafter.[85] The sum invested, £2,360,000, depreciated by £114,761 as the investment was progressively realised. An act of 1903 granted a further £1,790,000 for certain public works, but in fact only £1,675,000 were available, because of this deficit.[86] 'It is a serious matter to have to go to Parliament this year for any extension of capital account involving further borrowing', remarked a Treasury official mindful of the burden of war costs; 'but it seems to be "Hobson's choice"'. The capital sum included an additional £25,000 to cover an excess over estimate of some 12 per cent incurred in buying freeholds north of Great George Street.[87] Further difficulty arose when the funds of the National Debt commissioners proved insufficient to take up the terminable annuities issued under the 1903 act, and the Treasury had to be allowed to raise the moneys by sale of Exchequer bonds, a measure strongly attacked by the Liberals as setting an undesirable precedent and adding to the floating debt at a high rate of interest.[88]

The same choice between loans and annual Votes faced the Liberals in 1908, for completing the Great George Street offices, and again in 1911, for acquiring Whitehall Gardens for the Board of Trade [Pl. 141]. However, views of good financial practice had shifted somewhat in ten years. Austen Chamberlain as Conservative chancellor had concurred in parliamentary criticism of borrowing to fund naval and military works, and declared that 'this procedure should be reserved for exceptional occasions'; though he also put the case for loans for 'great capital expenditure . . . upon works of a permanent character':

> The system of charging upon the Estimates whatever sum was considered necessary often resulted in uneconomical administration. When a great work . . . of this kind was begun the quicker it was brought to completion the more economical it was as there were likely to be fewer alterations, the cost would be smaller, and the country would remain out of the enjoyment of the result of the expenditure for a shorter period. When the capital expenditure necessary for large works was charged upon the annual Votes it not infrequently happened that the sum provided was not the amount that could be economically and wisely spent in the year but the maximum amount which the necessities of the Chancellor of the Exchequer allowed him to allot for the purpose.[89]

His Liberal successor, Asquith, alarmed by an eleven-fold increase in such capital liabilities since 1896, while admitting they were represented by 'specific and tangible assets' and carried their own sinking funds, termed the policy 'a most unhappy chapter in the history of our national finance', which for defence works he would bring to an end as soon as possible. The system tended, as critics had claimed, to confuse the distinction between capital and revenue charges; encouraged 'crude, precipitate, and wasteful experiments' in the spending departments; and withdrew 'large items of annual expenditure from any effective Parliamentary supervision'. Asquith was cautious enough to admit that legitimate cases of temporary borrowing for capital works must arise occasionally.[90] Thus the government might fairly claim that their pledge did not extend to borrowing for building public offices (such borrowing had hardly been mentioned in debates). But that could open the door to resuming borrowing for 'really durable Naval and Military works'. Expenditure, unless very exceptional in character and amount, should be borne on annual Votes. Nevertheless Lewis Harcourt as First Commissioner informed the Treasury Secretary that 'The Chancellor of the Exchequer [Asquith] assures me that he had never intended that the New Block of Public Offices in Westminster, when erected, should be paid for out of annual votes, as he considers this to be a fit subject for a loan, as in the case of the block just completed.' The 1908 Finance Act, therefore, provided £600,000 for the completion of the Great George Street block out of the realised surplus of the year 1907/8, the 'Old Sinking Fund'.[91] The total sum provided for by the Public Buildings (Expenses) Act of 1908, £1,790,000, covered the War Office, the Admiralty, and the British and South Kensington Museums as well, Treasury borrowings being repaid by 30-year terminable annuities.[92]

Nevertheless, the issue of loan *v*. Vote remained a controversial one. The government had already decided to fund a new Stationery Office and an extension to the Patent Office by annual Votes, and to avoid an expected excess on the Expenses Acts (i.e. loans) by charging 'improvements of existing buildings at South Kensington' to Votes so far as necessary; Treasury officials had assumed (as had Works officials) that the new public offices would be paid for likewise.[93] When it came to buying further property to provide an adequate site for the Board of Trade, a Treasury official speculated that, applying Asquith's criterion, there might be something to be said for borrowing, if the proposals for new offices necessitated a very large expenditure in a very short period and would satisfy official demand for the next fifty years; 'But within the present and prospective growth of Government activity, it is impossible to regard a demand for £600,000 spread over six or seven years as anything more than a normal incident.'[94] Nor were loans necessarily an easy solution: 'When expenditure is chargeable to Votes', one official noted in 1908, 'the Treasury can sanction it to any extent. But when it has to be provided for by loan, we must cut our coat according to our cloth.' The savings banks, invented by Gladstone, offered a pool for government borrowing, but if the rate of interest were to be cut, nobody could foresee the result. Capital expenditure on the telephone system (loan-funded) was likely to increase, although the defence works loan expenditure was coming to an end; and all surpluses for some years to come were likely to be committed to financing Irish land purchases for creating peasant proprietorship.[95]

By 1911, with a new Board of Trade site under discussion, and a new First Commissioner in the Lords, the likelihood of another Works loan had become even more doubtful. A Treasury man offered five choices as to discharging the cost of sites:

1. Paying cash down: 'This course is unnecessarily heroic & may be dismissed.'

2. Creating terminable annuities for the freehold on a $3\frac{1}{2}$ per cent basis. Over a 35-year period, it would mean 5 per cent interest and sinking fund, working out at £25,000 p.a.; or over 50 years, $4\frac{1}{4}$ per cent, or £21,250 p.a. 'This is what I recommend. It is much better to buy the freehold even if the annual payment (to ourselves [i.e., because it was Crown land]) is slightly higher for the moment.'

3. Leasing at £16,555 p.a. for 99 years. After that, the rent might be raised to about £40,000 p.a.

4. Leasing for 999 years at about £18,000 p.a.

5. Borrowing half a million at 3 per cent, and repaying by annuities of £23,250 over 35 years, or £19,430 over 50 years (the Conservative course in 1898), which required statutory powers, and 'would be from a Parliamentary point of view far the worst way of "spreading"'.

Leaseholds and building costs of £380,000 over five years would be an average annual burden of about £60,000 charged to Votes. If £330,000 were borrowed, the country would be saddled with a 35-year annuity of £15,350. 'I really think that a rich country like this need hardly depart from the procedure of good finance for the sake of this annual difference, and, if we did so, the nemesis, politically, would be certain. For . . . such borrowing is difficult to reconcile with the pronouncements of the present Government and the case is not rendered easier by the fact that the buildings are required to house an inflated bureaucracy.'[96]

His senior colleague, J.S. Bradbury,[97] commented that from the Exchequer point of view the present moment was most unfavourable for borrowing on terminable annuities. The funding of Irish land purchases was mopping up Savings Banks funds, and if the Treasury were forced to borrow in the open market it would have a disastrous effect on the Consols market. Building on a 999-year lease would be acceptable, when the ground rent would be charged to parliamentary Votes year by year; but the purchase of the freehold by means of a terminable annuity would be more provident; there could be no objection to charging the annuity on annual Votes like a ground rent, and it was free of the objections to actual borrowing since there would be no demand on capital resources.[98] It was accordingly settled that the bill should provide for acquiring the whole Whitehall Gardens site for the new Board of Trade by means of a terminable annuity on a $3\frac{1}{2}$ per cent basis.

As this would appear every year on the Office of Works' Vote, one was in a sense back to the 'annual round', at least in principle, though a legal obligation was created by the act. The fate of the war-delayed new public offices (for the specific 'Trade' designation was abandoned) in 1931 showed how liable public works still were to the winds of the national economy.[99] Akers-Douglas's loan-financed programme of 1897 with the agnate acts of 1903 and 1908 represent the most successful programme of government building since Sir William Chambers' Somerset House.

11
The Golden Age of Competition

'WE LIVE in an age which has elevated competition into almost a religion, and has applied it very extensively to public life', remarked Edward Barry.[1] Competition (in which a cost figure was rarely stipulated, or even an estimate required) was the usual means of selecting an architect for great public buildings: the usual sequence of events was decision to build, choice of site, competition leading to selection of architect, provision of finance, revision of prize plan. Parliamentary critics tended to demand full plans, or even tenders, before voting funds, ignoring the difficulties involved. It is true that the government usually got its money, but the Treasury itself was so sharp a watch-dog that the full flowering of an architect's fancy seldom got past it.

Earlier nineteenth-century public works had commonly been executed by architects employed or retained by the state. The concept of a permanent government architect (then designated surveyor-general of the King's Works), which had dominated the eighteenth century, was discredited by the inefficiency of James Wyatt's administration, revealed after his sudden death in 1813. Government then retained the services of three leading architects (Nash, Soane and Smirke) until that arrangement collapsed after the death of George IV with the exposure of Nash's deficiencies and the relentless pressure for the adoption of the rule of the market-place: competition.[2] Nevertheless, government's need for a constantly available architect led it to make the fullest use of such a permanent official on a succession of major buildings despite public opinion's preference for competition in public building,[3] until the pressure of that opinion became irresistible or ministers became more responsive to it as the political nation grew in numbers.

Popular as it was with the public, Parliament and much of the profession, competition had its drawbacks, as we shall see. One of the difficulties of the 'market place' option was that English architects lacked the academic training that would have enabled them to handle large public commissions with facility: 'harmony and space', argued Arthur Cates of the Crown Lands, were 'neglected for the picturesque and the graceful'.[4] Towards the close of the century government turned to nominating architects, after taking professional advice, as well as making more extensive use of salaried architects for an increasing range of routine operations, such as county courts and post offices. But in the face of renewed criticism of these methods, the early twentieth century saw a return to competition for major works.[5]

We have already examined the structure of the Office of Works, and its employment of men with an architectural training, though for long termed 'surveyors'. We have seen also the need for men capable of advising ministers on designs obtained in the market-place and watching over their execution. We have now to turn to the ways in which the market-place concept functioned.

The starting point is the competition announced in 1835 for designs for New Houses of Parliament.[6] This established a model for subsequent competitions. It was successful in that the building that emerged was a masterpiece. It was unsuccessful in that the building erected was not the one that received the award. Alterations suggested artistic plagiarism, a charge which posed the question of the function of competition: essentially whether to choose a design or a designer. The common view was the former; but in practice it was the latter. Thus Beresford Hope, working to secure the appointment of George Gilbert Scott [Pl. 161] for the New Government Offices in 1858, suggested to the architect William Burn, a judge in the preceding competition, that the object of a competition was 'rather to select the best man than actually to select the design which is literally to be carried out'.[7] But Gladstone as a judge in the New Law Courts competition of 1867 asserted: 'The duty of the Judges of Design was rather to select a plan than

161. George Gilbert Scott, R.A. (1811–78), kt 1872, an advocate of the Gothic Revival who built his career on success in competitions. Only placed third in the Foreign Office competition of 1857, Scott, an able string-puller, nevertheless obtained the commission in 1858, and abandoned his stylistic principles to retain it on a change of ministry in 1859.

a man.'[8] Such confusion of purpose spread chaos through the subsequent developments.

Competition was liked by the public because it seemed the fairest way of obtaining the best possible design: inviting the nation's – or the world's – talent to display its skill; it was also cheap for the client, since the designs were worked out at the competitors' expense. It was disliked by many professionals because of the cost[9] and the high rate of risk: most competitors would work in vain for weeks or months; and also because it was – generally – submitting their work to an unprofessional and hence (they argued) an undiscerning jury. 'Many a showy design selected in competition has turned out in execution a poor and commonplace affair', complained Edward Barry: the design of an experienced architect that would be satisfactory in execution would not recommend itself to 'the highly-wrought expectations' of the judges. He must therefore either stand aloof, or 'wound his self-respect' with a design framed to please the taste of the judges, whose decisions often 'command no respect'.[10] It is not surprising that a correspondent in the *Builder* commented that 'the prosperous architect disdains competition'. Even if he did not 'disdain' it, an architect with a reasonable practice might find difficulty in undertaking a competition entry: John Prichard (1818–86)[11] remarked of the South Kensington Museums competition, 1864, 'What with work in hand, and a limited staff, and the short time allowed by Government to do it in, this too was a matter not to be lightly undertaken.'[12]

The architectural profession, however, was overcrowded; 'he who is not fully occupied, and may have active clerks and pupils to keep at work, feels that the advertisement [of a competition] . . . applies to him . . . and that, if he combined with others to ignore it, a tribe of a lower grade – surveyors, builders, and architects' assistants, – would soon fill up any blank in the number of competitors'.[13] The Victorian producer had always to bear in mind the 'dishonourable' end of his craft; the equivalent of today's third world.

Many other professionals welcomed competition for its triumphal possibilities. It was a means by which the young architect might make an effective start in professional life, normally a slow undertaking.[14] 'If he have used his time well, and have acquired the power of placing his designs on paper in an attractive manner, he is not likely long to want success', thought Edward Barry.[15] Competitors in government competitions were keen to exhibit their designs – in 1836, those unsuccessful in the Houses of Parliament competition mounted their own exhibition – and subsequently official exhibitions were arranged.[16] With the development of a professional illustrated press from the 1840s, extensive advertisement was available even for those who did not carry off a prize.[17] The *Architect* asserted in 1883 that pressure for a competition for the new War Office came from the 'legion' of architects who hoped, if not to win the commission, 'at all events to rank as a highly meritorious architect at the command of the public'.[18] The charge of a country's public works was the height of many architects' ambition, and with competition the road thereto even senior men were induced to compete. But the qualities likely to bring success in competition often contrasted with those needed for 'the satisfactory solution of grave problems in such a manner as to be worthy of the lasting approbation of posterity. . . . The temptation to promise impossibilities, to hide difficulties, and to make things pleasant all round, proves too often too great for any but the most robust artistic virtue.'[19]

Yet others saw competition as an invigorating activity, stirring the intellect to meet the needs of the age. There was 'no means so potent to give new life and vigour to art as public competition', declared the prolific writer Samuel Huggins, president of the Liverpool Architectural Society.[20] The 1857 Government Offices Competition was hailed for its stimulative effects on both the profession and the public generally.[21]

Too often, though, the system was abused: it was used to obtain designs or ideas cheaply, which were then entrusted to some favourite or cut-price huckster; or there might be corruption in the judging. Under George Godwin's editorship the *Builder* highlighted the all-too-common abuses, encouraging the Institute of British Architects (which took up the question in 1838) first of all in urging promoters to draw up a realistic programme to which they would adhere.[22] In 1850 the Architectural Association, embracing a sector of the profession perhaps more in need of competition than the grandees of the Institute, sought to improve competition by promulgating rules that protected the competitor and enhanced the position of the professional as far as possible. Needless to say, the government did not adhere to these rules, though it gradually became more responsive to them. The crucial demand was for a professional jury, and this was also the most controversial. The A. A. had proposed professional assistance to guide a jury in its choice; in 1872, after the chaotic government competitions of the 1860s, the RIBA published 'General Rules for the Conduct of Architectural Competitions' (considered below), urging the use of professional judges; and in 1880, a memorial signed by nearly 1300 architects called for a boycott of any competition that did not employ a reputable professional adjudicator.[23]

As architecture became a more narrowly and precisely defined profession, so it became necessary for architects to assert their monopoly of the design process.[24] Just as the solicitors claimed that the law suitors had 'no possible advocates in the matter' of choosing the best site for the New Law Courts 'except the profession of the Law',[25] so the architects claimed that they alone could select the best designs for public buildings. Indeed, with the change of a single word in a Law Society pamphlet, it might well have been the RIBA asserting that 'It is utterly idle and vain in the general public to imagine that non-professional persons, however, intelligent, can form any accurate opinion on the [style] and arrangement of the courts and offices.'[26] Such views were shared by few who were not professionals, where the fear was, on the contrary, that professional rivalries ruled out professional judges. Thus the determination of the Houses of Parliament competition was entrusted wholly to gentlemen with an interest in the arts.[27]

By 1856 professional men had acquired a higher social status and, influenced perhaps by the preachings of the *Builder* and the Institute, Sir Benjamin Hall, in resisting the 'clamour for intelligent despotism in the award of architectural commissions',[28] assembled a mixed band representing both Houses of Parliament, the arts fine and applied and the learned societies to judge his international competition for New Government Offices: the Duke of Buccleuch and his architect William Burn; a connoisseur of painting, Sir William Stirling, MP, and a professional artist, David Roberts R.A., celebrated for his sketches of ruins; Lord Eversley (a former Speaker) and an engineer, I.K. Brunel, with an eminent historian 'who had paid much attention to architecture', the president of the Society of Antiquaries, Lord Stanhope (formerly Mahon) as chairman. The names had been approved by Prince Albert, but while the list evidently satisfied Parliament, it did not meet the approbation of the professional press or, it may be supposed, the profession.[29]

As early as 1836, C.R. Cockerell had proposed to a parliamentary committee that the jury be composed of architects and artists to judge the design, scientists to assess the technical services, and a majority of intending users of the proposed building.[30] Hall had been a member of that committee, and it seems likely that the suggestion influenced his selection, which nevertheless was widely criticised.[31] The *Building News* was scathing about the 'all but universal incompetence of non-professional persons to judge of designs'; and at first claimed that Burn was unknown professionally – later, when his eminence as a country-house architect had emerged, criticising his connexion with Buccleuch.[32] (It was, however, perhaps his role as Lord Derby's architect that led to his nomination.[33]) A foreign architect, writing in the *Builder,* attacked the professional judges as 'of the old school, not familiar with aesthetical progress in practical forms'.[34] The judges called for the aid of professional men to check that competitors had complied with the instructions – which was, in some degree, to concede the RIBA's case – but they were treated strictly as assessors to take no part in the judging. It proved easier to introduce such men to the judging process than to control them, and assessors Angell and Pownall made their own assessments which, though not admitted by the judges, were ultimately to affect the choice of executant architect.[35]

Cockerell's suggestions in 1836 may have been influenced by his knowledge of how things were managed in France, a newspaper topic in the aftermath of the Parliament Houses competition, and similar to Soane's widely-reported suggestion for a jury of artists (a term then used to include architects) 'to determine on the relative merits' by giving reasoned written opinions, in a context of public exhibition.[36] Several decades later, under the autocratic Second Empire, when public architecture was generally determined by official nomination, in 1861 a rare competition was held for a major building, the new Paris Opéra, which attracted 179 entrants. The winner was to execute the building; second and third prizes of 6000 and 4000 francs were offered (£240 and £160). As in England, designs were submitted under the anonymity of mottoes, described as a useless precaution as the names of competitors and the character of their designs had been talked of many days before the exhibition of designs opened. A jury drawn from architects of the *Académie des Beaux Arts*, and the *Conseil Général des Bâtiments Civils*, presided over by a minister, decided that no design was sufficiently complete to be awarded the commission, but awarded prizes to five competitors, who were invited to engage in a further competition. The *Builder* criticised the plans for their inadequacy as theatres, i.e. in providing stage facilities and ventilation. 'The drawings do not induce the belief that such competitions are more productive of intended results with our friends the French than with ourselves.'[37] Inspired, doubtless, by the Opéra competition, César Daly, the French equivalent of George Godwin, then published a pamphlet on *Des Concours pour les Monuments Publics* in which he argued against limited competition as inconsistent with justice, the public interest, and art-progress; suggested that programmes should be more carefully prepared (though the *Builder*'s reviewer felt that 'minute instructions generally act counter to the intention of a competition'), adequate time given and a recompense paid comparable to the work involved; and called for a competent and impartial jury. There should be representatives of the different architectural schools and bodies, with nearly a third of the jurors elected by the competitors; they should be assisted by men especially acquainted with the uses of the proposed building. Competition was 'indispensable for ascertaining periodically and definitely the direction of architectural ideas'.[38]

After the fall of the Second Empire, Viollet-le-Duc considering the question in his lectures (1871) agreed in the desirability of establishing competition as a principle for 'all new architectural works', and took up the crucial problem of choosing a jury. To give useful results, competition required competitors. 'To secure really strenuous and productive competitions, in which undoubted tal-

ent will be displayed . . . we must therefore offer attractions to talent; but we cannot attract talent unless guarantees are presented that time and reputation shall not be sacrificed to rancour, rivalry, perhaps to mere imbecility of judgment or volition.' He suggested that if the Institute had not had 'the complete control of education' in France, 'the plan of having the jury nominated by the candidates themselves would offer sufficient security'. (Such a plan was sometimes suggested in England.[39]) But although in an increasingly democratic system competition was the accepted mode of selection, there was still, among those holding power, too much suspicion of the building world as corrupt and architects as self-interested for government to accept such a tribunal. It was therefore as unacceptable in England as in France.

Le-Duc's conclusion was that after a preliminary sifting of the designs, the relatively few meritorious ones should be put before a jury of 'persons of repute, who have not been architectural practitioners at all, or who have ceased for some time to be so', in whose presence the competitors would be examined about their designs by 'professional men of acknowledged capacity'. This was the procedure that, without the crucial interview, had been adopted in England in the Government Offices and Law Courts competitions. The complaint that 'the judges knew remarkably little about the subject' (made by Scott of the Government Offices competition) might apply to Viollet-le-Duc's jury, but he declared that such an objection was not tenable:

> Architecture is not one of those branches of knowledge which are full of mysteries, which bristle with technical terms and formulae incomprehensible to the bulk of intelligent people. There is no problem in architecture, difficult as it may be, that cannot be understood by educated persons, though strangers to the practical side of the profession, if it be clearly explained to them, with a reliance on that common sense which is essential to the appreciation of everything.

There would even be advantages in competitors having to explain their designs to such a jury.[40]

The selecting of judges was clearly one of the First Commissioner's most difficult tasks. The choice had to command confidence among architects and the public, but not every obvious candidate was willing to act. Fear of professional jealousies had confined the choice to connoisseurs in 1835; and again in 1857 Hall had ensured a majority of lay judges. *Building News* probably reflected professional views in its ambivalence on that occasion, first praising the type of judge that Hall promised to appoint from the elite of English society – men 'whose taste is refined by long study, careful observation, and extensive reading . . . which very few of the profession can equal', with no undue stylistic preference and no professional bias – and then attacking the specific nominees for their lack of known connexion with architecture.[41]

As First Commissioner from 1860 to 1866, Cowper followed his predecessors in arguing that judgement could not be left exclusively to the architectural profession, riven as it was by contentions and jealousies.[42] 'Two courses were open', he declared. One was that usually adopted by railway companies and public authorities: 'to select persons who had an interest in the building as the occupiers of it, and a responsibility in causing it to be erected, and to afford them the aid and counsel of professional architects'. The other was to include architects among the judges. The South Kensington Museums competition jury of 1864, chaired by Lord Elcho, included two architects. The New Law Courts competition jury, however, reflected the controlling interests of the royal commission and the Treasury: the First Commissioner, two Treasury nominees (the then chancellor, Gladstone, and the connoisseur MP Sir

162.   William Tite (1798–1873), sometime PRIBA, Liberal MP 1855–73, was an architect of the old Classical school. Profitably concerned in railway works, and a member of the Metropolitan Board of Works, he was a strong opponent of Scott's Gothic Foreign Office designs.

William Stirling-Maxwell) and two commissioners (Lord Chief Justice Cockburn and Sir Roundell Palmer) – men 'unbiased in their opinions by any of those predilections or prejudices which professional training almost necessarily engendered'.[43] This unprofessional team proved to need the assistance of two professional assessors, George Pownall (principally a surveyor) and John Shaw, who under pressure from the competitors and the support of the commission were finally added to the jury.[44]

Cowper promised that the National Gallery competition jury should include two architects; but the actual panel was named by his successor, Lord John Manners. In addition to the architects William Tite (1798–1873) [Pl. 162] and David Brandon (1813–97), a substitute for P.C. Hardwick, who declined, it included two artists (William Boxall,[45] and South Kensington's Richard Redgrave,[46]), William Russell, a trustee, the collector T. Gambier Parry,[47] Lord Hardinge,[48] and the MPs Beresford Hope and Lord Elcho.[49] Thus composed 'not only of Amateurs distinguished for taste and Artistic Knowledge, but also of eminent professional Architects' it might have been thought an ideal jury – indeed Manners found that he had 'anticipated the suggestions of the Institute [of British Architects]' in regard to the Gallery; suggestions forwarded by the IBA president, Beresford Hope, who favoured a jury of at least eight.[50]

The problem of juries was not, however, the only one confronting the would-be competitor. Another concerned the type of drawings to be admitted. It had long been agreed that coloured drawings corrupted the judges' eye; and it was feared that even sepia-tinted perspectives had the same effect. A correspondent in the *Builder* argued in 1857 that perspective drawings should be excluded altogether until after the judging; experienced perspective artists offered a better chance of winning, and the ordinary architect had to buy in their expertise. 'And there are few even professional architects who can wholly resist the favourable impression produced by views tinted as we have lately seen them; for example, the Liverpool Library and Constantinople Church.'[51] So perspectives in the Houses of Parliament competition had been limited to three, from specified viewpoints. In the Government Offices competition of 1856 the constraint was even more severe: only 'One perspective View, tinted with light brown Indian ink' was allowed for each office; the elevations were to be in line only.[52] (This of course did require that the judges should be sufficiently experienced to read line drawings.) A related question which much exercised the New National Gallery competitors in 1866, among others, was whether 'in line only' permitted line etching and shadowing.[53] Moreover, plans and sections needed to be examined with care, and in relation to elevations (to which they did not always correspond).[54]

Yet another matter of concern to competitors was the issue of anonymity: to some, the prescription of mottoes seemed pointless, as the identity of the authors was well known, because the designs were looked over by friends and discussed at dinner-parties weeks or months beforehand, and the experienced man would in any case recognise the hand of a well-established architect. But as one competitor pointed out, only the eminent could afford to dispense with anonymity.[55]

A further element in the competition question was the exhibition of drawings to the public. In the Houses of Parliament competition in 1836 this had been arranged by the unsuccessful competitors themselves, and the government had been reluctant to exhibit the winning entries.[56] The exhibition proved a success. Recalling these circumstances, no doubt, Hall decided on public exhibition of the New Government Offices entries before releasing the names of the judges. No fewer than nine thousand visited it on the first public day, and seven thousand the second. 'Architecture has become an art of the nation . . . it is now accepted as a national and popular art . . . it will no longer be possible to exclude the public from exercising a voice on the designs for public buildings', trumpeted the *Building News*, which a few weeks earlier had been asserting the exclusive inviolability of professional judgment.[57]

To the client the risk in open competition was that the winner might not have the experience or perhaps the skill to conduct the work. Thus the British government always refused to give an explicit undertaking that the winner would be appointed to the work. One solution of this problem was to stipulate a limited competition, in which the client could select experienced men likely to give him the sort of design he was seeking. Edward Barry, experienced in such competitions, thought the arrangement might have much to recommend it for first-rate cases. But a guarantee of good faith was essential. 'No one would think of inviting the Attorney General, with eleven other leaders of the bar, to work out a difficult case, on the promise that to one of them the professional conduct of it should ultimately be entrusted, nor would any one expect to obtain the opinions and advice of twelve eminent physicians, in order that he might choose one of them.' If architects, therefore, were to be expected to do what no other profession would tolerate, they had in return the right to the 'highest principles of justice and equity'. But agreements with architects were too often treated as binding on one side only.[58]

In the 1830s, most important government building had been entrusted to the man who won the Houses of Parliament in open competition, Charles Barry. The Office of Works Assistant Surveyor, John Phipps, drew up plans for enlarging the Board of Trade in 1844, but the First Commissioner, Lord Lincoln, found them unacceptable and asked Barry for designs that would both provide the accommodation needed and 'improve the Architectural appearance of the Building'.[59] This led to Barry's reconstruction of the Whitehall façade of Soane's offices, extended to incorporate the Home Office. He was then commissioned to execute another scheme suggested by Phipps, giving additional height to the Horse Guards buildings, though nothing came of his 'grandiose scheme'.[60] With the change of government in 1846, Barry rather lost favour, being held responsible for the delays and ever-increasing expense of the New Houses of Parliament. The comparatively small official works of the late 1840s (Museum of Economic Geology, Jermyn Street, 1846–8; New Ordnance Office, Pall Mall, 1850–1 [Pl. 33]) were accordingly undertaken by the permanent Surveyor to the Woods and Works, James Pennethorne.[61]

Pennethorne, a connection of Nash's wife, had been educated by that architect, and became his principal assistant in 1828; in 1833 he was first employed by the Woods and Works (as it then was) to deal with the Regent Street estate. In 1839 he was appointed joint architect (with Thomas Chawner) and surveyor of the metropolitan improvements under the act of 1839, and the following year, the whole of the professional business of the department, including any metropolitan improvements placed under the office by Parliament, was placed under their joint direction.

When Chawner's retirement in 1845 put the whole business in Pennethorne's hands, he was required to give up private practice, no change being made in his position when the Woods was separated from the Works in 1851. He continued to officiate as hitherto but answering to the separate offices. As seen in Chapter 2, he acted as architect and surveyor for the new London parks and all the metropolitan improvements, and, as we have said, for those public buildings undertaken at that time.

For years past, the security, against fire particularly, of the public records had been a cause of concern. In 1849 the active deputy keeper of the records, Sir Francis Palgrave, obtained plans from Inman, the Surveyor of Works, for a purpose-built record office, which the Treasury referred to the Woods and Works, so that they arrived on Pennethorne's desk. He probably shared the general opinion of Inman's inadequacy, and recommended a larger scheme, 'having regard to the strictest economy, excluding Ornament and Decoration', which was approved by the parties concerned. Parliament voting the funds in July 1850 – when warnings were sounded against putting any more work in Barry's hands –, the commission for the first stage of the Public Record Office was entrusted to Pennethorne [Pl. 165].[62] Similarly, when the extension of the Inland Revenue Offices at Somerset House was considered in 1849, Pennethorne was asked for a design [Pl. 163], ultimately approved in 1852.[63] He in fact claimed that 'according to the wording of the agreement,[64] legally and strictly, I am entitled

163.   Inland Revenue Offices, Somerset House West Wing, James Pennethorne, 1852–7 When the Inland Revenue required additional offices, Pennethorne as government architect was called upon to supply the need.

164. Design for New Government Offices, Downing Street, James Pennethorne, 1855. When First Commissioner Molesworth campaigned for new ministerial offices, he called on the Office of Works' architect to supply plans. Pennethorne understood from his successor that he was to work these up, but Sir Benjamin Hall, claiming he had not so instructed him, repudiated these designs and turned to public competition.

to be employed upon all the Government works that had not been commenced by other architects before 1845; but I have never advanced such a claim, nor expected a monopoly. I believe that all new buildings in London, from 1845 to 1856 . . . were placed in my hands.'[65]

Thus to Sir William Molesworth, contemplating the building of an entire new range of government offices, it seemed the natural thing to employ the architect of the Office of Works. Molesworth's successive instructions between December 1853 and December 1854 to Pennethorne to prepare plans for new public offices, culminating in a scheme arranged around 'Downing Square'[66] were standard procedure.[67]

However, when Hall succeeded Molesworth at the Works, he formed a disapprobatory view of Pennethorne. The extended operations in completing Victoria and particularly Battersea Parks aroused the new First Commissioner's ire as stated above.[68] He regarded Pennethorne as part of an *ancien régime* in the Works that was dead wood and must be cut away.[69] He accordingly brought in his own man as surveyor – Henry Arthur Hunt – and determined that the architects for new public offices should be chosen by competition. Pennethorne had already prepared 'very elaborate designs' for the new government offices in the vicinity of Downing Street,[70] and had also, by Hall's orders, prepared plans and a general estimate for offices to cover the Downing Street/Parliament Street/Great George Street/St James's Park site; of four proposals, Hall had chosen one on 17 September 1855 which, as Pennethorne believed, he was to draw out in more detail for submission to the Treasury. He therefore made 'elaborate designs, with plans, elevations, and perspective views', which he submitted to the First Commissioner in February 1856 [Pl. 164]. Pennethorne believed Hall to have 'expressed his approval of the plan, and suggested only some slight alteration in the elevations.'[71] These instructions had been given 'in a great measure, by private notes . . . but as with everything else which I was at that time doing,

I was content with verbal instructions from a First Commissioner without calling for them in writing'.[72] Hall however had a quite different recollection of events, which he set out in a letter to the Treasury that he read to the 1858 select committee:

'Mr Pennethorne procured a copy of a map or plan, which exhibited the district in question, and set out, with lines upon the map, what he considered to be a proper space to be built upon. The lines were not good,' that is to say, in my opinion, they were not good. 'I therefore directed a fresh outline, and desired Mr Pennethorne to give a rough estimate of what he considered would be the cost of the block so marked out. I also directed him to make a book of reference. Mr Pennethorne is wholly mistaken when he states that it was with my full knowledge and concurrence that he proceeded to make elaborate designs, with plans, elevations, and perspective views of a building. I was much surprised when he brought me some elevations of buildings, which he proposed to erect on the site I had marked out, and I certainly never expressed any approbation of the designs when submitted to me; on the contrary, I was satisfied, the very moment I saw them, that they were objectionable, and would never be accepted.'[73]

Hall told Pennethorne that he considered 'so great a work as the erection of public offices should be open to public competition'. Pennethorne subsequently again urged his claim to build the public offices, but Hall replied (and stated in the Commons) that 'I should (if the matter rested with me) throw the whole open to competition, not merely to the architects of this kingdom, but to the architects of the world'.[74]

Simultaneously, a similar argument was going on about designing a new War Office. Pennethorne had been responsible in 1850–1 for the new Ordnance Office in Pall Mall [Pl. 33], since 1854 part of the War Office. When a further new building was needed there, the department naturally turned to Pennethorne

165.   Public Record Office, east wing, towards Fetter Lane, James Pennethorne, 1856. North and west elevations. Pennethorne's unique design for housing the public legal records, built in stages 1851–8, was determined by considerations of safety against fire and against a rioting populace.

and in December 1855 the Works authorised him to communicate with the War Department 'for the purpose of preparing a plan for a large addition to the present Ordnance buildings'. He consequently designed a handsome Italianate palazzo [Pl. 166], which he estimated at £80,000.[75] On receipt of the estimate, Hall told him to confine himself 'simply to a probationary sketch' because 'as the work is to be a large one, and of a very prominent character as regards the metropolis, it may be considered to afford a good opportunity for competition'.[76]

In furtherance of this intention, Hall, having rejected Pennethorne's plan as dark and ill-ventilated – though the War Office people were perfectly satisfied with the plans[77] –, in order to 'obtain competition among first class architects in regard to a comparatively speaking small building' was obliged to resort to a limited competition.[78] On 13 March he invited eleven leading architects (including Pennethorne) to submit designs within six weeks (presumably in response to the War Office's known desire for speed), for which the government would pay each one hundred guineas. 'This act', he claimed, 'has been received with the greatest favor by the Profession.'[79] William Hosking (1800–61) had recommended this form of competition in 1842 in his introductory lecture as professor of architecture and engineering construction at King's College London.[80]

In truth, Hall doubted the wisdom of putting up an expensive building in Pall Mall when the concentration of the public offices on Whitehall was in contemplation. He therefore warned competitors that the work might not proceed.[81] Similarly he warned the premier on 20 March, 'I think it is very doubtful whether the new War Department Office will be proceeded with as I hope the Downing Street improvement will be carried out.'[82] Hall was obviously acting in response to War Office pressure, and attempting to cover all eventualities; but it presented to the world the appearance of a confused mind.

Others, however, were only too ready to assist the minister to clarify his views. 'Why, then, make two bites at the cherry?' demanded the Saturday Review. A competition like that of 1835 for a Palace of Public Administration was indispensable.[83] Two weeks after his invitation to the eleven architects, Hall wrote to the Treasury recommending that the Pall Mall proposal should stand over until the Commons had considered 'the whole question with reference to the concentration of public offices', and proposing a bill for the purchase of all the land between Downing Street and Great George Street.[84] Having successfully organised a select committee to report in favour of the proposed concentration, on 4 August he obtained the approval of a doubtful chancellor of the Exchequer to a more limited scheme for new War and Foreign Offices only.[85]

166. Design for a new War Office in Pall Mall, James Pennethorne, 1856. Pennethorne as Office of Works architect was called on by the War minister to design a new building in Pall Mall, but the First Commissioner, Hall, determined on a competition, later subsumed in that for New Government Offices in Downing Street. (*Collection Centre Canadien d'Architecture/Canadian Centre for Architecture, Montréal.*)

He then called a meeting of leading architects to discuss his proposed competition. In the face of criticisms he modified his proposals, but they still remained unsatisfactory.[86]

The government's invitation was for three designs, 'the first to comprise a scheme for the concentration of the principal Government Offices on a site lying between Whitehall and the New Palace at Westminster. The other two, designs for buildings which Her Majesty's Government have determined to erect forthwith as parts of such scheme; one for the department of the Secretary of State for Foreign Affairs, and the other for the Secretary of State for War.' [Pl. 167–73][87]

As contemporaries were not slow to point out, to make sense this clearly necessitated the master plan's being selected first, and the 'parts' being planned in accordance.[88] 'Hurry seems to have predominated over reflection in the Minister's mind', commented the *Saturday Review*, '. . . The grotesque and clumsy scheme . . . is what a child ought to be ashamed of.'[89] Hurry was doubtless one factor: a minister had always to make hay while the sun of a favourable Commons shone on him. Majorities were peculiarly volatile in the 1850s. Hunt, the Surveyor, admitted that if the block-plan competition had taken place first, 'great delay would have occurred'.[90] Hall was also cabined by unsympathetic superiors. He wanted to concentrate administration between Great George Street and Downing Street, but the chancellor, Sir George Cornewall Lewis, was prepared only to concede him two incontrovertibly necessary offices, though he was allowed to obtain a general layout.[91]

I cannot see [Lewis wrote to Palmerston] that, all of a sudden,

we are called upon to make this enormous expenditure for public offices. . . . The present accommodation is doubtless not altogether adequate, but these schemes seem to assume that we are living in the Rome of Romulus, and are in a moment to convert it into the Rome of Augustus. The fact is that we are not lodged in straw huts, and that we cannot immediately provide marble palaces for all the public departments.[92]

Clearly, Hall did not envisage everyone sending in three designs, to be judged as a unity, since seven prizes were originally specified for the War Office, five for the Foreign Office, and only three for the block plan, which was not part of the chancellor's programme.[93] Hall perhaps hoped that public opinion would make the case for the greater plan; meantime he had to secure what had been sanctioned: he could not afford to take the advice poured on him to do one thing at a time.[94] But the times were out of joint. The result was confusion.

The competition judges themselves were embarrassed:

With regard to the designs for the Foreign and War Departments, a difficulty presented itself in consequence of several of the competitors having sent in designs, combining in one building, more or less unfitted for subdivision, both the Public Offices, for which distinct prizes have to be awarded; whilst others have either confined their efforts to one of the buildings, or have given separate designs for each. It will be evident that these united designs compete under considerable disadvantage with the single designs, and that unless a united design should be superior in both departments to all its single competitors, it

167. a. Competition design for New Foreign Office (no. 94, *Utilitas*), 1857, awarded the first prize; Henry Edward Coe (1826–85) and Henry H. Hofland (b. ?1828). Coe produced an accomplished drawing strongly influenced by Visconti's New Louvre, but his inexperience in large-scale works was fatal to his hope of receiving the commission.

167. b. Paris: the New Louvre, L. Visconti, 1851–5. The success of Napoleon III's early regime and the Paris International Exhibition of 1855 ensured that the eyes of Europe were turned on his great building works.

168. a. Competition design for New War Office (no. 77, *Fortiter et fideliter*), 1857, awarded the first prize; Henry Bayly Garling (1822–1909). Like Coe, Garling turned to Paris for a model, choosing the Hôtel de Ville.

168. b. Paris: the Hôtel de Ville: centre by D. da Cortona 1530–51; wings by E.H. Godde and J.C.B. Lesueur, 1837–46; internal improvements 1854. A model for entries in the New Government Offices competition.

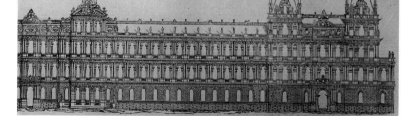

169. Competition designs for the New War Office, 1857, shewing strong French influence.:
a. Second prize, A. Botrel d'Hazeville (no. 75, *Deus atque jus*) 'Inspecteur aux Travaux du Louvre', Paris. Detail.
b. Third prize, John Thomas Rochead, 1814–78 (no.61, *Anglo Saxon*) of Glasgow. Despite his motto, he raided Lescot's Louvre for his design. Detail.

170.   Competition design for the Foreign Office, 1857 (no. 116a, *Nec minimum meruere decus vestigia Graeca ausi desirere et celebrare domestica facta*), awarded the third prize; George Gilbert Scott, A.R.A. French and Italian Gothic elements, regularly massed, modified to meet modern needs, and expressed in exquisite drawings.

171.   Gothic designs for the New Government Offices competition, 1857:
a (below). No. 140, *Cymru*, fourth prize for the War Office, by John Prichard (1818–86) and John Pollard Seddon (1827–1906) of Llandaff (Prichard claimed that the design was all his work). Perspective from Whitehall.
b (bottom). No. 35, *Thou hast covered my head in the day of battle*, fourth prize for the Foreign Office, by Thomas Newenham Deane (1828–99) and Benjamin Woodward (1815–61) of Dublin, shewing Ruskinian influence.

c (below). No. 54, *Suaviter Fortiter*, sixth prize for the Foreign Office, by Charles Buxton, MP (1823–71) assisted by W.G. and E. Habershon; the regularity and relative simplicity of the design may have recommended it to the judges.

172.   Classical designs for the New Government Offices Competition, 1857:
a (below). No. 20, *Corona*, fifth prize for the War Office, by Cuthbert Brodrick (1822–1905) of Leeds. The *Builder* thought it did not 'exhibit the character appropriate to government offices'. Brodrick (winner of the Leeds Town Hall competition of 1852, pl. 9b) made the giant order his hallmark, and repeated it in the limited National Gallery competition, 1866.
b (bottom). No. 17, *ZB*, fifth prize for the Foreign Office, by Thomas Bellamy (1798–1876), in Roman palazzo style. 'Capital drawings to a good Italian design' (*Builder*).
c (p. 171, top). No. 54a, *Au bon droit*, sixth prize for the War Office, by William G. Habershon and Edward Habershon, again inspired by the Louvre.
d. (p. 171, centre). No. 126, *Westminster*, seventh prize for the War Office (5th, 6th and 7th prizes were ranked equal), by John Dwyer (1820–58), yet again after the Louvre.

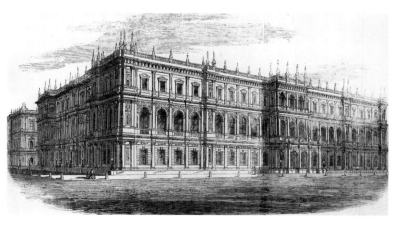

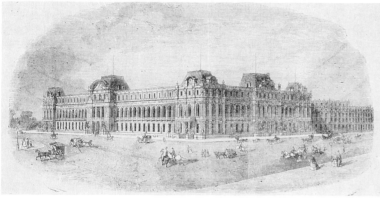

would not receive a prize, because one portion of it could hardly be executed without the other.[95]

The *Builder*, questioned by readers, had advised that it believed that there would be no objection to combining both offices in one building.[96] Its readers now expressed their disgust at the judges' decision.[97]

Hall's mishandling of the competition did not end with this fundamental blunder. Although he seemed keen for entries from foreign architects, the arrangements discouraged foreign entries. Five months was little time for so large and complex a project, and was in fact truncated because full particulars were not available till

173. Design for the New Government Offices competition, 1857, no. 112, *Omicron*, by Robert Kerr (1823–1904). Kerr's widely-praised design did not receive a prize. Kerr advocated a 'free or mixed Renaissance' style – what Viollet-le-Duc termed 'macaronic'.

the end of September.[98] Under pressure, Hall yielded an additional 20 days. The French foreign minister thought the premiums too low. Hall was unable to shift on this point, but granted an additional two weeks (to 4 April) for oversea entrants.[99] The scales of 16 feet and 44 feet to the inch (1:192 and 1:528) hardly eased the work of those accustomed to the metric scale. Nonetheless, the *Observer*, with which Hall had long had links, praised the proposal extravagantly: it was 'the very happiest means' of improving native talent. 'The simple fact that great national works are to be executed, and that whoever's plan is accepted will be sure to obtain European fame and make a rapid fortune, will afford such stimulus to exertion and the exercise of genius, that it will tend more to raise the character of the architectural profession than anything else ... the public ought to feel much obliged to the Chief Commissioner of Works for this innovation on old customs and prejudices.'[100]

Thoroughly familiar with the debates on the choice of designs for the New Houses of Parliament in 1835–7, in which he had taken part, Hall, while basing the terms of his competition on the earlier one, was obviously seeking to improve on it. Not only was the competition open to the world; every attempt was made to avoid jobbery: in contrast to 1835, the judges were not appointed until the designs were received, so that competitors could not flatter their prejudices. The designs were to be exhibited publicly (an enterprise, as already noted, undertaken by the competitors themselves in 1836). The draft conditions included a requirement for an approximate estimate of the cost of design, the omission of this element having been strongly criticised in 1836; but in the published terms, the demand was dropped, possibly because of the burden it imposed on entrants.[101] Nevertheless, the omission encouraged competitors to present extravagant schemes. Finally, a premiated architect employed to superintend the work would be paid five per cent on the outlay, so clearing away one of the most contentious issues about the Houses of Parliament.[102]

In the selection of judges, the same desire to improve on 1835 was exhibited: Hall had promised the Commons that he would mix professionals and laymen.[103] As in 1835, the role of the professional was highly contentious; often, he was seen as fatally biased by stylistic or personal considerations.[104] Hall's selection has been considered above (p. 162). Given the terms of the competition, it is hardly surprising that the judges and judging were criticised. After one meeting, the duke of Buccleuch was called to Scotland, and Eversley's wife having died, he too was absent from their final five decisive meetings. Having given themselves a week to examine the designs,[105] the judges asked for professional assistance to check their compliance with the conditions, a step that was to have unforeseen consequences. Hall recommended Samuel Angell and George Pownall. These experienced surveyors were not content with executing their limited function. A list of 67 designs chosen by the judges from the 218 entries was transmitted to them with instructions drawn up by Brunel; they checked both those and the other designs, submitted a mere 39 that satisfied the conditions, and compiled their own order of merit. The judges refused to accept this list, but it was later to escape into the public domain and prove a determining factor in the choice of architect.[106]

In their award, the judges observed that they had no knowledge of the sum that the government proposed to spend on the new offices, and that the designs were unaccompanied by estimates and did not admit of any accurate costing. They thus served notice that they declined any responsibility for the expensive character of the designs. They then explained, as quoted above, their difficulty in awarding premiums for the two offices in consequence of several entrants having combined both in a single building. So they had treated the lower prizes 'as marks of distinction for merit rather than . . . as fitted for separate construction'.[107] In other words, after the first three, the prize-winners stood on a level footing [Pl. 168–73].

The exhibition of the designs in Westminster Hall evoked much popular interest [Pl. 174]. In the first three days, some 27,000 people attended, and for the rest of the month the crowds continued to throng the Hall.[108] The professional and illustrated periodicals gave it much coverage. Benjamin Ferrey, an experienced Gothic architect, commented that it threw doubt on open competition as 'the right way of obtaining the best talent of the country': the most deserving designs were those of established men, whose 'style and manner' made them readily recognisable. He thought the most remarkable effect of the competition had been the development of some 'decidedly Italian Gothic designs', which bade fair to render English Gothic 'much more applicable to modern requirements'.[109] A foreigner (De Jong) thought the exhibition showed what England could produce: 'it is a contribution to popular education; a throwing off of all suspicion of secrecy, intrigue or partiality' – little did he foresee how it was to develop.[110]

It was ironic that despite Hall's desire to make his competition an improvement on that of 1835, it resulted in thorough confusion, the results were set aside, and eventually a lower-ranking prizeman was appointed by ministerial fiat after a long enquiry by a select committee. That the winners for the two offices were obscure, more or less, was what was to be expected from the process of competition[111] – indeed one of its aims was generally thought to be the bringing to light of hidden talent. But the choice did not engender confidence in the decision-makers, and made it easier to set aside the verdict. The decisive factor, however, was undoubtedly the grandeur and therefore the cost of the premiated designs. Before Parliament could vote the necessary funds, India had erupted into rebellion, and thunderclouds were gathering in both Persia and China. With emergency votes of credit for military purposes, it was not the time to embark on expensive schemes of metropolitan embellishment: a curious contrast perhaps with 1855, when despite the Crimean War many were so impressed by newly-seen Paris that they were prepared to contemplate making London more splendid.

Hall fought a brave rearguard action for his competition. When he was instructed in October 1857 to re-examine Pennethorne's Foreign Office plans with a view to executing them, he replied to the Treasury: 'It appears to me that in justice to the competitors the Government is bound, in the first instance, to consider the *premiated* designs . . . for if Mr Pennethorne's plans are adopted the competition will be wholly disregarded, and an architect who might have competed, but did not compete, would thus be substituted for the successful competitor.'[112] The Treasury admitted some force in Hall's argument, but insisted that the change of views in the Commons (following the exhibition of designs) which made it necessary to abandon the bill to purchase the Charles Street site obliged the government to produce a scheme for a new Foreign Office on the smaller site previously approved in 1855. The competitors' claims were satisfied by their prizes. If the principle of competition were to be adhered to, the government should invite a new general competition for the smaller site, because an architect who had achieved success for a large design might not be the best qualified to produce a simpler work.

The government did not think it expedient to adopt that course after the abandonment of the general design: 'considering the advantage which would arise from placing the architect to be employed . . . in communication with the officers of the department for the accommodation of which the building is to be erected', it was felt that the best course would be to employ the architect who had already made plans for the department, 'and

who from his official position in connexion with the Board of Works might be resorted to with the least invidiousness to the professional public'.[113]

Hall retorted that even were he to admit that the government was 'not fettered by the late competition', there were 'cogent reasons for not adopting' their proposed course. For a start, the new office must contain very much the same accommodation as had been specified in the competition. He insisted on the competitive principle he had laid down in March 1856 in respect of the proposed War Office in Pall Mall, 'as being alike advantageous to the public and the interests of the arts'. The monopoly exercised by a public architect was 'by no means advisable and is a source of discouragement to the profession'. However, as a way out, he suggested asking the competition winner for designs for the smaller site – the 'excellence of [his] internal arrangements' rather than external embellishment had placed him first. Otherwise, the profession's faith in the government would be imperilled, and when another competition might be necessary, as for a new National Gallery, eminent architects might decline: the premiums alone were no attraction, as they did not compensate for the time and labour involved.[114] But the Treasury insisted that the rejection of the bill for acquiring the additional site was 'a virtual abandonment of the whole scheme by the House of Commons'. There seemed, therefore, no reason why they should not revert to the plan that had been prepared before the great scheme intervened, i.e. Pennethorne's.[115] Thus matters stood when Palmerston's government fell. The further history of the Foreign Office competition, with the ultimate commissioning of George Gilbert Scott, who had taken only a third prize, is pursued in Chapter 13.

Hall's warning was pertinent, though, for it was not only government offices that were in need of improved accommodation: the British Museum and the National Gallery were filled to overflowing as purchases continued and gifts multiplied. The Law Courts were so over-crowded that in the summer work might become impossible. The new minority Conservative government of 1858–9 attempted to solve at least the National Gallery's problem by commissioning a new building on the northern part of the Burlington House site. Lord John Manners believed in fair play, so he nominated Banks & Barry (i.e. Robert Banks, long Sir Charles Barry's assistant, and his son Charles Barry), elbowed out of the Foreign Office job by Scott, whom they had beaten in the competition. On 9 December 1858 he discussed the problem of architec-

174. Exhibition of competition designs for New Government Offices, Westminster Hall, May 1857. Unparalleled public interest was aroused, and 27,000 persons came on the first three days.

175. Design for completion of the South Kensington Museum, 1864, Captain Francis Fowke, R.E. (1823–65). Henry Cole, moving power in the Department of Science and Art, preferred Royal Engineer officers to architects. Fowke was employed as departmental architect, designing the slow accretion of the museum's buildings. In 1860 he produced a plan for the completion of the museum, modified in 1863 and again in 1865 shortly before his early death. Although Fowke's 1860 estimate had been as much as £214,000, no competition was held. The museum's architecture remained in the hands of Royal Engineer officers until 1882, and it was not until 1890 that a limited competition for its completion was launched. When Queen Victoria laid the new foundation stone in 1899, she re-named the museum 'The Victoria and Albert'.

tural appointments with Lord Stanley, the Indian secretary, and agreed that

> You will confide the erection of the new India Office to Mr Scott with the view of securing harmony of design [with the adjoining Foreign Office] and public convenience; and I promise to use my best endeavours to secure for Messrs Banks and Barry the reconstruction of Burlington House, and the erection of all and every of the public buildings which may be executed on that site. Should a change of government occur, or should I leave office previous to giving effect to that agreement I should deem it my duty to leave a confidential minute behind me explaining the grounds on which it was formed, and on which I should request my successor to respect it.[116]

Banks & Barry were duly appointed in April 1859, though the Palmerston government abandoned the project in 1860 in face of parliamentary hostility.[117]

As Liberal First Commissioner for Works from 1861 to 1866, William Cowper adopted wholeheartedly the concept of competition as the means of obtaining designs for the surge of public buildings that he activated. When contemplating the question of new Law Courts in 1862 he indicated his intention of calling a general competition, 'the ordinary course taken in the erection of public building',[118] and in 1864 again referred to this intention. Practicalities however were to dictate that it should be a limited competition, as explained below. The first competition Cowper actually conducted was that for the huge Natural History and Patents Museums project in 1864.

Intense competition at the British Museum between books, antiquities and natural-history collections had provoked fierce public argument; several parliamentary committees, as well as a royal commission, had deliberated. At length, it was decided to move the natural-history collections to South Kensington.[119] To provide for them, and also for the public collection of patented inventions, Cowper proposed, accordant with his avowed policy, 'a general invitation to architects to submit a Block plan shewing an arrangement of the whole 17 acres in Museums, galleries and Courts for the purposes of Science and Art, and also an Elevation of a plan in detail of that portion of the whole building which will be required to contain the Natural History Collections about to be transferred from the British Museum, and the collection of Models belonging to the Commissioners of Patents'. He suggested three premiums, of £250, £150 and £100 (subsequently increased to £400, £250 and £100), as an incentive.[120]

The curious feature of this competition was that it was parthenogenic. Panizzi, effectively the administrator of the Museum, complained to the Treasury, 'I am not aware that the Trustees were ever asked' whether they wanted the increase of accommodation Cowper had specified for his competition, and suggested that 'the Trustees be informed, before Saturday next if possible, on what grounds such an additional extent of buildings is proposed, that they may give at once the whole subject the full consideration it requires'.[121] Cowper had based his instructions on plans prepared in 1862 by Richard Owen, superintendent of the natural history collections. He argued that 'it would have been unfortunate if the Trustees had been obliged to commit themselves to an opinion on the extent of space to be provided for exhibition, irrespective of other considerations'. 'The building', he insisted, 'should form part of a general design for laying out the whole of the site, and it should have the architectural dignity that is suitable to a National Museum.' When the plans were received, it would be possible to furnish the trustees with the information they required to express an opinion on arrangement, dimensions and number of rooms necessary for the natural-history collections.[122]

This concept of commissioning designs without reference to the client laid the ground for subsequent disputes between the several parties. Despite the Treasury's suggestion that Cowper should communicate with the trustees through the Treasury Board, which was 'not only responsible to Parliament generally for arrangements for providing fitting accommodation for the Collections of the British Museum: but as you are aware have in this particular case undertaken to confer with the Trustees previously to the adoption of any plan for providing them with additional space',[123] the First Commissioner drove his own furrow. His panel of judges, at least, might seem well chosen: Lord Elcho (an amateur who took a leading part in questions of public architecture for many years), William Tite, MP, sometime PRIBA, David Roberts, R.A., Pennethorne (the official architect) and James Fergusson (the leading historian of architecture of the day). But according to one competitor, John Prichard, 'Tite as an adjudicator upon Architecture would be a laughable farce, if unattended with mischief', though Fergusson was 'all very well'.[124] However, they had to consider only 33 entries from 32 architects.[125] They unanimously awarded the palm, as already mentioned, to Captain Francis Fowke, R.E., superintendent of construction of the South Kensington Museum [Pl. 175] (under the Department of Science and Art) [Pl. 104a]. The second and third prizes went respectively to Professor Robert Kerr [Pl. 104b] and Cuthbert Brodrick.[126] Gladstone's proposal to purchase Fowke's widely disliked 1862 International Exhibition building

176. New National Gallery, limited competition, 1866–7: C. Brodrick. A re-vamping of his War Office design of 1857 (cp pl. 172a).

[Pl. 103] had, as we have seen, provoked a furious revolt in the Commons the previous year which had led to the competition.[127]

Despite the Museum trustees' declared preference for Kerr's design, Cowper insisted that Fowke be commissioned. The trustees and officers had considered too exclusively the internal arrangements of the galleries and the means of lighting them, he asserted.

> I am convinced that the arrangement of no. 1 [Fowke's] is preferable in respect to the difference of light over the wall cases and Tables, to general convenience, and to grandeur of architectural effect and although I am bound to acknowledge that great deference is due to the opinion of the Sub-Committee of Trustees and of the Officers of the Departments of Natural History, yet it must be remembered that upon this occasion they do not appear to have had the advantage of the counsel and explanation of any architect; while the opinion of the judges who unanimously awarded the first Premium to no. 1 on the ground of its internal as well as its external arrangements carries with it the weight which is due on such a subject to eminence and experience in the profession of architecture.[128]

After a year's delay, the trustees gave way to Treasury pressure, and asked Fowke to consult the departmental officers in order to modify his designs. Unfortunately Fowke then died. Two months later, Cowper recommended the appointment of Alfred Waterhouse [Pl. 177] (who had won the Manchester Assize Courts competition in 1859 with a powerful Gothic design, and had opened a London office in 1864) to execute Fowke's designs. Waterhouse ultimately substituted his own.[129]

Like the Museum collections, the national collection of pictures had grown space. There had been much discussion since as early as 1844 about the possibilities of rebuilding the National Gallery, whether at Trafalgar Square or elsewhere.[130] The Commons having rejected alternative sites, there remained three possibilities in addition to a northern extension to the Trafalgar Square building: to rebuild it; to improve the façade; or to build a new façade in front of it. The official architect, James Pennethorne, had been closely involved in these proposals, in which Parliament and public took a keen interest; he had been employed to make additional galleries

177. Alfred Waterhouse, R.A. (1830–1905), sometime PRIBA. Originally from Manchester, where he made his reputation with Gothic assize courts, and then won the competition for the Town Hall, grandest expression of Victorian civic pride, he was brought in to execute Fowke's competition design for a Natural History Museum, and then nominated for the New Law Courts competition. As assessor of many late Victorian competitions, he exercised a powerful influence over the work of the period.

in 1860–1, and doubtless expected the commission for rebuilding. But after so many committees and commissions and parliamentary debates on the subject, Cowper dared not appoint him *mere motu*. In December 1864, when he received sketches from Pennethorne for a four-stage enlargement of the Gallery, Cowper specifically declined to name an architect.[131]

Clearly Cowper was already contemplating a competition – but what sort of competition? The South Kensington Museums experience had not been very happy. He looked about him, and borrowed an idea from the architectural market-place. Cowper was in a unique position in the mid-1860s because as well as the South Kensington Museums, the proposals to build new Law Courts and a New National Gallery had received parliamentary approval. At the Athenaeum he engaged the distinguished architectural critic and historian James Fergusson (a judge in the 1864 museums competition) in conversation about the prospect of limited competition for these great works. Fergusson was unhappy with the proposal, as he subsequently wrote:

If you name the competition be they 5, 10, 20 you virtually bind yourself to employ the successful candidate and I dont think there are half a dozen men in the profession I should like to see in such a position.

With unlimited competition the case is different – and I think the best men would compete for a 'national gallery' though they would not for the Law Courts. Every man fancies he knows all about so simple a matter as lighting pictures while few would dare to face the complication of law and law courts. . . . Penrose and Somers Clarke are both good and approved men and if their design was chosen there would be no objection to entrusting either of them with the execution – I would only add I hope their design *wont* be selected but that is another matter.

I shall at all times be delighted to assist either directly or indirectly in any manner in my power.[132]

Competition remained the lodestar; but 1856 had shown that not all the leading talent of the country was drawn by it, and in 1864 'none of the competitors were in the first rank of their profession'.[133] Therefore, despite Fergusson's disapprobation, Cowper introduced the concept of invited competition, such as was employed by 'railway companies or other corporations when they proposed to erect large buildings':[134] limited to a hand-picked selection of able architects, each paid a fee for his design. Such competitions had lately been used for the Chelsea Vestry Hall (1858), Grocers' Hall (1864), the Albert Memorial (1864) and the St Pancras Station Hotel (1865).[135] Its use by the government was a major change in official policy.

Parliament having authorised the purchase of additional land to the north of the National Gallery, in August 1865 Cowper asked Pennethorne to prepare site plans and sections to enable architects to consider how the existing structure might be married to an extension.[136] In a letter to the Treasury a few days later he remarked:

Under more ordinary circumstances I might be content to submit the formation of the plan to the Architect of this Office, but in this instance there are such special difficulties to be met and overcome that I am unwilling to restrict myself to the aid of a single architect however able he may be and it will be expedient to invoke the assistance of several of the most eminent and experienced architects in order to provide the materials for a careful consideration of the alternatives that may be adopted as to enable the Government and parliament to come to a deliberate and sound judgment on the subject.

I propose to invite 5 or 6 architects to submit Designs for laying out the ground and for the elevation of the intended Buildings. In the present preliminary stage of the proceedings I could not be expected to engage that any one of these Architects will be employed . . . but I propose to remunerate each of the persons who send in Designs for the time and expense devoted to the preparation of them; this course which has frequently been adopted of late in similar cases is found to be convenient since it encourages those who are invited to respond without unduly embarrassing those who have invited the Designs.[137]

Accordingly Cowper invited six architects to compete, allowing them three months, extended a week later to 31 October.[138] When parliamentary pressure compelled him to double the number of competitors for the simultaneous competition for the New Law Courts, he did likewise for the Gallery.[139] He proposed a sum of £200 to remunerate each competitor, a sum that, as Tite commented, 'would hardly pay for the paper and the framing and glazing of their drawings'.[140] Of the twelve architects ultimately invited, two[141] did not compete, 'probably from pressure of business and unwillingness to undertake labour without remuneration'.[142] The real inducement was obviously the commission for a new gallery. The instructions, despite Fergusson's recommendation, reserved freedom of action to the government: 'The First Commissioner does not engage himself to adopt any of the designs that may be sent in, but if one of the designs be adopted the author of it will be employed to carry it into effect, and will be paid the usual commission of 5 per cent on the outlay.' The competitors were asked to provide designs for remodelling Wilkins' building, as well as for an entirely new structure.[143]

Cowper, again anticipating the problem that arose with the Law Courts competition, assured the National Gallery competitors in June 1866 that the judges would include not more than two professional architects.[144] It was only after the competition was well under way, in November 1866, that Cowper's Conservative successor, Lord John Manners, named the panel of judges.[145]

Rumours that these judges (more numerous than hitherto) were not going to make an award led the competitors to appeal to Cowper, now in Opposition, as the commissioning minister; he accordingly wrote to the Secretary of the Office of Works on 15 February 1867 stating: 'The expectation held out to the architects to induce them to compete had always been that an impartial decision would be made and published between the competing designs, and that the successful competitor would be engaged as the architect of the building, even though the identical design was not adopted.' This, as Beresford Hope pointed out, was not consistent with the instructions, which referred to the execution of the prize design.[146] Cowper, having set up a competition to choose a design, then thought its function should be to choose a designer.

This ambiguity was not the only problem in the instructions. The government had been obliged by the Commons to retain the National Gallery in Trafalgar Square. The problem was therefore to design an architecturally distinguished building fit for 'the finest site in Europe' that should be 'specially adapted for the exhibition of pictures', i.e. lighted from the roof, a requirement inconsistent with the elevation required for architectural distinction and to compete effectively with Nelson's Column and St Martin's Church. The gallery had to accommodate crowds of holiday-makers and yet provide for the 'repose and concentration of mind required for the study of art'. These problems had to be resolved on a site of which one side was 230 ft and the other only 170 ft. Cowper accordingly, without discussing the problems with the National Gallery trustees, referred it to the selected competitors to decide the number of rooms, their size and manner of lighting.[147] He did however ask the Trustees to supply 'accurate information as to the amount of

178.   New National Gallery, limited competition, 1866–7: entry with most architectural merit: E.M. Barry. This precursor of the 'Wrenaissance' was too expensive to transmute into stone. Barry was employed in the 1870s to build additional rooms at the back of the old Gallery.

accommodation that ought to be provided . . . for receiving cleaning and storing pictures, and also for other purposes connected with the business of the Establishment', information that was circulated together with an account of Fowke's well-regarded Sheepshanks Gallery at South Kensington.[148]

However, Cowper's and Manners' combination of distinguished amateurs and eminent architects[149] proved even less effective than earlier state juries. Having found the instructions to the competitors too vague for their comfort, the judges asked the First Commissioner for written instructions for their own guidance. He responded that their primary regard should be 'suitableness to the important objects for which they are designed and their architectural elevations'; cost should not be considered. Under the competitors' instructions the judges were 'at liberty . . . to refrain from recommending any one of the competing designs for adoption'.[150] The judges therefore did so. The 'difficulties and the incompleteness of the instructions', said Hope, 'were too much for the competitors . . . they had not succeeded in making their bricks without straw'. Cowper, in Opposition, had urged that it was the judges' duty 'to declare the winner of the race even though they may form a low opinion of the running', and that – somewhat inconsistently – a non-award would 'inflict a heavy and undeserved professional stigma' on the competitors. The judges, on the contrary, declared (as Hope put it) 'that the running had been altogether creditable, but that, as the Jockey Club, represented by the late Commissioner of Works, had drawn up such an impossible set of conditions, the judges were bound to decide that the race was null and void. . . . The fact was the judges found entanglement, contradictions, and delusive expectations from the beginning to the end of the case.'[151] All they could do when pressed was declare Edward Barry's [Pl. 178] the best for a new gallery, and Murray's best for altering the existing one.[152] The entries were, said Tite, 'drawings of eminent beauty and excellent as works of high art', but not suitable for a National Gallery.[153]

The National Gallery submissions commanded less attention than those for the Law Courts. A correspondent in the *Spectator* declared that 'Mr Street's is the only respectable design in any style, and therefore it is, and not because it is Gothic, that its claims are urged.'[154] It is however comment-worthy that at a time when the

press was proclaiming the triumph of Gothic as a result of the Law Courts competition, only two entrants for the National Gallery, Street and Somers Clarke, submitted Gothic designs [Pl. 179]. 'It seemed to be assumed', wrote Street's son, 'either that Gothic was not suitable for the particular purpose, or that the surroundings in

179.   New National Gallery, limited competition, 1866–7: Entrance hall and stair, G.E. Street. The only competitor to submit a Gothic design, Street had visited the main Continental galleries to acquire technical information.

Trafalgar Square made the adoption of a style so different unadvisable.'[155]

Running in parallel in 1866–7 with the new National Gallery competition was, as mentioned above, that for new Law Courts. Despite Cowper's earlier intention of holding an open competition, when it was announced, it was limited to six invitees. The instructions for the Courts were of extraordinary complexity, yet the law judges were unwilling to have more than a few architects loosed on a study of existing courts. In the light of the 1864 Museums competition it seemed unlikely that established architects would be willing to go through the immense labour necessary; yet it was, as Fergusson suggested, unlikely that an unknown man would have the requisite experience to master the brief and produce a workable solution.

The Courts of Justice Commission, charged with the preparations for the new courts, therefore decided on 21 December 1865 that in order to secure the talents of leading architects, as well as avoiding as much as possible interference with the ordinary work of the courts, it was advisable to invite no more than six men to compete.[156] Pressure from the Commons however compelled a wider choice. Prompted by a press campaign led by the *Law Times*, the House demanded an increase in the number of competitors,[157] resulting in a doubling of the number.[158]

The extent of competition, however, was only one of three major factors in the competitive system: the choice of judges (considered above) and the selection of style were also controversial. Since the Houses of Parliament competition the question of style had been left open in those organised by government, but that had meant that the issue had to be faced at a later stage of proceedings. It might be that the judges as a body had a predilection for one particular style (as has been argued in regard to those of 1857),[159] so that unless their names were announced beforehand competitors choosing an unfavoured style were placed at a disadvantage. The usual official argument was that personal preferences among judges cancelled out.

Though 'vague and inconclusive in the most important particulars', the instructions for the New Law Courts were of unparalled minuteness.[160] In collaboration with the Treasury (which, under the enabling legislation, had ultimate control), the Courts of Justice Commission decided, as stated above, on a panel of five laymen to choose the best plan: two appointed by the Commission and two by the Treasury, under the chairmanship of the First Commissioner of Works. A Treasury Minute of 23 December confirmed the arrangements, giving the panel authority to determine on limited or unlimited competition and to choose the entrants.[161] Brownlee has argued that the predilections of these judges among the invited architects 'ultimately prevented them from reaching a conclusive decision'.[162] The same objection had been made to the judges of the Houses of Parliament competition of 1835, but their prejudices did not prevent their coming to a clear decision. Nor is it manifest that vagueness in the instructions inhibited the judges' determination. Rather it may be that the excessive scrupulosity characteristic of Gladstone (one of the Treasury representatives) produced their unfortunate decision in favour of one plan and another elevation.[163] Gladstone, as mentioned above, believed that his duty was to recommend a design, not a designer; and was doubtless influenced by the degree of competitors' adherence to the instructions as well as the attractiveness of the elevations.[164] What does seem clear is that the judges tended to favour the Gothic style.

Concerned at this predominance, Cavendish Bentinck, MP, had suggested that architecture and art should be represented among the judges; but the Reform Bill crisis caused the question to be dropped, and the new Conservative government assumed that the Commons acquiesced in what had been arranged. The architect MP Charles Lanyon backed a request from the competitors themselves that they should be permitted to nominate two additional judges from their fellow architects, but he was unable at first to carry the House with him.[165] However, the judges found they needed professional assistance, and George Pownall and John Shaw were appointed assessors. The competitors then requested that they be made judges, a request supported by the RIBA and pressed in the Commons until the Treasury conceded the point.[166] But in the end, all this manoeuvring proved pointless. The judges, assisted (or confused) by diverse reports from Shaw and Pownall and the various legal departments and organisations, decided that Barry's was the best plan, but Street's the best elevation [Pl. 180–1], so that the two should be invited to act jointly.[167] This

180. New Law Courts, limited competition, 1866–7: Plan of Court Floor:
a. E.M. Barry. Like most of the eleven competitors, Edward Barry adopted the concentric model, but reduced his central hall to a small space under his crowning dome. His plan was judged the best.
b. G.E. Street. Another concentric plan, Street's was dominated by his vaulted central hall, arranged east-west so that it would not act as a thoroughfare between the Strand and Carey Street.

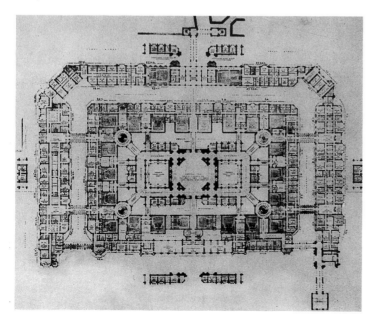

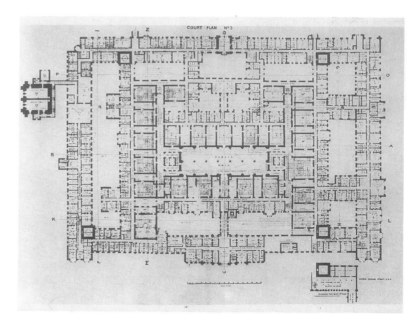

181. New Law Courts, limited competition, 1866–7: perspective:
a. E.M. Barry. Similar to his contemporary National Gallery design, and essentially classical in conception, this transmogrification into late Gothic was not greatly admired.
b. G.E. Street. Judged the best elevation, this also had a classical foundation. Street's superb drawing, Picturesque accents and powerful massing gave him the palm in a competition ostensibly to be determined by utilitarian considerations.

182.   Palais de Justice, Paris; J.L. Duc, 1857–68:
a. West front, exterior. A rationalist architect, Duc expressed the majesty of the law in architectural forms of classical derivation.
b. Vestibule de Harlay, interior; generally reckoned to be Duc's masterpiece.

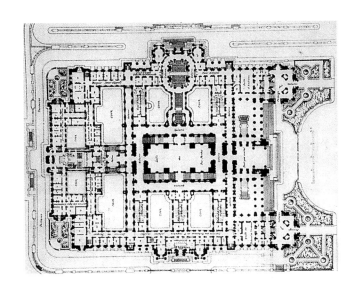

183.   Palais de Justice, Brussels; Joseph Poelaert, 1868–83:
a. Perspective view. This stupendous mass, recalling the exuberance of Roman architecture under the Empire, cost about three times as much to build as Street's Law Courts in the Strand.
b. The plan is a characteristic Beaux-Arts product, but provides comparatively little court space, so much being devoted to display features like the grand staircase.

controversial award[168] was at first accepted by Street and Barry, as by Scott, chairman of the competitors;[169] but Waterhouse, who had apparently previously initiated the series of reports, supplemented by photographs, that each competitor had submitted to the commission, now did 'his utmost to get the Commission to constitute themselves judges, & to set aside the award'.[170] This attempt failed, but the commission instead referred the award to the attorney-general, who declared it invalid.[171] In the changed circumstances, Edward Barry vociferously but vainly pressed his individual claim.

Faced with two inconclusive competition awards, Lord John Manners solved the problem[172] by appointing Barry to design the National Gallery, to which he had the best claim, and Street the Law Courts: 'the fairest decision possible'.[173]

12
Rival Modes of Selection

WE HAVE THUS SEEN that the two great competitions of 1866–7, designed to draw out the country's finest architectural talent, proved to be as great fiascos as that of 1856–7: limited competition appeared to be no more capable of providing what the country needed than had been open competition. How far it was the instructions, how far the judges, how far the weaknesses of the competitors themselves provided ample if tough joints for the profession and the public to chew over. 'They had seen enough of competition for public buildings', declared Sir William Tite, PRIBA, MP, who knew a good deal about the subject.[1] Nevertheless, in a world in which the virtues of competition still dominated, public opinion sounded no clear call for abandoning it in architecture, and the open character of the profession ensured that it remained a popular means of aiming at fame and success: only greater professional control was seen as the *sine qua non*.

An initiative by the Architectural Association eventually led to discussion at the RIBA general conference in 1871, in consequence of which a committee drew up 'General Rules for the Conduct of Architectural Competitions', which were, however, exhortatory rather than mandatory. They recommended the appointment of at least one assessor, who should draw up the instructions; stated grounds for excluding submitted designs; urged that all accepted should subsequently be exhibited, and that the winner be employed; and defined the size of premiums in relation to prospective costs.[2] In 1877 members' attention was again called to these rules, and the necessity of forwarding them to promoters of competitions at the earliest moment.[3]

Professional attention was further focused on the problem of competition in 1879–80, Thomas Porter,[4] himself a regular competitor, taking the initiative with a circular letter to members of the Institute in November, urging that the council act to minimise the evils of the existing practice. The *Builder* took up the issue, complaining of a want of cohesion in the profession which was a source of great weakness and loss of dignity. Competition brought little general benefit: 'It is very seldom indeed that a large competition, when conducted by competent judges, is gained by anyone who had been entirely unknown previously': an accurate statement if one reads 'entirely unknown' literally.[5] *Building News* condemned the system, but, as the mouthpiece of the avant-garde, viewed it rather as the Duke of Wellington saw the rotten boroughs in 1831. 'Competition has done much to place the product of an architect's skill on a level with other commodities. . . . The art has been brought to the level of a manufacture; . . . feats of draughtsmanship are mistaken for architecture, while the standard of professional morality has been considerably lowered by the practice of competing architects sending in designs far in excess of the real cost.' But if open competition were abolished, how would the 'less fortunate' advance themselves?[6]

In his campaign against the competition system,[7] Porter made four main points: the mania for competition, for small works as well as large, damaged not only the dignity but also the finances of the profession, for the cost was huge; promoters were not competent to select the best design, and it was essential to have not one assessor but at least two, to correct professional bias (the existence of which had always been used as an argument against professional judges);[8] disappointed competitors airing their grievances in the papers exercised a baneful influence; and – greatest evil of all – competition prevented the intimate connexion between client and architect which was essential from the outset for good design.[9] For very costly and important buildings only, competition might still be tolerated.

He hoped that the Fellows of the RIBA, relatively few though they were, would set an example by agreeing to refrain from open competition, or from a limited one in which a substantial honorarium was not offered to each participant. He believed this would kill off the system, raise the dignity of the profession, materially improve members' finances, and materially benefit office architectural assistants. The belief in the advantages of competition belonged, he thought, to the past generation, when the success of a few had given 'tremendous impetus' to the system. Furthermore, the Institute should introduce binding rules by which, for larger works, promoters might advertise for architects to send in their names and lists of works, from which a selection would be made in the proportion of one competitor for every £2000 to be spent. Each would be paid a suitable honorarium.

Discussion at the RIBA evoked general agreement that the conditions of competition needed to be made fairer, though whether it could be dispensed with was disputed. Its importance as a means of bringing forward young men without wealth or friends was stressed; but so too was the frequently corrupt nature of the exercise. Even the mottoes affixed to drawings to ensure anonymity were asserted to be a sham by Chatfeild Clarke; and Robert Kerr treated corruption drolly, suggesting that the 1864 South Kensington Museums competition (in which he had come second [Pl. 104]) had not been free of skulduggery: 'I have always thought it is of no use going into a competition unless you are sure to win! The man who knows how to win a competition does win, and the man who does not know does not win.' To win, he told the RIBA, 'you must go the right way to work to get the best "information". (Renewed laughter.) Ah, I see you know what I mean by that. Now, I got the best information at South Kensington, but, practically, Captain Fowkes [*sic*] got better. So, in addition to using the best information, the man who means to win must have "friends".'[10]

Ewan Christian, however, 'as one who owes all his success to competitions', contradicted Kerr, claiming that the only way to win was by 'taking the greatest possible trouble and making yourself master of your subject'. Charles Barry expressed his 'unlimited objection to competition', and his dead brother Edward (who had been a bitterly disappointed competitor in 1867) was quoted as denouncing it as bad for employers, bad for architects and bad for art in general.[11] But Barry's contrasting the treatment of architects with the greater respect accorded lawyers and physicians hints at their insecure professional status.[12] One Fellow pointed out that 'We have to remember that we live in the midst of competition; it is the rule everywhere. Whatever we may say or do in our capacity as members of a learned society, the outside public, and the corporations who pay for the buildings, eventually settle these matters.'[13]

As secretary of a committee appointed to consult the provincial societies and draw up a body of rules, Porter ensured that it embodied his proposals: architects were to send in their names, from whom a selection would be invited to submit sketches. In a two-tier competition, all those in the second stage would be remunerated. Except for the sketch competition, mottoes were to be abolished, as were premiums. A professional assessor, appointed at the outset, would draw up the instructions.[14] The RIBA general conference in May 1881 took up the issue, when it was argued that competitions could not be done away with – they afforded young men opportunities of thinking out something for and by themselves after office hours; but as at present conducted they were a scandal.[15] With differences within the organised body of the RIBA, then only a minority of architects, it was unlikely that any common line could be held in a profession that embraced a wide socio-economic range.

Thus, when in 1882 Shaw Lefevre as First Commissioner persuaded the second Gladstone administration to implement proposals for building the two great defence departments at the north end of Whitehall, professional opinion was ready to persist with competition, especially for such major works. As a good free-trader Lefevre promoted competition, despite the opposition of the permanent head of the Office. Algernon Mitford, Secretary from 1874 to 1886, was in favour of the Ayrtonian system of employing the Office 'surveyors' to draw the plans. 'There are no men in England so thoroughly cognisant of all the requirements of public departments', he told the 1877 select committee on public buildings. 'They are practically architects, and the only additional expense involved would be the hiring of a few temporary draughtsmen.' 'If our department were instructed to prepare plans, and were told by a committee of taste, Members of the House of Commons and others, who might be appointed, that the building was to be produced in such and such a style, I believe that it would be as well done in our department as it would be done outside.'[16] Pressed on the quality of architecture such officers might produce, Mitford admitted that 'in the event of our putting up a building of a national character, and which would court comment or criticism, not only in this country, but from abroad', it might be necessary to employ an outside architect. If so, however, 'I should say that architects are known by their works; and you could pick an architect; you would get the most talented architect of the day. I think that competition is a mischief altogether', he concluded weightily, 'whether limited or unlimited.'[17]

Despite his principal officer's view, in April 1883 Lefevre, who had been taking outside advice,[18] told the Commons that he proposed very shortly to invite a competition for designs.[19] The *Architect* suggested that competition had been chosen for two reasons: demand and supply – the hope that a better plan might be procured 'from outsiders of more ambitious pretensions' than the official architectural staff; and because there was 'an earnest demand on the part of such outsiders – whose name is legion – for permission to submit designs at their own risk'.[20] Lefevre nevertheless realised, as Cowper had done, that a fundamental problem about architectural competitions was how to persuade eminent architects to enter; while, if competition were restricted to a few of the great names, little encouragement was offered to the profession generally, and valuable new ideas or even young genius would be ignored. The two great limited competitions of 1866–7 had produced no more happy a result than the international competition of 1856–7. He told a select committee:

It was determined that the competition should be a double one, upon a new principle so far as the public offices were concerned, the object being to induce the principal architects to compete. It was represented to me that the labour and expense of making designs for a great public competition of this kind were so great that some of the principal architects would be very unwilling to enter upon them, and it was thought that by making what was a double competition, the first competition to be for sketch designs for the purpose of limiting the drawings in such a way as not to involve any considerable expense and labour, it might be possible to induce the principal architects to compete. The first competition under that plan was to be a secret one; it was to be open to all the world, but the names were not afterwards to be known. Out of the first competition 10 designs were to be selected, the authors of which were to compete in a second and more elaborate competition. . . .

There was to be a premium of £600 to be given to each of the 10 successful men in the first competition, which was supposed to be an inducement to them to compete, and would pay them the expense of the more elaborate designs in the second competition.[21]

The sketch designs, to be seen only by the judges and their officers, were to be submitted by 1 March 1884. In outline only, at the scale of 24 ft to the inch, they were to comprise a plan of each floor, at least two sections north-south and one east-west, and an elevation of each of the principal fronts and courts. The War Office was to be on the south side, adjoining the Horse Guards; and the rooms of the principal officers of both departments on the Park front. Plans for the second stage were to be of 16 ft to the inch, with a perspective drawing. The ten finalists might make 'reasonable modifications' to their sketch plans. The appointed architect would be paid £25,000 (including his second-stage fee of £600), for services 'to include all those usually performed by an Architect, except that he shall be relieved of all expense, trouble and responsibility in determining the times and amounts of instalments to the Builders, and in making up the accounts connected with the execution of the works'. Drawings and specifications were to be government property, the architect making at his own expense all necessary working copies.[22]

The two-tier arrangement, said to have first been employed in the Liverpool Free Public Library and Museum competition of 1856 at the suggestion of Wyatt Papworth,[23] had been embodied in the RIBA's competition regulations issued in 1872 and revised in 1883.[24] The chief contemporary objection was to the obligatory shrouding in secrecy of the unsuccessful sketch-designs – since publicity was a major aim of many entrants, and the influence of public opinion was thereby ruled out[25] –, and in the twentieth century professional opinion moved strongly against the two-stage competition.[26] But it had been used successfully for Manchester Town Hall (1866) and in the second competition (1881–2) for Glasgow municipal buildings, one of the most important of the time.[27]

Lefevre was happy with the outcome: there were 130 entrants for the elimination stakes, including one or two foreigners; 'a fair representation of the architectural talent of the country'.[28] Nevertheless, when one compares this field with that for the Glasgow municipal buildings (at £250,000 only a third of the proposed government offices' cost), with 110 runners, and considers that some 2500 sets of instructions at 5s. each had been sold, it looks less impressive.[29] The opacity of the instructions may have been partly to blame: 'The first perusal left as little impression on my mind as would the four faces of Cleopatra's Needle', commented one entrant.[30] The sheer workload of designing offices for 1800 persons in some 650 rooms within the limited space allocated must have defeated many.[31] A further excluding factor was the specifying a fee for the commission, £25,000, about £10,000 less than the five per cent commission required by Institute rules. Although the £600 each offered to the selected ten for the second stage 'sounded quite musical' to one Scot, and the larger sum 'made one's teeth fairly water', to many it was a stumbling-block.[32]

Among the judges were, in accord with RIBA views, two veteran architects, Philip Charles Hardwick, no longer in active practice,[33] and Ewan Christian PRIBA (1815–95), as well as three MPs: Lefevre himself, Childers, chancellor of the Exchequer and formerly head of both defence departments, and W.H. Smith, a similarly experienced Tory, representing the Opposition. Christian, who as architect to the Ecclesiastical Commissioners since 1850 had immense experience in examining plans, was not universally approved: a 'Goth', he was regarded as behind the times by the more progressive men, and an inappropriate choice for judging mainly Classical entries.[34] Some architects, indeed, objected to any non-professionals on the jury.[35] But the relatively avant-garde *Building News* admitted that Lefevre could not have been expected to collaborate with an Institute council headed by Horace Jones.[36]

Assisted by Mitford, Hunt, Taylor and J.T. Jones of the Office of Works, the judges surveyed the entries in three batches, taking between eight and ten from each for further consideration.[37] Their minutes suggest that the two professionals, with Taylor of the Works, were the dominant influences. They selected only nine entries for the second stage,[38] rejecting such distinguished men as Waterhouse, Graham Jackson and E.R. Robson [Pl. 184]. Of the nine, they recommended Leeming Bros, Verity & Hunt, and Webb & Bell, unanimously awarding the prize to John (1849–1931) and Joseph (1850–1929) Leeming, an almost unknown Halifax partnership [Pl. 186].[39] Despite avant-garde reservations about Christian, such a panel of judges should have satisfied Parliament, profession and public alike; choosing a design of architectural

distinction which should at the same time meet the requirements of the defence departments.[40] Yet there was considerable criticism: some reviewers felt the public had been defrauded by not being allowed to view the field. The *Architect* feared that the ban on the rejected exhibiting their sketches would frustrate their purpose in entering, and deplored the 'excessive secrecy'.[41]

The nine finalists' designs were put on show, but 'The exhibition of all the designs', wrote Beresford Hope in the *Saturday Review*, 'would have been the general guarantee of the fairness of the award. . . . As it is, the award is an unexpected and startling one. There is a moral certainty that there must have been a wide and distinguished representation of established architectural merit among the crowd of competitors, and yet the outcome is a little knot of extremely obscure men . . . by no means authors of designs of such superior merit as to present a self-evident explanation of the puzzle.' He suspected that the judges 'drifted into becoming slaves of their own rules and went to work justly and fairly according to preconceived resolves, but in a mechanical way . . . rejecting every definite shortcoming, and not showing mercy for any positive merits . . . until they found themselves reduced to the residuum which happened to conform to their arbitrary prepossessions'. The answer might be for competitions to include 'model block plans' drawn up by officials.[42]

Yet one of the prime merits of the competitive system was supposed to be its ability to throw up unknown men: 'whenever they win, a sense of satisfaction prevails among good-natured people, which it is a pleasure to experience'.[43] The 1884 competition brought forward not only the Leemings, but also Aston Webb (whose elevations were ironically the contemned Christian's preferred choice).[44] The other leading contenders were also mostly young; one in three, unusually, from the provinces; and the designs tend to the 'Wrenaissance' or neo-Baroque that was to characterise late-Victorian and Edwardian public building.[45] The failure of such busy leading men as T.G. Jackson or E.R. Robson may be accounted for by their inability to devote enough time to the problem,[46] but neither offered a really appropriate design

184. New Admiralty and War Office two-tier competition, 1884, Park front, elevations and perspectives:
a (Top left). A. Waterhouse.
b (Top right). T.G. Jackson. Lacking the panache which the judges obviously sought, neither Waterhouse nor Jackson was admitted to the final competition.
c (Bottom left). Thomas Porter. He was a determined critic of the competition system.
d (Bottom right). Malcolm Stark and James Lindsay of Glasgow.

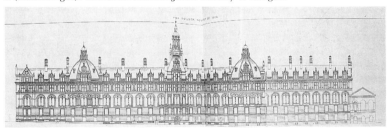

185.   New Admiralty and War Office competition finalists, 1884, Park front perspectives:
a (left). Aston Webb & Ingress Bell. Generally praised as the most beautiful entry, it was one of three finalists specially praised by the judges.
b (right). Thomas Verity & G.H. Hunt. Verity was a highly experienced theatre architect. This was the third of the recommended designs.

186.   New Admiralty and War Office competition, 1884. Leeming Bros of Halifax, unknown in the metropolis, were adjudged the winners on plan and elevation taken together.
a. The winning design, drawn by the Manchester perspectivist, Langham.
b. Revision: the First Commissioner required the reduction of the features overshadowing the Horse Guards, before submitting the design for parliamentary approval.

187. New Admiralty, Block III from Horse Guards Parade. Leeming Bros' revised competition design having been scrapped by a Commons' committee, they were commissioned to build an extension to the Old Admiralty, of which this was the third and final front. The use of red brick, with stone trim, was a departure from the tradition of Whitehall public offices, and was generally disliked.

[Pl. 184].[47] The preferring of Leeming Bros' design to those of Webb & Bell [Pl. 185a] or Verity & Hunt [Pl. 185b] may have been due in part to its superb draughtsmanship;[48] but largely, the judges' minutes and correspondence suggest, to Leemings' closer adherence, taking plan and elevation together, to the instructions, so Hope's analysis of their procedure may have been accurate.[49] Even a severe critic of their planning acknowledged that they had designed a light and airy, businesslike building.[50] Nevertheless, in elevation it was not the finest, nor in planning the ablest: 'either requisite must have stood in the light of a truly intelligent appreciation of the contrary merit', as Hope noted, wondering whether this difficulty were not 'fatal to the idea of selecting the builders [*sic*] of our public buildings by competition'.[51] Leemings' was a heavily-ornamented, – in Hope's view, 'uncomfortable' – expensive design, with a weighty tower frowning down the Horse Guards. It had a mixed reception from the professional journals. 'It is not a *great* building', declared the *Builder*.[52] Lefevre himself, though he was to champion it, required considerable modifications before putting Leemings' design to parliament.[53]

More significantly, although W.H. Smith (celebrated as a man of common sense) admitted that 'the internal arrangements of the building' were 'the main consideration which we had in view', he declared that he had never been satisfied with the specifications.

He campaigned successfully to prevent the erection of Leeming Bros' modified plans, though they had been definitively approved in April 1885 by the Commons at the First Commissioner's instigation.[54] The press attacks on the design and on Lefevre's architectural judgement probably helped to determine its fate.[55] Smith and his Liberal ally, Harcourt, dominated the committee which decided that Lefevre's project was unnecessary: for the Admiralty, extensions would be sufficient, that could be built quickly and economically. The War Office rebuilding was put off to another place and a later time.[56] However, the public honour was felt to be pledged to Leeming Bros, so that they were employed to execute the reduced scheme of Admiralty extensions [Pl. 133, 187] accepted by the government.[57]

Lefevre had greater success, however, in imposing his will in the so-called 'restoration' of Westminster Hall. The erection of the New Courts of Justice had involved a promise to demolish Soane's old courts immediately west of the Hall. Carried out in 1883–4, the demolition exposed to view the dilapidated west side of the Hall [Pl. 188]. What to do, Lefevre regarded as 'one of the most difficult [questions] which has ever fallen to an architect to solve'.[58] This might have been an interesting subject for competition, such as that *Country Life* has recently (1993) fostered for restoring Windsor Castle after the fire. But Lefevre chose what seemed an uncontroversial solution. He called in the leading church restorer of the day, John Loughborough Pearson (Scott had died in 1878), to consider 'restoration' of the walls and buttresses. But Pearson's old-fashioned idea of restoration[59] – reconstruction it might now be termed – brought down on him the wrath of William Morris's Society for the Protection of Ancient Buildings, as well as the enmity of Sir Charles Barry's friends, and those who favoured minimal restoration. Despite vigorous opposition and heated controversy, Lefevre arranged his select committee in 1884, carried Pearson's appointment (considered in greater detail in chapter 15), and had his design largely executed in 1886–90 [Pl. 188]. Pearson's national reputation had marked him out for this unusual and, as it proved, controversial task.[60]

Although this study does not include buildings for the police, we must refer at this point to the building of new headquarters for the Metropolitan Police. The rapid expansion of the force in the early 1880s called for a new headquarters. In 1883 a new Receiver, Alfred Richard Pennefather, was appointed for the Metropolitan Police District, and determined to secure an impressive, well-sited building.[61] In April 1886 he urged the responsible minister, the Home secretary, Childers, to purchase the site of the failed Opera House on the Victoria Embankment, first offered to the police three years earlier. The selection of an architect for so prominent a site was clearly a question of moment. Harcourt, the previous Home secretary, had wanted to employ a Royal Engineer, as the Department of Science and Art did at South Kensington. Pennefather now objected to this idea, and similarly opposed competition as wasteful and doubtful; he wanted to employ the experienced police surveyor, John Dixon Butler, supervised by 'an architect of standing'.[62] The decision to appoint R. Norman Shaw as supervising architect was taken by Childers' Conservative successor Henry Matthews, late in 1886, apparently orally after interviewing Shaw. He told the Commons that he had consulted 'high artistic authorities'; but Dr Saint suggests that the influence of W.H. Smith was crucial.[63] It was, of course, just at this period that Smith was co-operating with Harcourt to destroy the result of the 1884 Admiralty competition; he had himself employed Shaw at his country house in 1884–5.

After years of pressure from the Department of Science and Art, responsible for the government buildings at South Kensington, the cabinet decided in 1890 to authorise the completion of the South Kensington Museum.[64] Considerable activity was on foot there, largely encouraged by the 1851 Exhibition Commissioners, owners of the freehold. They were closely linked with the organising committee for the 'Imperial Institute' [Pl. 189] planned as the national memorial of Queen Victoria's golden jubilee.[65] In July 1887 the Exhibition Commissioners offered to lease some six acres in the centre of the old garden of the Royal Horticultural Society to the Institute for a nominal rent, a decision that destroyed the prospect of an axial layout between the Natural History Museum and the Albert Hall [Pl. 190].[66] Even before the site was obtained the Imperial Institute committee had formed a building committee that determined on a competition for a building to cost £250,000. The arrangements were largely decided by Waterhouse (a member of the building committee), who followed the RIBA proposals: architects were invited to submit their names; from 66 who did so, six were selected,[67] each to be paid £200; the jury was composed of three laymen, Sir Frederic Leighton PRA, and Waterhouse as assessor, an outside assessor being offered if the competitors should desire it. Waterhouse discussed the terms with the competitors,[68] but imposed his own preference for a perspective drawing on them.[69]

Given the ultimate fiasco of the 1884 Admiralty competition,

188. Westminster Hall.
a. Once Soane's Law Courts were removed in 1883, a tatterdemalion western flank was exposed, to which something had to be done:
b. Proposed restoration, J.L. Pearson, 1884. The leading church restorer of the day, Pearson was appointed first as consultant and then in 1884 as architect for the 'restoration', a highly questionable archaeological exercise. His additional storey to the towers, however, was never executed.
c. North Front from New Palace Yard, Sir Charles Barry, who had long before planned a range of parliamentary offices. His son revived the plan, but the minister had committed himself to Pearson's scheme.

189. Design for the Imperial Institute, South Kensington, by Thomas Edward Collcutt (1840–1924), who won a limited competition. Built largely in Portland stone, it cost about £354,000, the towers being modified in execution. It was to perpetuate a series of colonial exhibitions; a lively memorial of Queen Victoria's golden jubilee, funded by public subscription. But its endowment was inadequate, its role unclear. It served a variety of purposes simultaneously. Part accommodated London University when it moved out of Burlington Gardens in 1899, when alterations were made at the public charge. (Demolished, save for the tower, in 1957–65.)

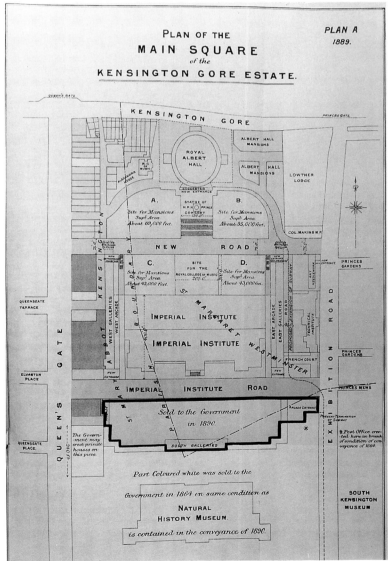

190. Plan of the layout of 'South Kensington' from the Natural History Museum northwards. The area marked 'Sold to the Government in 1890' became the site of the Royal College (later Imperial College) of Science. The opportunity of an axial layout between the Natural History Museum and the Albert Hall afforded by the existence of the Royal Horticultural Society's garden had already been lost.

and the weight of current RIBA opinion, any government might have been reluctant to risk an open competition for completing the South Kensington Museum.[70] Knowing the attitude of Smith and Matthews it may surprise us that a limited competition of invited architects was decided upon, four chosen by the First Commissioner and four by the RIBA. The explanation may lie in the success of the limited competition for the Imperial Institute.[71] Five of those now chosen had taken part in that contest.[72] The judges were to be five ministers, a representative of the Opposition, and a 'professional assessor', Waterhouse, who was told that 'the choice of design will probably proceed on somewhat broad considerations and it is not anticipated that the duties of the Assessor will entail any very minute or laborious examination of the plans'.[73] Only six months were allowed for preparation of entries, at which the competitors protested, whereon the number of drawings required was reduced. Although the competitors were known, their entries were still submitted under a monogram. In the result, Aston Webb [Pl. 191] was selected to complete what was to become the Victoria and Albert Museum, though the work was postponed for years and Webb's design greatly modified before and during execution.

Webb's success was welcomed by *A.A. Notes*, Webb being an active member of the Association, but its critic found the competition 'very disappointing', the competitors having 'failed to grasp the spirit and feeling that a building of such magnitude should have'. John Belcher's design [Pl. 252] had 'the most satisfying dignity'.[74] 'Taken as a whole', thought the *Architect*, 'the designs do not afford evidence in favour of limited competitions, unless on the ground that trouble was spared in the examination . . . the Government would have acted more wisely to have arranged for a general competition. It is true that the result in the War Office and Admiralty competition was not encouraging, but the circumstances are different with a scheme like the South Kensington one which has already given rise to much experimental designing.'[75]

Yet in many respects this was the most successful of the great government building competitions to date, and avoided the controversies that had rent or followed its predecessors.[76] The collaboration with the RIBA, the appointment of its president, Waterhouse, as assessor, and the assessor's dominance of the judging (thanks perhaps to the absence of connoisseurs from the jury) contributed to this result. So too did co-operation between the winner and the department. Asked whether Webb's design had been chosen as 'the best elevation from the picturesque point of view, or because it was the best arrangement inside', General Sir John Donnelly (1834–1902), as secretary of the Department of Science and Art, South Kensington's chief executive, replied: 'Well, I think for both reasons. . . . the plan as the building was eventually turned out after the competition, after it was modified, is as good as it could be.'[77]

Nevertheless Macvicar Anderson (1835–1915), VPRIBA, was simultaneously denouncing the whole competitive system as bad for the public and the profession alike: 'The probability is that out of a number of competitive designs, not one would be so good as that which a selected architect of experience would produce'; and competition prevented that intercourse between client and architect necessary from the outset. Only one man could be employed: it was not good that the others 'incur pecuniary loss, and suffer mental strain from working at high pressure in the absurdly insufficient time which is often allowed'. If there was any case in which competition should not be resorted to, it was, he insisted (contrary to the general professional view), government buildings. 'To subject works of national importance to the dubious and fortuitous chances of competition, appears to me unpardonable.' The government would consult the true national interest if they were to commission leading architects to carry out great buildings of the state,[78] just as Mr Alexander had chosen Ewan Christian for his gift of the National Portrait Gallery building (considered in chapter 15) [Pl. 192].

Meanwhile the government was employing its own salaried architects, Taylor and Tanner, for additions to the National Gallery (1884–7),[79] Bankruptcy Courts (1889–2),[80] Patent Office (from 1891),[81] Public Record Office (1892–5),[82] Land Registry (1900–5),[83] and somewhat obscure public buildings out of most MPs' habitual perambulations.

When the Liberal government in 1892 accepted an offer from Sir Henry Tate to finance the building of a new gallery for British art, a rather different set of circumstances prevailed. Tate was anxious to use his own architect, Sidney R.J. Smith (1858–1913).[84] But belief in the merits of competition was strong in the artistic community at large (at this precise time, architects were riven by the controversy whether architecture was a profession or an art),[85] and Sir Frederic Leighton, PRA, (in contrast with his view on the 1884 War Office and Admiralty commission) urged the chancellor of the Exchequer 'in the most earnest manner to stipulate for the choice of an Architect by *public competition*, a course to which Mr Tate cannot possibly make any legitimate objection and will certainly, more than any other, be in conformity with public feeling'. The chancellor was evidently doubtful, so Leighton took up the argument: 'It is perfectly true that competition does not *always* give the most satisfactory results – That is generally attributable to the assessors, but at least there is a considerable hope of a good work being secured.' Tate's negotiations with the preceding Conservative chancellor having broken down on this very point, Harcourt was understandably reluctant to offend him by insisting on competition, arranging instead that the plans [Pl. 193] should be approved by the Office of Works, which should also supervise their execution to ensure sound construction.[86]

The great new wave of public works which washed over London in consequence of Aretas Akers-Douglas's seismic upheaving of

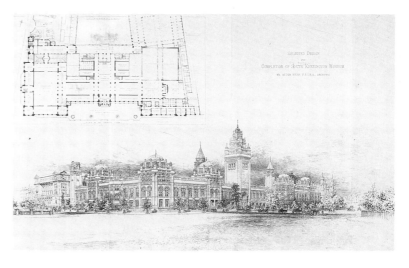

191.   Completion of the South Kensington Museum (later Victoria & Albert Museum). Two-tier competition, 1891, assessed by Waterhouse:
a. First prize: Aston Webb. Plan and elevation. No further steps were taken until 1899, and the design was then modified (cp pl. 251).
b. William Young (1843–1900) was another finalist, but the 'disciplined classicism' and repetitive towers of his 'very ambitious design' did not enthuse Waterhouse.

192.   National Portrait Gallery, Ewan Christian (1814–95). When Mr Alexander gave the funds for building a permanent home for the National Portrait Gallery, the government gave a site north-east of the National Gallery originally earmarked for its enlargement. On his east front, Christian continued the lines of Wilkins' Greek Revival style but for his free-standing north front he designed a Florentine Renaissance palace of considerable distinction.

public funding in the third Salisbury Administration from 1895 included the completion of the South Kensington Museum as well as new government offices – even that mirage, a new War Office. Webb's plan for the South Kensington Museum, well regarded by the authorities there after revisions, was brought into play, and he was also entrusted, without further competition, with new buildings for the Royal College of Science [Pl. 194], to be erected opposite the Imperial Institute.[87] But when the Carrington House

193.   Tate Gallery. Sir Henry Tate (1819–99), the donor, insisted on employing his own architect, Sidney R.J. Smith, who had designed several small public buildings, such as libraries, in South London.

194.   Royal College of Science, Aston Webb, 1900–6. The scheme for the college was at first considered in conjunction with that for the South Kensington Museum, so that Webb was commissioned to prepare designs. Not until 1898 was the large site on the south of Imperial Institute Road allocated to it, with £200,000 for the building.

and Great George Street sites were acquired, for a new War Office and Government Offices respectively, the problem of choosing architects again presented itself.

During the summer of 1897, Sir John Donnelly had told a select committee that limited competition, in which architects were invited to compete, was 'the constant practice now with regard to public buildings'.[88] But in November Akers-Douglas, the Conservative First Commissioner (somewhat unusually, a member of the cabinet) submitted to the Treasury a memorandum that had already been agreed between Reginald Brett (later Lord Esher), Secretary of the Office of Works, and Sir Francis Mowatt, the Treasury Secretary.[89] This described the South Kensington limited competition of 1891 as 'preferable for many reasons of a technical nature to an open competition', but recommended that 'If Her Majesty's Government desire to see erected a building of fine design, planned upon principles conducive to the comfort and convenience of the public servants who are to occupy it, without undue delay in carrying out the work,' the government itself should make a 'deliberate choice' of architects 'well known for their taste, skill, and efficiency'. Such a decision, controversial as it might be, would be 'no weightier than many which have to be taken by the executive Government'. It should be 'made imperatively clear' to the chosen architects that 'their designs are to follow, in their internal arrangements, the general lines laid down' by the Office of Works, 'and that the height and dimensions of rooms as well as of corridors are to be based upon the reasonable requirement of the public servants who are to ocupy them, as settled by this Department, further, that the elevations are to accord in point of style with the public buildings already erected in Parliament Street; and finally that the new offices are to be externally constructed entirely of stone' – the last, an implicit condemnation of the Admiralty extensions determined on by select committee. The memorandum concluded:

> In submitting this proposal . . . the First Commissioner is well aware of the nature of the responsibility which would be assumed by Her Majesty's Government should they undertake the thankless task of selecting the Architects to be employed. He is convinced, however, that no form of competition, unlimited or limited, is free from the gravest objections, if it is desired to erect buildings creditable to the nation, and serviceable for the future. Architecture is considered by its professors to be an art and not a commercial undertaking, so that a method of procedure which excludes from consideration the work of the most eminent architects, is one which the First Commissioner cannot bring himself to recommend.[90]

To secure their assent to his controversial proposal, Akers-Douglas circulated a memorandum to his cabinet colleagues in December 1897. He pointed out that in recent years a considerable range of government buildings had been carried out by the staff of the Office of Works; buildings which, 'designed by officers who are well acquainted with the accommodation and arrangement required, and who specially bore in mind the health, comfort, and convenience of those who would afterwards occupy them, have given general satisfaction'. However, he believed that for the major works now proposed public opinion 'would not indorse the architectural designing being intrusted absolutely to the staff of the Office of Works, even if its members were in a position to undertake the task'. On the other hand, 'when competition or limited competition has been adopted we have generally failed to get designs commanding final acceptance; great delays have arisen; and experience has certainly proved that buildings so designed have not given complete satisfaction'. Moreover, 'some of the best

known and most capable Architects decline to compete', even in limited competition. He therefore suggested that 'we should set aside competition in favour of deliberate choice, the responsibility of which should be taken by the Government'. There were, he pointed out, precedents in the appointment of Banks and Barry for the forecourt of Burlington House and Pearson for additions to Westminster Hall.

This bold suggestion, he realised, might be too much for his cabinet colleagues. Were that so, he proposed an alternative: to obtain from the RIBA a

> list of names of architects who in their opinion are qualified to carry out works of the magnitude and importance of those proposed, and who would agree to prepare plans upon information as to requirements, to be supplied by the Office of Works, on a classical design in keeping with other public buildings already erected in Whitehall. From this list the Government should make a selection of two Architects, and nominate one of them to prepare plans for the War Office . . . and another for the building on the Great George Street site. . . . When the plans for the various schemes have been prepared, I would propose that the two Architects to be selected, with Mr Aston Webb [architect of the South Kensington Museum], together also with the President of the Royal Institute of British Architects (the President of the Royal Academy) and Sir John Taylor [chief Office of Works architect], should act as a Committee to advise me in matters of general design in connection with the plans in question.
>
> I am aware [he concluded] of the nature of the responsibility which the Government would assume in undertaking the thankless task of selecting the Architects to be employed. At the same time, I am so convinced that no form of competition, unlimited or limited, is free from the gravest objections if it is desired to erect buildings creditable to the Government and well adapted to their requirements, that I can see no other course open than to adopt the plan which I have put forward after the most careful consideration with the officers of my Department, who have had prolonged experience of the difficulties attending the erection of public buildings such as those under consideration.[91]

The cabinet decided that 'deliberate choice' was too bold an option, preferring to consult the president of the RIBA. But Akers-Douglas's determination that government should make the choice was in keeping with the tendency of the age for the executive to make decisions, rather than deferring to select committees. His firm grasp of the rudder was made easier by the government's rosy financial situation, which enabled him to finance a large building programme without constant reference to the Commons.[92]

Questioned in the House, Akers-Douglas replied: 'It is certainly not the intention of the Government to go to public competition . . . because I think it is generally admitted that this practice has failed in the past, and that it is a rather dangerous policy'; instead, they proposed to ensure 'through Sir John Taylor, who will act as their assessor, that the interior of the offices is such as will meet the requirements of the case, and then appointing an architect for the purpose of clothing the building'.[93] But when his predecessor, Herbert Gladstone, urged him to 'induce Sir John Taylor to undertake the charge of the whole building', he explained that Taylor would not 'at his time of life . . . [undertake] so onerous a duty'; and he corrected his earlier statement: 'as Sir John Taylor knows more about what is required in the interior of public offices than anyone else, he should have control, and should work with the architect who is preparing the elevations'. George

Aitchison (1825–1910), R.A., PRIBA, 'acknowledged authority on classic architecture', would act as an additional assessor in carrying out the plans.[94]

The First Commissioner had in anticipation already, in January 1898, asked the RIBA to suggest a short list of architects of 'taste, skill and efficiency in Classical design'. The RIBA council in turn asked the provincial societies to recommend two classical architects each, with photographs of their works, from which a committee made a selection and added a list of London architects who were also asked to supply photographs. Out of 22 names chosen, the committee ballotted for twelve. Council added two more and ballotted for eight, whose names were forwarded to the government with supporting photographs.[95] When the government asked for more names, the next three in the ballot (who had obtained an equal number of votes) were added.[96]

The secrecy adopted in the selection of architects was criticised in the press, and the idea that they should merely 'clothe' the plans of official architects considered an insult.[97] However, the involvement of the RIBA in the matter was an astute move that went far to undermine professional objections.[98] The final selection, of John McKean Brydon (1840–1901) and William Young (1843–1900), was carried out by four ministers, including Balfour (leading minister in the Commons) and Lansdowne (the War minister) as well as Akers-Douglas; but Lord Wemyss (as Elcho had become) 'greatly influenced' the ministers' choice. As a young man, Young had fallen into the path of Wemyss (then Elcho), who was impressed by his efficiency, employed him extensively at Gosford,[99] and recommended him to his aristocratic friends. Young proved highly proficient in the complex planning of great country houses, experience useful for the even more complex Glasgow City Chambers competition of 1881. In preparing for that, he visited Rome and Florence; his success, and the magnificent structure he built in 1883–9 [Pl. 196][100] made him an obvious runner in the Whitehall stakes. Wemyss now further aided him by inviting Akers-Douglas to Gosford, and showing him Young's 'huge drawings' of Glasgow City Chambers.[101]

Brydon was less widely known. An enthusiast for English architecture of the seventeenth and eighteenth centuries, he gave two influential papers on that subject at the Architectural Association in 1889.[102] His Wren-inspired design had won the Chelsea Vestry Hall competition, 1885, and in 1891 he was triumphant in a competition for additions to Baldwin's Guildhall at Bath (1776); a picture-gallery and library were further added as a Jubilee memorial in 1897 [Pl. 195]. This work undoubtedly was a vital factor in his government appointment.[103]

The appointments were well received, chiming with the prevalent tone of British architecture. Moreover, the architects' instructions were less demeaning than the First Commissioner's original statement had suggested. They were now merely 'desired to follow in the internal arrangement ... general lines to be laid down by the Office of Works. The elevations will be of classical character ... to accord with those already erected in Whitehall.'[104]

Unfortunately, both Brydon and Young died before their designs were fully worked up. Young died in November 1900, aged 57. He had, for an agreed fee of £23,750 (5 per cent on the estimated cost of the War Office), 'kept an office of draughtsmen &c, superintended the work, and prepared all drawings &c'. By the time of his death, 'The general designs, and most of the drawings necessary for the structural building contracts', including ornamentation, had been made [Pl. 197]. A balance of £12,750 was left of his fee. The alternatives were either to find another architect to complete the work, which would cause delay and expense; or to leave the work with William's son, Clyde, 'not of a position or

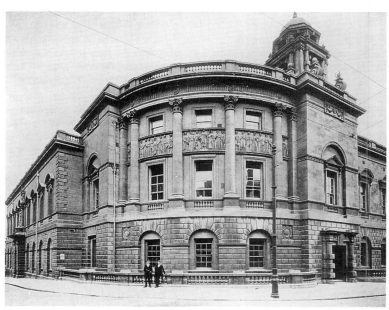

195.   Bath Guildhall. Brydon won a competition for additions to the guildhall in 1891. He added north and south wings to the eighteenth-century building, and then a new council room:
a. Council Room.
b. North wing: technical schools.

196.   Glasgow City Chambers, William Young, 1883-8. Product of a competition, Glasgow's immensely opulent town hall, 'the grand civic gesture *par excellence*', costing £540,000, established Young's reputation as a master scenic architect in the grand manner.

197.   Design for New War Office, William Young, 1899. He proposed repeating Inigo Jones's Banqueting House to the north. Appointed by the First Commissioner on the strength of his Glasgow City Chambers and completion of Gosford House for Lord Wemyss, Young did not live to complete the War Office.

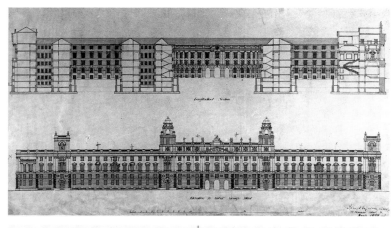

198.   Design for New Public Offices, Parliament Street, John McKean Brydon (1840–1901):
a. Elevation and section, Dec. 1898. Like Young, Brydon was appointed on the strength of his executed buildings, notably municipal buildings at Bath and Chelsea; like Young, he died before he could execute his greatest work. But Brydon, an early advocate of the 'Wrenaissance' worked more closely within the English Classical tradition, strongly influenced by Inigo Jones, Wren and Chambers.
b. Perspective, 1899. Brydon envisaged George Gilbert Scott's neighbouring block completed by the addition of corner towers – though not those designed by Scott himself (cp. pl. 53), but a version by John Oldrid Scott. Scott's offices actually top Brydon's, but the latter packed in more floors.

199.   New Public Offices, Park front. Designed by J.M. Brydon, 1898, drawing on his work at Bath (cp pl. 195); erected with modifications by Sir Henry Tanner, 1910–12.

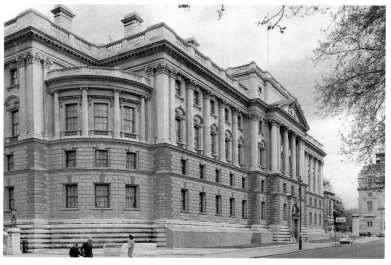

experience such as would justify the Works in leaving the job in his unassisted hands', assisted therefore by a senior architect, dividing the balance of the commission between them. Mowatt of the Treasury discussed the problem with Lord Esher (formerly Brett), the Secretary of the Office of Works, and proposed that Clyde Young should carry out his father's plans in association with Sir John Taylor, who would be paid £1100 a year out of Young's fee, so saving his pension of £700 a year; though the true advantage, to Mowatt's mind, lay in 'the exceptional ability, moderation, tact and energy of the man'.[105]

When Brydon died of a throat infection at the age of 60 in May 1901, he left no successor. Taylor, mindful of comments on the War Office, proposed that another outside architect be appointed to take over, on the grounds that the RIBA 'would not be satisfied with any other proposal, and might cause unfavourable criticism to be directed against [this] Department'. Akers-Douglas however thought that the work could be 'more satisfactorily and more economically carried out by his own officers' as the plans were 'complete except as to detail;[106] and . . . detail, especially internal detail, is a matter particularly within the cognizance of the Board's officials'. An outsider would want 'to give effect to his own ideas of taste and fitness' which would lead to 'contention, difficulty, and delay'; and would require a larger fee than the balance of £15,400 left from Brydon's. Akers-Douglas therefore proposed that the plans [Pl. 198] should be taken over from Brydon's executors (as provided for in his agreement) and the work be carried out by Taylor's successor as the Office's Principal Surveyor, Henry Tanner, FRIBA. Brydon's principal assistant ('who had, under that gentleman's personal direction', Akers-Douglas later told the Commons, 'prepared the greater portion of the drawings') should be engaged 'in order to secure, as far as possible, that Mr Brydon's designs may be executed in detail in their integrity, as public opinion will expect them to be'.[107] Despite criticism from Leonard Stokes, one of Brydon's executors and an applicant to succeed him,[108] and from the president of the RIBA and others, urging the appointment of a 'first-rate man entirely sympathetic with the class of work', Akers-Douglas stuck to a decision that he had taken only after careful consideration and the failure 'after some confidential inquiry' to find such a man.[109]

Now Tanner, although principal architect of the Works, Fellow of the Institute, and winner of the RIBA's Tite prize for Classical design in 1878, was unknown to the political world, whereas Taylor was widely acknowledged as an able public servant. Thus when the First Commissioner responded to the Commons on these matters, he presented them slightly differently, saying that he had tried 'to get an architect of note to undertake the work, but it was only possible on condition that the architect was given a free hand'. Taylor, therefore, would be in charge, having 'worked constantly both with Mr Young and Mr Brydon in the preparation of these plans, and was intimately acquainted with Mr Brydon's desires, and in sympathy with his views' [Pl. 199]. Akers-Douglas assured the Commons somewhat inconsistently that 'no variations at all would be permitted in the external elevations, and that they should only take place when approved by the President of the Institute of British Architects and the Consultative Committee'.[110] The undogmatic *Architect* implicitly supported the minister by reprinting from *The Times* a letter defending his decision.[111]

The national memorial to Queen Victoria in 1901 was not a governmental undertaking,[112] but funded by subscription [Pl. 200]; the organisers invited six architects to contribute designs. The concept of competition, however, continued to be viewed without enthusiasm in the Office of Works. Legislation hurried through in 1903 provided a second tranche of funds for public buildings, including a northern extension to the British Museum [Pl. 270]. The RIBA urged that the precedent of 1898 be followed: 'the architectural profession [*sc.* RIBA] should be consulted in the case of a work of such national importance'. The advisory committee on the new government offices recommended choosing an architect in private practice, although Tanner, who had already prepared designs for the Museum extension, warned:[113]

> the question of policy as to whether the work is to be entrusted to the officers of the Department or whether, the views of the Royal Institute of British Architects are to govern the action of the Board is, of course, not one upon which I should express any opinion, but the employment of Architects in independent practice has by no means been uniformly successful either as the result of competition or selection and has frequently occasioned an unnecessary expenditure without corresponding advantage.

The First Commissioner, Akers-Douglas's successor Lord Windsor, himself keenly interested in architecture,[114] having consulted the prime minister, obtained a panel of seven names supplied by the RIBA;[115] from which he and the advisory committee chose John James Burnet (1857–1938), again, like Young and Brydon, a Scot.[116] Son of a Glasgow architect, he had studied at the Paris *Ecole des Beaux-Arts*, working under J.-L. Pascal (1837–1920), an important influence in the late-nineteenth-century classical re-revival.

For the less important but nevertheless extensive Land Registry in Lincoln's Inn Fields, built from 1900 in two stages, Lord Windsor returned to his official chief architect,[117] Henry Tanner, a policy continued by his successors. Tanner, meanwhile, continued to be directly responsible for the new buildings of the General Post Office in the City, a sector in which he had long been an expert.

Work on the Great George Street offices continued under Tanner for another decade. When the project for a new Board of Trade was authorised in 1912, the First Commissioner, Lord Beauchamp, looked back at the precedents for nominating an architect, as far back as the choice of Banks & Barry for the extensions to Burlington House. His own inclination was 'strongly in favour of an open competition, to be settled by a fairly large committee – assisted by professional architects. The present trend of feeling in the House of Commons is certainly in this direction', he observed, 'and such a course obviates all the difficulties of choosing competitors or selecting a favoured few.' His view was perhaps influenced by the success of the London County Council

200. Admiralty Arch, Sir Aston Webb, R.A., 1905–10. This triumphal arch, part of the Queen Victoria Memorial linking a house for the First Sea Lord to Admiralty offices, ingeniously conceals the change of axis from the westward processional route of the Mall leading to the Queen's statue and Buckingham Palace to that eastwards of Charing Cross and the Strand (cp pl. 29b). Lewis Harcourt consulted the cabinet about the inscription.

in 1906 in holding a two-tier competition for its new County Hall, facing the Houses of Parliament, on the south bank of the Thames.[118] The difficulty was still, as his Commons' spokesman Wedgwood Benn commented, that 'the best architects refuse to enter a competition'.[119] What one tended to get was 'the swash-buckler gang and the swashbucklest being taken'.[120]

Professional opinion continued to be divided. A paper read at the Architectural Association in 1903 had called for a 'jury of [professional] assessors in place of the present one-man system, which has proved to be a dismal failure'. The speaker claimed that this jury system was now almost always applied to important competitions in America, where it had afforded a successful solution, as well as in France. In the discussion that followed, the competition principle found considerable support.[121] But what was becoming increasingly clear was the crucial role of the assessor, on which discussion began to focus. 'The ideal assessor has yet to be found', declared the *Building News* in 1906, and proceeded to analyse assessors' methods, recommending conscientious and laborious examination of entries, followed by a full published reasoned report, such as those delivered by judges in courts of law.[122] Important competitions in this era included the Birmingham Council House extensions, 1906–8, a two-tier affair,[123] and the Coventry Municipal Offices.[124] In 1913, forty architects competed in an open competition for a new exchange at Manchester, provoking an outburst against the system from the president of the Manchester Society of Architects. Let architects lacking other means of advancement compete if they wished to do so, retorted the *Builder*.[125]

The position at the end of our period was summarised by a leading article in the *Builder* a few months before the First World War: 'Competitions are bound to be a very large factor in architectural practice. . . . Let it be said at once that we should like to see every competition assessed by a capable architect, and if this had always been done we think the system would have been adopted without discussion by public bodies and the results accepted with unanimity by architects.' Alas! many distinguished architects lacked the necessary judicial quality of mind; others were unable to see the conditions from the competitors' point of view, and so imposed or accepted requirements that made a satisfactory outcome impossible: the best solution might – and often did – violate the conditions. Waterhouse had been an ideal assessor, possessing tact in managing promoters, wide experience in planning and design, and a fine judicial capacity. 'It may, we think, be fairly said that the great vogue the competition system has attained is in a large measure due to the fact that he was so constantly employed as an assessor.' 'The broad position [concluded the editorial] with regard to competitions is at present this: most public bodies who wish to put up buildings of any size institute architectural competitions, and, we are happy to say, in almost all instances ask for the appointment of an assessor by the RIBA, which very rightly (because it has the support of public opinion) bars those competitions in which an assessor is not appointed, and does not allow members of the Institute [a growing proportion of the profession] to compete in such instances – a course which has had excellent results.'[126]

Beauchamp was well informed about sentiment in the Commons. In 1911 there had been calls for competition for important public works; and criticism of the 'present practice of allowing the designs for the great Departments of State to be settled within the Office of Works' was voiced when in June 1912 the Vote for Public Buildings was considered in committee of Supply.[127] The select committee on Estimates, however, reported in July that while the usual remuneration for an architect was five per cent, official architects cost only 4.01 per cent and performed a variety of services for which market architects would charge additional fees.[128] Thus it is not surprising that the Office of Works was still pressing

in October for its own design for a new Board of Trade to be adopted.[129] But several MPs buzzed on persistently, attacking the Works' monopoly of public buildings. 'An enlightened opinion', declared one, 'supported by an unanimous Press, demands that our future public buildings shall be more worthy of the capital of the Empire.'[130]

A small committee was eventually formed for the proposed Board of Trade (including an Opposition representative, as 'helpful in any discussion in the House of Commons'),[131] which accepted Beauchamp's suggestion to follow the precedent of 1884 for a new Admiralty and War Office (employed also in 1906 for the LCC's County Hall): a two-tier competition; but one open only to British subjects, an interesting return to the nationalism of the Houses of Parliament competition of 1835. 'The fact that an open competition has been instituted for this building may be taken as some evidence that the Government is alive to the advantage of obtaining the very best ideas and employing the best available talent in the erection of public buildings', commented the *Builder* sententiously.[132]

The Office of Works demarcated the site in Whitehall Gardens [Pl. 201], furnished a schedule of accommodation to be provided on eleven floors, marking a decisive increase in the height of official buildings, made possible by the introduction of electric lifts, and indicated a cost limit of £570,000 for a two-part structure intended to cause the minimum of inconvenience to the work of the Board. In yet another reversion to an older practice, it made a stipulation also as to style, ruling out the general use of columnar treatment of the exterior. In the first instance only a sketch design under *nom-de-plume* was called for, consisting of plans of the ground and principal floors, with diagram plans for the other floors, north, east, and west elevations, and two complete sections, all drawn to a scale of 16 ft to the inch; a small-scale block plan, and two perspective sketches not more than 18 inches in length, showing the relationship to adjacent buildings. The competition was announced at the beginning of September 1913, the sketches to be submitted by 31 December.[133] Professional assessors would select ten from the sketchers, each of whom would be allowed four months to provide designs of 'a more complete and detailed character' and a fee of £300. Three assessors were appointed: Reginald Blomfield PRIBA, John Belcher, the government's own nominee,[134] and Aston Webb, R.A., nominated by the RIBA. (On Belcher's death in November 1913, Ernest Newton was substi-

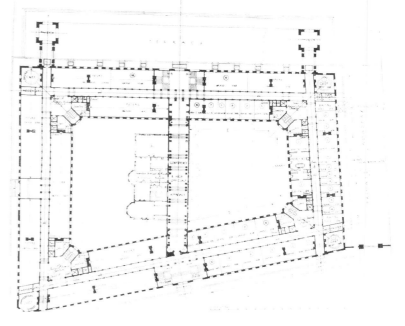

201.   Board of Trade, Whitehall Gardens; two-tier competition, 1914–15. Technological advances in both building and equipment enabled the government to adumbrate 100ft-high offices:
a (left). E. Vincent Harris, plan of Board of Trade design, showing position of 'fine rooms' preserved from Pembroke and Malmesbury Houses, previously on the site.
b (right, above). Percy Adams and Charles Henry Holden (1875–1960). Holden's 'affinity for cuboid masses' on a monumental scale 'pointed the design of large buildings in a new direction' (Service).
c. First prize: Emanuel Vincent Harris (1879–1971). Harris was a leader of the return to a purer classicism after the exuberance of Edwardian Baroque (as found in Young's work).

tuted.[135]) The architect selected by the assessors and approved by the Office of Works would be paid five per cent on his estimate – or if the designs were not proceeded with within a year, £5000. 'We trust this important competition will evoke an ample and satisfactory response from the architectural profession, as it should do', remarked the *Builder*.[136]

In fact, the profession had considerable cause for satisfaction, because the 'assessors' were the competition judges. For the first time the government handed over the power of judgment wholly to the profession, tacitly conceding the architects' claim that they alone possessed the necessary attributes. Yet further, the government abandoned its long-maintained right to dispense with the judges' award: the competition conditions stating specifically that the Commissioners of Works intended to entrust the author of the design placed first with carrying out the work.[137] The assessors chose Vincent Harris (1879–1971),[138] by this time a private in the Artists Rifles serving in France.

For the new offices of the Woods and Forests (1906–10) [Pl. 203], the department responsible for the Crown lands, which could finance its own headquarters, the presiding commissioner naturally turned to the department's own architect since 1904, John Murray (1864–1940). It was generally regarded as the best of the new government buildings.[139] When, however, after considerable parliamentary pressure,[140] the government decided to provide new premises to accommodate the whole of the scattered Board of Agriculture, on a side-street site between Whitehall Place and Great Scotland Yard, the Office of Works reverted to its own staff, appointing H.V. Hawkes, who had been responsible for the 1909–11 extension of the National Gallery [Pl. 293]. After his death in January 1911 the erection of the severe classical structure was supervised by another Works' architect, H.A. Collins.[141] Like the proposed Board of Trade, the Agriculture Board's offices [Pl. 204] were to be a high building. Rising some 95 feet above the pave-ment, it accommodated five floors in the main elevation, with two in the roof, and two in the basement.[142]

Similarly, the New Stationery Office and warehouse [Pl. 202], a vast building hidden away in Lambeth, on Waterloo Road and Stamford Street, was allotted to one of the brightest of the younger men in the Office, Richard Allison, Tanner's eventual successor as Chief Architect.[143] The new Science Museum at South Kensington, too, despite the demands for competition of the sponsoring department, the Board of Education, went to Allison.[144] The nine-floor Office of the Public Trustee, erected in the new LCC thoroughfare of Kingsway in 1912–14 at a cost of some £55,000, was designed by H.A. Collins and A.J. Pitcher, under Tanner.[145] [Pl. 140]

Thus despite professional and parliamentary pressures for competition, government tended to use its own resources whenever practicable. The transfer of buildings for most civil departments – particularly the county courts and post offices – to the Office of Works obliged it to build up a strong technical department, well capable of designing such routine structures. As it grew in strength it became increasingly attractive as a career prospect (as we have seen in chapter 5), and drew able architects into the security of its pensionable employment, men keen to stretch their sinews and tackle major design projects. Ministers were, however, too fearful both of being accused of establishing a government monopoly in public building, and also of criticism of the results, to entrust the highly visible external elevations of major new buildings to the Office of Works staff, however happy they might be to entrust the planning to their knowledgeable hands. They were therefore driven to choose one of the methods of selecting an architect available to the ordinary building promoter: to choose a specific man on the basis of recommendations; or to engage in one or another form of competition. Once again, fear of criticism, as well as external pressures, led them generally to invite competition for

202.   His Majesty's Stationery Office and Store, Stamford Street, R.J. Allison, 1912–14. The extensive use of reinforced concrete construction enabled this huge building to be erected relatively cheaply.

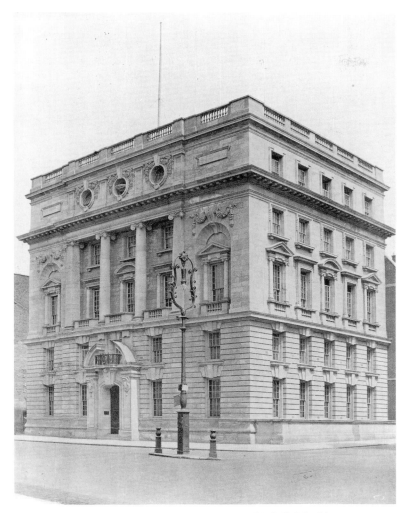

203. Office of Woods, Forests and Land Revenues, Whitehall, John Murray, 1909–10. Murray was the architect of this department, which administers the Crown estate; the *Architectural Review* thought his achievement 'best of all the new Government buildings in Whitehall'. Murray paid scrupulous attention to its context, taking care to balance the Banqueting Hall to the south of the massive new War Office, his immediate neighbour with which he aligned his cornice.

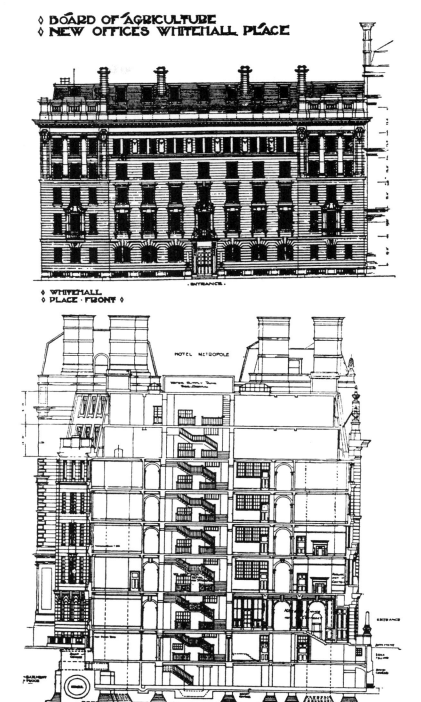

204. Board of Agriculture, Whitehall Place, H.V. Hawkes, 1912–14, elevation and section. For a relatively minor department, the Office of Works employed one of its staff architects; on account of his death, the execution was supervised by H.A. Collins, also of the Works. With seven floors above the pavement, these offices were the first in Whitehall to top one hundred feet. Reinforced concrete (Hennebique) was used extensively for weight-carrying members.

these major buildings. It is clear that in so doing, governments were not innovative: they adopted prevalent rules of procedure and tended to respond to professional pressure.[146] Despite successive modifications, however, the competition system time after time failed to produce satisfactory results, partly because of the well-nigh impossible conditions so often imposed in the cause of economy; partly because the architectural training obtainable in Britain gave little instruction in the problems of designing large-scale public works;[147] and partly because governments (and juries, too) did not know what they were looking for: a design or a designer.

While the ostensible purpose of the long series of competitions that we have studied had been to select a design, even when the winning architect was given the commission the building erected was not the embodiment of the winning drawings. The same truth is exhibited in other major competitions of the period – for instance that for the London County Hall, where Knott's winning design was drastically altered in construction, or that in 1903 for Liverpool Cathedral, in which a coadjutor was imposed on the winner.[148] In truth, what the competitive system produced was the choice of a designer, not a design. Beresford Hope had been right when he put it (as noted at the start of this chapter) to William Burn in the 1858 select committee on the new Foreign Office: 'in

an architectural competition, what you try for is to find the man who will give you the idea of his being the best fitted to carry out that particular work'; 'rather to select the best man than actually to select the design which is literally to be carried out'.[149] As Dr Bassin has pointed out, the key difficulty was that competitions were based 'on drawings alone. . . . The competition system tended to favor artistic rather than architectural skill, and to support . . . the notion of architecture as applied decoration.'[150]

13

The Battle of the Styles

Often as the 'Battle of the Styles' over the Foreign Office design has been recounted, no examination of government building of the Victorian era can ignore it. It was a vigorous illustration of national – indeed, international – contention about style, contention that continues today, though the specific alternatives on offer may have changed. John Steegman has argued that the eighteenth century saw a 'Rule of Taste . . . established and sustained almost entirely by the oligarchic control of wealth and by the extent to which aristocratic requirements and standards influenced society as a whole'. That Rule broke down at the end of the Georgian era, with 'the abandoning the signposts of authority for the fancies of the individual',[1] as we see exemplified in the Houses of Parliament competition of 1835.[2] Much of the architectural literature of the ensuing periods has been concerned, explicitly or implicitly, with attempts to reassert a Rule. Pugin popularised the idea that English architecture had taken a wrong turning in the sixteenth century,[3] and many practitioners took up the idea that they should return to earlier forms, out of which a more correct style, and one peculiarly appropriate to the nineteenth century, might evolve. 'The question of Gothic or Classic formed the architectural struggle of the age in which we live', the Revd Charles Boutell told an audience in 1857.[4] The intensity of the battle in 1858–62, however, owed much to the zealotry of the protagonist, George Gilbert Scott, an experienced publicist, and his antagonist Palmerston's immovable disdain of the new Gothic.

Whatever the individual's fancy, there was common agreement over the need for 'appropriateness'. That was an elusive quality: 'appropriateness', whether of function or locality, could appear in different guises. One had to decide, for a start, whether buildings should be autonomous or contextual. Autonomy may have been the rule in City streets,[5] but in the government quarter the cry was for buildings that acknowledged their neighbours. But whereas for Scott it was the Abbey and Houses of Parliament that established the context, for Charles Barry jnr and his partner it was the buildings around Horse Guards Parade.[6] Yet even here there were those, such as Samuel Angell, one of the professional assessors in the 1856 Government Offices Competition, who thought that 'very often very good effects are produced by contrasts', a view evidently shared by Sir Charles Barry, who 'for the sake of variety . . . should have preferred any style whose skyline dealt in curvilinear or spherical forms of outline' for the proposed public offices, 'as a contrast to what is done at the Houses' of Parliament.[7]

This may give the impression that in nineteenth-century England there was no common agreement on a style for public buildings. However, in the late 1850s most rational men would have agreed with Angell that 'the Italian style was the preferable style for business purposes' as giving 'a better disposition for light, and . . . more suitable to the streets, and to our City generally'.[8] Somerset House [Pl. 45] and the Whitehall Palace designs ascribed to Inigo Jones [Pl. 41] were constantly proclaimed, particularly by MPs, as ideal models for official buildings throughout the century.[9] Charles Barry jnr believed that the large unobstructed windows of the Italian style were, for public offices, 'in accordance with a very general opinion, and a very general taste'.[10] [Pl. 205]

It has been suggested that the choice of style for the New Government Buildings was determined by the imperial symbolism of the Roman style.[11] Evidence to substantiate this is hard to find. It is true that one pamphleteer in the controversy referred to the 'appropriate embellishment of that quarter of the metropolis which constitutes the very focus of the Empire'.[12] But the concept of Empire was not commonly seen in stylistic terms: 'dignity', 'nobility', 'appropriateness' could be achieved in either classical or Gothic styles, and for the only professional among the judges of 1857 the question of style 'did not operate': Burn 'merely attended to the designs before me, and endeavoured to give an opinion as to which were the best and the most suitable'.[13] Sir Benjamin Hawes, permanent head of the War Department, when asked, 'what is your view of the right style of architecture for public offices', responded: 'That is a very difficult question for me to answer'; given good planning, 'the plainer the building the better'.[14] For Hawes, as for Ruskin, style was something superadded to building. 'If it is thought better to make it highly decorative and ornamental, be it so; it will not make the office one bit more useful.'[15] Here is no sense that symbolic sculpture will strike dread into barbarian hearts, or fill brave Britons with martial ardour. What was commonly demanded was an expression of 'national character':

205. Banqueting House, Whitehall. Inigo Jones's Palladian masterpiece (1620–22) was admired throughout the Victorian era; though not all were prepared to accept that it should determine the stylistic tone of Whitehall.

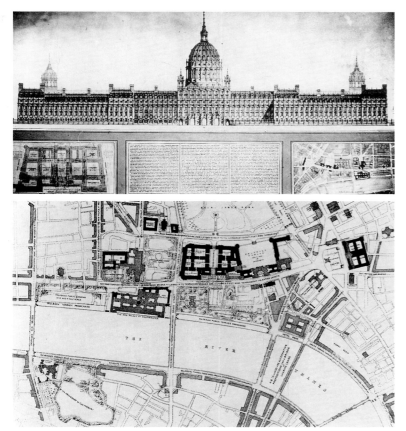

206. 'Palace of Administration', Sir Charles Barry.
a. Although the elder Barry was not a competitor for the New Government Offices in 1856–7, he shewed a design in the Academy Exhibition of 1858 for a Palace of Administration dominating Whitehall, to correspond to the Palace of the Legislature at Westminster. His recension of Soane's Board of Trade provided a basic unit.
b. Plan for improvement of Westminster, 1857.

In this age and this land, – in this heart of the greatest empire of the world . . . at this height of power, when England and the United States dominate the nations of the earth, we look forth for artists who are the ministers of the glory of their people, we expect to see on buildings which are to be monuments to after generations of Englishmen and foreigners some testimony that these are English works.[16]

In the 160 pages of evidence elicited by the 1858 committee on Foreign Office re-construction, about 12 are devoted to discussion of style, and that chiefly in terms of cost or convenience. 'Appropriateness' was seen in terms of the building's relationship with its neighbours, whether the classical buildings of Horse Guards Parade, or the Gothic of Westminster.[17] It was practical questions of cost, light and ventilation, and the terms and requirements specified in the competition, that exercised the committee. Similarly, the competitors whose voices were heard were concerned not with symbolism, but with the practicality of how to win. Coe, placed first for the Foreign Office, chose 'Italian' not 'from my own opinion, but more because I thought it would be liked'. Charles Barry jnr, second with his partner R.R. Banks for the Foreign Office [Pl. 207], was led by 'a great many considerations', but those he admitted, in addition to the influence of neighbouring buildings, were what he saw as the generally-received practical advantages of classical, and 'the strong desire' to see his particular version of Franco-Italian 'carried out on sufficient scale to give it a fair trial' in a London that lacked any such example.[18] His father, Sir Charles,

though not a competitor in person, had designed a palace of administration [Pl. 206], crowned with a massive dome in order to give variety in a skyline dominated by Gothic towers and spires.[19] The stylistic requirements were, then, in terms of 'dignity', and for appropriateness, a 'national' style. Whether Gothic or classic were the more national was the subject of argument.[20] Sir Charles Barry thought that 'feelings of historical and heraldic association' were 'not so pressing' for an administrative building as for the nation's legislature.[21] Anyway, if symbolism was a feature to be sought, it could be attained as well in Gothic as in classical style. In his influential *Seven Lamps of Architecture* (1849), Ruskin had insisted:

> In public buildings the historical purpose should be still more definite [than in domestic]. It is one of the advantages of Gothic architecture, – I use the word Gothic in the most extended sense as broadly opposed to classical, – that it admits of a richness of record altogether unlimited. Its minute and multitudinous sculptural decorations afford means of expressing, either symbolically or literally, all that need be known of national feeling or achievement.[22]

The Battle of the Styles over the New Government Offices was to be determined by practical men on practical grounds. Architecture as metaphor was a game for the intellectuals.

Prejudice and conviction of course played their parts. Scott, leader of a minority,[23] was almost as obsessional about Gothic [Pl. 207] as was Pugin, though he was of the evolutionist school, proclaiming the need to develop 'upon the basis of the indigenous architecture of our own country, a style which will be pre-eminently that of our own age, and will naturally, readily, and with right good will and heartiness, meet all its requirements, and embrace all its arts, improvements, and inventions'.[24] In discussing public buildings, Scott admitted that 'museums, public picture-galleries, and almost all classes of government offices' were 'in a great degree peculiar to our own day', and therefore had 'a pre-eminent claim to be treated in a manner at once new and characteristic of the age which they represent'. That ruled out equally the 'mediaeval Hotel de Ville, the Roman Palazzo, or the palace (*in nubibus*) of Inigo Jones'. It was impossible, Scott believed, deliberately to invent a new style, nor had the past 'made use of a style for one class of buildings different from what it applies to others'. What he advocated was 'the construction upon a gothic basis of a new *palatial* style' characterised by 'grandeur of sentiment', exhibiting stateliness and refinement, with costly materials, sculpture of the highest class, and lofty roofs.[25]

An important leader of opposition to Gothic public buildings was James Fergusson, 'in the public view . . . the most prominent of all' the contemporary writers on architecture.[26] Attacking revived Gothic in 1862, he declared: 'all our new buildings aim only at deceiving'. Art in Victorian Britain was 'little more than a dead corpse, galvanised into spasmodic life by a few selected practitioners, for the amusement and delight of a small section of the specially educated classes.'[27] For the style of the future he recommended Renaissance Italian as uniquely engaging our sympathies and 'by no means worked out or perfected'.[28]

Such views being widely accepted, competitors in Hall's government offices competition in search of a model, if not looking to Inigo, would probably turn to the admired purpose-built offices rising in Paris for the government of the Second Empire. Napoleon III had ordered the completion of the Louvre on a magnificent scale to house a range of official bodies, and imperial grandeur had wafted through even the Hôtel de Ville. With these imperial splendours the illustrated press, the ease of travel and particularly the 1855 Exposition had made the English public familiar. It was hardly surprising, therefore, that in the 1856

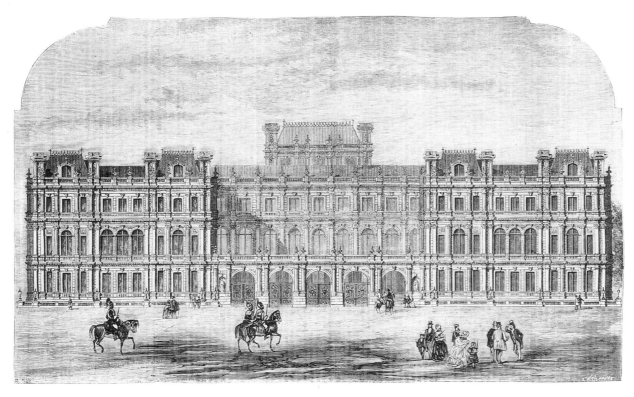

207. New Government Offices competition, 1857; the Foreign Office: a. Third prize, George Gilbert Scott: Gothic with a Continental flavour adapted for modern use. Scott had already, in 1855, experienced the complexities of designing a major public building, with his winning entry in the Hamburg Rathaus competition. b. Second prize, Robert R. Banks & Charles Barry jun. In the Roman style.

government-offices competition the overwhelming majority of the entrants offered designs that may loosely be called Italianate, in the Parisian mode.[29] What was more surprising was that the few Gothic submissions made such a good showing among the prize-winners.[30] 'Common rumour', according to the *Illustrated London News*, had it that Gothic designs were excluded 'from all chance of success'; while the *Building News* lambasted them as 'naked revivals of antiquated and disused forms'.[31] Yet Scott's [Pl. 170, 209] was origi-nally placed third for the Foreign Office, Deane & Woodward's [Pl. 208] fourth, Charles Buxton's (assisted by Habershon) [Pl. 171c] sixth, and Street's [Pl. 208] seventh; Prichard & Seddon's [Pl. 208] fourth for the War Office: a total of five out of fourteen prize winners (and out of eighteen Gothic schemes).[32] However, as Dr Bassin has pointed out, these were all, save Street's, marked by 'a basically Classical formulation', symmetrical in plan and generally so in elevation.[33] Of the other prize-winners, most of the designs

208. New Government Offices competition, 1857; designs awarded lesser premiums:
a. Prichard & Seddon, View from the Park. Regarded by the *Builder* as one of the four best Gothic designs.
b. G.E. Street's powerful masses were too 'churchy' for the general taste.
c. Deane and Woodward, detail (cp. pl. 171b). Woodward embodied Ruskin's theories, with permanent colour, and sculpture at a height easily readable; but *Builder* thought 'much of the ornament might have been thrown on the wall', like Turner's paint against canvas.

may be described as Second Empire,[34] only those of Brodrick (War Office) [Pl. 172] and Bellamy (Foreign Office) [Pl. 172] deriving from different Italianate traditions.

Coe & Hofland's winning design for the Foreign Office was very close to Visconti's New Louvre [Pl. 167]; Garling's for the War Office closer to the Hôtel de Ville [Pl. 168]. Banks & Barry's Foreign (second prize) [Pl. 207] and Botrel d'Hazeville's and Rochead's War Offices (second and third) [Pl. 169] were of similar character, along with Dwyer's (seventh, War Office) 'sterile reproduction of the Tuileries'[35] [Pl. 172]. Dr Toplis has suggested that this cluster of Second Empire prizes was 'deliberate promotion' by judges who 'felt that if they did not strongly press for this form of building, another, and less welcome style in their eyes, would be adopted'; 'large secular Gothic buildings of this type were an unknown quantity . . . a new approach to design . . . not controlled by a cultural elite . . . but by professionals'.[36] This is perhaps a reaction induced by over-concentration on the Gothic Revival. It takes no account of the power exercised over men's minds by the *grands oeuvres* rapidly reaching completion in Paris. The *Exposition Internationale* of 1855 had received immense publicity. Queen Victoria's visit was reported in all the papers; and thousands of her subjects of all classes followed in her train.[37] In 1856, before the Government Offices competition was mounted, the *Builder* pub-

lished illustrations of both the old and the new parts of the Louvre.[38] Paris possessed, in the *Conseil d'Etat* building on the Left Bank, the first purpose-built ministerial offices of the century [Pl. 12].[39] The newly-completed French Foreign Ministry [Pl. 12], with its sumptuous ministerial suite and reception rooms designed for the entertainment of the sovereigns of Europe, set a standard to which British architects might aspire, even though British ministers eschewed the presumption of Napoleon III.[40]

Dr Toplis, then, sees the judges' decision as 'an attempt by enlightened amateurs to retain their position as arbiters of taste in the face of these threats' from the professionals. However, this ignores the professional element among the judges themselves: Brunel and Burn clearly played a considerable role in the commission's work, and there is no reason to assume that Stanhope and Stirling (who alone among the judges after the defections of Buccleuch and Eversley were men of independent means) were especially concerned to maintain their rule of taste.[41] Stirling's statement that the judges felt that they could not, 'as unprofessional men', disagree with a selection agreed upon by three architects[42] must be seen in the Victorian context of duty: four officially-appointed judges attempting to perform the duty entrusted to them. Indeed, the disproportionate significance given to the Gothic designs in awarding the prizes suggests that the judges were deeply impressed by them. Burn specifically stated that the question of style 'did not operate' in his mind: he merely 'endeavoured to give an opinion as to which [of the designs] were the best and most suitable'.[43] Stirling avowed that 'he was fond of both styles of architecture'; thought that Scott should be allowed to 'employ the style to which he had given his particular attention'; and was to be active in the pro-Scott party.[44] Nor was Scott's avowed approach to design one that could adequately be assessed only by professionals; his attempt to produce an utilitarian Gothic to meet the needs of the time might have appealed to economy-minded parliamentarians, had it not been for their engrained hostility to the Palace of Westminster. Commentators in the professional press remarked on the marked evidence of architectural progress exhibited by the Gothic designs, which the ordinary classical had failed to develop, though professional bias cannot be discounted.[45]

Another commentator, Professor Morris, similarly sees the Gothicists as the party of progress fighting the upholders of the status quo.[46] That this is part of the truth is undeniable, though the hostility of the avant-garde *Building News* towards secular Gothic indicates that it is not the whole. As Fergusson argued, the Italian offered a base for progressive development. Morris fails to appreciate the distinction between, say, Tite (b.1798) of the old school and, for instance, Edward Barry (b.1830) of the younger classicists.[47]

Again, it is suggested that the lay judges 'must have been aware of the realities of the situation, and that there was little chance of the prize-winners being commissioned to carry out the work'.[48] That assertion cannot be proved. No doubt Stanhope and Stirling were aware that many of their parliamentary colleagues were taken aback by the scale and splendour of the designs, but equally they would have been aware of the real need for new government offices, and of Hall's commitment to choosing an architect by the competitive process. Whether the selected designs would ever be built might have seemed doubtful; but that was very different from throwing out the whole project.[49] Pennethorne was not a generally acceptable alternative, and the nomination of a non-prize winner would be too blatant jobbery to carry the Commons with it. Palmerston, it is true, would have been quite happy with a Foreign Office designed by Pennethorne; but Hall was immovably opposed.[50] It is fruitless to debate what might have happened had Palmerston remained in power: a change of government in February 1858 produced a new situation.

Lord John Manners, who became First Commissioner of Works in the new Conservative ministry, was an admirer of Gothic architecture.[51] So was Alexander James Beresford Beresford Hope, president of the RIBA 1865–7, and an MP (as a Conservative of independent views) from 1841 to 1852, March 1857 to April 1859 and 1865 to 1887 – more, an enthusiast. A rich landowner,[52] he had undertaken the rebuilding of St Augustine's Abbey, Canterbury, as a missionary training college from 1844, and from 1849 the rebuilding of All Saints, Margaret Street, as a model church, employing Butterfield in both works (though he later fell out with the architect), and he was to write a significant work on the appropriate character of church for the day.[53] In 1855, in partnership with John Douglas Cook,[54] he founded the *Saturday Review*, to which he was a frequent contributor on artistic questions. Scott dedicated his *Remarks on Secular & Domestic Architecture* (1857) to Hope 'in earnest trust that he will unflinchingly continue to press on to its natural results the cause he has so long and ably advocated'. Beresford Hope was to play a highly significant role in the

history of the Government Offices competition, not only publishing a pamphlet on the question,[55] but also moving an address to the Crown, 10 August 1857, for a royal commission on the proposed Government Offices. Hope's motion was overwhelmingly rejected (by 138 votes to 8), after a debate in which the sentiments generally expressed were hostile to expensive new buildings, effectively killing the competition designs.[56] Hope himself attacked both the sly way in which Hall had pushed forward his scheme, and the incompetent organisation of the competition; denouncing the winning Franco-Italianate designs as offices 'which would be finished in 1860, and which before 1861 had gone round we should devoutly pray that some earthquake would destroy'.[57] William Tite, a classical architect of the old school, joined in attacking the prize designs: they would 'create a great incongruity with Sir Charles Barry's building: what no man of taste would for a moment sanction'.[58]

The government then abandoned its larger plans. *The Times* with its facility for catching the opinion of the political nation promptly savaged the competition designs, protesting 'most earnestly against the adoption of any of those stupendous plans which were exhibited the other day, to the astonishment of all sober Englishmen. . . . What do we want with the Hôtel de Ville from Paris on the edge of St James's Park in order that a few hundred clerks may execute their daily tasks? The Colonies may be ruled from a building which is without the Pavillon de Flore at one extremity and the Pavillon Marsan at the other.' New offices were necessary for several departments, but the Treasury buildings offered an admirable model. 'By all means, however, let us have something better, if it can be done at a reasonable expense. There is surely a half-way house between a Gothic cathedral and a Union Workhouse.'[59] So advised, Palmerston revived the idea of a building by Pennethorne, which Hall's opposition blocked. The first three prize-winners for the Foreign Office meanwhile took to the press to trumpet their several claims.[60] One of them, that adept string-puller George Gilbert Scott, felt himself 'at liberty to stir'.[61]

When Manners came into office, he thus found matters at a deadlock.[62] Hope held a meeting at which Scott, Charles Barry and Digby Wyatt were present, when it was agreed 'to stir up the Institute'; in consequence a deputation of architects saw Lord John Manners.[63] It appeared to him, and the House agreed, that the problem were best referred to a select committee. Of that committee, Hope was chairman. He used his position to advance the case for a Gothic building.[64] When Scott was giving his evidence, Hope would intervene after a series of hostile questions (from Tite, for example), to make points in favour of a Gothic design and counteract any unfavourable impression that might have been created.[65] The Gothic case was also drawn out by two other supportive committee members, Manners himself, and Edward Akroyd, a Yorkshire industrialist who employed Scott to design All Saints Haley Hill, Halifax, one of his finest churches.[66]

In the examination of Burn before the committee, it emerged that Burn had constructed his own order of merit, and that the two assessors had also, in excess of their instructions, compiled a list. The two lists proved almost identical, but were not considered by the judges as a body.[67] Hope had taken no part in this questioning, but with these facts established, and the government's freedom to adopt any of the designs, he weighed in to establish the propriety of awarding the work to one of the leading prizemen. He then argued the case for design no. 116a (Scott's) as 'a special exceptional case of merit' because he came second, on Burn's list, for both offices (the judges, however, having laid down the principle that 'not more than one prize ought to be given to the same man').[68] Had Burn's list been accepted, 'the man who had obtained the second prize in both [offices]' would 'have been the most distinguished of any'[69] – an idea that Palmerston, employing the analogy of the racecourse, was subsequently to ridicule.[70]

This evidence enabled Hope to argue the case for Scott in his draft report and avow that Italian architecture possessed no advantage over Gothic 'as to cheapness, commodiousness of arrangement, or facilities for light and ventilation'.[71] The committee, however, rejected two important paragraphs (Draft 8 and 9), substituting a recommendation for 'a preference' being given to the successful competitors 'in the erection of the new Foreign Office' for Hope's more authoritative 'conviction that the architect of the new Foreign Office ought to be selected among those who were premiated'; and modifying Hope's vital third paragraph (Draft 10) to omit both the specific recommendation of either Banks & Barry or Scott, and also the crucial comment that Scott's ranking for both offices by the professionals indicated 'a sum total of remarkable merit'. Nevertheless, the report was sufficient to set the Scott band-wagon rolling. After the publication of the evidence, Hope's paper, the *Saturday Review*, carried an article (almost certainly Hope's work) on 'The Question of Architectural Style for the new Public Offices' which urged that Scott, who had 'fairly earned the most distinguished place' in the competition, should be appointed – or that there should be a second competition among all the prize-winners. The style should be 'the revived national style – a style so characteristic of our own age it is beginning to be called Victorian'.[72]

The report and the support it received in the press provided Manners with grounds for appointing Scott as architect for the new Foreign Office in November,[73] and thereby, it seemed, committing the nation to a Gothic building, a determination that was governed, he claimed, by the *genius loci*.[74] As noted above, he then agreed with the Indian Secretary, Lord Stanley, that he would 'confide the erection of the new India Office to Mr Scott with a view of securing harmony of design, and public convenience'.[75] When Hall raised in the Commons the question why the first and second premium plans had been passed over, he was answered by Hope's insistence that 'the sum total of merit in the competition rested with Mr Scott' as second for both buildings on the lists of Burn and the assessors; a design 'which had received the approbation of the leading journals, and of all thinking men'.[76] In the ensuing discussion, Palmerston expressed the prevalent feeling in the House, denouncing Gothic as barbarous; he suggested that Scott, as a 'person of great talent' who had studied Greek and Italian architecture should be able to make a handsome design in either of those modes.[77] Scott dashed off a letter to *The Times* defending the modernity of his design and its 'cheerfulness', superior to major contemporary works and even to Jones's Banqueting House [Pl. 205], an insensitive letter that nearly cost him the RIBA gold medal for 1859,[78] though the architectural press continued to support him.[79]

A week later, Hall resumed his assault on Manners, declaring that: 'If I could collect the expression of feeling on the part of the House, which was very decided when the subject was touched upon last Friday, I do think that feeling was most emphatically expressed against the building of a Foreign Office in the neighbourhood of Downing Street in the Gothic style.' He therefore asked for all three of the leading prize designs to be exhibited.[80] Manners repeated his former argument, stressing that the late Liberal government had declared itself not bound to any of the prize-winners, but had been too divided to come to a decision. Palmerston again concluded the discussion with an attack on 'dark and dingy' Gothic, an appeal for a building with a 'gay and cheerful outside, and light and airy' interior, and a recommendation of Pennethorne's harmonious, simple but sufficiently decorated de-sign [Pl. 119].[81] Scott's friends subsequently claimed that this time feeling in the House was much less hostile towards him.[82]

Scott's design [Pl. 170], beautiful as it was commonly acknowledged to be, did not receive universal approbation even from the Gothicists. John Henry Parker, glossarian of Gothic architecture, used the *Gentleman's Magazine* to advise Scott to 'get rid of the *foreign* look' and model his design on English thirteenth-century work.[83] He provoked, however, a defence from Street of the importance of Italian medieval domestic architecture as a model.[84] (Scott himself regarded his design as more French than Italian.[85]) Dean Liddell of Christ Church, Oxford, confessed that 'I do *not* much like Scott's ... Woodward ... would give you a much more artistic and genial Building.'[86] Scott, however, had naturally been required to revise his original designs in consultation with the departments. The competition design [Pl. 121, 170, 207] had provided for a Foreign Office facing the Park, arranged around three sides of a courtyard of which the fourth was formed by a War Office of similar U-plan fronting Parliament Street. In his revised block plan [Pl. 272], Scott reversed the War-become-India Office, so that the two quadrangles opened on each other.[87] To his elevations Scott imparted something of the Early French character that he had examined at Laon and Noyon in December 1857, of which he praised the 'vigour and ... masculine boldness'.[88] The revision [Pl. 209] showed rather less ornamentation, with a greater expanse of window-space.[89] These designs approved in April, the Office of Works called now for working drawings.

In the final report of the committee on the Foreign Office the paragraphs toning down Hope's strong pro-Scott line had been drafted by Lord Elcho, perhaps to secure wider support, for Scott looked upon Elcho as one of his principal supporters. He took a leading part in the campaign that Scott waged to retain his appointment and, if possible, build a Gothic design, after Palmerston's return to power in June 1859. Almost immediately after his latest drawings were put on view in the Commons library on 20 July,[90] Scott was sent for by Palmerston and told he must make an Italian design.[91] After reflection, Scott wrote at length to the minister, praying in aid moral, financial, practical and even political grounds: 'there exists throughout the country a great feeling of satisfaction at the prospect of the [Gothic] style being acted upon in this instance, and that a contrary result will be followed by very deep and widespread disappointment'.[92] Lord Elcho followed this up with a deputation, including members of the previous year's select committee, to express to Palmerston their views on the style of the new office, and their support for Scott.[93] In vain: the minister made clear alike to them and to Scott his unalterable opposition to 'gloomy looking Buildings in the Gothic style' – though assuring Scott that he entertained not 'the smallest doubt that an Architect of your known Talent and Ability will find it an easy task to design an Elevation in the Italian or Classic style'.[94]

The architect dreaded that he was about to lose his commission: he was alarmed lest the question come on in a morning sitting of the Commons when his supporters might be engaged in committees. 'I fear the consequence of this because I see that Charles Barry is making himself very active. He was decidedly canvassing for himself – in the room where my drawings are exhibited – yesterday – and this afternoon he was with Tite and Conyngham[95] in consultation. His notion is that if the style can be shaken he will be brought in. Pennethorne, Coe and Garling are also watching each for himself with the same hope.' Though Gladstone, at the Exchequer, was 'favourable to me personally and *tacitly* so to the style', he was '*terribly* set against the outlay'. Scott thought he could effect retrenchments 'as well or *better* in the same style than by changing it'.[96]

209.   a. Design for New Foreign
Office, Park front, G.G. Scott, 1859.
Having secured the Foreign Office
commission, Scott had to revise his
design to meet the newly-stated needs
of the department. In this view, the
influence of the Oxford Museum is
evident.
Palmerston's subsequent return to
power led to more drastic revisions.

209.   b. Oxford, The University
Museum, Deane & Woodward,
1855–60. Ruskin himself took a keen
interest in this work, which became
an influential model for civic
buildings.

Although Scott had already circulated a statement of his case to MPs, he besought Elcho to bring out in the debate a further point:

It is the extraordinary facility which the [Gothic] style offers for adapting the exterior to the interior. I have made two designs *with* and one *without* an official residence, and have now to make a second *without* it – but these changes give trouble alone in *internal* arrangement. I find none whatever arising externally – the style adapts itself at once to the changes without any effort whatever. Whereas in the Classic style all kinds of difficulties would occur. In my design I do not know whether you have noticed that nearly everywhere the grouping of the windows is dependent on the interior so that externally one is conscious of the internal divisions of the room. In short the exterior arises in great measure from the interior arrangements. Nor do I care how much they choose to alter the interior for in this style one is sure to fall on ones legs as to external design.[97]

The following day, 4 August 1859, the supply Vote for concrete foundations for the new Foreign Office was moved by the chancellor of the Exchequer. Scott had for years been on friendly terms with Gladstone, who declared that 'there was a material contest of opinion' about the nature of the design, for the building, 'and the Government were not prepared at this moment to propose a solution'. They were however willing to pledge that no decision would be taken during the parliamentary recess.[98] There was at this point no certainty that the newly-knit governing coalition of Whigs, Liberals and Radicals would hold, and ministers were clearly unwilling to risk their fate on such an issue.

However, Elcho informed the House that Palmerston's reply to the late deputation had been that 'Mr Scott's design was one of the most monstrous things he had ever seen – that it was more fitted for a monastery than anything else,[99] and that as long as he held office he would never consent to the adoption of Mr Scott's plans'.[100] Elcho pointed out the waste of labour, time and money if every new ministry, in an unstable parliamentary situation, 'were to play at see-saw with the subject'. He defended the Gothic style against the objections that it was dark within, costly and incongruous. The committee of 1858 had established that Scott's windows exceeded in size those in 17 public buildings; costs were similar in either style; and diversity in the town was 'grateful to the eye', as Edinburgh Old Town and Venice proved. Coningham, as Scott had expected, praised Palmerston's 'spirited resistance to any further invasion of the Goths and Vandals'. Scott had been chosen 'because the building was to be in the Gothic style, but the moment that decision was set aside then the question of the appointment of the architect should be fully and fairly considered'.[101]

Most of the other speakers, including Stirling, supported Scott's design, and Charles Buxton (1823–71), a competitor, asserted that 'a taste for Gothic was assuming a sway over people's minds', while the Italian style 'was becoming effete'.[102] Palmerston repeated Gladstone's pledge that 'nothing would be done with respect to fixing a plan until Parliament met again'; but also reiterated that, in or out of office, he would 'do all in his power' to prevent Gothic being used for a public official building, a style that 'might be admirably suited for a . . . monastery, or Jesuit college' – and we must remember the depth of popular antipathy at that time to such Roman institutions – but was 'wholly unsuited . . . either internally or externally' to public official uses. Imported from the Continent, it was national neither in origin nor by practice, as he showed by listing a great number of classical public buildings in London and the provinces.[103] On the last occasion the question had been discussed in the House, 'as far as the opinion of the House could be expressed, short of a division, by gentlemen on their legs, and by those who retained their seats, he never remembered a stronger expression of opinion elicited than was on that occasion manifested against Gothic'.[104] He concluded by suggesting that Scott could design a cheaper building, including a Colonial Office, in a different style. Lord John Manners, whom Palmerston had attacked for incurring expenses on plans without the sanction of the Commons, counter-attacked vigorously, adducing John Henry Newman's testimony that Gothic was less Ultramontane in spirit than the Italian style. Palmerston's course 'could only lead to increased expenditure, to certain failure, and to great individual wrong'; if they followed Palmerston's advice, 'the House might as well give up talking about science and art and the beautification of the metropolis; and they would have national galleries and public buildings erected to the disgust, sorrow, and astonishment of the nation'.[105]

Scott felt that the debate had substantially improved his position, a view shared by the *Saturday Review*.[106] The weight of speeches was two to one in his favour, and his opponents were only 'the old list';

whereas his supporters 'all were new speakers but one'.[107] But on Palmerston they made no impression, and on 22 August, backed by comment in *The Times* and support from a deputation of architects,[108] he saw Scott and threatened to appoint a coadjutor 'with the intention of acting upon *his* design'. Scott crumpled, although Palmerston had withdrawn his threat, undertaking to make another design which he trusted would be more to Palmerston's taste, 'only asking of your Lordship proper time for a work of such importance'.[109] He complained, however, '*extra-officially*' to Gladstone, condemning the idea of collaboration as impossible, and expressing his dread that he would be deprived of the commission despite his willingness to make a classical design. Gladstone reassured him as to his appointment, whatever might ultimately be decided as to style, but concluded with typically ambiguous advice: 'I am quite certain that you will undertake nothing except what you may feel & know your capacity to accomplish and that the widespread reputation you have acquired is to you too great a treasure to be hazarded for the sake of any particular employment.'[110] Scott then retired to Scarborough for a two-month family holiday, his first in 24 years, writing to Freeman of his wish 'to drift on to the next session without doing anything to foreclose the question'.[111] He realised that his strength lay in his supporters in the Commons; in the long parliamentary recess from mid-August to February he felt highly vulnerable – the more so as Palmerston had taken the Foreign Office question out of the hands of his First Commissioner, Henry Fitzroy.[112]

The Commons' debate had attracted considerable attention in the country, and one rural clergyman, Thomas James (1809–63),[113] wrote to Elcho to suggest a national memorial from 'men of art and literature' against dictating style to the selected architect. The local (Northamptonshire) architects were making their own protest,[114] but he had been in contact with many local societies which would support a lay protest.[115] This led to discussions with Henry Liddell (1811–98), Dean of Christ Church, who drafted such a memorial, avoiding the term 'Gothic' in order to 'get rid of the Ecclesiastical associations raised by the term, and encouraged (I must add) by Scott's designs'.[116] Instead of 'Gothic', he referred to the 'civil architecture of the Middle Ages in Italy': 'There is no plan, we sincerely believe, so plastic in details, so capable of every kind of modification, so easy to be adapted to the wants of English life.' James saw an objection to this, because 'with some the foreign element is the abhorrence'.[117] But the whole proposal faltered. By March 1860 it was clear that the friends of the Gothic movement generally thought that it was better at that moment not to bring the matter forward.[118]

Similarly, Scott's own project for a memorial from Gothic architects foundered for lack of sufficient support to make it worth while.[119] Scott however had also secured the aid of a powerful opponent of modern Classicism, his friend the historian E.A. Freeman (1823–92). In his youthful *History of Architecture* (1849) Freeman had praised Scott's St Nicholas, Hamburg, as 'the noblest work that three ages have produced'.[120] He now promised to write to *The Times*, though his 'admirable and exhaustive letter' (as Ruskin termed it), signed 'E.A.F.', did not appear until 19 October.[121] The letter was promptly reprinted in *Building News*, the *Gentleman's Magazine* and the *Ecclesiologist*. A request from Ruskin for the author's name infuriated Freeman, who believed Ruskin's advocacy of Italian Gothic had done enormous harm to English architecture.[122] He quarrelled with *The Times*, which closed its columns to further correspondence. Whether, in view of Scott's own critical giving ground, the loss of so influential a channel, 'the best champion of his cause' as T.G. Jackson termed it, was particularly significant we may doubt.[123] Ruskin himself, apart from this unfortunate intervention, played remarkably little part in the contro-

210. New Foreign Office: Park front from the Parade (State Paper Office on right); the amended 'Byzantine' version (1859–60), Palmerston's 'regular mongrel affair', that Scott put forward as a compromise between his Gothic and Palmerston's Classical convictions.

versy.[124] Freeman, however, contributed an article to the *National Review* in January 1860, after Scott had commented extensively on a draft.[125]

It was Scott's letter of 23 August 1859 to Palmerston that really marked his surrender. After long cogitation he produced what he regarded as a compromise by which he maintained the substance of his principles, but yielded the accident. He had, after all, written in 1857 of studying medieval Italian work 'to learn from it so much as will enable us to soften down the asperity of the contrast between our own Gothic and the mass of modern buildings'.[126] Realising that 'the earliest renaissance of Venice' contained an element cognate to the Byzantine found in twelfth-century Venetian palaces, he 'therefore conceived the idea of generating what would be strictly an Italian style out of these two sets of examples; Byzantine, in fact, toned into a more modern and usable form, by reference to those examples of the renaissance which have been influenced by the presence of Byzantine works'.[127] The new design [Pl. 210] was characterised by rows of round-headed windows on each floor, the two offices forming symmetrical open squares, with facing balustraded towers at the ends of the wings linked by a triple archway. The Park front, however, was distinguished by a domed tower, Parliament Street by an attic storey.[128] Scott was soon repenting of his apostasy. He explained elaborately to Elcho that his new design was '*defensive*'.[129]

> I merely wish to shew that if another style is demanded I am able to give it; but I wish at the same time to preserve my own consistency by not giving into the vernacular Palladianism of the day – I have said too much on the other side to allow of that – I merely wish to be pitted against *myself*, and to have a design of my own in *an* Italian style thought worthy of fighting my Gothic design against: but I wish to give heart and soul to the Gothic design after all.

He was the more defensive as he had heard that there was a 'movement' in favour of Pennethorne. But when he met the new First Commissioner, Cowper suggested a compromise.

> I accordingly laid aside the semi classic or classico-Byzantine design I had prepared and worked on an intermediate design. Since that, however, [he reported to Elcho] Mr Cowper has sent for me and told me that Lord Palmerston will have nothing to say to his suggestion and told him to say that if I was unwilling to make an 'Italian' design he should appoint a coadjutor to me.

I at once told him that I *had* already made an Italian design and could shew it to him at any time. I accordingly took it to him and, although very cautious owing to his recent rebuff, he was evidently pleased with it,[130] and said he would ask Lord Palmerston to name a time for me to shew it to him. This was nine days since and I have not heard from Lord Palmerston.

In the mean time I hear from various quarters that Mr Garling . . . is taking some measures in his own favour, and I fancy with Lord Palmerstons sanction and encouragement. I even *suspect* that he is privately sending him plans amended to his taste, but this is a guess only.

Scott emphasised the legality of his own position, remarking that he had 'prepared a design which though perhaps not to Lord Palmerstons exact taste, is *Italian* and I flatter myself has merits of a grade which ought to be sufficient to vindicate my position', so that he did not see that in justice he could be interfered with. He wanted to show Elcho not merely his 'Italian' design but also a large-scale model of part of his Gothic design.[131]

Though Elcho thought the 'Italian' or Byzantine design an improvement, and Scott after another interview with Palmerston thought his reaction not unfavourable, the architect was soon disillusioned, and, feeling 'in imminent danger of being jostled out of my appointment', wrote in agitation to Elcho on 28 May:

> I told you that Mr Cowper had informed me that Lord Palmerston did not like my new design. I have since seen Mr Cowper who tells me that Lord Palmerston thinks the grouping of windows in twos, threes and continuous arcades *Gothic*. Mr Cowper himself has, I am sure, no such feeling and I cannot but feel that it indicates on the part of Lord Palmerston a determination not to be pleased with anything I produce: indeed Mr Cowper told me that he considered that, as a new Government come into power since I was appointed, they had a right to recal [*sic*] the appointment and make a new one. This he said as an apology, apparently, from Lord P. rather than of his own motion. I was somewhat vexed and told him that I had reason to know that Lord Palmerston had already been in communication with another architect and that I considered this, as I held the appointment in the most distinct manner, to be unfair to me. I afterwards offered to make a number of sketches shewing varieties in design, which he very much approved and has since written urging haste as he says that *a decision must very shortly be come to.*

In the meantime I have received an intimation from an independent source (the *fourth* such intimation I have received all from different sources) that Lord Palmerston is in communication with Mr Garling who received the first premium for the *War Office*, indeed that a design is being made by him to meet Lord Palmerston's views. (his premiated design if you recollect was founded on the Hôtel de Ville at Paris and having high roofs would not be likely to meet Lord P's views). . . .[132]

Full of apprehension, Scott urgently attempted to meet Palmerston's requirements, and on 14 June 1860 (the day he was meeting William Stirling at the Commons to organise defensive moves)[133] submitted a report on both his Gothic and Byzantinesque designs to the Office of Works. Cowper invited C.R. Cockerell, Burn and James Fergusson, the architectural historian, to form a committee of reference to report on Scott's designs. This was a committee well-disposed to Scott, though Cockerell 'being a pure classicist, had the greatest difficulty in swallowing [Scott's] new style'. However, the others brought him round, and they made a largely favourable report.[134] Scott had meanwhile appealed to his friends, especially Gladstone, to support him against the premier's machinations; the chancellor, however, was careful to remain uninvolved.[135]

In accordance with the referees' comments, Scott now modified his work, among other changes substituting square-headed windows on the second floor for round-headed, reducing the number of grouped windows on each floor, and concealing the previously prominent dormers behind a balustrade.[136] The new elevation [Pl. 210] was exhibited in the Commons on 30 July, Scott telling Elcho:

> At last my two designs for the Foreign Office are exhibited in the 'Tea-room': if, indeed, I can call that *my* design which has been revised first to please Lord Palmerston, again to meet the views of the referees and a third time to meet Lord Palmerston again. I should not, however, have said this (*having conceded these alterations*) had it not been that I had always supposed that my first Italian design, which you have seen and which is more strictly speaking my own, would have been exhibited with the revised one: this was, in fact, agreed to and the permission withdrawn again on the ground that it would tend to confusion. I deeply regret this as I prefer in most respects the first design and it at least shews the extent of my endeavours to meet Lord Palmerston's views.
>
> I cannot but think that the Gothic design will approve itself to most of those who compare it with the thrice-revised Italian – and I do, more earnestly than I can express, trust that the former may be adopted.

He concluded by hoping that Elcho would afford him his 'powerful and, indeed, indispensable aid in the final issue of the business'.[137]

By this time, it was far too late in the session to consider voting money for the building; in any case, the government had not yet obtained possession of the site. Cowper gave the usual assurance that MPs would be able to discuss the style of the building when a supply Vote was proposed, and Palmerston had already given Manners a private assurance that he would allow the question of style to stand over until the next session.[138]

Meanwhile a paper war had been waging, opening with an article in the *Gentleman's Magazine* (January 1860), asserting that the national style had triumphed, and the classicists were losing clients and reputation. Freeman complained however that Ruskin's influence had perverted the revival, even Scott [Pl. 209] being bitten.[139] A number of pamphlets, mainly anonymous, tossed the ball to and fro,[140] but it is impossible to evaluate their effect on public opinion. Not very much notice was taken of them in the architectural press.

Yet more alarming to Scott than the lack of informed support

was the risk that the Secretary of State for India and his Council might withdraw from the arrangement that a new India Office be erected in juxtaposition to the Foreign Office, forming part of a homogeneous whole designed externally by Scott (though the interior was to be remitted to their own architect Matthew Digby Wyatt).[141] Hardly was this problem resolved when Hunt, the official Surveyor, warned Scott to comply with any instructions he might receive, or risk losing his appointment.[142] Cowper gave him verbal instructions on 7 September to prepare a block plan and an Italian elevation, and Palmerston then summoned him; he dismissed the new design as 'a regular mongrel affair' [Cp. pl. 210], and insisted on 'the ordinary Italian'.[143] He also told Scott that he had agreed with the Indian Secretary on a change of plan by which the two offices, rotated through 90 degrees, were to share the Park front, displacing Soane's State Paper Office, leaving the King Street or eastern side as a future work – and, importantly, reducing the need for immediate land purchases. Hunt claimed he had had difficulty in persuading ministers to retain Scott; Hunt and Wyatt between them persuaded him not to resign. 'I was in a terrible state of mental perturbation', Scott recorded, '– but I made up my mind – went straight for Digby Wyatt's [view] bought some costly books on Italian architecture and set vigorously to work to rub up what though I had once understood pretty intimately, I had allowed to grow rusty by 20 years' neglect.'[144]

Although Scott made so much, writing in 1864, of his mental turmoil at this point, it had, in fact, been his surrender a year

211.   The India Office, looking south, G.G. Scott, 1863–8. The secretary of state occupied the first-floor quadrant room. M.D. Wyatt may have influenced the design.

earlier that had marked the betrayal of the artistic principles he was commonly regarded as upholding, as the *Saturday Review* realised when the Byzantinesque design became public knowledge.[145] Toplis points out, however, that not only did Scott need the work to maintain his large office (and his family in their life-style at a time when other commissions were falling off), but that also he 'realized that he could change to a classical design without forsaking his principles'.[146] Had he not written in 1858: 'I am no mediaevalist'? The chief characteristic of his new palatial style was, he declared, 'grandeur of sentiment'. Of more material characteristics, he distinguished stateliness, and beauty and refinement of detail. Such features as porticoes, 'a more columnar style of decoration'; 'long ranges of covered arcading, not only on the lower story, but also above'; and noble cornices and balustrades. Noble quadrangles, costly materials, sculpture of the highest class, elaborate doorways, large windows, and roofs that 'rise fearlessly to the proper pitch' should be material features in the design.[147] Such a programme could be largely realised in the Italian style [Pl. 212].

'I was so determined to shew myself not behind-hand with the classicists that I seemed to have more power than usual', wrote Scott. 'The India Office, was wholly my *design*, though I had adopted an idea as to its grouping and outline suggested by a sketch of Wyatt's.'[148] Dr Toplis considers that sketches in the RIBA Drawings Collection that must date before a modification of the boundary line to the Park in 1862 are probably by Wyatt.[149] Certainly the irregular line of the Park façade [Pl. 211] derives from Wyatt's proposal to embrace the old State Paper Office within the site. An adjoining quarter-acre had also to be acquired, and the enabling legislation passed during the 1861 session.[150] Scott was probably completing his drawings in March,[151] though Cowper told the House on 2 May that he was still engaged on a revised elevation. His new designs were finally hung in the tea-room at the end of June 1861, Cowper yielding also to requests to display the earlier designs, to which was then added his Academy drawing of the new Park front in Gothic [Pl. 214].[152]

With the Italian designs at last on show, the government determined to bring forward a vote for funds for the building. Immediately beforehand, Lord Elcho moved, in a powerful and sarcastic speech,[153] that 'it was not desirable that the new Foreign Office should be erected according to the Palladian design now exhibited'. He recounted the history of the designs, criticising the way that 'our public works were often proceeded with in a very unsatisfactory manner' from the frequent changes of administration, which he contrasted with the stability in Paris. He described Scott as having become Lord Palmerston's draughtsman: the premier had 'succeeded in uniting those who had never agreed before; for those who differed as to Gothic and Palladian united in condemn-

213. Crown Life Assurance Office, Bridge Street, Deane & Woodward, 1856. In a Commons debate (8 July 1861), Lord Elcho circulated a photograph describing the house on the left as 'Palmerston pure', that on the right as 'Palmerston ornate', and Woodward's offices as 'What London would be if Palmerston would allow it'.

ing the plan'. What London needed was variety of colour and ornament, which could be obtained in Gothic. He emphasised his point by handing round the House photographs of the Crown Life insurance office near Blackfriars Bridge (by Woodward) flanked by two stucco buildings, one described as 'Palmerston ornate', the other as 'Palmerston pure'; while the Crown Life building was labelled 'What London would be if Palmerston would allow it.' [Pl. 213] If the exhibited design were built, the House would not be acting 'in accordance with the feeling and spirit of the country and of Europe in general'. Palmerston's popularity and power could lead them into a costly mistake they could not remedy.[154]

Elcho was seconded by Charles Buxton,[155] himself one of the competitors of 1857. Everyone agreed, Buxton argued, that the Palladian design was dull. 'No human being would ever be so deluded as to look up at it with that keen intellectual delight which was awakened by a really noble building'; whereas Scott's Gothic design 'glowed with thought and imagination, and would kindle the minds of those who looked at it'. He emphasised that great progress had been made in Gothic since Barry designed the Houses of Parliament – so unpopular with many of his auditors – so that a new Gothic office would not suffer from the same drawbacks; whereas the Palladian style was losing 'all hold on popular affection'. It was a matter of age; 'Men above sixty still loved Palladian;

212. New Foreign Office: Final Italian version, Park front, shewing arcade to prime minister's house (left), signed by Gladstone as chancellor of the Exchequer, early 1861.

214.   Scott's preferred design for the New Foreign Office, his final Italian version gothicised; diploma drawing on election as R.A.

men of taste below sixty hated it' (Pam was 77). So he appealed to Palmerston generously to 'sacrifice his own prepossessions in order to let this building harmonize with the feelings of the rising rather than the setting generation'.[156]

Other big guns firing against the Palladian design included Manners and Layard. Layard deplored the little advance the century had made in architecture; interiors whether Gothic or classic were still inconvenient. Although Palmerston told the Queen that 'Mr Layard was for neither, but seemed to wish that somebody would invent a new style of architecture',[157] Layard dealt trenchantly with the objections levelled against Gothic – its lack of light, ugliness, jesuitical character; and condemned Scott's Palladian as 'mean', and its acceptance as unjust to the classic competitors. The oppressive monotony of Paris showed 'how architecture illustrated the political condition of a people'; 'the whole was built on one plan'. On the contrary, we needed variety, beauty, colour, 'something that would interest people'.[158] Lord John Manners similarly denounced the groundless attacks on Gothic, and contradicted the First Commissioner's claim that Palladian was the only popular style by referring to recent Gothic work at the Inns of Court and in Manchester, Northampton, Perth and a number of other towns, as well as in the colonies and abroad. He concluded by reminding the House that Hall in 1856 had specifically stated that the government was unbiased and all styles would be carefully considered. Let Palmerston stand aside, and leave the question to the verdict of the House.[159] Another who asserted Gothic's capability of flooding an interior with light was Hon. Dudley Fortescue (1820–1909),[160] who stressed the great superiority of Gothic in being able to adapt 'the exterior of a building to its interior requirements'. Scott was 'a first-rate genius' and they should adopt his Gothic design.[161]

Ranged on the opposing side there stood, ministers apart, Sir William Tite and Bernal Osborne. Tite insisted on the darkness of Scott's Gothic rooms with their large window-heads; and artfully quoted Ruskin out of context appearing to praise the 'Roman Renaissance', the style 'most applicable to the uses of modern life' – an argument however that Ruskin set up only to destroy.[162] Bernal Osborne, usually the jester of the House, refused to comment on styles, wanted both plans rejected, and the building given 'to the man who gained the first premium'.

The ministerial opponents of Elcho's motion were Cowper, and Palmerston who wound up the debate. The First Commissioner had found a general opinion among men in the street and those 'practically versed in the science of architecture' in favour of Scott's Italian, 'better than any of the Italian designs exhibited in 1857'. Italian was the style 'best adopted for a public office, and most available for modern construction'. For Parliament, associational values had prescribed Gothic – the style 'connected with the period when the House of Commons first acquired its liberties'. Similarly, for the Foreign Office, 'the association to be desired was that of the period in which we lived, and the Italian style was that which by its breadth, simplicity, and symmetry best represented modern sentiments'. Such a building would group well with the buildings at the southern end of Whitehall – he dismissed the prospect of clearing the area between Charles Street and Great George Street. Italian was popular; it prevailed in Paris and the Continent. Part of the function of a public building was to furnish builders with a model for imitation; for one who would profit from a Gothic building, there were twenty 'who would profit by the example of a building in the Italian style'.[163]

The speech however for which the House had been waiting was Palmerston's. He started off with a fine sense of occasion: 'Sir, the battle of the books, the battle of the Big and Little Endeans, and the battle of the Green Ribbands and the Blue Ribbands at Constantinople were all as nothing compared with this battle of the Gothic and Palladian styles.' He attacked Manners, 'swayed by erroneous ideas in religion and taste';[164] pointed out recent major provincial buildings in classical style; denied that Gothic was national – 'the real aboriginal architecture of this country was mud

huts and wicker wigwams'; suggested that classical architecture was quite as characteristic; spoke of 'Great windows that exclude the light'; quoted Canova, who had told him, 'If London were only whitened it would be Paradise'; identified the variety of Gothic with the infinity of bad taste; recommended Scott's Italian as 'very beautiful', combining 'with sufficient beauty and ornament great moderation of expense'; and invited Elcho and Buxton to lay aside their prejudices and 'agree to lay the first stone of an Italian building', just as he had recently laid that of a Gothic library in keeping with the buildings of his old school.[165] After such a bravura performance, there could be little surprise that he carried the day by 188 votes to 95.

Immediately after the division the House went into committee to consider a vote of £30,000 for preliminary work on the new Foreign Office. In the ensuing debate a number of lesser lights who had not caught the Speaker's eye previously were able to contribute their mite to the now pointless discussion on style. Danby Seymour resurrected Pennethorne's design, referring to the success of his Museum of Practical Geology;[166] presenting Palmerston with the invidious task of talking down the very design he had earlier been so keen to build. With his usual jauntiness, the premier dismissed it as 'having a great deal more ornament' than Scott's.[167]

Thus ended the great debate. Charles L. Eastlake, writing some ten years later, remarked, somewhat inaccurately,

Mr Scott stood his ground till the last. He might, indeed, have taken one step which would have made him not only a cham-

pion but a martyr in the cause of the Revival: he might have resigned his commission. . . . From an aesthetic point of view it would have been a grand act. From a practical point of view it would have been Quixotic. Mr Scott would have been reckoned a hero, but we should not on that account have secured a Mediaeval Foreign Office.[168]

But, as we have seen, Scott was not the stuff of which martyrs are made. 'As it was,' continues Eastlake, 'the caprice and prejudice of a statesman who had no sort of claim to connoisseurship were allowed to prevail.' Whether such sweeping condemnation of Palmerston is justified we may beg leave to doubt; he displayed in the course of the years of debate a considerable knowledge of the contemporary architectural scene, even if he did fall into the romantic fallacy of describing Gothic architecture as 'jesuitical'. No doubt he was briefed by Donaldson; but he had grown up in an age when a knowledge of architecture was part of an aristocratic education. Looking at Scott's earlier designs and imagining them embodied in Whitehall – or seeing in the mind's eye some version of St Pancras translated thither – many today may think that Palmerston was right. Scott proved no mean hand at the Italian style, and achieved the effect at which he had originally been aiming. To Henry James, coming across the Park, 'the Foreign Office, as you see it from the bridge, often looks romantic [Pl. 215], and the sheet of water it overhangs poetic – suggests an Indian palace bathing its feet in the Ganges' (and of course half of it was an 'Indian palace').[169]

14
A Gothic Triumph

ALTHOUGH Henry Cole had advised Scott to copy Inigo Jones's Palace of Whitehall designs [Pl. 216] for the new government offices,[1] he had no intention of following such a programme himself at Brompton where the Department of Science and Art, under the ministerial aegis of the Lord President of the Council, was developing its 'culture centre'.[2] Cole and his team of 'ingenious practical men' sought 'an appropriate Victorian style for South Kensington, in a synthesis of Classical and Gothic'.[3] Captain Francis Fowke (1823–65) [Pl. 217], appointed 'Architect and Engineer' in the Science and Art Department in November 1856, was a Royal Engineer with a reputation for mechanical invention who 'saw his function as the direction and co-ordination of a design-office'. He had not trained as an architect, and was looked on sourly by many members of the profession. The dominant ethos of South Kensington was the Ruskinian concept that architecture was the superaddition of ornament to building, as evinced in the debate over the retention of the 1862 Exhibition building – though there the delay between building and decorating ran counter to Ruskin's ideals.[4]

The Sheepshanks Gallery, constructed in 1856–8 to house a collection of modern British paintings given to the nation with the intention that they would be displayed at South Kensington, provided an important development of the style.[5] The Gallery was a two-storeyed building of brick in various shades, grey, cream, blue and red, with pairs of round-arched blind windows, subsequently decorated in sgraffito, on the sky-lit upper floor; and a mansard roof, partly glazed, partly of coloured tiles. Internally, terracotta was employed for the first time at Brompton, in the form of a perforated ornamental frieze, which contributed to the ventilating system.[6] Godfrey Sykes (1824–66) seems to have been responsible for introducing the new material; a decorative artist influenced by Alfred Stevens: their work 'combined an unusually scholarly appreciation of the Italian Renaissance with a Gothic profuseness of material texture and of naturalistic observation'. This found expression in the South Court (1861–2), a 'synthesis of Gothic and Renaissance in metal [that] put South Kensington in the vanguard of what the Building News called "that convergence of opposite styles which seems to be taking place at the present day"'.[7] It was based on 'repeated first-hand study in Italy by the whole South Kensington team'.[8]

Terracotta was to become an extremely important material at South Kensington, not only in its decorative use in the Science and Art Department's buildings, but even more in the great Natural History Museum (1873–83) [Pl. 105, 150] where it was used as the principal facing material.[9] It was relatively cheap, it stood up to London's soot, requiring only to be washed periodically to exhibit its pristine colour, and the moulds, which could be re-used, reproduced, as Cole put it, 'the exact work of the artist'.[10] The South Kensington buildings were erected in piecemeal fashion, but a select committee in 1860 elicited the existence of a master-plan characterised by colonnades, loggias and pavilions to be built in-

crementally. The committee was encouraging, and Prince Albert's secretary described the proposed façade as 'beautiful'.[11] [Cp. Pl. 175]

After the success of the 1851 and 1855 International Exhibitions in London and Paris, Henry Cole had been extremely keen that London should mount a return, and he persuaded the Society of Arts to undertake the organisation.[12] A design for an exhibition building prepared by Fowke in 1860 was adopted, but subsequently modified: a leading feature was that it was fronted by picture galleries which could be retained if the rest of the building was discarded. Prince Albert was involved; and it was believed that the permanent quality of the galleries was intended to meet his wish to establish the National Gallery at South Kensington. The Exhibition Building as ultimately constructed [Pl. 103] occupied the entire Cromwell Road frontage between Exhibition and Prince Albert Roads, running back more than six hundred feet; it was marked by two vast dodecagonal glazed domes on octagonal crossings. The Building News described it as 'one of the ugliest public buildings that was ever raised in this country'. Beresford Hope (temporarily out of the Commons) referred in the Quarterly to its 'hideousness'.[13] The Art Journal denounced it as 'the most worthless and the vilest parody of architecture that it ever has been our misfortune to look upon'.[14]

Such was the building that in June–July 1863 the government proposed to purchase for the re-location of the natural history collections of the British Museum. Palmerston, although he had accepted the Opposition leaders' advice to separate the vote for the land from that for the buildings, mixed up the two in his speech proposing the purchase of the site, admitting that 'the many parts of the building which were constructed for temporary purposes . . . would require to be made more solid. Things that were now in wood would require to be made of something more durable.' Its glass domes would be reconstructed more solidly on a brick base. The exterior, 'plainly and simply constructed' (in accord with the South Kensington philosophy of adding ornament at

216.   Designs for Whitehall Palace. Many Victorian public men were enthusiastic admirers of the designs ascribed to Inigo Jones.

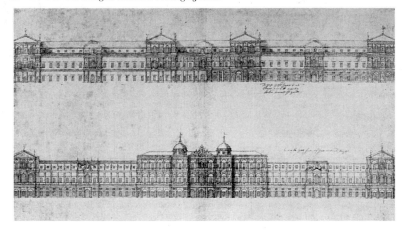

some convenient time) would be ornamented in stucco, 'durable and pleasing to the eye', a 'style of finishing' that admitted of 'the addition of pure ornamentation', with 'that higher degree of embellishment of which we see examples in the clubs of Pall Mall'.[15] William Gregory retorted that 'If hon. Members wanted to become acquainted with the effect of three-quarters of a mile of stucco, let them walk down Motcomb Street and look at the Pantechnicon and say whether it was possible for imagination to suggest anything more horrible.'[16]

Palmerston having made clear the government's intentions, opposition was organised to prevent the proposed purchase.[17] Thus feeling was already hostile when, a few nights later, Gladstone as chancellor proposed buying the building.[18] Reporting the architect Sydney Smirke's opinion that 'the outside of the Exhibition building is quite susceptible of being made extremely ornamental', he proposed that the galleries be preserved, with the northern arcade towards the Horticultural Society's garden; and that the adjoining $2^3/_4$ acres should be developed for the museum. The rest of the site would be left for future decision. The cost of adapting the buildings would be about £90,000.

As we have seen in chapter 6, Lord Elcho – whose stomach revolted against the idea – led the opposition to Gladstone's proposal, quoting from the *Spectator*: 'Let us not have the shrine of art set up in the Temple of Ugliness. The building stands condemned by the taste of cultivated Europe. . . . No patching, or stucco, or domes, or frescoes, or pillars, or gates of filagree iron can ever make the present building fit for anything but an International Dog Show, or a range of cavalry stables.' The RIBA, Elcho reported, condemned it as 'a grave discredit to the artistic reputation of England'. Like Tite in the Foreign Office debate, he quoted Ruskin: '. . . what is there but scorn for the meanness of deception? To cover brick with cement, and to divide this cement with joints that it may look like stone is to tell a falsehood.' Elcho believed that 'A great change was taking place in the spirit of British architecture. An earnest, truthful school was springing up, which abhorred pretences and used only bricks, stone, marble, and such materials as looked what they really were.' He concluded with a letter from Prosper Mérimée, the French authority on ancient buildings, who thought the Exhibition building 'detestable . . . it[s] proportions are bad . . . it belongs to no style of architecture . . . something with the pretensions of a monumental building without even the merit of being a commodious shed. . . . If you mean to apply it to several purposes, take care that you do not share the fate of those who buy a horse for a double purpose, and find that they have got one which will neither ride nor drive.'[19]

The elderly architect William Tite then joined in, agreeing that 'stucco was objectionable for a public building, for it was not truthful, like stone. Nor was it even economical, for it required colouring or painting every three years.' In an effort to rescue the position, the First Commissioner, Cowper, avowed that 'the Government had never seriously proposed to adopt stucco'; it was mentioned simply as 'a test of the expense of completing the front'.[20] Cavendish Bentinck in a savage attack enquired sarcastically whether the new buildings were to be 'Fowkean or Dilkhoosian' in style.[21] Frederick Doulton (1824–72),[22] the Lambeth pottery manufacturer, suggested Fowke might have been selected as architect to enable Palmerston to try his hand, 'as he had done with Mr Scott's work.' Lord Henry Lennox, however, a friend of Henry Cole, came to Fowke's defence, stating that 'Captain Fowke said that he should deeply lament the use of stucco'; Scott had suggested the use of 'rough brickwork, relieved by a dressing partly of stone and partly of terra cotta, with the addition of granite and other materials'. 'Provided always that the treatment of the design was artistic and trwell carried out', a most satisfactory and

economical building might be achieved.[23] Stafford Northcote, for the Conservative front bench, took a similar line, warning that Elcho and his supporters were really arguing for the ornamentation of the metropolis, which would lead to large expenditures. Joseph Henley (1793–1884),[24] another leading Conservative, turned this argument on its head by warning that the existing building itself might 'be treated in the most costly style'. Gladstone had reported that Smirke thought it 'susceptible' of great ornamentation. Henley recalled 'once seeing a mountebank with a black woman, who was susceptible of a great deal of ornamentation. He said, "I can make her white; and I can make her red; but do what I will, I can't make a handsome woman of her." I am afraid that Mr Smirke, do what he may to ornament the Exhibition building, must still leave it like that unhappy black woman: he cannot make it handsome.'[25]

Thus the arguments as to style played their considerable part in bringing about the government's overwhelming defeat, Elcho's motion being carried by 287 to 121. For all contemporary architects' concern about developing a contemporary style, when such a thing was put before the public, it was rejected. MPs, and the public generally, were looking for something they could recognise, be it essentially classical or gothic. South Kensington's utilitarian approach fell at the hurdle of public opinion.[26] The government was thus driven to an architectural competition for designs for the new buildings for Natural History and other purposes, in lieu of Fowke's unpopular building, which was demolished.

217. Site meeting at the South Kensington Museum, *c.* 1864. From the left: Henry Cole (1808–82), the powerful secretary of the Department of Science and Art, holding a plan with Captain Fowke, R.E., the museum's architect; Godfrey Sykes, designer of much of the architectural detail; and (?)John Liddell, a draughtsman who later claimed credit for Fowke's designs.

218. South Kensington Museum, Lecture Theatre building on north side of quadrangle, 1864, Francis Fowke, R.E.; ornamental details, G. Sykes; red brick and terracotta. The wings are a continnation of the design of the Residence Wing on the west side.

The chairman of the competition jury was none other than Lord Elcho, supported by the architectural historian James Fergusson, two architects of the old school, Tite and Pennethorne, and the sketcher of ruins, David Roberts R.A. The entry they unanimously chose as best turned out to be that of Captain Francis Fowke [Pl. 104a]: a terrible blow to the self-esteem of professional architects. 'I only hope that P[arliamen]t may be induced gradually to vote the money which will be required to begin and finish so beautiful and important a building', wrote Elcho.[27] Although Fowke's Early and High Italian Renaissance design was enriched with pavilions, cupolas, and a dome derived from that of St Peter's Rome, in essence it was closely related to the brick and terracotta design of the residences at the South Kensington Museum (1863),[28] described by Elcho as 'a model that London would do well to follow' [Cp. Pl. 218].[29] These were themselves an enriched development of the Sheepshanks Gallery, to which the façades of the 1862 Exhibition building had had a distinct resemblance.[30] It would seem, therefore, that it was essentially the utilitarian character (for which MPs were often calling), the lack of decoration of the structure that made the Victorian cognoscenti vomit. For Fergusson (one of the judges), hailed Fowke's competition design in print as 'neither Grecian nor Gothic, but thoroughly nineteenth century'.[31]

The South Kensington Museum was continued after Fowke's death more or less to his designs under another sapper, Colonel Henry Scott, who himself designed Science Schools (now the Cole Building of the Victoria and Albert Museum) on Exhibition Road in a similar manner [Pl. 219].[32] Although the sums provided for the purpose under the Science and Art Department vote were sometimes criticised in the Commons, there was no design before Parliament (other than the plan approved by the 1860 select committee) to invite comment and hostility: 'South Kensington' was able to build away in its own corner throughout the 1860s. [Pl. 218]

An intermission in new government building projects produced an apparent lull in the artistic war, but the Gothicists were consolidating their position in the country, despite Palmerston's success in ensuring irretrievably Palladian government offices, of which the Foreign Office occupied but a quarter, in Whitehall. The promised new War Office was shelved until completion of the Foreign and India Offices; so too various proposals for other new administrative offices. The *Companion to the Almanac for 1861* noted that Gothic was daily extending its conquests, though its eclectic character was criticised in 1863. By 1864 'Gothic is still the only wear; but it is a truly motley Gothic.'[33] But Renaissance too was strong. The uneasy relations between the advocates of the rival styles were shown by the skirmish over the new London University building.

The University of London was, until 1900, a purely administrative concept, responsible not for teaching (conducted by the constituent colleges) but merely for examining. The needs of the University were therefore limited to a range of offices, a chamber for the governing body, the senate, and examination halls. From 1856 these had been accommodated in and about Burlington House. Plans to locate the National Gallery on the northern part of the site were prepared by Banks & Barry in an Italianate style, but the idea was rejected by the Commons in 1859. After other false starts, in 1866 the government proposed a comprehensive plan for that site: London University should occupy a new structure on the north front; the Royal Academy was to be housed on the Piccadilly front, with the Learned Societies sandwiched between them.[34] The First Commissioner, Cowper, promised that, although the work might be executed in stages, 'the whole would be settled before any part was commenced. The Royal Academy building would be designed by their own architect [Sydney Smirke], subject to the approval of the Board of Works, and care would be taken that it harmonized in character and general arrangements with the University building. They need not be identical in style, but all the buildings that would cover the site would be viewed as one composition.'[35] Gladstone declared that the Vote was urgent because

219. The Science Schools, South Kensington, F. Fowke, H. Cole, R. Redgrave, J. Gamble and H. Scott, 1867–71. A Department of Science and Art project, the schools had a complex history before reinauguration as the Normal School of Science and Royal School of Mines in 1881, the former becoming in 1890 the Royal College of Science.

London University needed the building. The official architect Pennethorne was then directed to prepare specifications for the foundations.

The Conservatives then coming into office, Lord John Manners ordered Pennethorne to prepare a design as well. He presented alternatives, one Palladian and the other 'Italian Gothic'. Manners gave the Commons to understand that he had done this of his own volition, but a memorandum probably drawn up by the architect for the university states that he had in the course of preparing his plan drawn a 'plain Classic' detailed elevation,[36] which he submitted when Manners called for an elevation. The First Commissioner had then (according to the memorandum) asked for a different design 'suggesting also in very general terms the adoption of a character more Mediaeval or Renaissance; but without fettering the Architect as regards style'.[37] Manners invited the University authorities to express a preference, and the registrar and Pennethorne jointly reporting that 'they rather preferred' the 'Italian Gothic', work was put in hand and by April 1867 stood several feet high.[38] Meanwhile, discussions with the Academy had concluded with their being allocated Old Burlington House (to which they would add a storey and entrance arcade) with part of the garden behind on which to build galleries. The Learned Societies in consequence were to be housed in new buildings on the Piccadilly front for which the commission was given to Banks & (Charles) Barry [Pl. 99]. Pennethorne's Gothic design for the University was only revealed shortly before 5 April 1867, when Layard brought the matter before the Commons. Imperfectly informed, he impugned Manners' good faith as well as his taste.

Apart from the question whether Manners had violated pledges that the House should see the elevations before their execution, Layard focused on two issues: those of style, and of Old Burlington House. The Palladian architecture of the house was widely admired, but all the proposals for the site involved the demolition of its even more admired colonnade, the work of Gibbs. Layard argued that that eliminated one good reason for retaining the old house; 'to raise . . . lofty buildings round about it was like marrying a little short man to a very stout woman who would be smothered in her embraces'. So apparent was this absurdity that a storey was to be added to the old house, with a portico, so that it would lose its distinctiveness altogether; there ceased to be any point in retaining such an impediment to the replanning of the site.[39] With regard to style, he attacked the indeterminate 'Italian Gothic', and especially the conversion that he believed had taken place of the exterior façade from Classic, 'which was an anomaly, because the interior arrangements that would suit a Palladian building would probably not suit a Gothic building. The face of a building could not be changed without a corresponding change of the interior' – a view very different from that expressed by Scott a few years earlier,[40] and one now to be contradicted by the architect Tite in the ensuing debate.[41] Layard reported a resolution of the university's sub-committee:

They are, however, fully sensible of the disadvantage under which the architect has laboured in putting a Gothic casing upon an edifice planned for the adoption of an entirely different (and, indeed, antagonistic) style. Believing that ornament should be subservient to structural expression, they would gladly see the whole series of spires and pinnacles done away with. The sub-Committee also feel that the concealment of the roofs of the wings produces a want of harmony in the general effect, the centre having a high-pitched roof which is really picturesque.

Unable to persuade Manners to withdraw the elevation, the sub-committee had drawn on contextual and symbolic arguments, resolving 'That, having reference to the style of the adjoining buildings and to the character and purposes of the University of London . . . the modern style of architecture would be preferable

220. London University Building, Burlington Gardens, J. Pennethorne, 1866–70. In this free Classic design Pennethorne achieved work of European status.
a. Interior contract drawing, Upper Hall, 1868.
b. Exterior, in stone; the largely obscured sides are in two colours of brick.

either to the mediaeval or to the Italo-Gothic, for the elevation of the new building.'

The heated tone that Layard gave to this debate persisted despite a calming speech from Cardwell as a member of the university senate; although he attacked Pennethorne's design as 'a disfigurement to the metropolis', he remarked that it was not for London University, much less for its registrar, to decide 'how public money was to be spent in ornamenting or disfiguring the metropolis. That was a question for the House of Commons.' He hoped that a third design would be prepared. Beresford Hope on the other hand pointed out that it would be impossible, except from a balloon, to view the Academy building and the University building 'in the same *coup d'oeil*'. Medievalist that he was, he claimed that Pennethorne's design should be considered on its own merits:

if good, let it be adopted; if bad, corrected, for a bad Gothic design would raise a prejudice against the style ... make it as commodious and picturesque as possible, and if it could be made a new starting point for metropolitan architecture, so much the better. The time had come when the revolt was sounded against that monotonous repetition of Italian architecture in stucco and compo which had too long defaced our streets. Men were beginning to appreciate the picturesque forms of the Middle Ages so well adapted to the purposes of our present life.

In contrast, Tite thought that the three structures on the Burlington House site ought to be in one style (as proposed in Banks & Barry's 1859 project). He agreed with Bentinck and Elcho that works should be postponed until the House could consider the designs. Cowper ribbed his successor with the comments that he, Manners, had made a year earlier about the need for a harmonious scheme for the whole site, remarked that he had not himself ordered an elevation for the university because of his belief that it should be in harmony with the adjoining (though hidden!), yet-to-be-designed building for the Academy, and concluded that 'Italian-Gothic was a style in which beauty and variety might be successfully combined with grandeur of effect; but [echoing the university committee] that style was not appropriate to the position or the purpose of the building in question'.[42] In view of the general feeling, Manners then suspended the works for two weeks.[43]

When the supply Vote for the new university building was presented on 31 May 1867, Layard returned to the charge, insisting that all the buildings on the site must be in the same style: 'Ninety-nine men out of 100, if asked what should be the style of the new buildings, would say that it ought to be the same as that of Burlington House.' He thought that Pennethorne might produce another plan that might be referred to an eminent architect (as if Pennethorne were the veriest tyro). Manners produced a document signed by eminent architects, stating that 'there would not be the slightest architectural or other connection' between the Academy and the university buildings. In his old-fashioned way, he deprecated the canvassing of Members on this question by an outside body, which would lead to increased cost and delay and deprive the minister of his responsibility.

The debate that followed was largely a repetition of the earlier discussion. Cardwell repeated the argument that because the institution was novel, mediaeval architecture would be inappropriate. Hope retorted that 'some antecedent style or other must be

followed unless we invented an architecture of our own. Of this, indeed, there had recently been two examples, one at South Kensington and the other in Paris at the new Exhibition; but neither of them would, he imagined, be deemed satisfactory'. Pagan architecture had less affinity with the present day than had that of the Christian fourteenth century. He admitted that Pennethorne's design was not satisfactory, but suggested as a compromise, 'the adoption of that early [Renaissance] form of architecture embodying traditions of the Gothic period, of which the School of San Rocco at Venice was an example'. Tite regretted that the design had not been exhibited first, which would have saved a waste of money and obviated the stylistic difficulty: the general feeling of the House was opposed to Pennethorne's new style. Lowe, like Cardwell a member of the senate of London University,[44] agreed that 'with a unanimity which he had rarely witnessed, every one had disapproved the design . . . a façade of which everybody was inclined to be ashamed'. By a small majority in a thinnish House Layard carried his amendment against the two designs currently exhibited.[45]

Manners again bowed to the general feeling, which clearly favoured commissioning a new elevation, but he objected to the removal of the executed work, already standing 19 feet high. Layard however carried by 52 to 46 an amendment prohibiting any expenditure on either of Pennethorne's existing designs, and Manners gave way.[46] Whether any demolition was necessary is unclear; the *Survey of London* remarks that 'The sides and rear of the building are still very largely in the "Italian-Gothic" style, and abundantly justify the substantial objections . . . brought forward by the critics of Lord John Manners';[47] but the polychromatic character of the brickwork is not out of keeping with the romantic classicism of the façade that Pennethorne then devised. This ornamental High Renaissance design is one of his best buildings [Pl. 220], though somewhat depreciated by indifferent sculpture representing intellectual heroes.[48] It was doubtless these that the *Builder* had in mind when praising the building's expression of 'the nature of the purpose for which it had been erected'; Godwin recognised that though the detail was 'old-fashioned', and did 'not show sufficient individuality and originality of treatment to compel admiration in spite of fashion', it was 'far more thoughtful and artistic' than much contemporary Gothic. *The Times*, however, thought that the elaborate decoration was 'remarkable for a general character of flatness that is almost without parallel in any other important structure of the Victorian age'.[49]

Much larger schemes than London University were in gestation. The competition for a new National Gallery in Trafalgar Square was not generally regarded as very propitious ground for Goths; but the simultaneous competition for new Courts of Law, an even bigger affair, offered them an unrivalled opportunity.[50] The 'antique majesty of English law' had long been associated with the concept of 'our Gothic constitution', and all the nominees in the limited competition decided to submit Gothic designs.[51] The important Manchester Assize Courts competition, 1859 (a £70,000 work), had been won by Waterhouse's Gothic entry, which referred back to Scott's Government Offices design [Pl. 170], and hence to Woodward's Oxford Museum [Pl. 209]. Completed in 1864 and praised by the lawyers as well as by Ruskin, Waterhouse at Manchester pointed the adaptability of Gothic to contemporary needs.[52]

Sir John Summerson has suggested that the association of the courts with Gothic Westminster (they had, after all, been located in Westminster Hall itself until 1820) was one factor in the competitors' choice in 1866; that most architects of the right age 'had been caught young by the Gothic movement and had practised nothing else';[53] and that they felt that 'only the infinitely flexible Gothic

style' was capable of solving the complex problem presented by their monumental brief (of which an irregularly-shaped site was one significant factor).[54] That the architects of appropriate standing were mostly Goths is questionable. As we have seen, the selection of competitors was intended to be balanced, but Edward Barry (1830–80) 'departed from his usual style' in the competition,[55] as did H.B. Garling (1821–1909), while the classicist John Gibson (1817–92) – a pupil of Sir Charles Barry – withdrew, and P.C. Hardwick (1820–90) and T.H. Wyatt (1807–80) had declined. Other reputable architects of the Italian or eclectic schools 'of appropriate standing' included John Shaw (1803–70), J.T. Knowles (1806–84), F.C. Penrose (1817–1903), Digby Wyatt (1820–77), Cuthbert Brodrick (1822–1905), Charles Barry (1823–1900), W.H. Crossland (1823–1909), Robert Kerr (1823–1904), William Hill (1827–89), F.P. Cockerell (1833–78) and E.R. Robson (1835–1917).

Yet an eclectic Gothic universally pervaded the submissions in the limited competition of 1866–7 for the New Law Courts [Pl. 221–237]. 'It appears to have been understood from the beginning that the Law Courts were to be in the Gothic style', the editor of the *Builder* complained, a determination that deferred the development of a noble contemporary vernacular.[56] 'Of ten *bona fide* competitors names, seven were "Goths"', remarked Bentinck, 'and from this unfair appointment as well as for other reasons, the three "Non-Goths," and the artistic public inferred that no design, except one in the "Gothic" style would have any chance of success'. Beresford Hope, however, set him right: 'the original selection of architects had been fairly balanced between the parties, but some "Italians" withdrew'; they were replaced impartially, 'and yet, when it came to the scratch, not a single Italian architect was found to stand to his gun. With one consent, but with no mutual deliberation, each man for himself came to the conclusion that for the temple of traditional British law . . . an Italian or Grecian edifice

221. William Burges, A.R.A. (1827–81). A leader in the use of early-thirteenth-century French and Italian Gothic, which strongly influenced his widely plagiarised 1867 New Law Courts competition design.

would be a startling anachronism. . . . English Law Courts, built in English architecture, was what English common sense dictated.'[57]

'We presume the victory of Gothic over Classical architecture in this country may be dated from this event', declared the *Athenaeum*, with unconscious irony.[58] In his report on his Law Courts designs, Henry F. Lockwood (1811–78), well known in Bradford as a Classical man, explained that he had chosen Gothic because it was 'peculiarly adapted' for 'an Edifice combining such vast and varied requirements, and in which solemnity of character is essential. . . . Irregularities which would destroy the symmetry of a classical Building, in this Style contribute to its picturesque effect. A proper disposition of the masses will produce Dignity, and the harmony of the Façades will be in no way disturbed by the variety in the subordinate parts.' Nevertheless, it must be assimilated to present-day needs: 'A rigid adherence to crude and obsolete conventionalities is avoided, and the Style is carried out consistently with the improvements and innovations of the present Era. It has been sought to enter into the Spirit of the Style, rather than to reproduce mere Archaism [Pl. 222–3].'[59]

That had been Scott's contention for years past;[60] he naturally maintained the position he had defended for the Foreign Office: Gothic provided the most light and most easily admitted little irregularities [Pl. 233]. He also made use of the metaphorical argument which had been hardly applicable to his New Foreign Office. 'As a Mediaeval style, re-developed and modified at all points to meet the demands of the age, exactly symbolizes the English law, I cannot but think that both in idea and in its practical results it will approve itself . . . as the best suited.'[61]

For William Burges [Pl. 221] (1827–81) associationist philosophy was the key:

> In every other age but our own, but one style was in fashion at the time, and every artist designed in that style. Now, however, it is very different. When we consider the traditions with which our English laws and constitution are surrounded, we naturally seek for some style of architecture which will recall those traditions, and at the same time be the best of its kind. These conditions

222. New Law Courts limited competition, 1867, H.F. Lockwood (1811–78) of Bradford:
a (above). Plan shewing layout of courts and offices. This depicts clearly the concentric layout adopted by nearly all the competitors, screening the courts both from the noise of street traffic and from those merely visiting the offices. A high degree of segregation of the different categories of user was specified.
b. Perspective, Strand front. Lockwood's regular, symmetrical design, influenced by Barry's Houses of Parliament and Scott's Hamburg *Rathaus* design, was widely praised, though some critics doubted whether this Bradford man possessed the true Gothic spirit.
c (right). Main Entrance. This stair led to a Central Hall complete with hammerbeam roof copied from Westminster Hall.

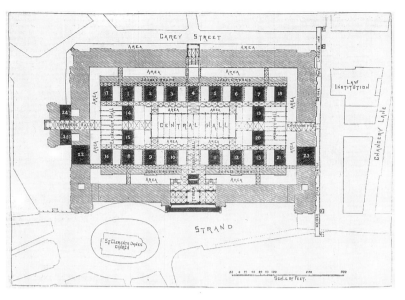

223. New Law Courts competition: Court interiors:
a. G.G. Scott: Appellate Court, for sitting of three judges.
b. W. Burges: a court in session.
c. H.F. Lockwood: a court with witness.
d. A. Waterhouse: a court in session. Note the extensive public gallery.

are fulfilled by the architecture of the thirteenth century. . . . In selecting the exact variety of the thirteenth century architecture to be adopted, we naturally give the preference to that of our own country

– though he employed the 'great broad masses' of Early French on the grounds that London's soot would destroy small-scale, cut-up English work [Pl. 224, 231].[62]

Similarly, Seddon's awe-inspiring design, 'pure English Gothic' – as he claimed, though clearly of Continental derivation in its silhouette – was 'treated with simplicity and large in its scale'. Waterhouse also (like Burges) had thought early-thirteenth-century Gothic especially appropriate, extreme delicacy in the exterior being unsuited to London's atmosphere. But 'the special and very peculiar requirements . . . have seemed in some respects to demand fresh expedients rather than recourse to precedent'.[63]

Thus the Crystal Palace was a possible source, as Hope recognised,[64] for his huge east-west central hall, 478×60 ft, rising 90 ft to a glass and iron roof, carried across a smaller north-south hall by a narrow bridge, and itself crossed at principal floor level by two narrow but ornamental bridges [Pl. 225].[65] Thus at least three of the competitors, Lockwood, Scott and Waterhouse, were consciously using an updated Gothic.

Contemporaries argued fiercely over their several merits; the more so perhaps because taste was changing swiftly over the years when the design was being finalised.[66] The *Builder* favoured Edward Barry; the more avant-garde *Building News*, Burges; *The Times* and the lawyers, Waterhouse; the *Athenaeum* and *Quarterly Review*, Street. Recent architectural historians have analysed and imposed their own classifications on the proposals.[67]

The problem was an exceedingly complex one: unprecedentedly voluminous instructions hampered rather than aided the competitors, who had to fit in no fewer than 1300 rooms of diverse functions on an inadequate site, and also achieve a high degree of monumentality in a 500 ft-long building that could be viewed only along a street (hence the bird's-eye competition perspectives). The only modern English building of comparable magnitude and importance was the Houses of Parliament, in which Barry's neoclassical planning had always been acknowledged as the fundamental element. It was requisitioned as a model by many of the competitors, its Picturesque elevation, and the disposition of elements in the river front readily discernible influences in many of the entries. Other possible models might have been found in some of the new public schools (e.g. Wellington); but Street and Deane were probably the only competitors with experience of them. The lunatic asylums of the 1840s and 1850s were often vast, though hardly as complex in their planning, but outwith the practice of most of the competitors.

Although universally Gothic in outward guise, the various designs were less uniform in their morphology. Summerson has pointed out the underlying neoclassicism of the older men's plans – Scott, Lockwood, Raphael Brandon – and Dr Hersey has seen a 'holdover from Neoclassical planning' in High Victorian Gothic civic architecture generally; 'In large buildings the logic and ease of Neoclassical planning overwhelmed the desire for variation and

224. New Law Courts competition: W. Burges, detail of arcade to Strand.

225. New Law Courts competition, 1867: Waterhouse's entry:
a. The ground-floor public hall rose through the entire building to an iron-and-glass roof derived from the Crystal Palace, perhaps via Mengoni's Milan Galleria, recently illustrated in *Builder*.
b. Plan of principal floor. Waterhouse solved the problem of controlling public access by designing two halls: the main east-west concourse (478 × 6oft) on this floor, limited to litigants and lawyers, crossed the public hall by a narrow bridge.

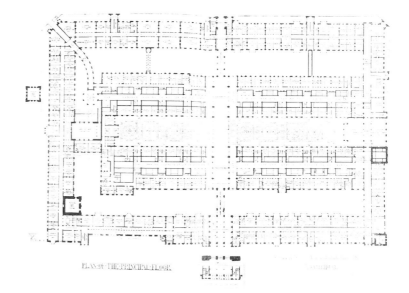

PLAN OF THE PRINCIPAL FLOOR

idiosyncrasy'.[68] Whether the stylistic label is helpful we may doubt: certain solutions were imposed by the necessities of the case. The contemporary critic James Thorne misunderstood these, condemning the competitors' approach as 'anything but according to Gothic principle and precedent', for all proceeded on the same idea of masking the 24 courts as one great symmetrical building.[69] It was a fundamental principle of architectural art, he argued, that 'a building shall distinctly declare its purpose'.[70] He failed to appreciate that the designs were indeed proclaiming the purpose of the law courts. The point of concentrating the Superior Courts of Law and Equity was to give physical expression to a conceptual union that had been the long-term aim of Victorian law reformers. Varying jurisdictions with differing procedures were gathered up into a comprehensive entity following one rule: the only difference between the courts was whether a judge sat alone or whether several judges sat together in Court of Appeal.

Thus the determining factors were practical: convenience, quietness, adequacy of natural light and air for the courts; for the offices, light, air and accessibility by the public; and for the whole range of users, lines of communication keeping distinct the several classes: judges, counsel, solicitors, their clients, witnesses, jurors, the general public. These practical considerations were, the instructions stated, to supersede 'so far as they may conflict, all considerations of architectural effect'. So far as elevations were concerned, the further determinants were the limit on height (for practical reasons); the situation between two streets of no great width; and the close vicinity to buildings east and (as originally planned) west. One other original requirement made a dramatic impact on most of the designs: that for a fireproof record or probate tower (subsequently abandoned).

To meet these several requirements, an obvious solution was to place the courts in the interior, ringing them with a wall of offices, as in an influential pilot plan made by H.R. Abraham, for his brother-in-law, attorney-general Bethell, in 1857: a repetition of small units imposing a high degree of external regularity. There were few distinct elements in the composition that could be developed in 'expressive High Victorian Gothic volumes'.[71] One such, however, was a central hall that could be used in organising the

226.   New Law Courts competition:
a. Perspective, Strand front, Henry Bayly Garling (1821–1909).
b. and c. Sections, shewing the complexity of design dictated by the provision of different services and the need for separate circulation system for different categories of user:
b. G.G. Scott, east-west section, looking toward Strand, shewing the internal streets separating public offices from the courts complex.
c. W. Burges, north-south section, looking east (the Strand on the right).

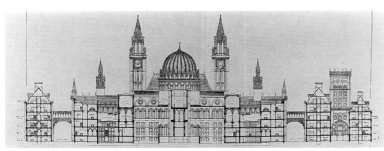

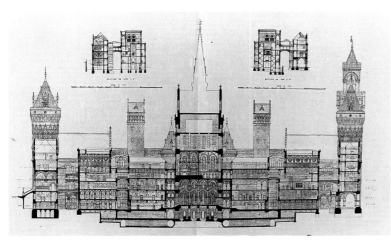

View of Alternative design for RECORD TOWER from Clement's Inn

227.   New Law Courts competition: record tower, G.E. Street (alternative, cheaper design). A fireproof tower for the kingdom's original wills was prescribed, but later abandoned. Street's immensely powerful but elegant, stripped-down tower was one of the finest elements of his entry.

distributive system, though Burges rejected it [Pl. 230a] as bringing the public into the heart of the building.[72]

Ironically enough, despite the clear injunction in the instructions, it was not planning but drawing that once again determined the ultimate outcome. As recounted in chapter 11, a joint award to Edward Barry (whose planning was much approved of) and G.E. Street (for his superbly drawn elevations, Pl. 181, 227) was not sustainable, and the commission was given to the latter. Thus the result justifies a fuller examination of the stylistic elements of the competition.

It was not in the planning alone that competitors broke the High Victorian canons of clearly articulated parts, independent volumes, expressive silhouettes, variety in plane and surface and openings. A number of reviewers diagnosed Lockwood's elevations [Pl. 222] as wanting in 'the true Gothic spirit';[73] and the same was true of his essentially classicist colleagues, Garling, hapless winner of the 1857 War Office competition [Pl. 226a],[74] and Edward Barry [Pl. 181]. Some of the younger men adopted the less regular massing generally favoured by contemporary opinion: Burges, of course; Waterhouse, who pushed further the Picturesque silhouette of the Houses of Parliament [Pl. 229]; and Seddon, whose tightly-packed plan gave rise to a highly controversial structure dominated by high pitched roofs of an almost Germanic fashion [Pl. 236], 'thoroughly Gothic' to the *Athenaeum*, but having 'little

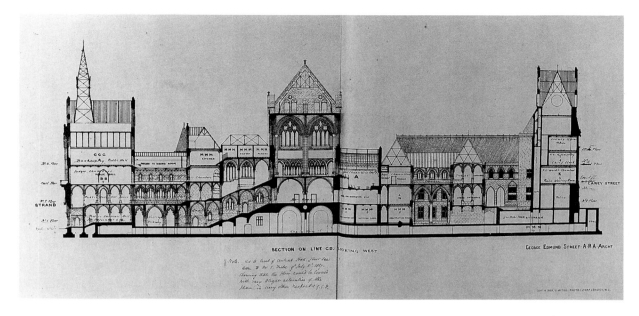

228. New Law Courts competition. G.E. Street, South-north section looking west (the Strand on the left), shewing difference in level between Strand and Carey Street.

consonance' with contemporary London for the *Builder*.[75] Abraham, deviser of the pilot plan, doubtless thinking that his only hope lay in a sharply differentiated scheme, arranged irregularly-shaped blocks of courts around a central circular domed record tower 310ft high. Deane also adopted an irregular layout [Pl. 237], breaking up his façade into several blocks of different heights, distinguishing the courts of common law from those of equity (a division legal reform was seeking to extinguish), as well as from the Admiralty and appellate jurisdictions.

Most of the entries were characterised by a very strong horizontality, expressing the three storeys of office accommodation on the outer face. Street and Burges were most successful in breaking it up, though Street did so while retaining the unbroken roof lines that had been characteristic of him since his Bloxham School design of 1854. Seddon's repeated vertical accents helped to break his horizontal continuities; and to some extent Deane by

breaking up his façade, as already mentioned, and Waterhouse by breaking forward his Strand façade and grouping his windows (a lesson he had learned from Scott's 1857 Foreign Office design) achieved a similar effect [Pl. 229, 237].

In no design was a highly picturesque quality more strongly evidenced than in that of William Burges [Pl. 224, 231].[76] His powerful drawings, with their strong Early French character,[77] made a marked impression on the public, and were awarded the palm in six of the fourteen periodicals that reviewed the designs,[78] Hope's *Saturday Review* being notably enthusiastic.[79] Although Burges's drawings caught the imagination of the day, several influential organs adversely remarked on their castellated and excessively medieval character. Rejected but extensively published, their influence was widespread.[80] The *Athenaeum*'s comment sums it up: a short-sighted man, 'standing near Mr Burges's proposed Law Courts, might well go wild with delight'; but 'delight in picturesque

229. New Law Courts competition, 1867. A. Waterhouse, perspective from the South Bank. Strongly picturesque in composition, and illustrated in superb tinted drawings, Waterhouse's design was criticised for its enervated elevations – 'drawing-room Gothic' (*Athenaeum*).

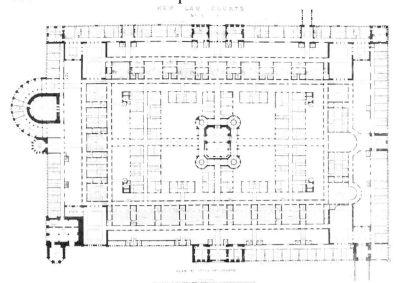

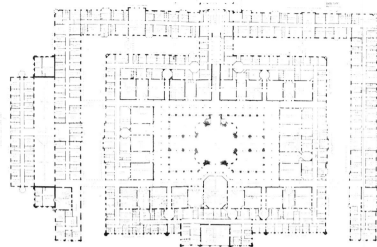

230.   New Law Courts, 1867: Competition plans, court floor:
a. Burges almost alone of the competitors abandoned a central public hall, though retaining the concentric organisation of the plan.
b. G.G. Scott: A well-conceived plan providing a two-storey "ambulatory" (the lower floor a constricted public route to the courts) around a central quadrangle in which was a small domed central hall.

effects and minor beauties' had mastered the architect's 'sense of fitness for the general character of the proposed structure'.[81]

Less flamboyantly worn, however, many other designs (even Street's) incorporated French elements.[82] Scott's eclecticism ranged from Brussels (town hall) to Venice (Doge's palace); in his domed central hall [Pl. 232] he sought to synthesise Byzantine classicism and French Gothic, just as he believed Classical characteristics like regularity and simplicity of form [Pl. 223] were desirable in public buildings: 'He is *only half* an architect who suffers Art to militate against practical convenience, or who, while meeting in

the best manner all practical requirements, fails to clothe them at all points in a garb worthy of the dignity of the edifice.'[83] Scott's synthesis, however, fell between two stools: he pleased neither the classicists nor the dominant Francophiles in the Gothic camp [Pl. 233].[84] Lockwood had assimilated much from Scott's earlier work; his design proved popular, but though the *Builder* liked its general outline, it damned the scheme with faint praise as 'decidedly municipal in character' [Pl. 222].[85]

Raphael Brandon (1817–77) and Street were alike thought too ecclesiastical. But Brandon's Puginesque design [Pl. 234] was *retardataire* copyism, a series of quotations drawn together by the axial planning that betrayed French training.[86] He saw the problem from an artist's viewpoint, remarking of his collection of medieval models, 'I have selected that date of style which showed the greatest amount of purity . . . and trusting to a faithful attention to the conveniences of arrangement, clothing the whole with artistic mantles, thus producing the effects naturally, bearing always in

231.   New Law Courts competition, perspective by W. Burges. His banner-waving for Early French (with Italian touches) earned him much applause, and the beauty of the drawings was greatly admired.

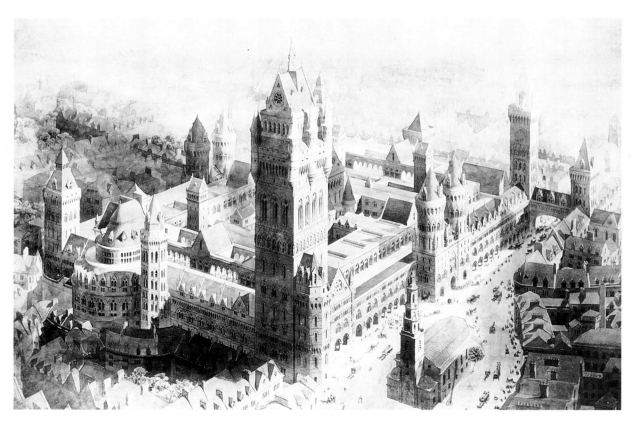

232 (above left). New Law Courts competition, details: G.G. Scott, Central Hall. Scott did not waste his 'Byzantine' Foreign Office scheme: Allom's drawing shows a mosaic Christ Pantocrator in the dome: an architectural form and a decorative material that Scott recommended for modern Gothic.

233. New Law Courts, 1867: G.G. Scott's competition entry: a. Carey Street entrance, with bridge to Lincoln's Inn. Scott's day was past. His planning was unadventurous, his façades monotonous; but features of his design did not lack nobility. b. Strand front, perspective.

234. New Law Courts competition, 1867, perspective:
Raphael Brandon (1817–77). Most magnificent of the entries, Brandon's was written off generally as too ecclesiastical.

mind the general outline and light and shade intended to be produced.'[87]

Street's return from French and Italian to largely English forms was more complex. Modern architectural historians disagree about its essential character. For Dr Hersey, who basically follows Hitchcock's identification of High Victorian with bold plasticity, asymmetrical massing, polychromy and structurally expressive detail,[88] to which he adds variety of fenestration, and associationism,[89] Street's competition design [Pl. 181] indeed has 'the germs of a more genuinely High Victorian Gothic solution', using much more expressive forms than his rivals: a towering great hall [Pl. 240] embedded in lower structures, like 'litigants walled in by squads of lawyers', and a variety of openings 'echoing the interior hierarchies of chambers and their occupants'.[90] Dr Muthesius identifies High Victorian rather with massiveness, heaviness, an emphasis on the horizontal, continuity of wall surface, and flat-plate tracery.[91] Thus for him Street's varied façades, contrasting 'concentrated groups of windows of different sizes' with extensive areas of blank wall [Pl. 227], preference for individual windows rather than arcaded rows, and lack of polychromy seem 'to lead away from High Victorianism'.[92] In his symmetrical fronts Street avowedly aimed at uniformity 'in their general character'; dominated by long, unbroken roof lines, they contribute to his desire 'to prevent the building looking trivial or frittered away', though rendering it sufficiently picturesque, principally by means of five towers; 'worthy of its object, the age, so rich a nation, and so great a city' [Pl. 181].[93] He thus achieved a synthesis of Gothic features with classical character.[94]

The professional and art press devoted itself to examination and

analysis of the competition entries as never before. The *Building News*, with its Radical *avant-garde* stance, viewed them with a jaundiced eye. Scott 'must surely feel by this time that his work has not kept pace with many of his *confrères* in quality'. Waterhouse gave evidence of having read *The Stones of Venice* more as an office duty than as an antiquary or an artist. His composition must 'end by setting the fashion to nearly all architects who think secondhand'. Edward Barry, Abrahams, Lockwood and Garling [Pl. 226a] were mistaken choices, treating us 'to the kind of Gothic in which Batty Langley and Horace Walpole delighted'. Street had been so busy on church work that he had never had the opportunity to learn all that was involved in a large public building. Deane's choice of Italian architecture, Gothic or not, was unsuitable; 'Mr Woodward's mantle has not fallen on Mr Deane'. But the eastern half of Burges's Strand front was 'the greatest result of the competition'.[95]

Somewhat more enthusiastic was the *Spectator*, which, although it had severe criticisms of individual entries, thought that even the least satisfactory attempt to solve a very difficult problem 'displays a great advance in mastery over the Gothic, made during the thirty years since the adoption of the prettiest, cheapest, and most practically manageable of all styles, for English public buildings, was settled by Sir Charles Barry's success; for we decline to hold the heavy mass in Downing Street more than an aberration, due to the old-fashioned taste of Lord Palmerston'.[96] Lockwood, 'almost alone of the eleven', had chosen 'the highly developed Gothic of France during the thirteenth century'. In general, the designs were too ecclesiastical; too often there was mechanical repetition of identical forms; or parts, pretty in themselves, were unsatisfactorily put together.[97] Burges's design was 'fairly bound together by the fine treatment of the arcaded sides presented towards the streets', but had a too medieval, too ecclesiastical look.[98] The Gothic of the Middle Ages must be elaborated; 'it must incorporate our physical science; it must answer to our civilized ideas; it must be defeudalized and demonasticized'. Waterhouse best met these tests.

Edward Barry's design [Pl. 181] was too strongly imbued with the late Gothic character of his father's Palace of Westminster to meet with much applause. Waterhouse's 'genuine civilized and civic Gothic' [Pl. 225], as the *Spectator* phrased it – a back-hander at Burges's *Castellum Juris* – and 'demonstrably the best exhibited', met 'at once the demands of taste and of common sense'.[99] But for the Ruskin-trained critic of the *Athenaeum* the 'comparatively feminine character' of Waterhouse's Gothic lacked 'that severity which pertains to our ideas of the Courts of Justice for a great empire'. It wanted 'Gothic expressiveness, even rudeness – if we must have that characteristic with purpose and strength of design'; his very attractive, tinted drawings were dismissed as 'the best examples of drawing-room Gothic we have seen'.[100] Preferred was Seddon's 'intensely honest and thoroughly Gothic design, rude, and even uncouth in some of its parts' [Pl. 236].[101] But Deane's Ruskinian Italian Gothic [Pl. 237], carried forward from his late partner Woodward's Government Offices, was now out of date and fashion. In contrast, Street's masses were skilfully grouped, his façade dignified with 'great simplicity of style . . . graces ample enough for the eye to rest on, and variety enough for its delight', possessing 'more of Fine Art' than any others, save Burges and Seddon, ruled out of court by cost.[102]

Describing the designs in considerable detail, and examining the plans and estimated unit costs with care, from February to May the *Builder* devoted a series of illustrated articles to the competition, but they were rather informative than critical. It gave scope however to Fergusson's criticism of the retrogressive character of the competition. He saw one ray of hope: 'No one is quite satisfied with it. In spite of all the talent employed, and the beauty of the drawings, it has been impossible to get up any enthusiasm about it in any quarter. . . . The general public, too, feel uneasy.' (J.T. Emmett in the *Quarterly* even wailed 'Architecture in England is dead.'[103]) Gothic spires and Grecian porticos, asserted Fergusson, were equally absurd in the nineteenth century.[104]

This attitude became pervasive, and by the time that another major government building was decided upon in the early 1880s both these 'absurdities' were out of the running. Street had built his Gothic Law Courts, surmounting tidal waves of criticism, but it was the last great Gothic public building ('the swan-song of the Gothic Revival', Goodhart-Rendel called it), and a more picturesque and less monumental Gothic than most of the competition entries, so that it was assaulted from more than one point of view. Furthermore, there was a generational change: Street was not the only competitor to die before the Courts were opened – six of his rivals were also dead. Waterhouse, a survivor, turned for his contemporaneous Natural History Museum to the *rundbogenstil* character of the premiated design of his deceased predecessor, Fowke, and its terracotta façades, though he handled them very differently, borrowing ideas from his own Law Courts design.

A recent commentator has fairly summed up the competition designs as 'efforts to unite the picturesque capabilities of medieval architecture with the stateliness and dignity that were considered classical'; remarking that 'The majority of entries either exaggerated the picturesque or adopted a kind of quasi-classicism.' But Professor Brownlee further suggests that this 'fragmented the Gothic movement'.[105]

235.   New Law Courts competition, Bar Library. This important room was given a high finish in competitors' drawings:
a. J.P. Seddon.
b. A. Waterhouse.

237.   New Law Courts competition, 1867, perspective:
T.N. Deane. His design was far more expressive of function than his rivals', allocating the different judicial divisions to distinct blocks. He echoed the no longer fashionable stylistic treatment given by his late partner, Woodward, to their Government Offices entry of 1857.

236.   New Law Courts competition, John Pollard Seddon (1828–1906):
a. Perspective of model. Seddon's powerful massing and bold Early French detail (diplomatically described as 'pure English') cloaked a crowded and inconvenient plan.
b. Principal refreshment rooms, below Central Hall. Seddon was criticised for failing sufficiently to segregate the various types of user.

The Gothic movement, of course, never possessed the unity imposed on it by historians of architectural style. It was from the first riven between those who believed in copying the past, and those who (like Scott) used the past as a point of departure. The *Ecclesiologist* had perhaps succeeded temporarily in uniting these two parties by its insistence on the use of 'Middle Pointed' in order thoroughly to master the style before allowing new development. But Clutton & Burges and Street had defied this *fiat* in the Lille Cathedral competition (1855–6), in which they took the first and second prizes respectively, and made the 'vigorous' early-thirteenth-century French Gothic the vogue in England.[106] Scott himself saw that competition as the moment of disintegration of the Gothic movement, marking a return to the earlier eclecticism.[107] His concept of a palatial Gothic style embraced precisely that 'quasi-classicism' that Brownlee sees as cleft-making.[108] The concept of an architecture 'universal in it applicability . . . *one* commanding, comprehensive, and all-pervading style', which Scott and his compeers had sought,[109] was abandoned, and the classical style – which had never surrendered – reclaimed its mastery of the monumental field. Nor is it surprising to find classical qualities among the competitors of 1867 when we remember that several of them hardly belonged to 'the Gothic movement'. Edward Barry, for instance, believed that: 'Whatever may be the local result of any battle of the styles, designs based on classical traditions will hardly disappear from the practice of the modern world.'[110]

The simultaneous New National Gallery competition showed that those traditions were still alive. The chosen competitors were invited to submit designs for (a) an entirely new Gallery; (b) an adaptation of the existing building. At a time when the press was proclaiming the triumph of Gothic as a result of the Law Courts competition, only two entrants for the National Gallery – Street and Somers Clarke – submitted Gothic designs. Street avowedly attempted to give the National Gallery 'so much simplicity, dignity, and classicality of effect' as would ensure 'its having a sufficiently grave and monumental character' [Pl. 179].[111] 'It seemed to be assumed', wrote Street's son sadly, 'either that Gothic was not suitable for the particular purpose, or that the surroundings in Trafalgar Square made the adoption of a style so different unadvisable.'[112] The judges declined to make an award, ultimately conceding that Edward Barry's designs for a new Gallery [Pl. 238] and James Murray's for adapting the old one 'exhibited the greatest amount of Architectural merit'.[113]

Nonetheless, the National Gallery designs excited some interest in the professional press. The *Athenaeum* carefully reviewed all the designs for a new gallery, while the *Builder* analysed them in even

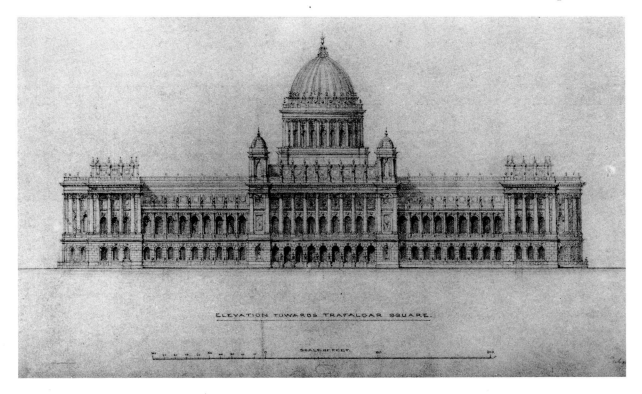

238. New National Gallery design, 1869, E.M. Barry. Disappointed of the Law Courts commission, Barry was appointed to design a new National Gallery by Lord John Manners in 1868. Financial considerations reduced this to adding a number of rooms to Wilkins' gallery. Barry's rich classical design was itself reduced from his competition entry (cp pl. 172).

ELEVATION TOWARDS TRAFALGAR SQUARE.

SCALE OF FEET.

greater detail.[114] Owen Jones's suggested to the *Athenaeum* 'the Venetian Renaissance of the sixteenth century'; although elegant and elaborate, 'there is nothing in its exterior either striking for itself or proper to a picture gallery'. As was to be expected of an authority on architectural colouring, he proposed to use terracotta of varied colour. Brodrick's characteristic Greek columnar design was 'at once admirable and objectionable; it reminds us of some of the better qualities of Soane's finer designs – it is dignified, but eminently unfitted to . . . our climate'. While the *Builder* criticised Street for insisting on a Gothic solution, the *Athenaeum* thought it impossible not to admire his courage in furnishing a 'purely Gothic design for a building to which that style is popularly believed inapplicable'. It was almost 'free from asceticism or quaintness, very rich and grand in its parts, and aptly decorated according to the construction'. 'If a Gothic design can be accepted by the public, – and, prejudice apart, we see no reason against its being so, – it would be hard to find a more beautiful or better adapted work than this.' But to the *Builder*, the Trafalgar Square front resembled 'a church that has lost an aisle, where piers and arches have been filled in with new walling and windows'.

'Enormously deep, round-headed bays' lighting 'a single lower range of rooms' on the principal front vitiated M.D. Wyatt's entry, another that sought a polychromatic effect through using terracotta. Charles Barry & Banks, who had had the advantage of designing a gallery when it was intended to place it on the Burlington House site, offered much the same: 'monotonous, not to say extremely commonplace' Italian, with 'ranges of colonnades on the front and dumpy towers with pinnacles on the roof' would 'neither enliven or dignify Trafalgar Square' (*Athenaeum*); while the *Builder* found it deficient in novelty, and lacking differentiation from offices or palaces. Somers Clarke offered both Italian and Gothic, both with 'enormously lofty campaniles at their north-east corners': they might do for a town hall, but not for the horizontal lines required of a picture gallery (*Athenaeum*). The Venetian Gothic version presented a mass of wall, resembling the Doge's Palace; 'Surely those who copy should at least select' (*Builder*). Murray's Greek Corinthian entry, 'not without grandeur and

grace', which the *Builder* recognised as modelled on Schinkel's Berlin Museum, was preferable to his Roman alternative, with 'detestable rustications, and those hideous pillars which put one in mind of tea-chests and Cheshire cheeses placed one on the top of the other'. Commonplaces such as the bearded masks decorating keystones ought not to be tolerated in a new public building (*Athenaeum*). 'This is not the sort of design that we wish to see carried into effect', remarked the *Builder*. 'If a building that is new be an art-work, there must be novelty in it.' Penrose's designs were dismissed by both *Builder* and *Athenaeum* as lacking character, and Cockerell's similarly by the latter; for the *Builder*, 'there is almost too much of building up, merely to get sky-line'. Edward Barry's 'very fortunate modification of Roman and Palladian' met the *Athenaeum*'s favour, possessing 'much elegance and splendour', though not without trivial features. 'On the whole', concluded the *Athenaeum*, 'this display cannot but serve to raise the reputations of those English architects, who show ability even greater than might have been expected.'

Parliamentary comment on style was relatively restrained, questions of funding, cost and site now proving far more controversial. Cavendish Bentinck won little support when he complained that the non-representation of architecture and art among the Law Courts' judges left the country with an insufficient choice, 'for no design in the modern style had been exhibited. . . . The designs exhibited were very curious, no doubt, as illustrations of Gothic cathedrals, feudal castles, and other mediaeval monuments, but they were most extravagant in their character, costly in their estimates, and barbarous in their details.'[115] The extreme improbability of any of the National Gallery designs being executed probably explains the lack of parliamentary comment thereon.

Lord John Manners's decision to award the Law Courts' commission to Street was by no means the end of the argument over style. A change of government within the year was followed by months of contention about moving the new Courts to the Thames Embankment.[116] Even when this matter was resolved in favour of the Strand, Street had to revise a design that was too big for the ground allocated, and then to contend for years with the penurious First Commissioner, A.S. Ayrton.[117] Thus it was four years from his appointment that work began, four years when taste was changing in which powerful critics could train their guns on Street's proposals. Not that Street himself was immune from stylistic development: Professor Brownlee has charted the enthusiasm that he expressed for the boldness of French Gothic in 1866 shifting to a growing appreciation of the poetry, importance, and finally supremacy of English, a shift that aligned him with the leaders of what was to emerge as the 'Queen Anne' movement.[118] The quasi-French grouping of masses had won admiration in the competition, but their Picturesque quality could be secured in the English style; the cost was the abandonment of Classical regularity [Pl. 239].

After the abandonment of the Embankment site, Street had prepared revised designs for accommodating the Law Courts on the Carey Street site without the additions he had originally hoped for. These involved a complete rearrangement of the main blocks, with the office wing on the east, and the central hall rotated through 90 degrees, to run north-south, so providing a principal feature in the Strand front. For the south front of the hall, Street adapted the north (entrance) front of Westminster Hall, an appropriate allusion to the old seat of the courts.[119] The other principal accent of the simplified façade was a great clock-tower at its eastern end (recalling Barry's asymmetrical treatment at Westminster), which was excised by the economy-obsessive First Commissioner.

In February 1871 Street submitted a 'very hasty sketch' of his revised scheme. Captain Galton's report which the Treasury called for in March 1871 was highly critical. 'It does not enter into the functions of this Board [remarked the subsequent Treasury letter] as a general rule to give opinions upon matters of taste and art, but, supported by the professional opinion of the responsible adviser of the Office of Works, they cannot, on the present occasion, hesitate to express the conviction, at which they had independently arrived, that great and just disappointment will be experienced by the Public if the elevation fronting the Strand is executed according to the present design.' Street was ordered to 'reconsider his plan for the Strand front so as to render it more worthy of the importance of the Building and of its position in the Metropolis'.[120]

When Street sent in his 'long since revised' elevation, with a *flèche* over the central hall, and two flanking ventilation turrets, providing vertical accents, though 'generally an improvement', it still failed to satisfy the Treasury: 'They are sure [it] will disappoint the just expectations of the Public'. Street had realised what the Treasury clearly had not: the long façade of the Courts would be seen only in perspective. He protested that his revision was a great improvement on his competition plan, implied that part of the difficulty was the Treasury Board's inability to read geometrical drawings, pointed out that he had been ordered to omit the 'urgently required' clock tower, which provided a 'striking break in the general horizontal line', and promised to send a perspective drawing. 'I feel very sure that seen in perspective it will be an effective and fine front, quite worthy of the building. I have intentionally made it comparatively simple in its detail, but in London I hold that the effect which is best worth obtaining is that which is produced by good light and shade, and by effective disposition of the shapes of the building.'[121] He sent working drawings of the whole front at the scale of one-eighth of an inch to the foot, together with a photograph of the whole on 7 July. The Treasury approved them on 4 August.[122]

These worked-up revised designs were then exhibited to the Commons.[123] They provoked an extraordinary outburst of hostility. Cavendish Bentinck was a leader in the parliamentary opposition to them, but because of the pressure of government business so late in the session – and, it was said, Ayrton's snubbing and sneering at MPs who criticised – the real attack came in the public prints,[124] primarily from the authoritative James Fergusson. Probably primed by his friend Galton of the Works, Fergusson, bitterly anti-medievalist and a zealot for a truly contemporary architecture,[125] led off with an attack on their medieval and Picturesque qualities published in the *Builder* (1 July 1871), which became a persistent opponent of Street. He condemned both Street's general façade ('the meanest design . . . proposed in our day'), and his stone-vaulted central hall ('an imperforate, gloomy, solid vault') [Pl. 239–40]. The professional press followed with uniformly unfriendly comment, though the more generalist *Athenaeum* praised Street's work.[126] In August *The Times* chewed up the façade as lacking the 'pure and noble form, exalted dignity, entire unity' requisite in the 'Courts of Justice of an Imperial City'; but rather resembling 'a street in some collegiate town', exhibiting merely 'a certain picturesqueness': 'we want much more than this in a great building devoted to a great purpose, a building which is intended to stand for ever, in the centre of a metropolitan city, as the chief credential of its empire and pre-eminence'. There should be a new competition.[127] It then gave ample space to hostile correspondents.[128] Their principal objections were to the 'utter want of unity' and appropriate dignity,[129] a view shared by a modern critic for whom 'It represents the pathetic collapse of an overstrained imagination.'[130] In fact, as Goodhart-Rendel appreciated,[131] it is a brilliant exercise in constructing a 500ft-long street façade (visible only in enfilade) for a great public building: with two symmetrical and overlapping divisions indicating the internal organisation of courts and offices respectively.[132] [Pl. 239b]

The Times' correspondents were fertile with suggestions for what they saw as appropriate models – the town hall at Piacenza, the Cloth Hall at Ypres, and the inevitable Inigo Jones's Whitehall.[133] More hostile letters were followed by a less unfriendly but still severely critical leading article about a month later: public taste had 'set too strongly in the direction of Gothic revival to be easily diverted'; Street's 'extravagances of varied form . . . intended to be picturesque' were 'merely grotesque'; 'We require the majesty which can alone be supplied by unity of plan, severe simplicity of form, and imposing grandeur of mass.' The matter should be held over until next year for parliament to decide.[134]

Street was by no means without his supporters, notably the trenchant architect and writer E.W. Godwin (1833–86), who rallied to his support in articles in *Building News* and the *Architect*. These periodicals then published other supportive articles.[135] Realising the importance of winning over professional opinion, Street used the viewing of his drawings as a weapon: he enabled some of his elevations (in which he had re-introduced a revised clock-tower) to be published in *Building News* and the *Architect* in November and December 1871.[136] He invited the initially hostile *Law Journal* to examine the designs and so won them over; and on 23 December 1871 he opened his drawing office to members of the RIBA.[137] The inimical *Builder*, which had not been given the same facilities, was not slow in venting its spite ('. . . not pass muster in a suburban villa; . . . utter want of . . . anything like the dignity which should mark an important public building').[138] *The Times* published a further brutal attack ('ecclesiastical . . . frivolous . . . fatal fertility . . . meanness . . . only relieved by the monstrosity . . . and the studied deformity'): Street might have got rid of the ridiculous, but he could not achieve the sublime. 'We require a building of a fair and goodly front, along which from end to end shall be written as clearly as though in letters a yard high: "These are the Courts of Justice of a great Empire".'[139] Hostile letters from architects and cognoscenti followed.

Beresford Hope however brought the *Saturday Review* to Street's defence,[140] and the *Athenaeum* continued its support.[141] Thus with a

239. New Law Courts, G.E. Street, perspective of revised Strand front:
a. Western portion, 1871. Appointed architect for the New Law Courts, Street had to re-design them for a site on the Embankment, and then again for a return to Carey Street, but without the extra land he had originally included. By this time, he realised the impracticality of a uniform symmetrical front of some 500ft in a narrow street, and therefore broke it up into two overlapping, approximately symmetrical units, achieving a highly picturesque composition.
b. Artist's drawing of whole front, showing its complex double symmetry (ABCBADAE) about the two entrance axes (C,D).

now friendly *Building News* and *Architect*, of the five journals specifically dealing with artistic questions, only the *Builder* remained hostile. Street also aimed for securing wide support in the political nation at large by supplying a large perspective drawing to the *Illustrated London News* with its huge middle-class readership, published (with favourable comment) on 20 January 1872 [Pl. 239].

The editor of the *Architect*, Roger Smith (1821–91), was another contemporary who appreciated what Street was doing. He referred to two 'canons of street architecture': 'that a large building in a street' first will 'be seen as a whole when seen from up or down the street, but will be extremely foreshortened, and must be designed so as to look well when so foreshortened'; and secondly 'be seen only piecemeal when seen from the opposite side of the street, and must be designed so as to look well when seen in detail'.[142] Street solved both these problems with the overlapping symmetries of his two-centred front and the strong terminal accent (cut off by the Treasury) [Pl. 239b].

The literary battle, perhaps the most intense of all the architectural battles in the press, reached a climax at the end of 1871, with Fergusson's publication of another article, more sarcastic than ever, in *Macmillan's Magazine*, an angry denunciation of the Gothic movement reprinted in *The Times* and *Building News*.[143] Fergusson's cup of vitriol[144] not merely scarified the ecclesiastical medievalism of Street's work, his vaulted hall un-Gothic and unnecessary, but

240.   New Law Courts, G.E. Street, central hall, 1871. Street was determined to build the first stone-vaulted hall erected in England since the middle ages. He pursued a long and ultimately successful struggle against architectural and official critics, finally appealing to the cabinet against the First Commissioner of Works.

Waterhouse, but they were victims of a thoroughly vicious system: 'Archaeology is not Architecture.'[145]

Street published his own defence, *The New Courts of Justice: Notes in Reply to Some Criticisms*, directed principally against Fergusson; and friendly Beresford Hope published another powerful article in the *Saturday Review*.[146] When parliament reassembled early in 1872, the persistent press attacks through the autumn and winter bore sour fruit in a motion by Cavendish Bentinck that Street's designs ought not to be executed.[147] He found little support. The spring had arrived. Hope defended the Strand elevation as 'composed of a well-balanced and dignified main pile, with an *annexe* for the judicial offices eastward. The crowning mass was the Central Hall.'[148] Roundell Palmer threw his great legal weight likewise into the scales in favour of Street's design. Elcho complained that questions of taste were 'usually contested by partizans of the classical and the Gothic style; whereas the question ought to be the suitability of a building for its purpose, and the wise expenditure of the public money'. The First Commissioner, Ayrton, replying, remarked that 'There was no national style to which every one was expected to conform. The style was therefore determined by the selection of an architect who was distinguished for his pre-eminence in some particular style.' It was four years too late to make a change.[149] Members' refusal to join the critics suggests that, as the *Athenaeum* claimed, professional and lay opinion alike supported Street, the marked hostility of *The Times* perhaps provoking a sympathetic reaction.[150]

When Cavendish Bentinck returned to the attack some three months later, Ayrton told him that 'while great difference of opinion and much dissatisfaction had been expressed' about the Strand elevation, 'there had been no such general disapproval as would render it necessary for the Office of Works to take any steps on the subject'.[151] Despite further sniping by Cavendish Bentinck, Ayrton continued to support Street's appointment and qualifications for the work.[152] Professional and public opinion may well have been alienated by the virulence of the attacks on Street, and many, genuinely impressed by the merits of the designs when explained, had rallied sufficiently strongly to ensure that Street retained his commission. Ayrton, for all his ruthless insistence on keeping down the cost, appreciated Street's professional skill. Nevertheless, when the opened tenders showed in March 1873 sums considerably in excess of Street's estimate, Ayrton's comments to the Treasury, based on Galton's report, reproduced some of the strictures that had appeared in the press the year before.

> In my opinion, however, the excess . . . is to be ascribed to the character of Mr Street's Plans and designs in the following particulars. The Central Hall, though an exact reproduction of an ancient mode of construction, is an extravagant building unsuited to the purpose for which it is to be constructed, and prejudicial to the buildings on either side of it.
>
> In order to exhibit a part of the Gable end of the Hall, which is not in the centre of the Southern front, the Southern elevation is broken up in an irregular and costly manner to produce a picturesque effect. But this cannot be seen on account of the narrowness of the road [the precise reason for not having a uniform front], which is not likely to be widened. A more uniform elevation of simple grandeur would be better adapted to the side of the Street, and would admit of more convenient arrangements within the building. The extension of the building in other parts is unnecessarily irregular, and adorned with carving and useless pinnacles, and additions which are assumed to be ornamental.[153]

After further correspondence with the Treasury, the Office of Works wrote to Street himself in similar vein, remarking that the

also questioned the legitimacy of his appointment (driving Street into print to defend himself). With almost every qualification for a great architect, Street had thrown it away to follow the chimera of reproducing thirteenth-century Gothic art – as reasonable as to design our warships like galleys. Probably no great harm would have been done, however, if it had stopped with the Law Courts: they would serve as a warning to posterity. But we were threatened with worse: the Natural History Museum was too instructive an illustration of the system to be passed over. An effective innovatory architect, Fowke, having died, his designs were superseded by Waterhouse's undoubtedly modern building garbed in a pretended and inaccurate 'Norman'. Street's, however, failed from the opposite quality: 'It is the accuracy of imitation pervading every detail that makes it so perfectly intolerable.' For this 'Joshua of architects' the sun of art had stopped in 1377. The vaulted hall should go; that would enable the introduction of a central feature, with appropriate wings. But even that would not remedy the fundamental error inherent in the design – 'suitable for barefoot friars in some remote, sparsely inhabited Midland valley'. There were probably not in Europe two architects of greater ability than Street and

241. New Law Courts, G.E. Street, 1873—82.
a. Eastern portion of the Strand facade. Street was attacked for his loose composition, but the façade can be viewed only in perspective.
b. Tower at corner of Carey Street and Bell Yard.

First Commissioner had no doubt that he could prepare a design 'more suitable to the site', that would reflect credit on him and be 'more generally acceptable to the public than that which it may supersede'.[154] However, the disputes from this point onwards were essentially about cost rather than style. Street was sufficiently politically worldly-wise by this time to exploit the tensions in the government between Ayrton and the Treasury to secure more generous treatment that enabled him to retain such important features as the central hall and the clock-tower.[155]

Fergusson had also denounced Waterhouse's Natural History Museum, as seen above [Pl. 242]. Captain Fowke, brought up as a military engineer, had learned at the country's expense to become an architect, declared Fergusson in his *Macmillan's Magazine* article. He had won the Museum competition (Fergusson a judge) with a design 'neither Grecian nor Gothic, but thoroughly nineteenth century' that would have marked an epoch in the history of architecture in England. After his death, Waterhouse was appointed to execute his design; his 'position as an architect did not allow of his carrying out any other person's design, much less that

242.   Natural History Museum, South Kensington, A. Waterhouse, 1873. Although he had been appointed to execute Fowke's competition design, suitably revised, in the end it was Waterhouse's own design that was built. The employment of a *rundbogenstil* and extensive use of terracotta are, however, legacies of Fowke's design.

of a soldier-officer'; so after discussion with Museum personnel Waterhouse decided to substitute new designs of his own, though retaining the general concept of a round-arched style and the use of terracotta for the facing.[156] Fergusson might have been thought sympathetic to this treatment, but as one of the judges who awarded Fowke the palm, he regarded Waterhouse's version as a corrupt 'Revival' style – Norman, not Gothic – substituted for Fowke's genuine nineteenth-century style. In his *Macmillan's Magazine* article cited above he attacked Waterhouse's professional arrogance, condemned his Norman, 'or according to the more fashionable euphuism, the "Bizzantine" style', which was no more Norman than the British Museum was Greek. 'It is a modern building, with large openings filled with plate-glass. The roofs are filled with skylights; swing-doors, modern fire-places, plate-glass cases, and every other nineteenth-century contrivance is sought to be introduced; but he escapes from the difficulty of designing details appropriate to the present age, under the pretext that the rude clumsy ornament he is using is correct Norman.' Just to make

sure of quashing it, he concluded that if it really were Norman it would be intolerable.[157]

When Parliament reassembled, it was once again Cavendish Bentinck who led the attack, trying to unsettle Waterhouse's design. He was joined by Lord Elcho, another of the 1864 competition judges, who wished to reinstal Fowke's. When Waterhouse's 'abomination' was finally displayed in the Commons' library, it was – as usual – too late in the session to make an effective attack. The critics resumed operations in the 1872 session. But Mrs Fowke refused to assist the campaign, and Elcho handed back the matter to Cavendish Bentinck.[158] Ayrton, though, was a tough parliamentary performer, and however much he might bear down on his architects, he was not prepared to allow interference from backbench MPs. His arrogance and sarcasm served thus on occasion to protect the very architects of whose claims to design artistic and stylistic masterpieces he was so contemptous. 'Style' being an unnecessary ingredient, he would not tolerate parliamentary cooks revising the recipe.

15
Classicism Revivified

THE COST of these on-going operations ensured that it was well into the next decade before the government undertook further major building. During the fallow years there was a decisive shift of taste away from Gothic, save for churches. Barrow (1882) and Middlesbrough (1883) are the last great Gothic town halls. Norman Shaw (1831–1912) was greeted as the leader of a new revival style, 'Queen Anne', termed by some 'Flemish Renaissance', characterised by red brick, gabled façades, windows with glazing-bars, employed as early as 1873 for thriving Leicester's new town hall. But Italianate styles continued popular for civic dignity,[1] and the 1880s saw a renewed enthusiasm for the work of Wren and his school,[2] which with a tincture of Beaux-Arts developed into 'Edwardian Baroque', a style 'symbolically consistent with the various designers' intents – nationalism, traditionalism and dynamism all captivated in a single approach, without the moral overtone of gothic revival or indeed, the international aspect of a purer classicism'.[3] (The Office of Works had itself kept the classical flag flying, for instance in Williams's GPO West [Pl. 243], 1869–73, and Taylor's Bow Street Magistrates' Court, 1874–80, and Bankruptcy Courts, 1890–2.) The constantly-deferred new premises for the defence departments were authorised by legislation in 1882. A two-tier competition, overwhelmingly classical in entries, produced three leading designs in 1884, those by Leeming & Leeming of Halifax, awarded first prize, and those of two London practices, Verity & Hunt and Webb & Bell [Pl. 185], as mentioned above.

Leeming Brothers divided their principal elevation, towards Whitehall, into two symmetrical units, reflecting the plan [Pl. 246]: the site, approximately a rectangle with its longer axis along Whitehall, had the north-east corner cut out by Biddulph's Bank (thought too expensive for the government to buy), and the south-west corner similarly cut out to avoid to encroaching on Horse

Guards Parade; thus the main courtyard could not sit squarely in the centre of the block. The façade rose to 90 ft, generally regarded as too high for Whitehall, here narrowing towards Charing Cross, and terminated with the strong vertical of a high tower overshadowing Horse Guards (no doubt an appropriate symbol). Over a plainly rusticated basement, its ground floor was richly rusticated, with square-headed windows in arched panels divided by piers on which rose a giant Corinthian order uniting the first and second floors; above the entablature rose an attic and 'roofs of tolerable steepness, though not conspicuous enough' for the Architect's taste.[4] The Times's conclusion was that the most elastic term was the best to describe its style: Renaissance, for it was not Gothic, French or Palladian (in the Somerset House sense), nor yet a mixture as was the Brussels Palace of Justice [Pl. 183].[5]

The Architect thought that it was the Law Courts Competition result over again. The best plan was that of Verity & Hunt, the best elevations 'those in the beautiful design of Messrs Webb & Bell' [Pl. 185], but their plan [Pl. 244] was defective and the height of their building excessive. 'The judges have fallen back upon a design which, though extremely well planned, does not quite equal the best plan, and though full of architectural merit is distinctly below the best in those indications of originality, power, and effectiveness which display architectural genius.'[6] The progressive British Architect on a cursory first view agreed that 'we are unable to indorse the decision arrived at by the judges', a view that it subsequently maintained both in editorial comment and through its correspondence columns, though admitting that Leemings' 'beautiful figure drawing and finished outline work' were 'worthy of a great competition'; it regarded Webb & Bell's plan as the best, but their elevation, 'assuredly the most skilful architectural design of the whole', lacked the 'solid dignity that would most befit a war office'.

243. GPO West, St Martin's-le-Grand, J. Williams, main elevation, contract drawing. An additional storey was added in 1884 to accommodate the newly-nationalised telegraph service.

Leemings' design was styled a 'somewhat ordinary treatment of a sort of Roman Classic'.[7] However, one of the judges, the architect Philip Charles Hardwick, told a Commons' committee that 'there was not the slightest doubt about it, that Messrs Leeming's design, both in the internal arrangements and in the elevation, was the best of all those that were submitted to us'.[8]

The *Builder*, never enthusiastic about the Leemings' design – 'unquestionably picturesque in general effect and grouping, but it is not a *great* building, and none of the improvements in detail which are quite possible ... will make it so' – after a month of reviewing the other eight second-stage entries expressed its clear hostility. It gave detail elevations of the three finalists [Pl. 245]. 'We fear such a comparison cannot possibly be favourable to the selected design, which consists of more or less pretty bits with no coherence whatever, and the columnar order is, as used here, as complete a piece of architectural sham as could be seen; a ponderous base, and a great column and cornice carrying nothing but a single statue.' Verity (French-trained) & Hunt's entry [Pl. 185, 247] exhibited 'far more knowledge and capacity in what may be

THE BUILDER, OCTOBER 4. 1884.

244. Admiralty and War Office competition, 1884. Of the nine finalists in this two-tier competition, three were recommended. The irregularity of plan was determined by the decision not to include two banks and adjoining property fronting Charing Cross (on the right), but to include the Whitehall frontage from the Admiralty to the Horse Guards (on the left):
a. Verity & Hunt. This shewed how much had been learned from experience. All the main rooms were lighted from the exterior or the large central court, and the corridors from internal courts.
b. Webb & Bell. Their even larger central court aimed at the same objects of providing light and air. Central corridors received light from top-lighted halls. The requisite accommodation was obtained by a mezzanine floor.

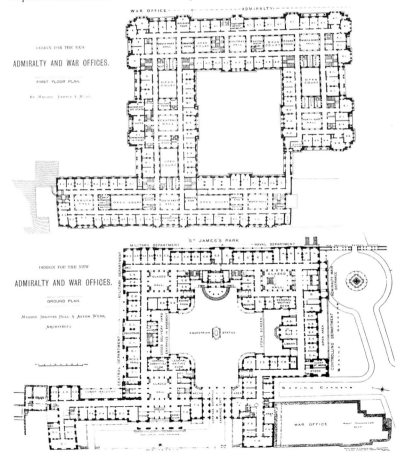

245. Admiralty and War Office competition, 1884. The relative merits of the elevations of the three recommended contestants were compared by the *Builder*:
a (above). Webb & Bell: "by far the most refined in detail', but not appropriate to a war ministry.
b (p. 235, top left). Verity & Hunt: 'there is a massive stability ... expressive of its purpose', but it was 'old material suitably worked up by a practised hand'.
c (p. 235 top right). Leeming Bros: a 'singularly piecemeal' elevation, consisting of 'well-worn details ... not combined or worked up into a whole'.

called the technique of Classic design than the selected design evinces, though it would probably not be considered so generally attractive'.[9] The *Architect* similarly criticised Leemings' 'fussiness': 'rows of absurd piers and columns – as ugly and baneful as they are useless'. The models [Pl. 246] exhibited in August 1885 were merely 'Pimlico palatialized in real stone', with statuary that no House of Commons would advance a penny for, and 'without which a perpendicular excrescence of solid block, column and attic, will appear a motiveless obstruction'.[10] *Building News*, so often striking a different line, commented that Leemings' Spring Gar-

246 (below).   Admiralty and War Office competition, 1884. The palm was awarded to Leeming Bros, perhaps because they transgressed the instructions the least.
a. Plan: Leemings sacrificed the advantage of a really large central court in order to secure ample corridor lighting from a series of smaller courts.
b. A model was made of Leemings' winning design.

dens elevation [Pl. 186] would, 'we think, convince any impartial reader that the character of the work itself is of a high order, and that its authors can very well afford to ignore the somewhat incoherent criticism to which it has been subjected'.[11]

Writing anonymously in the *Saturday Review*, Beresford Hope disapproved of the results generally. One design was too like a

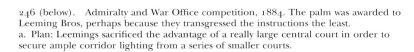

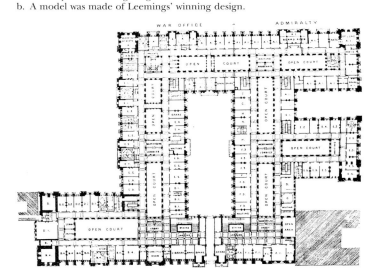

247.   Admiralty and War Office competition, 1884. Great court, Verity & Hunt. Although the exterior was somewhat severe, the internal façades were to be rich in statuary.

large hotel, another, a Borrominesque 'wilderness of incongruities and enormities', a third 'thin and commonplace', others 'a rather agreeable academic study', or 'covered . . . with an exuberance of delicate Gothic lacework . . . little in correspondence with its surroundings', or merely of 'elaborate French style . . . by no means unpleasing' [Cp. Pl. 248].[12] Of the three prizemen, he favoured the third, Webb & Bell's 'quick and lifelike French Renaissance . . . treated with a gravity and self-control which does not lose hold of the picturesque capabilities of the style, and yet eschews its often exuberant ornamentation'. (Webb himself wrote: 'the building should be dignified and discreetly ornate as befitting its imperial character'.[13]) Verity & Hunt's, Hope damned with faint praise; but for Leeming Brothers' he sharpened his hatchet: it was 'uncomfortable', with 'odd combinations', 'a centre without character', 'unsatisfactory devices'. 'There is no lack of ornamentation . . . but it is ornament which with all its book correctness fails to give pleasure from its pervading want of originality.'[14]

Hope used his seat in the Commons to lash out at the character of Leemings' design: 'It was vulgar, commonplace, overloaded with ornament, and absolutely fantastic in such originality as it possessed, for that certainly appeared in a form which no one else would have conceived – that of elongated four-sided cupolas, standing in a row upon the top line of the structure . . . the building was to be overloaded with columns.' He suggested that the plan should be re-clothed 'with artistic features of a different character. . . . It was not a question of style, Gothic or Italian, but peculiarly and emphatically one of taste, and the design ought to be as simple as possible.' He made much of the fact that Leeming Brothers were young, unknown architects, and doubted their capacity at that time to design something better.[15] Hope's views about ornament had undergone a change since the 1850s and 1860s, when he had campaigned relentlessly in favour of Scott's Gothic Foreign Office design; but his attack on Leemings was strongly reminiscent of the dismissal of the claims of young Coe & Hofland, who had taken first prize in the Foreign Office competition. Shaw Lefevre retorted that 'In every way Messrs Leeming's designs were distinctly and decidedly the best.' Compared with the Houses of Parliament or the Law Courts, their design was 'very conspicuous for its simplicity of treatment and

absence of . . . fantastic details'. Furthermore, the designs had been considerably revised, the Whitehall front being 'completely modified', the columns 'having been thrown back more than the building itself', and the overbearing tower moved back to the Parade. Another stalwart in aesthetic matters, William Gregory, back from governing Ceylon, agreed with Hope in finding the elevations 'somewhat overloaded with ornament . . . a rather large number of columns designed for the purpose of ornament which could very well be dispensed with without spoiling the architecture'.[16]

Although the Liberal government carried the vote on that occasion, dissatisfaction with the designs became more widespread. The RIBA put forward its own proposals, involving the re-planning of northern Whitehall.[17] The question of cost assumed mounting importance against a background of rising national expenditure, and at length a committee was appointed to reconsider the project. As we have seen in chapter 10, it concluded that a new Admiralty was unnecessary, an extension to the existing building being sufficient, while the War Office could be postponed.[18] Leeming Brothers prepared new plans for the committee, a plain brick building harmonised with the existing Admiralty.[19]

The committee's report caused the competition plan to be entirely abandoned. Instead, an extension in red brick with stone dressings was constructed along the north and west sides of the Admiralty garden;[20] the front to Horse Guards Parade, at first intended to be closed merely by a screen, was then erected in the same style [Pl. 187]. These new Admiralty buildings were the first nineteenth-century government buildings in the Whitehall quarter to be faced mainly in brick, and they came under general condemnation.[21] The RIBA council addressed a perceptive letter to the First Commissioner protesting that the select committee's scheme was 'not worthy of a great public undertaking . . . the result . . . is not likely, even financially, to realise the expectations that have been formed'.[22] Lefevre, who had promoted Leemings' original design, called this 'a miserable piece of patchwork' that 'no architect in the kingdom' approved – 'which even the designers themselves are ashamed of'.[23] Herbert Gladstone, Liberal First Commissioner involved in the Admiralty extension, warned his successor to 'keep a free hand . . . as far as he can. . . . When any considerable number of eminent individuals begin to interest

248. Admiralty and War Office competition, 1884. The triumphant revival of Classical architecture was indicated by the general shunning of Gothic by the nine finalists.
Perspectives:
a. Hall & Powell: although the façade precisely indicated the planning, it was thought 'monotonous and commonplace' (*Builder*).
b. Maxwell & Tuke: High Renaissance, with a grand twin-towered central feature that led only into a glazed court. Leemings later borrowed the square corner domes for their Admiralty extension.
c. Glover & Salter: the sole Gothic entry among the finalists, hopelssly outdated. The Whitehall front in two divisions with a central recessed gable recalls Street's Law Courts Strand front.
d. Spalding & Auld: *Builder* found their elevations 'suggestive of a Crystal Palace bazaar, and their perspectives too terrible both in design and drawing to be described.'

themselves in questions of this sort, the result generally is one of muddle and chaos, and that is illustrated by the external appearance . . . of the new Admiralty buildings. There is mess and muddle in regard to the external design.'[24]

By late 1894 the red-brick and Portland-stone west block, 'handsome and well worthy of its fine position', was externally complete [Pl. 249]; 'a fenestrated type of Italian Classic architecture, three-quarter columns being introduced at salient points to afford appropriate relief', reported the *Architect*. 'Careful consideration has been given to the skyline, with the result that, while adopting Classic detail, picturesque effect has been obtained, each feature of ornamentation being utilised for practical purposes, such as those of ventilators and watertanks.'[25] Opinion in general was less favourable. Lord Wemyss called the new blocks 'unworthy of the dignity of the offices which they contain. In their architecture they are weak where they should be strong, there are useless pediments which are not needed, pillars where they are not required, and there is a sort of trimming at the top which looks as if it was made out of the bricks from a child's toy box.'[26] Another MP

declared: 'The new Admiralty is the most unsightly building in London.'[27]

Before the overthrow of his defence ministries scheme, Lefevre had, as mentioned in chapter 12, set in progress one small but important work: the construction of a new west front to Westminster Hall. Aware that it was 'almost a Parliamentary bargain' that Soane's unloved Law Courts should be demolished when Street's work in the Strand came into use, he had already in 1882 contemplated the possible visual effects, suggesting that the Hall should probably be left open to view rather than follow Barry's idea of masking it with offices.[28] With the demolition of the Courts in 1883–4 the dilapidated west side of the Hall was exposed [Pl. 188a], probably for the first time since it had been reconstructed and buttressed by Richard II – 'a perfect eyesore', Ayrton called it.[29] A portion of the original wall had also been uncovered, bearing Norman masons' marks. A tidying-up was clearly necessary, and protection of the ancient marks desirable. Lefevre called in the surveyor to Westminster Abbey, John Loughborough Pearson

249.   Admiralty Extension, Block III, to Horse Guards Parade, Leeming Bros, 1901. A galimatias, with domes borrowed from Maxwell & Tuke, the centre influenced by Verity, and touches of Wren in its attic.

(1817–97), 'to examine the walls and buttresses with a view to the restoration of them'.[30] Pearson's view on the restoration of churches, his principal field of activity, was 'to make the church "a very effective building"'.[31] He applied the same technique to the Hall.

This thorough restorer defined his object as 'consistently with present requirements to recover the aspect which [the Hall] presented in Richard II's time; also to retain the existing evidences of earlier and later historical work'. He therefore proposed, on the basis of the evidence (both physical and graphic) as he read it, to build between the Riccardian buttresses an open cloister with gallery over, crowned with an embattled parapet, declaring: 'In fact, but little of the Restoration is conjectural.' The open cloister would be a stand for carriages – or the arches might be traceried and glazed to create a set of rooms similar to those he proposed for the gallery above. The difficulty of terminating this feature to the north, beside the entrance front of the Hall, he proposed to overcome by building out at right angles a two-storeyed structure on foundations of a building of Henry III's time. As there was no evidence of its original appearance, he employed the same style as for the gallery and cloister. At ground level it would provide much-needed standing for MPs' horses – 'parking' is not exclusively a modern problem – replacing an existing shed; while above would be a large room. Access to the upper levels of both parts of the new building would be from the Hall by new stone staircases. Pearson also proposed modifications to the Hall itself: the modern dormers should go (thereby ensuring the present internal gloom), and the northern front, a restoration by Soane in 1820–3 which exuded 'an air of spuriousness', should be remodelled so as to harmonise 'Barry's elaborate architecture', immediately adjoining, 'with the severer work of the Hall' – this to be achieved principally by

altering the windows and niches, and raising the towers to 'render them worthy of their position' [Pl. 188b].[32]

Pearson's proposals aroused a great deal of controversy. His restoration work at Peterborough Cathedral and elsewhere had already brought him under the hostile scrutiny of William Morris and the Society for the Protection of Ancient Buildings (S.P.A.B.).[33] The upshot was reference in November 1884 to a select committee chaired by Lefevre, with Beresford Hope, Sir John Lubbock, and W.H. Smith among its members. Although said to be hand-picked, and certainly lacking expert members apart from the Scottish architect J. Dick Peddie (1824–91) and the dogmatic amateur Hope, it proved a notable battle-ground.[34]

Pearson now found his proposals under a twofold attack. His old enemies the S.P.A.B. denounced them, calling for a distinctly modern wood-and-plaster structure purely to protect the ancient wall.[35] Charles Barry, as a witness, urged that the Hall should be concealed behind the range of committee rooms that Sir Charles Barry had proposed years before (abandoned by the government in 1866). He was supported by Peddie and the *Builder*, who fought vigorously for a much more conservative treatment of the Hall than Pearson advocated.[36] But the overwhelming weight of professional opinion was that 'the grand and severe lines of Westminster Hall combine well with the more florid work of Sir Charles Barry; and that it would be a grave mistake to erect any building in front of it so as to shut it out from view'. Ewan Christian, Waterhouse, Blomfield and John Oldrid Scott generally supported Pearson's proposals, though the former two at first wanted a lower building, showing more of the flying buttresses. When canvas and plaster models of the alternative heights were set up they found they preferred the original scheme, as 'it gives greater dignity to the side of the Hall than the lower building, while it leaves open to view from a distance more than they expected of the upper line of windows, and of the flying buttresses'. The committee by a large majority opted for Pearson's original over-scaled design for the west front, with the wall slightly lowered and a plain instead of an embattled parapet, with 'the date, or some other distinctive mark' placed on some of the stones (thus far the S.P.A.B. had made an impact). But his heightening of the Hall's north towers, which the *Builder* had favoured as the only genuinely architectural element, was deferred for further consideration.[37]

Lefevre's bias in favour of Pearson's plan was evident in the committee, where he was supported by Walter of *The Times* and Hope of the *Saturday Review*, both papers being used to advocate Pearson's scheme.[38] In his report, Lefevre successfully discredited his opponents, lumping Peddie and Barry together with Morris & Co. as a 'distinct school of archaeological opinion' that insisted that any additions to the Hall should 'be of a markedly modern character . . . purposely made incongruous'. His well-chosen committee readily fell in with his views.[39] The work was carried out in 1886–90, in accord with the committee's recommendations. Time is still testing the effect on the Hall's north front. Internally, Pearson's design required access staircases that intruded into the Hall, a feature that was strongly objected to, without success, by members of both Houses:

> We have had a building put up more like a second-rate dissenting church than anything else – a structure which is a disgrace to this House, which has no perspective, and which is as defective in architectural beauty as an average dissenting church. As to the interior of Westminster Hall, I would ask whether it would not be possible to reduce the meretricious piece of architecture which has been called 'Spurgeon's pulpit' there?[40]

> Look at Westminster Hall! Its whole character has been destroyed by the erection of the monsters that guard the entrance to the stairs in the centre of the north wall, begotten of the nightmare imaginings of Mr Shaw Lefevre, who has also at the outside West End entrance of the Hall destroyed Sir Charles Barry's work by building a buttress against one of the Gothic pillared sides of the Tower, in the centre of which he had placed the doorway that led to the Hall.[41]

But Westminster Hall was *sui generis*. The general reassertion of Renaissance style was strikingly encapsulated in a building to house the National Gallery of Portraits,[42] designed by Ewan Christian (1814–95), a leading Goth and extensively-employed church architect. In 1889 Mr W.H. Alexander offered to pay anonymously for the long-desired permanent accommodation, if government would provide a site, duly found in Hemmings Row, just north of the National Gallery.[43] Christian, chosen by the donor, designed an early Florentine Renaissance palazzo [Pl. 192], a work of considerable distinction; when in 1891 the government funded an eastern extension, he worked with equal skill in Wilkins's Greek style, continuing the contiguous east front of his National Gallery.

At South Kensington, architects were far freer in their designs than they could be in Whitehall. There was little unity of style between the Natural History Museum, the Imperial Institute and the Science Schools, the near neighbours of the South Kensington Museum. A competition for the Museum's completion was held in 1891.[44] Façades were required along Exhibition and Brompton Roads, meeting at a corner, and simultaneously visible from a certain standpoint, from which the competitors had to provide a perspective view. The statement of its requirements produced by the Department of Science and Art has been described by the Museum's historian as 'extraordinarily perfunctory'.[45] It was there-

fore hardly surprising that the winning design, by Aston Webb, 'was eventually much modified in the light of practical necessity'.[46] The only restriction on the competitors as to style had been a suggestion that the new building should resemble the 'South Kensington' style of the existing portions of the Museum designed by Fowke and Henry Scott.

Most entries were in an eclectic style to which it is difficult to attach an historic label, but suggest the growing significance of the classical tradition in end-of-the-century British architecture,[47] albeit markedly characterised by yearnings for the picturesque, as exemplified in John Belcher's Institute of Chartered Accountants (1888–93) [Pl. 250].[48] The *British Architect* thought that Aston Webb had 'hit off very successfully the sort of design and grouping which is appropriate to the site and its surroundings', questioning whether he would have been so successful 'without his previous experience in actual building', which brought 'the needful restraint and sobriety' into the design [Pl. 191].[49] The *Architect* remarked somewhat disparagingly that 'the successful design no doubt gained approval partly by the respect for economy which it exhibits. Mr Webb is not afraid of repetition.'[50] Webb had obviously looked at Waterhouse's neighbouring Natural History Museum[51] – doubtless the more so as Waterhouse was the professional assessor in the competition – and one critic identified Webb's design as 'a rich variety of Romanesque', though another distinguished the 'grace and playfulness of Spanish Renaissance' as an additional element. To a third, 'The composition is a direct result of continuous nineteenth-century thought, and the product of our Gothic and Renaissance revivals. . . . We can take a tower from Spain, a campanile from Italy, and a dome from Constantinople, and so combine them with some definite quality in one design that they shall look homogeneous and dignified. . . . We are eclectic, but we are not unmindful of character; we think of the past and its traditions, but we wish to be progressive and to work to modern requirements.'[52] Webb's main hall strongly echoed that of the Natural History Museum, and in his explanation Webb remarked that he had considered his general outline in conjunction with that building, and pointed to its towers and that of the Imperial Institute [Pl. 189] as determining his own central tower [Pl. 251], designed to

250. Institute of Chartered Accountants, Moorgate Place, John Belcher, R.A. (1841–1913), with help from Beresford Pite (1861–1934), designed 1888, built 1890–93. Here 'began the modern expression of the cavalier spirit in architecture' (James Bone).

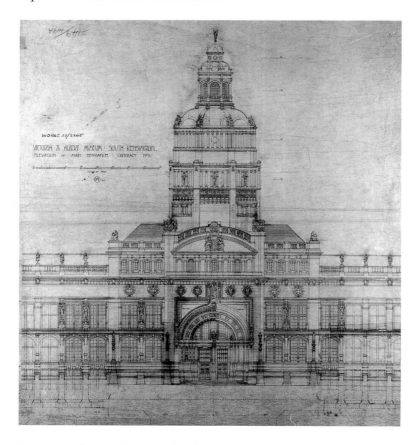

251. Victoria and Albert (formerly South Kensington) Museum, Aston Webb.
a. Main entrance and central tower, contract drawing *c.* 1904. Faced with Works'
hostility to large towers, Webb had drastically remodelled his design by 1899;
subsequently, rapidly changing departmental requirements produced a series of
modifications.
b. As completed 1909, from Exhibition Road (south).

'group well with them, and assist to form a crown of towers almost
unique in Europe'.

Runner-up was John Belcher (1841–1913), whose solecistic classicism [Pl. 252] evoked Claudian palaces or even the visions of
John Martin – or, as the *Building News* commented, 'the ruins of
some stately edifice in the Venetian Lagoons'.[53] This anticipation
of Edwardian Baroque in red brick and Portland stone (like
Leeming Brothers' Admiralty extension) 'showed strikingly the
direction in which fashion was moving'.[54] To a 'young lion' of the
Architectural Association, Belcher came nearest to his 'idea of a

large public building' with his dignified design, handled broadly
and simply.[55] William Emerson (1843–1924) proposed red brick
and terracotta, perpetuating the South Kensington tradition in
his loosely Renaissance design [Pl. 253], with spiral staircases
on the corners, after that at Blois; but central dome and corner
tower fought for predominance. Closely rivalling Emerson in
Waterhouse's assessment, William Young's many-towered, grandiose, repetitive classicism [Pl. 191] was derived from his swaggering
Glasgow City Chambers (1883). T.G. Jackson's was equally eclectic,
with early French and Italian Renaissance features modifying his
habitual Jacobethan, dismissed by the *Builder* as 'deficient in
marked character'. Thomas Collcutt, the architect of the nearby
Imperial Institute, offered something of similar type, with a notice-
able flavour of contemporary work of the British Raj in India – in
addition to which the *Building News* identified 'Chinese hats' to the
terminal towers and a Byzantine-looking central dome. Sir Thomas

252. South Kensington Museum
competition 1891, neo-Baroque
design by John Belcher. Perspective,
drawn by W.B. McGuiness. Runner-up
in the competition to Webb, and the
'most original' design (Waterhouse).
For the passer-by, the Cromwell Road
front would mask the higher parts
further back.

253. South Kensington Museum competition 1891.
a. William Emerson: perspective.
b. Deane and Son: central hall.

Deane (whose firm was a survivor of the 1857 Government Offices competition) offered a style based on the Certosa of Pavia in terracotta and brick, lacking the towers that were a feature of the preceding entries [Pl. 253]. A design totally apart was Mervyn Macartney's 'new Newgate' (as the *British Architect* put it), praised for its plan, but 'severe and uncompromising to a degree which few Britishers would ever tolerate', built in Portland stone and completely ignoring its context.[56]

When Henry Tate provided funds for a Gallery of British Art on Millbank in 1892, he was allowed to choose his own architect. Sir William Harcourt, the Liberal chancellor, thought Sidney R.J. Smith's first elevation 'rather nice . . . somewhat after the fashion and dimensions of the Fitzwilliam at Cambridge', comparatively simple and without 'gingerbread ornamentation'; but he disapproved of a second version in 'the pretentious style so much in favour in the modern debased municipal architecture, which predominates in provincial public building': 'I thought the addition of the pretentious dome and cupolas of a gimcrack order of decoration anything but an improvement'. Harcourt advised Smith to visit the Fitzwilliam Museum, 'one of the few successful edifices of the last half century. The severe exclusion of meretricious decoration is its signal merit.' The designs were referred to the Office of Works, and the First Commissioner amended the specifications. 'Most anxious' not to interfere with Tate's discretion as to the style and character of the gallery, the Works confined its criticism to points that might affect maintenance: 'The Board [of Works] are now, and have been for some years past, incurring heavy expenditure in remedying original defects of construction' at the Foreign Office and the Law Courts. Their objection here was chiefly to the roof and the glass domes proposed over the towers at the end of either wing. After discussion with Taylor of the Works, Smith 'much simplified' his design, which was then approved.[57] The *Architect* thought that the galleries were well adapted for the display of art, but criticised the site as too low for a 'severely Classical' building of one storey on a basement [Pl. 193].[58]

At South Kensington, Aston Webb was given further commissions once work had actually begun on the Museum. The new

254. Royal College of Science, South Kensington, Sir Aston Webb, detail of façade, 1900—6. (dem. 1973—4). The library on the first floor forms the central motif of the design.

building for the Royal College of Science, sited immediately south of the Imperial Institute, was entrusted to him. By that time, at the end of the century, Classicism was again thoroughly in vogue. Webb's design was a lesson in contextual good manners [Pl. 254]. He devised a façade closely in harmony with its neighbour opposite, each 'tending to help the effect of the other': though in a classical style, its rhythm echoed that of the Institute, the main block of each (lying immediately opposite) being of shallow E-plan. 'The domes which flank the screen walls of the corridors on either side [of the main block] will be repetitions of those that Mr Collcutt added to the similar features ranging right and left of the Imperial Institute', reported *Building News*. Webb solved the problem of an 'imperative need for window space', by creating a succession of emphatic verticals, which the reviewer thought he handled so as to ensure a 'sense of breadth and becoming monumental dignity'.[59]

It was Aretas Akers-Douglas who, as First Commissioner, decided on the classical style for the new public offices agreed upon in 1896: a new War Office on the Carrington House site on the east of Whitehall, and those on the corner of Great George Street and Parliament Street. They were to be of stone (unlike the Admiralty extension) and in keeping with their surroundings.[60] Akers-Douglas thought that they would 'add largely to the architectural beauty of the Metropolis'; but the Liberal leader, Harcourt, was less sure from his twenty-year experience of public buildings, recalling Byron's line, 'The most recent was the least decent' – ironically enough, as it was partly Harcourt's penuriousness that was responsible for 'the most recent', the Admiralty extension.[61] The battle of the styles appeared to be over: members called only for 'buildings of an ornamental kind', in harmony with their great surroundings: 'State buildings ought to have some stateliness'.[62]

When the appointments of Brydon and Young to design the new

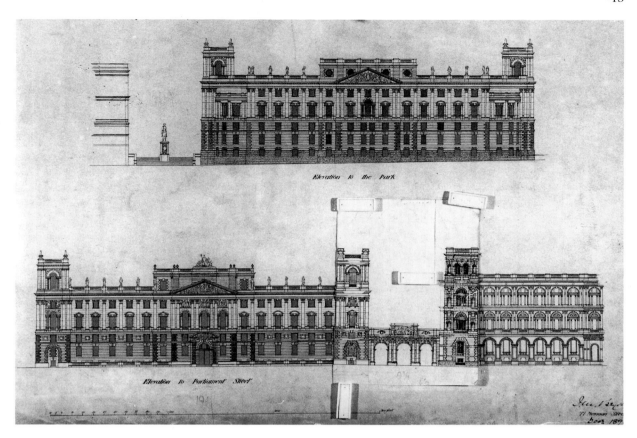

255. New Public Offices, Westminster, J.M. Brydon, 1898. Elevations to the Park and the Parliament Street, with flyer shewing alternative treatment of corner tower, and addition to Scott's Home Office of a corresponding tower. The use of a mezzanine enabled Brydon to provide an additional floor in a building somewhat lower than Scott's.

government offices were announced in July 1898, the *Architect*, which had already called for 'a magnificent appearance', suggested that 'The time is ripe for an effort which will recall the old glories of the art', but it was essential to allow architects time to mature their designs: it was not easy for 'any architect who always endeavours to be at his best' to surpass all his former works. If the new buildings would 'serve as correctives to much of what now passes as advanced architecture, they will be worth the money expended on them, regardless of their use as offices'.[63] Exhibited in the Commons' tea-room early in 1899, the designs were well received. 'What first engages attention is the manifest effort to enhance the interest of the existing buildings' – Scott's Home and Colonial Offices were given corner towers (though not Scott's original version), arches were thrown across Charles and Downing Streets, the Banqueting Hall was duplicated north of the War Office. Brydon's more rectangular, larger site, enabled him to produce more impressive elevations with an Ionic order [Pl. 255, 264] than Young could achieve in Corinthian [Pl. 197, 256] on his more awkward site.[64]

One in particular who found no satisfaction in Young's War Office design was that enthusiastic Volunteer, Lord Wemyss, despite his having chosen Young to complete his own Scottish seat, Gosford, in baroque magnificence.[65] His efforts to secure a different design provide an interesting tailpiece to this history of attempts to influence official decisions on architectural matters by pressure in and out of parliament.

Wemyss worked hard, first to persuade Young to base his designs on the 'Inigo Jones' designs for Whitehall, and then to prevail on the government to accept his own version, culminating in an appeal to public opinion.[66] He presented to the prime minister a weighty memorial, with 139 signatories (including peers of both parties), praying the government to have models made for public exhibition of both Young's design and Inigo Jones's Whitehall

256. New War Office, Whitehall; William Young, 1899. Perspective from Whitehall. Young took care to respect the neighbouring Banqueting House, which he suggested repeating to the north.

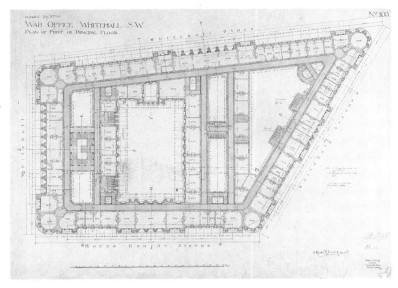

257. New War Office, William Young. Contract drawing: plan of principal floor, shewing Young's able handling of an awkwardly-shaped site. The great court is architecturally treated; the lesser is very plain, with two lavatory blocks projecting into it a third being conveniently sited across a narrow intermediate court provided to light corridors. At a period when electric lighting produced a satisfactory resolution of the problem of dark interior corridors, architects had succeeded in devising plans to do away with them. The secretary of state's office overlooked Whitehall, the commander-in-chief's, Whitehall Place.

Palace [Pl. 41], which 'might, without difficulty, be made to meet all War Office requirements, while it would present a more imposing symmetric and extended front – immediately facing the Horse Guards'. The objection that Jones's design was for a palace he met with the retort that Somerset House was 'the finest, most palatial building in London – and yet it is devoted to government offices'; architects could adapt Jones's for the War Office site. It would not overshadow the Banqueting Hall any more than in the original design of which the Hall was part. The arches across the road to Whitehall Mansions would be wider, higher and lighter than those of the Horse Guards under which the diamond jubilee procession had passed. The objection that rooms over archways were objectionable was childish: at Stanway (his Gloucestershire seat) there was a gatehouse by Jones, and Jones's Whitehall Palace consisted of a series of courts entered through archways with rooms over. Nor would it 'defame' Jones's memory – indeed, it would transform the Banqueting Hall from a museum of old uniforms into a hall fit for government receptions.[67]

Having published the designs in March, when the public verdict had on the whole been 'exceedingly favourable', the government held, five months later, that it was now too late to halt developments; and in any case Jones's designs with their thirty-foot-high rooms were unsuitable for a public office [Pl. 216]. Only in one way could they be adapted: 'by dividing these lofty rooms horizontally by means of a floor, with the result that you would give one half of these big windows to the top floor and the other half to the lower floor. . . . The men on the lower floor would get the bottom half of the window, and could not possibly see out of it; while the men in the room above would have the top half of the window,

258. New War Office. Section north-south from Horse Guards Avenue, through principal staircase. After Young's death in 1900, the work proceeded under his son, Clyde Young.

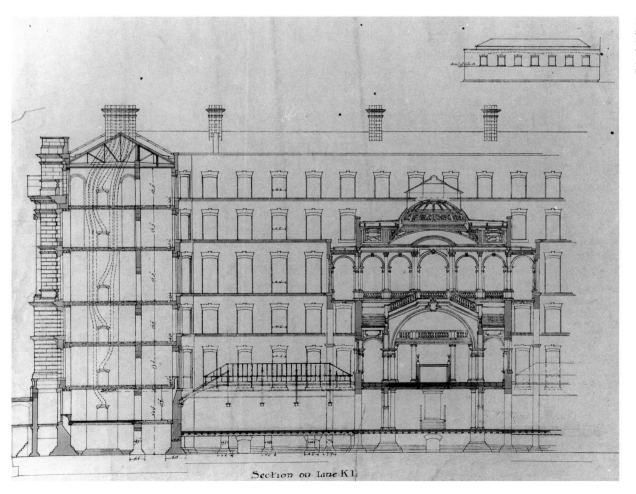

Section on Line KL

259. New War Office, Whitehall:
a. The Secretary of State's room, overlooking Whitehall.
b. Quadrangle, north-west corner.

which would be close to the ground, with the result that it would throw no light into the room.'[68]

Unsurprisingly, the *Builder* was hostile to Wemyss's memorial.[69] Wemyss then turned to *The Times*. But there too the editor refused to support him: the matter was too far advanced, the official design though not 'a great success' was not 'so great a failure', and Wemyss's design involved the 'artistic mistake' of 'fitting the inside to a façade, instead of developing a façade as a consideration of the internal requirements'.[70] Nor was the president of the RIBA more helpful: 'he admired the design, but said "If this is adopted there will be nothing to show the architecture of the 19th OO"', to which the octogenarian earl replied, 'D— the architecture of the 19th OO. I prefer Inigo Jones.'[71]

Wemyss then 'appealed to Caesar', seeking to stir up public opinion with the aid of the latest technology. At the Palace Theatre, the latest news items filmed for Bioscope programmes were a regular feature of the evening's entertainment for a popular audience, along with performing sealions and '*poses plastiques*'.[72] Wemyss thought film might be 'a valuable means . . . of giving publicity to intended public buildings of sufficient importance which is now wanting. I hope [he wrote to Morton, manager of the theatre] we may see this new most valuable feature in future form part of yr wonderful entertainment, when such occasions arise. . . .' But alas! 'I am sorry the machinery does not suit – Would it not *take* [Wemyss asked] to have stationary photos: of objects of great and passing interest?'[73] Scarcely surprisingly, Morton appears not to have taken up this diverting proposal, and Wemyss' publicity campaign was still-born.

'The result of the method adopted by the Government is, upon the whole, satisfactory', declared *Building News* when the designs were unveiled in March 1899. Many would prefer Brydon's 'English Renaissance' to Scott's neighbouring Italian. Both new designs were 'eminently well adapted for the purposes intended', and would 'unquestionably . . . enhance the architectural dignity of London'. Though neither was 'brilliant or dashingly original', both

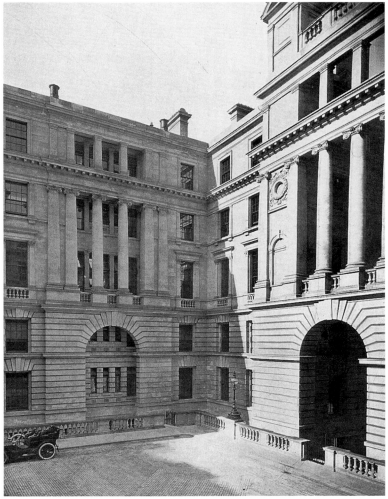

262.   New Public Offices, Westminster: Principal Stair, executed in Mazzano marble by Messrs Farmer & Brindley.

261.   New Public Offices, Westminster, Brydon and Tanner:
a. Exterior view, contractor's advertisement, 1908.
b. Loggia in Charles Street.

were 'distinctly removed from the mediocrity of the commonplace' [Pl. 197–8]. Subsequently reviewing the course of English architectural development, Goodhart-Rendel saw them as 'historically significant in marking the return of English civil architecture to the European neo-Classical convention'.[74]

The sudden deaths of Young in 1900 and Brydon six months later left their more-or-less complete designs to be carried out largely by Office of Works architects Taylor and Tanner,[75] the First

Commissioner stating that confidential inquiries had been unable 'to discover anyone sufficiently in sympathy with Mr Brydon's artistic ideals to subordinate his own inventive genius to that of the original designer' – a remark that substantiates Goodhart-Rendel's argument that the lack of an academic architectural education encouraged those who 'wished, with the romantic egotism of their age, that every man should make his designs notably different from those of every other man'.[76]

When the hoardings came down, the new buildings received a not unfriendly welcome from the professional press. The *Architect* acknowledged that the government had been 'conscious of their duty to erect a building not altogether unworthy of the claims of the nation to be one of the most enlightened and leading forces of the world'. Brydon's building, however, was no 'marble palace', as a critical MP had complained: 'The exterior [Pl. 261] is substantial rather than rich'; the interior 'of a severely businesslike character', except for the entrance hall and the two reception apartments for delegations [Pl. 262–3], 'treated with restrained richness'.[77] *Building News* was rather cooler: it criticised such details as the heavy keystones that were out of keeping with the delicate architraves of the windows, and the corner towers designed for effect rather than use, but liked the graceful cupolas and the monotony-breaking use of Venetian windows in the long south front. 'But . . . considering the importance of the occasion and of the situation, and the large sum expended on it, one might have hoped for something of higher architectural interest.' This contrasts with the praise poured on Brydon's designs in 1899, and suggests a change in taste as much as a comment on Tanner's touches: an influence, perhaps, of the freer treatment and more developed neo-baroque of Rickards as displayed at Cardiff or Deptford.[78]

260 (left).   New War Office, William Young. Principal stair, the walls and pilasters in Painswick stone, with alabaster balusters, and imposts to the arches; Piastraccia marble steps, and Brescia marble columns, executed by Farmer & Brindley, 1904–6.

263. New Public Offices, Westminster: Board of Education, Deputation Room (now the chancellor of the Exchequer's room):
a. Contract drawing signed by Henry Tanner, Office of Works.
b. The room, wainscotted by Messrs Farmer and Brindley, on completion in 1908.

The external differences between the elevations signed by Brydon in December 1898 [Pl. 255, 264] and those signed by Esher and Tanner [Pl. 264–5] are not great: the most substantial, the substitution of rustication for channelling in the stonework of the ground floor and mezzanine, with the introduction of heavy keystones in both ranges of windows similar to those Brydon employed in his upper ranges. There was also a modification of the Parliament Street frontispiece, including the attic.[79] The most conspicuous alteration was Lewis Harcourt's decision to omit the shade-casting towers on the Charles Street front; changes were also made in the arch connecting Brydon's with Scott's offices. But Tanner's real changes lay in the construction.[80]

By 1910, however, opinion was blaming Tanner for an aesthetic failure: the *Architectural Review* liked the circular court [Pl. 266–7], clearly derived from Jones's Whitehall Palace designs, but decided that 'on the whole the building is not a successful achievement . . . shorn of some features which would have added greatly to its dignity, while the intrusion of another hand less inspired than the

original designer is plainly evident'.[81] A quarter-century later, a classically-minded critic harshly observed that: 'It is obvious that had [Brydon] been as competent as Sir William Chambers he would have built as Chambers built, without any variation. It can leave no doubt . . . that he thought much more highly of Chambers than Chambers would have thought of him.'[82] But Chambers was only one, and not the principal, of the English classicists so admired by Brydon.[83]

The westward extension of Brydon's public offices was necessarily continued in the same style when work began in 1912 – he had, in fact, drawn out the design for the whole site. Growing disenchantment with his style was plain. The president of the RIBA in his opening address (1912–13) described 'the whole of the work done by the Office of Works as poor from an architectural standpoint'.[84] One MP called the Whitehall buildings – 'this rigid type of architecture' – 'a degradation to the country', though he admired the more Frenchified *dixhuitième* design for the new County Hall, seat of the LCC on the south bank opposite the Houses of Parliament. 'We lose sight entirely of the idea that the most beautiful things are the simplest things', he remarked, perhaps influenced by recent continental work. Lord Robert Cecil, however, preferred 'the more

264. Public Offices, Westminster. Entry to Charles Street from Parliament Street:
a. Brydon's original design, 1898, with proposed completion of Scott's Home Office tower by J.O. Scott.
b. Modified design by the Office of Works, 1903. After Brydon's death in 1901, the work was formally entrusted to Sir John Taylor, the government's principal architect, but in fact largely executed by Henry Tanner, Taylor's successor. The First Commissioner had promised that no variation from Brydon's design would be allowed unless first approved by a special advisory committee. Scott's tower was never carried out.

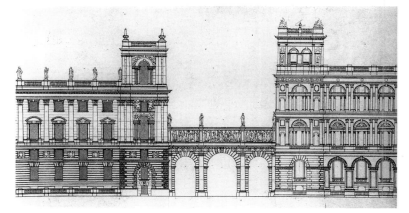

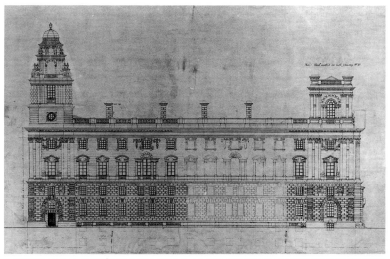

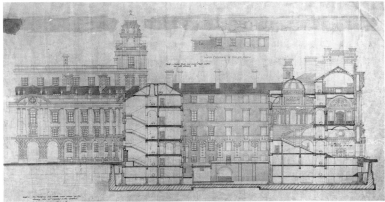

265. New Public Offices, Great George Street. Contract drawings, initialled by Henry Tanner, January 1902:
a. Elevation. This differed in certain details from Brydon's original design: the base is rusticated instead of merely channelled, keystones in the window traverses are enlarged (and introduced in the mezzanine) and the second-floor windows ornamented.
b. Section, shewing the two basement floors, principal staircase, and doorway to reception room.

266. New Public Offices, Westminster, plan, J.M. Brydon, 1898. A great central court 161ft in diameter was inspired by Inigo Jones's Whitehall Palace plans. Large subordinate courts ensured light and air to the offices, and single-sided corridors were lighted from smaller courts as in the Leemings' Admiralty plan.

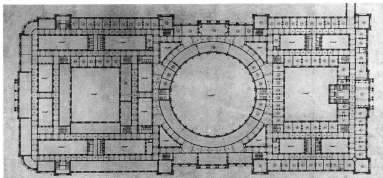

267. New Public Offices, Westminster, J.M. Brydon and H. Tanner, Central Court, from photograph, 1908.

official style . . . however ugly, if it is practical for the purposes for which it is built'. But then he was

> an agnostic. . . . I cannot help feeling . . . that anything which was built ten or twenty years ago is always ugly; anything that was built fifty or sixty years ago is moderately beautiful; and that when you get further back than that the thing is always extremely desirable and beautiful. The modern building which has just been put up has a certain prestige, because the architect is still alive, and his friends do their best to praise it. As soon as the architect is dead, and his friends have disappeared, the thing is always ugly. . . . If buildings now are ugly it is because there is no architect at the moment capable of erecting beautiful public buildings.[85]

French *dixhuitième* influence was also observable in Aston Webb's work at either end of the Mall in connexion with the publicly-subscribed Queen Victoria Memorial. We have seen in chapter 2 that Webb won the limited competition for the architectural works. His ingenious triumphal arch with converging faces neatly resolved the problem of turning the Mall into the Strand, and was embodied in a fourth block extending the Admiralty, which permitted the use of public funds in completing the design [Pl. 268]. A balance of some £50,000 from the subscriptions enabled refacing the decaying Caen-stone east front of Buckingham Palace in Portland

268. Admiralty Arch, Aston Webb, 1905—10. Elevation to Charing Cross.

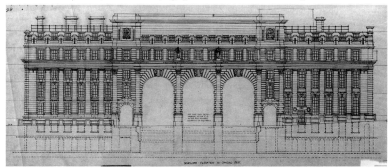

269.   Buckingham Palace, refronting to Mall, Aston Webb, 1913.

Scotland showed his skill in 'the chastest Beaux-Arts style', which he maintained in the King Edward VII Galleries at the British Museum: only part of a larger design that was never completed [Pl. 270].[89] The façade was hailed by Walter Godfrey in 1938 as 'by common consent one of the most important contributions to the architecture of this century', and Summerson observed that it was 'directly in the tradition of Duc's Palais de Justice'; more recently it has been described as combining 'the scale and dignity of Smirke's work with the qualities of profile and finish which derive from modern materials'.[90]

Although new offices for the Commissioners of Woods and Forests (the Crown estate) with a 75-ft frontage in Whitehall, on the other side of Whitehall Place from Young's War Office, were designed with scrupulous care to maintain the alignment of that powerful building's storeys and cornice, and with respect for the Banqueting House on its southern flank, nonetheless John Murray (1864–1940) exhibited rather more of a French character in his elegant Baroque detailing [Pl. 203]. The *Architectural Review* in 1910 hailed it as the 'best of all the new Government buildings in Whitehall'.[91] A more marked departure from Edwardian Baroque was observable in the adjacent offices for the Board of Agriculture in Whitehall Place [Pl. 204], designed by another government architect, H.N. Hawkes (d.1910) in 1909 and completed by his colleague H.A. Collins. Largely executed in reinforced concrete, using the Hennebique system, this seven-storey 13-bay block employed columnar decoration only in its upper reaches. The apparent height was reduced by putting two floors in a mansard roof, and the façade stonework was channelled, in a manner which owes much to Frank Verity's 'Champs Elysées'-style apartments in Cleveland Row.[92]

Tanner had in fact already introduced the Hennebique system in order to reduce the cost of a new General Post Office Building on the site of Christ's Hospital, near the GPO complex in St Martin's-le-Grand, in 1906. He was followed by his colleague Richard Allison in the design of the new Stationery Office and

stone. The work, carried out in the summer of 1913 with extraordinary celerity, preserved the disposition of Blore's fenestration, but changed the style to *dixhuitième* [Pl. 269], perhaps influenced by Maquet's new Royal Palace in Brussels.[86] King George V and Queen Mary took a close interest in Webb's proposals.[87]

When the 1903 Public Buildings Expenses Act provided funding to augment a bequest to the trustees for the extension of the British Museum,[88] the 1898 precedent for choosing an architect was followed, as noted in chapter 12. John James Burnet (1859–1938) had been trained in a French *atelier*, and notable works in

270.   British Museum Extension (Edward VII Galleries), Montagu Place; John James Burnet (1857–1938). The grandeur of effect achieved by this French-trained Scot is slightly diminished by the Museum's demand for an entrance at ground level.

a. Original design, March 1905. The large dome is that of the Reading Room.
b. Revised design, June 1905, with omission of decorative sculpture.

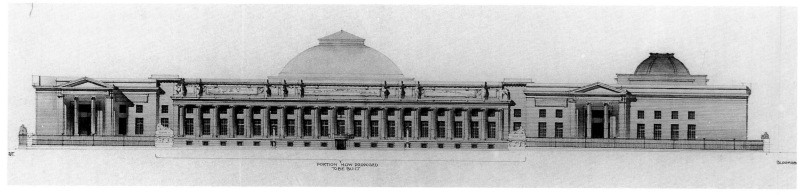

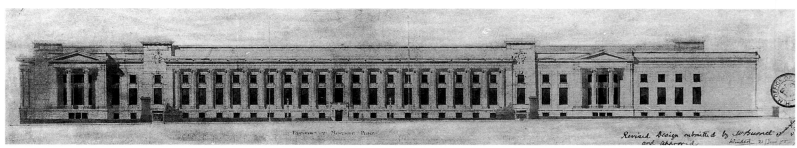

NEW OFFICES FOR THE BOARD
OF TRADE

HALF INCH DETAIL

warehouse in Stamford Street in 1912. Crown exemption from the provisions of the London Building Acts enabled the Works to experiment in this way, but imitation by the building industry at large had to await post-war legislation.[93]

A two-tier competition for new £570,000, eleven-storey Board of Trade offices in 1913 marked the abandonment of Young's and Brydon's grand manner. Edwardian Baroque, after its brief reign was now officially pronounced dead: 'For the external elevations the columnar treatment is to be avoided except in isolated features.'[94] The Office of Works, with its large staff of qualified architects, increasingly subject to the influence of contemporaries' work, was escaping from the historicism of the past century. As the sketch-designs of the 177 first-stage entrants[95] were in the usual manner returned unexhibited to their authors, we cannot comment on the general run of designs.

It was 1915 before the second stage of the Board of Trade competition was judged. The ten finalists included Percy Adams & C.H. Holden, Robert Atkinson and Edwin Cooper. Vincent Harris's winning design [Pl. 201] was characterised by 'business-like simplicity'. Unlike previous government buildings, this was to rise over one hundred feet, containing eleven floors, including basements. Several of the finalists had created a quasi-basement above ground, placed three floors between this and the main entablature, and inserted one floor in the frieze, another in the attic, and two in the roof. Harris simplified his elevations, including six floors between base and cornice, and grouping two upper storeys with pilasters and balcony [Pl. 271]. Despite the height, the limited site required tight planning, as the *Architect* observed, and to secure a decent court rather than the mere wells offered by some others Harris had to adopt the central-corridor plan, with rooms on either side. But the introduction of electric light had transformed the situation since the days of Scott, or even of Leemings, and made central corridors acceptable.[96]

Harris's victory was compared with that of Knott for the London County Hall, where the plainer and less expensive had been preferred to the richly-decorated. 'In dealing with the external treatment of a huge workshop with many small rooms and some large ones, with a basement and ten other floors above, competing architects had a knotty problem to solve in avoiding a barrack-like effect on the one hand, or on the other of making their office building appear like a big hotel.' Harris's inclusion of six floors between 'qua-basement and main cornice' was thought to afford 'a great accession of dignity', avoiding monotony by 'grouping two upper storeys together by means of an order of pilasters and balcony'.[97]

> Once again [remarked the *Architect*] we see the victory of economical planning over clever attempts at Architecture with a capital A. As is usually the case the most simple and obvious-looking plan, when achieved, is the winner. In conformity with the invariable English custom, the site for the building is far too exiguous to permit of any display of fine planning such as we see in the academic designs of architectural students in the Ecole des Beaux-Arts, or even as is possible in actual buildings on the Continent of Europe or that of America.

Nevertheless, the ten designs (of which Holden's [Pl. 201], with its 'feeling for solid masses' was the most forward-looking) formed 'an exhibition of the high standard of present day British architecture, alike in design and draughtsmanship'.[98]

271.   New Board of Trade competition 1914. Detail, Vincent Harris. A marker that Edwardian Baroque was dead.

16
Hazards of the Building Process

Between the parliamentary approval of a new major public building project, and the handing over of the completed work to the department concerned, three conceptually distinct stages intervened. First was a process of discussion involving the relevant department, the Office of Works and the outside architect, with occasionally an intervention from the Treasury. This stage concluded with a design agreed between the parties at an estimate furnished by the architect. The second stage, involving the preparation of working drawings and specifications, directed towards putting the work out to competitive tender, was one essentially for the architect's own office. If the lowest tender exceeded the estimate, the architect had to negotiate with the Works, and probably the Works with the Treasury, so that the second stage would be prolonged: particular circumstances, such as a rise in costs during the preparation period, might be accepted as a valid reason for increasing the sum allocated; but frequently the architect had to revise his plans in order to get the price down. (Thus any prolongation of the second stage switches the scene from the architect's office back to Whitehall, or even to Westminster.) The third stage commenced with the acceptance of a builder's tender, and comprised the actual work of building. During this stage, the Office of Works insisted that the entire responsibility for the work lay with the architect, and was scrupulous that any intervention on its part should not diminish that responsibility. The contract might be for the entire building, but often the foundations were taken separately while the working drawings for the superstructure were elaborated. Thus, taking the building as a whole, there might well be an overlapping of stages. Once the carcass was up, the fittings could be installed, but work on external embellishment by way of statuary or carving might continue. The building phase terminated with the formal handing over of the completed structure to the department, though pressures on accommodation might be such that the department, as with the Home Office in 1875, moved in before the architect gave his certificate.

In practice, the pressure for keeping costs down ensured that these stages can seldom be clearly distinguished. The Office of Works or the Treasury might intervene at any point short of the actual signing of the contract, to set the handle back to 'start'. These departments, especially the Treasury, could also control the rate of building by the amount of funds they chose to allocate each year for a given project, as we have seen.

The first stage, leading to official acceptance of a design and estimate, could well be a lengthy one. The winner of a competition would learn how wide was the gap between his premiated design and a building that met the precise needs of the client. Moreover, to draw a chemical analogy, those needs might be unstable, whether because of the growth or the reorganisation of a department, or because the client had changed his mind. The parliamentary system promoted planning instability: a hostile vote might compel the Treasury to demand changes, or a change of government might bring in men of different views from their predecessors. In a sense, one might say that the client himself had changed, because, although the client was still 'the government', that government was different from that which originally commissioned the architect.

Foreign and India Offices

Thus Scott found that the change from a Conservative to a Liberal administration in 1859 forced him to abandon his Gothic designs and prepare wholly different ones if he were not to lose the commission. This naturally prolonged the preparatory stage – the more so on that occasion as he vainly used all means in his power to persuade the new premier to accept his own ideas. Some time, however, was rescued, by setting to work on the foundations while the superstructure was taking final design shape.

Scott was appointed to design the new Foreign Office in November 1858; he submitted an outline plan [Pl. 272], and was instructed on 17 January 1859 to prepare detailed drawings and an approximate estimate, which he submitted on 3 March. Two weeks later he was instructed to proceed with working drawings and furnish a list of builders who would tender, which should have marked the commencement of stage two.[1] Shortly after the change of government, the tenders were submitted in July 1859, the lowest at £232,024 from John Kelk, a railway contractor anxious to secure more prestigious commissions for social advancement.[2] However, the new government's stylistic predilections moved operations back to stage one. Scott had also entirely to recast his plan when Palmerston agreed that the new Indian secretary should occupy the second proposed office, which should share the Park front with the Foreign, so dividing the site east-west in place of the original north-south division.[3] [Pl. 272b]

While Scott fought out his lengthy battle with Palmerston, officials were clearing the way to move things forward. Temporary accommodation for the Foreign Office was found in two houses in Whitehall Gardens, Pembroke House (used by government since 1851) and Malmesbury House, the move taking place in August and September 1861. During August Scott prepared a specification for the foundations, contracted to Kelk at £19,577, though he did not sign the contract until May 1862. The delay in starting the foundations may well have been a result of the discovery that an additional 5000 sq.ft of the Park would have to be acquired in order to accommodate the offices as planned.[4] A similar foundations contract for the India Office had been agreed at £19,990, so that the whole site could be developed in one operation. Work began on 19 May 1862, excavating to a depth of twenty feet or more; a raft of concrete 12 ft thick was then laid, to the same specification as the 'Barry raft' at the Houses of Parliament, using the same old-fashioned method of throwing the concrete in from a height of ten feet. Despite the theoretical objection that this technique lets air into the material, in practice the rafts have been found to be well compacted.[5]

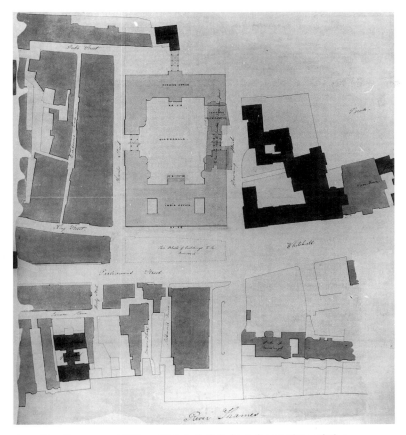

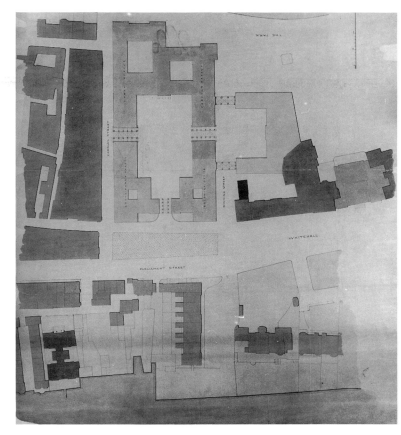

272.   New Government Offices, Whitehall; G.G. Scott, layout plans, 1858–9:
a. Late 1858, with India Office on Whitehall, Foreign Office on the Park, and Colonial Office on Downing Street.
b. Mid 1859, with India and Foreign Offices sharing the Park front, incorporating the site of Soane's State Paper Office, now moved to share Whitehall front with the Colonial Office.

Meanwhile, Scott's new Palladian design had been approved, and he was instructed on 6 August 1861 to prepare working drawings[6] and specification, tenders being invited a week later. However, the bill of quantities was still being drawn up when Kelk finished the foundations, in March 1863. At this point there was a divergence in the arrangements for the two offices, the India Office [Pl. 273] – constructed on the authority of the secretary of state, paid for from Indian funds, and not the responsibility of the Office of Works – going ahead on the basis of a contract for three months' work on prices negotiated with Kelk, the commission being transferred to a new partnership between Kelk's manager, Taylor, and George Spencer Smith, who had in reality carried out the foundations contract. But for the Foreign Office the First Commissioner insisted on a contract in gross, i.e. for the whole structure,[7] for which Scott's drawings and specification were a *sine qua non*, forthcoming only on 29 May 1863. The Works calculated that Scott's estimate of £200,000 (based on Kelk's original tender) would be exceeded, and proposed that 'some of the more costly decorations' should be omitted. It was a month before Scott completed his revisions. Cowper asked for further alterations, tenders being called for on 14 August. Of the eleven tenders received, ranging narrowly from £209,615 down to £195,573, the lowest was that of Smith & Taylor, the on-site contractors. It was mid-November before work began on the Foreign Office superstructure, marking the start of the third stage, by which time parts of the India Office were probably already up to first-floor level. Work continued there on a series of contracts on the basis first of Kelk's original prices, and then of those of the Foreign Office contract.[8]

Some information about the building of the Foreign Office

273.   India Office, Matthew Digby Wyatt, *c.* 1864. Plan of roof of Principal or 'Muses' staircase, shewing ironwork.

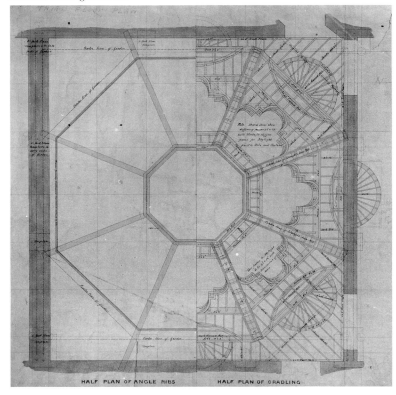

HALF PLAN OF ANGLE RIBS   HALF PLAN OF CRADLING

emerged in the course of examining witnesses before the Royal Commission on Trades Unions in 1867, when both trades unionists and employers were heard. George Francis Trollope of one of the large public contracting firms showed that the textbook picture of the public-works contractor turning to speculative house-building in order to keep his workforce together between contracts is not to be relied upon: he spoke of a contractor, 'Mr Smith, for instance, at the Foreign Office', beginning with 400 or 500 men to dig the foundations, discharging them gradually as the work goes on, and taking on bricklayers and labourers, 'and so it goes on through the whole work'.[9] Smith himself explained that if he wanted '500 men next Monday, we should take the usual means of making it known, and if we did not get the necessary number of men within a reasonable interval we must raise our price'. Trollope commented that in such a situation he would have to offer 6d. a day extra, whereupon 'the men would flock to us'.

The commission's questioning brought out the basic antagonism between the employers and the unions, Smith complaining that unions had slowed down the rate of working, and Trollope that 'the effect of the unions is to induce [the men] not to do anything for my benefit', so that 'many masters' now said: 'I used during the winter to keep on as many men as I could even at my own personal loss, but now these men care nothing for me.'[10]

Smith admitted he employed two sub-contractors, Wilkinson and Bone, to execute brickwork by piece-work. They gave him a price at which they would do brickwork: so much per rod up to a certain height, and higher rates as the building rose and the labour consequently increased, the work being measured three times during the progress of the building, but the sub-contractors being paid sums weekly on account. They then paid their men by the day. Edwin Coulson (d.1893), secretary of the Operative Bricklayers Society, alleged that this was a pretence, 'a swindle against the men and a swindle against the Government', the so-called sub-contractors being merely foremen who hoodwinked the workmen into believing that it was let as piece-work to them; paying the men by the day; and exaggerating the hours worked, or engaging inexperienced men at sub-standard wages, so that they could pocket the difference. (This was to argue that they were also hoodwinking their alleged employers.) The consequence, Coulson claimed, was inferior workmanship, such as the dry-packing of bricks (i.e. not laying them in mortar) [Pl. 274], or leaving 'pockets' in walling.[11]

The unions' opposition to piece-work was lucidly explained by George Potter (1832–93), president of the London Working Men's Association and a leader in the 1859 building strike: he saw it as a means by which employers forced down prices, and drove the men to make inferior articles.[12] Smith naturally denied such accusations of inferior workmanship. One of his clerks of works had suggested that they might be ascribed to 'a report that may have got abroad, as to some hollow walls . . . in consequence of certain parts of the building having to be kept fireproof, some of the walls had to be built upon iron girders, and, in order to lessen the great weight upon those girders, they have been built hollow, and are so shown upon the architect's drawing'. Only a few weeks previously, the department requiring a rearrangement of rooms (the Office had not yet been formally handed over), 'a great many of the walls have been cut through . . . They are all perfectly solid.'[13] The building was in fact executed with the best technical devices of the day to ensure fireproof and secure construction, with wrought-iron joists supporting concrete flooring.[14]

Completion fell behind schedule: the India Office was due to be finished by 1 April 1866, and the Foreign Office five months later. An extension to 1 May 1867 was granted for the latter in October 1866. Tenders for gas fittings and grates were let in May and June 1867, lifts and internal painting in August, and decorative painting

of the reception rooms (Clayton and Bell) in September. Two events marked the approaching completion of the two offices: on 19 July 1867, a ball to which 2500 guests were invited was held in the Durbar Court of the India Office [Pl. 275], to mark the visit to London of the Sultan of Turkey, 'the greatest state reception that London had ever seen', the Council Room being set aside for the Sultan's supper.[15] On 25 March 1868 the premier's wife gave a grand reception in the foreign secretary's room, the Foreign Office reception rooms not being sufficiently complete. The foreign secretary himself gave a dinner there for the Queen's Birthday on 23 May [Cp. pl. 276]; the Office was displayed to peers and MPs on 27 June, and the officials began to move in two days later.[16]

Meanwhile, the government had been considering the eastward completion of the block towards Parliament Street. The Devon sub-committee of the 1866 Manners Treasury commission allocated the site to the Colonial and Home Offices and their dependencies, and the commission itself recommended that they 'be erected without delay'.[17] Scott on 12 February 1868, following a conversation with Manners, called attention to the desirability of laying all foundations for the eastward extension at one and the same time: 'The buildings are erected on so unfavourable a foundation that the entire surface occupied by building, – with a margin round the same, – has to be excavated to a very great depth and a continuous stratum of concrete laid to a thickness, I think, of about twelve feet.' As with the Foreign Office, much time might be saved if the foundations were laid while the superstructure plans were preparing. A week later, the Treasury approved his formal appointment as architect for the work.[18] But not until July did the two departments supply the requisite information about accommodation 'in tabular form'; after which Scott 'spent weeks in going from office to office consulting every head of every department as

274.　Shoddy building practice: dry packing of bricks exposed in a Victorian wall.

275 (right).　India Office: Matthew Digby Wyatt, Durbar Court. A state ball for the Sultan of Turkey was held here on 19 July 1867, with 2500 invitees, "a happy identification of imperial with metropolitan pride' (F. Harcourt). So successful was it, that the court was then glazed over (1867–8), and became the setting for many state functions.

to his own accommodation' and endeavouring to carry out his wishes,[19] work that one might have expected to have been already done by the Office of Works to enable it, or the Treasury, to establish a specification.[20]

Nevertheless, the general outline of his plan must already have been established: the squaring-off the block externally eastward, with internally the great courtyard completed on a symmetrical plan except for a large rectangular bay to the east between the two new offices, giving on a carriage entrance from King Street [Pl. 129].[21] This appears on two of the plans published with the report of the Treasury Commission [Pl. 126], and furthermore the contract for foundations was let to Smith & Co. on 30 July 1868, at £20,709, priced at the same rate as for the Foreign Office: though wages had risen, they now had a favourable opportunity of disposing of the spoil.[22] Scott submitted his estimate of £352,372 (exclusive of commission and fittings) to the Works on 9 December, the day of Layard's appointment as First Commissioner in Gladstone's ministry.[23] With another £55,000 to cover the omitted items, the total, soaring above £400,000, was too much for an administration pledged to 'retrenchment'.[24] Once again, the first stage had to be re-run.

Layard promptly set up a departmental committee (Trevelyan, Stephenson and his new architectural adviser, Fergusson) to examine Scott's plans. Their report indicated the weakness of the procedure followed:[25]

When we directed our attention to the building, the principle

276.   Foreign Office, Downing Street, G.G. Scott 1863–8. State staircase dressed for ministerial reception, 1896.

upon which the Foreign and India Offices had been planned presented a great difficulty. They have been designed upon a plan more of a palatial, than of an official character. The size and height of the rooms in the two principal floors are such, that if the remainder of the building were completed strictly according to the same plan, there would be a great loss of available space for official purposes.

Therefore the great question was whether the normal heights of the different storeys, 'as expressed by the external architecture', be modified in the new part without damaging the architectural effect.

After full consideration, we arrived at the conclusion that this would involve a modification of the exterior lines, and a degradation of the character of the principal front, which would be justly regarded as a permanent disfigurement, and would not be tolerated in a building occupying such a position.

We were the more inclined to accept this result, as we saw reason to believe that, even if the front towards Parliament Street were finished according to the Foreign and India offices proportions, it would not involve the necessity of adopting the same standard in any buildings for public offices which may eventually be erected as wings to this central block, either on the south side of Charles Street, or on the north of Downing Street.

Accepting, then, the need to maintain the external lines of the Foreign Office [Pl. 277], the committee turned to find means of obtaining more accommodation:

Here we were chiefly dependant upon . . . Mr Scott, who cordially entered into our views . . . by making an addition to the area of the building on the eastern side of the quadrangle, and omitting a proposed carriage entrance; by introducing an entresol into a portion of the first floor; by making the basement and third floor available for ordinary official accommodation; and by a careful attention to economy in all the arrangements for laying out the interior of the building, additional office room can be obtained equal to at least a third of that for which provision had previously been made.

We have endeavoured, not only to place those offices which are most connected with each other in business in the closest proximity to each other, but also to arrange the rooms within each office in accordance with the official relations subsisting between the officers for whose use they are intended.

Thus, compared with the Foreign Office, there was to be a fourth office storey; the building area, too, was extended [Pl. 129]. By these means they were able to provide in the new block for the entire Colonial and Home Office staff, and all the offices connected with them, including the Lunacy Commission and the Poor Law Board, which would not have been accommodated in Scott's original plan – 'a *new* design greatly differing from the former one; comprising several more departments and covering much more ground'.[26] It was at this stage that Scott advanced his east front across King Street, aligning it with the front of Barry's so-called Treasury Buildings [Pl. 122].

On 4 June 1869 Scott was authorised to proceed with the rest of the foundations, so far as the ground was available (some of the King Street houses not having yet been demolished). The secretaries of state having approved the plans, Scott was on 12 August ordered to prepare working drawings. But stage one was again prolonged: towards the end of November the First Commissioner went over the drawings with him, giving him certain additional instructions: any prospect of rebuilding north of Downing Street was excluded [Cp. pl. 212]; he was to construct two fireproof divisions; provide a kitchen and coffee room; and go through the

277.   Charles (now King Charles) Street, G.G. Scott, 1863–76, shewing on the left the continuous floor levels throughout the entire India and Home Offices block, necessitated, according to Scott, by the height of the state reception rooms of the Foreign Office.

plans again with the departments. The plan and elevation must nevertheless be entirely Scott's responsibility. The specifications for tender were to be submitted as soon as possible.[27] Scott duly submitted the working drawings, specifications, and revised estimate of £379,968 for the building (1 s.5½ d. per cu.ft) and £56,500 for fittings, etc., on 14 December.[28] Asked to estimate likely expenditure, Scott reckoned £3500 to the end of March (instead of the £10,000-worth of concreting he had hoped for), because of the difficulty over the site, but £100,000 in the new financial year – a sum the Office cut down to £80,000.[29]

A ruthless economist, A.S. Ayrton, had taken over the Office of Works from Layard. In response to a Treasury demand for further information about Scott's estimates, Ayrton commented with heavy significance: 'The plans and elevations of the buildings shew that they will be of a highly ornate character externally. . . . It is proposed to adorn them with statues along the parapet, the height of which from the ground will render it necessary that they should be colossal, and with cupolas at the corners'. He had already directed that these features should be estimated for separately. Scott supplied further statistics, but suggested leaving the calculations until the tenders were submitted. Ayrton insisted. Scott jibbed, 'as the quantities are not in any such condition as to facilitate my making a corrected estimate'; with the aid of his surveyor he 'assumed a sum which we think probable', viz. £350,000.[30]

Disputes between Ayrton and the Treasury then prolonged the planning stage still further: Ayrton, regarding the designs as too elaborate and expensive, wanted to send Scott back to the drawing board. At the same time, he recognised Scott's standing as an architect, and resisted for a time the Treasury's demand for a report from one of his own officials, Galton, the Director of Works, on Scott's existing designs.[31] On the basis of that report, the Treasury required Scott to diminish the opulence of his designs, reduce the height of the rooms, and replan the corridors to avoid using borrowed light.[32]

Responding rapidly to his new instructions, Scott within two weeks reduced the architectural features of the east front, omitted the cupolas, cut out the grand stair of the Home Office, simplified the interior finishings, and arranged satisfactory corridor lighting. But the perennial problem of room height he was able to solve only to a limited degree. The Foreign Office, with its state apartments, he insisted,

gives the key to the entire block . . . without making an architectural monstrosity the same general lines and levels must be continued wherever the parts now to be executed are in conjunction with those already erected. . . . I have, wherever they cease to be visible together, modified this by a redivision of stories and the introduction of mezzanines; while, through a considerable portion of the Parliament Street front which is occupied by the Libraries, the height becomes advantageous and is utilized by means of Galleries. There is however a remainder in which I have failed to devise any means of meeting the objection. . . . I have done all which I see my way to do in this respect. . . .

The result of this 'work of *radical change* in many portions of the building' and remodelling the quantities was a reduced estimate calculated at £264,000, with the hope that tenders (inclusive of foundations) might be received as low as £250,000.[33]

On this basis the Works' officials recommended going to tender. Treasury authority was granted on 18 August, and 14 tenders were received on 15 September, ranging from £279,860 down to £242,323, a sum which, remarked Scott, 'after adding the cost already incurred for foundations, is somewhat less than Mr Lee [his surveyor]'s calculation [viz. £264,000] though the chances of competition (perhaps influenced by the [Franco-Prussian] war) have not been so exceptionally in our favour as he had indulged a hope that they *might* be'. The successful firm, Jackson & Shaw, of Earl Street, Westminster, were Scott's contractors for the Grand Midland Hotel, St Pancras.[34] Scott supplied general contract drawings and specification on 19 October, but as the drawings lacked figures and some were without scales, they had to be returned. By 1 November 40 drawings had been received. The contract was signed on 26 November, the building to be completed within three years from obtaining possession of the site.[35] The last portion of the site, the houses in King Street, was cleared by 26 January 1871.[36]

As in the Foreign Office, Scott specified a fireproof construction, though here employing Dennetts' plaster arches on wrought-iron beams for ceilings, overlaid with concrete flooring, rather than Barrett's system which required more ironwork as well as permanent timber shuttering; so obtaining a lighter and more economical, as well as potentially sounder, construction.[37] In May 1872, the Home Secretary called for the plans, because 'some changes have been made in the arrangements of the Office, for which it may be necessary to make special provision'. Galton pointed out that the work was 'so far advanced that no structural alterations can be made', to which Ayrton added 'and it is hoped will be completed nearly within the contract time'.[38]

However, at that precise period Jackson & Shaw were the object of a builders' strike, to which they responded with a lock-out. When the masons accepted the London Master Builders' terms in mid-July, the strike fizzled out. However, it led to a 12 per cent increase in wages. At the same time, prices of building materials were rising. Scott had to provide not only for additional works required by the Home Office, but also for altering the projection from the Colonial Office into Downing Street, where originally an arcade to proposed new buildings on the northern side had been envisaged [see Pl. 212]. Despite the First Commissioner's statement that the Privy Council Office would remain, Scott had left open the possibility of constructing an arcade, a point that Galton had missed in examining the plans in 1870. Although the contractors priced this at only £544, they asked for a 15 per cent increase on the cost of additions in view of higher prices. Scott commented that the rises varied greatly by material and type of work, but thought they had a claim.[39] Despite earnest pleas by Jackson & Shaw that they had 'suffered very heavy loss already, upon the original contract, and must suffer still more', and that they were threatened with another strike in July 1874, the Works stuck rigidly to the terms of the contract.[40]

Further additions to the contract in April–May 1873 embraced a subway under the basement corridor and channels for pipes in the corridors on all floors, to facilitate access to pipes after completion of the building.[41] In December 1874 Scott reported that the two offices were virtually complete, save for part of the sculpture: the busts in the tympana of the first floor windows with their foliated spandrels had been 'delayed owing to the excessive difficulty in the selection of a series of persons to be represented'; a difficulty he had only just overcome with the help of friends and the two sculptors (Armstead and Philips). The persons selected are explorers (for the Colonial Office) and philosophers and scientists (for the Home Office) [Pl. 278–9]. Also the terminations of the corners had been left unfinished, pending determination whether the cupolas were to be erected. Authorised extras totalled £5282.[42]

Fitting up the new offices occupied the whole of 1875, and the architect had not given his certificate of completion when the officials began to move in about the end of that year. One consequence was considerable official criticism, as faults emerged that there had been no time to rectify. Chief of these was the offensive smells. In part this resulted from a suggestion made by Galton that the drain pipes should not be buried underground, but be kept within sight and convenient access in a sub-basement. Cracks from small settlements eventuated, 'soil' spread over the floor so as to 'create a nuisance in the room above'. Though such faults could easily be remedied (and the drains were eventually covered in concrete), once the officials were in they reported defects to the Office of Works, instead of to Scott's clerk of works at the building, so that rectification became embedded in the bureaucratic process.[43]

The Gladstone ministry had also undertaken a number of other building projects, of which the New Law Courts and the Natural History Museum were the largest and proceeded more or less contemporaneously. In both the planning stage was prolonged and problem-ridden, largely because of the financial limitations imposed on them. The planning of the New Law Courts saw a battle royal between Ayrton as First Commissioner and the architect, Street, that was ultimately resolved in the latter's favour by the intervention of the cabinet. Waterhouse at the Museum had not established the relationships that assisted Street to ride his troubles successfully – and his building was less a focus of public interest – and he had to yield more.

The New Law Courts

Of all the great nineteenth-century public buildings, the Law Courts experienced the most vicissitudes. Street was appointed architect by a Treasury minute of 30 May 1868. He was required to revise his plan in consultation with the Courts of Justice royal commission.[44] Entirely recasting his plan – borrowing ideas from Waterhouse's entry [Pl. 225] – Street concentrated on achieving the efficient plan that the competition had called for. He gathered nearly all the courts around an elongated central hall on the high level of Carey Street. By tauter planning he was able to save 37,000 sq.ft., though the 'great plan' as it was called covered no less than eight acres – half an acre more than the site offered.[45] A key change was his abandonment of symmetry on the Strand front, perhaps influenced by Burges's design: the presence of St Clement Danes on its island in the Strand being acknowledged by a slight recession in the western part of the front.[46] In view of the general election and change of government, November–December 1868, it is scarcely surprising that the Treasury did not respond quickly to the plans submitted by the commission, to which Street made a full report on 11 January, asking permission to proceed with the elevations.

The new First Commissioner, Layard, was keen (as Street knew) to transfer the New Law Courts to the Thames Embankment;

278.   New Government Offices, G.G. Scott, 1868—75: Parliament Street front. The Home Office occupied the left and central parts, the Colonial Office that on the right.

279.   Statuary on the Whitehall front:
a.   Colonial Office, the principal floor, with busts of imperial heroes in the window soffits: from the left, David Livingstone, William Wilberforce, Sir John Franklin, probably by Farmer & Brindley.
b.   Colonial Office, the ground floor, allegorical figures of the Continents in the spandrels: from the left, Africa, America, Australasia, by H.H. Armstead.

280.   New Law Courts, G.E. Street. Design for Carey Street front, January 1871.

Lowe, at the Exchequer, was determined to keep the entire cost within the total million and a half authorised by the 1865 act. Following the Commons' debate of 20 April, Layard asked Street to prepare new plans for the Howard Street site [Pl. 112] designated by Lowe.[47] Longer but narrower, it obliged Street to abandon the concept of enclosing the courts and their immediate adjuncts with a protective shell of offices, which he now removed to the east end of the site (as he was to do ultimately at Carey Street) [Pl. 114]. When required to provide a comparable plan for the existing Carey Street site, he did little more than shift the office block to the south side of the courts complex [Pl. 114].[48] The commission resolved against the Embankment on 23 June, a day after Gladstone had agreed to remit the site question to a select committee, which narrowly decided in favour of Carey Street.[49] On the last day of 1869 Layard's successor, Ayrton, instructed Street to prepare plans for Carey Street 'within the limits of the site prescribed by the Act passed in 1865, also within the limits of the funds . . . provided by the act passed in the same year'.[50]

Street's 'entirely fresh plan' [Pl. 114] was an attempt to shrink the 'great plan' to fit the restricted site, to the disadvantage of light and ventilation. His suggestion for the demolition of St Clement Danes was a forlorn hope. At the Office, Galton and Hunt criticised the new plans, particularly objecting to 'the crowded position of the courts and their accessories around the Central Hall'.[51] Street's response was to abandon, as at Howard Street, the concentric formation, placing his main office block now to the north, along Carey Street.[52] Galton and Hunt approved this unenthusiastically, pointing out that an addition to the west of the site was necessary. Ayrton, in submitting this report to the Treasury, scribbled one of his annihilatory glosses: there were 'some architectural features of an extremely expensive character which do not in the least affect the purposes for which the buildings are to be erected and which it may be found desirable to modify or dispense with altogether'.[53] Lowe, himself a keen retrencher, thus alerted, scrutinised the plans; refused the request for additional land; proposed that the central hall be diminished and the complex separation of categories of users simplified; and ridiculed Street's estimate of £750,000.

Within six days of learning of the Treasury's rejection, Street had come up with a solution that was to prove definitive: he merely turned his plan on its side[54] [Pl. 281]. The central hall now ran north-south. The fear of creating a new thoroughfare between Carey Street and the Strand had hitherto blocked this solution, but it allowed Street a substantial hall [Pl. 240], longer than his competition plan (though shorter than the great plan and its immediate successors) around which he could locate 18 courts, with a grand entry from the Strand recalling the north entrance of Westminster Hall, its avatar. Office blocks lay to east and west, though in an afterthought Street deleted the western block. Reporting on his new design he argued strongly to retain the central hall: 'solidity

281.   New Law Courts, G.E. Street. Final plan, November 1870. Street rotated his central hall to run north-south, flanked by the courts, and to the exterior, ranges of offices, the principal office block being moved to the east.

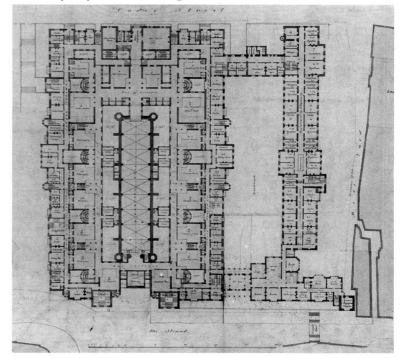

282.   New Law Courts, G.E. Street, contract drawing. Main entrance from the Strand, with flanking towers and central hall gable behind.

and good arrangement', he claimed, were his keynotes, 'of much more importance than an excess of rich and costly architectural detail'.[55] The royal commissioners at their penultimate meeting fell in line with government thinking: they desired the building 'should not be imperfect in . . . architectural character'; but were still keener not 'to sacrifice the complete usefulness . . . to architectural ornament'. They were therefore prepared to change the central hall if that was the most effectual means of attaining that 'complete usefulness'. At their final meeting on 3 August 1870 they approved the slightly modified design now formally laid before them by the Treasury and became *functus officio*.[56]

All ought now to have been plain sailing, but two serious problems emerged. One was the endemic issue of cost, to which we will return; the other, the hostile trend of public taste. Warning shots were fired over the Embankment design [Pl. 113] by the *Builder*, never enthusiastic about Street's competition design, and the *Building News*: they disliked its picturesque irregularity, a characteristic, too, of the new plan for which Street now set about preparing the elevations.[57] [Pl. 280]

In the meantime, however, Street urged that work should start on the foundations (again overlapping the stages of planning and execution), following the precedent of the New Government Offices, where the foundations contract had been separated from the superstructure; he also suggested a contract for prices, instead of the by now conventional contract in gross requiring a full set of drawings and specifications. Although the Works rather grudgingly accepted the separation of foundation and superstructure, it insisted on a lump-sum contract for the foundations. Thus it was not until late December 1870 that the first invitation to 21 contractors went out; one that was bedevilled by difficulties about deadlines

and, more importantly, by the terms of contract imposed by the Office of Works.[58] Ayrton gave way to pressure from the great contractors, and 19 tenders were ultimately received for the foundations on 20 January 1871, the highest astonishingly double the figure of the lowest, Dove Brothers, awarded the contract at £36,775.[59]

To return to Street's superstructure, the principal features of the Strand front, which could not of course be viewed axially, were the entrance to the great hall, to the west, and on the eastern corner a massive clock tower. Galton and Hunt objected to the latter as not providing useful accommodation, and Street at Ayrton's request substituted enlarged office space, though retaining a much smaller tower.[60] In forwarding the plans to the Treasury, Ayrton once again fired a Parthian shot: the vaulted roof of the hall should be further considered. The Treasury made its routine reference to Galton, who was hostile, not only to the vaulted roof, but also to the elevations, in which he echoed widespread press criticism.[61] The Treasury accordingly required Street to reconsider his design.[62] Thus while the foundations were constructing, the superstructure was still in the planning stage. Unfortunately, his alterations, with a large spire instead of a ventilating tower over the central hall [Pl. 282], were not acceptable to Lowe. Street, complaining that he was required 'to amend the design in accordance with the views of the Treasury' which he had no means of ascertaining, demanded to be put in direct communication with that office, thereby escaping for the time from Ayrton's occasionally supportive but generally stifling toils.[63]

Street now worked rapidly to supply the Treasury with a set of drawings of a somewhat simplified design, including perspectives and a large photograph joining up the several drawings of the

Strand front. These seem to have done the trick, and Treasury approval was given on 4 August 1871.[64] Street then pushed on with preparing contract drawings [Pl. 282–4], in which he made further revisions, including an enlarged clock tower at the eastern end of the Strand front, though not as emphatic as his original proposal. These changes were accepted by Lowe on 5 February 1872 and, despite the press controversy and wide hostility to Street's designs,[65] the architect was able to continue with the lengthy preparation of the drawings necessary for putting the superstructure to tender.[66]

The quantity surveyors had started as early as May 1871, working closely with Street, who incorporated his answers and explanations to their queries in a book from which he formed the complete specification for the building.[67] Though 'every drawing for the building' was in their hands by mid-June, it was not until December 1872 that specification and plans were ready. Street had made 'such complete . . . drawings that every portion . . . is shewn in detail', which entailed the surveyors in precise measuring, involving greater labour and responsibility than the conventional presentation.[68] He suggested that the work be divided (as Nash had done at Buckingham Palace in the 1820s), into two contracts to obtain quicker results, and tenders were invited on that basis, as well as for a single contract. Instead of charging for the 'extremely voluminous' bill of quantities, to prevent undesirable builders from tendering, as Street suggested, the Office preferred to ask contractors whether they would accept an invitation to tender.[69] Twenty-four contractors, including, in accord with Works' practice at that time,

five provincial firms, were invited to tender. Although the range of responses was less extreme than for the foundations, there was still a quarter of a million between the lowest, Joseph Bull & Sons of Southampton at £744,344, and the highest.[70] The wide gap of nearly ten per cent between Bulls and their next competitor, the reputable firm of George Baker & Son,[71] however was a danger signal ignored by a Works' regime dominated by the competitive ethos; and Street's concern to realise his master work may have inhibited his casting doubt on Bulls' capacities. Professor Brownlee has described Bulls' standing and limitations.[72] Their employment on the Law Courts resulted, as noted above, in contention, delay and bankruptcy.

Even so, Bulls' tender, allowing for foundations, heating and

283. New Law Courts, G.E. Street. Constructional details from contract drawings:
a. Public staircase, Strand front, Nov. 1872. The construction is in traditional materials.
b. Public and jury stairs, Strand front, shewing that alterations were being made as late as October 1879.

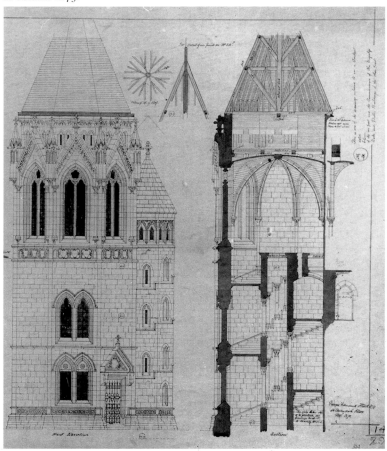

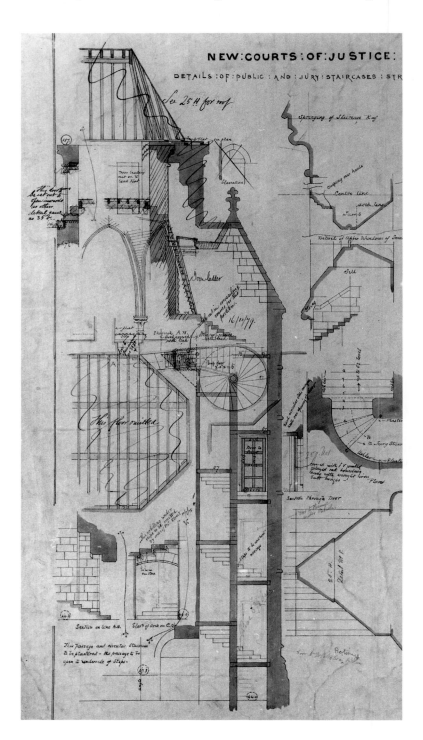

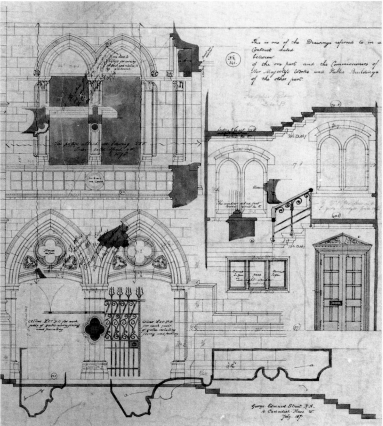

284.   New Law Courts, G.E. Street:
a. Southern Bar Room: windows. One of the richest pieces of detailing.
b. Detail of west front, marked with alterations in April and June 1878

lighting, came out at £108,000 more than the £710,000 allocated for the building.[73] This immediately threw Street's plan once more into jeopardy. The attack focused on his darling central hall. Hunt suggested that it should go. The Treasury likewise, unable to stomach the increased cost, suggested converting it to an open court, possibly surrounded by a cloister to protect against 'inclement weather'.[74] Ayrton (influenced perhaps by Waterhouse's Great Hall [Pl. 225]) told Street that an iron and glass structure would serve. 'Unfeignedly surprized and hurt', Street rejected this as 'incompatible with the whole scheme of the building'; the hall was the entrance to all the courts, and if any portion of the building was to have an architectural character, it should be this. 'Experience does not warrant anyone in assuming that rapid decay can be prevented where glass and iron are combined in roofs and consequently no one has yet succeeded in making such works dignified or fine in their Architectural character.' To eliminate this most important feature would be to ensure 'complete and disastrous failure', 'an act of artistic suicide'. The Natural History Museum had been allowed to add 15 per cent because of rising costs; he asked for the same treatment. He could save about £34,000, by omitting a ventilating turret, using cheaper stone inside, reducing the quantity of carving, and so forth, while the £18,000 provided against extra works could be struck out.[75]

Galton preferred the simplicity of striking out the central hall, to save £80,000. Ayrton instructed Street to consider this, which would improve the Strand front, in which also the clock tower was 'wholly unnecessary'; he had no doubt that he was able to design something 'more suitable to the site ['the side of a street somewhat narrow'] and more generally acceptable to the public'. Street bitterly rejected Ayrton's assertions point by point. To make a contract with Bulls and leave the question of the central hall to be settled later would invite trouble and expense. He must be told exactly what reductions he might make; to carry out Ayrton's suggestions would result in a building 'grievously maimed and mutilated'. In the angry correspondence that ensued, Ayrton ignored a significant letter from the Treasury, which had modified its stance remarkably: a saving of a half of the excess, i.e. some £54,000, would now be sufficient.[76]

Street was now clearly playing for time. On 13 March, Gladstone had resigned following a narrow defeat in the Commons. Although he resumed office five days later, he doubted 'whether either the administration or the parliament can again be what they were'.[77] It seemed unlikely that the administration would survive much longer. If Street could delay a decision long enough, the abominable Ayrton would be swept away. But Ayrton and his advisers were playing it tough and demanding the deletion of the central hall and alteration of the Strand front. He had therefore to fall back on his personal contacts with Gladstone and Lowe. His appeal to the prime minister proved unnecessary, for Lowe told him, face to face on 27 May, that the Treasury had already agreed to allow a £54,000 increase to cover rising prices.[78]

Secure in this knowledge, Street firmly refused to make the reductions required by the First Commissioner, but declared that there was 'no difficulty in reducing the cost by about £54,000', so bringing it down to the Treasury figure. With the Works still rigorous, Street negotiated with Bulls, who agreed to his reductions to arrive at a contract for £704,901 – 'no opening for the re-measurement of the work, no uncertainty as to its real cost, no more delay in its execution, and no departure from the plan signed by Lord Hatherley for the Commission and approved by the Treasury'. He then informed Ayrton that he was appealing from the First Commissioner's decision to the Lords of the Treasury – in fact had already done so several days earlier. He had, of course, no doubt of the outcome. My Lords upheld his appeal. Accordingly, on 2 July

1873 the Office informed Street that he should revise his drawings to provide for a contract price of £704,901 instead of £758,816, the very reduction of £54,000 that he already suggested.[79] The central hall was saved.

It was not yet possible to sign a contract, however. Bull & Sons had bitten off more than they could chew, and almost immediately, as Street had feared, began to wriggle. As Professor Brownlee points out,[80] they were clearly under-capitalised for such a huge work which was on the scale rather of the major railway or docks contractors, than that of their provincial church and town-hall practice. Bulls had had time, as Street had feared, to repent of their rash offer, and now raised difficulties: they wanted compensation for four months' wasted in discussion at a time of rising wages; and insisted that, since there were drawings for only one of the 18 courts, the cost of the remaining 17 must be ascertained by measurement at a schedule of prices – precisely the sort of situation that Street was struggling to avoid. The government would lose the advantages of a lump-sum contract, and the door would be opened to dispute. The real problem was that Bulls had made an error of £300 in pricing the oak fittings for the specimen court, and could not afford to increase this seventeen-fold.[81]

Bulls also wanted a clause added to the contract, providing that the government should pay for the cost of valuing any departures from the contract plan.[82] The Works rejected these contentions, but Bulls persisted. 'They have been advised that if they sign a contract for the eighteen Courts without drawings they will be obliged to execute whatever I give them to do', reported Street, adding that they were anxious their priced schedule should not be printed, lest it become public property – an idea rejected as 'extremely objectionable: it might be called for in parliament, or by the Treasury, and considering the number of copies required, filling in prices by hand would require much labour and possibly lead to mistakes'.[83]

A meeting achieved little progress: Bulls pushed for alterations to the contract 'which could only be made', remarked Street, 'for the sake of their profits'. Instead of the squared bolted timber scaffolding used on public works since the Houses of Parliament, they wanted to use 'common pole scaffolding where it is sufficiently strong. But the sense of the word sufficiently', noted Street, 'is just what I and they would probably not agree upon'. They also wanted liberty to work stone anywhere (instead of solely on site): in view of their sample of inferior quality, Street feared such permission 'might open the door to any amount of quarrelling'. Bulls' demands also indicated their lack of working capital, as mentioned in chapter 12.[84]

Unacceptable as such claims might be, the faults were not wholly on Bulls' side, as the Office surveyor, Hunt, pointed out in a lengthy report. The unclear division of duties between Hunt and the director of Works, Galton, referred to above, resulted in Hunt's not being consulted on the form of tender, in which ambiguities existed that Bulls were exploiting. Hunt also pointed out that Ayrton's obstinate determination to follow his own course, instead of accepting Bulls' tender in its integrity (as Hunt, as well as Street, had urged), had enabled the contractors to set up their claims. Ayrton's supersession by the more tactful William Adam enabled a compromise to be reached that maintained the substance of the Works' requirements, while allowing Bulls an additional sum on the court fittings and extending the time for completion. The contractors still pressed for compensation for the delay, which they claimed had caused them a loss of at least £10,000, and for other concessions. Ultimately the Office Solicitor advised giving them a new copy of the complete specification, conditions and draft contract (omitting the fittings of the courts), and asking them if they

would or would not execute it. Even then, it was not until 7 February 1874 that the contract, for £693,429, was actually signed.[85]

This, however, was but a prologue to a lengthy chapter of misfortunes. Bulls were slow to gather a sufficient work-force or enough machinery on the site. They disputed Street's certificates for work completed (as he had foreseen), involving him and the government in frequent and expensive measurings; they did not maintain their equipment satisfactorily, and failed to pay sub-contractors. They had, through no fault of their own, also to contend with a masons' strike in 1877–8, necessitating the recruitment of Italian and German labour. Inevitably in a building of such scale, despite his immense care in preparing the huge number of working drawings (there are over two thousand in the Public Record Office), Street made frequent modifications during the course of the works [Pl. 283–4], which gave the contractor grounds for dispute.[86] But Bulls' inadequacies contributed significantly to an over-run of nearly two and a half years over schedule. Despite government subsidy, Bull and Sons, as mentioned above, went into liquidation soon after Queen Victoria opened the Courts.[87]

The Natural History Museum

The planning stage of the new museum for the Natural History collections of the British Museum was prolonged by the death of Captain Fowke, winner of the 1864 competition for designs [Pl. 104]. The competitors had been issued with copies of the plan prepared in 1862 under the directions of Professor Richard Owen, superintendent of Natural History at the Museum, in which two-storeyed side-lighted galleries 40 ft wide were separated by 20 ft lighting areas [Pl. 285].[88] This was intended as a general guide only, but had been closely followed by Kerr in the design awarded second prize [Pl. 104]. Kerr's was, not surprisingly, preferred by the trustees to Fowke's design, in which a continuous series of 63 ft-wide galleries were lighted from above.[89] Despite reports from departmental officers and the arguments of a sub-committee of trustees and officers, the First Commissioner, Cowper, insisted on the advantages of Fowke's design for diffusion of light over the exhibits, general convenience, and architectural effect.[90] Suggestions about internal arrangement and lighting from the officers could be easily adopted. When, after Fowke's early death, Waterhouse was appointed his successor, his brief was to provide

285. Proposal for Natural History Museum on two floors, by Professor Richard Owen, 1864, which provided a basis for competition entries.

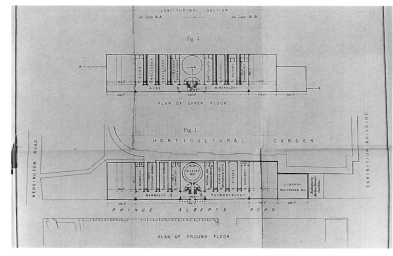

the working drawings and estimate, giving careful consideration to such suggestions from the officers.[91] A change of government in mid-1866 further delayed progress, as the Conservatives, seeking to establish their credentials as an economy-minded administration, deferred any vote for the new museum until the 1868/9 estimates. They also cut out the proposed Patents Museum that had been part of Fowke's scheme.[92] (This element was to disappear until the creation of a Science Museum.[93]) Obviously, Waterhouse would have to make considerable changes to Fowke's design. The elevation he proposed was approved by the Museum trustees, but in June 1868 was rejected by the Treasury, which thereupon postponed the question to the next financial year. By that time the Liberals were back in power, with a First Commissioner, Henry Layard, keen to line the new Thames Embankment with magnificent public buildings. Waterhouse obliged with a splendid design [Pl. 105]. Public and parliamentary opposition to poaching open space needed for public recreation killed the scheme.[94] It was not until May 1870 that the government finally decided to locate the Natural History collections at South Kensington.[95]

By this time, a changed regime held power at the Office of Works under Layard's successor, Ayrton. That minister characteristically objected to Waterhouse's plans as of an expensive character, needing careful reconsideration, especially regarding space for study, mode of lighting, rooms for staff and the most economical use of space. Adequate buildings could be built much more cheaply. Discussions with the architect produced a design estimated at £350,000, based on the principle of future extension, only one architectural front, that towards the Cromwell Road, being provided, and that apparently a return to the 1868 design [Pl. 105].[96] After further discussions, Waterhouse undertook in November to prepare new designs to cost £330,000 only, furnishing sketch plans by the new year, and contract plans within six months of receiving notice to proceed.[97] Waterhouse's sketch plans received qualified approval from the trustees, who wanted the rear galleries constructed half on one plan and half on another. Waterhouse had reverted to Owen's 1862 system of galleries 40ft wide, separated by reserve galleries of half the width [Pl. 286]; but the keeper of geology (for which the west wing was destined) wanted considerable changes.[98] The Office of Works, insensitive to departmental needs, sought to impose uniformity in both wings.[99] Waterhouse placed his museum 150ft from the dust of the Cromwell Road, occupying about three and a half acres in the centre of the 16½-acre site. Thus the incorporation of the Royal Horticultural Society's galleries to the north, a feature of Fowke's design, was abandoned. The front building, 670ft long, contained three floors of galleries above a basement of offices and workshops which, because the ground was five feet below the street level, stood above ground level.[100] Ayrton objected to the 170-ft high central towers [Pl. 287]. The Treasury upheld him, and Waterhouse was instructed to reconsider their elevation and proportions.[101]

In May 1871 the Commons called for the plans and a model.[102] A Vote of £30,000 was made for beginning the work. General approval of the sketch plans was given on 5 May 1871, and the specification and working drawings submitted in mid-December. Three weeks examination of the specification in the Office led to further modifications. In accord with Treasury criticism, the museum was moved nearer the Cromwell Road, and some differences between the plans of the two wings were introduced to meet the wishes of the keeper of fossils.[103]

As chairman of the judges in the 1864 competition, Lord Elcho was naturally interested in preserving Fowke's design. Fergusson, another member of the jury, brutally attacked Waterhouse's design in *Macmillan's Magazine* in January 1872.[104] Elcho, after consulting

Henry Cole, sought unsuccessfully to raise the question in the Commons.[105] The public seemed unconcerned. Waterhouse, however, did not entirely obliterate Fowke's ideas. In elevation, traces of Fowke's design were distinguishable in, for instance, the lower-storey windows of the wings and the turrets of the end pavilions [Pl. 242]. Moreover, he retained Fowke's intended use of terracotta as facing material, which he extended to the whole façade.

With the specifications at last about to go to tender, Waterhouse, as observed in chapter 9, warned the Office that prices had risen 10–20 per cent since 1870. Although his instructions did not require the architect to revise his plans unless the tenders were too high, Ayrton on Galton's advice nonetheless insisted that Waterhouse make preliminary reductions.[106] He accordingly reluctantly omitted his hoop-iron bond courses except above second-floor level, substituted Portland stone for granite in the enclosure works and for Craigleith in parts of the interior, and reduced the thickness of wainscot flooring and the cost of tile paving.[107]

It was therefore the end of August before invitations to tender went out.[108] Waterhouse, as noted above, had had serious doubts about the merits of competitive tendering; and he had also suggested dividing the terracotta work among two or three firms, a proposal condemned by Hunt.[109] Despite Waterhouse's reductions, of 17 contractors who sent in tenders, the lowest was (allowing for warming and other expenses) £83,000 above the authorised £330,000. But unlike the New Law Courts, the range from Baker & Son at £395,000 to George Myers at £458,210 was relatively narrow, and the firms of known capacity. The small number of terracotta manufacturers[110] seems to have been part of the problem, and to bring Bakers' tender down to £352,000 Waterhouse, at Galton's suggestion,[111] substituted Portland stone and brick for some terracotta, as well as slates for lead roofing, and reduced the height of the central portion containing the index museum, replacing the central towers with low spires.[112] He also omitted a smoke tower, and adopted a plaster ceiling for the index museum instead of a wooden one.[113]

Nagged by the trustees of the British Museum, the Treasury, conscious that the failure to use any of two successive years' votes of funds would invite parliamentary criticism, nagged the Works, and, assured that £10,000 might be spent before April, authorised acceptance of Bakers' tender at £352,000 on 13 December 1872.[114]

Waterhouse promised a revised specification, but reported that there were so many alterations and so much to be re-written that it would be 'some little time' before the final copies were ready. The contract was signed on 8 February 1873, with completion due three years later. But progress was slow. Out of a vote of £40,000, only £4180 were spent by 5 April. Ten weeks were lost partly because of the First Commissioner's indecision about the position of the Museum in relation to the Cromwell Road: it was eventually placed nearer the road than originally intended – as the Treasury, looking to the value of the land, had suggested – fuller investigations having revealed problems with the northerly strata.[115]

Progress continued slower than Waterhouse had expected: in October 1873 he was blaming the delay on an insufficient number of workmen; in January 1874 on a delay in the supply of terracotta.[116] Delivery of ironwork for the ground floor was very delayed, which prevented proceeding with the brickwork (and correspondingly would have prevented fixing the terra-cotta). By January 1876, within a few weeks of the due completion date, little more than half, only £173,000 worth of work, had been done. The unfamiliar material was largely to blame: terracotta was being used on a hitherto unheard-of scale.

The manufacturers experienced difficulties in making the blocks – as many as 30 per cent sometimes being rejected for

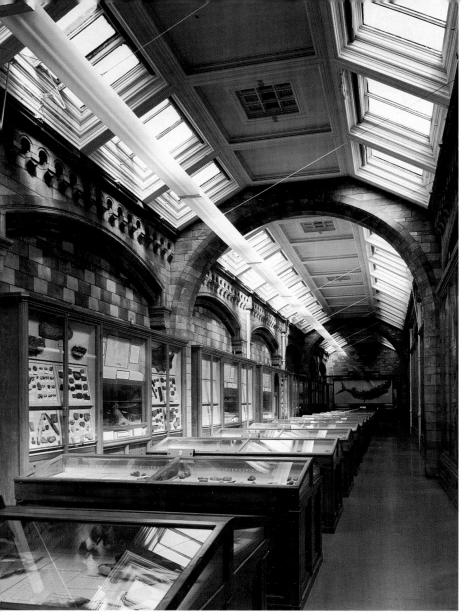

defects occurring in firing – and the contractors in handling them, material new to the workmen. A great improvement in quality and in the rate of production was achieved, however, by early 1876. In the spring, over a hundred bricklayers were employed on site.[117] But later in that year a serious quarrel developed between the architect and the contractors about alterations from the contract drawings. The terracotta contract lay between Bakers and the manufacturers, Gibbs & Canning of Glascote, Tamworth, who complained that 'the character of the Work has been so entirely different from that contemplated' as to cause expense and delay, so that they had had to proceed in a piecemeal manner greatly enhancing the cost of the building.[118] Waterhouse retorted:

> I do not consider that I have exceeded the ordinary latitude of an Architect in revising from time to time the details of the Terra Cotta. Some portions of it have been made simpler than was originally intended, and other portions have been enriched. The precise difference in value forms one of the subjects of investigation by the Surveyors who are now engaged in adjusting the value of the variations as between the Government and the contractors.

All the detail drawings and models had been delivered to the contractors at least eight weeks and usually eight months before the receipt of the terracotta.[119]

The extensive use of this unfamiliar material ultimately led to serious contention between architect and contractors over payment. Waterhouse had sought to represent the building's function in its decoration, the terracotta of the western, zoological wing exhibiting extant animals, and that of the fossil or geological wing, extinct ones. His drawings, based on material supplied by Owen, were modelled by Dujardin of Farmer & Brindley, and the terracotta then cast from the models.[120] According to Waterhouse's retrospective report (20 July 1881), because of the difficulty in obtaining satisfactory blocks of blue-grey colour, he had omitted a large quantity of them, substituting an increased amount of surface ornamentation in buff. A reduction in size of blocks (which facilitated firing) meant that more were required (60,000 pieces of decorated terracotta, 100,000 in jambs, etc., and a large number of

286. Natural History Museum, South Kensington, A. Waterhouse.
a. Gallery designed for staff and students, with access to showcases in adjoining public gallery.
b. Public exhibition gallery; the archways opening to the study gallery behind have been subsequently blocked up.

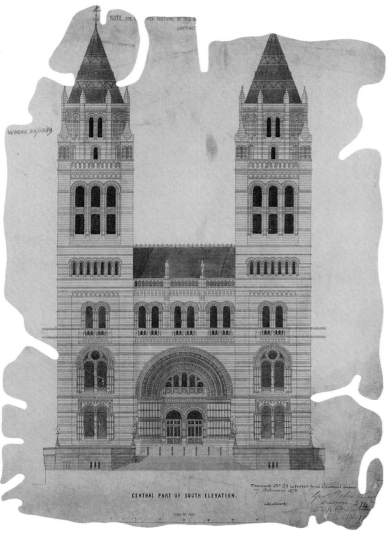

287. Natural History Museum: Central Towers.
a. Waterhouse's original design for the towers was rejected by First Commissioner Ayrton as too expensive, but Captain Shaw of the London Fire Brigade urged their reinstatement to hold reservoirs for fire-fighting. They were further modified to meet departmental requirements.
b. The towers after cleaning, 1981. One of the advantages claimed for terracotta was that it would resist the fatal London soot, needing only occasional washing down.

interlocking pieces in voussoirs, and chequers), though handling was made easier. They were filled with cement concrete instead of carrying bricks into the cavities to the fullest extent possible, for which he would allow £2206 extra, as well as 6d. for fixing each additional block. In the character of the brickwork in the wall behind there was little difference.[121]

The contractors' quantity surveyor, Charles B. Trollope, not surprisingly took a different view:

Two distinct classes of Terracotta illustrating past and present Natural History have been introduced and the varieties [?] in the decoration have been crossed [?] regardless of cost, making the work a gigantic puzzle. Archways are altered in shapes, Enriched work introduced where none was intended, and omitted where shewn on original drawings, Two colors introduced to the arches, The contract drawings for jointing the terracotta altogether varied, The contract for brickwork backing to the terracotta entirely changed. . . . I defy anyone to say whether at increased or diminished cost.[122]

He claimed some £21,000 for extra expense of sorting and setting terracotta, nearly three times the sum allowed by the architect's surveyor, Thomas Rickman.

Although concerned at the unsatisfactory progress of the Museum, the Office of Works was reluctant to move in the matter. Sir John Karslake, the late attorney-general, was consulted, but advised that to recover the contractual penalties for non-completion it would be necessary to prove special damage, which would be impossible. It was best to facilitate progress as much as possible to ensure completing the carcase. If Bakers then broke down, it would be easier to make fresh contracts.[123]

Further delay resulted from a decision to reinstate the central towers [Pl. 288], cut down by economy-minded Ayrton and a cost-cutting Treasury, as mentioned above, recommending that the

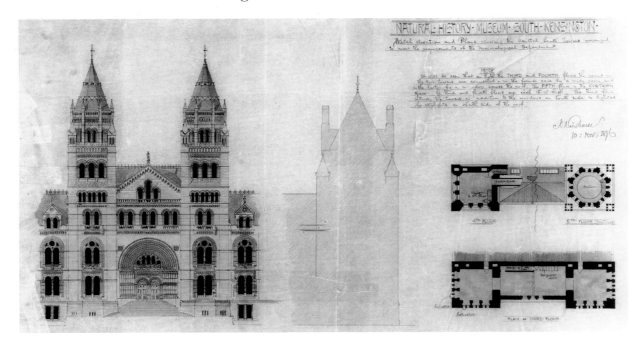

288. Natural History Museum, South Kensington, A. Waterhouse. Revision of towers to meet requirements of Minerological department and Fire Brigade, November 1876.

towers be treated 'with a view to a better architectural effect, especially in reference to their elevation and proportion'.[124] Captain Shaw of the London Fire Brigade however (as mentioned in ch. 9) recommended that they should be restored to their original height (170 ft) in order to hold 12,000-gallon water tanks. Lord Henry Lennox, First Commissioner in Disraeli's 1874 ministry, assented: but he too disliked Waterhouse's original version. The terracotta sector was therefore reduced in height, the main gable increased, and the length of the windows modified to meet the wishes of the trustees[125] [Pl. 288].

As Bakers had already received payment about equivalent to the sum value of work executed and unused materials, Waterhouse proved unwilling to issue further certificates for additional payments. From August 1876 there was continual dissension between architect and contractor. The dispute centered on payment for skylights and ventilators prepared but not delivered, advances made on account of plant, and the reserve sum held back to guarantee completion. Bakers argued that 'had the contract been carried out under the conditions on which we undertook it, the whole of the plant and the retention money would at this time have been released'.[126] Early in 1879 they agreed that the parties' surveyors should investigate the deviations from contract, omissions as well as extras, about which they had shown 'such disinclination . . . as to preclude these necessary investigations being made during the greater part of the progress of the Building'.[127] In March, Waterhouse admitted his dilemma: any certificate would trench on the reserve, but Bakers could not go on without money. The situation was similar to that experienced with the over-extended Law Courts' contractors. Out of a reserve of some £4700, Hunt recommended an advance of £3000.[128] But in May Waterhouse finally refused another certificate, the Office refused any further advance, and by July Bakers, like Bulls, were bankrupt.[129] The works were concluded by Bakers' trustees.

South Kensington Museum

Circumstances were at first rather different in the neighbouring South Kensington Museum, on the eastern side of Exhibition Road. A Government School of Design had been set up in 1837 as a result of public concern about the inadequacy of British indus-trial design. Although encouraged by Prince Albert, the School with its Germanic involvement with the 'commercial requirements of craft processes' was disliked by the aristocratic connoisseurs and their parliamentary connections, and commonly regarded as a 'job'.[130] Henry Cole pressed through the Society of Arts for the re-organisation of the School, and in the aftermath of the 1851 Exhibition succeeded in establishing a Department of Practical Art in 1852 under the Board of Trade to administer art education nationally. This blossomed in 1853 into the Department of Science and Art. A museum of manufactures was set up at Marlborough House, subsequently developing into a museum of ornamental art.

When Marlborough House had to be cleared in preparation for the Prince of Wales' coming-of-age, the art school and the museum were put in adjacent premises on the 1851 Commissioners' estate at Brompton (renamed by Cole 'South Kensington'), linked by a cheap structure designed by Pennethorne and executed by Kelk.[131] In November 1856 Captain Francis Fowke, R.E., was appointed architect and engineer to the Department of Science and Art,[132] and thereafter the department was responsible for its own buildings until 1870. Kelk, and his successors, Smith & Taylor, were generally employed to carry out the building works, with no attempt at competitive tendering until the 1860s, a situation governed by the small and uncertain annual Votes.[133] A select committee in 1860 scrutinised 'South Kensington', reporting favourably on the whole, and recommending £44,000-worth of urgent works, new buildings to be capable of being worked into a general plan for the site – such as Fowke had produced. His plan for the completion of the museum in the area bounded by Exhibition and Cromwell Roads was the basis for the later plans. The northern range of Lecture Theatre buildings, completed in 1869 after Fowke's death, is nevertheless his work.[134] Fowke's 1865 plan showed a doubling of the cubic capacity compared with his 1860 design; expenditure so far had been some £93,000 out of an estimated £214,000. An estimate for completing the permanent buildings, submitted in December 1865, provided for an additional 9,000,000 cu.ft (as against nearly 4,000,000 already built) at a cost of £368,000.[135] The most important works were estimated at £220,000. As a result, the Treasury approved an expenditure of £195,000 spread over six years, of which £89,000 were spent by April 1870 [Pl. 96, 175, 218–19].

Revised plans put forward in 1869 for an additional 4,000,000 cu.ft, costing £463,000, more ran into obstruction from the new regimes of Lowe at the Exchequer and Ayrton at the Office of Works, under whose control South Kensington's buildings were now placed.[136] The cabinet decided that no new building should be started until a revised plan had been drawn up.[137] The chancellor of the Exchequer in the succeeding Conservative administration agreed that completion should be 'in a manner befitting its purpose and contents' and Colonel Henry Scott (1822–83), Fowke's successor in the Department of Science and Art, prepared a £500,000 design. Working drawings were authorised in August 1875, but in early 1876 completion was postponed and a limited scheme (including an Art Library) to cost £80,000 substituted in July.[138] Even then, Henry Scott's designs lay in the Treasury for most of 1877. Tenders were advertised for (a new development, invitations to tender for major works having previously been sent to selected firms) in January 1878, Perry & Co. winning at £45,000. The structure was complete by 1882, when Taylor of the Works complained of the deflection of the roof caused by inadequate principals so that it had to be strengthened at a cost of £300.[139]

Gladstone's return to power in 1880 marked the resumption of the policy of centralisation. The Science and Art Department's independent architectural office was abolished and Scott dismissed in March 1882; funds authorised by the Treasury were blocked by an unsympathetic First Commissioner, Shaw Lefevre; and in 1885 the Treasury itself disallowed further expenditure in favour of the defence ministries project and the new General Post Office.[140] By 1890, however, a Liberal Unionist chancellor, Goschen, was persuaded by the congestion in the museum of the need to complete it, and authorised an architectural competition for designs.[141] With the return in 1892 of Gladstone and Lefevre, the Treasury stopped all preparations for new buildings.[142] Not until the Conservative Akers-Douglas's major public works scheme under a system of loan finance came into being was work resumed, partly at least under the influence of a select committee in 1897 on the South Kensington Museums which drew urgent attention to the fire risks from inflammable temporary buildings and private residences.[143] In a second report, the committee again stressed the importance of 'immediate action' against fire, and the need to complete the buildings east of Exhibition Road for the 'safe deposit and satisfactory exhibition of the art collections (including the Indian section now on the west side of the road in a hired building)'.[144] A resumed committee the following session recommended that the whole area east of Exhibition Road be devoted to art, with science on the west side.[145] Externally completed in 1906, the 'Victoria and Albert Museum' was opened formally in June 1909 [Pl. 289].

289. Victoria and Albert (formerly South Kensington) Museum, A. Webb: final plan, 1904. He had in 1899 aligned the western side with Exhibition Road, curved the 720ft Cromwell Road front, and introduced a long eastern and western halls immediately behind the front galleries, for large architectural exhibits. He now made changes in detail, including designing the octagon court.

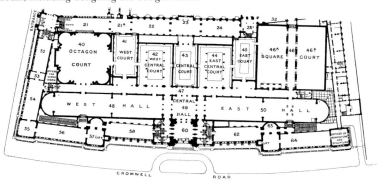

Admiralty Extension

Perhaps sorriest of all the building sagas of our period, however, was that of the Admiralty Extension. As we have seen, Lefevre as First Commissioner had persuaded the second Gladstone administration to undertake a new Admiralty and War Office in juxtaposition on the site of the Old Admiralty in Whitehall and premises to the rear in Spring Gardens [Pl. 132]. 'Economists' in both parties, led by W.H. Smith for the Conservatives and Sir William Harcourt for the Liberals, obtained a select committee that overturned the previous decisions,[146] recommending the quick fix of an additional block to the Old Admiralty building, which professional advisers suggested could be built for between £120,000 and £160,000 within two or three years [Pl. 133].[147] The new War Office was deferred.

Leeming Brothers, the disappointed architects of the big scheme, were recommended for undertaking the small one, and produced a rapid plan and an estimate of £192,600, including £7600 for alterations to the Old Admiralty.[148] On this basis, the Commons approved the change of scheme. The new block at nearly 45,000 sq.ft would more than treble the Old Admiralty, and would take about three years, allowing six months for preparing plans and quantities, nine months for the foundations (known to require 'a great amount of work'), and 21 months for the building itself.[149] This was to be a plain building, organised on the 'bank parlour system' for large numbers of clerks working together under a supervisor – particularly applicable to the accountant-general's office, hitherto in old houses in Spring Gardens.

To avoid a double remove, the Admiralty then decided that the extension would have to be built in two stages, naturally prolonging the operation. The Admiralty's changes of mind have been described in chapter 9. Because of the changes of plan, only £2600 was spent of the 1888/89 Vote. When the Works applied for £30,000 for 1889/90, the Treasury cut the Vote to £5000, of which £5 11s.2d. were spent by 31 December 1889, shortly after the tender for foundations of Block I had been accepted at £21,485. In the next 12 months expenditure rose to nearly £16,000. The excavators had to go to a great depth to secure a firm foundation, costing an additional £17,800, but furnishing a second basement, and taking about 15 months to complete as against the estimated nine. A revised estimate was submitted of £226,000, including the architects' commission, previously omitted through some confusion in the Office. 1891 was marked by a six-month strike and lock-out in which the Amalgamated Society of Carpenters and Joiners scored a partial victory over the London Master Builders, leading to an all-round increase in wages, which held up preparation of tenders for the superstructure. To the end of November only £1838 had been spent, though by April the year's total was nearly £10,000. In February 1892 the Treasury cut an allocation of £50,000 for 1892/93 by £10,000 because of 'heavy demands upon the Exchequer'; and for once the whole sum was used up.[150]

Work on the superstructure by new contractors, Shillitoe & Son, amounting to already nearly £27,000 had been done by 15 November 1891, and the architects put in a second revised estimate of no less than £291,000, of which £110,000 were for Block II, joining the western Block I to the Old Admiralty [Pl. 133]. Leemings explained this by the ten per cent advance in building wages as a result of the strike, their too sanguine view of the foundations, and their lack of adequate information until a contract had been let for the superstructure. The estimate submitted to the Treasury in December was £304,000, the Office deploring Leemings' lack of foresight but arguing that 'the condition of the building trade during the last three or four years has been so disturbed that it has been extremely difficult to reckon on the prices at which Builders

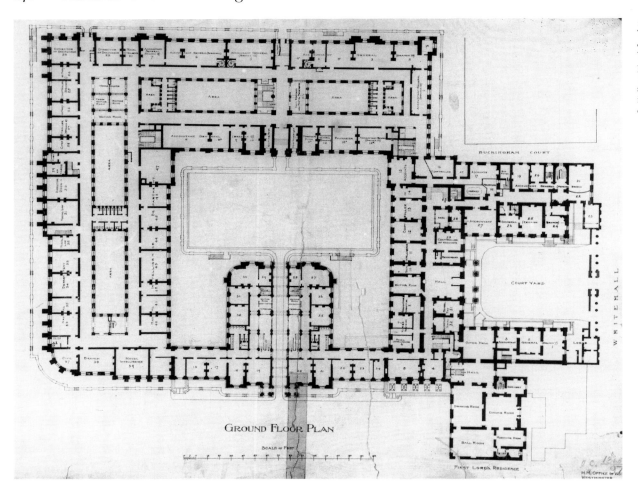

GROUND FLOOR PLAN

SCALE OF FEET

290. The Admiralty, Plan, 1905. The Old Admiralty is on three sides of the eastern courtyard opening on Whitehall, the First Lord's House projecting southwards. On the left (west) is Leemings' Block I Extension; Block II on the north connects it with the old building; and Block III closes the quadrangle on the south.

would venture to tender for works of great magnitude'. Block I was finished in November 1895 at a total estimated cost of £163,700.[151]

The site for Block II[152] was not cleared until mid-1896. A tender from Mowlems of £103,000 plus £2500 for the most recent increase in wages was accepted in July. Once again, there were difficulties with the foundations, those adjoining the old building proving far worse than anticipated. Similarly, pinning down the Admiralty to a definite assignment of rooms proved onerous, the hydrographer (as in Block I) especially troublesome. By December, the Office was taking £340,000 as a provisional estimate for the entire job. The architects' gruesome experiences with Block I at least assisted them in coping with Block II; expenditure rose from £18,000 in 1896/97 to £40,000 in 1897/98, and £50,000 the following year.[153]

With the invention of the cordite-firing gun it had been necessary to launch a new naval building programme, initiated by Lord Spencer in 1894–5; but the new battleships rapidly became obsolete; more secure bases were needed, and new barracks. Between 1886 and 1900 the naval estimates doubled.[154] To handle the additional work-load imposed by the Naval Works Loans Act of 1895 and the much enlarged department of the Director of Works, there was a very large demand for new offices. Under the Public Buildings Expenses Act of 1897, £150,000 was allocated for a further extension of the Admiralty headquarters, but commencement was delayed by a fierce argument between the Admiralty, pressing for building on the Charing Cross front, and the Office of Works, which preferred the ampler solution ultimately adopted after reference to the cabinet.[155] A wing, linking the southern end of Block I with the Old Admiralty and turning the Admiralty garden into a courtyard, was commissioned in December 1900, a

decision that involved raising the central dome of the northern Block II several feet so that it might be seen from the Park, raising the southern cupola on Block I, and creating a balancing cupola at the south-east angle of the building [Pl. 187]. Leemings were instructed to proceed 'with the utmost possible despatch', on an estimate of £140,000 plus five per cent commission.[156]

Tenders for the foundations were advertised for 'in the usual papers' in April.[157] The successful bidders were J. Chessum & Sons of Monier Street, Bow, at £15,926 (the highest, Foster Bros. at £39,885).[158] Work could not begin before 18 June because of the distribution of medals for the South African War on Horse Guards Parade, but it then soon became evident that the foundations were once again to give trouble: in one corner of the site where a test borehole had not been made, the level of the London clay – to which the foundation must be taken – varied in a 'most remarkable manner'. Although, warned by experience, Leemings had allowed the large sum of £20,000 for foundations, by February 1902 they were having to ask for another £3600 for underpinning the excavation adjacent to the Old Admiralty in addition to £3000 that they thought could be assimilated in the original estimate: the clay was 11 ft 6 ins lower than had been anticipated.[159]

A dispute had already developed in January between the architects and the contractor over discontinuing pumping operations that Leemings believed might endanger the Old Admiralty, which was built on piles. Chessums called in expert opinion, sought to repudiate responsibility in carrying out the architects' instructions, and complained that all the underpinning works were completely different from those shewn in their contract.[160] During the summer, the same question arose again, and Leemings also insisted on the need for piling being set beneath the excavations. Chessums prevaricated, complaining that setting the piles would cause further delays that might take them into the bad weather which would increase the cost. Serious settlements developed in the Old Admiralty in July 1902, and the contractors finally obeyed instructions. Nevertheless, disagreements continued. Chessums claimed more than £11,000 for extra and stronger timbers, 'excessive shoring', and piling and strutting to the under-pinning, which led in February 1902 to the appointment of an arbitrator. E.A. Gruning's award was generally favourable to the official argument, and he finally awarded Chessums an additional £2861, bringing expenditure on Block III foundations to some £23,000.[161]

It was consequently July 1903 before the superstructure contract for Block III was let to Holloway Bros at £87,700.[162] The superstructure was erected without further problems. Thus, when the extension was completed in 1905, not less than £400,000 and 18 years had been spent on what was intended to be a cheap and speedy operation. In architectural terms, too, the result was a disaster, 'one of the most deplorable buildings ever seen in this country'.[163] Yet the Admiralty's appetite for space was still unsatisfied: the 1903 Public Buildings' Expenses Act provided another £100,000, which was used in 1907–14 in conjunction with Aston Webb's design for a triumphal arch between the Mall and Charing Cross (part of the Queen Victoria Memorial) to supply new houses for the first lord and senior naval lord (subsequently modified to create office space).[164] Once again, foundations caused delay: a disused six-foot sewer was discovered which had to be bricked up, and one crossing the site that could not be diverted gave 'infinite trouble'.[165] Difficulties in obtaining possession of part of the site caused further long delay, and it was not until 1908–09 that much progress was made on the buildings.[166]

Public Offices

Under the regime of Akers-Douglas, First Commissioner 1895–1902, and those of his successors before the First World War, important improvements were made. Akers-Douglas introduced a long-term system of financing public buildings by borrowing a lump sum from surplus revenue,[167] so that a coherent programme

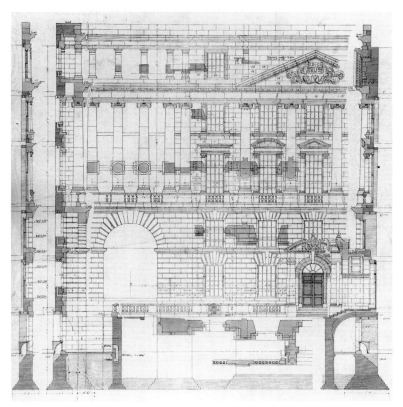

292. New War Office, W. Young. Detail of west side of main courtyard.

could be undertaken free from the vicissitudes of parliamentary changes of mind. Thus the great blocks of the new War Office [Pl. 292], nearly opposite the Horse Guards, and the New Public Offices on Parliament and Great George Streets [Pl. 291] could be undertaken successfully. To ensure completion on schedule, much overtime was worked, especially carpenters and joiners engaged in internal works.[168] Ministers in this period also developed the Technical Branch of the Office of Works, and were able to entrust to it a considerable number of sizeable projects, including the Chancery Lane front of the Public Record Office (from 1893), the Land Registry in Lincoln's Inn Fields (in two stages), a western extension of the Royal Courts of Justice, large extensions to the Patent Office and the National Gallery [Pl. 293], the Science Museum at South Kensington, offices for the Board of Agriculture in Whitehall Place and for the Public Trustee in Kingsway, and a new Stationery Office, mostly undertaken between 1906 and 1913.[169]

The use of new building materials and techniques enabled very large buildings to be carried out at moderate cost. Tanner's King Edward Buildings, for the new Post Office headquarters in the City (1907–11), were constructed in reinforced concrete according to the Hennebique system of which Mouchel & Partners were the English agents, the first large-scale use in London.[170] The Stationery Office of 1912, partly offices, but largely a warehouse, on an inexpensive South Bank site, followed suit.[171] The same system was also employed for the important weight-bearing members of the Board of Agriculture.[172] New techniques were similarly employed in the Public Trustee Office, built in the London County Council's Kingsway in 1912–16, but there steel framing was employed. No great problems emerged in the use of these relatively experimental processes, and the Office of Works was praised for its innovatory achievements [Pl. 202, 204, 140].

These projects were not immune from the serious labour disputes of the years just before the Great War. Previously, although

291. New Public Offices, Westminster, J.M. Brydon and H. Tanner. Detail of centrepiece to the Park: elevation and section.

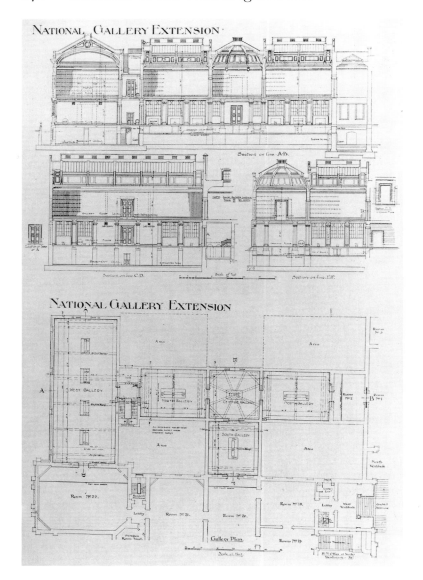

293.   National Gallery western extension, H.N. Hawkes, 1907—11:
a. Plan and section shewing five new galleries built over St George's barrack yard.
b. A gallery, shewing lighting from roof and general reticence of decoration.

strikes had interrupted public works, as at the Houses of Parliament in 1841 and the New Law Courts in 1877–8, the contractors had been able to obtain substitute labour and continue the works. The carpenters' and joiners' strike of May 1891,[173] mentioned above, followed by a general lock-out by the master builders,[174] affected work on the Patent Office as well as the Admiralty extension; and an engineers' strike delayed iron work on the Public Record Office in 1897–8.[175] But the growth of unionisation in the early twentieth century, particularly in the transport industries, meant that trade disputes could disrupt public works even without the contractors being directly involved, and without their being able to affect the issue. The Stationery Office was delayed by the coal and dock strikes of 1912, and the very great difficulty thereby caused in obtaining materials; it was further delayed by the London building trades dispute of 1914, which also adversely affected the Public Trustee Office and the new Science Museum, a dispute that was abruptly ended with the outbreak of war.[176]

Envoi

W E H A V E A N A L Y S E D the principal factors affecting English government building in London during the Victorian and Edwardian periods, building brought pretty well to a halt by the First World War. What conclusions can be drawn?

The most obvious, perhaps, is that parliamentary government was a messy way of setting about the job. The House of Commons had a 'mischievous propensity' for taking a practical part in the regulation of details 'entirely beyond its grasp'.[1] Parliamentary government today with the large 'payload' vote dominating the governing party, and a strict regime of party whipping is no doubt a different creature from that which existed in mid-Victorian England before the obstructive tactics of Irish nationalists forced governments to acquire greater control over the parliamentary timetable. But even in today's highly organised system it is difficult to fit into the parliamentary session all that ministers wish. In the period we have been examining, time after time bills were launched only to be abandoned because of lack of time, or because of threats of opposition that would cause disruption of the whole ministerial programme. As Lefevre remarked of works in hand in 1882,

> in the present state of business of the House of Commons it is impossible to find time for an adequate explanation . . . ; to attempt to do so would infallibly wreck them [the works], for the smallest sympton of opposition would, for want of time, avail to prevent any measure, not of the first political necessity, being passed. An administrator under the present scheme of things must above all things court silence, and avoid presenting more opportunities for criticism, favourable or unfavourable, than is absolutely necessary.[2]

Activity was often determined by the outlook of ministers. Even in periods of flourishing revenue (as under Goschen in 1888–92), little might be done, which suggests that something depended on the energy and capacity of the Works Minister. Once set in motion, building schemes might run into a minefield of connoisseurship or a heavy barrage of commonsensical cost-cutting or, in the later years of our period, Irish obstructionism. There was every justification for the accusation that the House of Commons was 'the worst building committee in the world'.[3] On the other hand, ministers did not encourage efforts to establish an advisory council for public buildings, recognising that the Commons must have the ultimate voice.

In the 1850s and 1860s particularly, governments could not be certain of their majorities, and interested parties could whip up opposition on a particular issue enough to upset government policy, especially if they could attract the support of *The Times*, as over the purchase of the 1862 Exhibition building, or the siting of the National Gallery. Building questions were too contentious to be embarked on while they could be avoided. Questions of sanitation apart, there was remarkably little internal pressure for new offices, partly, no doubt, because of the usually spacious accommodation afforded senior officials, partly because of the usually short working day, but also because of the lack of unionisation. Those who experienced the worst working conditions were 'temporary' staff, even though in some establishments they might have been serving for years on end.

In an age of low taxation and strictly balanced budgets, eliminating the capital cost of a new building could well provide the required budgetary savings; few would complain; and it was an easy course for a harassed chancellor. But what of external pressures? The influential quarterlies evinced no enthusiasm for the development of a comfortably-housed bureaucracy, though they might occasionally push for more gallery-room or museum-space. The powerful *Times* spoke with forked tongue,[4] swaying often with opinion in the clubs as often as it swayed that opinion. Much of improvement urged could be dismissed as 'metropolitan', to be funded, if they chose, by the metropolitan ratepayers. The views of the professionals could be shrugged off as self-interested. The RIBA represented only a small number of architects until about the turn of the century; the professional press was seldom united. Large-circulation illustrated periodicals in the style of the *Illustrated London News* might widen public knowledge of designs, but offered no editorial policy that might influence governments.

It is not surprising in these circumstances that the third Salisbury administration was able to adopt a non-popular policy in its building concerns; to abandon the architectural competition which to an uninformed public seemed the best means of securing the best designs; and to select its architects for itself – with judiciously invited assistance from the profession's formal leaders. Fortunate in coming into office at a time of successive large annual revenue surpluses (thanks in part to the unexpectedly large proceeds of Harcourt's controversial death duties), and when ministerial control over the House had been tightened, it was even able to establish long-term funding for a major programme of public buildings to overcome years of hesitation and neglect, and to remove it from the obstacle-course of annual supply Votes.

At the same time, the very extensive run-of-the-mill new building work called for by the revenue services and above all the Post Office, and for the county courts, at once obliged and enabled the establishing of a government architectural service capable of designing and carrying out large-scale works of a standard certainly equal to the generality of similar work in the private or municipal sector. Moreover, thanks to Crown exemption from inhibiting regulations of the London Building Acts, the Office of Works was capable of instructive technical innovation, such as large-scale reinforced-concrete structures. The *Builder*, noting that the new Post Office headquarters in Newgate Street was 'the first example of reinforced concrete construction on an important scale undertaken in the metropolis', commented:[5]

> Therefore the building stands as an authoritative demonstration of the fact that the new system of construction need no longer

be regarded as an experiment in any sense of the term. The enlightened policy displayed by H.M. Office of Works in thus adopting reinforced concrete is particularly commendable, and it is to be hoped that one result will be the abandonment of the vexatious restrictions hitherto placed on the employment of the same material by the Local Government Board. The new building certainly constitutes a valuable object-lesson for architects, and demonstrates also the advantages which can be secured by reinforced concrete construction when unfettered by regulations such as those contained in the London Building Act. . . .

Our period was also one that, however heterogeneous stylistically, was homogeneous in its prevalent conviction that a concentration of purpose-designed offices was the most efficient means of governing, in terms of both cost and administrative time. Because ministers sat in parliament, that concentration had to be in Westminster. Other sectors of governmental activity also had their foci: the Post Office in the centre of the business area; the Law Courts removed from Westminster to the legal quarter, between the inns of court, with close at hand such cognate functions as the Record Office (originally for legal records), the Land Registry, the Patent Office, and the office of a new legal functionary, the Public Trustee. Although the National Gallery remained in Trafalgar Square, thanks in part at least to improvements in the microclimate, and the Royal Academy not far away in Piccadilly, a greenfield site supplied by the commissioners of the 1851 Exhibition provided such a focus for institutions of Art and Science, a location made possible by the improvements in metropolitan communications offered by the underground railway.

The closing decades of the nineteenth century saw also the development of a popular awareness of Britain's role as the centre of a world-wide empire, much of it settled by men of British race, governed from London; an awareness, too, of the nation's vast increase in wealth,[6] even if characterised by a shift from manufactures to trade and finance. This consciousness was embodied in such imperial spectacles as the Jubilees of 1887 and 1897 and the coronations of 1902 and 1911; and also in the palaces of the great imperial financial and trading enterprises. Little wonder, then, that the early twentieth century saw governments responding with their own imperial administrative palaces. 'Maintenance of Empire', it has been suggested, was seen as 'the only way to keep Britain at the forefront of world affairs'; governments were therefore concerned to 'keep Britain at the centre of her empire'; and saw 'the symbolic presentation of Britain as an Imperial power' as a means to that end.[7] Let there arise a new Whitehall for imperial administration, a new South Kensington for an imperial culture-centre of art and science.

But war unparalleled interrupted the wide-ranging plans. If half-hearted efforts saw some continuation at South Kensington, disturbed economic conditions between the two World Wars ensured that at Westminster the halt on government building imposed in 1915 was prolonged. The consequence was a back-sliding to Victorian circumstances. An official leaflet, c.1969, remarked that

> Only 30 per cent of the Civil Servants working in central London occupy buildings owned by the Crown; the remainder are in leased offices which impose a heavy and increasing burden of rentals on the taxpayer. Many of these leases will terminate during the next twelve years; the Ministry cannot expect to retain all these offices and will have to pay higher rents for those it keeps. Even the few office buildings which the Government owns are obsolescent; 80 per cent of them are over 50 years old. A considerable amount of Government headquarters' work has been dispersed and plans are in hand to move more. . . . But the Whitehall area is the centre of the country's administration; Ministers and their staffs must be near Parliament; and the staff who have to work in central London must be properly housed for efficient working. Moreover, land in Whitehall is too expensive to waste.[8]

Similar problems of congestion were facing the National Gallery, the Public Record Office, and the national museums – most notably in respect of the British Museum library, of which the proposed extension involved lengthy controversy with the local authority and conservation groups.

Although the 1950s and 1960s had seen the realisation of the great Whitehall Gardens project (originally conceived for the Board of Trade, but actually occupied by the expanded administration of a shrinking defence force), the further proposal for comprehensively redeveloping (i.e. clearing and starting from scratch as in previous schemes) the southernmost quarter, between the new offices and the Houses of Parliament, envisaged in 1969–72, was abandoned because of economic circumstances, and a highly successful refurbishment substituted with a small measure of admirable new building. Whether more central offices will be demanded in the foreseeable future is problematical. Just as new technology influenced the location of Victorian galleries and museums, so today the telephone, fax machine and computer have facilitated the removal from London of large offices engaged in routine operations to areas in which the decay of basic industries left many unemployed. Furthermore a new ethos of government aims at handing over tasks once performed by civil servants in their ministries to independent or semi-independent 'agencies' located out of the capital; indeed, an anti-London culture seems to have developed in governing circles, so that London is in danger of losing features long regarded as proper attributes of a capital city.

A final question that calls for assessment is one that each generation will answer for itself: what measure of success did the English system of public building achieve between 1850 and 1915? Summerson has roundly condemned it, at the same time praising the dubious achievement of a Beaux-Arts architect in a minor Continental neighbour.[9] The lack of formal educational training in England was undeniably a handicap when architects were called upon to design a large-scale complex structure such as a major ministry. But the English system encouraged an originality not always evident in the Beaux-Arts tradition. Viewed as townscape, Whitehall is at least respectable. No one building may display the brilliance of Louis Duc's western façade of the Palais de Justice in Paris [Pl. 182], but we have a range of handsome buildings that declare themselves the ministries of a great power. The Law Courts are a remarkably original solution, effective probably only in Gothic, to the perennial problem of creating a monumental building along a narrow street. And the British Museum and the institutions of Science and Art at South Kensington present a catalogue of innovations in design and materials that stand comparison with Continental rivals.

APPENDIX 1

First Commissioners of Works, 1851–1915

1 Aug. 1851	Lord Seymour (L)
4 Mar. 1852	Lord John Manners* (C)
5 Jan. 1853	Sir William Molesworth, Bt* (L)
21 July 1855	Sir Benjamin Hall, Bt (L)
26 Feb. 1858	Lord John Manners* (C)
18 June 1859	Hon. Henry Fitzroy (L) Died 22 Dec. 1859
9 Feb. 1860	Hon. William Cowper (L)
6 July 1866	Lord John Manners* (C)
9 Dec. 1868	Austen Henry Layard (L)
26 Oct. 1869	Acton Smee Ayrton (L)
11 Aug. 1873	William Adam (L)
21 Mar. 1874	Lord Henry Lennox (C)
14 Aug. 1876	Hon. Gerard Noel (C)
3 May 1880	William Adam (L)
29 Nov. 1880	George Shaw Lefevre (L)
13 Feb. 1885	Earl of Rosebery (L). Also Lord Privy Seal*
24 June 1885	Hon. David Plunket (C)
17 Feb. 1886	Earl of Morley (L)
16 Apr. 1886	Earl of Elgin (L)
5 Aug. 1886	Hon. David Plunket (C)
18 Aug. 1892	George Shaw Lefevre* (L)
10 Mar. 1894	Herbert Gladstone (L)
4 July 1895	Aretas Akers-Douglas* (C)
11 Aug. 1902	Lord Windsor* (C)
10 Dec. 1905	Lewis Vernon Harcourt* (L)
3 Nov. 1910	Earl Beauchamp* (L)
6 Aug. 1914	Lord Emmott* (L)
25 May 1915	Lewis Vernon Harcourt* (L)

* with seat in Cabinet

Sources: C. Cook & B. Keith, *British Historical Facts 1830–1900* (1975), 55; D. & G. Butler, *British Political Facts 1900–1985* (1986).

C: Conservative   L: Liberal

APPENDIX 2

Secretaries of the Office of Works, 1851–1915

Aug. 1851	Trenham Walshman Philipps (1795–1855), private secretary to Chief Commissioner of Office of Woods and Works from 1827; ret. 6 Nov. and d.27 Nov. 1855
Nov. 1855	Alfred Austin (1805–84)
1 Jan. 1869	George Russell (1830–1911), res. 22 Apr. 1874
10 Aug. 1874	Algernon Bertram Mitford (1837–1916)
June 1886	Henry Primrose (1846–1923)
June 1895	Hon. Reginald Brett (1852–1930), suc. as Lord Esher, 1898
June 1902	Hon. Sir Schomberg McDonnell (1861–1915)
May 1912	Lionel Earle (1866–1948)

a. Major Government Building Works, 1850–1915

Department	Date	Building cost, £000s	Architect	Main Contractor Foundations	Superstructure
Admiralty Extensions					
Block I (West)	1888–95	167	Leeming	W. Webster	Shillitoe & Son
Block II (North)	1896–1901	146	Bros	J. Mowlem & Co.	
Blocks III & IV (South & Mall)	1901/2–1912/13	350	Leemings/Webb	J. Chessum	Holloway Bros (III only)
Residences (Mall)	1905/6–13	76	A. Webb	J. Mowlem & Co. (IV also)	
Agriculture, Board of	1910/11–14/15	58	H.N. Hawkes & H.A. Collins	Holloway Bros	
					Higgs & Hill Ltd
Bankruptcy Buildings, Carey St.	1890–2	70	J. Taylor	Foster & Dicksee	
British Museum,					
Reading Room	1854–60	61	S. Smirke	Baker & Fielden	
'White' Building	1882–4	—	J. Taylor	G.W. Booth	
Edward VII Galleries	1906/07–14/15	152	J.J. Burnet	C. Wall Ltd	W.E. Blake Ltd
Buckingham Palace, ballroom etc.	1854/5	91	J. Pennethorne	Thomas Cubitt	
Re-fronting	1913	50	A. Webb	J. Mowlem & Co.	
Burlington House,			R.R. Banks &		Mansfield & Price (failed)
Learned Societies	1868/9–76/7	159	C. Barry jnr	G. Trollope	Perry & Co.
Foreign Office	1862/3–68/9	285	Geo. G. Scott	J. Kelk	G. Smith & Taylor
General Post Office,					
West	1869–75	—	J. Williams		
North	1888–97	220	H. Tanner	J.T. Chappell	
Edward VII Building	1907–13	323	H. Tanner	Holloway Bros	
Post Office Savings Bank, Hammersmith	1899–1905	298	H. Tanner	Foster & Dicksee	Kirk & Randall
Home & Colonial Offices	1868/9–78/9	307	Geo. G. Scott	Jackson & Shaw	
Houses of Parliament completion	1852–60	261	Sir C. Barry	John Jay	
	1865–7	33	E.M. Barry	William Field	
India Office	1862/3–68/9	350	Geo. G. Scott & M.D. Wyatt	J. Kelk	G. Smith & Taylor
Land Registry,					
Block I	1902/3–06/7	58	H. Tanner	T.H. Kingerlee	
Block II	1911/12–13/14	31	R.J. Allison	F.T. Thorne	
National Gallery,					
Alterations	1860/1–61/2	16	J. Pennethorne	W. Cubitt & Co.	
East	1870/1–76/7	98	E.M. Barry	G.W. Booth	
North	1884/5–87/8	49	J. Taylor	J. Mowlem & Co.	J. Stephens
West	1907/8–11/12	38	H.N. Hawkes	J. Allen & Sons	F. & H.F. Higgs
National Portrait Gallery	1890/1–94/5	96	E. Christian	J. Shillitoe & Son	
Natural History Museum	1872/3–84/5	696	A. Waterhouse	Geo. Baker & Son	
New Public Offices, Great George Street					
(I)	1899–1908	650	J.M. Brydon &	J. Mowlem	Spencer, Santo & Co.
(II)	1911/12–1914/15	182	H. Tanner	F.G. Minter	Holloway Bros
Ordnance Office	1851/2–53/4	22	J. Pennethorne	W. Holland	
Patent Office	1892/3–1904/5	137	J. Taylor	B.E. Nightingale*	
	1905/6–07/8	29	H.N. Hawkes	J. Smith & Sons Ltd (1905)	
	1908/9–12/13	91	H.N. Hawkes	E. Lawrance & Son (1911)	
Public Record Office,					
North	1850/1–58/9	86	J. Pennethorne	Lee & Son	
East	1863/4–67/8	53	J. Pennethorne	Piper & Whealer	
Tower and North-east	1868/9–71/2	59	J. Pennethorne	Jackson & Shaw	
West, Block A	1891/2–95/6	77	J. Taylor	Brass & Son	Foster & Dicksee
Block B	1895/6–1900/1	54	J. Taylor	Foster & Dicksee	
Public Trustee Office	1912/13–14/15	55	A.J. Pitcher & H.A. Collins	Kingerlee & Son	Galbraith Bros
Royal College of Science	1900/1–05/6	304	A. Webb	Leslie & Co.	
Royal Courts of Justice	1871/2–84/5	1013	G.E. Street	Dove Bros	J. Bull & Sons
West Block	1908/9–14/15	94	H. Tanner	Foster & Dicksee	Spencer, Santo & Co.
Somerset House West	1852/3–57/8	88	J. Pennethorne	J. Kelk	
South Kensington Museum,†					
Cast Courts	1868–73	35	H. Scott	Geo. Smith & Co.	
Science Schools	1867–74	31	H. Scott	Geo. Smith & Co.	
Art Library	1878/9–83/4	65	H. Scott	Perry & Co.	
Completion	1899/1900–1910/11	897	A. Webb	Leslie & Co.	Holliday & Greenwood
Stationery Office, conversion	1853–5	26	J. Pennethorne	T. Piper	
	1910/11–14/15	126	R.J. Allison	Perry & Co. Ltd.	
New University of London	1866/7–71/2	98	J. Pennethorne	Jackson & Shaw	
War Office, Whitehall	1899/1900–1907/8	672	W. Young	J. Mowlem & Co.	Foster & Dicksee
Westminster Hall,					
Restoration	1886/7–90/1	44	J.L. Pearson	J. Shillitoe & Son	
Woods & Forests, Office of	1907–10	—	J. Murray	J. Mowlem & Co.	

*J.T. Chappell secured the second contract (1893) but relinquished it to Nightingale, who held the first (1892) and third (1895, 1896) contracts. H.H. Bartlett executed the Library contract (1899) and Perry & Co. the 1903 extension.
†Buildings between 1855 and c.1867 executed in a series of small contracts.

Sources: PP Appropriation Accounts; PRO, Work 13 *sub* contract.

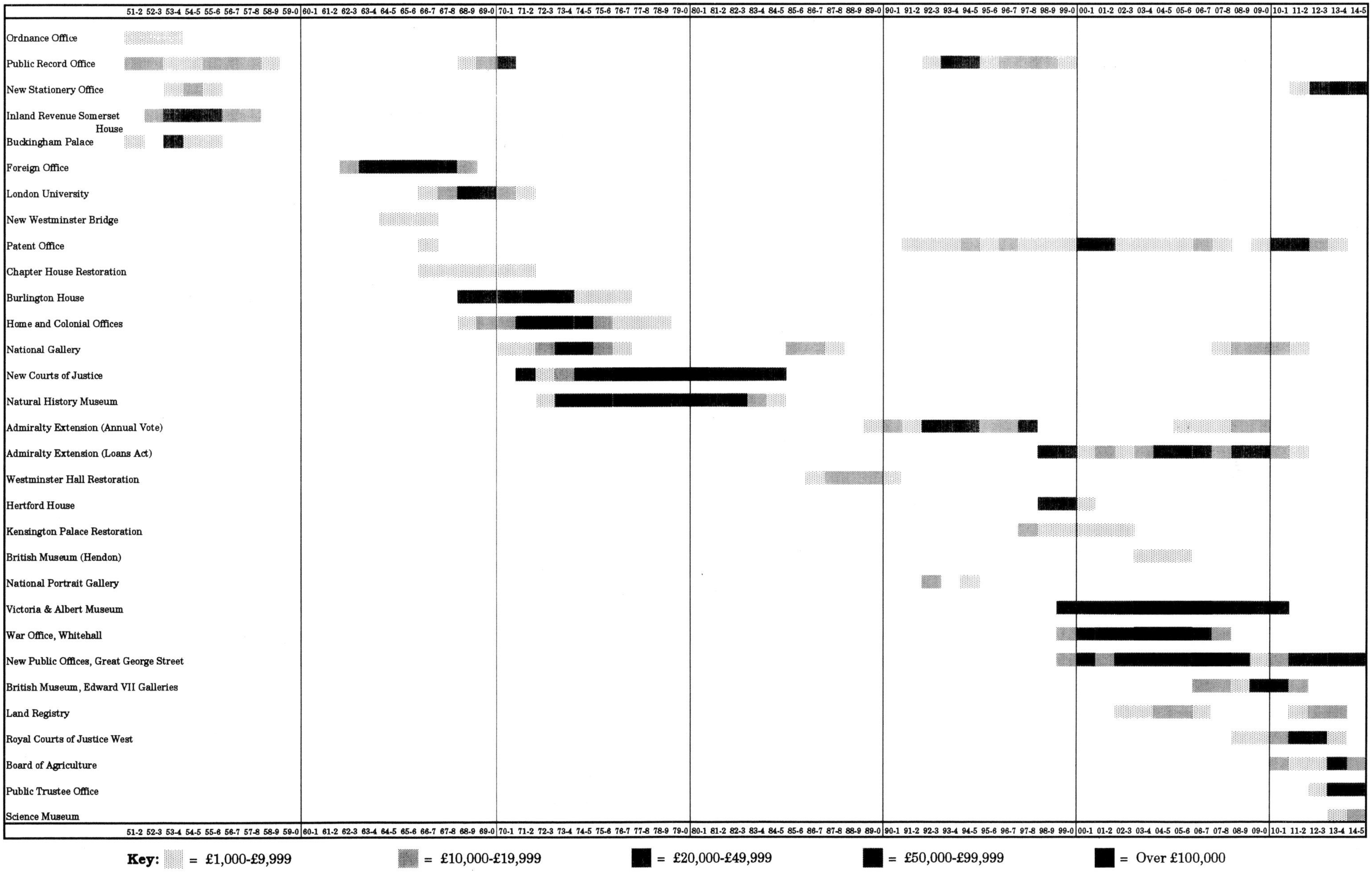
Ordnance Office
Public Record Office
New Stationery Office
Inland Revenue Somerset House
Buckingham Palace
Foreign Office
London University
New Westminster Bridge
Patent Office
Chapter House Restoration
Burlington House
Home and Colonial Offices
National Gallery
New Courts of Justice
Natural History Museum
Admiralty Extension (Annual Vote)
Admiralty Extension (Loans Act)
Westminster Hall Restoration
Hertford House
Kensington Palace Restoration
British Museum (Hendon)
National Portrait Gallery
Victoria & Albert Museum
War Office, Whitehall
New Public Offices, Great George Street
British Museum, Edward VII Galleries
Land Registry
Royal Courts of Justice West
Board of Agriculture
Public Trustee Office
Science Museum
51-2 52-3 53-4 54-5 55-6 56-7 57-8 58-9 59-0 60-1 61-2 62-3 63-4 64-5 65-6 66-7 67-8 68-9 69-0 70-1 71-2 72-3 73-4 74-5 75-6 76-7 77-8 78-9 79-0 80-1 81-2 82-3 83-4 84-5 85-6 86-7 87-8 88-9 89-0 90-1 91-2 92-3 93-4 94-5 95-6 96-7 97-8 98-9 99-0 00-1 01-2 02-3 03-4 04-5 05-6 06-7 07-8 08-9 09-0 10-1 11-2 12-3 13-4 14-5
Key: = £1,000-£9,999
= £10,000-£19,999
= £20,000-£49,999
= £50,000-£99,999
= Over £100,000

Notes: 1) Between 1896/7 and 1914/5 more than £5,000,000 were expended under the Public Buildings (Sites/Expenses) Loans Acts (including some £3,500,000 on building), while works on the annual Parliamentary Vote were occasionally proceeding simultaneously (as on the Admiralty). Post Office and Police buildings are excluded from this diagram.
2) So far as is possible to distinguish, site costs have been excluded. New building at the British & South Kensington Museums has been omitted because it is not distinguished from annual maintenance.

b. Annual expenditure on new public buildings in London, 1851–1915.
Source: PP, Appropriation Accounts.

APPENDIX 4

The Leading Characters

AKERS-DOUGLAS, Aretas, 1851–1926. *Educ.* Eton & Univ. Coll. Oxford. *Suc.* to estates of kinsman James Douglas 1875. MP (Cons.) 1880–1911. Opposition whip 1883; Treasury sec. 1885–6, 1886–92; Opposition chief whip 1892–5; FCW (Cabinet) 1895–1902; Home Sec. 1902–05. *Cr.* Viscount Chilston, 1911. Industrious, tenacious, discreet; a dextrous politician of good judgement.

AYRTON, Acton Smee, 1816–86. Born at Kew, practised as solicitor at Bombay, returning 1850. Barrister (M.T.) 1853. MP (Rad.) 1857–74 (Tower Hamlets). Chaired s.cs. on metropolitan questions, notably local govt & taxation 1861, 1866). Treasury sec. 1868–9; FCW 1869–73; Judge-adv.-gen. 1873–4. A zealous economist, brusque in manner, he alienated the aesthetic interest, but introduced important reforms at OW.

BAILLIE COCHRANE, Alexander Dundas Wishart Ross, 1816–90. S. and h. of Admiral Sir T.J. Cochrane, G.C.B. *Educ.* Eton & Trinity Coll. Camb. MP (Cons.) 1841–6, 1847–52, 1857, 1859–68, 1870–80. Member, Young England, figures as 'Lord Buckhurst' in Disraeli's *Coningsby. Cr.* Baron Lamington 1880. Trustee N.P.G. 1876–d.

BARRY, Charles, 1795–1860. Architect. Articled to Middleton & Bailey, surveyors. Grand tour 1817–20 included Near East. Designed several churches for Church Building Commn; Travellers' Club (Italianate), 1829; Reform Club 1837. Won competition for New Houses of Parliament, 1836, and employed thereon until d. Laid out Trafalgar Square 1842–5; reconstructed BoT and H.O. 1846. Also Bridgwater Ho. 1847, Halifax Town Hall 1860, and considerable country-house practice. Kt 1852.

BARRY, Charles, jnr, 1823–1900. Architect. Eldest s. of preceding; assisted fa. until 1847, when entered partnership with R.R. Banks (1813–72). Competitors for New Govt Offices 1856–7, awarded 2nd premium for F.O. Appointed to design accommodation for Learned Socs, Burlington House, 1860, 1868 (built 1869–74). Also Dulwich Coll. 1868–70; Institution of Civil Engineers, Gt George St, 1896. PRIBA 1876–9; gold medal 1877.

BARRY, Edward Middleton, 1830–80. Architect. Yngr s. of (Sir) Charles BARRY. Articled to T.H. Wyatt, then joining his fa.'s practice; suc. him as architect at Houses of Parliament 1860, until 1869, when dismissed by AYRTON. A.R.A. 1861, R.A. 1869; prof. of architecture 1873–83. Selected for limited competitions for Albert Memorial 1863, N.G. 1866, and New Law Courts 1866; judged to have architecturally the most merit for N.G., and best plan for Law Courts. Awarded commission for enlarging N.G. 1868. Also rebuilding Covent Garden Theatre 1857; Cannon St (1864) and Charing Cross (1866–71) Sta. Hotels; grand stair, R.A., Burlington Ho.

BEAUCHAMP, William LYGON, 7th Earl, 1872–1938. Gd-s. by mo. of Lord Mahon, historian (5th E. Stanhope). Landowner (1883, estates of 17,600 acres, worth £25,000 p.a.). *Suc.* fa. 1891. *Educ.* Eton & Ch. Ch. Oxford. London School Board 1897–9. Gov. New South Wales 1899–1902. A Free-trader, joined Lib. Party. P.C. 1906; Lord Steward 1907–10; pres. of Council 1910; FCW (Cabinet) 1910–14; pres. of Council 1914–15. Leader, Lib. Party, HL, 1926–31. K.C.M.G. 1899, K.G. 1914; lord warden of Cinque Ports 1913–33. *M.* sis. of 2nd Duke of Westminster 1902. In 1931, having been denounced to the king by his bro.-in-law as a homosexual, res. offices and went to live in Italy. Provided E. Waugh with a model for Lord Marchmain in *Brideshead Revisited.*

BERESFORD HOPE, see HOPE.

BRETT, Hon. Reginald Baliol, 1852–1930. S. of W.B. Brett, 1st Visc. Esher, MR; *suc.* fa. as 2nd Visc. Esher 1899. *Educ.* Eton & Trinity Coll. Camb. Priv. sec. to Lord Hartington 1878–85. MP (Lib.) 1880–5. Sec. OW 1895–1902. CB 1897, K.C.V.O. 1900, K.C.B. 1902, G.C.V.O. 1908, G.C.B. 1908; dep. constable Windsor Castle 1901, constable 1928; chairman, W.O. Reconstruction cttee 1904; trustee, B.M. In charge of diamond jubilee celebrations, and Q. Victoria's funeral. Co-founder, with LEWIS HARCOURT of London Mus. 1911. *M.* dau. of former Belgian Minister to U.K.

BRYDON, John McKean, 1840–1901. Architect. Articled to David Bryce, Edinburgh. Subsequently with J.J. Stevenson, W.E. Nesfield and R. Norman Shaw. FRIBA 1881, VP, 1899, 1901. Won competitions: Chelsea Vestry Hall, 1885 (Wren Revival); Bath Municipal Buildings, 1891. An influential advocate of reviving style of 17–18 C. Eng. architecture. Appointed for New Public Offices, Great George Street 1898.

BURNS, John Elliot, 1858–1943. 16th child of an engine-fitter, left school at 10, later apprenticed as engineer. Active in labour movements. Worked in W. Africa and studied labour conditions in Europe. Soc. cand. in 1885 gen. election. Tried for seditious conspiracy & acquitted 1886, but imprisoned for public order offence, 'Bloody Sunday', Trafalgar Sq. 1887. Leader, London dock strike 1889. Member LCC 1889–1907. MP (I.L.P.; Lib. from 1906) Battersea 1892–1918. Pres. LGB (Cabinet) 1905–14; pres. BoT 1914, res. on declaration of war. An enthusiastic Londoner.

CHARTERIS, Hon. Francis Richard, 1818–1914; styled Lord ELCHO, 1853–83; Earl of WEMYSS from 1883. S. and h. of 7th (9th but for attainder of 1746) E. of Wemyss. *Educ.* Eton & Ch. Ch. Oxford. MP (Cons.) 1841–6, 1847–83 (Lib.-Cons. from 1855). Jnr lord of Treasury 1853–5. Trustee N.P.G. 1856–66. His two chief interests as MP were the Volunteer Movement and public buildings. Successfully opposed removal of N.G. to Kensington Gore 1856. Chaired s.c. on Hungerford Bridge & Wellington St Viaduct, 1869. Dismayed by AYRTON's appointment as FCW. Patron of W. YOUNG. Fought to have Inigo Jones's Whitehall Palace design adopted for New W.O. 1898–9.

COLE, Henry, 1808–82. *Educ.* Christ's Hosp. Clerk, Record Commn 1823, then sub-commr; asst kpr, PRO 1838–51. Promoted 'Felix Summerley's Art Manufactures' in 1840s. Chairman, Soc. of Arts, 1851–2. R. Commr for Exhibition of 1851. Sec., Dept of Practical Art 1852, Dept of Science & Art 1853–73. Promoted R. Albert Hall 1865–71. K.C.B. 1875. Amiable in private, but widely unpopular as the directing force of 'S. Kensington'.

COWPER (afterwards COWPER-TEMPLE), William Francis, 1811–88. 2nd s. of 5th E. Cowper, and his w. Emily, sis. of 2nd Visct Melbourne (prime minister) – subsequently (1839) w. of 3rd Visct Palmerston (q.v.), who was often said to be Cowper's real fa. *Educ.* Eton. Army, 1827–35. Priv. sec. to Lord Melbourne as prime minster 1835–41. MP (Lib.) 1835–80. Minor office 1841, 1846–Mar. 1852, Dec. 1852–55; pres. Bd of Health 1855–8 with VP of Council (Education) 1857–8; VP BoT 1859–60; FCW 1860–66. Inherited Palmerston's estates on mo.'s d. 1869, taking additional surname Temple. *Cr.* Baron Mount-Temple 1880. A friend of Ruskin.

DISRAELI, Benjamin, 1804–81. S. of Isaac Disraeli, historian of literature. Privately educ. MP (Cons.) 1837–76. Critic of Sir Robert Peel in 1840s, when wrote political novels. Cons. leader in Commons from 1848. Ch. of Exchequer 1852, 1858–9, 1866–7; prime minister 1867–8, 1874–80. *Cr.* E. of Beaconsfield 1876.

ELCHO, Lord: see CHARTERIS.

FERGUSSON, James, 1808–86. *Educ.* Edinburgh High Sch. Spent ten years in India as a merchant, and began study of Indian architecture. Advocated earthwork fortifications 1849; R. Commr, Defences of U.K. 1857. Gen. manager, Crystal Palace Co. 1856–8. Published *Illustrated Handbook of Architecture*, 2 vols., 1855; *Hist. of the Modern Styles of Architecture*, 1862; revised as *Hist. of Architecture in all Countries, from the Earliest Times*, 3 vols., 1865–7; *Hist. of Indian and Eastern Architecture*, 1876. Competed for New Government Offices, 1856–7; judge in Kensington Museums competition 1864. Sec. for public works and buildings (later, inspector of,) in OW 1869. Controversialist in public works issues in 1870s, attacking Street's Law Courts designs, and those of Waterhouse for Nat. Hist. Mus.

GALTON, Douglas Strutt, 1822–99. Yngr s. of a gentry family, cos. of 1st Lord Belper. *Educ.* Rugby, R.M.A. Commissioned in R.E. 1840. Sec. Railway Commn 1847; sec. Railway Dept, BoT, 1854; inspected N. American rlys with Robt Lowe 1856; govt referee on Met. main drainage 1857; R.C. Sanitary Condition of Military Barracks & Hospitals 1858–61; R.C. Thames Embankment 1860; asst inspector-gen. Fortifications 1860; permt asst under-sec. War 1862–9; Director of Public Works & Buildings, OW, 1869–75 (post abolished). F.R.S. 1859. C.B. 1865, K.C.B. 1887. Jt gen. sec. Brit. Assoc. for Advancement of Science 1871–95, pres. 1895. Leading sanitary engineer of his day, designed barracks and hospitals. *M.* favourite cos. of Florence Nightingale; left personalty sworn at £93,000.

GLADSTONE, Herbert John, 1854–1930. Ygst s. of the prime minister. *Educ.* Eton & Univ. Coll. Oxford. MP (Lib.) 1880–1910. Priv. sec. to fa. 1880–1; minor office 1881–5, 1886, 1892–4; FCW 1894–5; Home sec. 1905–10. Gov.-gen. Union of S. Africa 1910–14. *Cr.* Visct Gladstone 1910.

GLADSTONE, William Ewart, 1809–98. Yngr s. of Liverpool merchant. *Educ.* Eton & Ch. Ch. Oxford. MP (Cons.) 1832–46; (Lib.-Cons.) 1847–68; (Lib.) 1868–95. VP Bd of Trade 1841–3, pres. 1843–5; Col. sec. 1845–6; ch. of Exchequer 1852–5, 1859–66, 1873–4; prime minister 1868–74, 1880–5, 1886, 1892–4.

GREGORY, William Henry, 1817–92. Irish landowner. *Educ.* Harrow & Ch. Ch. Oxford. MP (Lib.-Cons.; from 1866 Lib.) Dublin City 1842–7; Co. Galway 1857–71. Gov. of Ceylon 1871–6. K.C.M.G. 1875. Racehorse owner to 1853. Chairman, s.c. on British Museum 1860. Trustee, N.G. 1867-d.

HALL, Benjamin, 1802–67. Welsh landowner. *Educ.* Westminster & Ch. Ch. Oxford. MP (Whig) 1831, (Lib., with Radical views) 1832–59 (representing St Marylebone from 1837). *Cr.* Bart. 1838; Baron Llanover 1859. Pres. Bd of Health 1854–5, FCW 1855–8. Introduced legislation creating Met. Bd of Works to deal with Metropolitan problems of sewerage and roads, 1855. Reformed OW organisation and promoted open competition for public works.

HARCOURT, William George Granville Venables Vernon, 1827–

1904. Gd-s. of Abp of York, and h. to Harcourt estates (*suc.* 1904). *Educ.* Trinity Coll. Camb. Barrister (I.T.) 1854; counsel for MBW over Thames Embankment scheme 1861; Q.C. 1866; prof. of International Law, Camb. 1869–87. MP (Lib.) 1868-d. Sol.-gen. 1873–4; Home sec. 1880–5 (introduced bill on London govt 1884); ch. of Exchequer 1886, 1892–5; Lib. leader in Commons 1894–9. A keen retrencher; introduced death duties 1894. Kt 1873.

HARCOURT, Lewis, 1863–1922. Known as 'Loulou'. S. and h. of preceding. *Educ.* Eton. Priv. sec. to fa. 1881–1904. MP (Lib.) 1904–16. FCW (Cabinet) 1905–10; Col. sec. 1910–15. *Cr.* Visct Harcourt 1917. Founder, with Lord Esher (see BRETT), of London Mus. 1911; trustee, Wallace Coll., N.G., B.M. Encouraged private benefactions for public uses. Committed suicide.

HOPE (afterwards BERESFORD HOPE), Alexander James Beresford, 1820–87. Yngst s. of Thomas Hope, writer on art. Inherited estates of step-fa., Marshal Visct Beresford 1854, and took additional surname of Beresford. *Educ.* Harrow & Trinity Coll. Camb. MP (Cons.) 1841–52, 1857–9, 1865-d. P.C. 1880. Chairman, S.C. on Foreign Office Reconstruction 1858, working for appointment of Geo. G. Scott as architect. Advocate of Gothic architecture; purchased ruins of St Augustine's Abbey 1844 and restd them as college for missionary clergy; paid for building of All SS, Margaret Street, as model church for Camden Soc. 1849–54; published pamphlets supporting Gothic designs for New Government Offices. Co-proprietor, *Sat. Rev.* from 1865. PRIBA 1865–8; trustee B.M. 1879-d. *M.* sis. of 3rd M. of Salisbury (prime minister) 1842.

LAYARD, Austen Henry, 1817–94. MP (Lib., with Radical sympathies) Aylesbury 1852–7; Southwark 1860–9. Under-sec., Foreign Affairs, 1853, 1861–6. FCW, Dec. 1868–Oct. 1869. Minister to Madrid, 1869–77; ambassador to Turkey 1877–80. G.C.B. 1878. Trustee, N.G. 1866-d. Excavated Nimrûd 1845–7, 1849–51, believing it to be Nineveh, and published an account. Collector of Italian painting (lived much in Italy); writer on art – 'He knows the whole subject from a Nineveh Bull to a Raphael Madonna' (Earl Russell, who considered appointing him Commons' spokesman for a department of literature and art, *Later Corr. of Lord John Russell*, ed. G.P. Gooch, II (1925), 343.)

MCDONNELL, Schomberg Kerr, 1861–1915. Yngr s. of 5th E. of Antrim. Priv. sec. to Lord Salisbury as prime minister. Fought in S. African War 1900–02. Sec. OW 1902–12. Re-joined army 1914, insisted on going to front line 1915 and killed in action.

MANNERS, Lord John James Robert, 1818–1906. *Educ.* Eton & Trinity, Camb. Active member, Cambridge Camden Soc. Grand tour 1839–40. MP (Cons.) 1841–7, 1850–88. Member of 'Young England', and figured in Disraeli's *Coningsby* as 'Lord Henry Sidney'. FCW 1852, 1858–9, 1866–8; P.M.G. 1874–80, 1885–6; ch. of duchy of Lancaster 1886–92. *Suc.* bro. as 7th Duke of Rutland, 1888.

MITFORD (afterwards FREEMAN-MITFORD), Algernon Bertram, 1837–1916. Gd-son of 3rd Earl of Ashburnham. *Educ.* Eton & Ch. Ch. Oxford. Ent. F.O. 1858; early friend of Prince of Wales; served in China and Japan 1865–70. Secretary, OW 1874–86. 1886, *suc.* to estates of cos. Earl of Redesdale. MP (Cons.) 1892–5. *Cr.* Baron Redesdale 1902.

MOLESWORTH, William, Sir, bart., 1810–55. *suc.* fa. as 8th bart. 1823. *Educ.* Edinburgh Univ., Trinity Coll. Camb. Grand tour 1828–31. MP (Rad.) 1832–41, 1845 (Southwark)-d. FCW (Cabinet) 1853–5. Col. Sec. 1855.

PALMERSTON, Henry John TEMPLE, 3rd Viscount (I.), 1784–1866. S. of 2nd viscount, Irish and English landowner, *suc.* fa. 1802. *Educ.* Harrow, Univ. of Edinburgh, St John's Camb. MP (Ministerialist/Canningite, joined Whigs 1830) 1807–65. Sec. at War 1809–28; For. sec. 1830–34, 1835–41, 1846–51; Home sec. 1852–5; prime minister 1855–8, 1859-d. *M.* 1839, Emily, dau. of 1st Visc. Melbourne and wid. of Earl Cowper.

PENNETHORNE, James, 1801–71. Architect. Related to w. of John Nash, who trained him as his successor. Jt Surveyor OW 1840, sole 1845–56; salaried Surveyor and Architect OW 1859–70. Planned many Met. street improvements and public buildings, incl. Mus. of Economic Geology 1846–50, Public Record Office 1850–68, Univ. of London 1868–71. Designs for New Government Offices and War Office 1856 superseded by FCW's decision to go to competition. RIBA gold medal 1856. Kt 1870.

PLUNKET, David Robert, 1838–1919. 3rd s. of 3rd Lord Plunket. *Educ.* T.C.D. Barrister, Q.C. (I) 1868. MP (Cons.) Dublin Univ. 1870–95. P.M.G. 1880; FCW 1885–6, 1886–92. *Cr.* Baron Rathmore 1895.

RUSSELL, George, 1830–1911. Gd-s. of Lord William Russell (bro. of 6th D. of Bedford). *M.* dau. of 6th D. of Roxburghe 1862. Treasury clerk 1851; priv. sec. to Financial sec. 1855–6; Asst Sec. OW 1856–68, Sec. 1868–75; quarrelled with Galton about respective powers; res. because of accusation about cheating at cards.

SCOTT, George Gilbert, 1811–78. Architect. S. of a cleryman. Articled to J. Edmeston; in office of H. Roberts 1832. Partnership with W.B. Moffatt; built many union workhouses; began to specialise in church work, enthused for Gothic by Pugin's writings and the Cambridge Camden Soc. Developed largest arch. practice of the day; sought to design a Gothic applicable to modern secular needs. Entered many competitions; placed 3rd for F.O. in 1857, but with help of friends (including BERESFORD HOPE) obtained the commission, though obliged by Palmerston to build in Italian style. Unsuccessful in limited competition for New Law Courts, 1866–7.

SHAW LEFEVRE, George John, 1831–1928. Son of Sir J.G. Shaw Lefevre, Clerk of the Parliaments, and nephew of Speaker Shaw Lefevre, Visc. Eversley. *Educ.* Eton & Trinity, Camb. Barrister. MP (Lib.) 1863–85, 1886–95. Minor office 1866, 1868–74; FCW 1880–3; P.M.G. (Cabinet) 1883–5; FCW 1892–4; pres. LGB 1894–5. Member, LCC 1897–1912. *Cr.* Baron Eversley 1906. A keen retrencher; founder, Commons Preservation Soc.

SMITH, William Henry, 1825–91. Newsagent. Member, MBW 1855. MP, Westminster/Strand (Cons.) 1868-d. Sec. to Treasury 1874–7; first lord Admiralty 1877–80 (satirised by W.S. Gilbert in *HMS Pinafore*); War sec. 1885; Irish sec. 1886; War sec. 1886; first lord of Treasury & leader HC 1887-d.

STREET, George Edmund, 1824–81. Architect. S. of solicitor. Articled to O.B. Carter of Winchester. Worked in G.G. SCOTT's office for five years, set up own 1849. Worked purely in Gothic; authority on Italian and Spanish forms as well as English. Second in competition for Lille cathedral, France, 1855. Received a lesser premium in Government Offices competition, 1857. Invited to compete for New N.G. and New Law Courts 1866–7; latter elevation recommended as best, and he received the commission 1868 (built 1873–82 after prolonged struggle with FCW). A.R.A. 1866, R.A. 1871; RIBA gold medal 1874. Also nave, Bristol Cathedral; St James the Less, Westminster.

TAYLOR, John, 1833–1912. Architect. S. of a joiner. Asst to Asst Surveyor for London OW, 1859; Surveyor, London Dist. OW 1865. In effect, principal official architect from *c.*1876, responsible for additions to N.G., PRO, Patent Office, &c.; closely concerned in all major govt met. building works except P.O. until retirement in 1901. C.B. 1894, K.C.B. 1897.

TANNER, Henry, 1849–1935. Architect. Clerk to Asst Surveyor, OW, 1871; promoted 1873, 1877. Charged with Post Office branch of OW, designing many Crown post offices. Principal Surveyor 1887; designed GPO North, 1890–5, and GPO King Edward Buildings, 1907–11. Principal Architect in succession to TAYLOR, 1901–13; modified designs for Gt George St Offices after BRYDON's d. in 1901, and supervised erection 1902–14. Kt 1904; C.B. 1911. An authority on the use of reinforced concrete.

TITE, William, 1798–1873. Architect. S. of a Russia merchant. Pupil of David Laing (1774–1856). Competitor, Royal Exchange 1840; received commission (£150,000) 1841–4. Much involved in planning and construction of railways and design of stations. PRIBA 1861–3 and 1867–70. MP (Lib.) 1855-d. Member MBW from 1855. Took active part in F.O. style (opposed Gothic), Thames Embankment, and New Law Courts site controversies. Kt 1869.

WATERHOUSE, Alfred, 1830–1905. Architect. Articled to R. Lane, archt of Manchester. Own practice 1853. FRIBA 1861, gold medal 1878, pres. 1888–91; A.R.A. 1878, R.A. 1885. Won competitions, Manchester Assize Cts (Gothic) 1859, Manchester Town Hall (Gothic) 1867. Appointed to execute Fowke's design for Nat. Hist. Mus., S. Kensington, 1865, but evolved his own design, built 1873–85. Competitor, New Law Courts, 1866–7. Extensively employed as competitions assessor. Other buildings include Eaton Hall for M. of Westminster 1870–97 (£603,000); Prudential Insurance offices, High Holborn, and Univ. Coll. Hosp., London.

WEBB, Aston, 1849–1930. Architect. Articled to Banks & Barry 1867. Own practice 1873. Pres. Arch. Ass. 1884; PRIBA 1902–4; gold medal 1905. A.R.A. 1899, R.A. 1903, P.R.A. 1919–24. With Ingress Bell competed unsuccessfully for New Admiralty & W.O. 1884, Imp. Institute 1887; successfully, Birmingham Law Courts 1886, Christ's Hosp. Horsham 1891. Won limited compn for completion of S. Kensington Mus. (Victoria & Albert) 1891, executed 1899–1909. R. Coll. Science 1900–6. Won Q. Victoria Mem. limited compn 1901 (architectural layout of Mall; Admiralty Arch 1905–11; re-fronting Buckingham Palace 1913). Also Met. Life Assurance Co. Moorgate 1890, R. Naval Coll. Dartmouth 1899, Univ. of Birmingham 1906. Kt 1904, C.B. 1909, K.C.V.O. 1914.

WEMYSS, Earl of: see CHARTERIS.

WINDSOR, Robert George WINDSOR-CLIVE, 14th Baron, 1857–1923. *Suc.* gd-mo. in barony 1869. *Educ.* Eton & St John's Camb. Cons. P.M.G. 1891–2; FCW 1902–5. Trustee, N.G. 1900-d. *Cr.* Earl of Plymouth 1905. *M.* Alberta Victoria, dau. of Sir A.B. Paget, amb. to Italy, by his w. Ctss Walburga v. Hohenthal. Landowner (1883: 37,454 acres worth £63,788 p.a.), artist, and patron of art and architecture.

YOUNG, William, 1843–1900. Architect. Articled to James Lamb, Paisley. Worked in office of Surrey Co. surveyor, attracting attention of Lord Elcho (q.v.) in connexion with erecting marquee for Nat. Rifle Brigade, which led to his employment by magnates, including ELCHO (later E. of Wemyss) at Gosford, Scotland. 'No man knew more the requirements of a great country house or how more effectively to carry them out' (Brydon). Won competition for Glasgow City Chambers, built 1883–9 (£540,000), after visit to Italy. Thus chosen for new W.O., Whitehall, 1898.

Notes

Abbreviations

In addition to commonly received abbreviations, the following have been employed in the notes:

A.A.	Architectural Association	N.G.	National Gallery
BL	British Library	N.P.G.	National Portrait Gallery
BN	*Building News*	n.s.	new series
BoE	*Buildings of England*	NHM	Natural History Museum
BoT	Board of Trade	NLC	New Law Courts
ch.	chancellor	OW	Office of Works
cl.	class	P.M.	Prime Minister
CC	Cole Correspondence	P.O.	Post Office
C.O.	Colonial Office	*PD*	*Parliamentary Debates*, preceded by *3*, *4*, or *5* to indicate
corr.	correspondence		which series.
cr.	created	*PP*	*Parliamentary Papers*
C.R.O.	County Record Office	PRA	President of the Royal Academy
CWFLR	Commissioners of Woods, Forests and Land Revenues	PRIBA	President of the Royal Institute of British Architects
dep.	deposit	PPRIBA	Past President, &c.
DNB	*Dictionary of National Biography*	PRO	Public Record Office
F.O.	Foreign Office	q.	question
FCW	First Commissioner of Works	RA	Royal Archives
GLRO	Greater London Record Office	R.A.	Royal Academy
GPO	General Post Office	R.C.	Royal Commission
H.O.	Home Office	RIBA	Royal Institute of British Architects
HC	House of Commons	S.C.	Select Committee
HL	House of Lords	SAD	Department of Science and Art
ILN	*Illustrated London News*	SRO	Scottish Record Office
I.O.	India Office	*Survey*	*Survey of London*
K.B.	King's Bench	T.	Treasury
King's Works	*History of the King's Works*, general ed. H.M. Colvin.	T.M.	Treasury Minute
		temp.	temporary
LCC	London County Council	VAM	Victoria and Albert Museum
LGB	Local Government Board	W.A.	Windsor Archives, on permanent loan to the 1851
MBO	Metropolitan Buildings Office		commissioners
MBW	Metropolitan Board of Works	W.O.	War Office
MoD	Ministry of Defence		

Conventions

Parliamentary Papers. Listed by year, followed by sessional number (in round brackets) or Command number (in square brackets), and volume number in Roman numerals. A number immediately following in Arabic numerals is the MS page number as in British Library volumes.

Dates have been made uniform, thus: 1 Jan. 1890.
The form 1890/91 refers to a financial year.

1. Introduction

1 J. Summerson, 'The Victorian Rebuilding of the City of London', *London Jnl* 3 (1977), 163–85; J. Booker, *Temples of Mammon* (Edinburgh, 1990), 128–37.
2 J. Summerson, *Victorian Architecture: Four Studies in Evaluation* (New York & London, 1970), 115.
3 For a list and explanation, see *PP* 1861 (211) VIII, qq. 387–413, and app. 12.
4 See D. Owen, *The Government of Victorian London* (Cambridge, Mass., & London, 1982), 24–5; D. Fraser, *Urban Politics in Victorian England* (Leicester, 1976), ch. 4.

2. Imperial City

1 M.-L. Biver, *Le Paris de Napoléon* (Paris, 1963).
2 B.A. Ruble, 'From Palace Square to Moscow Square', in W.C. Brumfield, ed., *Reshaping Russian Architecture* (Cambridge 1990).
3 G. Riemann, 'Schinkel's Buildings and Plans for Berlin', in M. Snodin (ed.), *Karl Friedrich Schinkel: A Universal Man* (New Haven & London, 1991), 16–25.
4 H.-R. Hitchcock, *Architecture: Nineteenth and Twentieth Centuries* (Harmondsworth, 1958), ch. 2 & 3.
5 C.S. de Krey, *A Fractured Society* (Oxford 1985), 3.
6 See, inter alia, P. Earle, *Making of the English Middle Class* (1989), pt 1; A.L. Beier & R. Finlay, eds, *London 1500–1700* (1986).
7 D. Defoe, *A Tour through England and Wales* (3 vols., 1724–6).
8 See F. Sheppard, *London 1808–1870* (1971), ch. 1.
9 See J. Summerson, *Georgian London* (new edn, 1988), 46, 105–7.
10 Ibid., ch. 7, 12, 14; D.J. Olsen, *Town Planning in London* (New Haven & London, 1964).
11 Defoe, *Tour*, Everyman edn, 1928, I, 314–15.
12 F. Sheppard et al., 'The Middlesex and Yorkshire Deeds Registries', *London Jnl*, 5 (1979), 194.
13 See A. Saunders, *Regent's Park* (1969), 75–8.
14 J. Summerson, *Life and Works of John Nash Architect*

(1980), ch. 5.

15 1st Report CWFLR, app. 12A, 88–90, cited Summerson, *John Nash*, 77.

16 Ibid., 82.

17 *King's Works*, VI, 176–8.

18 See T.H. Shepherd & J. Elmes, *Metropolitan Improvements; or London, in the nineteenth century* (1827).

19 Ibid., 1–2.

20 J.F. Robinson (later Lord Goderich) when chancellor of the Exchequer required Soane to change the Order of his Board of Trade Offices from the Ionic of the Temple of Vesta at Tivoli to that of the Temple of Jupiter Stator at Rome, not only 'allowed to be among the finest specimens of the Corinthian order', but also 'the richest order in all the remains of Antiquity'. See *King's Works*, VI, 553.

21 *King's Works*, VI, 403, 430, 481, 504, 512, 551.

22 Ibid., 158–78.

23 *PP* 1831–32 (614) V, *S.C. on improving approaches to the Houses of Parliament and Buckingham Palace.*

24 *PP* 1835 (598) V; 1836 (569) IX, *S.C. on Arts and Manufactures.*

25 *King's Works*, VI, 462.

26 Ibid., 463.

27 Ibid., 463n.; W.H. Leeds, *Public Buildings of London* II (1838), 190.

28 *PD* XL, 234, 1437.

29 M.H. Port, ed., *The Houses of Parliament* (1976), ch. III.

30 *King's Works*, VI, 403–10.

31 See E. Miller, *That Noble Cabinet* (1973).

32 *PP* 1836 (517) XX, *S.C. on Metropolis Improvements*, q. 120.

33 Ibid., qq. 255, 264.

34 *PP* 1837–8 (418) XVI, *First Report of S.C. on Metropolitan Improvements*, qq. 307–10.

35 *PP* 1837–8 (418) XVI, p. 5.

36 Ibid., (661) XVI.

37 *PP* 1839 (136) XIII, *First Report of S.C. to consider the several Plans for the Improvement of the Metropolis*, p. v.

38 Ibid., p. vi.

39 *PP* 1840 (410) XII, *First Report of S.C. on Metropolitan Improvements.*

40 Ibid., p. v.

41 *PP* 1840 (354) and (554) XII.

42 *PP* 1841 (398) IX, *S.C. on Metropolitan Improvement.*

43 *PP* 1844 [15] XV.

44 PRO, Crest 35/2496.

45 F.W. Trench, *Collection of Papers relating to the Thames Quay* (1827); *Letter from Sir Frederick Trench to Viscount Duncannon, First Commissioner of Woods and Forests* (1841). See F. Barker & R. Hyde, *London As it might have been* (1982), 8, 81–94. For Trench see *DNB*, and R.G. Thorne, ed., *The House of Commons 1790–1820* (1986).

46 Cp *PP* 1882 (235) VII, *S.C. on Artizans' and Labourers' Dwellings Improvement Act*, vi–viii and qq. 512–18, 526–30, 546, 583–96, 662.

47 See *DNB*.

48 *PP* 1844 [15] XV, *First Report of Royal Commission on Metropolitan Improvements*, pp. 7–42.

49 *PP* 1845 [348] XVII, *Second Report of R.C. on Metropolitan Improvements.*

50 *PP* 1845 [619] XVII, *Third Report of R.C. on Metropolitan Improvements.* See also *PP* 1831–32 (614) V.

51 *PP* 1845 [619] XVII, q. 289. As the MBW found when it embarked on slum clearance.

52 *PP* 1846 [682] XXIV, *Fifth Report of R.C. on Metropolitan Improvements*, pp. 3–5.

53 Ibid., p. 6.

54 *PP* 1856 (193) LII, *Reports by Mr Page and Mr Pennethorne on Thames Embankment and Battersea Park.*

55 J.F.B. Firth, *Municipal London* (1876), ch. 13, 14; Firth, *Reform of London Government* (1888), ch. 1–3.

56 *3PD*, CXXXVII, 702–15 (16 Mar. 1855); Firth, *Municipal London*, ch. 7, 10–12.

57 *PP* 1854–55, X.

58 18 & 19 Vict., c. 120.

59 Usually limited to £40 ratepayers, but reduced to £25 for poorer parishes.

60 Metropolis Management Act (18 & 19 Vict., c. 120), 1855, s. 144; Act 21 & 22 Vict., c. 104, s. 25.

61 *PP* 1866 (186) XIII, *First Report of S.C. on Metropolitan Local Government, &c.*, app. 6.

62 The assessments were carried out periodically by surveyors appointed by the local authorities, and subject to local influences. See M.H. Port, 'The Life of an Architectural Sinner: Thomas Wayland Fletcher, 1833–1901', *London Jnl*, 15 (1990), 64.

63 *PP* 1866 (186) XIII, *S.C. on Metropolitan Local Government*, app. 6. Rich St George, Hanover Square (with some 88,000 inhabitants in 1861, and 10,421 inhabited houses, and a valuation of £944,000) had the lowest rate in the £ at 2s.1d., raising approx. £115,000; the S. London suburb of St Mary, Newington (with 82,000 inhabitants, 12,815 inhabited houses, and a valuation of £240,000) at 5s.4d. in the £ raised only £65,000; while Rotherhithe in S.E. London (24,500 inhabitants, 3529 houses, £83,500 valuation) required a rate of 7s.4d. in the £ to raise £31,000. (Valuation and census figures from *PP* 1861 (372) VIII, *2nd Report of S.C. on Metropolis Local Taxation*, app. 14). See also A. Offer, *Property and Politics 1870–1914* (Cambridge, 1981), 171ff.

64 *PP* 1861 (436) VIII; 1866 (186) XIII; 1867 (135 and 268) XII.

65 *Valuation of Property (Metropolis) Act* 1869, 33 & 34 Vict. c. 67.

66 See Offer, loc. cit.; Owen, *Government of Victorian London* (cited ch. 1), 314, 322. In 1867 the Metropolitan Poor Act established a common fund from which the poorest parishes could be subsidised.

67 For a history of these, see *PP* 1861 (476) VIII, *3rd Report of S.C. on Metropolis Taxation*, xiii–xv. The duty on coal imported into London, by far the most important, consisted of a charge of 4d. per ton received by the City corporation (amounting to £74,824 in 1860–1), and charges of 8d. per ton (for metropolitan improvements, paid over to the FCW) and 1d. per ton (for special objects), totalling £168,561 in 1860–1 (ibid.).

68 An act of 1871 commuted the metage duty for one on weight, which in 1874 produced £17,400, Firth, *Municipal London*, 188.

69 The total tax of 13d. a ton yielded about £450,000 in the late 1880s, see Firth, *Reform*, 147; also *Municipal London*, 187.

70 *PP* 1836 (517) XX. The reformer Joseph Firth had a different view, see *Reform*, 87.

71 The dues were charged on all coal coming into the port of London, were easy to collect and difficult to evade, but they increased the price of coals to the poor by a small degree, and also bore on the inhabitants of the neighbouring counties whose coal was supplied from London. See *PP* 1852–53 (916) XXII, 125ff. *S.C. on Coal Duties*; and 1889 (228) IX, 473ff. *S.C. on Coal Duties Abolition Bill.*

72 Statute of 1845. See also *PP* 1861 (476) VIII, *3rd Report of S.C. on Metropolis Local Taxation.*

73 L. Griffin, 'An Imperial City', *Pall Mall Mag.*, 1 (1893), 668. (I owe this reference to Mr R. Hyde.)

74 Owen, *Government of Victorian London*, 165–8.

75 F. Sheppard, 'London and the Nation in the Nineteenth Century', *Trans. R. Hist. Soc.*, 5 ser., XXXV, 64–9.

76 P.J. Waller, *Town, City, and Nation* (1983), 26.

77 See C. Fox, ed., *London World City 1800–1840* (New Haven & London, 1992), passim.

78 Cp K. Baedeker, *London and its Environs* (1905), 33–4.

79 I. Morus, S. Schaffer & J. Secord, 'Scientific London', in C. Fox, ed., *London World City 1800–1840*, pp. 134–5.

80 H.J. Dyos & D.A. Reeder, 'Slums and Suburbs', *Victorian City* (1973), H.J. Dyos & M. Wolff, eds., I, 360.

81 Joseph Chamberlain, quoted by Waller, 54.

82 D.J. Olsen, *The City as a Work of Art* (New Haven & London, 1986), 4.

83 'Within a short time very great advances have been made in the character of our civic buildings: the leading thoroughfares and defiles have been adorned with many edifices of a style and pretensions hitherto unknown. The [Royal] Exchange was the first grand innovation [1842]; then the Coal-Exchange [1851]; the various palatial insurance offices; the Hall of Commerce; then club chambers', asserted the *Builder*; but it wanted now a 'great central duct' 100ft wide between the City and Leicester Square, with a viaduct across Farringdon Street, 17 May 1856, p. 269.

84 Cp W.L. Burn, *The Age of Equipoise* (1964), 26–30.

85 W. Howitt, 'Holidays for the People. Michaelmas', *People's Jnl*, II (1846), 171, quoted by H.J. Dyos & D.A. Reeder, 'Slums and Suburbs', *Victorian City*, I, 380.

86 Cp *PP* 1889 (326) LXVI, *Annual Report of the MBW*, 1888, p. 26: 'In 1855 such thoroughfares as the Strand and Cheapside were congested. They are congested in 1888. Yet within the last 20 years the Victoria Embankment and Queen Victoria-street have been made, and a broad stream of traffic now passes along them between east and west, whilst more to the northward another stream is conveyed in the same direction through the new main channel from Oxford-street to Old-street.'

87 S. Walpole, *History of 25 Years*, I (1904), 459–60, contrasts the inconvenience of London in 1860 with the position forty years later.

88 See F. Sheppard, *London 1808–1870: the Infernal Wen* (1971), 139–48.

89 J. Booker, *Temples of Mammon: the Architecture of Banking* (Edinburgh, 1990), 128–37. James Thorne, reviewing the architecture of 1861, remarked: 'The [City] Insurance Offices have added within the last few years some of the most distinctive examples of civic architecture', *Companion to the Almanac*, 1861, p. 256.

90 Summerson, 'Victorian Rebuilding' (cited ch. 1), 163–85.

91 J. Thorne, *Companion to the Almanac*, 1862, pp. 243, 273.

92 See Owen, *Government of Victorian London*, ch. 11; Waller, *Town, City, and Nation*, 54–8; Firth, *Reform*, ch. 1. The difficulty of satisfactorily defining what was a 'metropolitan member' is illustrated by a dispute over membership of a select committee on the Thames Embankment, 14 May 1860. Paxton had proposed 15 names, as was usual; only three sat for London constituencies, though others, including Alderman Cubitt (then lord mayor) and William Tite, served on metropolitan local authorities – Paxton claimed that there were seven 'metropolitan members' and resisted any change. A subsequent proposal to add Lord Fermoy (Marylebone) and Locke (Southwark) was rejected. *3PD* CLVIII, 1176–7; 2039 (4 June 1860).

93 Southwark, formerly only 'the Borough', now took in Christchurch and St Saviour's parishes, as well as Bermondsey and Rotherhithe. The new constituencies were Marylebone, Finsbury, Tower Hamlets, Greenwich and Lambeth.

94 Cowper remarked to Prince Albert's secretary that 'the Metropolitan members are not acceptable' in the House, at a time when the radical QC Edwin James was MP for Marylebone, shortly before he was disbarred with debts of £100,000 (*Dod's Parliamentary Companion*, 1861). RA, Add. MSS Q. 554, 27 July 1860.

95 Hackney was split off from Tower Hamlets, and Chelsea was created out of Middlesex.

96 RA, Add. MSS Q. 528, 12 Sept. 1857.

97 C. Seymour, *Electoral Reform in England and Wales* (1915), app. 3–5.

98 *Times*, 2 Mar. 1886, p. 9.

99 Curiously enough, the most explicit statement of the doctrine that the metropolis must pay for its own embellishment came some years later, from ministers determined to secure the use of Coldbath Fields prison site for the Post Office, rather than yield it to the new LCC for open space. The Postmaster-general declared it was 'the duty of the Government to see that the taxpayer is not fleeced or robbed or deprived of his rights. This principle has been so much recognized by the House of Commons in this very Parliament – that certain charges, which . . . were defrayed by the taxpayers at large in connection with the London Parks, have been transferred to . . . the ratepayers of the Metropolis'. The Home secretary, appealed to by London MPs to assist in London improvements, stated: 'We refuse to do so out of funds that do not belong to London.' *3PD* CCCXXXVIII, 942–4, 1764–9 (19, 26 July 1889).

100 *3PD* CLV, 917 (4 Aug. 1859). See also *PP* 1856 (59) LII, *Accounts, Office of Works*, pp. 26–7; (318) LII, . . . *Report to the FCW . . . on New Westminster Bridge*.

101 See pp. 168 below.

102 *3PD* CL, 1112 (28 May 1858). Lewis was hitting notably at Sir Charles Trevelyan (see below, p. 117), as well as Hall (a metropolitan member of long standing).

103 *Builder*, 22 Aug. 1857, p. 478.

104 *PP* 1860 (483) IX, *S.C. on Miscellaneous Expenditure*, q. 949.

105 Ibid., q. 887.

106 *PP* 1861 (372) VIII, *2nd Report of S.C. on Metropolis Local Taxation*, q. 3587.

107 *3PD* CLVIII, 736–46.

108 *PP* 1860 (494) XX, *S.C. on the best means for providing for the increasing traffic of the Metropolis by the Embankment of the Thames*, qq. 61, 93, 281.

109 *3PD* CLXI, 1225 (1 March 1861).

110 Radical MP for Tower Hamlets, 1857–74. A caustic-tongued barrister who had worked in Bombay for several years, Ayrton was a leading campaigner for metropolitan reform. For his career as FCW, see below, pp. 65–8.

111 *3PD* CLXI, 1228–9 (Ayrton), 1232 (Locke).

112 Owen, *Victorian London*, ch. 4.

113 *Sol. Jnl*, 1869, pp. 402–3.

114 PRO, Work 22/2/18, confidential minute by A.H. Layard, 4 Nov. 1869. Baillie Cochrane had put forward a similar idea some years earlier in the Commons; and Thorne, in *Companion to the Almanac*, 1866, had commented; 'By the beauty of the site, convenience of access, and quiet, it seems self-designated for a series of stately public buildings . . . devoted to public use, and worthy alike in purpose and architecture of the site and the country' (p. 142).

115 *Builder*, 1868, p. 581.

116 *Architect*, Jan. 1869, p. 1; 2 Apr. 1870, p. 159.

117 D. Van Zanten, *Designing Paris* (1987), 71; M.-L. Biver, *Le Paris de Napoléon* (Paris, 1963), 277.

118 A. Gabriel, *Guide de l'Architecture des Monuments de Paris/Guide to the Architecture of Monuments in Paris* (Paris, 1991), 150; *3PD* CLV, 935 (4 Aug. 1859).

119 The so-called 'apartements du Duc de Morny', which, having survived to our own day, are being restored as part of 'le projet Grand Louvre'. In describing Queen Victoria's visit to Paris, the *Daily News* stressed the new splendours of the Hôtel de Ville, 25 Aug. 1855.

120 See A. Sutcliffe, *Autumn of Central Paris* (1970), 12–13.

121 Ibid., 23–30.

122 Ibid., 31, 36, 38.

123 RA, Add. MSS Q, 247, Hall to Phipps, 3 Dec. 1855.

124 Hall, when First Commissioner, visited Paris, with a view to examining the public buildings, with which he was 'much pleased', and was able to consult Haussmann, since 1853 prefect of the Seine. RA, Add. MSS Q, 241, 244, 247 (Hall to Phipps, 5, 26 Nov., 3 Dec. 1855).

125 See below, p. 172.

126 *Builder*, 1876, p. 725.

127 Cawston, *Comprehensive Scheme*, 19–22, quoting F.R. Farrow's paper to RIBA, Dec. 1887; G.R. Marek, *The Eagles Die* (1975), 171–2, 177; Olsen, *The City as a Work of Art*, ch. 5.

128 Marek, 121–8.

129 K. Baedeker, *Munich and its Environs* (1956), 63–4.

130 See Riemann, 'Schinkel's Buildings and Plans for Berlin', in Snodin, *Karl Friedrich Schinkel*, 16–25; also 124–32.

131 Cawston, 22–3, 27.

132 *PP* 1877 (312) XV.

133 *Builder*, 18 Aug. 1877, p. 825.

134 Ibid., 25 Aug. 1877, p. 852. Godwin took the occasion to publish two long articles on the recent history of the Office of Works, *Builder* 1877, pp. 852–6, 897–9.

135 See S. Koss, *Rise and Fall of the Political Press in Britain: I: The Nineteenth Century* (1981), 121–2, 411–12, 417–18.

136 *Builder*, 11 July 1896, pp. 23–4. H.H. Statham fought the battle persistently. See *RIBA Jnl*, 3 ser., IV (1897), 289–312; also *Murray's Mag.* v (1889), 68–84; *Fortnightly Rev.*, LXVI (1896), 879–93; *Nat. Rev.*, XXIXC (1897), 594–603.

137 *Builder*, 26 Feb. 1887, p. 309.

138 Ibid., 9 Apr. 1887, p. 532.

139 Ibid., 11 Apr. 1885, p. 505.

140 Ibid. For more critical comment on Poelart's Palais de Justice see *Builder*, Apr. 1885, p. 512; *Architect*, 28 Oct. 1883; *Quarterly Rev.* CLXXVI (1893), 40–72. See ch. 12, n. 147.

141 See p. 163.

142 J. Summerson, *Victorian Architecture* (New York, 1971), 115; D. Cannadine, 'Context, Performance and Meaning of Ritual', in E. Hobsbawm & T. Ranger, eds., *Invention of Tradition* (Cambridge, 1983), 112–13.

143 Cannadine, loc. cit.; *Fortnightly Rev.*, II, 102.

144 *Civil Engineer and Architect's Jnl* was wide-ranging, 1837–68. *Builder*, 'An illustrated weekly magazine for the architect, engineer, archaeologist, constructor, sanitary reformer, and art-lover' had been running very successfully since 1842; *Building News*, with a similar content, since 1854. The *Architect*, aiming to be the voice of the profession, was founded in 1869, *British Architect* in 1874 (in Manchester, moving to London c.1882). All these were published weekly at 6d. or 4d., along with the *Illustrated London News* from 1842 and the *Graphic* (1869), wide-circulation family picture papers giving considerable attention to architecture. More specialised were *Ecclesiologist* and *Church Builder* (quarterly from 1861), and the weekly trade papers such as *Engineer and Building Times* (1870), and *Building World* (1877); and more generally concerned with the arts, *Athenaeum* (1828) and *Art Journal* (1849). *Academy Architecture* and *Architectural Review* (1896) followed, setting new standards of illustration, pub. monthly and more costly than the others. These periodicals were not emphemera; most ran into the second half of the twentieth century.

145 *Builder*, 1857, pp. 261, 269, 317.

146 See H. Parris, *Constitutional Bureaucracy* (1969), esp. chap. IX.

147 D. Olsen, *Growth of Victorian London* (1976), 329.

148 Ruskin had in 1849 urged the importance of expressing historical meaning in the ornamentation of public buildings, *Seven Lamps of Architecture*, VI, paras. iii and vii.

149 A. Briggs, *Victorian Cities* (1963), 163–4, quoting the spokesman of the 'cultured classes', Dr Heaton, speaking in 1854. See also J.H.G. Archer, *Art and Architecture in Victorian Manchester* (Manchester, 1985), 128–30.

150 Summerson, *Victorian Architecture* (cited ch. 1), 4–5, 115–16.

151 Prince Albert had suggested an advisory council in 1848, when reform of the Woods & Works was being discussed, PRO, 30/22, Russell Papers, 7D, Morpeth to Russell, 26 Sept. 1848.

152 *King's Works*, VI, part I.

153 See below, p. 153 and ch. 10.

154 *Times*, 2 Mar. 1886, p. 4.

155 See app. 1.

156 See M.H. Port, 'An Ædile for London?', *London Jnl*, 12 (1986), 57–64. As early as 1850, *Builder* had welcomed the prospect of an endowed commission for public buildings, 2 Feb. 1850, p. 52. See below, p. 59.

157 *King's Works*, VI, 211.

158 *Sat. Rev.*, 8 May 1869, p. 615. Lord Elcho, having seen his plan for an advisory council dropped (see below), supported this, *Architect*, 6 Nov. 1869, p. 227.

159 In any case, Lord John Manners had been in the cabinet as First Commissioner (1858–9 and 1866–8), as Shaw Lefevre was in 1892–4 and Akers-Douglas in 1895–1902. Much depended on the intrinsic weight of the man.

160 A view shared by many Londoners; but whereas the country party expected Londoners to foot the bill, Londoners looked for subsidies from the taxpayer to underpin their metropolitan functions.

161 *PP* 1868–69 (387) X, *Second Report of the S.C. . . . on Hungerford Bridge and Wellington Street viaduct*, iii–vii; qq. 3373, 3377–80, 3384–5, 3409–11, 3412, 3428, 3448.

162 See below, pp. 158–9.

163 See P. Edwards, *History of London Street Improvements 1855–1897* (1898).

164 See A.S. Wohl, *The Eternal Slum: Housing and Social Policy in Victorian London* (1977), ch. 4, 5.

165 Edwards, *Street Improvements*, 49–61.

166 Owen, *Government of Victorian London*, 115.

167 The key Avenue de l'Opéra (1876–7), the completion of the Boulevards St-Germain and Henri-IV (1876–9), and the Rue Réaumur (1893–5) were important post-Haussmann works. A. Sutcliffe, *The Autumn of Central Paris*, ch. 2, 3.

168 LCC [L. Gomme], *Opening of Kingsway and Aldwych* (1905).

169 Ibid., 26, 40.

170 Ibid., 9–12, 39.

171 Cp *Arch. Rev.*, 7 (1900), 118–21.

172 R. Blomfield, W. Flockhart, E. George, H.T. Hare, M. Macartney, E.W. Mountford, E. Runtz & Co., and L. Stokes (*Builder*, 3 Nov. 1900, pp. 379–81). Each was paid £250, and the LCC worked closely with the RIBA.

173 See A. Saint, *Richard Norman Shaw* (New Haven & London, 1976), 346–50.

174 *Builder*, 1900, pp. 379–81.

175 *Australia House* (1918), unnumbered (kindly made available by Dr Bernard Attard), on which this paragraph is based.

176 The secretary of the Commonwealth department of External Affairs expressed bitter disappointment: 'The architects don't seem to have risen to the occasion at all. Everything internal seems to me to have been sacrificed to an attempt at grandeur which . . . might have equally well been achieved without the sacrifice of utility . . . of about one third of the whole site we get practically no

return. It is all taken up with the great doorway and wall at the eastern end.' National Library of Australia, MS 52 (Atlee Hunt Papers), item 843, Hunt to R.M. Collins, 11 Sept. 1912. I owe this reference to Dr Bernard Attard.

177 The foundation stone was laid 24 July 1913; though delayed by the war, building continued, part was occupied in 1916 and the whole completed in 1918. *Australia House*.

178 N. Pevsner, *BoE, London I* (Harmondsworth, 1973, 3rd edn, rev. B. Cherry), 367.

179 Cawston, *Comprehensive Scheme*, 3; Berlin's death rate had decreased by 12 per thousand, the Hague's by 7, and Rome's by 3.9. London's was 2.2 down, Paris's only 0.8.

180 Ibid., 6–7. The number killed and injured in London's streets rose from 3527 in 1881 to 5784 in 1891.

181 Sutcliffe, *Central Paris*, 49–55; B. de Buffévent, ed., *Centenaire de la Réconstruction de L'Hotel de Ville de Paris* (Paris, n.d.).

182 W.H. Mallock, *The New Republic* (1877; new edn 1879, reprinted Leicester U.P., 1975), 260–1.

183 Cawston, 82–8.

184 *Times*, 14, 21 Jan. (pp. 12), 5, 6, Mar. (pp. 9, 12), 4, 7, 16 Apr. (pp. 12, 7, 10); *3PD* CXLI, 768 (10 Apr. 1856).

185 RA, Add. MSS Q, 213–14, 7, 9 Aug. 1855.

186 Ibid., 229, 231, 253 (11, 27 Sept., [24 Dec.], 1855).

187 Ibid., 275, 284, 295 (Hall to Phipps, 15 Feb., 4 Mar., [19 Mar.]); 285 (Phipps to Hall, 4 Mar. 1856).

188 *PP* 1856 (85) VII, 387, *S.C. on St James's Park*; *3PD* CXLII, 1134–41 (6 June 1856).

189 RA, Add. MSS Q, 295; 333, 336 [14, 19 June 1856]. See *PP* 1856 (85) VII, 387. The suggestion for a footbridge over the ornamental water was Prince Albert's (RA, Add. MSS Q, 213, 7 Aug. 1855). Disraeli had carried an amendment to Hall's draft committee report to the effect that there were 'grave objections to any considerable increase of traffic through the Royal Parks', loc. cit., p. vi.

190 *3PD* CXLII, 1559–69, 16 June 1856.

191 RA, Add. MS Q, 456, 12 Nov. [1857].

192 Ibid., 554, 556 (July 1860).

193 Ibid., 665–697, Dec. 1861–Mar. 1862.

194 Ibid., 692 [1 Mar. 1862], holograph note; 694, Cowper to Phipps (1 Mar. 1862). General Charles Grey (1804–70) was Private Secretary, but Queen Victoria used several of her courtiers as secretaries, including Sir C.B. Phipps (1801–66, keeper of the Privy Purse), and Sir T.M. Biddulph (1809–78, master of the Household).

195 Ibid., 764, 3 Jan. 1865.

196 H.L. Malchow, 'Public Gardens and Social Action in late Victorian London', *Victorian Studies* 29 (1985), 103.

197 W. Robinson, *The Parks, Promenades, and Gardens of Paris* (1869), xx.

198 The following account is based primarily on RA, Add. MS Q, Office of Works III 1863–76, and *PD* CCVII–CCXXI, CCXXIII–CCXXXII: 27 Mar., 8 June, 6 July, 3 Aug. 1874, 12 Apr., 7 June, 2 July, 4 Aug. 1875, 21 (HL), 24 Feb., 26 May, 8 June, 14 Aug. 1876, 14 (HL), 23 Feb. 1877.

199 RA, Add. MS Q, 787, 31 July 1866.

200 Blair Adam MSS, 4/423, Gladstone to Adam, 12, 18 Nov. 1873; to Marquis of Westminster, 28 Dec. 1873.

201 RA Add. MS Q, 857, Lord Henry Lennox to Biddulph, 17 July 1874.

202 Ibid., 919, 30 Nov. 1875.

203 Lord Redesdale, *Memories* (1915), II, 694–5.

204 The following paragraph is based largely on Shaw Lefevre MSS, Gordon of Haddo Papers, 1/8, bundle 2.

205 G. Shaw Lefevre, 'Public Buildings in London', *Nineteenth Century*, 1888, Nov., 717–18.

206 RA, L 19/128, 6 Mar. 1882.

207 Lefevre persuaded a discouraging Gladstone that the removal of a reservoir from the north-west corner of Green Park, which his scheme required, to a better position in Hyde Park at a cost of £3000, was 'adequate public cause'. BL, Add. MS 44153, Shaw Lefevre to Gladstone, 17 Mar. 1882, Gordon of Haddo MSS 1/10, bundle 5, 20 Mar. 1882.

208 Ibid., 1/9, bundle 1, 25, Mar. 1882.

209 Ibid.; BL, Add. MS 44153, ff. 116–25, Aug.–Sept. 1882. Gladstone in the end supported Lefevre's plan, ibid., f. 125.

210 *Times*, 29 Nov. 1882.

211 See J. Physick, *The Wellington Monument* (1970), 2–19.

212 Gordon of Haddo MSS, 1/8, bundle 2, 17 Apr. 1883.

213 *Times*, 5 June; *Builder*, 23 June 1883, p. 839.

214 *3PD* CCCXXXI, 181, 1340–5, 3 July, 13 July (HL) 1883.

215 Press cutting, October, Gordon of Haddo MSS, 1/51. In fact, the plan seems essentially to have been that devised by the Secretary, Mitford. See Lord Redesdale, *Memories*, II, 694–5. A subsequent Secretary, Esher, devised a sequel; the widening of the western end of Piccadilly in 1901–2, Esher Papers, 5/12; Chilston Papers, C.6/257, 374, 384, 409, 429–33, and C 198/1.

216 Gordon of Haddo MSS, 1/8 bundle 2, Lefevre to Gladstone, 24 Sept. 1883.

217 Ibid., Gladstone to Lefevre, 24 Aug., and memo. 23 Aug. 1883.

218 Ibid., Lefevre to Gladstone, 24 Sept. 1883. Gladstone replied that he had not known of the proposals until a few days before he wrote. He stressed the need for a river crossing at Charing Cross, and concluded: 'My opinion has always been that these large questions connected with the Parks Palace & official London should be settled by the Cabinet & not departmentally. But as matters now stand I will not do more than refer the papers to Granville, & learn Childers's views; not carrying the matter further if they think it should proceed without further impediment in its present course.' Ibid., 1/10, bundle 2, 26 Sept. 1883.

219 An Act of 1887, extended in 1890 and 1892, gave a private company power to acquire land bounded by Charles Street, Parliament Street, Broad Sanctuary and Delahay Street for erecting new buildings, but the Acts lapsed because of the promoters' inability to raise the necessary funds. BL, Add. MS 46089, ff. 45–7.

220 BL, Add. MS 46089, ff. 54–65, draft, FCW to Treasury [June 1895].

221 *PP* 1896 (310), X, iii, and app. 1.

222 Ibid., qq. 337–435. Herbert Gladstone laboured without much success to obtain from the superintendent an endorsement of his (and his father's) plan for taking the Victoria traffic into a distinct roadway, qq. 385–95.

223 *PP* 1897 (335) X, iii, vii.

224 Ibid., qq. 28, 98.

225 Ibid., qq. 142, 146, 31.

226 Ibid., q. 106.

227 Ibid., qq. 112–15.

228 There seems to have been no opposition to the RIBA scheme on the grounds of the picturesque unfolding of the townscape by the existing curve of the road.

229 See below, pp. 243, 245, 247–8.

230 R. Shannon, *Crisis of Imperialism* (St Albans, 1976), 107.

231 D. Wormall, *Sir John Seeley and the Uses of History* (1980), 154, 155.

232 See *Survey*, XXXVIII, ch. xv.

233 R.C.K. Ensor, *England 1870–1914* (Oxford, 1936), 177.

234 *Survey* XXXVIII, 221.

235 PRO, T. 1/9453B/18588. Aston Webb made additions, including a new entrance, in 1899–1900 on an estimate of £11,450 (ibid.), not mentioned in the *Survey* account.

236 B. Semmel, *Imperialism and Social Reform* (1968 edn, Garden City, N.Y.), 46.

237 L. Griffin, 'Imperial City', *Pall Mall Mag.*, I (1893), 656–68. (I owe this reference to Mr R. Hyde.)

238 Queen Victoria's jnl, 22 June 1897, quoted E. Longford, *Victoria R.I.* (1966 edn), 688.

239 Esher Papers, 5/7, f. 68, 23 June 1897.

240 Ensor, op. cit., 240–1.

241 A.P. Thornton, *The Imperial Idea and its Enemies* (1959), ix.

242 P. Garside, 'Representing the Metropolis – The Changing Relationship between London and the Press, 1870–1939', *London Jnl*, 16 (1991), 157.

243 Ibid., 160; 161, quoting L. Brown, *Victorian News and Newspapers* (Oxford, 1985).

244 Esher Papers, 19/5, p. 89.

245 Esher Papers, 14/5, *Report of Queen Victoria Memorial Com.* (1911), on which the following account is based; meetings of 19, 21 Feb. 1901.

246 Ibid., 25 Feb., 11 Mar. 1901; 19/5, pp. 90–1, 92 (18 Feb., 11 Mar. 1901); Lord Esher, Final Report, Queen Victoria Mem. Com., RA, George V, O. 109, Queen Victoria Memorial. See also PRO, Work 20/20 and, for drawings, Work 35/125–80.

247 Princess Louise unsettled the king's mind temporarily; said to be angry because she had not been consulted (she was a competent sculptress), she suggested that a large open space before the palace would expose it to risk from riotous mobs, Esher Papers, 2/10, Esher's journal, 8 Apr. 1901.

248 But Austen Chamberlain at the Exchequer said he could not find the sum in 1905/06. He also declared it to be impossible to finance related works in Green Park, which the king urged on 'as a means of providing work for the unemployed', but this small charge seems to have been met, RA, George V, O. 109, Queen Victoria Memorial, nos 4, 4a (5 Aug. 1904), 5, 6 (6, 7 Jan. 1905).

249 PRO, T. 1/10071/1778. The government also contributed the land thrown into the street to a value of about £105,000. *Architect* 1913, i, 186; ii, 100.

250 Esher Papers, 14/5, p. 7. See *Arch. Design*, 48 (1978), 322–3.

251 Webb was restricted by the instruction that no alteration was to be made to the interior, so that Blore's fenestration had to be preserved. The work was executed with extraordinary rapidity, men working day and night Aug.–Oct. 1913. King George V wanted a straight front to the palace, and no curtailment of the area of the central balcony, as it was 'used from time to time when the King and other members of the Royal Family wish to show themselves to the People'. The superstructure over the central pediment, designed to hide the high chimneys at the back, was also a feature about which there was considerable discussion with King George and Queen Mary. RA, George V, O. 109, Queen Victoria Memorial, nos. 20–31, 50. The cost of the refronting appears to have been about £50,000, ibid., no. 39.

252 *4PD* CLXXXVII, 732 (2 Apr. 1908).

253 *Architect*, 15 Mar. 1884, p. 167. Cp *Builder*'s proposal to remodel London as 'the seat of a Federated Imperial Government', 5 Jan. 1912, pp. 11–13.

3. The Case for Public Buildings

1 The Office of Works was responsible for supplying furniture, coals, candles, soap, etc. Each individual house had its own housekeeper, office-keeper and messengers, *PP* 1856 (368) XIV, *S.C. on Public Offices*, q. 118.

2 Built 1733–7; see *King's Works* V, 431–3. 'Even Kent's solid building was unable to withstand the vibrations of a mangle operated by the Treasury housekeeper in her laundry: the Revenue Room ceiling collapsed', M. Wright, *Treasury Control of the Civil Service* (Oxford, 1969), 5n.

3 Sir L. Guillemard, *Trivial Fond Records* (1937), 19.

4 H. Roseveare, *The Treasury* (1969), 210.

5 Guillemard, loc. cit.

6 Sir E. Hertslet, *Recollections of the Old Foreign Office* (1901), 18.

7 *PP* 1839 (466) XIII, *S.C. on Public Offices (Downing Street)*, iii. Between 1839 and 1857 the number of F.O. despatches trebled; between 1827 and 1860 the number of foreign envoys doubled. See also *3PD* CXLV, 1705 (12 June 1857) for increase of work at F.O. and BoT in recent years.

8 *3PD* CXXXIX, 1576, 31 July 1855.

9 Lord Malmesbury, *Memoirs of an ex-Minister* (1884), I, 334; *3PD* CXXXVIII, 2015, 15 June 1855. Macaulay was said to have noted the progressive subsidence of one of the Cabinet-room windows (1846–7), ibid. See also *PP* 1859 (136-sess. 1), *Report by Mr John Phipps on the state of the buildings now occupied as the Foreign Office*.

10 See *Survey*, XXIX, 359–77.

11 *PP* 1877 (312) XV, *S.C. on Public Offices and Buildings*, q. 1801; *3PD* CLXVI, 1044 (29 Apr. 1862); H. Gordon, *The War Office* (1935), 74–5. Lord Northbrook (1826–1904), under-sec. for War 1861 and 1868–72, confessed that 'he could never find his way to the office of the Commander in Chief without a messenger to guide him', *PP* 1887 (184) VII, *S.C. on Admiralty and War Office (Sites)*, q. 2036. A similar account is given by A. Griffiths, 'The War Office Past Present and to Come', *Fortnightly Rev.*, LXXIX (1903), 665–78.

12 *Reminiscences of Lord Kilbracken* (1931), 4. Kilbracken's father, J.R. Godley, was the assistant under-secretary in question.

13 Gathorne Hardy, MP (Cons.) 1856–78; War Sec. 1874–8; cr. Vct Cranbrook 1878, earl 1892.

14 RA, E. 21/214, Biddulph to the Queen, 14 June 1875; E. 23/8, 'copy', Queen Victoria to Biddulph, 14 Jan. 1877; *PP* 1877 (55) XXVII, 687, *Report of Committee to inquire into Sanitary State of War Office*.

15 *Pall Mall Gazette*, 15 Jan. 1877.

16 William Jenner (1815–98), F.R.C.P. 1852, pres. 1881–8; bt 1868; established distinct identities of typhus and typhoid fevers.

17 One w.c. was used by 25 men of the printer's department, which itself was permanently lighted by gas, PRO, T. 1/7632B/18736, no. 3285.

18 *PP* 1877 (312) XV, q. 502.

19 PRO, T. 1/7632B/18736, 5 Mar. 1877.

20 *PP* 1887 (184) VII, qq. 1584, 1634–5; *Times*, 19 Aug. 1875, p. 7.

21 *PP* 1856 (368) XIV, *S.C. on Public Offices*, p. iii; qq. 157, 187–8.

22 *PP* 1857–58 (417) XI, *S.C. on Foreign Office Reconstruction*, q. 2023.

23 *PP* 1877 (312) XV, *S.C. on Public Offices*, q. 1796.

24 PRO, T. 1/8723A/3241, F. Bergne, 19 Oct. 1892.

25 *PP* 1887 [C. 5226] XIX, *R.C. to inquire into the Civil Establishments*, p. x.

26 *PP* 1887 (184) VII, q. 1568. Abortive plans were made in 1852 for rebuilding the Admiralty to accommodate the civil departments in Whitehall, MoD Library, Admiralty, Da 0123. For an account of the Old Admiralty see *Survey*, XVI, 57–8.

27 Sir J.H. Briggs (ed. Lady Briggs), *Naval Administrations 1827 to 1892: the experience of 65 years* (1897), 164–5. (I owe this reference to Professor Paul Smith.)

28 *PP* 1887 [C. 5226] XIX, *R.C. to inquire into the Civil Establishments*, paras. 27, 106.

29 E.g. A.C. Morton (an architect), *4PD* XXIV, 954 (21 May 1894).

30 E.g. Sir John Trelawney said 'he would rather see great men in little offices than little men in great offices', *3PD* CXLVI, 1422 (13 July 1857).

31 A.V. Dicey, *Law and Opinion in England* (1905), lect. VII; O. MacDonagh, *Pattern of Government Growth* (1961), 344.

32 *Civilian*, 23 Aug., 6 Sept. 1884.

33 But it was more expensive to build, and the courts providing light cut off rooms on one side from those on the other. *PP* 1887 (184) VII, *S.C. on Admiralty and War Office (Sites)*, qq. 1058–64.

34 A. Trollope, *The Three Clerks* (1858), ch. xviii.

35 *PP* 1887 [C. 5226] XIX, p. x.

36 There were no typewriters in the Admiralty, one of the largest Whitehall departments, in 1899. Lady Murray, *Making of a Civil Servant: Sir Oswyn Murray . . . Secretary of the Admiralty 1917–36* (1940), 46. Brett appears to have introduced them to the Office of Works when he became Secretary, 1895.

37 *Working conditions in the Civil Service. Report by a study group appointed by H.M. Treasury* (1947), 7. See also F. Duffy, 'Office buildings and organisational change', in A.D. King (ed.), *Buildings and Society* (1980), 255–80.

38 *PP* 1856 (368) XIV, *S.C. on Public Offices*, 34; 1857 sess. 2 (152) XLI, *New Government Offices*, 4–12; 1877 (312) XV, *S.C. on Public Offices*, app. A, Standard of accommodation.

39 *PP* 1854 [1713] XXVII, *Report on the Organization of the Permanent Civil Service*.

40 O. Anderson, *A Liberal State at War* (1967), 51.

41 *PP* 1856 (368) XIV, *S.C. on Public Offices*.

42 Ibid., cited, q. 118.

43 Ibid. Hunt calculated the rental of houses occupied as public offices and held on lease at £22,000 p.a., ibid., qq. 78, 198.

44 Ibid., qq. 119, 126–7.

45 Ibid., q. 148.

46 Ibid., q. 5.

47 Ibid., qq. 157–70.

48 Ibid., q. 192.

49 Ibid., qq. 171, 173. The permanent establishment at the Treasury had been reduced to about 70, ibid., q. 147. Another civil servant of extensive experience who was convinced of the economy and efficiency of concentration was Sir Richard Bromley (1813–66), accountant-general of the navy, who produced his own plans to house 1512 officers and clerks and 356 office-keepers and messengers 'now scattered over London' in a building 1910 × 240 ft, costing £1,386,166 at 11d. per ft cu. *PP* 1861 (103) XXXV, 227; Broadlands Papers, WFC/B 33–5 (Mar.–May 1862).

50 *PP* 1856 (368) XIV, app. 1.

51 *Times*, 3 Nov. 1883, quoted by W.H. White, *Architecture and Buildings* (1884), 157.

52 See C. Cook and B. Keith, *British Hist. Facts 1830–1900* (1975), 150: Totals of civil servants for:
1851   39,147
1861   31,943
1871   53,874 (including some workmen)
1881   50,859 (excluding telegraph and telephone services)
1891   79,241
1901   116,413 (including the General Post Office)
1914   280,000 (including Scotland and Ireland).

53 *PP* 1904 (75) LIV, *Estimates etc. for Civil Services for the year ending 31 March 1905*, pp. 110–11, 113, 130–1, 147–8.

54 *PP* 1856 (368) XIV, pp. iii–iv, and qq. 6, 10, 11, 18, 19, 56–62, 77–9, 194–7.

55 Broadlands Papers, GC/LE 74, Lewis to Palmerston, 20 Aug. 1856.

56 Ibid., 75, 26 Aug. 1856.

57 Lewis to J. Wilson, n.d. [?Sept. 1856], E.I.

58 Barrington, *Servant of All*, I (1927), 313–14. Arguments for a state residence (strongly opposed by the economic party), as facilitating a choice of non-aristocratic ministers, had earlier been put to the S.C. on Official Salaries, *PP* 1850 (611) XV, qq. 94, 250, 328 (citing Burke).

58 Broadlands Papers, 198, Palmerston to Lewis, 25 Sept. 1856.

59 PRO, Work 12/86/1, 'New Government Offices', Instructions to architects, 8: 'One State Dining Room to accommodate 50 Persons, with Apartments adjoining for occasional Supper and Tea Rooms, Library, Morning Room, &c. Five Reception Rooms, en suite, on the First Floor, to accommodate 1500 Visitors. . . . About 12 or 14 Bed Rooms, with a suitable number of Dressing Rooms. All the other requirements of a Nobleman's Town House.'

This provision aroused much ire among economically-minded MPs and the popular press. It had already caused the rejection of Palmerston's first attempt to secure a new Foreign Office; *3PD* CXXXIX, 1574–8 (31 July 1855). But Jupiter thundered: 'It is thus that our democrats fight, by their narrow parsimony, the battle of the aristocracy, and, to save a small sum to the public, confine the higher offices of the State to a small and wealthy circle', *Times*, 1 Aug. 1855, p. 8. After considerable shilly-shallying, the residence was finally dropped from Scott's definitive plans, only the three reception rooms surviving.

60 *PP* 1887 (184) VII, q. 2047. Isaacs (F.R.I.B.A., M.I.C.E.) was somewhat ambivalent about the Clearing House ('of a very simple character') as a model, however, describing it first as 'the nearest approach to the class of building that we should follow in the proposed addition to the Admiralty' (q. 2047), but when an MP asked: 'The Clearing House is not the sort of building, I presume, that would be wanted for public offices?' he replied: 'No, of course not . . . I know it to be one of the most modern description of buildings erected for a large number of people' (q. 2072). It cost 6½d. per cu.ft. (and for St Thomas's 9d.), against Leemings' estimate of 11d. for a plain extension in the character of the Old Admiralty (q. 1796).

61 *4PD* CXC, 1172 (G.F.S. Bowles, 19 June 1908); cp W. Rutherford, 28 May 1908, *4PD* CLXXXIX, 1395.

62 *Architects' Mag.* I (1900–1), 196.

63 *PP* 1887 (184) XII, qq. 1970, 1978, 1989, 2000, 2003.

64 *PP* 1856 (368) XIV, q. 158.

65 *3PD* CXLVI, 799 (2 July 1857).

66 Instructions to competitors, PRO, Work 12/86/1, no. 41.

67 *3PD* CXLVII, 364 (24 July), 1301 (10 Aug. 1857).

68 As the history of Leemings' victorious design in the 1884 War Office & Admiralty competition was to show, see pp. ••• below.

69 The problem was evident in the 1960s over the Greater London Council's contribution to running the Museum of London, see F. Sheppard, *Treasury of London's Past* (1991), 168–9.

70 See p. •••.

71 PRO, Ed. 84/55, 9 Jan. 1882, cited J. Physick, *Victoria and Albert Museum* (1982), 177.

72 PRO, Ed. 84/55, 26 Jan. 1885, cited Physick, 180.

73 PRO, Work 17/25/2, 2 Dec. 1886, cited Physick, 181.

74 PRO, Work 33/1399–1418.

75 Where it had been added to the Sheepshanks Collection of modern British paintings, donated in 1856 on condition that it was housed in an exhibition building at South Kensington, a development of a scheme for placing the nation's pictures there, see Broadlands Papers, GC/ST/15, 24 (Lord Stanley of Alderney to Palmerston, 29 June 1855, 19 Oct. 1856).

76 PRO, Work 33/1521–45.

77 Sir Charles Holmes and C.H. Collins Baker, *Making of the National Gallery 1824–1924* (1924), 57–60.

78 *3PD* CCCXXXVI, 645 (6 May 1889).

79 Holmes and Collins Baker, 61–3.

80 Drawings of the Gallery in 1869 by George Scharf, the first secretary (who also lived in the house) are in BM Print Room, 200. c. 6.

81 *3PD* CCCXXXIV, 1117–25; XXXCCCV, 493–4, 1192 (Apr.–May 1889). Alexander, a recluse, was owner of the valuable eponymous estate in Kensington (ex info. Dr J. Hayes).

82 Another outstanding example of private philanthropy was Lady Wallace's bequest to the nation in 1897 of her late husband's great art collections (inherited from his father the 4th Marquis of Hertford), on condition that the government built a new museum for them in central London. A committee reported in favour of retaining the collections at Hertford House instead (*PP* 1897 [C. 8445]), trustees were appointed, the freehold purchased, the out-buildings converted to galleries, and various internal modifications completed, in 1897–1901 at a cost of nearly £130,000 (*PP, Appropriation accounts; Wallace Collection Catalogues. Pictures and Drawings* (15th edn, 1928), pp. xvi–xxv). The Treasury secretary wrote to his Works' compeer, 14 Aug. 1900, 'Hertford House – and be hanged to it! I have seen the Trustees, the Secretary and what is more important the Bills. The long and short of it is that the Trustees have outrun the constable to the tune of about £5000, without any authority. . . . It goes without saying that the Trustees bought in a very dear market.' What was properly Works' expenditure, the Treasury would authorise; the rest must be put in a supplementary vote 'over which I expect the Chancellor will damn all the art out of Alfred Rothschild's hair and whiskers' (Esher Papers, corr. 5/10, ff. 145–6. Rothschild was a trustee).

83 Montague Smith (1809–91): MP (Lib.-Cons.) 1859–63; Q.C. 1852; judge 1863; kt 1865.

84 *3PD* CLXXII, 605–7, 10 July 1863.

85 MP (Cons.) 1852–65; Q.C. 1849; kt 1867; judge 1875–81.

86 *3PD* CLXXII, 607–8.

87 Public expenditure for such a purpose might be justified under either the second or third functions of the state (after defence), as defined by Adam Smith: the maintenance of internal order, and the 'erecting and maintaining certain public works and certain public institutions, which it can never be for the interest of any individual, or small number of individuals, to erect and maintain'. A. Smith, *The Wealth of Nations* (1950 edn), ii, 184–5.

88 Where by 1884 they had attracted nearly 5,800,000 visitors, including 275,696 in 1883. *PP* [c. 4164] XXVIII, 785.

89 *PP* 1864 (504) XII. *S.C. on the Patent Office Library and Museum*, report, and qq. 35–7, 96–8.

90 *PP* 1859 – sess. 2 (120) XIV, *Report of Commissioners of Patents for Inventions, 1858; 1872*, XXIV, 232ff. Pennethorne built an extension in 1866–7.

91 For the Victorian Post Office, see M.J. Daunton, *Royal Mail* (1985).

92 PRO, Work 30/5880–91.

93 *PP* 1884–85 [C. 4267] XXII, 561, *Report of committee appointed by the Treasury to examine the subject of central Post Office buildings and establishments*. The increase of labour was tabulated (app. A):

Year	Letters, newspapers, &c.	Registered letters	Staff
1868	341,679,548	1,945,138	1431
1873	481,813,236	3,184,968	1911
1878	624,383,728	4,663,844	2078
1883	775,391,380	7,325,509	2423

The number of telegrams had risen from 5,086,132 in 1870–71 to 15,458,563 in 1883–4 (app. B); and the profits from P.O. business from £1,128,000 in 1868 to £2,740,000 in 1883 (app. C).

94 PRO, Work 30/5902–3.

95 *PP* 1884–85 [C. 4267] XXII, app. C.

96 Ibid., p. 6.

97 PRO, Work 30/5892–901. 'The most vivid proof of the prodigious development of the British Empire under the sway of Queen Victoria will be the fact that it has been found necessary to raise in succession three such pites [as the GPO buildings] . . . each dwarfing its predecessors', J. Henniker Heaton, MP, 'Ten Years' Postal Progress', *Contemporary Rev.* 1895(2), 1–14.

98 Regarded by some as 'altogether extraneous to the proper functions of the Post Office', *4PD* L, 1771–2 (26 July 1889).

99 The disused Coldbath Fields Prison was made available (now known as 'Mount Pleasant'). See *4PD* L, 942–7 and 1754–89 (19, 26 July 1889); *PP* 1889 (323) XI, *S.C. on Post Office Sites Bill*. The old buildings, badly ventilated and heated, were blamed in 1894 for much sickness, and even deaths, among the staff, *4PD* XXIV, 949–54, 21 May 1894.

100 PRO, Work 30/4749–67.

101 *PP* 1860 (441) VII, p. xxi.

102 *PP* 1887 (184) VII, q. 1567.

103 *PP* 1867–68 (281) LVIII *[Treasury] Commission to inquire into . . . the Accommodation of Public Departments*, 6.

104 (1818–1904), 2nd s. of 5th D. of Rutland; depicted as 'Lord Henry Sidney' in Disraeli's *Coningsby* (1844); MP (Cons.) 1841–7, 1850–88; suc. as 7th. D. of Rutland 1888; FCW (in cabinet) 1852, 1858–9, 1866–8; P.M.G. 1874–80, 1885.

105 *PP* 1867–68 (281-I) LVIII, *[Treasury] Commission . . . [on] Accommodation of Public Departments*, report of sub-committee, app. A.

106 Ibid., pp. 1–2.

107 Ibid., (281), 1–2.

108 Ibid., q. 161. Sir J.H. Briggs, Chief Clerk of the Admiralty, claimed in 1892 that Corry became 'thoroughly convinced, from the rapidly increasing business of the Admiralty, that the time had arrived when a building should be erected capable of embracing within its precincts all the various branches under Admiralty control', *Naval Administration 1827 to 1892*, 164. (I owe this reference to Professor Paul Smith.)

109 MP (Cons.) 1837–74; sec. for War & Cols 1852; First Lord of Admiralty 1858–9 and 1866–7; War sec. 1867–8; cr. Lord Hampton 1874.

110 *PP* 1867–8 (281-I) LVIII, qq. 277–9, 287, 289.

111 Ibid., qq. 85, 87.

112 *PP* 1877 (312) XV, app. 2. The Emigration Office and the Crown Agents were under the Colonial Office, while under the Home Office were: Privy Seal Office, Irish Office, Lord Advocate for Scotland, Local Government Office, Commissioners in Lunacy, Friendly Societies Registration Office, Directors of Convict Prisons, Inspectors of Prisons, of Reformatories, of Constabulary, of Factories, of Anatomy, of Burial Grounds, Poor Law Board, Parliamentary Bill Office and temporary commissions.

113 *PP* 1887 (184) VII, q. 1581; 1877 (312) XV, qq. 1159–66.

114 Ibid., app. 2.

115 *PP* 1872 (200) I; 1873 (40) I.

116 The Coinage Act of 1870 made the chancellor of the Exchequer Master of the Mint, bringing him into direct communication with the executive head of the Royal Mint opposite the Tower of London. As it was also desirable to renew the Mint's machinery, the idea of moving the whole establishment to a situation on the Embankment just west of Blackfriars Bridge, more convenient for both the Bank of England and Whitehall, was found attractive. Hunt, the Surveyor, calculated that the move could be financially profitable. See *PP* 1871 (295) XXXVII, 311, *Letter from T. to FCW about removal of Royal Mint to Thames Embankment, 7 Nov. 1870*; 1871 (334) XI, *S.C. on New Mint Building Site Bill*; 1871; IV, 351, 359 (*Mint Building Site Bill*); 1874, IV, 1 (*Mint Removal Bill*); 1881 (304) IX, 537, *London City Lands (Thames Embankment) Bill* [H.L.]; *Royal Mint, 12th Annual Report*. See also *3PD* CXCIX, 425–6 (17 Feb.), 1626–7; CCIII, 382ff. (18 July 1870); CCVI, 134–44 (4 May 1871); and C.E. Challis, ed., *New History of the Royal Mint* (Cambridge, 1992), 518, 522–30.

117 *PP* 1877 (312) XV, qq. 517–34.

118 *4PD* LV, 121 (17 Mar. 1898).

119 See below, pp. 127–9.

120 *PP* 1877 (312) XV, qq. 14, 21, 68. The net rental of offices which could be concentrated in new buildings in Whitehall was £20,080.

121 Ibid., qq. 214–19, 229–31, 234–5, 641–9, 849–54, 1927.

122 Ibid., qq. 32, 50, 451, 475.

123 Ibid., qq. 314, 316.

124 Ibid., qq. 319–23, 399–400, 406–7.

125 Ibid., qq. 416, 453.

126 Ibid., qq. 1916, 1919, 1933–5.

127 Ibid., qq. 955, 965, 973, 980, 1010, 1398, 1413.

128 Ibid., qq. 1398, 1920, 1936, 1954–64.

129 Ibid., evidence of Col. Pasley, qq. 955ff; of H.W.R. Walker, qq. 1397–8, 1419.

130 Ibid., q. 1914. A problem familiar to researchers at the PRO.

131 Ibid., qq. 1968–72.

132 Ibid., q. 1398.

133 Ibid., q. 576.

134 Ibid., qq. 1398, 1405. See also q. 266 for Mitford's praise of Somerset House.

135 Ibid., qq. 539–42, 546.

136 Ibid., qq. 48–9, 111–12, 845–7. Sir William Harcourt complained in 1898 that 'Even on a midsummer day, when you come from the public offices in Whitehall and wish to go to the Foreign Office, you cannot get there except by going through a passage lighted by gas', *4PD* LV, 116 (17 Mar. 1898).

137 *PP* 1896 (310) X, *S.C. on Government Offices (Appropriation of Sites)*, q. 588. By the time in the 1890s that Leemings' Admiralty extensions were being built, with their corridors looking on to courts on one side, the argument against the central corridor had been very much weakened by the introduction of the odourless electric light, ibid.

138 *PP* 1877 (312) XV, qq. 48, 213–18, 641–9.

139 Ibid., qq. 20, 129, 167, 215, 480–1, 855, 877, 1832, 558; *PP* 1887 (184) VII, q. 408.

140 Ibid., qq. 410–11, 1255.

141 'In many cases the rooms occupied by one official entitled to the sole use of a room are exceptionally large, but, owing to their situation, difficult to allocate otherwise', PRO, Work 12/237, report on F.O., 23 Jan. 1924.

142 See *ILN*, 24 May 1878. Gladstone could not bear the 'size and magnificence' of the new Foreign Office, and preferred the Cabinet room in no. 10 Downing Street, Sir Algernon West, *Contemporary Portraits* (1920), 49. Lord Salisbury, however, held his cabinets in the Foreign Office (Esher Papers, Corr. 5/10, ff. 125–6, Esher to Mowatt, 17 July 1900); and he used the cabinet room and the two adjoining reception rooms as an office after he had given up the Foreign secretaryship (ibid., ff. 188–9, 194, Akers-Douglas to Esher, 1, 5 Nov.; M.V. Brett, ed., *Jnls and Letters of . . . Vct Esher* (3 v. 1934), 268, 9 Nov. 1900). Salisbury's secretary then asked for 'a bolt to be put on the inside of Lord Salisbury's door so that he can exclude his Colleagues and his Secretaries when he has had

enough of them . . . of course there is a lock on the door already; but Lord Salisbury is dreadfully destructive to keys!' (ibid., ff. 208–9, 13 Nov. 1900).

143 J. Tilley & S. Gaselee, *The Foreign Office* (1933), 141.

144 Sir C. Parkinson, *The Colonial Office from Within 1909–1945* (1947), 12–13, 18.

145 Sir Robert Anderson, 'The Lighter Side of my Official Life', *Blackwoods Mag.*, Nov. 1909, p. 606ff. (I owe this reference to Dr Jill Pellew.) The extra floor in a building that necessarily followed externally the lines of the adjoining Foreign Office was of course introduced to meet criticisms of the earlier building, and assessed by the architect with Galton of the Works and departmental officials.

146 *PP* 1877 (312) xv, qq. 20, 126, 128, 132, 134–5. Scott complained of the abuse of his plans, especially in the Home Office: 'when I had struck out my first plans . . . I spent weeks in going from office to office consulting every head of every department as to his own accommodation . . . but the internal constitution of those apartments [*sic*] has been changed, and it is very often the case that a department for which a group of rooms was planned, does not occupy it at all, and if it does occupy it, that their internal arrangements are so altered that the same rooms do not fit, so that it is a wonder to me that they were able to shake together at all in this building, for, practically speaking, a considerable portion . . . was planned for different uses from what it is appropriated to' (qq. 676, 716–20, 799).

147 *PP* 1856 (368) xiv, qq. 148, 150, 152.

148 *PP* 1877 (312) xv, qq. 225–6, 881.

149 Ibid., qq. 225–6, 441.

150 'In all recently erected banks, and other places of business [the clerks are grouped in large numbers] to a much greater degree than used to be the case. A private room is reserved for the partners, but . . . all the other officers and clerks of the establishment work together in a single great office, with glass partitions separating the more important heads from the other clerks.' Lefevre to Lord Hartington, 4 Apr. 1883, *PP* 1887 (184) vii, q. 2036.

151 Characteristic of Smith's line is the following exchange with Mitford: 'Is there a single instance within your knowledge in which a new building erected within the last 20 years has proved to be more convenient than, or even equally convenient with, the old building which it replaced? – No, I do not know of any one. – There is no instance within your knowledge in which a new building has been equally convenient with the old one which it has replaced? – Certainly not.' *PP* 1877 (312) xv, qq. 241–2.

152 Ibid., qq. 483–7; *PP* 1887 (184) vii, q. 1324.

153 *PP* 1887 (184) vii, qq. 1304–10, 1316.

154 Ibid., q. 2036.

155 Ibid., qq. 1672–4, 1711.

156 Ibid., qq. 640–1.

157 Ibid., Lord George Hamilton, q. 641; *PP* 1877 (312) xv, q. 1417.

158 *PP* 1887 (184) vii, qq. 1250, 1500. Existing rooms in the Admiralty for 13 clerks were said to measure 28 × 24 ft, ibid., q. 1251.

159 Ibid., qq. 539–40.

160 Ibid., q. 1075. But the 1887 report of the R.C. on the Civil Establishments 'strongly recommended' the provision of large rooms in both War Office and Admiralty, *PP* 1887 [C. 5226] xix, p. x.

161 PRO, Work 12/92/1, ff. 1–3, Instructions, second or final competition of architects, 1884.

162 *Civilian*, 16 Aug. 1884, pp. 237, 241.

163 Ibid., 23 Aug., p. 250; 6 Sept. 1884.

164 *PP* 1897 (335) x, *S.C. on Government Offices (Appropriation of Sites)*, qq. 739–44; PRO, T. 1/9185A/15177, no. 8579, 22 May 1897; PRO, Work 12/

89/1, f. 22, abstract of Admiralty requirements.

165 *PP* 1896 (310) x, *S.C. on Government Offices (Appropriation of Sites)*, qq. 9–21, 102–7. The other offices were those of the Privy Council, the Parliamentary Counsel, the Civil Service Commissioners, the Inspector of Reformatories and the Lunacy Commissioners. The Board of Trade proposed to keep its Standards Department in the Jewel Tower, Old Palace Yard, and the Electrical Department in its recently fitted-up accommodation in Richmond Terrace, ibid., qq. 35–6, 132–6.

166 Ibid., qq. 295–305, 311, 317, 330–5; app. 2, 3. App. 3 gives an undivided total of 268 for messengers and attendants of various kinds; but as Taylor explained, in a large department like the Admiralty and War Office, 'their staff was changing almost daily', qq. 126–7.

167 J. Carswell, *The Civil Servant and His World* (1966), 114.

168 MP (Cons.) 1892–1906; (Lib.) 1910. Founder of *Vanity Fair* 1868.

169 *4PD* lv, 668, 671 (4 Mar. 1898).

170 'We rarely have a year in which there is not some legislation which involves and necessitates the increase of some of the large departments' – Sir John Taylor, *S.C. on Public Offices (Sites)*, *PP* 1897 (335) x, q. 789.

171 *4PD* lv, 117–20 (17 Mar. 1898).

172 *PP* 1889 [C. 5831] *Treasury committee to inquire into the Science Collections at South Kensington*.

173 Because of Treasury obduracy. See p. 269 below.

174 *4PD* lv, 1262 (29 Mar. 1898).

175 Ibid., 1135–6 (28 Mar. 1898).

176 MP (Unionist) 1895–1906, 1910–22; LCC 1907–25; pres. N.U.T. 1894; kt 1925.

177 *4PD* lv, 1270 (29 Mar. 1898).

178 Physick, *Victoria and Albert Museum*, 204–9, quoting PRO, Work 17/25/8, 21 Oct. 1895; *PP* 1899 xlv, *S.C. on College of Science (Building and Site)*.

179 E.W. Cohen, *Growth of the British Civil Service 1780–1939* (1941), 163–4.

180 So *Survey*, xxxviii, 253. Roscoe (vice-ch. of London Univ.) commented on 7 Mar. 1908, after seeing the pres. of the Bd of Trade, that it was a favourable moment for erecting a science museum because it was essential for the working of the new Imperial College of Science, 1851 Comm. file 68.

181 Set up in 1837, and established in Jermyn Street in 1851, see *King's Works*, vi, 460–1.

182 Bodleian, Harcourt dep. MS 459, f. 19, preliminary report of Bell committee.

183 Ibid.

184 *PP* 1911 xviii; 1912–13 xxii.

185 *Survey*, xxxviii, ch. xix.

186 *4PD* cxxvi, 812; cxxvii, 774 (29 July, 10 Aug. 1903). As early as February 1899, Esher could see that there was no realistic prospect of housing the BoT in Great George Street because of the growth of LGB, H.O., and Education, Esher Papers 5/11, ff. 211–19.

187 *4PD* lxxxii, 397, 1214 (1, 10 May 1900); lxxxiv, 297, 1351–2 (18, 28 June, 1900); cxi, 539–50 (12 June 1902). The cost of the Colindale depositary (including £2623 for the site) was £20,092, *PP*, *Appropriation accounts*, 1903/06.

188 *4PD* lxxxii, 397–9 (1 May 1900).

189 Ibid.; and lxxxiv, 297–8 (18 June), 1351–2 (28 June 1900); xc, 1025 (8 Mar. 1901).

190 *4PD* cix, 73, 539–52 (9, 12 June 1902); cx, 639, 788 (2, 3 July 1902).

191 *4PD* clxxxvii, 737–9 (2 Apr. 1908).

192 Described in 1894 as 'a disgrace to the smallest country in Europe . . . a strange and motley group of buildings with long dark passages and small and inconvenient rooms', *4PD* xxiv, 954–6.

193 MP (Cons.) 1892–1906 (Peckham), 1906–24 (City of London); chairman, Estimates committee.

Stockbroker; chairman of Gt Northern Rly; cr. Bt 1902, P.C. 1916, Baron Banbury of Southam 1924; 'able to talk at any moment at any length on any subject' (*Complete Peerage*, xiii, 398).

194 *4PD* clxxxviii, 1177, 1185–6 (13 May 1908).

195 *4PD* cxc, 1172 (19 June 1908).

196 Sir L. Earle, *Turn over the Page* (1935), 92.

197 Carswell, *Civil Servant*, 114.

198 PRO, t. 1/10960b/22783, 15 May 1908 (9080/08). t. 1/11161/25329, 17 Dec. 1909.

199 7 Nov. 1908.

200 A trawl of the *Civil Service Gazette*, *Civilian* ('The Accredited Organ of the Civil Service') and *Civil Service Times* ('The Representative Organ of the Civil Service', pub. 1886–92 only) for June–Dec. in 1877, 1884, 1887, 1897, 1903, 1908 and 1912, periods when reports or legislation on public buildings were under discussion in the press in general, produced almost no comment on these matters, save for a rare remark about sanitation. They were largely concerned with grading, pay, and pensions, particularly in the numerically dominant Revenue departments.

201 *Appropriation accounts* for 1909/10 and 1912/13, *PP* 1911 (7) l, and 1914 (55) lvi.

202 PRO, t. 1/11219/13629, 16 July 1910.

203 Earle, *Turn over the Page*, 91.

204 PRO, t. 1/11219/13629, memo. by J.H. Hillier, 14 June 1910; by Sir G. Murray, 24 Apr., and Lord Beauchamp, FCW, 11 Apr. 1911.

205 PRO, t. 1/11322/16991, OW to Treasury, 21 July 1911 (14244/11). A marginal note observes: 'I believe Sir R. Chambers [Treasury permanent secretary] does not altogether share this view'; Chalmers was notorious for his economical views.

206 The 1909 Labour Exchanges Act and the 1911 National Insurance Act 'involved a great increase of staff, and the creation of such elaborate administrative machinery, that it was necessary to create a special "Labour Exchange and Unemployment Department"'; and just before the outbreak of war in 1914, 'the staff of the Board of Trade was exactly fifty times as numerous as in 1867', Sir H. Llewellyn Smith, *The Board of Trade* (1928), 182–3, 238–9. In general, there were about 28,000 more non-industrial established civil servants in 1911 than in 1902. E.W. Cohen, *Growth of the British Civil Service*, 163–4.

207 *5PD* xl, 1782–1831 (9 July), 2072 (11 July 1912).

208 *5PD* ccxlviii, 800 (16 Feb.); ccl, 1133–66 (1 Apr. 1931); ccliv, 1030.

209 *Working conditions in the Civil Service* (1947), 17.

210 Ibid., 7.

211 Ibid., 16.

212 Parkinson, *Colonial Office from Within*, 23.

4. The Office of Works 1851–1873

1 See Owen, *Government of Victorian London* (cited ch. 1).

2 *PP* 1889 (326) lxvi, *Annual Report of the Metropolitan Board of Works for 1888*, p. 9.

3 For the MBO see A.G. Ruffhead, 'Office of Metropolitan Buildings, London, 1840–1855', M. Phil. thesis, Univ. of London, 1973.

4 *PP* 1889 [326] lxvi, 10.

5 Ibid., 29.

6 Ibid., 26.

7 By 14 & 15 Vict. c. 42, *An Act to make better Provision for the Management of the . . . Land Revenues of the Crown, and for the Direction of Public Works and Buildings*.

8 D. Van Zanten, *Designing Paris* (Cambridge, Mass. & London, 1987), 121.

9 14 & 15 Vict. c. 42.

10 See below, p. 70.

11 *PP* 1914 [Cd 7416] xlix, para. 4; PRO, Work 22/2/17, 'Report on the Office of Works', 12 Mar. 1867.

12 Lord Henry Lennox, FCW, to Treasury, 20 Jan. 1875, PRO, Work 6/413, 'Memo. as to certain Matters concerning the Office of Her Majesty's Works', 8.

13 *3PD* CCCXXXVIII, 679. The 'one' is undoubtedly Henry Layard.

14 Rosebery (Lib.), Plunket (Cons.), Morley (Lib.), Elgin (Lib.), Plunket (Cons.). See app. 1.

15 It was on several occasions seen as a first ministerial appointment for a former chief party whip – Adam in 1873, Plunket in 1885, Akers-Douglas in 1895.

16 *3PD* CCCXXXVIII, 686.

17 Ibid., 683.

18 See M.H. Port, 'An Ædile for London?', *London Jnl*, 12 (1986), 58–64; *Times*, 23 June 1858, letter, p. 6, 'S.D.O.'

19 *PP* 1860 (483) IX, *S.C. on Miscellaneous Expenditure*, qq. 1365–6, 1369–70.

20 Ibid., qq. 1412–13.

21 Ibid., q. 1432.

22 See M.H. Port, ed., *The Houses of Parliament* (1976), 187ff.

23 *PP* 1860 (483) IX, qq. 1548–9. So that it would not be necessary to teach the history of current business to successive First Commissioners.

24 Port, 'An Ædile for London?'

25 *PP* 1868–69 (387) X, *2nd report of S.C. on Hungerford Bridge, etc.*, qq. 3283–5, 3311–17, 3347, 3933.

26 Ibid., qq. 3427–9, 3448.

27 Ibid., vii. The report did recommend that any company or corporate body promoting a private bill for executing works or buildings in the metropolis should deposit plans at the Office of Works, and the First Commissioner report on them to parliament, ibid., iii. Ayrton attempted to oblige the MBW to do so, PRO, Work 1/89, p. 365, 5 Jan. 1870.

28 *PP* 1860 (483) IX, qq. 1420–8, 1448, 1482, 1487–8.

29 *PP* 1868–69 (387) X, q. 3933.

30 *King's Works*, VI, 217–18.

31 Former private secretary to Lord John Russell. He moved in the circle of the Prince of Wales. Lowe thought him socially 'rather too grand' for his post (BL, Add. MS 44301, f. 43). Debrett's *Peerage, sub* Bedford; J.C. Sainty, *Office-holders in modern Britain: I. Treasury officials, 1660–1870* (1972), 148; *Times*, 10 Sept. 1884, p. 8f. See appendix 4 and M.H. Port, 'A Contrast in Styles at the Office of Works', *Hist. Jnl*, 27 (1984), 155n.

32 BL, Add. MS 44419, ff. 271–3, Layard to Gladstone, 23 Mar. 1869.

33 H.H. Statham, 'How our public improvements are carried out', *Fortnightly Rev.*, 1882, p. 816.

34 See appendix 4. For a full account of Pennethorne's career, see G. Tyack, *Sir James Pennethorne and the making of Victorian London* (Cambridge, 1992).

35 These consisted chiefly of the Museum of Economic Geology and the Public Record Office (*King's Works*, VI, 460–1, 471–6), and the west wing of Somerset House for the Inland Revenue. He had also been instructed in 1854 to prepare designs for new public offices in Downing Street. *PP* 1857–58 (417) XI, *S.C. on Foreign Office Reconstruction*, 184–5.

36 See appendix 4.

37 See appendix 4 and *DNB*.

38 See below, p. 66.

39 Cp. Summerson, *Victorian Architecture* (cited ch. 1), 115.

40 John Phipps (*c.*1796–1868), Assistant Surveyor, London District, in charge of all the major public offices, best-paid official architect, Pennethorne apart, received £800 p.a. at the end of his career. He retired in 1866 after 16 years service, aged 72. PRO, Work 2/29, p. 442. When an official 'meas-

urer' (quantity surveyor), William Albon, retired in 1866, his average remuneration over the preceeding three years was calculated at £279, which Hunt judged 'extremely moderate when compared with the payment made for similar services in private practice', ibid. 31, p. 171.

41 Calculation from *PP*, annual appropriation accounts, see bibliography.

42 PRO, Work 2/32, p. 385 (11 Jan. 1869).

43 Pennethorne's appointment did not contradict this for reasons explained below, p. 165.

44 *PP* 1854 [1713] XXVII, *Report of Committees of Inquiry into Public Offices*, 328.

45 Ibid., 322–7.

46 See *King's Works*, VI, 220.

47 *PP* 1860 (483) IX, *S.C. on Miscellaneous Expenditure*, q. 1337.

48 According to Austin, Hall had pulled into shape a highly disorganised office, instituting a register of correspondence and laying down 'stringent rules' that were 'just what was needed', requiring only a period in which to mature. *PP* 1856 (304) VII, 65, *S.C. on Civil Service Estimates*, Class 7, qq. 8, 9, 16, 17. As a country gentleman, Hall was notoriously mean, an ungenial and dictatorial host, see A. Fairfax-Lucy, ed., *Mistress of Charlecote: the Memoirs of Mary Elizabeth Lucy* (1985 edn), 95–8.

49 See F.M. Boase, *Mod. Eng. Biog.*, 1 (Truro, 1892).

50 See *PP* 1856 (193) LII, *Progress reports on . . . Battersea Park*.

51 *PP* 1863 (483) IX, q. 1338. See also 1857, sess. 2 (130) XLI, *Report by FCW on Metropolitan Improvements*, 2–3.

52 (1810–89). Son of a builder, quantity surveyor for Barry in preparing estimates for his Houses of Parliament design; much employed by railway companies – designed stations for N. Staffs Rly. C.B. 1871; kt 1876.

53 *PP* 1860 (483) IX, q. 1046, 1517.

54 Ibid., q. 1049.

55 Ibid., qq. 1528, 1659.

56 Ibid., q. 1539.

57 Ibid., q. 1365.

58 M. Wright, *Treasury Control* (Oxford, 1969), 195, 339.

59 Ibid., 201–4, 223–4.

60 PRO Work 6/413, Report of the Committee of 1857. Since efficiency depended on the Secretariat, they recommended increasing its personnel from 2 clerks (£150 × £15 – £400), a registrar and 3 supplementary clerks to 2 first-class (£400 × £20 – £600) and 3 second-class (£250 × £15 – £350). The Accounts Branch, not properly organised since the split in 1851, needed supplementary clerks and hourly-paid copyists.

61 *PP* 1857–58 (417) XI, q. 482 and app. 4.

62 Ibid., app. 4, pp. 186–7, 191–5.

63 PRO, T. 1/6693A/3774.

64 *PP* 1857–58 (417) XI, app. 4, p. 196.

65 Composed of Arbuthnot, Blackburn (a lord of the Treasury, and a Mr H.J. Holland of Liverpool, PRO, T. 1/6703A/4213, 30 Mar. 1859.

66 *PP* 1868–9 (336) XXXIV, p. 3.

67 Broadlands Papers, GC/LA/34/enc. 1, memo. by Samuel Laing, 6 Jan. 1860.

68 *3PD* CLX, 1360 (16 Aug. 1860).

69 It was probably the saga of the National Gallery that Gladstone had most particularly in mind, see pp. 84–91 below.

70 R. Shannon, *Gladstone*, 1 (1982), 418–19, 445.

71 Cp. ibid., 446, 452.

72 *PP* 1860 (483) IX.

73 See appendix 4.

74 *PP* 1860 (483) IX, *S.C. on Misc. Expenditure*, qq. 792, 855.

75 T.A. Jenkins, ed., *Parliamentary Diaries of Sir John Trelawny, 1858–1865* (1990), 214–15 (27 June 1862).

76 PRO, Work 22/2/17, 'Report on the Office of Works', 12 Mar. 1867.

77 *PP* 1860 (483) IX, q. 1300.

78 PRO, Work 22/2/22, 'Memo. for the Commissioners', Feb. 1875, app., T.M. 12 May 1874.

79 Hall's papers appear not to have survived. Cp M. Fraser, 'Sir Benjamin Hall in Parliament in the 1850's', *Nat. Library of Wales Jnl*, XV, (1967–8), 310–24, 389–404.

80 PRO, Work 22/2/18, no. 6, confidential memo. by Layard, 4 Nov. 1869.

81 According to Mitford, 'The First Commissioner would certainly consult his advising officer, the consulting surveyor, upon any plans.' *PP* 1877 (312) XV, q. 261.

82 *PP* 1860 (483) IX, qq. 1548–9, 1559.

83 See appendix 4.

84 See Olive Anderson, *A Liberal State at War* (1967), 112–16.

85 PRO, Work 22/2/18, Layard's confidential memo., 4 Nov. 1869; 2/33, p. 41, 11 Mar. 1869, Layard to Treasury. Layard intended that every architect of an important public building should furnish a model as well as drawings; and he had a large model of Westminster and the Embankment made, on which proposed buildings might be tried out (memo., 4 Nov. 1869).

86 *PP* 1868–69 (336) XXXIV, *Papers relating to the recent changes in the Establishment of the Office of Works*, p. 6.

87 Ibid., p. 4.

88 PRO, Work 22/2/18, no. 6, confidential memo. by Layard, 4 Nov. 1869, p. 1.

89 PRO, Work 2/33, p. 41.

90 PRO, Work 2/32, pp. 378–9, Layard to Treasury, 4 Jan. 1869.

91 Ibid., 22/2/18, no. 6, p. 2.

92 Employed in India in youth; wrote on principles of beauty and on fortifications, 1849; *Handbook of Architecture*, 1855; *Hist. of the Modern Styles of Architecture*, 1862, revised 1873; RIBA gold medal, 1871.

93 Hamilton is an obscure figure, described as 'the arch-pragmatist' and 'especially prone to tendentiousness', who 'moved anonymously, tactfully, and with great discretion, though not less powerfully on that account'. Wright, *Treasury Control*, 255, 134, 22. 'He has a genius for adaptation and arrangement', remarked Lowe when at the Exchequer, BL, Add. MS 44301, f. 63, Lowe to Gladstone, 7 Aug. 1869.

94 *PP* 1868–69 (336) XXXIV, p. 4.

95 Ibid., p. 5.

96 Ibid., p. 6.

97 Ibid., pp. 7–9, Layard to Treasury, 11 March 1869.

98 Ibid., p. 9, 16 March 1869. After Pennethorne requested an extension, it was agreed he should retire on 30 June 1870, though he should complete the works on which he was engaged, even after that date (ibid., pp. 10, 13, Treasury minute, 3 July 1869).

99 BL, Add. MS 44421, ff. 158–61, 12 Oct. 1869.

100 BL, Add. MS 38949, f. 84, 21 Feb. 1871.

101 *PP* 1860 (483) IX, *S.C. on Miscellaneous Expenditure*, qq. 991, 1433.

102 See appendix 4.

103 PRO, Work 22/8/9 (Fergusson to Russell, 15 Dec. 1869); 6/413, memorandum of 18 Dec. 1873.

104 PRO, Work 2/33, p. 409, Ayrton to Treasury, 11 Jan. 1870.

105 Ibid. Ayrton's own draft is Work 22/2/20, ff. 1–15.

106 The MBW at first paid its architect, Marrable, £800 p.a. He resigned in 1861 because they offered him only an additional £200 p.a., Owen, *Government of Victorian London*, 43.

107 BL, Add. MS 44301, ff. 118–19, Lowe to Gladstone, 22 Jan. 1870.

108 *PP* 1868–69 (387) X, *S.C. on Hungerford Bridge etc.*, app. 3.

109 Edward Strutt (1801–80), cr. Baron Belper 1856, cotton master, friend of J.S. Mill, Liberal MP, and substantial landowner.

110 For his career, see DNB, and PRO, Work 2/45, pp. 293–5 (Treasury minute on Galton's superannuation, 12 Aug. 1875). He had visited the USA in 1856 with Lowe to inspect the railways. Layard, who also knew him, thought him 'a good man of business' who would 'no doubt, be useful in the mere work of cutting down and controlling expenditure', but he was 'without any architectural knowledge or experience whatever', BL. Add. MS 38949, ff. 11–13, 33. Layard bought some of his pictures in June 1889 for the Dublin Gallery, ibid., 38950, f. 99.

111 PRO, Work 6/413, memo, 18 Dec. 1873.

112 BL, Add. MS 44538, f. 105, 15 June 1870; PRO, Work 1/92, 87–8 (13 June 1870), 195, 197–200. Faced with some 40 applicants, the Secretary recommended public competition. Candidates should be able to design and superintend the execution of new buildings; additions, alterations, repair and maintenance of existing buildings; have knowledge of strength of all building materials, their nature, and the principles and methods of employing them, their prices and the value of labour; understand architectural drawing, the making of working plans and specifications, taking out quantities, estimating work to be done, measuring executed work and abstracting and bringing it to bill in detail; and be able to make technical reports properly composed and spelt.

113 PRO, Work 6/413, FCW to Treasury, 20 Jan. 1875.

114 PRO, Work 12/96/2, ff. 145, 153, 161, May–June 1870.

115 Ibid., 6/413, p. 9.

116 PP 1877 (312) xv, S.C. on Public Offices, qq. 623–6.

117 Born 15 Nov. 1833; appointed assistant to John Phipps (?1796–1868) assistant surveyor for London, 27 June 1859 (PRO, Work 2/40, p. 733); suc. him, 1866. K.C.B. 1897; died 30 Apr. 1912 (DNB).

118 PRO, Work 22/11/1, f. 6. Galton wanted three elements added to those in which Tanner had been examined, viz. levelling and chain surveying; drainage and water supply; applied chemistry.

119 PRO, Work 22/8/7, ff. 6, 8, 11–24, 33–46.

120 BL, Add. MS 44640, f. 175, Cabinet note by W.E. Forster, 1873.

121 Kimberley Jnl (1958), 39 (28 June 1873). See below, pp. 260–2.

122 3PD CCXVII, 1123, 28 July 1873, on a supply vote for acquiring a site adjoining the Houses of Parliament.

123 Ibid., 1268–9, 30 July; Times, 29 July 1873. See M.H. Port, 'A Contrast in Styles at the Office of Works', Hist. Jnl, 27 (1984), 172–4.

124 PRO, Work 2/36, 9 May 1871.

125 PP 1873 (131) VII, 1st Report of S.C. on Civil Services Expenditure, q. 428.

126 Ibid., qq. 430–4.

127 Even a subject for theatrical satire, cp. W.S. Gilbert's very successful The Happy Land (1873).

128 Companion to the Almanac for 1888, 138.

129 W.H. White, Architecture and Public Buildings, 146.

130 It also pleased the Postmaster-General.

131 BL, Add. MS 38949, f. 87, 23 Feb. 1871.

132 PRO, Work 22/2/20, FCW to Treasury, draft, 11 Jan. 1870. Ayrton had already seized upon this issue in his previous post as financial secretary of the Treasury, see ibid., 2/33, p. 207, Ayrton to FCW, 27 July 1869.

133 PRO, Work 1/90, p. 417, 22 Jan. 1870.

134 This was intended to secure the government against a repetition of the controversy with Sir Charles Barry over measuring at the Houses of Parliament. Waterhouse was shaken to discover that he was committed to the measuring of works at the Natural History Museum, which he

had never supposed to come 'within my duties as an Architect', PRO, Work 17/16/2, ff. 216–17, 30 July 1874. See Port, Houses of Parliament, 151–4.

135 PRO, Work 2/33, pp. 426–31, FCW to T., 17 Jan. 1870. Many copies of the memorandum are to be found in PRO Work, e.g. 2/35, after p. 344; 17/16/2. G.G. Scott, completing the Whitehall offices, was not willing to sign, ibid. 12/96/2, f. 257, 15 May 1871.

136 Ayrton agreed that Col. Henry Scott should continue as architect at South Kensington to complete the buildings already authorised; and regulations were drawn up settling the relative duties of the Science & Art Department and the Works, PRO, Work 2/34, pp. 223–5, 343–5, FCW to T., 26 May and 9 Aug. 1870. See also BL Add. MS 44617, confidential print 8 July 1871.

137 So J. Physick, Victoria and Albert Museum (1982), 164–6. Henry Cole, appearing before the Elcho committee on proposals for the Embankment, had confidently asserted the superiority of the Science and Art Department's employment of R.E.s, and other methods, PP 1868–69 (200) x, 1st Report S.C. on Hungerford Bridge &c., qq. 2209, 2212–13, 2216–20, 2226, app. 3. But writing to Layard after the transfer, Cole remarked, 'Unless I am very wrong, I think our buildings will go on more quickly than before! – and I am like Mark Tapley in my feelings' (17 Mar.). His confidence was justified, for although Ayrton did not sanction the completion plan (Physick, 166), he secured £20,000 (as Cole enthusiastically informed Layard) to roof in the Science Schools and finish the South Court (28 Oct. 1870), BL, Add. MS 38997, ff. 296–7, 341–3. Mr Physick sees the Works' surveyor, John Taylor, as a hostile influence (94, 175, 179–80, 203). But it was Lowe's and the Treasury's 'malevolent meddling' that Cole blamed for cuts in funding in 1872, BL, Add. MS. 39,000, f. 224, Cole to Layard, 25 Feb. 1872.

138 PRO, Work 2/34, pp. 90–3, FCW to T., 7 Mar. 1870.

139 Ibid., 2/34, pp. 90–3, FCW to T., 7 Mar. 1870; p. 121, T. to FCW, 22 Mar. 1870, 2/35, pp. 529–31, FCW to T., 3 Jan. 1871. A clerk to the Assistant Surveyor was appointed at the same time, one Henry Tanner (see below), ibid., and Work 2/37, p. 371, FCW to T., 14 Oct. 1871.

140 PRO, Work 2/34, pp. 104, 265 (14 Mar., 24 June 1870); Work 2/35 (commenced 11 Aug. 1870); T. 1/7415B/8028, draft Treasury minute, 12 May 1874; Work 2/35, p. 661 (23 Jan. 1871); Work 22/8/7, ff. 46–7, Treasury to FCW, 10 June 1873. For the Order in Council, see N. Chester, The English Administrative System 1780–1870 (1981), 160–1.

141 PRO, Work 2/37, p. 40, 25 July 1871.

5. The Office of Works 1873–1915

1 PRO, Work 17/16/3, ff. 155–6, 19, 26 Feb. 1873, relating to line of pavement, NHM.

2 Scottish landowner; Liberal whip, 1868–73; re-appointed FCW Apr. 1880; governor of Madras 1880–1.

3 See M.H. Port, 'A regime for public buildings: Experiments in the Office of Works, 1869–75', Arch. Hist., 27 (1984), pp. 74–85.

4 VAM, Cole Diary, 26 Nov., 6, 8 Dec. 1872.

5 SRO, Blair Adam MS 4/569, Russell to Adam, 'Private', 6 Nov. 1873.

6 PRO, Work 12/40/3, ff. 190–201 and 202–3 (Sept. 1873, for Hunt's sour comment that the FCW had not taken his advice about the NLC contract, and Galton's riposte that the FCW had acted on a full consideration of the matter, presumably

on Galton's advice); 6/413, 18 Dec. 1873.

7 Ibid., 'Paisley Post Office'.

8 Cp the similar circumstances of Trollope's Adolphus Crosbie, secretary of the General Committee Office, The Small House at Allington (1864), ch. II, LVI.

9 Bodleian, Hughenden Papers, B XIV/B/14.

10 Russell was certified by Dr Prescott Hewett on 14 Apr. 1874 as 'suffering from great disturbance of the nervous system his memory is impaired so that he is unable to bring his mind to bear upon any subject for more than a few minutes together – his nights restless and sleep is obtained only by means of medecines and as a consequence his general health is broken. Under these circumstances . . . I have advised him to give up all employment, to leave Town, and to go and live in some quiet place in the country.' PRO, T. 1/7415B. His letter of resignation (ibid.) is dated 22 Apr. 1874. Although he had more than 20 years' service, Russell did not apply for a pension. See also Civilian, 2 May 1874, p. 408.

11 Bodleian, Hughenden Papers, B/XIV/24a; C/X/A/3, 12.

12 Lord Blake, Disraeli (1966), 326–7. See also Quarterly Rev., CLXXXV (1897), p. 165.

13 A.B. Freeman-Mitford, Lord Redesdale, Memories (1915), ii, 683. Lennox claimed that ill-health interrupted his work, and that Galton's eight-week absence hindered him (Hughenden Papers, B/XX/LX/411, 414).

14 According to the civil service organ, Civilian, 16 May 1874, p. 447, Disraeli first offered the post to his erstwhile 'Young England' colleague, Alexander D.W.R. Baillie-Cochrane (1816–90), the 'Buckhurst' of Disraeli's Coningsby, cr. Baron Lamington 1880. Baillie-Cochrane, MP (Cons.) 1841–6, 1847–52, 1857, 1859–68, 1870–80, often spoke in the Commons on questions of public works, and was hailed as the 'Apostle of the Thames Embankment' for his early advocacy of its merits as a site for public buildings.

15 See appendix 4.

16 Bodleian, Hughenden Papers, B/XX/LX/413 (Lennox to Disraeli, 14 Apr. 1874); 418 (Lennox to M. Corry, 27 Apr. 1874). Robert John Callender, auditor-general of Ceylon (£1500 p.a.), but an absentee on account of his health, was strongly recommended by Childers and Stansfeld as 'an excellent man of business' who had shewn 'ability, energy and zeal' in the discharge of official business. BL, Add. MS 44419, ff. 271–3, Layard to Gladstone, 23 Mar. 1869.

17 E. Gosse, in his introduction to Lord Redesdale's Further Memories (1917), xii, refers to Mitford's 'vividly social nature'.

18 Redesdale, Memories, ii, 703.

19 PRO, Work 6/413, Lord H. Lennox, 'Memorandum as to certain matters concerning the Office of Her Majesty's Works', Feb. 1875. Personnel had increased from 85 in 1870–1 to 151 in 1874–5, Work 22/2/22, Treasury minute, 12 May 1874.

20 PRO, Work 6/413, Lennox memo, pp. 5–6.

21 Nancy E. Johnson, ed., Diary of Gathorne Hardy, later Lord Cranbrook, 1866–1892: Political Selections (1981), 205.

22 PRO, Work 6/413, Lennox memo, Feb. 1875, pp. 1–2, 6 (interim report of departmental committee, 9 June), 7 (Treasury to FCW, 10 Aug.; FCW to Treasury, 7 Dec. 1874; Treasury to FCW, 14 Jan. 1875), 8–12 (FCW to Treasury, 20 Jan.); 12–13 (Treasury to FCW, 27 Jan. 1875); Redesdale, Memories, II, 703.

23 Bodleian, Hughenden Papers, B/XX/LX/447, 27 Feb. 1875.

24 Marquis of Zetland, ed., Letters of Disraeli to Lady Bradford and Lady Chesterfield (1929), i, 184, 24 Dec. 1874.

25 Johnson, *Hardy*, 229 (27, 28 Feb. 1875).

26 The unique example of the Board being called upon to act. Cp Cowper's evidence, *PP* 1860 (483) IX, q. 852.

27 Redesdale, *Memories*, ii, 703; Zetland, ed., *Letters of Disraeli*, i, 202; Johnson, *Hardy*, 229.

28 Bodleian, Hughenden Papers, B/XX/LX, 439, 440, 444 (Lennox to Corry, 26, 28 Jan., 7 Feb. 1875); 448 (Lennox to Disraeli, 31 Mar. 1875: 'Here is the Paper; I hope it will carry out your wishes and restore Harmony'); PRO, Work 2/44, pp. 143 (24 Mar. 1875), 294 (14 Apr. 1875).

29 PRO, Work 2/45, pp. 293–5 (Treasury minute, 12 Aug.); 337 (19 Aug. 1875).

30 Zetland, *Letters of Disraeli*, i, 298.

31 Bodleian, Hughenden Papers, B/XX/LX, ff. 410, 411 (18, 30 Mar. 1874), 440, 444 (28 Jan., 7 Feb. 1875); RA, Vic. Add. Q, 913.

32 *PP* 1877 (312) XV, *S.C. on Public Offices and Buildings*, qq. 2157, 2160–3.

33 Bodleian, Hughenden Papers, B/XX/LX/488 b, c, 15 July 1876; *Times*, 14 July 1876, p. 10.

34 *Times*, 18 July 1876, p. 9.

35 Mitford wrote that 'Lord Henry took very little interest in the business of the office', recalling one occasion when, 'after vain endeavours on my part to coach him in the details of the various votes [of supply], he gathered up his papers at the last moment, and saying: "Impudence befriend me!" put on his hat and hurried away' to the House. Lord Redesdale, *Memories* (1915), II, 683.

36 Second s. of 1st E. of Gainsborough. Army 1842–51; MP (Cons.) Rutland 1847–83; Treasury offices, 1866–8; FCW 1876–80; m. sis. of 3rd. E. of Lonsdale.

37 *PP* 1875 [C. 1113] XXIII.

38 Sir W.H. Stephenson of the Inland Revenue, R.C.G. Hamilton, assistant secretary in the Financial Department of the Board of Trade, and Mitford to represent the Works.

39 The new establishment for England consisted of Secretary (£1200 p.a.); Assistant Secretary (£800 × £50 − £1000); Corresponding Branch or Secretariat (2 first-class clerks at £450 × £25 − £700; 4 second-class at £315 × £15 − 400; and 2 third-class at £100 × £10 − £200 × £15 − £300); Accounts Branch (clerk in charge, £400 × £20 − £600; one second- and one third-class clerk, and 7 Lower Division clerks); Examiners Branch (chief examiner, £600 × £25 − £800; 2 second-class and 11 junior clerks); Furniture Branch (3 clerks and 3 other officers). The 13 classified clerks composed the Playfair Commn's Upper Division, characterised by intellectual rather than mechanical work. Technical Branch (Consulting Surveyor, 12 surveyors of different sorts, 18 clerks of works, 10 junior clerks). PRO, Work 2/46, 894–902, Treasury to FCW, 30 Mar. 1876; PRO, Work 22/3/7, ff. 1–10, 30 Mar. 1876. Cp. J. Pellew, *The Home Office 1848–1914* (1982), 28–30, 93ff.

40 W.H. White, sec. of RIBA, also condemned Hunt's position, valuing properties &c while his partners Stevenson and Jones were involved in the market, *Architecture and Public Buildings*, 163–4.

41 PRO, Work 22/3/7, ff. 1–10 (Report of departmental committee, 1 Mar. 1876).

42 PRO, Work 22/8/7, ff. 54–5, T. to FCW, 1 Nov. 1877.

43 *Architect*, 15 Mar. 1884, p. 167.

44 See appendix 4.

45 Redesdale, *Memories*, II, 687.

46 In offering him the post, Gladstone remarked: 'The only objection I can anticipate to this arrangement is that the office will not find employment sufficient for the energies which you have at all times shown in the discharge of public business.' Gordon of Haddo Papers, bundle 1/10, 27 Nov. 1880.

47 *Times*, 20 Apr. 1928, p. 11, with a heading, 'An aedile of taste'. See also his articles in *Nineteenth Century*, XII (1882), 667–86; XVIII (1888), 703–18.

48 'Ape' cartoon, *Vanity Fair*, 29 May 1880. (I am grateful to Mr Charles Plunket for communicating this to me.) Plunket was created Lord Rathmore in 1895.

49 Gordon of Haddo Papers, bundle 1/10, Gladstone to Lefevre, 16 Aug. 1892, 'Secret and immediate'. Gladstone had had a stormy encounter with him over Home Rule, see Morley, *Gladstone*, III, 139–41.

50 R. Harcourt Williams, ed., *Salisbury-Balfour Correspondence 1869–1892* (Herts Rec. Soc., 1988), 348. I owe this reference to Mr Harcourt Williams.

51 *PP* 1877 (312) XV, *S.C. on Public Offices and Buildings (Metropolis)*, q. 245.

52 Ibid. q. 247.

53 Ibid. q. 251.

54 Ibid. q. 252.

55 Ibid. qq. 258–60, 256.

56 Ibid. qq. 261–3, 275–7, 281–2, 283, 285, 289.

57 Ibid. q. 264.

58 Ibid. qq. 274–9.

59 Ibid. qq. 609–12, 621–2, 632, 635–8.

60 Ibid. qq. 623–6.

61 Ibid. q. 266.

62 Ibid. qq. 266–9, 273.

63 PRO, Work 33/1523–45.

64 W.J. Reader, *Professional Men: the Rise of the Professional Classes in Nineteenth-Century England* (1966), 202.

65 The FCW tried vainly to obtain a knighthood for Taylor in 1887 after his 'great services', working 'night & day' in superintending the execution of his designs for temporary galleries in Westminster Abbey for the Jubilee service. Plunket also referred to his 'large amount of useful & ornamental work in connection with our Public Buildings generally, & at this moment he has just brought to completion a considerable addition to the National Gallery from designs of his own making'. Plunket to Salisbury, 23 June 1887, Salisbury MSS, Hatfield, 'Plunket' no. 10. Taylor had to wait for the next Jubilee for his knighthood, though awarded a C.B. in 1894.

66 PRO, Work 30/4651–75; 2685–715; and 2524–33, 2536–60 respectively.

67 PRO, Work 17/25/2, 9 Dec. 1886, cited, Physick, *Victoria and Albert Museum*, 181.

68 PRO, Work 22/2/23, 1–5 (Mar.–Apr. 1883).

69 Redesdale, *Memories*, II, 698.

70 Grandson of 4th Earl of Rosebery. Treasury 1869; priv. sec. to Lord Ripon as Viceroy of India 1880–4, to Gladstone 1886; sec. OW 1886–95; chairman of Customs 1895–9, of Inland Rev. 1899–1907; K.C.B. 1899.

71 PRO, Work 22/8/7, ff. 62–3, 6–8 Feb. 1884.

72 PRO, T. 1/8185B/13206, 14 May 1885.

73 PRO, T. 1/8721B/2272, T. memo., 20 Jan. 1893.

74 Ibid., memoranda on 1011/93; Work 22/2/25, ff. 1–8 (19 July 1889). Some element of Ritchie's duties appears to have fallen to Taylor, Surveyor for the London District, PRO, Work 12/88/2, ff. 38–40.

75 PRO, Work 2/35, pp. 529–31, 3 Jan. 1871.

76 Tanner was first appointed as clerk to the assistant surveyor on 16 Mar. 1871 (PRO, Work 2/37, p. 371). As Principal Architect, he was to be influential in promoting the use of reinforced concrete construction, see *RIBA Trans.*, 1910.

77 PRO, Work 22/8/7, ff. 71–4, 28 Nov. 1893.

78 Gordon of Haddo Papers, 1/9, bundle 4, T. to FCW, 16 Feb. 1882 and associated unfoliated papers.

79 PRO, Work 22/8/7, ff. 128–30, 20 Oct. 1902.

80 PRO, Work 12/88/3, ff. 76–8, 10 Jan. 1893.

81 PRO, T. 1/8721B/2272, memo. by J.T. Hibbert, financial secretary, 23 Jan. 1893.

82 *PP* 1887 (184) VII, qq. 172, 197–8.

83 PRO, Work 12/88/1, ff. 22–4, 17 Jan. 1888.

84 Ibid., ff. 33 (10 Feb. 1888); 38–40, Lefevre to T., draft, 22 Feb. 1893.

85 *PP* 1887 (184) VII, qq. 307–12, 1073; PRO, Work 12/88/2, ff. 2–8, Taylor to FCW, 29 Nov. 1892.

86 Ibid., ff. 10–18, FCW to T., 14 Dec. 1892.

87 PRO, Work 12/88/2, ff. 23–30, 23 Dec. 1892; T. 1/8723A/3241, 1010/93, F.A'C. Bergne's minute of 20 Jan. on FCW's letter of 18 Jan. 1893.

88 PRO, Work 12/88/3, ff. 92–6, n.d., draft by FCW to T., [?2 Feb. 1893].

89 According to a contemporary, F.W. Hirst, in *DNB*.

90 H.G. Hutchinson (ed.) *Private Diaries of Rt Hon. Sir Algernon West* (1922), 245. West was Gladstone's private secretary.

91 Cp PRO, T. 1/8721B/2272.

92 Gordon of Haddo Papers, 1/10, bundle 4, Primrose to Lefevre, 7 Oct. 1892.

93 J. Lees-Milne, *The Enigmatic Edwardian* (1986), 99. On 22 Feb. 1895 Harourt wrote to Brett: 'Won't you let *me* try to get the Office of Works for you? or don't you like the place?' Esher Papers, 10/16.

94 R. Rhodes James, *Rosebery* (1963), 354–5. Rosebery had for several months beforehand been pondering whether he could bestow the commissionership of Woods and Forests on his friend. Esher Papers, 10/16, Harcourt to Brett, 22 Jan., 4 Apr. 1895; Harcourt MSS, L.V. Harcourt's journal, 23 Feb. 1895.

95 Bodleian, Harcourt MSS dep., L.V. Harcourt's journal, 23 Feb. 1895; Esher Papers, Corr. 5/6, f. 55, 2 June 1895.

96 M.V. Brett, ed., *Journals and Letters of Reginald Viscount Esher* (3 vols., 1934), I, 192.

97 Among other things, their sexual proclivities were markedly different, Brett being being addicted to a succession of boy favourites, see Lees-Milne, passim. Brett's father, a notable lawyer, had established the family.

98 For an excellent account of Esher at work in a particular field, the London Museum, see F. Sheppard, *The Treasury of London's Past* (1991).

99 The Queen, the Prince of Wales, and the Treasury alike were anxious that his accession to the title should not oblige him to resign; Balfour (first lord of the Treasury) wrote to Mowatt (the permanent secretary), 'So far as I am able to judge he does his work admirably'; Mowatt told Esher that he was a colleague 'with whom I can work, and in whom I can trust'. Brett, *Journals and Letters*, I, 235, 248–9; see also 234, 266, 285.

100 Chilston Papers, c.198/3, Esher to Akers-Douglas, 29 Jan. 1902; Lees-Milne, 135; Esher Papers, 5/16, p. 48, 10 July 1902. Lord Balcarres, who disliked Esher as a 'whisperer', was told, however, 'by the two senior men on the Public Accounts Committee' that Esher 'was the most incompetent official who ever had to explain his departmental finance', J. Vincent, ed., *Crawford Papers* (Manchester, 1984), 59, citing Balcarres' diary, 26 Apr. 1904.

101 PRO, Work 22/8/7, 85–8, Brett to FCW, 10 Aug. 1895.

102 Ibid., ff. 90–3, Brett to T., 22 Nov. 1897; 97, 99, Brett to Tanner, 28 Feb. 1898.

103 Ibid., ff. 106–10, Brett to Tanner, 7 Apr. 1899.

104 Ibid., f. 119, 20 Dec. 1901.

105 PRO, T. 1/9375/18011, 10 Aug., 11 Oct. 1901.

106 H. Parris, *Constitutional Bureaucracy* (1969), 254.

107 *Times*, obituary, 16 Jan. 1926, p. 12; Esher Papers, 10/16, L. Harcourt to Brett, 3 July 1895. Akers-Douglas was created Viscount Chilston in 1911. See appendix 4.

108 Taylor's new staircase at the National Gallery had been hailed in 1888 as 'one of the best architectural works of the year in London'; The design of

his new galleries was thought to contrast 'favourably with the overdone ornamentation and darkened skylights' of Edward Barry's work of the 1870s. *Companion to the Almanac for 1888*, pp. 128–9. A decade later, though, after he had completed the Bankruptcy Buildings and the PRO, the *Architect* damned him with faint praise: 'His work, on the whole, is above the ordinary official standard, but it shows no pretension towards novel effects or to provoke comparison with adjoining work. . . . Sir John Taylor's buildings are well adapted to accommodate a large number of permanent and temporary clerks, who cannot be made more efficient by any outlay on ornamental masonry', 1 Apr. 1898, p. 202.

109 PRO, T. 1/9266B/11099, 14 Mar. 1898.
110 Ibid., no. 19129, 23 Nov. 1897.
111 Ibid.
112 PRO, T. 1/10815/8956, Mowatt to ch., 13 Nov. 1900.
113 Esher Papers, 5/13, ff. 162–3, Arthur Ellis to Esher, 30 Nov. 1901.
114 PRO, T. 1/9375/18011, 31 Aug. 1901.
115 SRO, HH 45/47 'New Government Offices'. (I am grateful to Dr Andrew Saint for drawing this to my attention.)
116 Esher confided to his journal, 6 July 1902, 'I am glad to be free of the Office. After 6 or 7 years one has done all the work that is possible in an office of that kind', Brett, *Journals and Letters*, I, 338.
117 McDonnell obtained leave from Salisbury to fight in the South African War in 1900. When the First World War broke out, he became an Intelligence officer for London region; but then, aged 53, insisted on transfer to the front-line Infantry; he died of wounds received in action. PRO, Work 22/9/4. See appendix 4.
118 Esher Papers, 10/16, 24 Nov., 10 Dec. 1905.
119 Bodleian, Harcourt dep. MS 453 ff. 34–7, McDonnell to L.V. Harcourt, 6 Feb. 1907.
120 PRO, Work 22/8/7, ff. 128–30, 20 Oct. 1902.
121 On pay scales of £310 × £15 − £400, and £150 × £10 − £300 respectively.
122 *PP* 1914 [Cd 7416] XLIX, *Report of Committee of Inquiry into the Architects and Surveyors' and Engineering Divisions of H.M. Office of Works, London*, paras 79–81.
123 Some MPs thought they should sacrifice sleep, too: Sir Brampton Gurdon, in the Public Accounts Committee, 1903, criticised the payment of £400 to Tanner for his supervision of the Parliament Street offices, when 'the whole of the 24 hours were at the service of their Lordships' of the Treasury (q. 2291). Powell Williams made the same point, asking 'whether it is not reasonable and right in the case of a public servant to ask him to take the rough and the smooth, and to fulfil additional duties when the exigencies of the service call upon him to do so?' – to which McDonnell replied: 'If the rule were to apply to this kind of case, I would have great difficulty in obtaining a principal Architect at all, because I do not think we should get one in the London market that would be worth having' (q. 2323). *PP* 1903 (74, 140, 212, 304, 305) V, 31ff.
124 PRO, Work 22/3/7, ff. 11–47.
125 B. Kaye, *Development of the Architectural Profession* (1960), 143; *A.A. Notes*, 1889, p. 157.
126 *PP* 1914 [Cd 7416] XLIX, para. 64.
127 It is significant that the original design of 1901 for the Queen Victoria Memorial – the *place* in front of the palace, and the processional way in the Mall – was sketched out by a 'young draughtsman', R.J. Allison (promoted Assistant Architect 1st class in 1908, later to become Chief Architect). Esher Papers, 19/5, pp. 90–1, 18 Feb. 1901; *Whitaker's Almanac*, 1908.
128 *PP* 1914 [Cd 7416] XLIX, para. 64. A growing

tendency for public bodies to appoint salaried architects in the interests of economy was deplored at this time by members of RIBA: the immediate effect was to reduce the amount of work for the outside architect, 'and that of the most profitable kind'. See report of debate, *Arch. Rev.*, Jan. 1907, p. 69 (and comment that 'bad art still predominates' whether in or outside the RIBA). But in 1899, when the LCC had been unable to find a satisfactory architect at £1500 p.a. (out of 27 applicants), and raised its offer to £2000 p.a., the *Brit. Architect* commented that men of good practice and constantly increasing income were not likely to be tempted to forego independence for the position of a salaried municipal official liable to dismissal at any time and certain to be turned off without a pension, 3 Feb. 1899, p. 71.
129 *PP* 1913 [Cd 6740] XVIII, *App. to 3rd Report of the R.C. on the Civil Service*, qq. 17571–6, 17658.
130 *PP* 1914 [Cd 7416] XLIX, para. 26. Although the senior French state architects also spent most of their time on 'administration', it was largely a matter of examining and reporting on designs by colleagues, so that they were, although under a rule of 1832 each was confined to one major public work at any given time, much more active in design matters than their English counterparts. D. Van Zanten, *Designing Paris* (1987), 116–17.
131 For Post Office complaints of a 'level of meanness of appearance' in OW designs, see Post 30/3062, E.16286/1914, file VI, P.O. to Treasury, 28 July 1913. (I owe this reference to Professor M. Daunton.)
132 *PP* 1912–13 (277) VII, *S.C. on Estimates*, p. vi.
133 D. Van Zanten, *Designing Paris* (1987), 121–2, 130–5.
134 Even now, the Royal Fine Arts Commission is hardly a piranha. W.H. White asserted in 1884 that one FCW had said he could not consent in his own department to be superseded by such a committee, *Architecture and Public Buildings*, 170–1.
135 *PP* 1912–13 (277) VII, qq. 182, 210–12, 217.
136 Bodleian, Harcourt dep. MS 453, loc. cit.
137 Ibid., f. 43, same to same, 12 Feb. 1907; PRO, Work 22/3/7, ff. 48–63. The committee was composed of Sir H.W. Primrose of the Inland Revenue (a former Works Secretary), T.L. Heath (1861–1940) of the Treasury (who with Lord Esher had formed the 1902 committee), McDonnell of the Works, John Gavey, Engineer-in-Chief to the Post Office, and John Belcher, PRIBA.
138 PRO, Work 22/3/7, ff. 18 (Nov. 1905), 48–50 (26 Feb. 1906), 64–8 (8 Feb. 1907).
139 A select committee in 1907 recommended that the P.O. should ultimately take over its own buildings. The question was considered in 1912–14 but shelved on the outbreak of war, Post 30/3062, E. 16286, file XIV. (I owe this reference to Professor M. Daunton.)
140 PRO, T. 1/11270/4357, no. 16054/10 (OW to Treasury, 25 Aug. 1910).
141 Ibid. Harcourt took the same line in opposing Post Office proposals for setting up its own works organisation, 28 May 1908 and 5 Oct. 1910, 'Post Office Buildings', Post 30/3062, E. 16286/1914. (I owe this reference to Professor M. Daunton.)
142 *PP* 1913 [Cd 6740] XVIII, qq. 17675–80.
143 *PP* 1914 [Cd 7416] XLIX, para. 51.
144 *PP* 1914 [Cd 7416] XLIX. See p. 79.
145 In 1912, four Architects, four Assistant Architects 1st cl. and six 2nd cl. were employed entirely upon Post Office work, supported by five 1st cl. and seven 2nd cl. Architectural Assistants, 35 clerks of works and 53 draughtsmen. Treasury committee (Sir F. Cawley) on P.O. Buildings, 1912–13, Post 30/3062, E. 16286. (I owe this reference to Professor M. Daunton.)
146 *PP* 1914 [Cd 7416] XLIX, para. 66.

147 New GPO East and proposed rebuilding in Bath Street; extension of Land Registry, Lincoln's Inn Fields; building for Public Trustee, Inland Revenue, etc., Kingsway; New Science Museum; New Stationery Office and rebuilding on existing site; new offices next Admiralty, and in Parliament Street, ibid.
148 PRO, Work 22/8/7, ff. 146–7, 24 Nov. 1909. In March 1911 he suggested that the figure should be reduced again, to £1000, but no such action was taken, ibid., f. 153.
149 In 1908 these were the Great George Street Public Offices extension (£500,000), Strand Law Courts extension (£100,000), New GPO (£300,000), South Kensington PO and Meteorological Office (£30,000), Recruiting Station (£27,500), and Duke of York's School and Public Offices (£70,000). PRO, Work 22/8/7, ff. 141–2, 10 June 1908.
150 Ibid., ff. 141–2; PRO, T. 1/11270/4357, no. 19303/10 (OW to Treasury, 26 Oct. 1910); minutes by RFW[ilkins] and Sir George Murray (16 Dec.) on no. 16054/10.
151 *PP* 1914 [Cd 7416] XLIX, *Committee of Inquiry into the Architects and Surveyors' and Engineering Divisions of H.M. Office of Works, London*.
152 Engineer; chairman Irish Board of Public Works 1901–13; K.C.B. 1911.
153 *PP* 1914 [Cd 7416] XLIX, para. 3.
154 Ibid., paras 8, 13–15, 22–5, 38–9, 66–8, 85.
155 Ibid., described and assessed in detail, in paras 27–32.
156 Ibid., paras 43–8.
157 SRO, HH 45/47, 'New Government Offices'; *RIBA Trans.*, 1910; *Builder*, XCVI (1909), 394, 427–31.
158 SRO, HH 45/47, 'The British Museum' (I owe this reference to Dr Andrew Saint); PRO, Work 17/5/1, 17/6/4–8.
159 *PP* 1914 [Cd 7416] XLIX, pp. 31–2.
160 Ibid., p. 32.
161 Cp. p. 69 above.
162 Respectively W. Pott, R.J. Allison, and F. Baines. Harcourt MS 459, 1914/15 staff list. *PP* 1914 [Cd 7416] XLIX, para. 17.
163 Ibid. Post 30/3062, E.16286/1914, Cawley committee on Post Office Buildings (Apr. 1913), gives slightly different figures for some ranks (29 Assistant Architects 2nd class; 27 Architectural Assistants, 28 Clerks of Works). Cp. n. 145 above.
164 *PP* 1914 [Cd 7416] XLIX, paras 87–90. See W.H. White, *Architecture and Public Buildings* (1884), 179, on the refusal of the OW to guarantee figures of quantities taken out by their own men.
165 *PP* 1914 [Cd 7416] XLIX, para. 93.
166 Bodleian Harcourt MS dep. 459, 1914/15 staff list.
167 See appendix 4.
168 *Times* obituary, 8 Mar. 1923, p. 12.
169 Hewell Grange, Tardebigge, Worcs., by Bodley & Garner, 1884 (see Pevsner, *BoE, Worcestershire* (1968), 39, 277–8); and the palatial 54 Mount Street, Mayfair, 1896–9 by Fairfax B. Wade (see *Survey*, XL, 324–5).
170 See p. 25. He remained on the managing committee until the work was completed.
171 See appendix 4.
172 L. Earle, *Turn over the Page* (1935), 86.
173 Sheppard, *Treasury of London's Past*, 33, quoting Mus. of London, DC11/6, p. 24. Harcourt married a niece of Pierpont Morgan in 1899, and inherited the Nuneham Park estate from a cousin in 1904.
174 Bodleian, Harcourt dep. MS 453, ff. 29–30, 26 Jan. 1907.
175 E. David, ed., *Inside Asquith's Cabinet: from the Diaries of Charles Hobhouse* (1977), 229. Hobhouse also thought him 'subtle, secretive, and not very reliable or *au fond* courageous, does not interfere often in discussion, but is fond of conversing with the P.M. [Asquith, next to whom he sat at Cabinet]

in undertones', 23 Mar. 1915. An earlier assessment, 13 Aug. 1912, noted that he had 'many attractive qualities: charming manners when he likes, a temper under good control, a hard worker, but no one trusts him, and everyone thinks that language is only employed by him to conceal his thought', p. 121.

176 Bodleian, Harcourt dep. MS 424, f. 271, 21 Feb. 1896.

177 Sheppard, *Treasury of London's Past*, 36.

178 See p. 100 below.

179 Earle, *Turn over the Page*, 92. Charles Hobhouse, p. 229, regarded him as 'a nonentity of pleasant manners, a good deal of courage, and a man of principle, but with no power of expression'.

180 Vicary Gibbs, editor of the *Complete Peerage*, attacked him as a political 'rat', who (being a convinced Free Trader) had gone over to the Liberals after governing New South Wales (1899–1902) as a Conservative appointee. *Complete Peerage*, II (1912), 43–4. Gibbs' hostility may have been influenced by knowledge that Beauchamp (like Esher and Loulou Harcourt) was homosexual. In 1931 his brother-in-law, the Duke of Westminster, denounced him to King George V, and he was obliged to leave England. He inspired Evelyn Waugh's 'Lord Marchmain' in *Brideshead Revisited*. See C. Sykes, *Evelyn Waugh* (1975), 114, 168–9, 252; M. Amory (ed.) *Letters of Evelyn Waugh* (1980), 46.

181 Asquith's nickname for him, see R. Jenkins, *Asquith* (1964), 334. (See *King Lear*, III, vi.)

182 See pp. 196.

183 Earl of Oxford and Asquith, *Memories and Reflections 1852–1927* (1928), II, 15–16; G.E.C., *Complete Peerage*, XIII, 156, quoting *Times* obituary, 14 Dec. 1926. Charles Hobhouse (p. 229) found him 'honest, slow, laborious, and has a whining mechanical voice which detracts from a good and sober judgement and hard work'.

184 Educ. Marlborough; Paris and Gottingen Univs; Merton Coll., Oxford; asst sec., R.C. on the Paris International Exposition, 1898–1900; K.C.B. 1916, K.C.V.O. 1921, G.C.V.O. 1933. His mother was a niece of 4th Earl of Clarendon, Foreign Sec., d. 1870, and his aunt married 1st Earl of Lytton, viceroy of India.

185 Earle's competitors were Lord Basil Blackwood (1870–1917) and Bernard Mallet (1859–1926), Registrar-general, 1909–20; K.C.B. 1916. Earle, *Turn over the Page*, 82–3, 90. Mallet had been private sec. to Akers-Douglas, 1886–91, and subsequently to A.J. Balfour as First Lord of the Treasury.

186 Ibid., 91.

187 *PP* 1914 [Cd 7416] XLIX, para. 3.

188 Entered OW 1889 as temp. draughtsman; Assistant Architect 2nd cl. 1901; Architect 2nd cl. 1911; Principal Architect 1914 in charge of science and art buildings; Chief Architect 1920–34; FRIBA 1919; kt. 1927.

189 Principal Architect 1914 in charge of palaces and public buildings to 1927; kt. 1918, K.C.V.O. 1928.

190 See p. 194.

191 *PP* 1912–13 (277) VII, p. vi. The percentage of cost for architectural staff at that time was only 4.01 of outlay, and included 'a variety of services . . . for which architects are entitled to charge additional fees, and a very large amount of work is done in "maintenance" of buildings all over the world', ibid. A clause was however inserted in the report by 3 votes to 2, noting that the committee had not had sufficient time 'to enquire as closely as they would have wished into the organisation of the Architects Department, and recommend this to the consideration of the Treasury'. An unsuccessful amendment listed points of enquiry: 'whether the present organisation is efficient and economical; whether the staff is overmanned; whether much of the work done by highly-paid and qualified professional men might not be done as well and more cheaply by clerks of works and foremen'; whether the Post Office work might not be done better by a permanent Post Office architect; and, surprisingly, whether outside architects should be 'called in so frequently, and, if so, on what terms', ibid. The chairman, Sir Frederick Banbury, endorsed their report in the House, 30 July 1913: 'I believe a considerable sum of money is saved for the State by the methods which are pursued by the Office of Works.' 5*PD* LVI, 680.

192 Sir Harold Emmerson, *Ministry of Works* (1956), 139.

193 PRO, Work 22/30, memo. 1917.

194 *PP* 1913 [Cd 6740] XVIII, *App. to 3rd Report of R.C. on the Civil Service*, qq. 17464–5.

195 Ibid., ff. 26–31, 'Financial powers of the Office of Works'.

196 *PP* 1912–13 (277) VII, *S.C. on Estimates*, q. 217 (R.F. Wilkins).

6. Art and Science

1 *PP* 1857 sess. 2 [2261] XXIV, *R.C. on National Gallery Site*, q. 2820.

2 *King's Works*, VI, 405–11.

3 E. Miller, *Prince of Librarians* (1967), 273–4. From the mid-1850s, Smirke's great colonnade was disfigured by a 'row of extremely unsightly and incongruous wood and glass sheds', housing newly acquired antiquities, *Nature*, 14 Apr. 1881, p. 549.

4 *King's Works*, VI, 464, n. 3.

5 See *Survey*, XXXVIII, ch. v; Q. Bell, *Schools of Design* (1963); and J. Physick, *Victoria and Albert Museum* (1982), ch. I and II.

6 Minutes of the 1851 Comm., 13 Aug. 1851 (file VIII, nos 9, 9a, 10, 13 and 14), cited by W. Ames, *Prince Albert and Victorian Taste* (1967), 97.

7 *Survey*, XXXVIII, 85.

8 Physick, 22–3; VAM, CC 14, 30 June 1855.

9 A body chaired at first by Prince Albert, to administer the profits of the Great Exhibition.

10 1805–60. MP (Lib.) 1847–59; financial sec. to Treasury 1852–8.

11 Physick, 24, quoting *Third Report of the 1851 Comm.*, (1856), App. T, p. 265; 1851 Comm. box, XII, 64, 65, 70; VAM, CC 14/179 (10 July [1855]); 1851 Comm. letters 182, 195 (24 July, 8 Dec. 1855).

12 Lord Derby commented on Cole's exceptional unpopularity (1851 Comm. box XX, 65, 19 Dec. 1864); and John Bright was reported to consider South Kensington 'something of a humbug' (VAM, Cole Diary, 21 July 1859).

13 *Survey*, XXIX (1964), 272ff.

14 *King's Works*, VI, 471–6. The Master of the Rolls was already custodian of many judicial records, and he proposed erecting a repository for the nation's records on the estate attached to his office.

15 Set up in 1852 by the Patent Law Amendment Act, in the office of a master in Chancery, in Southampton Buildings, which cuckoo-like it took over.

16 See D.J. Olsen, *Town Planning in London* (1964).

17 Cp 3*PD* CLXXXIV, 55, 67.

18 See *Survey*, XXXVIII, chap. iv.

19 Cited, *Survey*, XXXVIII, 49.

20 *PP* 1850 (612) XV, *S.C. on National Gallery*, p. iii. The minutes of the Morpeth committee were not published until they were included with those of the 1850 (Seymour) committee. Barry's plan and elevation are appended.

21 *Report of Commission on the state of the pictures* in *PP* 1850 (612) XV, 67–9, app. A. Thomas Uwins (1782–1857), Keeper of the Gallery, told the 1848 committee: 'I saw some people, who seemed to be country people, who had a basket of provisions, and who drew their chairs round and sat down, and seemed to make themselves very comfortable; they had meat and drink; and when I suggested to them the impropriety of such a proceeding in such a place, they were very good-humoured, and a lady offered me a glass of gin, and wished me to partake of what they had provided.' On Mondays 'a large number of the lower class of people assemble there, and . . . bring their families of children, children in arms, and a train of children around them and following them, and they are subject to all the little accidents that happen with children, and which are constantly visible upon the floors'. *PP* 1850 (612) XV, app. D, evidence . . . 1847–8, qq. 82, 83.

22 *Times*, 14, 20, 27 March, 19 Apr. 1850.

23 3*PD* CIX, 645 (11 Mar.), 1367–8 (25 Mar.); CXI, 895 (7 June 1850).

24 FC of Woods & Works 1850–1, FCW 1851–2; suc. as 12th Duke of Somerset 1855; first lord of the Admiralty 1859–66.

25 *PP* 1850 (612) XV, iv–v. The connoisseurs Baring Wall (1795–1853) and Henry Hope (1808–62) were doubtful whether a suburban site would offer much relief from smoke, p. vii. That there was force in this argument is suggested by the occasion, 5 Dec. 1879, when Robert Maclagan took his son to the top of the new spire of St Mary Abbot's, Kensington: 'It was a very clear day, but on the whole the effort was unrewarding, as under a cloudless sky, smoke at a low level hid so much. In the direction of the Albert Hall and the new Natural History Museum, nothing could be seen.' Carola Oman, *An Oxford Childhood* (1976), 25.

26 Nicholas W. Ridley Colborne, bro. of Sir M.W. Ridley, Bt; MP (Whig) 1805–12, 1818–26, 1827–32, 1834–7; trustee, N.G. from 1831; cr. Baron Colborne 1839.

27 *PP* 1851 (642) XXII, *Report of Commissioners appointed to consider the Question of a Site for a New National Gallery*.

28 Ibid., 545.

29 3*PD* CXXIII, 1020–6 (6 Dec. 1852).

30 See *Survey*, XXXVIII, 52, based on papers of the 1851 Commissioners. (The grant is incorrectly ascribed, however, to the Coalition government that succeeded the Conservatives.)

31 *Survey*, XXXVIII, 52–5.

32 *Art Jnl* n.s. V (1853), 117, 101–2.

33 Ibid., 264.

34 1818–78; MP (Cons.) 1852–68, 1874–8; suc. uncle and assumed name of Maxwell 1866. See *DNB*.

35 1798–1860; MP (Cons.) 1853–7, 1859–60; inherited estates of Robert Vernon (1774–1849), noted collector of contemporary British art, who gave his paintings to the nation, 1847 (see *DNB*).

36 1809–85; MP (Cons., then Lib.) 1837–62; cr. Baron Houghton 1863. See *DNB*.

37 A constant speaker on art and military questions. See appendix 4.

38 *PP* 1852–53 (867) XXXV, xixff.

39 As President of the Academy, Eastlake also had an interest in securing the arrangement that would best suit the Academy – which was to remain in Trafalgar Square.

40 *DNB*, q.v.

41 *PP* 1852–53 (867) XXXV, qq. 4691 (Eastlake); 7490–9 (Dyce); 7943–4 (Ford); 9437–9, 9465–7 (Wellesley).

42 President, Soc. of British Artists (an anti-Academy body) 1840–69. He was a pupil of Beechey and Lawrence; see *DNB*.

43 *PP* 1852–53 (867) XXXV, qq. 7058, 7100, 7131, 7153 (Hurlstone); 7224, 7355–6, 7390–2 (Foggo); 10012–14, 10020 (Moore); 8428, 8444, 8448 (Fergusson). Hurlstone and Foggo were presumably the '*croutistes*' denounced by the *Art Jnl*, V (1853), 175 as instigators of the Mure committee.

44 *PP* 1852–53 (867) XXXV, xv–xvii.

45 Ibid., xli, xlvi–viii. According to Lord Elcho in 1856, Mure's draft report condemned the Kensington Gore site, *3PD* CXLII, 2101 (27 June 1856), but this does not emerge from the draft as printed.

46 *Art Jnl*, V (1853), 264.

47 *PP* 1857 sess. 2 [2261] XXIV, *Report of R.C. on National Gallery*, qq. 2786, 2793–5. See also Treasury Minute, 25 Apr. 1856, embodying the government's decision to build at Kensington Gore, *PP* 1856 [2106] XXXVIII, 507.

48 G.P. Gooch, ed., *Later Correspondence of Lord John Russell* (1925), ii, 216, 6 June 1856. This was a measure of the prince's concern, as he was usually very chary of seeking to influence Commons' voting.

49 SRO, Wemyss MSS, RH4/40/4, 2 Aug. 1860, E. Oldfield to Elcho.

50 *3PD* CXLII, 1393–4, 12 June 1856, second reading of National Gallery Site Bill postponed. The bill was further deferred until Elcho's motion for a royal commission was debated.

51 *Times*, 21 June 1856, p. 9.

52 Broadlands Papers, RC/F/734, 21 June 1856.

53 Ibid., 735, 26 June 1856; *3PD* CXLII, 2154; *Times*, 23 (p. 10), 24 (p. 12), 25 (p. 12), 26 (p. 12) June 1856.

54 *3PD* CXLII, 2098–2154. The ch. of the Exchequer in his evidence to the National Gallery R.C. of 1857 set out in even greater detail the objections to the sites named by Elcho, *PP* 1857 sess. 2 [2261] XXIV, qq. 2806ff.

55 *Art Jnl*, 1856, pp. 243–4. E.A. Bowring, sec. to the 1851 Comm., blamed Elcho 'more than any other human being' for thwarting 'the original great design of the Prince Consort and the Commission', *Nineteenth Century*, Aug. 1877, p. 70; see also ibid., June 1877, p. 577.

56 *Observer*, 30 Nov. 1856, 14 Dec. 1856.

57 *3PD* CXXXV, 797–9, 874–80 (26, 27 July 1854).

58 *Survey*, XXXII, 413.

59 *BN*, 26 June 1857, p. 652; *3PD* CXLVI, 75–88, 19 June 1857.

60 1798–1867; 2nd baron; astronomer; Poor Law commissioner 1833. See *DNB*.

61 1799–1873; MP (Cons.) 1835–7, 1844–73; financier. See *DNB*.

62 1788–1864; kt 1850.

63 Broadlands Papers, GC/LE 65 (5 July 1856).

64 Ibid., GC/LE 72, 73, Lewis to Palmerston 11 Aug., 19 Aug. 1856.

65 Ibid., GC/LE 75, 25 Aug. 1856.

66 Ibid., 81, 21 Oct. 1856.

67 Ibid., 82, 24 Oct. 1856. According to *DNB*, Milman was 'highly esteemed in society', a man of intellectual superiority, though lacking in creative imagination.

68 Broadlands Papers, GC/LE 83, 25 Oct. 1856.

69 Ibid., 84, 31 Oct. 1856.

70 Further problems about the Commission's personnel are discussed in Lewis's correspondence with Broughton, B.L., Add. MS 47299, ff. 163–6 (1 Dec.), 167 (3 Dec.), 172 (5 Dec.), 174 (9 Dec.), 177 (10 Dec. 1856) and 191 (17 Jan. 1857).

71 Broadlands Papers, GC/HA 34, 17 Aug. 1856.

72 Ibid., 190, 191, Palmerston to Lewis, 1, 7 Oct. 1856.

73 Physick, *Victoria and Albert Museum*, 33–9.

74 E.g., *PP* 1857 sess. 2 [2261], XXIV, qq. 3292, 3304–5; 3221, 3226, 3230; 3268–9, 3295–6.

75 1851 Commn, box XIV, 18, quoted by *Survey*, XXXVIII, 52.

76 *PP* 1857, sess. 2 [2261] XXIV, *Report*.

77 *Art Jnl*, 1857, p. 329.

78 Sir John Taylor Coleridge (1790–1876), justice of K.B. 1835. See *DNB*.

79 *PP* 1857, sess. 2 [2261] XXIV, *National Gallery Site Commission*, app. III.

80 *BN*, 14 Aug. 1857, p. 842; *Builder*, 15 Feb. 1857, p. 59.

81 *PP* 1857, sess. 2 [2261] XXIV, pp. 169–70.

82 *BN*, 17 July 1857, p. 733, insisting that 'the public mind is quite made up not to tolerate the pauper occupancy of its own premises by the Royal Academy, or any other trading corporation of showmen'.

83 See, e.g., *Times*, 10 Feb. 1859, a leader criticising the absurd inadequacy of the existing gallery: 'There is hardly a second-rate provincial town on the Continent that has not a better Gallery for its pictures'; and urging that 'If Trafalgar-square will bring twice as many visitors during this and the next four centuries, that more than compensates for the loss of those that come after.'

84 *3PD* CLI, 1380–84 (13 July 1858).

85 *3PD* CLII, 181–4 (8 Feb. 1859).

86 *Survey*, XXIII, 413.

87 VAM, CC box 1, [9] Aug. 1856.

88 *BN*, 6 Feb. 1857, p. 140; G.M. Ellis (ed.), *Letters of Sir William Hardman* (1925), ii, 37; VAM, Cole Diary, 6 Mar. 1861.

89 *3PD* CLXXI, 902 (15 June 1863); VAM, CC 14, 16 Nov. and 4 Dec. 1858.

90 Physick, 40–4.

91 *3PD* CLX, 1014 (16 July 1861); *PP* 1860, XL, 123, *Drawings and report by Capt Fowke for making the National Gallery more available*. Fowke's proposals were laid before the public in the *Cornhill Mag.* 1 (1860), pp. 346–55.

92 *3PD* CLX, 1533–5, 1541, 1544 (18 Aug. 1860); when according to Bernal Osborne, 'there were barely forty Members' in the House (ibid., CLXXV, 1330). For Pennethorne's plans, see PRO, Work 33/1336–86; for a description and illustration, *Builder*, 6 Apr. 1861, pp. 231–3. See also G. Tyack, '"A gallery worthy of the British people". James Pennethorne's designs for the National Gallery, 1845–1867', *Arch. Hist.* 33 (1990), pp. 127–9.

93 Broadlands Papers, HA/J/2, n.d., PM/A, Cowper's list of requirements for N.G.

94 E.g., *3PD* CLI, 1382 (13 July 1858); CLX, 1315 (14 Aug.); 1591 (20 Aug. 1860). See also S.C. Hutchison, *History of the Royal Academy* (2nd edn, 1968), 104–6.

95 *3PD* CLX, 1591 (20 Aug. 1860).

96 *3PD* CLXVIII, 602ff (21 July 1862).

97 *PP* 1863 [3205] XXVII, *Commissioners appointed inquire into the present position of the Royal Academy in relation to the Fine Arts*, p. xxi.

98 Ibid. The commissioners, chaired by Lord Stanhope, included Lord Elcho and William Stirling.

99 SRO, Wemyss MSS, RH4/40/7, 3 Sept. 1864, Elcho to C. Bruce Allen.

100 *PP* 1860 (181) XVI, qq. 364–6, 373, 424–30. Fowke's plan and elevation are given in app. 2.

101 One of the codicils to Turner's will allowed ten years from his death (in December 1851) for building a gallery for his pictures, *PP* (HL) 1861 (201) V, app.

102 *PP* 1860 (181) XVI, qq. 345, 358–9, 404. Lord Overstone urged the merits of Burlington House for the Gallery, and won Eastlake's support, qq. 350–1, 395–7, 429–442.

103 *3PD* CLXXV, 1329, 6 June 1864.

104 P. Guedalla, ed., *Gladstone and Palmerston* (1928), 262, 10 June 1863.

105 PRO, Work 1/76, p. 20.

106 *3PD* CLXXV, 21.

107 Ibid., 1297–1332.

108 Ibid., 1636–9.

109 PRO, Work 1/78, pp. 33, 116, 186; 1/79, pp. 131, 206.

110 Ibid. p. 428.

111 Ibid. 1/80, pp. 5, 31, 163, 194, 203–4, 392.

112 *3PD* CLXXXIV, 1304.

113 Sir C. Holmes & C.H. Collins Baker, *Making of the*

National Gallery 1824–1924 (1924), 62–3. See, for E.M. Barry's unrealised plans (1867–9), PRO, Work 33/1388–97, and for his executed plans (1871), ibid., 1398–1409; for Taylor, 1885, ibid., 1521–45; for Hawkes, 1907–11, *Arch. Rev.* XXIX (1911), 226–30.

114 See appendix 4.

115 George Augustus Frederick Cavendish Bentinck (1821–91), MP (Cons.), a frequent speaker on questions of public art.

116 *3PD* CLXXXIV, 51–75, 8 June 1866.

117 *Builder*, 16 June 1866, p. 456.

118 *3PD* CLXXXIV, 1308–22, 23 July 1866.

119 R. Academy, 'Statement made by Sir Francis Grant P.R.A. to the General Assembly of the Royal Academy', 29 Aug. 1866.

120 BL, Add. MS 38949, ff. 10–11. *Survey*, XXXII, 414–21.

121 For accounts of the history of the British Museum see Edward Miller, *That Noble Cabinet* (1973), and J.M. Crook, *The British Museum: a case-study in architectural politics* (Harmondsworth, 1972).

122 Pückler-Muskau, H.L.H. V, *Tour in Germany, Holland, and England in the Years 1826, 1827, & 1828* (4 vols., 1832), III, 69.

123 Refugee from Modena; assist. librarian, B.M., 1831; chief keeper, printed books 1837; chief librarian 1856–66; KCB 1869. See E. Miller, *Prince of Librarians: the Life and Times of Antonio Panizzi of the British Museum* (1967).

124 Miller, *That Noble Cabinet*, 180, citing *PP* 1850 XXIV, *R.C. on British Museum*, q. 10217.

125 *PP* 1852 (557) XXVIII, 201, *Copy of all Communications made by the Architect and Officers of the British Museum to the Trustees, respecting the Enlargement of the Building . . .*, p. 2.

126 Miller, *That Noble Cabinet*, 174–182, citing *PP* 1850 XXIV, p. 31.

127 *PP* 1852 (557) XXVIII, 201ff., pp. 6–15.

128 Ibid., pp. 17–19. See also E. Miller, *Prince of Librarians*, 154–6, 176–8, 207–8.

129 *PP* 1852 (557) XXVIII, 201ff., pp. 26–35; Plans H–L; 1852–53 (42) LVII, 317ff., *Copy of all Communications made by the Architect and Officers . . . respecting the Enlargement of the Building . . .*, pp. 1–2.

130 For some account of them, see Crook, *British Museum*, 168–77.

131 *Quarterly Rev.*, XCII (1852) 175–82.

132 *PP* 1857–58 (379) XXXIII, *Copies of all Communications . . . respecting the want of Space for exhibiting the Collections . . .*, p. 3, 6 Dec. 1853; Miller, *That Noble Cabinet*, 187.

133 Miller, *Prince of Librarians*, 210–11.

134 See complaints by keepers, 1854–57, in *PP* 1857–58 (379) XXXIII, pp. 3–32.

135 Ibid., 7, 10, 28.

136 Ibid., 12 (1852); 4–5 (1858).

137 R. Owen, *On the extent and aims of a national museum of natural history* (1862), 42–3, 65, 69, 70.

138 *PP* 1852–53 (867) XXXV, qq. 7845–6. Lord Ellesmere had in 1846 suggested to Peel moving the fossils to the Hunterian Museum under Richard Owen; Peel had suggested that 'the stuffed birds and beasts' might go with them, and discussed the question with Owen. BL, Add. MS 40586, ff. 248–50, cited Miller, *That Noble Cabinet*, 234–5; *DNB sub* Owen, Richard.

139 *PP* 1857–58 (379) XXXIII, 373ff. (pp. 38–47).

140 BL, Add MS 38988, f. 145, to Layard, 25 May 1862, cited by Miller, *That Noble Cabinet*, 220–1.

141 Broadlands Papers, GC/LE 188, Palmerston to Lewis, 6 Aug. 1856.

142 F.R.S. 1834; Hunterian professor of Comparative Anatomy 1836–56; superintendent, B.M. Nat. Hist. collections 1856–83; K.C.B. 1884. An acerbic controversialist. See *DNB*.

143 *Survey*, XXXVIII, 201. But the memorial was written by Sir Roderick Murchison, *PP* 1868–69 (200) X, q. 2369.

144 *PP* 1857–58 (28) XXXIII, 499–503, *Copy of a Memorial addressed to Her Majesty's Government by the Promoters and Cultivators of Science....* 'As the chief end and aim of natural history is to demonstrate the harmony which pervades the whole, and the unity of principle which bespeaks the unity of the Creative Cause, it is essential that the different classes of natural objects should be preserved in juxtaposition under the roof of one great building.' They suggested 'the prolongation of the present building northwards' in 'halls requiring little embellishment', p. 3.

145 Crook, *British Museum*, 198.

146 *PP* 1857–58 (379) XXXIII, *Copies . . .* , 25, 28.

147 *3PD* CL, 1572, 1578–9 (4 June 1858).

148 *PP* 1859 XIV, 514, *Papers relating to the Enlargement,* 22. See Miller, *That Noble Cabinet,* 239–40.

149 *3PD* CLIII, 250–272 (17 Mar.), 384–5 (18 Mar. 1859).

150 Ibid., 262.

151 Ibid., 265.

152 *3PD* CLV, 438.

153 *3PD* CLXVI, 1903–06, 19 May 1862. Prevented from developing the financial potential of their estate by governmental indecision, the 1851 Commission itself had asked for the partnership to be dissolved, *Survey*, XXXVIII, 61.

154 *3PD* CLIII, 252; CLV, 432.

155 Owen, *Extent*, 114.

156 *Survey*, XXXVIII, 201; Owen, *Extent*, 116–17.

157 Owen, *Extent*, 117.

158 Ibid. 124.

159 *PP* 1868–69 (200) X, qq. 2407, 2403.

160 *PP* 1860 (87) XXIX, 265ff. *Copy of all Communications . . . respecting the want of Space . . . ,* pp. 6, 7, 11, 20. The presence of *ex officio* ministerial trustees on 21 Jan. 1860 alone assured Palmerston of his majority.

161 *PP* 1860 (540) XVI, 173ff., *Report on the British Museum.* Lowe, the minister responsible for the South Kensington Museum, vainly sought to include a reference to 'the applicability of the principle of division of labour to museums', as well as other reasons on account of which the committee 'cannot recommend the retention of the Natural History collections at Bloomsbury as a permanent arrangement' (p. xli).

162 Ibid., p. iv.

163 Geologist; F.R.S. 1826; kt 1846; dir.-gen. Geological Survey 1855; bt 1866.

164 SRO, Wemyss MSS, RH4/40/3, Murchison to Elcho and reply, 30 Mar., 8 Apr. 1860.

165 *PP* 1862 (97) XXIX, 169ff. *Copy of the Correspondence between the Treasury and the British Museum, on the subject of providing Additional Accommodation . . .*

166 *PP* 1860 (87) XXIX, p. xxvii; app.

167 SRO, Wemyss MSS, RH4/40/4, 2 Aug. 1860.

168 *PP* 1862 (97) XXIX, 169ff. pp. 4–5.

169 BL, Add. MS 44397, ff. 17, 26, 76.

170 *PP* 1864 (117) XXXII, 167ff. *Copies of Correspondence between the Treasury and the British Museum on the subject of providing Additional Accommodation for the several Collections . . .* (1862–4).

171 *3PD* CLXVI, 1903–33 (19 May 1862); the bill was lost by 163 votes to 71.

172 *Survey*, XXXVIII, 203, citing records of the 1851 Commission.

173 *Times*, 21 May 1862, p. 5.

174 MP (Lib.) 1850–68; jt.-sec., Bd of Control 1855–8.

175 *3PD* CLXVI, 1903ff., 19 May 1862.

176 *Times*, 21 May 1862, p. 8.

177 E. Ashley, *Life of . . . Palmerston* (1876), ii, 222; J. Morley, *Life of . . . Gladstone* (1903), ii, 48–50, 62.

178 *Times*, 21 May 1863, p. 8. The *Warrior* was the first ironclad warship.

179 1851 Commn. box XIX, 32, 50, 51, Bowring to Grey, 26 Jan., 18, 20 May 1863; VAM, Cole Diary, 23 Mar. 1863; P. Guedalla, *Gladstone and Palmerston*

(1928), 262, 10 June 1863.

180 *3PD* CLXXI, 899ff. (15 June 1863). The cost of land for the Coventry Street/Long Acre improvement scheme (1843) had been nearly £120,000 an acre; and £10–£12 a sq. yd (equivalent to £50–60,000 an acre) were commonly paid in Manchester for warehouse sites: Broadlands Papers, HA/J/8, excerpted from 1851 Comm. *2nd Report.*

181 H.R. Fletcher, *The Story of the Royal Horticultural Society 1804–1968* (1969), I, 186, 191; *Survey*, XXXVIII, ch. vii; *PP* 1863 (382) XXIX, 381ff., *Observations on Plans for the International Exhibition Building and the mode of Completing it as a Permanent Museum.*

182 G.E. Buckle, ed., *Letters of Queen Victoria*, 2nd ser. (1926), i, 89, Queen Victoria to Lord Derby, 10 June 1863.

183 P. Guedalla, 262, n. 176.

184 1851 Commn. W.A., XIX, 75, Grey to the queen, 11 June 1863. Elcho warned of the 'very strong hostility' of the Commons to the exhibition building, so that, wishing to see the Natural History collections at South Kensington, he tabled an amendment for buying the site only, ib. 78, 12 June 1863.

185 *3PD* CLXXI, 922–3. It was indeed the Queen's desire to see achieved her husband's project of bringing the National Gallery to Kensington, R. Fulford, ed., *Dearest Mama* (1968), p. 68, Queen Victoria to Crown Princess, 7 June 1862.

186 *3PD* CLXXII, 130. The Queen had made known to each of the 1851 Commissioners her wish that the government should buy the site; had herself written to Lord Derby; and the royal secretaries had been busy in late May endeavouring to 'bias' MPs, and persuaded Disraeli to stop Opposition whips canvassing against the vote; but they were afraid that if word of their activities got out, it would do more harm than good. (Lord Granville recalled that Prince Albert had always stressed 'being extremely careful in ever using the Queen's name to influence others. This principle especially applies to a question of obtaining a vote of money from the H of C.') Lord Elcho was also persuaded that the purchase of the building would be a 'great bargain'. VAM, CC box 12, 27 May 1863; 1851 Comm., W.A., XIX, 48, 49 (Grey to Disraeli, 13 May, and Disraeli to Grey, 15 May), 73, 74 (Queen to Derby and reply, 10 June), 76 (Granville to Grey, 12 June), 80 (Bowring to Grey, 16 June); 1851 Comm. letters, 425–6, Grey to Bowring 22 and 24 May 1863.

187 *PP* 1860 (181) XVI, app. 1.

188 *3PD* CLXXI, 929 (15 June 1863). Cowper, at the Office of Works, was anxious to see a station at South Kensington close to the purchased property, BL, Add. MS 44401, f. 154, 29 Oct. 1863. Gladstone subsequently (9 June 1865), damning any expectation of a favourable (i.e. cheap) purchase of additional land in Bloomsbury, suggested that the growth of the Museum's collections was far from ended, remarking: 'the principle of diffusion, reasonably applied, within certain proper and well-defined limits, appeared to him on the face of it a more rational principle' than concentration. *3PD* CLXXIX, 1354. By 1865/66, the South Kensington Museum was attracting as many visitors as the Brit. Museum and the Nat. Gallery put together, *PP* 1871 (447) XXXVII.

189 T.A. Jenkins. ed., *Parliamentary Diaries of Sir John Trelawny,* 261.

190 J. Vincent, ed., *Disraeli, Derby and the Conservative Party: Journals and Memorials of Edward Henry, Lord Stanley 1849–1869,* p. 199.

191 *3PD* CLXXII, 75–91. Palmerston was absent through illness, G.E. Buckle, ed., *The Letters of Queen Victoria*, 2nd ser. (1926), i, 97. Lennox to Grey, 1851 Commn. box XIX, 105.

192 VAM, Cole Diary, 2 July 1863; Earl of Malmesbury, *Memoirs of an ex-minister* (1884), ii, 300.

193 *3PD* CLXXII, 92–102. See also SRO, Wemyss MSS, RH4/40/7, Kerr to Elcho, 4 July 1863.

194 'One of the most wasteful, one of the most extravagant, and one of the most unjustifiable proposals ever submitted to the House' (G.W.P. Bentinck, *3PD* CLXXII, 107); 'an invention on the part of the Government to hoodwink the country' (Cavendish Bentinck, ibid., 114); 'great and culpable . . . ignorance . . . [or] a palpable deception' (Gregory, ibid., 122).

195 *Letters of Queen Victoria*, 2nd ser., i, 96–7, Disraeli to Gen. Grey, 3 July 1863; Malmesbury, *Memoirs*, ii, 300.

196 Vincent, *Journals*, 199.

197 *Letters of Queen Victoria*, 2nd ser., i, 99, 3 July 1863; 1851 Commn. W.A., XIX, 113. The Liberals were divided, 101 for and 129 against the government's proposal. 'As for the Conservatives, they jumped at an opportunity of giving Gladstone a slap in the face', T.A. Jenkins, ed., *Parliamentary Diaries of Sir John Trelawny*, 262n, citing Broadlands Papers, GC/BR/19, 4 July 1863.

198 *Letters of Queen Victoria*, 2nd ser., i, 98, 3 July 1863.

199 Lord Derby remarked to General Grey that 'Cole . . . is undoubtedly one of the most generally unpopular men I know', 1851 Commn. W.A., XX, 65, 19 Dec. 1864.

200 Vincent, *Journals*, 199.

201 SRO, Wemyss MSS, RH4/40/6. To the Comte de Laborde, Elcho was writing: 'Let us build a handsome brick and stone receptacle worthy of a nation awakening to a sense of its late architectural and monumental sins.' Ibid. 28 June 1863. General Grey however was emphatic that the rejection of the purchase proposal had been activated by general opposition to the 1851 Commissioners' plans for South Kensington, 1851 Commn. XLVIII, 432, 15 May 1864. Grey also, in his distress on learning of the hostile vote, had sent ironical congratulations to Elcho, 'wishing him a long life, that he might have plenty of time to moralize over the waste to which his vote has condemned this ground, and to say every time he passes the hoardings that will surround it for the next 20 years "This is my work."' 1851 Commn. W.A., XIX, 42, 3 July 1863.

202 1851 Commn. W.A., XIX, 116, 20 July 1863.

203 BL, Add. MS 44401, ff. 235–7, 249 (11 Dec. 1863).

204 Miller, *That Noble Cabinet,* 242, citing BL, Add. MS 38996, f. 114.

205 1851 Commn., *Fifth Report*, app. D.

206 See p. 173.

207 See app. 4.

208 *PP* 1868–69 (200) X, v; q. 1467.

209 Ibid., q. 1467.

210 Ibid., q. 1481.

211 Ibid., qq. 1512, 1521.

212 Ibid., qq. 2202, 2323, 2369–94, 2403.

213 An early exercise in cost-benefit assessment: based on the Embankment's saving 6*d.* per head in time and fares over South Kensington, Ayrton calculated the public gain at £18,245 p.a., or a capital sum of £456,000. PRO, Work 17/16/2/, ff. 103–9, 4 Mar. 1870.

214 Ibid., ff. 112–13, 14 May 1870.

215 *3PD* CCII, 1361 (4 July 1870).

216 See p. 211.

217 PRO, Work 17/60, unfoliated, confidential printed memo. by F.S.P [arry] of the Treasury, July 1891. The following account is based principally on this, and a continuation memo., July 1892. These are also to be found in Bodleian, Harcourt dep. MS 192, ff. 118–24, together with a chronological 'history', ff. 115–16. Mitford's contemporaneous plan for a National Portrait Gallery building

in Delahay Street was blocked by the Treasury.

218 See *DNB*.

219 An example of the 'blighting influence' of the 'particularly peppery' F.A'C. Bergne, a Treasury principal clerk whom even his chief, Mowatt, classed among 'lower animal organisms [that] become more and more irritating as one gets on in life'. H. Roseveare, *The Treasury* (1969), 225; PRO, Work 17/60, memo. by W.L. J[ackson], MP, financial sec., 12 Jan. 1890; Esher Papers, corr. 5/10, ff. 111–12, to Esher, 9 July 1900.

220 George Joachim Goschen (1831–1907), MP (Lib.) 1863–86, (Lib.-Unionist) 1887–1900; ministerial posts 1865–6, 1868–74; ch. of Exchequer 1887–92. See *DNB*.

221 Thomas Humphry Ward (1845–1926), fellow of Brasenose College, Oxford.

222 George James, 9th earl (1843–1911), MP (Lib.) 1879–80, 1881–85; suc. uncle, 1889; artist; trustee, N.G.

223 Sir Francis Chantrey (1781–1841), R.A., sculptor, left the reversion of his estate to the R.A. for the purchase of the best works of painting and sculpture executed by artists residing in Great Britain.

224 Bodleian, Harcourt dep. MS 192, ff. 85–94, Lord Carlisle to Sir W.V. Harcourt, 5 Nov. 1892. Unfortunately, the Law Officers advised that the Sheepshanks collection could not be removed from the South Kensington Museum and the National Gallery trustees refused to give up their paintings. (See PRO, Work 17/60 and *3PD* CCCLV, 1193.)

225 Bodleian, Harcourt dep. MS 192, ff. 85–94.

226 Ibid., ff. 121–4 (memo. by F.S. Parry of the Treasury, also in PRO, Work 17/60).

227 Sir William Agnew (1825–1910); MP (Lib.) 1880–6; cr. bt. 1895. See *DNB*.

228 So destined by the recommendation of S.C. on Museums of Science and Art Department, *PP* 1898 (175) XI, *First Report*, as essential to good administration, satisfactory results and efficiency in museums and science schools.

229 Secretary of the Science & Art Dept 1855–8; MP (Lib.) 1868–92; 1869 commr, 1851 Exhibition Commission (1883–9, sec. of management committee, when he transformed its finances); jnr minister, 1873–4, 1886; 1880–3, chmn, HC committees; K.C.B. 1883; cr. Baron Playfair 1892.

230 To consist of Gregory (a N.G. trustee), Plunket (FCW), Armstrong (Art Director at South Kensington), H. Ward and W. Agnew (friends of Tate), and those present at the meeting of 24 July 1890: Lords Carlisle and Hardinge (chairman of N.G. trustees), Layard (another trustee), Sir F. Burton (Dir. N.G.), Sir F. Leighton PRA, Sir J. Gilbert and Sir J. Linton (watercolourists), Sir G. Scharf (director, N.P.G.).

231 See p. 10.

232 *4PD* v, 1555 (20 June 1892).

233 Bodleian, Harcourt dep. MS 458, 1, memo. 15 May 1908.

234 Ibid., MS 192, ff. 52–3, R. Welby to Harcourt, 23 Sept.; 55, Harcourt to Ward (copy), 8 Oct.; 61, Ward to Harcourt, 13 Oct. 1892.

235 Ibid., ff. 64–5, 69, 74–9 (Harcourt to Leighton, 25 Oct.), 80–1 (memo. of meeting, 25 Oct. 1892).

236 Ibid., ff. 82–4, 96–7, 107–10, 153–4. PRO, Work 17/60, 17/96. See also *Magazine of Art*, 1893, pp. 145–9.

7. Courts of Justice

1 *King's Works*, VI, 504ff.

2 M.H. Port, 'The new Law Courts competition, 1866–67', *Architectural History*, 11 (1968), 75 ff.; D.B. Brownlee, *The Law Courts* (Cambridge, Mass., & London, 1984), 50–2; *Arguments for the removal of the Courts of Law and Equity from Westminster . . .* (1841), p. 33.

3 J. Stow, *Survey of London* (1603; ed. C.L. Kingsford, Oxford, 1971 edn) II, 42–3; W.J. Hardie, 'Hist. of the Rolls House and Chapel', *Middlesex & Herts. Notes & Queries*, II (1896), 49–68; Sir R. Megarry, *Inns Ancient and Modern* (1972).

4 BL, Add. MS 39053, ff. 130–1, Petition of Lincoln's Inn against bill for new site for Law Courts, 1869.

5 For an account of the Law Society's campaign, largely waged in the *Law Times*, for new courts, see Brownlee, *Law Courts*, 52–3, 60–4.

6 E.g., PRO, Work 12/32/3, no. 1, *Arguments for the removal of the Courts of Law and Equity from Westminster to Lincoln's Inn Fields being a response of a pamphlet entitled Facts for the consideration of Parliament, before the final adoption of a plan perpetuating the Courts of Law on a site injurious and costly to the suitor (1841)*.

7 *3PD* LVII, 1162; *PP* 1842 (476) X.

8 *PP* 1842 (476) X, *S.C. appointed to consider the Expediency of erecting a Building in the Neighbourhood of the Inns of Court, for the sittings of the Courts of Law and Equity, in lieu of the present Courts. . . .*

9 *3PD* LXVII, 1073–4, 16 Mar. 1843.

10 *PP* 1845 (608) XII, *S.C. on Courts of Law and Equity.*

11 PRO, Work 12/32/4, ff. 1–3, 8.

12 PRO, Work 12/32/3, ff. 2–9.

13 Brownlee, *Law Courts*, 64, reproduces a perspective sketch, reputedly from *PP* 1859 sess. 1, x.

14 Brownlee, *Law Courts*, 65, quoting Inc. Law Soc., *Observations on the Proposed Concentration of the Courts of Justice . . .* (1859).

15 PRO, Work 12/32/4, no. 12, *Observations in favour of the Concentration of the Courts of Justice and all the requisite offices in the Vicinity of the Inns of Court and on the means of defraying the expense* [1858].

16 Sir John Taylor Coleridge, justice, K.B. 1835–58.

17 *PP* 1860 [2710] XXXI, 89ff. , *Report of Commissioners appointed to inquire into the expediency of bringing together into one place or neighbourhood all the superior courts of law and equity, the probate and divorce courts, and the high court of admiralty and the various offices belonging to the same; and into the means which exist or may be supplied for providing a site or sites, and for erecting suitable buildings, for carrying out this object.*

18 Q.C. 1840; MP (Lib.) 1851–61; sol.-gen. 1852–6; att.-gen. 1856–61; lord chancellor as Lord Westbury 1861–5; a passionate law reformer with a sarcastic tongue. See *DNB*.

19 See *DNB* for his influence as a law reformer.

20 See p. 152.

21 *PP* 1860 [2710] XXXI, q. 700. The surveyor H.R. Abraham told a select committee in 1861 that 'I do not think that there is a worse locality; the persons who occupy the houses are an erratic sort of people; costermongers, thieves, prostitutes, and such class of people to a great extent; the buildings 'perhaps of the very worst description in London'. *S.C. on the Courts of Justice Building Act (Money) Bill, PP* 1861 (441) XIV, qq. 170, 100.

22 *PP* 1865 (124) XII, *S.C. on Courts of Justice Site bill*, qq. 22–3, 36–9, 189–90, 197, 201, 206–8, 210, 221, 248–9, 290, 297. See also *PP* 1865 (74) XLV, 45, *Return of number of houses etc. in the New Law Courts site.*

23 *PP* 1860 XXXI, *Report*, p. xxx.

24 PRO, T. 26/3, f. 51, 25 Oct. 1860. Although the preliminary steps for introducing legislation were approved, 15 Nov. 1860, the Treasury again warned that the government 'is to be in no way considered as pledged to the adoption of the Commissioners plan or any part of it', and that they would institute enquiries as to the costs and possible sources of funding, ibid., f. 58.

25 *3PD* CLXII, 800, 1562; CLXIII, 1159–60, 1169, 1480, 1682–4; CLXIV, 174, 191, 1188, 1507.

26 PRO, T. 26/3, f. 181, 4 Dec. 1861.

27 As the attorney-general pointed out, 27 June 1864,

28 *3PD* CLXXVI, 368–70.

29 *3PD* CLXVI, 796–826.

30 PRO, Work 12/32/4, f. 10.

31 Ibid., 12/1, f. 67.

32 *PP* 1864 [3280] XXIX; *3PD* CLXXVI, 368–70.

33 PRO, Work 1/77, p. 135.

34 PRO, Work 12/1, ff. 119–20. Pennethorne's proposal to include Grays Court was rejected by FCW, ibid. 1/78, p. 27, 11 Nov. 1864.

35 T. Sadler, *Edward Wilkins Field: A Memorial Sketch* (1872), 39, cited by Brownlee, *Law Courts*, 74. Field's firm was entrusted with the actual purchase, PRO Work 1/78, p. 354.

36 *3PD* CLXXVI, 372.

37 Lord Selborne, *Memorials Pt II: Personal and Political 1865–1895* (1898), i, 24.

38 *3PD* CLXXVIII, 490, 30 Mar. 1865. See also Selborne, *Memorials Personal and Political* (1898), i, 22.

39 *3PD* CLXXVII, 929, 934.

40 See p. 177.

41 *PP* 1871 [C. 290] XX, *Report of the Commissioners appointed to advise and report as to the buildings proper to be erected . . . for the New Courts of Justice*, 40–1, 52.

42 Ibid., 113.

43 PRO, Work 12/36/2, f. 23, Aug. 1868. The Conservative ministry was then in its final months. Their chancellor of the Exchequer said that the government did not hold itself responsible for the commission's scheme, and but for the change of ministry would have formally recorded its objections, *PP* 1868–69 (381) X, q. 3045.

44 See p. 177.

45 Professor Brownlee has failed to understand the full complexity of Layard's role, *Law Courts*, 183–4.

46 See M.H. Port, 'From Carey Street to the Embankment – and back again!', *London Topographical Record* XXIV (1980), 167–90.

47 *3PD* CXCII, 362–4, 368 (15 May), 1045 (29 May 1868).

48 *Times*, 22 July 1868, p. 9.

49 See p. 177.

50 *3PD* CXCIII, 335–6.

51 BL, Add. MS 38996, f. 40, Street to Layard, 20 Jan. 1869.

52 BL, Add. MS 38949, ff. 7–9. Layard to Gregory, 20 Aug. 1868.

53 BL, Add. MS 39053, ff. 73–5.

54 PRO, Work 12/1, ff. 280–1.

55 PRO, Work 12/1, ff. 280–1 (14 Dec. 1868); fully summarised by Brownlee, *Law Courts*, 184.

56 BL, Add. MS 38996, ff. 6 (6 Jan.), 42 (21 Jan. 1869).

57 Ibid., ff. 3–4, (5 Jan.), 15 (6 Jan. 1869).

58 Ibid., ff. 5–6 (5 Jan.), 42–3 (21 Jan. 1869); Brownlee, *Law Courts*, 188, quoting Street's speech in Soc. of Arts debate.

59 Brownlee reports a letter in the *Law Journal*, 1 Jan. 1869 (pp. 11–12), commenting favourably 'on the rumor that a committee would be formed to study the Embankment site for the law courts', *Law Courts*, 186.

60 See p. 117.

61 *Times*, 6 Jan. 1869, p. 9.

62 *Daily News*, 11 Jan. 1869.

63 BL, Add. MS 38996, f. 104 (25 Feb. 1869).

64 Ibid., ff. 38–43, 49 (Jan. 1869).

65 See PRO, Work 12/32/3, no. 10, *The New Law Courts. Statement by the Council of the Incorporated Law Society on the subject of the suggested change of site* (Feb. 1869).

66 Brownlee, *Law Courts*, 187.

67 Soc. of Arts, *Proceedings of a Committee appointed by the Council of the Society of Arts to report upon the best way of dealing with the Thames Embankment* [1869], of which there is a copy in PRO, Work 12/32/4, no. 161. It met on 9, 16 and 23 Mar. 1869. It had 33 members, but fewer than a third attended on

67 BL, Add. MS 39053, ff. 114–15. One such model letter is of interest as an early specimen of the genus:

Dear Sir,

The second reading of Mr Layards Bill (Thames Embankment Site) is fixed for   June next. You will personally oblige me if you can attend the House on that occasion. I am enabled by my professional experience to urge strong reasons in favor of the Carey Street Site. They are:

1. That it has been purchased under an Act of Parliament for the express purpose of erecting the Courts of Justice.

2. That it has been cleared so that the proposed new buildings might be at once commenced.

3. It is undoubtedly the most advantageous site for the convenience of the profession and of the Suitors.

4. It will be accessible by Fleet Street and the Strand without necessarily purchasing any other property.

5. It consists of $7\frac{1}{2}$ acres of ground, six of which will contain the new Courts of Justice and the Offices necessarily connected therewith leaving $1\frac{1}{2}$ acres unoccupied for light and air.

6. The building when completed will have a very imposing effect and will be visible to the myriads who are daily passing east and west and from its elevated position will be almost as commanding as St Paul's Cathedral.

The obvious reasons against the Embankment Site are

1. That the Site has to a considerable extent to be obtained and the purchase made.

2. That although the approximate value of the property to be purchased may be ascertained it is impossible to calculate the compensation to be paid to owners and occupiers for goodwill, loss of trade &c.

3. That the buildings if erected there will be visible only from the bridges and to the passengers comparatively few in number who go up and down the river.

4. That the erection of the Courts of Justice must necessarily be delayed for an indefinite period.

I may add that no branch of the profession has the slightest pecuniary interest in preferring the Carey Street site, but all are actuated solely by an anxiety to increase the facilities for transacting business, and in the interests of the Suitor. [Marginal note by Layard: 'This is the most audacious assertion of all.'] Ibid. f. 116.

68 Ibid., ff. 118, 124. The figures given were highly disputable.

69 Ibid., f. 126. See also Port, 'From Carey Street . . .', 175–6 for a most arrogant Law Society pronouncement that 'It is utterly vain and idle in the general public to imagine that non-professional persons, however intelligent, can form any accurate opinion on the position and arrangement of the courts and offices best adapted to the transaction of the business of the suitors.'

70 BL, Add. MS 39053, f. 120, claiming that 5000 out of 6000 solicitors in the legal district had offices (or those of their town agents) on the north of the Strand. But of 2126 members of the society, only about three-quarters practised in London, according to Layard's note.

71 Ibid., f. 128.

72 *Solicitors' Jnl*, xiii, 402–3, 20 Mar. 1869.

73 *PP* 1868–9 (48) XLVII, 651 (widely summarised in the press, e.g., *ILN*, 17 Apr. 1869).

74 BL, Add. MS 39053, ff. 95–9, 27 Feb. 1869.

75 BL, Add. MS 38996, ff. 50, 61, 70, 104, 106, 132,

160 (20 Jan.–13 Apr. 1869).

76 So Lowe stated, *3PD* CLII, 1256.

77 Ibid., 1202 ff.

78 BL, Add. MS 38996, ff. 164–5 (to Fitz-Roy Kelly, 21 Apr. 1869).

79 *3PD* CXCV, 1699 (27 Apr.); CXCVI, 538–60 (10 May 1869).

80 BL, Add. MS 38949, ff. 11–12, Layard to Gregory, 13 May 1869; partly printed in Selborne, *Memorials, Part II: Personal and Political, 1865–1895*, i (1898), 25.

81 *3PD* CXCVI, 549, 557 (10 May 1869).

82 BL, Add. MS 38996, f. 186 (to Fitz-Roy Kelly, LCB, 11 May 1869).

83 Ibid., ff. 188–9, 11 May 1869.

84 BL, Add. MS 38949, ff. 11–12.

85 BL, Add. MS 44536, f. 125v., 9 Mar. 1869.

86 *3PD* CXCVII, 458–60. Gladstone never forgot his defeat over the proposed purchase of the 1862 Exhibition building, see above, p. 98.

87 BL, Add. MS 38996, ff. 192–3, 194–5.

88 Ibid., ff. 281–2, 12 June 1869. The letter in question, ff. 210–11, sent to Buxton's MP uncle, Charles, urges objections of taste and expense to the Embankment, and asserts that the Metropolitan Railway promoted petitions against Carey Street because it hoped to prevent the construction of a much-needed railway under mid-London. The petition with 7500 signatures presented by Gregory on 20 Apr. 1869 lay 'for about a week' at the Metropolitan Railway stations, and was signed by 109 barristers and 143 solicitors, BL, Add. MS 39053, f. 110.

89 BL, Add. MS 38996, ff. 226–7, 25 May 1869. They had moved a boundary 40ft. outwards.

90 Ibid., ff. 290–1, 16 June 1869.

91 Ibid., f. 200, 18 May 1869.

92 PRO, Work 12/32/2, ff. 74 *Courts of Justice (New Site)*, 35, 59, 60.

93 BL, Add. MS 38996, ff. 166–8, 174–5, 178–9 (28 Apr., 5, 6 May 1869).

94 Ibid., ff. 202–3, 19 May 1869.

95 Reproduced in *BN*, 28 Apr. 1871.

96 BL, Add. MS 38996, ff. 204–5, 20 May 1869.

97 Ibid., ff. 219, 270–1 (25 May, 5 June 1869).

98 Ibid., ff. 292–4 (20 June), 299–300 (24 June 1869).

99 *PP* 1868–69 (381) X. J.R. Mowbray, R. Gurney, W. Hunt and W. Williams were Inner Temple, G.O. Morgan Lincoln's Inn.

100 PRO, Work 12/32/2, ff. 52 (13 May 1869), 58.

101 BL, Add. MS 38996, ff. 265–7, 297–8 (3, 4, 21 June 1869). See also *PP* 1868–69 (274) XLVII, *Report of Committee appointed by Courts of Justice Commission to examine all plans submitted to the Commission, with a view to ascertain the Dimensions and measurements*.

102 PRO, Work 12/32/2, f. 80.

103 BL, Add. MS 38996, ff. 253–6, 3 June 1869.

104 Ibid., ff. 301, 305, 311, 313, 315 (25 June–3 July 1869).

105 *PP* 1868–69 (381) X, qq. 1241–57, 1267–82, 1411, 1504–8.

106 Ibid., qq. 3060, 3089, 3118–19, 3134–5, 3167–9.

107 Ibid., qq. 2123–5, &c.

108 BL, Add. MS 38949, f. 12, Layard to Gregory, (2 Aug. 1869).

109 Sat for Chippenham 1865–85; cr. bt 1880; a leading freemason; (two of his sons were barristers).

110 *PP* 1868–69 (381) X, iv–v.

8. Government Offices

1 See *Survey*, XIV (1931), pll. 79–98; XVI (1935), ch. 2.

2 Ibid., XIII (1930), ch. 11, 21; XIV, ch. 6.

3 George Scharf's minutely detailed pencil drawings

of Delahay Street and King Street (1859 with later annotations) are in BM, Print Room, 200. c. 6, ff. 24, 31–33 (I am grateful to Mr Peter Jackson for drawing them to my attention.)

4 *King's Works*, VI, 551ff.

5 PRO, Work 30/972–4.

6 *PP* 1839 (466) XIII.

7 *King's Works*, VI, 560–1, 572.

8 *PP* 1857–58 (417) XI, q. 356.

9 *3PD* CXXXIII, 1278 (8 June 1854).

10 *PP* 1854 [1713] XXVII, 328–9, reprinted in 1856 (368) XIV, 13–14.

11 *PP* 1854–55 (382) VII, *S.C. on Downing Street Public Offices Extension Bill*; PRO, Work 30/975; PRO, T. 1/6693A/3774.

12 *PP* 1854–55 (382) VIII, p. 10, report of Inman and Phipps.

13 PRO, Work 12/84/1, ff. 11, 26.

14 PRO, Work 30/977.

15 *PP* 1854–55 (382) VII, appendix.

16 PRO, Work 12/84/1, ff. 34–6, 40–2; *3PD* CXXXIX, 1574.

17 *PP* 1854–55 (382) VII; the committee amended the bill to compensate the Crown estate for the loss of the north side of Downing Street.

18 *3PD* CXXXVIII, 2014.

19 *3PD* CXXXIX, 1574–8.

20 *PP* 1857–58 (417) XI, *S.C. on Foreign Office Reconstruction*, app., p. 176; PRO, T. 1/5997A/10002 (correspondence; and geometrical elevation for Pall Mall by Pennethorne, rather more severe than that reproduced in Pl. 166).

21 See pp. 168–71 below.

22 *PP* 1856 (368) XIV.

23 Ibid., qq. 18–31.

24 Ibid., qq. 55–6.

25 Ibid., qq. 156, 158, 162, 190; PRO, Work 30/982.

26 RA, Add. MS Q, 326, Hall to Phipps, 2 June 1856.

27 *PP* 1856 (368) XIV, p. iii.

28 Ibid.

29 See p. 168.

30 See H. Parris, *Constitutional Bureaucracy*, ch. ix.

31 RA, Add. MS Q, 416, Hall to Prince Albert, 16 July 1857.

32 I.O. Collns, L/SUR/2/3–4. See Sir G.V. Fiddes, *The Dominions and Colonial Offices* (1926); *King's Works*, VI, 561.

33 *3PD* CXLVI, 1422 (13 July); *PP* 1857 sess. 2 (50) (111) IV, 295, 335; 1861 (150) (137) III, 869, 875; 1862 (189) IV, 697.

34 PRO, Work 2/29, p. 200 (24 Aug. 1865).

35 *PP* 1865 (192) XLVII, 169.

36 *PP* 1867–68 (281) LVIII, 257.

37 Ibid. (281-I) LVIII, 311.

38 See p. 32 above.

39 *PP* 1867–68 (281) LVIII, qq. 277–8.

40 Ibid., qq. 158–63.

41 Ibid., qq. 428–57.

42 Ibid., plan facing p. 5.

43 Ibid. Scott's evidence, 27 July 1867. Unfortunately the names of the interrogators are not given, but it is clear that Manners, Trevelyan and Ward Hunt were among them. Much of Scott's appearance before the commission was taken up by the advocates of the alternative plans seeking to secure his endorsement for their proposals.

44 *PP* 1867–68 (281) LVIII, qq. 192–205, 214–15, 233–42.

45 See *DNB*.

46 *PP* 1867–68 (281) LVIII, app. 'Lt Colonel Clarke's Plan of 1865–6'. See also *Builder*, 13 Mar. 1868, pp. 200–2.

47 *PP* 1867–68 (281) LVIII, pp. 45–6. A model of Clarke's proposed buildings is illustrated in J. Physick & M. Darby, *'Marble Halls'* (1973), p. 44.

48 MP (Cons.) 1857–77; financial sec. 1866–8; ch. of the Exchequer 1868; first lord of the Admiralty, 1874-d.

49 *PP* 1867–68 (281) LVIII, qq. 502–09, 521–2, 530.

50 Belvoir Castle MSS, cabinet diary of Lord John Manners.

51 *PP* 1868–69, x, 871, *S.C. on Public Offices Concentration Bill.*

52 Cp Sir Thomas Biddulph's recollection of seeing 'a Procession of I believe 50,000 men pass down Whitehall and occupy the Street for all the morning', RA, E. 17, no. 50, 16 Apr. 1870.

53 The Earl of Redesdale, a relation of Mitford, Secretary of the Works, advocated buying up the whole site between the new offices and Great George Street, and had been particularly concerned about the island of shops and houses between King Street and Parliament Street, *3PD* CXCII, 102–3 (24 Mar. 1868).

54 PRO, Work 12/96/2, ff. 11–12, 21 Mar. 1868.

55 Class I civil estimates (Public Works and Buildings) had risen from some £943,000 in 1867–8 to £1,267,000 in 1868–9, and thereafter remained above £1,200,000. M. Wright, *Treasury Control of the Civil Service 1854–1874* (1969), 374.

56 PRO, Work 2/34, pp. 59–61; 12/96/2; 30/665, 666.

57 BL, Add. MS 44637, ff. 44v, 63, 97, 100. One idea for consolidating the War Office was the purchase of Dover House. A cabinet committee was appointed, but on 9 Aug. 1869 adjourned to November without any decision arrived at.

58 RA, E. 16, no. 39.

59 W. Verner, assisted by E.D. Parker, *Military Life of H.R.H. George, Duke of Cambridge* (1905), 409–10, 5 Dec. 1869.

60 RA, E. 16, no. 41, 2 Mar. 1869.

61 See W.S. Hamer, *The British Army: civil-military relations, 1885–1905* (Oxford, 1970).

62 RA, E. 16, no. 69, 1 May 1869; cp. PRO, Work 30/980.

63 RA, E. 16, no. 70, copy, 2 May 1869.

64 Gladstone annotated his copy of the paper, 'What hurry?', BL Add. MS 44611, ff. 45–6.

65 RA, E. 16, no. 83, Biddulph to Grey, 4 June 1869. 'I must confess', Biddulph continued, 'that a plan by which the Commander in Chief would be using two separate Establishments for the transaction of public business, does not appear to be a convenient one – the difficulties attending the creation of a War Department adjoining the Horse Guards, arise from the expense of buying Dover House (estimated at £60,000) on one side, and the want of space owing to the Admiralty buildings on the other.'

66 BL, Add. MS 44611, ff. 45–6, confidential print [Aug. 1869].

67 Ibid.; Add. MS 44538, f. 45, 7 Jan. 1870.

68 1804–70; yngr s. of 2nd Earl Grey, the prime minister; the Queen's secretary, having been secretary to Prince Albert 1849–61.

69 RA, E. 17, no. 16, 16 Feb. 1870. H.C.G. Matthew, *Gladstone Diaries*, VII, 19 Feb., 17 Dec. 1870.

70 Verner & Parker, *Military Life of . . . Duke of Cambridge*, 413, 26 Dec. 1869.

71 Ibid., 415–16, 27 Dec. 1869.

72 Ibid., 415–16 (Cambridge to Cardwell, 27 Dec. 1869); RA, E. 17, no. 15, Grey to Cambridge, [16 Feb.]; no. 20, Cambridge to Grey, 24 Feb. 1870.

73 RA, E. 17, no. 20, Cambridge to Grey, 24 Feb. 1870. Grey was wholly sympathetic to Cambridge: 'Had I any power to reform, my mode of doing it would be, to bring the Secretary *for* War back to the Secretary *at* War's offices [in Horse Guards]', ibid. no. 18.

74 Ibid., no. 23, Cardwell to Grey, 26 Feb. 1870.

75 Ibid., no. 27, 28 Feb. 1870; BL, Ad. MS 44638, f. 154.

76 *3PD* CCII, 1786 (8 July 1870); BL, Add. MS 44538, f. 189, Gladstone to Cardwell, 12 July 1870.

77 *3PD* CCII, debate, 1753–86.

78 RA, E. 17, nos. 163, Cardwell to the Queen, 20 Dec.; 164, Ayrton to Ponsonby, 21 Dec. 1870.

79 Morley, *Gladstone*, II, 360–1.

80 1825–95. Major-gen. 1868; priv. sec. to Queen on death of Grey, 1870; P.C. 1880, G.C.B. 1887.

81 RA, E. 17, no. 166, 26 Dec. 1870.

82 Ibid.; nos. 167 (26 Dec.), 168 (28 Dec. 1870). See also A. 40, no. 87 (Gladstone to the Queen, 17 Dec.); E. 59, nos. 20 and 21 (Ponsonby to Cambridge, 23 and 28 Dec. 1870).

83 Ibid., E. 18, nos. 8 (Cardwell to ?Biddulph, – Jan.), 11 (Biddulph to Cambridge, 22 Jan.), 13 (Cambridge to Biddulph, 'Private and Most Confidential', 23 Jan.), 15 (Cardwell to the Queen, 25 Jan. 1871); BL, Add. MS 44539, Gladstone letter books, f. 59v, to Cardwell, 21 Jan. 1871.

84 He was allocated his own entrance, attended by sentries, next to Schomberg House (occupied by the minister). But Mr Secretary Hardy admitted that 'he goes up one of the worst passages and staircases that I think any high official does', though to 'a nice room'. *PP* 1877 (312) XV, q. 1885.

85 RA, E. 18, nos. 13 (23 Jan.), 61 (7 Mar. 1871).

86 Ibid., E. 18, nos. 54 (Cambridge to the Queen, 17 Feb.), 61 (Cambridge to Biddulph, 7 Mar.), 64 (Biddulph to the Queen, 11 Mar.), 66 (the Queen to Gladstone, 13 Mar.), 72 (Gladstone to the Queen, 16 Mar.), 73 (Cardwell to Gladstone, 14 Mar.), E. 59, no. 29 (Biddulph to Cambridge, 7 Mar. 1871); BL, Add. MS 44539, Gladstone letter books, f. 141v, to Cardwell, 21 Jan. 1871.

87 RA, E. 17, nos. 84 (Cardwell to Biddulph, 9 May), 85 (Gladstone to the Queen, 13 May), 87 (Biddulph to Cardwell, 17 May 1871); BL, Add. MS 44639, f. 40 (13 May 1871).

88 RA, E. 19, no. 6, Biddulph to Cambridge, 7 Sept. 1871).

89 R.C.K. Ensor, *England 1870–1914* (Oxford, 1936), 20–1; Morley, *Gladstone*, II, 363–5, 373.

90 Morley, II, 383–7.

91 *PP* 1872 (200) I, 13.

92 RA, E. 19, nos. 28 (3 Oct., Cambridge to the Queen), 29 [3 Oct. 1871] (Biddulph to Gladstone), 171 (Cambridge to Biddulph, 'Private', 11 July), 173 (Cambridge to Biddulph, 20 July 1872); A. 42, no. 84a (Gladstone to the Queen, 17 Dec. 1871); Q. 12, no. 10 (Ponsonby to the Queen, 1 Feb. 1872); E. 59, no. 52 (Biddulph to Cambridge, 19 July 1872).

93 Ibid., E. 59, nos. 59 and 62 (Biddulph to Cambridge, 20 Jan., 8 Apr. 1873); A. 45, Gladstone to the Queen, 22 Mar. 1873.

94 See appendix 4.

95 RA, E. 20, no. 32, 22 Mar. 1873.

96 Ibid., E. 20, nos. 32 (22 Mar. 1873), 33 (Biddulph to the Queen, 24 Mar.), 42 (Cambridge to Biddulph, 9 Apr. 1873).

97 A proposal that had 'met with considerable opposition in the House of Commons', PRO, T. 1/7376A/10198, 7 Oct. 1873.

98 *PP* 1877 (312) XV, app. 2.

99 PRO, T. 1/7376A/10198, Noel (Admiralty) to T., 6 Nov.; Campbell-Bannerman (W.O.) to T., 27 Oct. 1873.

100 Bodleian, Hughenden Papers, B/XX/LX/424, Lennox to Disraeli, 28 May 1874; Belvoir Castle MSS, Cabinet diary of Lord John Manners, 6 June 1874; N.E. Johnson, ed., *Diary of Gathorne Hardy, later Lord Cranbrook, 1866–1892: Political Selections* (Oxford, 1981), 209, 212 (7, 30 June 1874); PRO, T. 1/7376a/10198, 22 June 1874.

101 RA, E. 21, nos. 53 (Biddulph to Hardy, 2 July), 57 (Hardy to Biddulph, 3 July 1874).

102 Ch. of Exchequer, War sec. (Hardy), Admiralty (Ward Hunt), Lord John Manners, Cave (P.M.G.), Sclater Booth (LGB), FCW, and representatives of W.O. and Admiralty permanent staffs, PRO, T. 1/7376/10198, draft minute, 22 June [1874].

103 Commissioner of public works, Victoria 1855; dir. of works, Admiralty 1873–82; see *DNB*.

104 R.E. 1839; dir. of works for fortifications 1862; K.C.M.G. 1874; col. governorships, 1875–89.

105 PRO, Work 30/984.

106 *PP* 1877 (312) XV, qq. 517, 520, 531, 534.

107 See *PP* 1877 XXVII, 687–91. Hardy noted in his diary, 24 July 1875, 'H.R.H. has been extravagantly absurd on the insanitary condition of his room (!) & those of his staff & declaring he will go. I have written that the Cabinet & myself will not have a separation for which he is really straining everything & putting all sorts of secret machinery into operation. . . . The office is bad & parts close & perhaps unhealthy but there is nothing against the upper parts of the building.' But six days later: 'I shall have trouble about the W.O. as the Sanitary Comee. has sent in a most unfavourable report by some strange pressure I fancy.' *Loc. cit.*, 245, 246.

108 PRO, T. 1/7559B/19767, 19 Aug. 1875.

109 RA, E. 21, no. 232, Cambridge to Biddulph, 31 Oct. 1875. Meanwhile, efforts had been made to mitigate the unsanitary conditions in Pall Mall, ibid., nos. 214, 225.

110 PRO, T. 1/7559B/19767, no. 7981, 9 May 1876.

111 Ibid., 1 Jan., 1 June, 23 Oct. 1876; 7632B/18736, 29 Jan. 1877. Trollopes' properties were 13, 15, 15½, and 16 Parliament St and 53 King St. For their lease of no. 15 and disturbance, government paid an additional £6768. See also *PP* 1864 (186) XXXII, 287, *Crown and Government Property (Westminster)*.

112 PRO, T. 1/7632B/18736, no. 3285/77. See above, p. 27.

113 N.E. Johnson, ed., *Diary of Gathorne Hardy*, 250.

114 'The Queen has frequently spoken to Lord Beaconsfield, and *urged him*, in the strongest manner to have the New War Office built, or even commenced, on account of the extreme insalubrity of the offices, which is really intolerable. But nothing has been done! Mr Hardy assured The Queen, that a number of Clerks, have been removed, and that the bad *smells* (which are said again *now* to be quite awful) was caused by new Carpets!! This however is *not* the case. . . . The Queen is *quite* determined that *something* should be done, for the poorest people now a days, are *not* allowed to remain in Lodgings subjected to dreadful smells. . . . [Sanitary experts should inspect and report to her.] The Queen must *insist* on its being done . . . it will only strengthen the hands of the Govt for proposing to Parliament, what is necessary to build new Horse Guards and War Offices.' Ibid., E. 23, no. 8, 14 Jan. 1877.

115 PRO, T. 1/7632B/18736, T. Minute, 5 Mar. 1877.

116 Pennethorne had drawn up plans in 1868 for the profitable laying-out of this area, where the leases were reverting to the Crown, PRO, Work 38/249–50.

117 PRO, T. 1/7632B/18736, no. 4699, 14 Mar. 1877.

118 RA, E. 23, nos. 28 (Hardy to Ponsonby, 9 Mar.), 29 (Cambridge to ?, n.d.), 30 (Biddulph to the Queen, 12 Mar.), 31 (Biddulph to Hardy, 13 Mar. 1877); PRO, T. 1/7632B/18736, 14 Mar. 1877.

119 *3PD* CCXXXII, 1042 (26 Feb. 1877).

120 *PP* 1877 (312) XV, *S.C. on Annual Expenditure on Public Offices and Buildings*, p. iii.

121 PRO, T. 1/7632B/18736, no. 11736/77.

122 *PP* 1877 (312) XV, *S.C. on . . . Public Offices and Buildings*.

123 *PP* 1877 (312) XV, app. 9; qq. 1499–1508, 1525.

124 Ibid., app. 8; PRO, Work 30/985.

125 *PP* 1877 (312) XV, qq. 1680–7, 1892, 1699–1706, 1723–4, 1774. Though there was 'a good deal of personal communication between [the War Office] and the Admiralty', it was 'very limited' to a

few individuals, according to the War Office chief clerk, qq. 485–6.

126 PRO, Work 30/984.

127 *PP* 1877 (312) XV, app. 7; qq. 1085, 1088, 1101–05, 1125–7, 1139, 1141, 1155–6, 1158–9.

128 Ibid., q. 1632.

129 See above, pp. 42–3.

130 Ralph R.W. Lingen (1819–1905); sec. committee of Council on education 1849–69; perm. sec. Treasury 1869–85; K.C.B. 1878; cr. Baron Lingen 1885. Gladstone eulogised him as 'a ferocious economist, parsimonious with public money, looking upon the chief of each spending department as an enemy against whom he defended the public treasury'. A. West, *Contemporary Portraits* (1927), 76. See *DNB*.

131 PRO, T. 1/7632B/18736, no. 11736, 8 Nov. 1877.

132 Ibid., no. 17491, 8 Nov. 1877.

133 G. Shaw Lefevre, 'Public Works in London', *The Nineteenth Century*, 1882, pp. 667–86.

134 BL, Add. MS 44131, f. 164, Childers to Gladstone, 25 Sept. 1884; *DNB*.

135 BL, Add. MS 46056, ff. 28–9, GSL memo. 22 May 1895. The purchase of the site was estimated at £600,000, of which £250,000 represented property already in government possession. Lefevre told an 1897 select committee that the cabinet also thought that 'it was not wise that the Government should monopolise so much of the sites within easy reach of the Houses of Parliament'; and one cabinet member wished to preserve the antiquarian interest of King Street, *PP* 1897 (335) X, q. 319.

136 Gordon of Haddo Papers, 1/9, bundle 1, Lefevre to Gladstone, 7 July; bundle 4, Cabinet confidential print, 20 July 1881; PRO, Work 30/986.

137 *3PD* CCLXVII, 1794–6. Property between Charles Street and Great George Street to the extent of £242,000 had already been purchased, *PP* 1882 (253) XII, on *Public Offices Site Bill*, p. 3.

138 *Companion to the Almanac for 1888*, 125. Sir H. Verney supported the RIBA plan, *3PD* CCLXXI, 1606 (6 July 1882), urged again in 1886, when Lefevre insisted that the traffic in Whitehall did not justify widening it, and asked who could justify spending half a million (or even half that) for 'obtaining a better view of a new building' and widening the approaches to parliament, *Times*, 5 Mar. 1886, p. 13.

139 *3PD* CCLXXI, 1605–6.

140 *PP* 1882 (253) XII.

141 *3PD* CCLXXII, 429–37, 836–43 (14, 18 July 1882).

142 *3PD* CCLXXVII, 1481 (5 Apr.), CCLXXXIII, 1317–19 (20 Aug. 1883).

143 See pp. 182–4 below.

144 *3PD* CCXCVI, 1167–1216, 9 Apr. 1885; PRO, Work 30/4154.

145 PRO, Work 30/989, 22 Feb. 1886.

146 *3PD* CCCII, 1170 (25 Feb.), 1999 (4 Mar.); CCCIII, 113 (8 Mar. 1886).

147 *3PD* CCXCVI, 1106; CCCIV, 449; BL, Add. MS 44153 ff. 226–7, Lefevre to Gladstone, 20 May 1886.

148 *3PD* CCCV, 1638, 21 May 1886.

149 1845–1927, 3rd s. of 1st Duke of Abercorn. MP (Cons.) 1868–1906; jnr minister 1874–80; first lord of the Admiralty 1885–6, 1886–92; Indian sec. 1895–1903. See *DNB*.

150 *PP* 1887 (184) VII; PRO, Work 30/988, plan for W.O. on Carrington House site, 1887.

151 PRO, Work 30/4171, 5821–4.

152 PRO, T. 1/9185A/15177, no. 8579, 22 May 1897; T. 1/9425B/15440, 9 Aug., 4, 25, 29 Sept. 1899; Work 12/89/1, 1–34, passim; Chilston Papers, C6/195; C236/11, 12.

153 *3PD* CCCXXVI, 759–92 (31 May 1888).

154 BL, Add. MS 41227, ff. 195–8, Lefevre confidential memo. 15 Nov. 1892.

155 PRO, T. 1/8723A/3241, no. 15900, Lefevre to Treasury, 17 Oct. 1892. Carrington House had

156 been demolished in 1886; see *Survey* XVI, 177.

156 PRO, Work 12/91/3, ff. 2–6 (MS); a printed version, sent to the War minister, is in BL, Add. MS 41227, ff. 195–8; and another copy in Add. MS 46089, ff. 1–4 (Herbert Gladstone Papers).

157 PRO, T. 1/8723A/3241, nos. 15900/92 (memo, HWP 30 Nov., and Harcourt, 9 Dec.), and 18953/92 (Lefevre to Treasury, 14 Dec., and Harcourt draft reply, 29 Dec. 1892). See also Lefevre's comments to Campbell-Bannerman (War sec.) on his 'very hot correspondence' with Harcourt – 'rather an amusing specimen of Harcourtianea', BL, Add. MS 41227, f. 199, 16 Jan. 1893.

158 PRO, Work 12/91/3, f. 11, 2 Jan. 1893.

159 PRO, T. 1/8723A/3241, no. 15900, Bergne (19 Oct.); Hibbert (21 Oct. 1892).

160 A history of this protracted scheme is among Herbert Gladstone's papers, BL, Add. MS 46089, ff. 43–8.

161 Bodleian, Harcourt MSS dep., box 186, ff. 1–2, 1 Jan. 1895.

162 BL, Add. MS 45992, ff. 19–21, Harcourt to H. Gladstone, 5 Jan. 1895.

163 Bodleian, Harcourt MSS dep., box 186, ff. 11–17, 1 Mar. 1895; PRO, Work 30/3991–6, 38/76.

164 Bodleian, Harcourt MSS dep., box 186, ff. 23–4, Harcourt to Hamilton, 17 Mar. 1895; BL, Add. MS 46089, f. 18, Hamilton Memo. 13 Mar. 1895. Hamilton recommended 'a War Office parallel to the south west side of Parliament Street', which would allow more space at the back of the War Office for other departments, saving £2000 p.a. in rents.

165 Bodleian, Harcourt MSS dep., box 186, ff. 56–9, 17 May 1895.

166 BL, Add. MS 46056, ff. 28–30, 17–22 May 1895.

167 BL, Add. MS 45992, ff. 42–3, 31 May 1895.

168 *4PD* XXXIV, 611–25, 30 May 1895.

169 Bodleian, Harcourt dep. MS 419, Journal of L.V. Harcourt, 10 and 11 June 1895.

170 *4PD* XXXVI, 993, 1102–3, 1371, 1582, 1674, 1742 (27, 28, 30 Aug., 3, 4, 5 Sept. 1895).

171 *4PD* XL, 511.

172 Kent R.O., Chilston Papers, Diaries, 5, 25 Feb. 1896; *4PD* XXXIX, 906, 1233 (14, 17 Apr.); XL, 151–2, 510–16 (29 Apr., 4 May 1896). George objected on general principles to such important matters being passed by the House at half-past five o'clock on a Wednesday afternoon.

173 *PP* 1896 (310) X.

174 Ibid., qq. 24, 32–4, 37, 39–40, 48–9, 63–4, 77, 79, 96, 98, 102–4, 107; app. 1.

175 *Builder* however (3 Oct. 1896, p. 261) attacked the pentangular Carrington House site as 'a surveyor's plan', 'like all the plans that come out of the Office of Works'. Filling up irregular sites left by traffic lines was one of 'the most wretched and paltry ways of building even minor Government offices', and would not be acceptable in Berlin or Paris.

176 Already in 1889 *Manchester Guardian* had protested against demolishing King Street, with its 'thousand interesting associations', *Brit. Archt*, 17 Feb. 1889, p. 112.

177 *PP* 1896 (310) X, qq. 194, 204–14, 370–3, 474–5, 494–500, 516–18; qq. 370–3.

178 Ibid., qq. 156–66, 532–3.

179 See appendix 4.

180 *PP* 1896 (310) X, qq. 588–92.

181 Ibid., qq. 619–26.

182 Ibid., qq. 643–54.

183 Ibid., iii–v.

184 *PP* 1897 (335) X, *S.C. on the manner in which the Sites available for the erection of the New Buildings required for Government Offices may best be appropriated for that purpose*.

185 Ibid., qq. 4, 155, 190, 405, 552, 252–3.

186 Kent R.O., Chilston Papers, C. 5, f. 274, Akers-Douglas to Col. Edis, 21 May 1897.

187 *PP* 1897 (335) X, qq. 155, 157, 414, 418–19, 421, 426, 551, 562.

188 Ibid., qq. 12–26, 28, 31.

189 Ibid., iii, iv.

190 Ibid., q. 793.

191 *4PD* XLVIII, 327–34, 1 Apr. 1897.

192 PRO, Work 12/81/19, f. 7 'Confidential', 23 June 1898.

193 Ibid., ff. 14–15, [Oct. 1898].

194 *4PD* LXVIII, 1328, 20 Mar. 1899. The risk was that freeholders would grant new leases and put up new but flimsy buildings, in order to extract a higher price when government wished to buy.

195 *PP* 1897 (335) X, q. 343. James Lowther had in the debate on the Public Buildings (Expenses) Bill, 2R, 28 Mar. 1898, urged the government to buy the whole area down to the Park, as it would be 'at a very much less cost than must inevitably be involved if the matter is delayed a considerable time' (*4PD* LV, 1284).

196 In his designs dated December 1898 Brydon was treating the entire rectangle, including the southwest quadrant, as part of his building plan, PRO, Work 30/1002–08.

197 PRO, T. 1/9979B/13557, Office of Works to Treasury, 20 Mar. 1903; Public Offices (Expenses) Act. Cp. PRO, Work 30/3937. Any prospect of disposing of the BoT site in Whitehall Gardens had disappeared as early as 1899, see ch. 3, n. 186.

198 PRO, T. 1/10960B/22783, Office of Works to Treasury (9080/08), 15 May 1908.

199 *PP* 1908 (108) X, 991, *S.C. on Public Offices Sites (Extension) Bill*, pp. 5–6, qq. 2–22. Opposition came from 'one of the most eminent firms [of solicitors, viz. Nicholsons] in London', which had nine years of a lease still to run, ibid. Although the S.C. accepted the government's case, the Lords did not (8 Edw. VII, c. 112). In the Commons, William Rutherford had moved the rejection of 2R on the ground that much cheaper sites near parliament (slum property at Millbank) were available for public offices, *4PD* CLXXXVIII, 1182–3, 13 May; CLXXXIX 1395–6, 29 May 1908.

200 PRO, T. 1/11219/13629, OW to Treasury, 16 July 1910, referring to earlier letter of 13 July 1909.

201 Ibid., Cabinet confidential print, FCW, 11 Apr. 1911.

202 PRO, T. 1/11322/16991, OW to Treasury, 21 July 1911.

203 *5PD* XXXIX, 89 (4 June); XL, 1824, 1829–30 (9 July 1912); *PP* 1912–13 (204) IX, 175, *S.C. on Public Offices (Sites) Bill*.

204 Info ex. Dr Andrew Saint, English Heritage.

205 *5PD* LI, 693 (3 Apr. 1913); PRO, Work 12/481, 482.

206 PRO, Work 12/347.

207 The Commissioners of Patents from 1862 to 1875 annually urged the Treasury to allow them to buy, from surplus revenue, a site opposite the Horse Guards, running down to the river, to provide for Office, Library, and their projected Museum. Banks & Barry had included a new Office in their abortive plans of 1859 for the Burlington House site. See *Reports of Patent Commissioners*, *PP* 1859 sess. 2, XIV, 679ff.; 1872 XXIV, 232ff.

208 H. Harding, *Patent Office Centenary* (1953), 35–6; PRO, Work 30/2513–23 (Pennethorne), 2524–33 (Taylor, 1897), 2536–40 (Taylor, 1891), 2541–4, 2546–53 (Taylor, 1892), 2554–60 (Taylor, 1894–5).

209 *PP*, *Appropriation accounts* (see bibliography).

210 *5PD* XXXIX, 90 (4 June 1912).

9. The Costs of Building

1 *PP* 1887 (184) VII, q. 683.

2 Those for Waterhouse's Natural History Museum added greatly to the total cost.

3 *BN*, LIII (1887), 423–4.

4 Ibid.; cp *PP* 1887 (184) VII, *S.C. on Admiralty and War Office (Sites)*, qq. 1079–85, 1538–42. Examples of costs per foot cube given to the committee included Scott's Foreign and Home Offices, 1s.0½d.; Barry's Houses of Parliament, 2s.6d.; Smirke's British Museum, 1s.6d. (Taylor's additions, 10d.); Royal Exchange (Tite), 11d.; St Thomas's Hospital (Currey) 9d.; Bow Street Police Court (Taylor) 11d.; Williams's GPO West 8½d. (qq. 1141, 1088, 1154).

5 *4PD* XLVIII, 332, 1 Apr. 1897.

6 The First Schedule of the *Public Offices Extension Bill* shows Upper and Lower Crown Streets, Crown Court and Charles Street to be largely occupied by weekly tenants, PRO, Crest 2646.

7 *PP* 1877 (312) XV, *S.C. on Public Offices (Sites)*, q. 1982.

8 *PP* 1882 (235) VII, *S.C. on Artizans' and Labourers' Dwellings Improvement Acts 1875 and 1879*, q. 528: 'Is it not a fact that before the standing arbitrator, and before juries the claimants' witnesses put in valuations greatly in excess of the real value of the property taken, and can you quote some instances of such excessive valuations? – It does not advance one's estimate of human nature when one has much to do with compensations; the elasticity of the consciences of surveyors is something awful.' Evidence of F.W. Goddard, Surveyor of the MBW.
 Referring to leasehold interests, he said 'we have great difficulty when proceeding in Lands Clauses compensation cases to get a jury to look at it in the way in which it practically should be looked at', ibid., q. 513. Every free- or lease-hold interest was entitled to a jury.

9 The *1897 Post Office London Directory* lists 15 distinct occupiers at these addresses.

10 PRO, Work 12/170.

11 Ibid.

12 PRO, T. 1/10960B/22783, 13 May 1908 (9610/08).

13 PRO, T. 1/8723A/3241, no. 15900, Oct. 1892. See p. 136.

14 19 Mar. 1853, p. 131.

15 *PP* 1877 (312) XV, evidence of A. Cates, qq. 1509, 1543, 1548; *PP* 1887 (184) VII, qq. 674–6, 748.

16 BL, Add. MS 41227, ff. 195–8, 15 Nov. 1892.

17 *4PD* LV, 108 (17 Mar. 1898).

18 *PP* 1882 (235) VII, q. 639.

19 *Survey*, XXXVIII, 54–7.

20 Ibid., 64, 69.

21 *PP* 1877 (312) XV, q. 1083; *PP* 1854–55 (382) VII, p. 9. But FCW reported the cost of the site to the Treasury, 4 Mar. 1864 as £278,366, of which £86,766 was for the India Office, PRO, T. 1/6703A/4213. The F.O. cost £285,473, so that the site cost 40 per cent of the total (PRO, T. 1/7009B/20313, 26 Feb. 1870). See also *PP* 1864 (186) XXXII, 287.

22 PRO, T. 1/6703A/4213, 22 July 1858. M.D. Wyatt's calculations about site costs in 1860 give a price of about £8819 per acre (£1.82 per sq ft) for the original New Government Offices site, and roughly twice as much for the King St. – Parliament St. island, I.O. Collns, L/SUR/2/4, f. 26.

23 *PP* 1856 (368) XIV, qq. 18, 56; 1877 (312) XV, q. 1077. Hunt did not define the western boundary of the smaller site, whether Delahay Street or the Park.

24 *PP* 1896 (310) X, *S.C. on Government Offices*, q. 79 and app. 1.

25 *PP* 1887 (184) VII, *Admiralty and War Office (Sites)*, qq. 247–9; *PP* 1896 (310) X, qq. 82–6.

26 PRO, T. 2/Office of Works, no. 1061 (17 Jan., for nos. 27–30, 32–34, and 35A Great George St. and 2 Delahay St.); no. 11525 (30 June 1903). See also Work 12/170 for purchases under the 1896 Act.

27 *5PD* XXXIX, 89–90 (4 June 1912).

28 *PP* 1860 (483) IX, q. 1546.

29 PRO Work 12/40/3, ff. 50–6, Street to FCW, 1 May 1873; Work 17/16/3, ff. 49 (Waterhouse to FCW, 2 July), 111ᵛ–12 (Galton's report, 6 Dec. 1872); Work 12/96/2, ff. 301–2, Scott to FCW, 7 Feb. 1873. The contractors for the Home and Colonial Offices had claimed 15 per cent extra, arguing that the labour strike of 1872 had caused a 12 per cent increase in wages, and that building materials had cost 30 per cent less in 1870, ibid., ff. 314, 316 (Jackson & Shaw to Scott, 29 Jan., 16 Apr. 1873).

30 PRO, Work 12/88/3, f. 79ff., 17 Jan. 1893.

31 For problems with a large lump-sum contract in the 1950s, see Jean Imray, *The Mercers' Hall* (1991), 421–5.

32 See p. 269.

33 PRO, Work 30/1012, PRO, Work 30/3509–11.

34 PRO, Work 30/3511.

35 *King's Works*, VI, 264–77.

36 *3PD* CXXXIV, 1063.

37 *3PD* CXXXIX, 1576.

38 *3PD* CLXIV, 544 (8 July 1861).

39 *3PD* CLXIV, 535 (8 July 1861); CLXVI, 1929 (19 May 1862).

40 *3PD* CLXXI, 911 (15 June 1863).

41 *3PD* CCXCVI, 1179 (9 Apr. 1885).

42 PRO, Work 17/60, memo. by Harcourt, 22 Feb. 1893.

43 PRO, Work 12/88/3, ff. 76–8, T. to FCW, 10 Jan. 1893.

44 *4PD* CLXXXVIII, 1181 (13 May 1908).

45 *5PD* LIII, 2005 (13 June 1913). A similar proposal had been rebutted by the FCW in 1860: *PP* 1860 (483) IX, q. 942.

46 *5PD* LIII, 2016.

47 PRO, Work 17/16/2, ff. 186–92 (Galton's report, 4 Apr.), 194–5 (T. to FCW, 2 May), 198, 203 (Ayrton, 5 May), 212 (Waterhouse to FCW, 26 July 1871); 17/18/4 (8 Mar. 1876 and Dec. 1877); 17/17/1, ff. 152–3, accounts, 1879; ff. 103–4, 299 (Waterhouse to OW, 9 Jan. 1877, 26 Jan. 1881).

48 *PP* 1887 (184) VII, *S.C. on Admiralty and War Office*.

49 PRO, Work 12/88/1, ff. 5–6, 12 May 1887: 'With better designed structural arrangements [than in the approved plans of 1884 for a new building], considerable improvements could be carried out in regard to the working of the department' – though it seemed to represent a major change for a department in which 82 officers out of 99 had rooms to themselves, as did 35 clerks (out of 719), while there were only five rooms in which there were more than ten clerks, ibid., f. 3, 11 May 1887.

50 Ibid., f. 20, 8 Dec. 1887.

51 PRO, Work 12/88/1, ff. 33 (10 Feb.), 38 (11 Apr. 1888).

52 Ibid., ff. 48–9. See also MoD Library, Vt 1, 8' to 1" plans of Admiralty Extension, Blocks I–III.

53 PRO, Work 12/88/3, ff. 51–3, 56–7.

54 PRO, Work 12/91/3, ff. 2–6, memo. FCW to T., 14 Dec. 1892; 12/88/3, ff. 51–3 (16 Dec. 1892, OW to T.).

55 PRO, Work 12/91/3, ff. 2–6.

56 Ibid.

57 PRO, Work 12/88/2, ff. 10, 14 Dec.; 19–22, – Dec. 1892.

58 M.H. Port, 'The Office of Works and building contracts in early nineteenth-century England', *Econ. Hist. Rev.* 2 Ser., XX (1967), 94–110.

59 The French *Bâtiments Civils* appears to have been more successful than the Office of Works in keeping expenditure on new public buildings down to its very carefully prepared estimates. See D. Van Zanten, *Designing Paris* (1987), 130–1.

60 As at the New Houses of Parliament, New Law Courts and Natural History Museum.

61 Similar problems with contemporary general contracts in France are graphically depicted by E. Viollet-le-Duc, *Lectures on Architecture*, translated by B. Bucknall (1881), II, 409–14. In England the practice came in for much criticism as well as commendation when it was relatively new (see *King's Works* VI, 161–2, and M.H. Port, 'The Office of Works and early 19th-century building contracts'); later criticisms affecting public buildings proved difficult to substantiate, *PP* 1867 [3873] XXXII, *1st–3rd Reports R.C. on Trades Unions*, qq. 1522, 2762 ff., 2814; 1867 [3952] XXXII, *4th Report*, q. 7369; 1892 [c.6795-VI] XXXVI (2), *R.C. on Labour, Group C*, q. 18,936. See also *Beehive*, editorial, 20 Feb. 1864.

62 Nevertheless Hunt, as Surveyor of the OW from 1855, is said to have been a strong advocate of lump-sum contracts, *Civil Engineer*, 1859, p. 249. As late as 1892, a builder's foreman was still insisting that 'one great evil in the [building] trade is the system of contracting for public works . . . the system upon which the public and even private contracts are given to the lowest tenderer. That is really, I consider, one of the main causes for the sweating and driving of *employés*, so many masters contend for a given piece of work . . . that, in order to turn out that work at anything like a profit to himself, he has to rely upon sweating and driving his workmen and putting in inferior materials.' *PP* 1892 [c.6795-VI] XXXVI (2), *R.C. on Labour, Group C*, q. 18,936.

63 *3PD* CCCL (13 Feb. 1891); *PP* [c.6795-VI] XXXVI-II, *R.C. on Labour, Group C*, qq. 17407–24a; App. 29. The FCW told an MP in 1907 that all OW contracts included the following clause: 'The wages paid by the contractor to workmen employed by him in the execution of works shall be those generally accepted in each trade for competent workmen in the district where they are employed . . .', *Builder*, 10 Aug. 1907, p. 170.

64 PRO, Work 12/33/2, ff. 8–12, 13 Dec. 1869.

65 See W. Papworth, ed., *Gwilt's Encyclopaedia of Architecture* (1899 edn), 751ff.

66 PRO, Work 12/40/2, f. 60 (14 June 1872); 12/34/2, ff. 13–16.

67 *3PD* CLXIV, 541–3 (8 July 1861); Toplis, *Foreign Office*, 97; Broadlands Papers, WFC/JJ3 [1863], WFC/s4 (21 Aug. 1863).

68 I. Toplis, *The Foreign Office* (1987), 138.

69 *PP* 1861 (137) III, 875 (24 & 25 Vict. c. 33).

70 Toplis, 139–41.

71 25 & 26 Vict. c. 74, Act to vest part of St James Park in OW for Public Offices.

72 PRO, Work 12/96/2, ff. 3–4. M.D. Wyatt had earlier recommended splitting the I.O. foundations and superstructure contracts to economise time while completing working drawings and taking out quantities, I.O. Collns, L/SUR/2/4, f. 395.

73 The following paragraph is based on Toplis, 143–4.

74 Toplis, citing PRO, Work 6/307, ff. 46, 50. For the contract drawings, see PRO, Work 30/914–71, dated from 30 May to 21 Aug. 1863, and RIBA Drawings Coll.

75 Toplis lists the tenders, the highest at £209,615, but seven below £200,000, p. 235, n. 62.

76 *PP* 1867 [3873] XXXII, *1st–3rd Reports, R.C. on Trades Unions*, qq. 1522–47, 2765, 2770–1, 2797–2802, 2812–14.

77 Ibid., [3952] *4th Report*, qq. 7368–9.

78 Ibid., [3873], q. 2785.

79 PRO, Work 12/96/2, ff. 1, 108.

80 Ibid., f. 316, 16 Apr. 1873.

81 PRO, T. 1/7009B/20313, 21 Jan. 1870.

82 PRO, Work 12/96/2, ff. 170–1, T. to FCW, 22 July 1870; 175ff. Scott to FCW 6 Aug. (endorsed by Galton 9 Aug. 1870); 267–72, Scott to FCW, 22 July 1871.

83 Ibid., ff. 189, 304, 323–4.

84 PRO, Work 12/40/2, ff. 1, 2 (4, 7 Aug. 1870).

85 Ibid., ff. 23, 26; *Builder*, 28 Jan. 1871, p. 71.
86 PRO, Work 12/40/2, ff. 45, 57, 67 (16 Mar., 6 June, 14 Dec. 1872). For Dove Bros' record, see Brownlee, *Law Courts*, 292.
87 PRO, Work 12/40/2, ff. 10, 26. There seems to have been difficulty in persuading provincial firms to involve themselves, though the Works was anxious to include them. See also PRO Work 17/16/3, f. 18, addition of provincial builders (including Bull) to list of those invited to tender for the Natural History Museum, 5 Jan. 1872.
88 Bull & Sons' tender was £744,344 as against the £816,675 of the next lowest, Baker & Son (Dove Bros' tender at £924,100 suggests that their experience with the foundations had not been happy), PRO Work 12/40/3, f. 117.
89 PRO, Work 2/40, pp. 151–6 (FC to Treasury, 3 Apr.), 157–62 (Street to FC, 27 Mar. 1873).
90 Ibid., pp. 157–62 (Street, 27 Mar.), 329 (FC to Treasury, 13 May), 422–3 (Treasury to FC, 20 May), 528 (Street's schedule, 11 June), 557 (Treasury to FC, 1 July 1873); 12/40/3, 112 (OW to Bulls, 31 May), 122 and 134–8 (Street to OW, 6 and 16 June 1873).
91 PRO, Work 12/40/3, ff. 190–240.
92 Ibid., ff. 174 (Bull & Sons to OW, 15 Aug.), 182–4, 187–9 (Street to Galton, 5 and 6 Sept.), 190–201 (Hunt's memo. 15 Sept. 1873).
93 Brownlee, *Law Courts*, 297–305.
94 PRO, Work 12/33/2, ff. 170–1, 183 (3 Aug. 1884, 24 Feb. 1887).
95 PRO Work 17/16/3, ff. 1, 4–5 (27 Nov., 19 Dec. 1871).
96 Ibid., f. 49, 2 July 1872.
97 Ibid., ff. 53, 54, 56, 62 (4–11 July 1872).
98 Ibid., ff. 9, 27 Dec. 1871; 70, 12 Aug. 1872.
99 Ibid., ff. 89–90.
100 A sudden increase in export demand in 1871 for iron, and the effects of the Franco-German war, caused the price to shoot up, rising from £7.10s. to over £10 per ton, reaching its highest level since 1828 in 1873; it then sagged, and by the 1880s was low again. S.G. Checkland, *Rise of industrial society in England 1815–1885* (1964), 46.
101 PRO, Work 17/16/3, ff. 99–100 (14 Oct.), 103 (28 Oct.), 106–7 (28 Nov.), 109–10 (5 Dec., Bakers' revised tender), 117 (6 Dec.), 122 (13 Dec. 1872).
102 There was uncertainty in the building industry about fixing this new material. Was it 'as a substitute for stone or as a more prestigious type of brick. Partly as a result of such contention there was considerable inconsistency in the way that blocks were filled and fixed. Cement, brick-bats and flints were all used for filing hollow blocks' on the South Kensington Museum. Different types of cement were used for fixing blocks, 'among which . . . hard Portland cement often caused failure, with blocks shattering as the cement expanded'. M. Stratton, 'Science and Art Closely Combined: the organisation of training in the terracotta industry, 1850–1939', *Construction History*, 4 (1988), 46–7.
103 PRO, Work 17/16/2, ff. 216–17, 30 July 1874 (see also ff. 218ff.); 17/17/1, ff. 112–13, 13 Feb. 1879. The Works had disallowed the charge of the surveyor who had measured the deviations in the basement, but it had been sanctioned on arbitration. Since then, the Office had allowed the builder to include half the measuring fees in his bills, but Hunt insisted that if the architect's share were also met, 'the Architect has no interest in adhering to his original plan, & might, commit us to a large expenditure for measuring up works', a characteristic Works' view of the lack of integrity of professional men, and typical, too, of Hunt's 'poacher turned gamekeeper' attitude. (See p. 61 above.) Ibid., 17/16/2, ff. 218–19 (13 Aug.

1874), 234–5 (1 June 1875).
104 Samuel Baker, founder of the firm was Sir Robert Smirke's brother-in-law, and much employed by him.
105 *Survey*, XXXVIII, 213, and sources there cited.
106 *King's Works*, VI, 109.
107 Ibid., VI, 197–8, 237–9; M.H. Port, ed., *The Houses of Parliament* (1976), 151–4.
108 Broadlands Papers, GC/HA/30, 4 Aug. 1856.
109 PRO, Work 2/33, p. 207, 27 July 1869.
110 PRO, Work 2/33, 1 Jan. 1870.
111 PRO, Work 12/33/2, ff. 1–4 (18 Nov. 1869), 13–14 (1 Jan. 1870).
112 This was to ignore the amending act of 1866, see p. 106.
113 PRO, Work 12/33/2, ff. 16–22 (FCW, draft, 17 Jan.), 23–5 (Treasury, 18 Mar.), 31–2 (Hunt, 23 Mar.), 33–7 (Galton, 24 Mar. 1871).
114 Ibid., ff. 43, 47, 49, 50 (Street, 20 Nov. 1872, 13 Aug., 25 Sept., 26 Sept.), 54 FCW, (30 Sept.), 64 (Hunt and Galton, 4 Nov. 1873).
115 Ibid., ff. 72–131, *passim*. Street's disagreements with the Office did not end here: he long argued, but in vain, that warming and ventilating services for the east wing were not included in the agreement of 1870 (ff. 153–5, 11 June 1880) and in 1878 he claimed surveyor's fees for the measuring necessary for certificating the contractor's work, at 10s. per cent; on the total of £732,509, a matter of £3662 – this was finally settled after Street's death by a payment of £1500, ibid., 12/35/1, ff. 1–3 (6 Nov. 1878); 12/33/2, ff. 162 (15 May), 167 (21 July), 170–1 (3 Aug.), 172 (23 Dec. 1884).
116 See M.H. Port, 'A Regime for Public Buildings. Experiments in the Office of Works, 1869–75', in J. Newman, ed., *Design and Practice in British Architecture* (1984), 74–85.
117 Among these was the striking out the towers at either end of the Whitehall façade. Scott fought for years to reinstate the towers, without which the front was, he thought, 'reduced to an idealess mass' and rendered 'dull and almost featureless' (BL, Add. MS 44441, Scott to Gladstone, 8 Dec. 1873, endorsed by the private secretary, 'He must be mad?' – having earlier minuted, 'The question of economy seems unappreciable compared with that of saving London from such erections', PRO, T. 1/7329A/20026). See also Blair Adam MSS 3/433, Gladstone to Scott (copy), 23 Dec. 1873; Scott to W.P. Adam, FCW, 5 Jan. 1874; draft, FCW to T., supporting Scott, 2 Oct. 1873 – also copy in Hughenden Papers, B/XX/LX/422b, together with Scott to Lord Henry Lennox, 14 Apr. 1874 (422a) and supporting letters to Disraeli's private secretary, 25 and 27 May 1874, nos. 421, 422. The battle was resumed in the 1890s by his son, J. Oldrid Scott, and J.M. Brydon as architect of the adjoining New Public Offices (see PRO, Work 30/1007); and as late as 1910 an MP returned to the question, the FCW replying that financial exigencies prevented completion 'at present' (5PD XIV, 1133).
118 PRO, Work 2/36, pp. 718, 861 (10 June, 3 July); 2/37, pp. 7, 51, 52–7, 106 (19, 27, 22 July, 8 Aug. 1871).

10. Financing the Costs

1 J. Ruskin, *The Seven Lamps of Architecture* (1849), I, 1.
2 3PD CCII, 1752–6 (8 July 1870).
3 Ibid., 1762, 1769–72; BL, Add. MS 44538, f. 189, Gladstone to Cardwell, 12 July 1870.
4 See ch. 2, n. 99 above.
5 Witness Charles Dickens's *Bleak House* (1852–3).
6 E.B. Sugden (1781–1875), MP (Tory) 1826–32, 1837–41; sol.-gen. 1829–30; lord chancellor of Ireland 1835, 1841–6; lord chancellor (G.B.)

1852; cr. Lord St Leonards 1852. A cautious law reformer, but an overbearing judge.
7 BL, Add. MS 38996, f. 177, 4 May 1869.
8 See above, p. 105.
9 William Page Wood (1801–81), Q.C. 1845; MP (Lib.) 1847–53; vice-chancellor 1853; lord justice of appeal 1868; lord chancellor 1868–72; cr. Baron Hatherley 1868.
10 *PP* 1860 [2710] XXXI, 89ff. *R.C. on concentration of Courts of Law and Equity*.
11 He had already, 19 Dec. 1860, warned the principal mover, Sir Richard Bethell (later lord chancellor as Lord Westbury), that he would 'object to placing any charge whatever on the public' for new law courts without first ensuring the thrifty management of court funds, BL, Add. MS 44337, ff. 187–91.
12 BL, Add. MS 44636, ff. 55–8, 27 Apr. 1861.
13 *PP* 1860 [2710] XXXI, para. 94.
14 *PP* 1861 (440) LI, 667, Treasury minute, 16 July 1861.
15 *PP* 1862 (164) XLIV, 397, *Memorial of the Incorporated Law Society*, 5 Nov. 1861.
16 BL, Add. MS 44337, ff. 197–8, 12 Feb. 1862.
17 3PD CLXVI, 796–826, 10 Apr. 1862. 'The cost seems to be on a lavish scale. . . . The House begins to be a little cautious, & high time too!' one country squire confided to his journal. T.A. Jenkins, ed., *Parliamentary Diaries of Sir John Trelawny* (1990).
18 PRO Work 12/32/5, 25 Oct. 1862.
19 See above, p. 106.
20 3PD CLXXVI, 363–70, 27 June 1864.
21 *PP* 1864 (448) XLVIII, 431, Treasury minute, 18 June 1864.
22 Quoted, T.A. Nash, *Life of Richard Lord Westbury*, II (1888), 100.
23 1851 Comm. file 68. Slightly less stringent economies were the norm: 'I may say, every year something is postponed, which it would be desirable, on its own account, to perform', W. Cowper, FCW, to S.C. on Misc. Expenditure, *PP* 1860 (483) IX, qq. 787, 924.
24 Lord Henniker, 3PD CCCXXXIV, 1122–5.
25 'Things often turn out differently in the House of Commons to what one expects . . .' remarked Lord Clarendon to the Duchess of Manchester, 6 Feb. 1860. A.L. Kennedy, *'My Dear Duchess'* (1956), 89–90. It was doubtless from his unhappy ministerial experience that Lord John Manners recommended loan finance, as for fortifications, to fund his master plan of 1867 – the policy ultimately adopted in 1898: *PP* 1877 (312) XV, q. 1169.
26 See pp. 182–4.
27 MP (Lib.) 1880–1906; trade union leader, and chairman masons' committee in 1872 lock-out; worked as a mason on Houses of Parliament briefly in 1850s.
28 3PD CCXCVI, 1106 (31 Mar. 1885).
29 BL, Add. MS 44153, ff. 226–7, Lefevre to Gladstone, 20 May 1886.
30 3PD CCCIV, 449 (1 Apr. 1886).
31 Lefevre complained to Gladstone of the unusual composition of the 1886 committee, with four Liberal front benchers and three Conservative out of a total of 16 members. 'According to the usual etiquette the members of the Government below the rank of Cabinet Ministers are bound to vote with their leaders in the Cabinet and consequently a decision on the Liberal side will practically rest with Sir W. Harcourt; who I believe is strongly opposed to the present scheme. As Mr W.H. Smith and Lord George Hamilton are also declared opponents to the present plan, but were overruled by their colleagues in the late Government in their attempts to upset it, it is obvious that a combination between Harcourt and Smith would practically carry the Committee. . . . I should be alone and unsupported. What I have to suggest is that Mr

Childers should be substituted for one or two of the Junior Members of the Government on the Committee . . . his presence . . . would ensure my having a fair hearing and trial.' BL, Add. MS 44153, ff. 227–31, 20 May 1886. But when the committee was reappointed in 1887 (under Conservative aegis), Childers was omitted.

32 *PP* 1887 (184) VII, *S.C. on Admiralty and War Office (Sites)*.

33 Ibid., qq. 1–119, 2036–45.

34 Ibid., qq. 1564–1689.

35 Ibid., qq. 1690–1766.

36 Ibid., qq. 1283–1370, esp. 1286–7, 1290, 1292–4.

37 Ibid., qq. 1629–30.

38 PRO, T. 1/8297B/11930, 20 July 1887.

39 See pp. 269–70.

40 PRO, Work 12/88/3, f. 2, 11 Jan. 1889.

41 *4PD* CXLVII, 1091–2 (20 June 1905).

42 *4PD* XL, 514–15, 4 May 1896.

43 *4PD* XLVIII, 327, 1 Apr. 1897.

44 M.H. Port (ed.), *The Houses of Parliament* (1976), 88.

45 See p. 7 above.

46 *King's Works* VI, ch. viii.

47 Port, *Houses of Parliament*, 101–3, 109, 115–17, 156–7, 218–31.

48 *PP* 1849 (404) XXX.

49 Port, *Houses of Parliament*, 151–6.

50 Ibid., ch. xii.

51 Ibid., 149, 161.

52 E.g., *3PD* CXLVI, 149, 155, 157 (Willoughby, Drummond, Briscoe, 22 June 1857).

53 E.g., *3PD* CIV, 857–8 (26 Apr. 1849); CVIII, 270 (4 Feb. 1850).

54 E.g. *3PD* CXIII, 726ff. (debate, 2 Aug. 1850); CLXIV, 550 (Lindsay, 8 July 1861); CLXXXVIII, 165 (Bright, 20 June), 536 (Headlam, 25 June); 1695 (Neville-Grenville and O'Loghlen) and 1701 (Seymour, 13 July 1867); CXCV, 271, 299 (Manners, Walter, 6 Apr. 1869).

55 E.g., *3PD* CLIV, 1346 (Pease, 15 July 1859); CLXXXVIII, 653–9 (House of Lords, 28 June 1867).

56 E.g., *3PD* CXIX, 231ff., 400ff. (debates, 6, 11 Feb. 1852); CLIV, 1339–41, 1345 (Ayrton, Verney, Coningham, 15 July 1859); CLVIII, 1699 (Ayrton, 18 July 1867).

57 E.g., *3PD* XCVII, 139 (Osborne, 2 Mar. 1848); CXXIX, 1313 (Hume, 4 Aug. 1853).

58 Lord Claud Hamilton, *3PD* CXLVI, 158.

59 Port, *Houses of Parliament*, 162–5. Several MPs recognised their own share in the responsibility (e.g., Osborne: 'all the mischief occasioned in this building has been entirely created by Committees of this House', *3PD* CXIX, 400, 11 Feb. 1852); and ministers tended to blame the lack of executive control (e.g., ch. of Exchequer: 'Parliament had never effectually committed the responsibility for these works to the Executive Government', *3PD* CXXXIII, 1282, 8 June 1854).

60 The average Vote over the four years 1855/6–1858/9 was nearly £132,000. That for 1859/60, last year of Sir Charles Barry's life, was £58,525. In 1867/8 the Vote was still as much as £45,137; in 1868/9 £47,936; and in 1869/70, £34,026 – *3PD*: CL, 1201; CLIV, 1338; CLXXXVIII, 1695; CXCII, 299; CXCVII, 679.

61 *PP* 1867–68 (451) VIII, *House of Commons arrangements*; *3PD* CXCV, 258ff. (6 Apr. 1869).

62 Salviati had revived the art of working in enamel mosaic, and was employed at St Mark's, Venice. At the 1862 Exhibition he came to England, and was then employed by the queen. He established a school of young artists in Venice, but by 1867 was in need of additional capital. Layard, as well as encouraging the artists, helped find subscribers for the Venice and Murano Glass and Mosaic Co. Ltd, taking two shares himself, which he sold on taking office. *3PD* CXCII, 712 (26 July 1869).

63 *3PD* CXCVII, 679–85 (28 June 1869).

64 Ibid., 1429–45 (8 July 1869).

65 *3PD* CXCVIII, 708–20 (26 July 1869) – Layard was bitterly hurt by the attacks, see BL, Add. MS 38949, ff. 22–4, Layard to W.H. Gregory, 5 Mar. 1870. Gladstone's harsh view was that Layard did 'not seem very thoroughly to understand pecuniary responsibility and the management of Estimates', A. Ramm (ed.), *Political correspondence of Mr Gladstone and Lord Granville* (1952), I, 45 (18 Aug. 1869); so he got rid of him. See M.H. Port, 'A Contrast in Styles at the Office of Works', *Hist. Jnl*, 27 (1984), 151–76.

66 *Builder*, 26 Jan. 1850, p. 39. Godwin, the editor, was campaigning at this time against the tendency of popular leaders to act as 'checks and drawbacks' upon the spirit of improvement, spoiling great public works by 'begrudging the needful cost . . . to display it to full advantage', and depriving 'the industrious mechanic and artisan' of employment. Legislators should rather 'bestow more attention in securing . . . the utmost completeness of design in the first instance, and then address themselves to reducing the estimates to the lowest cost compatible with the carrying out of this principle'. Cp 2 Feb. (p. 52) and 1 June 1850 (pp. 258–9).

67 *Builder*, 28 Sept. 1850, p. 457.

68 P. Guedalla, *Gladstone and Palmerston* (1928), p. 117 (15 Dec. 1859).

69 See J. Morley, *Gladstone* (1903), II, 42–8.

70 Guedalla, *Gladstone and Palmerston*, pp. 172–3; R. Shannon, *Gladstone*, I (1982), 407, 419.

71 BL, Add. MS 44538, f. 89, 4 Mar. 1870.

72 *3PD* CCXCVI, 1202, 1214; 1213.

73 BL, Add. MS 46089, f. 18, 'Confidential', 13 Mar. 1895.

74 Bodleian, Harcourt MSS dep., box 186, ff. 23–4, 17 Mar. 1895.

75 *PP* 1896 (159) VI, 383, *Public Offices Westminster (Site) bill*; 1897 (223) VI, 531, *Public Offices (Whitehall) Site bill*.

76 *4PD* XXXVI, 993 (27 Aug. 1895); 59 Vict., c. 5, *Public Offices (Acquisition of Sites) Act*, 1895 sess. 2.

77 59 & 60 Vict., c. 6. The measures were to provide improved harbour defences, barrack accommodation, &c.

78 60 & 61 Vict., c. 27, *Public Offices (Whitehall) Site Act*, 1897.

79 61 Vict., c. 5.

80 *4PD* LV, 107–11 (17 Mar. 1898). The Treasury had decided against the western extension of the Great George Street Offices, structural alterations in Downing Street, building (for the Civil Service Commission) in Spring Gardens, and the completion of the Home Office towers. The completion of the PRO, the GPO, and Hertford House (for the Wallace Collection) were to be included in the customary estimates for 1898/99, PRO, T. 1/9202B/17790, 13 Dec. 1897.

81 *4PD* LV, 1285–6, 29 Mar. 1898. The chancellor explained that works long in execution resulted under the previous system in large balances building up in the Treasury, on which no interest was received, ibid., 1287.

82 (1832–1918). Held minor office (Lib.) 1880–4, including financial sec. of Treasury; dep. Speaker and chairman committees 1886–92 (Lib. Unionist); cr. Baron Courtenay of Penwith, 1906.

83 (1857–1934). MP (Lib.) 1892–5, 1896–1923; property developer; pres. Rural Dist. Councils Assoc.; bt 1910.

84 *4PD* LV, 121–2, 125, 17 Mar. 1898. See also the criticisms of Gibson Bowles, ibid., 1292–4.

85 *4PD* CXXVII, 773–4 (10 Aug. 1903).

86 PRO, T. 1/11075/17428, OW to T., 20 Aug.; Work 12/122/3, ff. 3–4, T. to OW, 3 Sept. 1909. On the other hand, £257,000 was received in dividends and interest before 1 Apr. 1908, PRO, Work 12/122/3.

87 PRO, T. 1/9979B/13557, Minute, 'EWH' [Hamilton], 4 Apr. 1903 (5315/03).

88 *4PD* CXXXIX, 650–68 (2 Aug. 1904).

89 *4PD* CXXXVIII, 1079–80, 1083 (25 July 1904); CL, 821 (28 July 1905).

90 *4PD* CLVI, 289–90 (30 Apr. 1906).

91 8 Edw. 7, c. 16, s. 9. See PRO, T. 1/10960B/22783, L. Harcourt to Murray, 8 Feb. 1908 (2967/08); Arthur T. Thring to Bradbury, 15 May 1908 (8734/08). The act was amended by the Public Buildings Expenses Act of 1913 (3 & 4 Geo. 5, c. 14), which authorised the application of £145,000 to a Home Office Industrial Museum (£25,000), additional accommodation at the Admiralty (£55,000), and the Coll. of Art, South Kensington (£65,000).

92 *4PD* CXXVI, 807–8 (29 July 1908).

93 PRO, T. 1/10960B/22783, Murray to First Commissioner, 3 Feb. 1908 (569/08); memoranda accompanying 2967/08.

94 PRO, T. 1/11322/16991, Minute, 'JB' [Bradbury], 12 Oct. [1911].

95 PRO, T. 1/10960B/22783, Minute 'WB' [Blair], 25 Mar. in 5428/08.

96 PRO, T. 1/11322/16991, Minute, 'RFW' [Wilkins], 7 Oct. 1911.

97 John Swanwick Bradbury (1872–1950); private secretary to the chancellor, 1905–8; head of division 1908–13; joint. sec. of the Treasury, 1913–25; K.C.B. 1913; cr. Baron Bradbury 1925. Gave his name to £1 notes issued in First World War.

98 PRO, T. 1/11322/16991, Minute, 'JB' [Bradbury], 12 Oct. [1911].

99 See p. 56.

11. The Golden Age of Competition

1 E.M. Barry, *Lectures on Architecture* (1881), 135.

2 *King's Works*, VI, ch. III–VI.

3 See G. Tyack, *Sir James Pennethorne and the Making of Victorian London* (Cambridge, 1992).

4 *Architect*, 23 Dec. 1887, p. 381.

5 Joan Bassin, *Architectural Competitions in Nineteenth-Century England* (Ann Arbor, Mich., 1984), asserts that 'Between 1882, when the first compulsory examinations took place for Associateship, and the passing of the Architect's Registration Act in 1921, the competition system was virtually destroyed by the crippling restraints which the RIBA placed on both promoters and competitors' (p. 15). This assertion is contradicted by the annual lists given in R.H. Harper, *Victorian Architectural Competitions* (1983) for the years to 1900, and subsequently by the evidence of the professional periodicals.

6 M.H. Port, ed., *The Houses of Parliament*, ch. III.

7 *PP* 1857–58 (417) XI, q. 1174. Burn dodged the issue by responding: 'Sometimes you do not get the best man along with the best design.'

8 *3PD* CXCII, 370.

9 'For the embarking in extensive competitions . . . is an expensive luxury', commented one well-reputed architect, John Prichard, SRO, Wemyss MSS, RH4/40/7, 11 Apr. 1864.

10 E.M. Barry, *Lectures on Architecture* (1881), 176.

11 Architect of Eatington Park, Llandaff Cathedral, several churches, etc., and entrant in the Government Offices and South Kensington Museums competitions.

12 SRO, Wemyss MSS, RH4/40/7, 11 Apr. 1864.

13 *Builder*, 14 Dec. 1861, p. 866.

14 This was Norman Shaw's view of the function of competitions, GLRO, LCC Establishment Cttee minutes, 26 July 1906 (7), cited by Andrew Saint, *Richard Norman Shaw* (1976), 346.

15 E.M. Barry, *Lectures on Architecture*, 135.

16 Thus in 1867, the New National Gallery drawings were exhibited in the Royal Gallery, Houses of Parliament. Photographs were sent to the Paris Exhibition; E.M. Barry substituted photographs in order to exhibit his entry at the Royal Academy; and a selection from the entries was shown at an Architectural Association exhibition during the summer. PRO, Work 1/83, pp. 124, 215, 359, 373; 1/84, pp. 2, 24, 402.

17 The widely-circulating *Illustrated London News* (founded 1842) also gave extensive coverage to new architecture and to major competitions.

18 *Architect*, 6 Oct. 1883, p. 201.

19 E.M. Barry, *Lectures*, 140.

20 *Builder*, 23 May 1857, p. 289.

21 *Companion to the Almanac*, 1858, pp. 222–3; *BN*, 12 June 1857, p. 598.

22 Bassin, *Architectural Competitions*, ch. 1.

23 *Builder*, XXXVIII (1880), 662.

24 For the consequences for architects unable to live by their control of the design progress, see M.H. Port, 'The Life of an Architectural Sinner: Thomas Wayland Fletcher, 1833–1901', *London Jnl*, 15 (1990), 57–71.

25 *Solicitors' Jnl*, 13 (1869), p. 402, secretary, Metropolitan and Provincial Law Association. ·

26 Statement by Law Society council reported in *Solicitors' Jnl*, vol. 13, 273–5, 6 Feb. 1869.

27 Port, *Houses of Parliament*, 25–7.

28 *BN*, 20 Feb. 1857, p. 177.

29 Broadlands Papers, GC/HA/46, Hall to Palmerston, n.d.; *Builder*, 16 May, p. 269; 13 June, p. 336 (Buccleuch, whose Montagu House – about to be rebuilt – adjoined the site, and his architect, Burn, were considered interested parties); *BN*, 15 May, 'Judgment required in Judges'; 22 May, pp. 529–30; 29 May, pp. 546, 560.

30 *PP* 1836 (568) IX, q. 2201.

31 Beyond the professional press, see *Ecclesiologist*, 1857, pp. 172–3, 187; *Sat. Rev.*, 9 May 1857; *Athenaeum*, 1857, p. 628.

32 *BN*, 15 May 1857, 'Judgment required in Judges'; 22 May 1857, pp. 529–30.

33 Derby MS 133/7, 1839–55. (I am indebted to Lord Blake for permission to see this.)

34 *Builder* 1857, p. 359.

35 See below, p. 171.

36 *Morn. Chronicle*, 14, 17 Feb. 1836.

37 *Builder*, 1861, 85, 141, 192. Alphonse-Nicolas Crépinet (1826–92), who shared the second prize for the Opéra, won the first prize for the block plan in the British government-offices competition in 1857, and his partner Botrel is presumably the same as the Botrel d'Hazeville who took third prize for the War Office. Crépinet, who was employed on the New Louvre 1852–60, went on to a career as *architecte-en-chef*, D. van Zanten, *Designing Paris*, 123, 283.

38 Cited Bassin, 78; review in *Builder*, 25 May 1861, p. 352.

39 John Shaw urged Hall in 1856 that the competitors be invited to report on the best three designs, as in the Liverpool library competition, *Builder*, 27 Sept. 1856, p. 521.

40 E. Viollet-le-Duc, *Lectures on Architecture*, trans. B. Bucknall (1881), II, 309–409.

41 *BN*, 'The Judges in the Great Architectural Competitions', 20 Feb. 1857, p. 177; 'Judgment required in Judges', 15 May 1857.

42 *3PD* CLXXXIII, 182 (30 Apr. 1866).

43 *3PD* CLXXXVI, 2019.

44 M.H. Port, 'New Law Courts Competition', *Arch. Hist.*, 11 (1968), 89.

45 1800–79; R.A. 1863; director N.G. 1865–74; kt 1867.

46 1804–88; R.A. 1851; art superintendent 1852, inspector-gen. Govt School of Design from 1857, and director, dept of Science & Art 1874–5; sur-

47 veyor of queen's pictures 1857–80.

47 1816–88; authority on decorative painting; see *DNB*.

48 1822–94; 2nd viscount; under-sec. for War (Cons.) 1858–9.

49 PRO, Work 1/83, pp. 14 (28 Nov.–13 Dec.), 67 (14 Dec. 1866).

50 *Ecclesiologist*, XVIII, 173.

51 'Light Brown Indian Ink', *Builder*, 18 Apr. 1857, pp. 221–2. Samuel Huggins, a prolific contributor to the periodical press and president of the Liverpool architectural society, complained of the importance given to these drawings; a colleague had been deterred from entering the competition: 'You must make up your mind . . . to spend £50 for getting up of the drawings, or you have no chance with those London men', ibid., 23 May 1857, p. 289.

52 Instructions to Architects, 30 Sept. 1857, PRO, Work 12/86/1, no. 41; also in *PP* 1857 sess. 2 (152) XLI, 205ff.

53 *Builder*, 2 May 1857, p. 246, 'A competitor'; 27 June, p. 360, 'A correspondent' understood 'in line only' (the Office of Works refusing a definition) as 'that simple mode of drawing, half outline, half etching, which has of late years become one of the commonest and . . . one of the very best systems of making elevations at once simple in execution and readily intelligible', slight suggestions of shadow indicating projection and recession. See also *BN*, 30 Jan., pp. 114–15 (T. Allom's lecture); 6 Feb. 1857, p. 138, where the rule against shading is criticised because of the difficulty caused in reading drawings; PRO, Work 1/81, p. 434, instructions, 29 June 1866; 1/82, pp. 210, 237, 241, 245, corr. with Street, Murray, and E.M. Barry, and circulars to N.G. competitors, Sept. 1866 – there was no objection to shadows in elevations being etched in lines, but tinting was forbidden.

54 See *Builder*, 20 June 1857, p. 347, 'R'.

55 Ibid.; 'Renardus P.C.', *Builder*, 25 Apr. 1857; cp. 18 Apr., pp. 221–2; 9 May, p. 261; 16 May, p. 269.

56 Port, *Houses of Parliament*, 73, 79–80.

57 *BN*, 8 May, p. 447; 12 June 1857, p. 598. Cp. 15 May, 'Judgment required in Judges'.

58 E.M. Barry, *Lectures on Architecture* (1881), 137.

59 *King's Works*, VI, 560, citing Lincoln's letter-book, Nottingham Univ., Newcastle MSS, Ne C 12053.

60 *King's Works*, VI, 571.

61 For Pennethorne's career, see Tyack, *Sir James Pennethorne and the Making of Victorian London*.

62 *King's Works*, VI, 474–6; *3PD* CXIII, 270.

63 PRO, Work, 12/99/6, ff. 1–6, 19, 51.

64 Apparently referring to the minute of Commissioners of Woods & Works, 22 June 1840, printed in *PP* 1857–58 (417) XI, S.C. on Foreign Office Re-construction, app. 5; or the Treasury letter of 18 Dec. 1845, ibid.

65 Ibid., q. 1791.

66 See PRO, Work 12/86/1, ff. 1, 11, 26, 40–2; T. 1/6693A/3774.

67 *PP* 1857–58 (417) XI, app. 4, pp. 184–5, Memorial of Pennethorne to the Treasury.

68 See p. 61.

69 He may well have been confirmed in this opinion by a savage article by Hope, denouncing 'hands of proved incompetence' in government architecture, *Sat. Rev.*, 17 Nov. 1855, pp. 48–9.

70 PRO, T. 1/6693A/3774; *PP* 1857–58 (417) XI, p. 185.

71 Ibid.

72 Ibid., evidence, q. 1909.

73 Ibid., q. 1913.

74 Ibid., q. 1913.

75 See PRO, T. 1/5997A/10002.

76 *PP* 1857–58 (417) XI, app. 4 (p. 176ff.), where the correspondence is printed.

77 Ibid., q. 1979.

78 Broadlands Papers, GC/HA/15, 20 Mar. 1856.

79 RA, Add. MSS Q, 297, Hall to Phipps, 14 Mar. 1856.

80 *Builder*, 5 Apr. 1856, p. 190. By his advice the method was employed for King's Coll. Hospital, five architects being invited, the winner to be employed at 5 per cent, the others to receive 80 guineas each.

81 *PP* 1857–58 (417) XI, app. 4, pp. 188–91; qq. 762, 768.

82 Broadlands Papers, GC/HA/15.

83 22 Mar. 1856, p. 412.

84 *PP* 1857–58 (417) XI, qq. 666–9.

85 Ibid., app. 1, p. 164.

86 Ibid., qq. 686–704; app. 1, pp. 164–5.

87 Ibid., q. 736.

88 Sir Charles Barry remarked: 'I think it was a great mistake in the original instructions that the competition should have been simultaneous for a block plan, and for specific buildings under certain conditions', ibid., q. 1516. The *Builder* commented: 'The course adopted, prompted by desire for expedition, can scarcely be considered the best calculated to obtain a grand whole. A design should first have been obtained for laying out the whole of the land . . . and *then* designs should have been sought for the two structures named, to occupy such positions as might be most consistent with the best distribution of the whole.' *Builder*, 30 Aug. 1856, pp. 468–9. See also 9 May 1857, p. 261.

89 *Sat. Rev.*, 6 Sept. 1856, p. 416.

90 *PP* 1857–58 (417) XI, q. 263. The architect and competition judge William Burn, however, admitting that the block plan competition was a 'total failure', thought it of no importance, because the position of the F.O. was prescribed in the instructions, ibid., qq. 1199, 1233.

91 *PP* 1857–58 (83) XLVIII, p. 2, *Minute of interview between ch. of Exchequer and FCW*, 4 Aug. 1856.

92 Broadlands Papers, GC/LE 74, 20 Aug. 1856.

93 *PP* 1857–58 (417) XI, app. 1, p. 164.

94 E.g., *Sat. Rev.*, 6 Sept.; *Times*, 7 Oct.; *Builder*, 25 Oct., p. 577.

95 Quoted, *PP* 1857–58 (417) XI, p. iv.

96 *Builder*, 27 Dec. 1856, p. 696.

97 Ibid., 18 July 1857, p. 408, 'A Disgusted Competitor'.

98 The discrepancy between the number applying for particulars and the number of designs submitted is notable: at least 1791 sets of conditions were despatched, including 270 overseas (*3PD* CXLIX, 348–50, 9 Feb. 1857), but only 218 entries were received, of which 21 were from foreigners: of these only 39 (representing 28 different competitors) satisfied the conditions. There were in all about 84 entries for the Foreign Office and 80 for the War Office. (*PP* 1857–8 (417), XI, app. 2; I. Toplis, *The Foreign Office* (1987), 35; see *Designs for the Public Offices* (H.G. Clarke & Co., 1857). But cp. ch. 12, n. 29.

99 PRO, Work 12/86/1, ff. 158–65; 12/86/4, ff. 7, 8.

100 *Observer*, 31 Aug. 1856.

101 PRO, Work 12/86/4, ff. 9–12.

102 See Port, *Houses of Parliament*.

103 *3PD* CXLIV, 701–2, 16 Feb. 1857.

104 See, e.g., *Sat. Rev.*, 21 Feb. 1857, cited by Toplis, *Foreign Office*, 37.

105 Toplis, 39, refers to 'the general inertia pervading the early proceedings of the panel'. It is however specifically stated in the judges' minutes that the adjournment of a week was to enable the members severally to study the designs: there were some 2000 drawings. Far from being inert, the judges must have had to work very hard; from their plea for professional assistance it is clear that they found the task overwhelming.

106 PRO, Work 12/86/3, passim.

107 PRO, Work 12/86/3, ff. 23–8, report of the judges, 27 June 1857.

108 *Builder*, 9, 16 May 1857, pp. 261, 269.

109 Ibid., 16 May 1857, p. 272.

110 Ibid., 27 June 1857, p. 359.

111 Henry Edward Coe (1826–65), a pupil of G.G. Scott, had set up his practice in 1848. He designed some houses at Sydenham and, in partnership with one Goodwin, an infirmary at Dundee (£15,000); he had also erected some churches. Taking pupils evidently contributed to his income. *PP* 1857–58 (417) XI, qq. 827–8, 843–8. Though winning second place in a competition for Caterham Junction Royal Hospital for Incurables (R.H. Harper, *Victorian Architectural Competitions*, 203), he remained obscure. His partner, Henry Hofland, a former assistant of Scott's erstwhile partner W.B. Moffat, is even more obscure (see PRO, Work 12/86/4, ff. 69–70).
Henry Bayley Garling (1821–1909) also had little to record; though afterwards a more substantial figure, invited to compete for the New Law Courts in 1866, he achieved nothing of significance. When a new War Office was actually undertaken, he claimed the work, Chilston Papers, c. 6, July 1898.
Their fate may be contrasted with Continental experience. The unknown Ludwig Hoffmann (1851–1932) won the 1884 competition for the Imperial Supreme Court building at Leipzig (119 entrants) on the strength of his planning. He was encouraged to revise his commonplace elevations (at enhanced cost), and given technical assistance in executing the £300,000 commission, which led to his appointment as City Architect of Berlin, 1896 (*Builder*, 4 Jan. 1896, pp. 11–12). Alexander von Wielemans (1843–1911) similarly won the competition for the Vienna Justiz-palast, 1874, and was given the commission.

112 *PP* 1857–58 (83) XLVIII, p. 8, Hall to Treasury, 5 Nov. 1857.

113 Ibid., pp. 9–10, 28 Nov. 1857.

114 Ibid., pp. 10–11, 28 Dec. 1857.

115 Ibid., pp. 11–12, 1 Feb. 1858.

116 Belvoir Castle MSS, Lord John Manners's Letter Book, f. 20, to Lord Stanley, 10 Dec. 1858. Manners added a note that he had placed a memorandum in the drawer of his bureau, so as to cover a change of ministry.

117 They were again employed when a revised proposal for the site was made in 1863, and they successfully claimed the commission when a final determination was made in 1866. PRO, T. 1/6649B/17865.

118 *3PD* CLXVI, 802 (10 Apr. 1862).

119 See p. 98 above.

120 PRO, Work 17/16/1, ff. 1, 8; *PP* 1864 (254) XXXIV, 135ff., *Instructions . . . for Plans and Designs for Public Buildings to be erected on Land used . . . for International Exhibition . . .* , with plan of site.

121 PRO, Work 17/16/1, ff. 17–18.

122 Ibid. ff. 23–4, draft 1 Feb. 1864.

123 Ibid. ff. 25–6, 3 Feb. 1864.

124 SRO, Wemyss MSS, RH4/40/7, 11 Apr. 1864.

125 The number of entrants is given variously in *Builder* as 33 or 39, or 31 submitting 33 designs; in fact, as the list in *Survey*, XXXVIII, 203n. shows, there were 32, of whom Sang submitted two designs; the confusion arises from the similarity of name of two competing Glasgow firms: A. & G. Thomson (i.e. 'Greek' Thomson and his brother), and the unrelated A.G. Thomson: see A. Gomme & D. Walker, *Architecture of Glasgow* (rev. edn, 1987), 46n., 93n., 301. Other competitors included Garling, F.P. Cockerell, F. & H. Francis and T. Porter.

126 PRO, Work 17/16/1, f. 74, 2 May 1864. Brodrick had won the Leeds Town Hall competition, 1851, was fourth for the War Office in the 1856–7 com-

petition, and an invitee in the National Gallery competition, 1866. Kerr's design in the New Government Offices competition had been unplaced, but much praised in the press.

127 See p. 98 above.

128 PRO, Work 17/16/1, f. 139, 9 May 1865.

129 PRO, Work 2/29, p. 376 (14 Feb. 1866); 1/85, p. 365 (8 Jan. 1868); 2/32, p. 132 (15 June 1868). See *Survey*, XXXVIII, 205–6.

130 See G. Tyack, ' "A gallery worthy of the British people": James Pennethorne's designs for the National Gallery, 1845–1867', *Arch. Hist.*, 33 (1990), 121–31.

131 PRO, Work 1/78, p. 116.

132 Broadlands Papers, WFC/F, 1, n.d. [1866].

133 *3PD* CLXXXIII, 1181 (18 May 1866). The unsatisfactory results of the Brussels Law Courts competition 1861–2 may also be noted; see *Builder*, 31 May 1862, pp. 367–8.

134 *3PD* CLXXXIII, 1181.

135 R.H. Harper, *Victorian Architectural Competitions*, 93, 95; G. Stamp & C. Amery, *Victorian Buildings of London 1837–1887*, pp. 73, 80.

136 PRO, Work 1/80, p. 31.

137 Ibid. 2/29, p. 212 (11 Sept. 1865). The number of competitors was doubled when parliamentary pressure compelled the doubling of the number of competitors for the New Law Courts.

138 PRO, Work 1/81, pp. 50, 71, Circulars, 15, 22 Feb. 1866, to Scott, E.M. Barry, Banks & Barry, M.D. Wyatt, Street and Brodrick. On 11 Aug., the time limit was again extended to 1 Jan. 1867, ibid. 1/82, p. 133.

139 F.P. Cockerell, Gibson, Somers Clarke, S. Smirke, Owen Jones and Penrose were added; PRO, Work 1/81, pp. 141, 145, 185, 241, 252, 279. As Gibson had also been invited to compete for the Law Courts, he did not accept for the Gallery, ibid. 156–7, and was replaced by Murray (p. 434). Henry Hofland (co-winner of the 1857 Foreign Office competition) was refused permission to enter, ibid. 152.

140 PRO, Work 2/29, p. 212; *3PD* CLXXXVI, 833 (29 Mar. 1867). But Street wrote to his sister, when he received his invitations to compete for this and the Law Courts '. . . they pay enough to each architect to make it no loss of money to make the designs', A.E. Street, *Memoir of G.E. Street*, 51. The Law Courts competitors received £800 each.

141 S. Smirke and G.G. Scott withdrew. PRO, Work 17/13/15, 11–12.

142 William Cowper, *3PD* CLXXXVI, 828 (29 Mar. 1867).

143 PRO, Work 17/13/15, 10: Instructions to architects, 15 Feb. 1866. On 29 June, competitors were informed they might send in perspectives, but only in Indian ink; and that the judges would include not more than two professional architects. On 11 Aug., the time was extended to 1 Jan. 1867. Ibid.

144 The circular was dated 29 June 1866, a day after the Conservatives had taken office, but it is unlikely that the new FCW, Manners, would have given the instructions.

145 See p. 164.

146 PRO, Work 17/13/15, in 10 (Cowper to Austin, 15 Feb. 1867); *3PD* CLXXXVI, 831.

147 Ibid., 827–9.

148 PRO, Work 1/81, pp. 416, 434 (22, 29 June 1866).

149 PRO, Work 1/83, p. 67.

150 Ibid., p. 162, 17 Jan. 1867. The designs were returned to the competitors; Street's south elevation is in VAM; his hall and staircase drawing, and Brodrick's perspective drawing, in RIBA Drawings Coll.

151 *3PD* CLXXXVI, 832. Boxall, Redgrave, Tite and Brandon signed a memorandum that because lighting from the roofs was necessary, towers,

domes, spires, turrets, etc. were undesirable, PRO, Work 17/13/15, 67. The surveyor W.J. Gardiner, called in to report whether competitors had complied with instructions, calculate the area of picture galleries provided by each, and show how they were to be lighted, stated that those of Jones, Brodrick, Murray, Clarke and Banks & Barry extended beyond the given site (i.e., over the Barrack Yard, which competitors had been told *might* be obtainable ultimately); Clarke's design was coloured; and Brodrick and Cockerell had not provided lavatories, ibid., 65; Work 1/83, p. 206.

152 PRO, Work 17/13/15, 1–9 Minutes of National Gallery judges, 1867, 18 Feb. Hope and Tite had apparently disagreed with the recommendation of Murray (*3PD* CLXXXVI, 833), and Hope and Russell had proposed unsuccessfully that Street's and Cockerell's ground plans had points worthy of commendation. Printed descriptions of the designs by Brodrick, Street, M.D. Wyatt, Banks & Barry, E.M. Barry, Clarke, Jones and Murray, and MS descriptions by F.P. Cockerell and Penrose are contained in PRO, Work 17/13/15, 98ff.

153 *3PD* CLXXXVI, 834. M.D. Wyatt, as chairman of the majority of competitors, protested to the FCW against the judges' decision, 12 Mar. 1867, PRO, Work 17/13/15, 92.

154 A.E. Street, *Memoir of G.E. Street*, 52.

155 Ibid., 51.

156 *3PD* CLXXXIII, 181 (30 Apr. 1866).

157 *3PD* CLXXXII, 775–96. On 17 Mar. 1866 Cowper, anticipating the outcome of Bentinck's motion for increasing the number of competitors for the Law Courts (debated 22 March), proposed increasing the number of National Gallery competitors to ten; on 23 April, in line with the Treasury decision on the Law Courts, this was further increased to 12. PRO, Work 2/29, p. 418; 2/30, p. 32. Bentinck tried unsuccessfully on 18 May to secure a further increase in the number of competitors, supported by Sir G. Bowyer who urged open competition, 'for it might be that the best man of all was one as yet unknown to fame' (*3PD* CLXXXIII, 1181).

158 See D.B. Brownlee, *The Law Courts* (1984), 90–8. The arrangements were intricately connected with those for the National Gallery, but whereas Cowper appears himself to have nominated the competitors for the Gallery, those for the Law Courts were named by the judges' panel, the additional entrants after informal discussions only. When Cowper invited Gibson to compete for the Gallery (19 Apr. 1866), he was not aware that he had already been invited to compete for the Courts, PRO, Work 1/81, pp. 156–7.

159 See p. 201.

160 'Lincolniensis', 'The New Law Courts', *Times*, 18 Nov. 1867, p. 11, cited by Brownlee, *Law Courts*, 86.

161 PRO, Work 12/33 (1), 40–1.

162 Brownlee, 86. Cowper told the Commons that 'The reason why the Commission originally was composed exclusively of unprofessional men was that it was suggested that they would be unbiased in their opinion by any of those predilections or prejudices which professional training almost necessarily engendered.' This suggests that Cowper's willingness to name professional judges had been over-ridden by the commission. *3PD* CLXXXVI, 2019 (3 May 1867). Brownlee in his argument takes no account of the subsequent addition of two professionals as judges.

163 Brownlee hypothesises at length on the judges' attitudes, basing his argument on accounts by H.S.P. Winterbotham, MP (1837–73), in *3PD* CXC, 337 (29 June 1868); and *Architect*, 2 Sept. 1871, p. 113.

164 See *3PD* CXCII, 370.

165 *3PD* CLXXXIII, 1178–87 (18 May 1866); CLXXXV,

814–18 (22 Feb. 1867); CLXXXVI, 728 (28 Mar. 1867).

166 Ibid., 2018 (3 May 1867); *PP* 1871 [C. 290] XX, p. xxiii and Min. 61, 67.

167 Port, 'The New Law Courts Competition', 89–90.

168 The press was highly critical; see *Times*, 19 Nov., p. 7; *BN*, 6 Dec., p. 841; *Eccl.*, 1867, p. 292. See also correspondence in *Times*, 15 Aug., p. 9 (E.W. Pugin), 20 Aug. 1867, p. 10 (E.W. Godwin). *Builder* was ambivalent, supporting the joint award, but attacking Street's elevations (cp. 28 Dec., p. 936).

169 *PP* 1868–69 (317), XLVIII, 683ff.; 1871 [C. 290], XX, 106.

170 RIBA, MS Sc GGS/4/4/6, 7, Burges to Scott (20 Nov. 1867), Street to Scott (12 Dec. 1867).

171 This was provided for in the original instructions, and decided upon by the Courts of Justice Commissioners in mid-December; if the award was confirmed, the majority of commissioners were in favour of accepting it, Belvoir Castle MSS, Lord J. Manners' letter-book, Manners to Derby, 17 Dec. 1867. Manners reports a dispute between Cockburn (pro) and Palmer (anti) on the validity of the award that casts some doubt on Brownlee's analysis of the judges' opinions, *Law Courts*, 156.

172 That this was Manners' own solution as early as 9 Dec. 1867 is made clear in his 'Cabinet Diary', Belvoir Castle MSS.

173 *3PD* CXCIII, 342 (29 June 1868).

12. Rival Modes of Selection

1 *3PD* CXCV, 273 (6 Apr. 1869). Tite had emerged the victor from the murky competition for the Royal Exchange, 1840, see H.M. Colvin, *Biographical Dictionary of British Architects* (1978). He had also been a member of the jury for the 1864 Kensington Museums competition, and of the select committee on the rebuilding of the F.O., 1858.

2 *RIBA Trans.*, XXX (1879–80), 88–9.

3 Ibid., 88.

4 Porter was one of the finalists for the Admiralty and W.O., 1884, see below, p. 182.

5 *Builder*, 8 Nov. 1879, pp. 1223–4.

6 *BN*, XXXVIII (1880), 307.

7 *RIBA Trans.*, XXX (1879–80), 65ff.

8 'The relationship between the design approach of the successful entrants and the design approach of the assessors . . . is obviously one that needs more careful study', R.H. Harper, *Victorian Architectural Competitions* (1983), xxiv. Harper calculates that between 1843 and 1900, six assessors judged 134 competitions between them. By Nov. 1884 an RIBA committee had obtained undertakings from some 1350 architects not to enter public competitions unless professional assessors were appointed, *Times*, 10 Nov. 1884 (10a).

9 As Scott, T.H. Wyatt, Waterhouse and Edward Barry had argued in respect of the New Law Courts competition, 3 Mar. 1866, quoted Port, 'New Law Courts Competition', *Arch. Hist.*, XI (1968), 83.

10 *BN*, 30 Jan. 1880, pp. 126–7. It is interesting to compare the version given in *RIBA Trans.*, XXX, 92: 'The winner . . . must in the first place produce the best plan, and to do this he must go to work so as to get the best information; that is to say, it is only by getting the very best information – you know what I mean – that you can start at all. I got the best information at South Kensington [in 1864], only Captain Fowke somehow got better. In the next place the winner . . . must produce the best exterior; if he cannot do it himself he must get somebody else to do it for him. Lastly, he must have a friend at court, as that is essential.'

11 *RIBA Trans.*, XXX, 92.

12 Cp. B.H. Jackson (ed.), *Recollections of T.G. Jackson* (1950), 212. Edward Barry had himself been ad-

13 *RIBA Trans.*, XXX, 89.

14 Ibid., XXXI (1880–1), 266, 268.

15 Ibid., 269–73. Waterhouse went against the trend in arguing for coloured perspectives, which promoters understood better than line drawings, but he complained that entrants' standards of morality were low, many letting their pencils run wild and showing domes 30 or 40 feet higher than they were capable, as shown by their sections, of rising. As an experienced assessor, he thought that instructions were often too full, binding too tightly or sometimes leading astray.

16 *PP* 1877 (312) XV, qq. 265, 267.

17 Ibid., qq. 269, 273.

18 Sir F. Leighton, PRA, wrote to him: 'I have been thinking over the subject of our conversation and it occurs to me that in one respect I may not have conveyed to you quite what I meant on the subject of competitions – I doubt whether even for a *limited* competition you could obtain the assent of some of the older men and as you wish to employ such a one I do not think that the scheme is one which will conduce to your ends – but in *principle* – and supposing the task were not of a very special kind and requiring a particular order of experience and accomplishment – I think that a competition limited to men whose ability to carry out the work on a large scale is known from their performance is not a bad thing – I myself on one occasion proposed it's being tried. Meanwhile I repeat the doubt remains whether you could get men to assent to this arrangement – the *open* competition would be a grave error in my opinion.' Gordon of Haddo MSS, 1/10, bundle 2, 'Saturday' [?1882]. Leighton seems to have changed his opinion of competition later, see below, p. 187.

19 *3PD* CCLXXVII, 1481, 5 Apr. 1883.

20 *Architect*, 6 Oct. 1883, p. 201. The 1880s were said to be a slack period for architects.

21 *PP* 1887 (184), VII, qq. 49, 53.

22 PRO, Work 12/92/1, no. 6, Sept. 1883.

23 *RIBA Trans.*, XXX (1880), 108, cited J. Bassin, *Architectural Competitions* (Ann Arbor, Mich., 1984), 102. Although the form had been used in several important provincial competitions, and included in the RIBA 'rules', Christian, who was a church specialist, evidently believed it was an innovation suggested to him two or three years previously by Clutton – an open competition for sketch-plans – 'just little plans which could be prepared in the course of a day or two, and yet fully illustrate the architect's intention' – from which a few might be selected for developing.

24 H.V. Lanchester, 'Competitions', in J.A. Gotch (ed.), *Growth and Work of the RIBA* (1934), 110. That the regulations had made little impact is suggested by Ewan Christian's remarks at the 1880 RIBA meeting, *RIBA Trans.*, XXX, 92.

25 Hope (*Sat. Rev.*, 9 Aug. 1884, p. 172) was only one among several critics of the arrangement.

26 See H.V. Lanchester & P.E. Thomas, 'Competitions Past and Present', *RIBA Jnl*, 3 ser. XL (1933), 525–42. Lanchester remarked that 'Almost its sole use is in placing before promoters a series of definite solutions from which they can realise how they have failed to express all that they had in mind' (530). Thomas thought that 'practically every competition of this character is won in the initial stage, and that the other competitors in the second stage are merely elaborating designs which have already lost' (534). One doubts whether this were so in the 1884 competition.

27 *BN*, XL (1881), 562. *Builder* (30 Mar. 1867, p. 223), had hailed the Manchester conditions (in which the second-stage competitors were to re-

ceive £300 each) as 'for the age and the country, an immense innovatory stride', cited J.H.G. Archer, 'A Classic of its Age', in Archer (ed.), *Art and Architecture in Victorian Manchester* (Manchester, 1985), 130.

28 *PP* 1887 (184), VII, qq. 56–8. Only 128 entries were accepted, as two arrived late, PRO, Work 12/115/4/1, Minutes of judges of designs, 3 Mar. 1884. Among the unsuccessful entrants were Waterhouse, T.G. Jackson, Voysey, E.R. Robson, Darbishire, Worthington, Corson, Ricardo, J. Rhind, Truefitt, E.T. Hall, Garling, Sang, F. & H. Francis, John Giles, Giles & Gough, Spiers, F.H. Fowler, Sedding, Macartney, Belcher, I'Anson & Baggallay, Emerson and Cheers. PRO, Work 12/115/4/1, pp. 55–63, list of competitors.

29 Harper, *Victorian Architectural Competitions*, 54 (*Builder*, LVII, 1889, p. 260 refers to 125 entries for Glasgow); *BN*, XLVI (1884), 423, 'Nemo'. Sheffield Town Hall competition (also two stage), 1889, at only £80,000, elicited 179 entries, Harper, 147. About one entrant for every ten applications for details was not unusual, C. Cunningham, *Victorian and Edwardian Town Halls* (1981), 106–7.

30 *BN*, XLVI (1884), 462, 'A Scottish Competitor'. A 'leading architect' was said to have taken a month's study to grasp the particulars, and another man 'isolated himself in an obscure part of the Isle of Wight for some weeks in order to solve the enigma', ibid., 423 'Nemo'.

31 One competitor claimed that another, 'half killing himself', had worked 'late into the morning ever since the particulars were published', and employed five men for two months on the drawings – and this was only the first stage, for sketch-plans. A third, with his coadjutor and a qualified assistant, reckoned to have spent 1600 hours on the project; a fourth, with his staff, 2300 hours. But others spent as little as 300 hours, while a man who cut out strips of paper representing the specified departments, which he moved around his outline plan until he found the best arrangement, completed it in about 100 hours. *BN*, XLVI (1884), 423 'Nemo', 388 'A Competitor', 461 'Honour to Merit', 462 'A Scottish Competitor', 498 'Nemo'.

32 Including William Young, victor in the Glasgow municipal buildings competition, 1882. *BN*, XLVI (1884), 613. See also, ibid., 'Hastings'.

33 See H. Hobhouse, 'Philip and Philip Charles Hardwick', in J. Fawcett (ed.), *Seven Victorian Architects* (1976).

34 *BN*, XLVII (1884), 326. The *Civilian*, 26 July 1884, p. 195, stated: 'We believe that the feeling of the Committee [of judges] was originally in favour of a set of Gothic plans, but it was subsequently found impossible to hope to get the Army and Navy successfully administered from among minarets, vaulted roofs and pointed windows.' The judges' minutes, however, lend no substance to this story. Christian, incidentally, had in 1835 assisted W. Railton with his premiated design for New Houses of Parliament, *Builder*, 2 Mar. 1895, p. 170.

35 *BN*, XLVI (1884), 423 'Nemo'.

36 *BN*, XLV (1883), 433. Jones (1819–87), who had started his career developing suburban estates, was architect to the City of London, responsible for Smithfield, Billingsgate and Leadenhall Markets, additions to Guildhall, and Tower Bridge; PRIBA in 1882–3, he was knighted in 1886.

37 PRO, Work 12/115/4/1, Minutes of the judges, 12, 17, and 21 Mar. 1884.

38 Those of Thomas Porter, Maxwell & Tuke (Manchester), Stark & Lindsay (Glasgow), Leeming & Leeming (Halifax), Webb & Bell, Spalding & Auld, Glover & Salter, Henry Hall & Powell and Verity & Hunt. (Of three border-liners, Porter was included, Robson and Hunt & Steward & Knight were rejected.) Ibid., 27, 31 Mar. 1884; pp. 55–63,

list of competitors. The instructions for the second stage were made more precise; they were to include a plan, elevation and section of a representative bay 'drawn to the scale of a quarter of an inch to a foot', and particular attention was to be given to the sanitary arrangements, ibid., 31 Mar. 1884, pp. 27–9.

39 Ibid., 11, 16, 18, and 23 July 1884; *PP* 1887 (184), VII, qq. 51, 61–4. Although Christian concurred with Hardwick that 'on the whole, guided by the instructions and taking plans and elevations together', Leemings' design was the best, he told Lefevre that 'viewing them separately, I consider the plans of Messrs Tuke and Maxwell to be superior in respect of general internal arrangement, and that the elevations produced by Messrs Aston Webb and Ingress Bell are more beautiful, and more elastic and capable of adjustment to necessary improvements of plan than any others submitted in the second competition', PRO, Work 12/115/4/1, pp. 82–3, 17 July 1884.

40 *PP* 1887 (184), VII, q. 50. It was specified that 'The architectural features of the new building . . . shall be subordinate to its main purpose of a great public office, and not the determining cause of its interior arrangements.' (ibld.).

41 *Architect*, 6 Oct. 1883, p. 201. The judges had reconsidered this question on 18 July 1884, and concluded that as it was unlikely that all the competitors would return their drawings for exhibition, no such exhibition should be held, PRO, Work 12/115/4/1, minutes of the judges.

42 *Sat. Rev.*, 9 Aug. 1884, p. 173.

43 *Architect*, 21 Aug. 1891, pp. 106–7. In 'A letter to the Rt Hon. J.G. Shaw-Lefevre MP on the models for the new Public Offices', 4 Sept. 1885 (pp. 140–2), the *Architect* observed: 'It was your object, I know, to find a young genius, who having nothing to lose, would consent to the tutelage of Her Majesty's Office of Works.'

44 See n. 39 above.

45 Aston Webb (see appendix 4) became PRIBA in 1902 and PRA in 1919; Malcolm Stark of Stark & Lindsay, from Glasgow, won the Belfast City Hall competition in 1896, having been placed second (to Leemings) in the Edinburgh municipal buildings competition, 1887 (not built). Thomas Verity (1837–91) in contrast was a well-known theatre architect, who with Hunt won the 1882 Royal Agricultural Hall, Islington, competition, and the 1883 Nottingham municipal buildings competition (£100,000). For trends in public building architecture, see Cunningham, *Victorian and Edwardian Town Halls*.

46 As suggested by a correspondent in *BN*, XLVI (1884), 613 'Hastings'.

47 *Builder*, 16 Aug. (Robson), 224, 234–5 (elevations), 238–9 (plans); 20 Sept. 1884 (Jackson), 388–95.

48 '. . . the drawings of Messrs Leeming and Leeming are probably the best set that has been seen for many a day', 'Utility', *BN*, 15 Aug. 1884, p. 280. Leeming Brothers were assisted in their drawings by R.F. Farrer, who had served articles with them, and some of the sculpture was drawn by one Powell, a Leeds mural artist; the perspective was drawn by a specialist, Langham of Manchester. *BN*, XLVII (1884), 326.

49 PRO, Work 12/115/4/1, minutes of the judges, 23 July; pp. 82–3, Christian to FCW, 17 July 1884.

50 *BN*, XLVII (1884), 280–1 'Utility'.

51 *Sat. Rev.*, 9 Aug. 1884, p. 172.

52 *BN*, XLVII (1884), 153, 197–9, was moderately favourable; *Builder* consistently hostile, XLVII (1884), 6 Sept., 320; 4 Oct. 1884, 454. See below, p. ••.

53 PRO, Work 12/115/4/1, minutes of the judges, 21 Apr. 1885. Leemings were asked to move the tower from Whitehall to the Park front, modify the attic storey to Whitehall, and reduce the ornamentation. In Sept. 1885, the *Architect* (pp. 140–2) invited Lefevre, by then in Opposition, 'to denounce the amended designs', the change of government having 'nipped in the bud the flowery promise of your rule. Instead of making a clean sweep of rows of absurd piers and columns – as ugly and baneful as they are useless – they are still preserved to darken the light of day, and increase the fussiness of each façade.'

54 *PP* 1887 (184) VII, qq. 50, 68, 85, 1216–17, 1327–31. Smith had been absent from four of the judges' ten meetings. Models of the revised design [Pl. 228b] were exhibited (*Brit. Arch.*, 21 Aug. 1885, p. 82), but the feeling was still a need for something better (ibid., p. 91).

55 *Builder*, 26 Feb. 1887, termed the design 'commonplace' and Lefevre 'an incompetent amateur "person of taste" who did not know the difference between drawing and architecture'; see also pp. 532 and 595.

56 *PP* 1887 (184) VII, *Report of S.C. on the Admiralty and War Office (Sites)*. See p. 236.

57 See below, p. 269.

58 Lefevre, 'Public Buildings in London', *Nineteenth Century*, Nov. 1888, pp. 703–4.

59 A. Quiney, *John Loughborough Pearson* (New Haven & London, 1979), 186.

60 *PP* 1884–85 (166) XIII; see pp. 237–9 below.

61 See Susan Beattie, 'New Scotland Yard', *Arch. Hist.*, 15 (1972), 68–81, on which this paragraph is largely based.

62 A. Saint, *Richard Norman Shaw* (1972), 266, citing PRO, HO 45/9765/B841A/1 and 45/9630/A23696/12.

63 *3PD* CCCXLIII, 1814–15 (1 May 1890); Saint, 266.

64 See J. Physick, *Victoria and Albert Museum*, pp. 176–85.

65 See *Survey*, XXXVIII, 220–1. The commissioners also offered several smaller sites for the Royal College of Music (1887–91), again at a nominal rent. In 1888 an architectural competition was planned for a building costing more than £30,000, but was abandoned the following year and (Sir) Arthur Blomfield appointed as architect, ibid., 228.

66 Ibid., 221.

67 R.R. Anderson, A.W. Blomfield, T.E. Collcutt, T.N. Deane & Son, T.G. Jackson and Webb & Bell, ibid., 222.

68 B.H. Jackson (ed.), *Recollections of T.G. Jackson* (1950), 210.

69 *Survey*, XXXVIII, 222.

70 Donnelly, Secretary of the Department of Science and Art, told a select committee in 1897 that limited competition 'is the constant practice now with regard to public buildings. . . . Open competition has not been found to be very successful', *PP* 1897 (341) XII, *S.C. on Museums of the Science and Art Department*, qq. 477, 479.

71 See *BN*, 24 June (p. 977), 1 July 1887 (pp. 3–7, 35); *Builder*, 2 July, pp. 1–3; *Brit. Arch.*, 1, 8 July (pp. 1–6, 21).

72 Several of those nominated declined or resigned; the full list was Aston Webb,* Anderson, Deane,* Collcutt,* Jackson,* Shaw, Emerson,* Belcher,* Macartney,* Bodley & Garner, and Young* (final entrants asterisked). Young was specifically chosen as a Scotchman. Waterhouse, who as PRIBA nominated half the entrants, had intimated to the FCW that he did not wish to be invited, and was accordingly appointed assessor. PRO, Work 17/23/9.

73 PRO, Work 17/23/9, f. 43, cited J. Physick, *The Victoria and Albert Museum* (1982), p. 185. The judges nominated were the Ld Pres. of the Council (ministerial head of Dept of Science and Art), Lord Cranbrook; First Ld of the Treasury, W.H. Smith; ch. of Exchequer, G.J. Goschen (who did not act, because of pressure of work); FCW, D. Plunket; Vice-Pres. of the Council, Sir W. Hart Dyke; and A.J. Mundella, MP, representing the Opposition. PRO, Work 17/23/9.

74 *A.A. Notes*, VI, Sept. 1891, p. 56.

75 *Architect*, 21 Aug. 1891, pp. 106–7.

76 'Limited competitions have advantages, but they always excite less interest than those which are general. . . . When the contest is between a few men, it is only partisans who can feel much excitement about the result'; hence, the indifference displayed about the South Kensington competition (ibid.). Moreover, the Treasury had refused funding for carrying out Webb's designs; Chilston Papers, C5/65.

77 *PP* 1897 (341) XII, *Second Report from S.C. on the Museums of the S.A.D.*, q. 480.

78 *RIBA Jnl*, ns VII (1891), 247–9 (9 Apr. 1891). True to his ideals, Anderson had refused an invitation to compete for completing the S.K. Museum, PRO, Work 17/23/9, no. 25, 23 Nov. 1890. However, he served as assessor in no fewer than ten competitions, 1881–1900: Harper, *Victorian Architectural Competitions*, 180–1.

79 PRO, Work 33/1521–45.

80 PRO, Work 30/4656–75.

81 Ibid., 2524–33, 2536–77.

82 Ibid., 2669–700, 2742–54.

83 Ibid., 5287–323.

84 Smith was employed by Tate to design a number of public libraries that he contributed to South London, and became a specialist in that field. See *Builder*, 4 Apr. 1913, p. 411.

85 R. Norman Shaw & T.G. Jackson (eds.), *Architecture: a Profession or an Art* (1892). See B. Kaye, *Development of the Architectural Profession in Britain* (1960), 135–41.

86 Bodleian, Harcourt MS dep. 192, ff. 96–7 (9 Nov.), 98–9 (11 Nov. 1892), 80–1, 109–110.

87 *Survey*, XXXVIII, 243.

88 *PP* 1897 (341) XII, q. 477.

89 PRO, T. 1/9198C/17136, 23 Nov. Brett to Treasury; 24 Nov. 1897, Mowatt to Chancellor of Exchequer.

90 Ibid.

91 Ibid., 9 Dec. 1897.

92 See p. 159.

93 *4PD* LV, 123 (17 Mar. 1898).

94 Ibid., 1155–6 (28 Mar. 1898).

95 Charles Barry, Belcher, Brydon, Burnet, Deane, Drew, Lynn and Young. 'It was understood that the selection would be made mainly on consideration of the successful buildings actually erected by the competitors in a *Classic style* of architecture. We make no further comment', reported *BN*, 13 May 1898, LXXIV, 692. Later it did comment: 'We felt how singularly inadequate these nominations really were, the omissions being even more remarkable than the inclusions of some names which . . . had very little to recommend them. . . . Nor have we now any objections to urge against any of the eight architects in question, except in connexion with the style and character of the buildings to be erected.' 22 July 1898, LXXV, 92.

96 *Architect*, 29 July 1898, p. 65, from *RIBA Jnl*.

97 *Architect*, 22 July 1898, p. 50; 25 Mar. 1898, p. 185; *BN*, 11 and 25 Mar. 1898, LXXIV, 362, 403.

98 Though *BN* neutrally declared that the RIBA council 'in no way represents the architectural profession', 8 Apr. 1898, p. 513. *Builder*, 30 July 1898, refers to criticism of the appointments in the *Morning Post*.

99 *BN*, 12 Aug. 1887, 3 Apr. 1891; *Architect* LIII (1895), 272–3; *Country Life* XXX (1911), 342ff.

100 See A. Gomme & D. Walker, *Architecture of Glasgow* (2nd edn 1987), 191–4. For a contemporary account, see *BN*, 16 Jan., 1 May 1885; 16 Sept. 1887; 20 Apr. 1888; 29 Mar. 1889; 3 Oct. 1890.

101 SRO, Wemyss MSS, RH 4/40/14, Wemyss to

Douglas, 'Sunday' [July 1898]; to Young, 17 July 1898; 40/13, Lansdowne to Wemyss, 1 July [1899]; Wemyss to Balfour, 6 Sept. 1899.

102 These were extensively reported; see *Architect*, 22 Feb., 1 Mar. 1889, pp. 100–2, 121–3; *Brit. Archt*, 31 (1889), 151–2, 169; *Builder*, LVI (1889), 147, 149, 168; *BN*, XVI (1889), 263.

103 *Brit. Archt*, 27 Nov. 1885, pp. 230ff.; W.J. Loftie, 'Brydon at Bath', *Arch. Rev.*, XVIII (1905), 3–9, 50–9, 146–9.

104 *4PD* LXII, 96 (18 July), 296–7 (19 July 1898).

105 PRO, T. 1/10815/8956, 15 Nov. 1900, 19968. 'I think we are "sweating" Sir John Taylor', noted the ch. of the Exchequer. By November 1901, Arthur Ellis of the Lord Chamberlain's Office was complaining (as noted in ch. 5) that 'Dear old Taylor . . . hasn't the physical *push* in him to get things forward', Esher Papers, 5/13, pp. 162–3.

106 'Complete plans, elevations and sections, to the scale of 10 feet to an inch; also full, careful and clearly drawn half-inch scale details of all the important parts'. Akers-Douglas to Sir John Aird, MP, 2 Dec. 1901, printed in *Architect*, 6 Dec. 1901, p. 357.

107 PRO, T. 1/9735/18011, 17 June (10401), 10 Aug., 31 Aug. 1901 (13805); *4PD* CXII, 103 (29 July 1902). Stokes, one of Brydon's executors, complained that 'this young gentleman is now . . . with others engaged in altering Brydon's design', letter to *Times*, quoted *BN*, 10 Sept. 1901, p. 402. Stokes claimed that the drawings handed over to the Works were incomplete drawings for the carcass of the building, as Brydon had been instructed to obtain tenders for the carcass only, leaving the finishings for a second contract. A number of ¹/₂-inch scale drawings existed, but many of them had been made hurriedly to help the quantity surveyors obtain a tender. Brydon 'kept but a small staff, preferring to do his own work'. *BN*, 16 Aug. (p. 227), 20 Sept. 1901 (p. 402).

108 Esher Papers, 5/12, ff. 185–91, Akers-Douglas to Esher, 17 Aug. [1901].

109 *BN*, 16 Aug. (p. 227), 23 Aug. (p. 263, quoting PRIBA's letter to *Times*), 6 Dec. 1901 (p. 760).

110 *4PD* CXII, 103–4 (29 July 1902). The consultative committee seems to have been an idea of Esher's: the non-official members were Aston Webb and John Belcher; see Esher Papers, 5/13, ff. 38–9, Akers-Douglas to Esher, 21 Sept. 1901; PRO, Work 17/5/1, f. 39; Work 30/1019 and 3758; Chilston Papers, C. 6, ff. 432–3, Akers-Douglas to Lord Balcarres, 14 Jan. 1902. For the alterations that were made, see below, p. 248.

111 *Architect*, 6 Sept. 1901, p. 151.

112 See p. 24 above.

113 PRO, Work 17/5/1, f. 41, Tanner to McDonnell, 22 Feb, 1904.

114 He employed Bodley & Garner to build the 'lavish' Hewell Grange (1884–91), and Fairfax Wade for his 'exuberant' and very opulent London house, 54 Mount Street, an amalgam of Wren-period motifs 'with hints from French classicism', and Arts & Crafts features. See *Survey*, XL, 324–5.

115 Sir R.R. Anderson, J. Belcher, R. Blomfield, J.J. Burnet, T.E. Collcutt, H.T. Hare and J.W. Simpson. PRO, Work 17/5/1, ff. 53–4 (5 May 1904). Windsor was influenced by H.C. reaction to Tanner's exhibited designs, protests from the RIBA, and the fact that the proposal was for a major, three-frontage extension of a national building, ibid., ff. 45–6, FCW to P.M., 16 Mar. 1904.

116 PRO, Work 12/204; 17/5/1, passion. For Burnet (ARA 1921, RA 1925; kt. 1914) see A.S. Gray, *Edwardian Architecture* (1988 edn), 128–31. Burnet was chosen unanimously on the strength of his executed work in Glasgow and Edinburgh, which shewed that he 'had sympathy with, and was capable of the refined treatment of the severe classical style of Smirke's British Museum'; Tanner reporting favourably on his Glasgow buildings, 'particularly of the internal work', ibid., f. 111, 13 Dec. 1904, FCW to P.M.'s priv. sec.

117 As Akers-Douglas had done in 1897 for the alterations to Manchester House to make it a suitable public museum for the Wallace Collection. For Land Registry, see PRO, Work 12/149.

118 See *Survey*, Monograph 17, *County Hall* (1991), ch. III.

119 PRO, Work 12/204, Beauchamp to Benn, 12 Mar.; Benn to Beauchamp, 13 Mar. 1912.

120 Lethaby to Sydney Cockerell, 9 Nov. 1905, quoted by A. Saint, *Richard Norman Shaw* (1976), 351.

121 *Architect*, 13 Mar., pp. 177–8; 20 Mar. 1903, pp. 194–6.

122 *BN*, 9 Feb. 1906, p. 193.

123 *BN*, 27 Apr. 1906, p. 600. Webb & Bell assessed 124 first-round entries.

124 *BN*, Apr. 1906, p. 568.

125 *Builder*, 31 Oct. 1913, p. 444.

126 Ibid., 24 Apr. 1914, pp. 487–8.

127 *5PD* XXVI, 1065–6 (Whitehouse, Noel Buxton, 31 May 1911); XXIX, 1850 (Noel Buxton, 15 Aug. 1911); XXXIX, 88 (4 June 1912).

128 *PP* 1912–13 (277) VII, p. vi.

129 PRO, Work 12/204, memo. by L[ionel] E[arle], 15 Oct. 1912: 'I have been impressed by the design that I have seen prepared in this office & I hope the Com^ee if appointed may see fit to adopt our design.'

130 *5PD* XL, 1308 (Goldsmith, 4 July), 2072 (Noel Buxton, Goldsmith, 11 July); XLI, 1344, 2907 (Goldsmith, 25 July, 6 Aug. 1912); LI, 694–7 (Hogge, Goldsmith 3 Apr. 1913); LIII, 2007–8, 2010 (Whitehouse, Lord Robert Cecil, 13 June 1913); LVI, 677, 1491 (Bennet-Goldney, 30 July, 6 Aug. 1913).

131 Lord Beauchamp (FCW), D. Lloyd George (Exchequer), L. Harcourt (late FCW), S. Buxton (Board of Trade), A. Lyttelton (Opposition), T. McKinnon Wood (Sec. for Scotland, included because of possibility of a new Inland Revenue building in Edinburgh). Austen Chamberlain and Lord Balcarres declined invitations to serve. PRO, Work 12/80/8, ff. 1–8.

132 *Builder*, 7 Nov. 1913, p. 488.

133 The details were published in *Builder*, 5 Sept. 1913, pp. 241–3.

134 A member of the government's advisory committee on the Great George St. offices, Belcher, PRIBA 1904–6, RA (1909), had executed a number of prestige office buildings in London, the grandiose baroque Ashton Memorial, Lancaster, 1906, and with his partner J.J. Joass designed buildings for the British section of the Franco-British Exhibition at White City, 1908. He was also co-author of the influential *Late Renaissance Architecture in England* (1901). See A. Service, *Arch. Rev.*, CXLVIII (1970), 282–90.

135 PRO, Work 12/80/8, ff. 8–20, 50. Newton, ARA (1911) was principally a country-house architect; he had been R. Norman Shaw's assistant, and as PRIBA in 1914 was one of an official panel of advisers on the rebuilding of the Regent Street Quadrant. See H. Hobhouse, *History of Regent Street* (1975), 120–2.

136 *Builder*, 22 Aug. 1913, p. 189.

137 PRO, Work 12/80/8, ff. 27–34.

138 Harris, who served in the LCC Architect's department, 1901–4, had won (with his partner T.A. Moodie) the Glamorgan County Hall competition, 1909, on classic Roman, rather than Baroque lines. See A.S. Gray, *Edwardian Architecture*, 206–7.

139 *Arch. Rev.*, XXVIII (1910, 2), 54–61; *Builder*, 8 Jan. 1910. The building now houses the Ministry of Agriculture.

140 *5PD* XXIII (21 Mar. 1911).

141 Construction of the foundations was delayed by discovery that the Regent Street sewer ran under a corner of the site, necessitating a modification of the plans; and the superstructure was delayed by preparations for the coronation of King George V. *PP* 1911 (7) L, *Appropriation account*; *5PD* XXVIII, 1137 (5 July 1911).

142 *Builder*, 17 Apr. 1914, pp. 473–4.

143 *BN*, 29 Dec. 1905 (illustrations after p. 898); 9 Feb. 1906 (interior views, pp. 204–5); 13 Dec. 1912, 829–30 (illustration after p. 832).

144 *Survey*, XXXVIII, ch. XIX.

145 *Arch. Rev.*, XXXVIII, 131.

146 It is also noteworthy that, between 1843 and 1900, government competitions for major buildings seem not to have affected the number of competitions generally, to judge by those listed in *Builder*. R.H. Harper, *Victorian Architectural Competitions*, 'annual lists'.

147 Summerson is particularly severe on 'the astonishing insularity of Victorian architecture', praising the Brussels Law Courts (contemporary with Street's) by Joseph Poelart: 'powerful, accomplished, worldly, the confident heir of a great tradition . . . a superb example of success', *Victorian Architecture* (1970), 115–16. But the *Architect* made the same comparison in 1883 (3 Nov., p. 263): though remarking that 'England has gone about her work in a spirit so wholly ungenerous, and Belgium with much lavish magnanimity', it also noted that superb, grand, and imposing as Poelart's *Palais de Justice* might be, his classicism was 'clumsy and incoherent'. (Cp also C. St John Wilson, *Architectural Reflections* (1992), 225, attacking Poelart's 'mindless pomposity', echoing therein J.T. Emmett's 'a contemptible imposture', *Quarterly Review* CLXXVI (1893), pp. 40–72. Comments on current Continental designs occur often in contemporary architectural periodicals.

148 See *Survey*, monograph 17, *County Hall* (1991); Bassin, *Architectural Competitions*, chap. 6.

149 *PP* 1857–88 (417) XI, qq. 1175, 1174.

150 Bassin, *Architectural Competitions*, 112.

13. The Battle of the Styles

1 J. Steegman, *Consort of Taste 1830–1870* (1950), 3–4.

2 M.H. Port, ed., *The Houses of Parliament*, ch. III.

3 A.W.N. Pugin, *Contrasts* (1836, 1841), *True Principles of Pointed, or Christian Architecture* (1841), 7–9.

4 *BN*, 12 June 1857, pp. 613–14.

5 *Builder*, 8 Dec. 1855, p. 585.

6 *PP* 1857–58 XI, *S.C. on Foreign Office reconstruction*, qq. 947, 872.

7 Ibid., qq. 1267, 1408.

8 Ibid., qq. 1246–7; and C. Barry jnr, q. 873. Cp *Blackwood's Mag.*, XCI (Jan.–June 1862), p. 301: 'The style of the Italian Renaissance is specially fitted for palaces, grand public buildings, and private domestic buildings.'

9 'Let a Government building of any scale be projected, and at once a cry is raised for the realisation in some form of this grand ideal' [i.e. Whitehall Palace], *Builder*, 6 May 1899, p. 431. *Architect*, 11 Aug. 1899, dismissively remarked, 'According to Lord Wemyss and his friends, there is no progress in architecture' (p. 81). Cp, e.g. *Times*, 7 Oct. 1856 (Government Offices); *3PD* CLII, 1265 (Lowe, 20 Apr. 1869, for Law Courts); *PP* 1877 (312) XV, S.C. on Public Offices, qq. 372–3; *4PD* LXXV, 1432 (Lord Wemyss, 4 Aug. 1899, for War Office); *5PD* XLVIII, 940 (12 Feb. 1913, for Board of Trade). 'Inigo Jones's' Whitehall designs, redrawn from the set at Windsor by Maurice Adams, were published in *BN*, 19 Dec. 1884, after p. 976. Even

Waterhouse thought at first of modelling his Admiralty and War Office competition entry on Jones's palace.

10 *PP* 1857–58 (417) XI, q. 873.

11 E.K. Morris, 'Symbols of Empire: Architectural Style and the Government Offices Competition', *Jnl of Architectural Education*, XXXII, no. 2, Nov. 1978, pp. 8–13.

12 A Practical Man, *Remarks on the Designs proposed for the New Government Offices* (1857), 9, quoted by Morris, 8–13.

13 *PP* 1857–58 (417) XI, q. 1211.

14 Ibid., q. 2011.

15 Ibid., q. 2017.

16 *BN*, 8 May 1857.

17 *PP* 1857–58 (417) XI, qq. 872, 947, 1272, 1408.

18 Ibid., qq. 785, 872–5.

19 Ibid., qq. 1408, 1496.

20 Ibid., qq. 958, 1068, 1547.

21 Ibid., qq. 1555–6.

22 *Seven Lamps*, VI, Memory, VII. In the following para. VIII, Ruskin postulates an India House 'massively built . . . chased with bas-reliefs of our Indian battles', sculpted with 'groups of Indian life and landscape, and prominently expressing the phantasms of Hindoo worship in their subjection to the Cross'.

23 So, I think, for opinion in general; though in the tiny RIBA of the day, the parties were more even, witness the very narrow majority by which Tite was elected PRIBA, 1857, followed by the uncontested election of his opponent, Beresford Hope, on the next occasion.

24 G.G. Scott, *Remarks on Secular and Domestic Architecture, Present and Future* (1857), ix–x.

25 Ibid., 202–8.

26 R. Kerr, ed., J. Fergusson, *History of the Modern Styles of Architecture*, 3rd edn (1891), I, xiii.

27 Ibid. 49.

28 Fergusson, *History of the Modern Styles of Architecture* (1862), 488–9.

29 *BN*'s assessment that out of some 217 entries, about 20 were Gothic and Elizabethan and 15 Renaissance. 22 May 1857, p. 501. 'The style of the Tuileries in particular finds numerous followers' remarked *Ecclesiologist*, XVIII (1857), 173. (*Builder* had illustrated Tuileries/Louvre on 11 Mar. 1854 (p. 131), 5 Jan. (p. 7) and 17 May 1856 (p. 275).

30 It is highly unlikely that the judges were influenced by public lectures denouncing classical architecture (*Builder*, 17 Sept. 1857, p. 622, letter signed '*Δ*'); though Rev. C. Boutell's lecture, Binfield Hall, Clapham, was avowedly 'to excite sympathy for the Gothic and National style' (*Builder*, 23 May 1857, p. 283).

31 *ILN* XXXI (1857), 275; *BN*, 5 June 1857, pp. 569–71 (cp also pp. 572, H.L.W., 'What Style?' and 573, O.U., 'General design of the new offices'). *BN*'s hostility to Gothic emerges in a review of an anticlassical pamphlet, 20 Feb. 1857, p. 180.

32 PRO, Work 12/86/3, p. 37.

33 J. Bassin, *Architectural Competitions in Nineteenth-Century England* (Ann Arbor, Mich., 1984), 85.

34 It should be noted, however, that Coe & Hofland declared that their design, first for the Foreign Office, was 'pure Italian', displaying 'some novelty' in its treatment; and that it did not have a single point in common with the Paris Hôtel de Ville 'nor (with the exception of the curved roofs) with any single one of the many other fine buildings which are the glory and pride of that beautiful city'. *Times*, 20 Aug. 1857, p. 11.

35 *Ecclesiologist*, XVIII (1857), 236–7.

36 I. Toplis, *The Foreign Office* (1987), 58–9.

37 E.g., *Times*, 16, 17, 18, 21, 29 May, 9 Oct. 1855; *Observer*, 19 Oct. 1856, p. 3.

38 See n. 29.

39 Ordered by Napoleon in 1810, begun by J.C.

40 Bonnard in 1814 as Foreign Ministry, and carried to completion as Ministry of Interior by J. Lacornée (1779–1856) in 1821–35; allocated to *Conseil d'Etat* and *Cour des comptes*, 1838.

41 Designed 1844 by Lacornée, with a ministerial *hôtel* facing the river, and offices and archives running back to the rue de l'Université; first stone laid, 29 Nov., 1845; buildings covered by Nov. 1847; work suspended under the Second Republic; resumed 1852, and hastened by Napoleon III's intervention, 1853. As in Whitehall, unstable ground required a concrete raft. See M. Hamon-Jugnet & C. Oudin-Doglioni, *Le Quai d'Orsay* (Paris, 1991). Count von Hübner, *Neuf Ans de Souvenirs d'un ambassade a'Autriche à Paris . . . 1851–1859* (2 vols., Paris 1904), entry for 9 Feb. 1854, describes the minster's first reception in 'le nouvel hôtel du quai d'Orsay, palais somptueux et je dirais presque présomptueux, dans le goût de la fausse Renaissance', cited in *Le Quai d'Orsay*. (I owe this reference to Mlle A. Croizat.)

42 The dialogue in the 1858 select committee between Burn and Stirling suggests that it was Brunel or Roberts who opposed Burn's suggestion that the assessors' list should be received with the remark: 'You had better appoint them judges; and then I will retire, because I see no use in having them to act in the same capacity in which we are acting ourselves' (qq. 1124–5).

42 *PP* 1857–58 (417) XI, q. 1125.

43 Ibid., q. 1211.

44 *3PD* CLII, 928–9 (4 Aug. 1859); SRO, Wemyss MSS, RH4/40/3, Scott to Elcho, 28 May 1860.

45 *Builder*, 16, 23 May 1857, pp. 272 (Ferrey, Pugin's friend), 284 ('A Competitor'). But cp 4 July, p. 371. A complete list of the 218 entrants is given in *BN* III, 8 May 1857, pp. 441–3, 445, 447. Toplis, *Foreign Office*, app., lists those whose identity is known.

46 E.K. Morris, 'Symbols of Empire: Architectural Style and the Government Offices Competition', *Jnl of Architectural Education*, XXXII, 2, Nov. 1978, pp. 8–13. The attempt, however, to identify the contest between *avant-garde* medievalists and *status-quo* classicists with the political one; 'Whigs (conservatives) and Tories (liberals or progressives)' is a risible mis-reading of the situation, ibid., p. 11.

47 Ibid., 13.

48 Toplis, 56.

49 Burn told the 1858 select committee that 'I certainly should not have undertaken any part of the duty of a judge . . . had I not thought that some member of the profession who gave designs would be employed to carry them into effect', *PP* 1857–58 (417) XI q. 1170. Discussions of the competition in the press do not convey and suggestion that the exercise was a farce, cp especially *BN*, 12 June 1857, p. 598, 'the feeling of the public is that the conditions of the competition have been too restrictive, and that the dignity of the nation requires the provision of a great monumental building. . . . Working in sympathy with public feeling, there will be no objection to an adequate provision for the administrative service.' Not until 10 July did *BN* talk of 'battling against the luxurious imagination of the future architects of the Government offices', pp. 705–6.

50 *3PD* CLII, 517–18; *PP* 1857–58 (83) XLVIII, 331, *Correspondence between FCW and T., in relation to Erection of Public Offices.*

51 *3PD* CLII, 938 (4 Aug. 1859); CLXIV, 527–31 (8 July 1861).

52 Youngest son of Thomas Hope, the banker and connoisseur, he inherited the estates of his stepfather, Viscount Beresford, in 1854; m. dau. of 2nd Marquis of Salisbury 1842.

53 *The English Cathedral of the Nineteenth Century* (1861).

54 1808?–1868, editor of the *Morning Chronicle* and subsequently of the *Saturday Review*.

55 *Public Offices and Metropolitan Improvements* (1857), which apparently ran to three editions.

56 *3PD* CXLVII, 1295–1312.

57 Ibid., 1298.

58 Ibid., 1309. It is not clear whether Tite was referring to the Houses of Parliament (the most likely, but the argument then becomes one he is unlikely to have preferred), or to the so-called Treasury Buildings that Barry had refronted in 1846.

59 *Times*, 12 Aug. 1857, p. 9.

60 Ibid., 20 Aug. (Coe and Hofland, p. 11); 21 Aug. (Banks and Barry, p. 10); 26 Aug. 1857 (Scott, p. 9).

61 G.G. Scott, *Recollections*, 180.

62 *3PD* CLII, 518 (18 Feb. 1859).

63 G.G. Scott, *Recollections*, 180.

64 E.g., *PP* 1857–58 (417) XI, q. 902, 910–15, 950, 954–86.

65 E.g., ibid., qq. 1047, 1051–3, 1055–7, 1060–5.

66 Ibid., 1172–3; cf qq. 991–3, 1239; 1069–70, 1600, 1604–05.

67 Ibid., app. 2; qq. 1102, 1113, 1116–20.

68 Ibid., qq. 1185–90, 1182.

69 Ibid., q. 1189.

70 'What would be said if it were applied to horse-racing, and the horse which ran second in two heats were held to be entitled to the cup?' *3PD* CLII, 270 (11 Feb. 1859).

71 *PP* 1857–58 (417) XI, pp. xii–xiii, paras 8–10.

72 *Sat. Rev.*, V, 303, cited by Toplis, *Foreign Office*, p. 75, as are many of the references that follow.

73 *PP* 1859 sess. 2 (122-II) XV, 367.

74 *3PD* CLII, 264–5 (11 Feb. 1859). In an undated memorandum Manners noted: 'During recess carefully considered report & evidence. In autumn recommended that notices for acquisition of that property be given, & that merits of 3 competitors being equal, the rival styles being equal, the site decided question of style & virtually of architect. Site is bounded on North by Downing Street & trends southwards toward Abbey. Style being National, Scott naturally became Architect.' Belvoir Castle MSS (cited by Brownlee, 'That "regular mongrel affair"; G.G. Scott's design for government offices', *Arch. Hist.*, 28 (1985), 168).

75 Manners to Stanley, 10 Dec. 1858, Lord John Manners's Letter Book, Belvoir Castle MSS. Manners promised to leave a confidential minute in his office explaining the grounds of the decision, of which the memo. cited above may be a copy.

76 *3PD* CLII, 266–9.

77 Ibid., 271–2.

78 *Times*, 14 Feb. 1859, p. 6 (quoted by Toplis, p. 85; see p. 86 for an account of Donaldson's reaction).

79 *Builder*, 19 Feb., p. 125; *BN*, 18 Feb., p. 153, 25 Feb., pp. 175–6; *Civil Engineer*, XXII, 75. (For details, see Toplis, p. 88.)

80 *3PD* CLII, 515–16 (18 Feb. 1859).

81 Ibid., 516–20, 523–4.

82 See below ••.

83 *Gent. Mag.*, ns VI (1859), 62–5; in *Builder*, 1 Jan. 1859, Parker urged the merits of French as much more desirable than Italian, pp. 5–6. Cp also, Parker's review of Sir F.E. Scott's pamphlet, *Shall the New Foreign Office be Gothic or Classic, Gent. Mag.*, ns IX, Sept. 1860, pp. 306–8.

84 *Builder*, 1859, 22–3.

85 'I did not aim at making my style "Italian Gothic"; my ideas ran much more upon the French, to which for some years I had devoted my chief study. I did, however, aim at gathering a few hints from Italy, such as the pillar-mullion, the use of differently coloured materials, and of inlaying. I also aimed at another thing which people consider Italian – I mean a certain squareness and horizontality of outline. This I consider pre-eminently suited to

the street front of a public building. I combined this, however, with gables, high-pitched roofs, and dormers.' G.G. Scott, *Recollections*, 178.

E. Blau has remarked on the influence of Deane and Woodward's Oxford University Museum (1853), which 'established a new image of monumental secular Gothic architecure that was to influence the design of almost all major public buildings in England . . . in the second half of the nineteenth century'. She argues that its essential classicism immediately made it a prototype for government buildings. Its influence on Scott's first F.O. designs is clear, contributing that 'squareness and horizontality' combined with high-pitched roofs and dormers that Scott claimed as his own. It was also a parent, as Blau notes, of Waterhouse's Nat. Hist. Museum and Scott's New Law Courts entry. E. Blau, *Ruskinian Gothic* (Princeton, 1982), 44–6, 79–80. See also G. Hersey, *High Victorian Gothic*, 198, 203.

86 SRO, Wemyss MSS, RH4/40/3, 15 Aug. 1859.
87 PRO, Work 30/898. Scott also sketched other possible layouts, some showing a Foreign Office without a major quadrangle: one has a south-western arm, another with a large re-entrant on the Parade corner. In all, there is some form of connexion with the State Paper Office. RIBA, Drawings Coll., illustrated Brownlee, 'Scott's Design', pl. 5a.
88 Brownlee, 'Scott's Design', 169, citing Scott's 'On the Present Position and Future Prospects of the Revival of Gothic Architecture' 923 Sept. 1857), *Associated Architectural Socs Reports and Papers*, IV (1857–8), 75.
89 Cp plates 2b (Competition design) and 6a, Brownlee, 'Scott's Design'.
90 Described and illustrated, *Builder* (1859, pp. 535–7, 601); *Building News* (1859, pp. 756–7); *Civil Engineer* (1859, p. 249).
91 G.G. Scott, 'Recollections', MS II (RIBA), 193–4.
92 Broadlands Papers, GC/SC/18, 23 July 1859. (Toplis quotes from and extensively summarises this letter, Palmerston's reply, and Scott's comeback, pp. 95–7.)
93 SRO, Wemyss MSS, RH4/40/2, Elcho to Palmerston, 26 July [1859]; reported at length, *Builder*, 1859, pp. 515–17 (summarised, Toplis, 98–9) – Palmerston rehearsed his speech for the forthcoming Commons' debate.
94 Broadlands Papers, GC/SC/21, 28 July 1859.
95 William Coningham (1815–84), Liberal MP for Brighton, and a picture collector.
96 SRO, Wemyss MSS, RH4/40/2, Scott to Elcho, 3 Aug. 1859.
97 Ibid.
98 *3PD* CLII, 918–20.
99 Palmerston's use of anti-papist rhetoric was a constant feature in his argument against Gothic.
100 *3PD* CLII, 920.
101 Ibid., 927.
102 Ibid., 930.
103 Doubtless furnished by his architectural adviser, T.L. Donaldson, who also supplied him with notes on Gothic architecture and architectural aphorisms by E.B. Lamb, Broadlands Papers, GC/DO/4.
104 This hardly emerges from the report of the relatively short debate, *3PD* CII, 515–24, 18 Feb. 1859. Tite and Coningham took the opportunity to make their usual anti-Gothic speeches, as did Palmerston himself; Manners defended his decision at length. The only other speaker, Hall, who introduced the subject, certainly asserted that in the previous week's debate (*3PD* CLII, 260–73, 11 Feb.) 'feeling was most emphatically expressed against the building of a Foreign Office in the neighbourhood of Downing Street in the Gothic style'. Manners however denied that on the second occasion the opinion of the House 'was expressed in anything like

the same sense' (ibid., 936).
105 *3PD* CLII, 935–9, 941.
106 *Sat. Rev.*, VIII, 190. *Builder* published a view, plan and description of Scott's Gothic design, 13 Aug. 1859, pp. 535–7.
107 SRO, Wemyss MSS, RH4/40/2, Scott to Elcho, 5 Aug. 1859.
108 *Times*, 6 Aug.; *Builder*, 1859, pp. 562–3. Godwin stood rather aloof in the battle; but Palmerston's reception of the deputation was attacked in *Building News* (1859, pp. 767–8) and *Sat. Rev.* (VIII, 253–4), and gave rise to much correspondence.
109 Broadlands Papers, GC/SC/20, 22 Aug.; Scott, *Recollections*, 190.
110 BL, Add. MS 44392, ff. 139–48 (23 Aug.); 44530, ff. 67ᵛ–68 (30 Aug. 1859). D.B. Brownlee, *The Law Courts* (1984), 173 quoting the latter, says Gladstone 'suggested that the architect resign rather than yield on the question of style'. That would have been far too straightforward advice for Gladstone to tender.
111 Brownlee, 173, quoting Freeman Papers, John Rylands Lib.
112 'Many Members know how keenly the late Mr Fitzroy [who died in Dec. 1859] felt the slight which was put upon him by the Noble Lord [Palmerston] taking out of his hands the responsibility, indeed all voice in the decision of this chief question appertaining to the Office he held' – notes for speech, Lord John Manners, 4 Aug. 1861, Belvoir Castle MSS.
113 Secretary of the Northampton Archdeaconry Architectural Society (which Scott, a member, regarded as the best of the provincial societies), *Ecclesiologist*, XXII (1861), 227.
114 See Toplis, *Foreign Office*, 89.
115 Oxford Archaeological Soc. was the first to memorialise the competition judges in favour of Gothic, *Eccl.*, XVIII (1857), 176, 250.
116 He remarked that 'a continued study of Scott's design more & more disgusts me . . . I think it would effectively damage the prospects of a better Architecture.'
117 Cp J.H. Parker in *Gent. Mag.*, ns VI (1859), 62–5.
118 SRO, Wemyss MSS, RH4/40/2, James to Elcho, 16 Aug. [1859]; RH4/40/3, James to Elcho, 8 Feb.; Elcho to James, 10 Feb.; Liddell to Elcho, 21 Feb.; James to Elcho 25 Feb., 13 March [1860].
119 See Toplis, 106, 227.
120 E.A. Freeman, *A History of Architecture* (1849), 452; Toplis, 107.
121 *Times*, 19 Oct., p. 19; 21 Oct. 1859, p. 7.
122 See report of Freeman's attack on 'Ruskinism', *Eccl.*, XVIII, 247; *Gent. Mag.*, ns III (1857), 75.
123 Basil H. Jackson, ed., *Recollections of Thomas Graham Jackson* (1950), 74. Toplis, p. 108, misinterprets Jackson's comment as applying to Freeman, rather than *The Times*.
124 Ruskin recommended Gothic as the appropriate style for government buildings in introducing G.E. Street as lecturer at a meeting of the Architectural Photographic Society (*Builder*, 19 Feb. 1859, p. 126, quoted by M.W. Brooks, *John Ruskin and Victorian Architecture* (1989), 154). Kenneth Clark quoted Ruskin's letter of Aug. 1859 to E.S. Dallas: 'Nice sensible discussion you're having in England there about Gothic and Italian, aren't you? And the best of the jest is that, besides nobody knowing which is which, there is not a man living who can build either. What a goose poor Scott (who will get his liver fit for a *paté de Strasbourg* with vexation) must be not to say at once he'll build anything! If I were he, I'd build Lord P. an office with all the capitals upside down, and tell him it was in the Greek style, inverted to express typically Government by Party. Up today, down tomorrow.' *Gothic Revival* (2nd edn 1950), 288. Brooks points out that Ruskin elaborated this in a subsequent letter

to Dallas, 10 Sept. 1859, expressing his view of Scott as 'an able and admirable architect – as far as architects reach these days' but that all modern architecture was 'spurious' until architects became sculptors, which would not depend on the adoption of any particular style (pp. 155–6). So Ruskin regarded the 'battle' as irrelevant.
125 Brownlee, 'Scott's Design', 181, citing Freeman Papers, John Rylands Lib.
126 G.G. Scott, *Remarks on Secular & Domestic Architecture*, 273.
127 G.G. Scott, 'Recollections', MS, II (RIBA), 213–14, cited, Toplis, 112.
128 RIBA, Drawings Coll.
129 SRO, Wemyss MS 4/40/3, 16 Feb. 1860.
130 But according to Scott's 'Recollections', Cowper 'only hummed and hawed and said civil things', MS, II, 215–16.
131 SRO, Wemyss MS 4/40/3, 16 Mar. 1860.
132 Ibid., 28 May 1860. On 13 June Scott wrote again to say that his fears about Garling had been confirmed; he had even obtained a builder's estimate.
133 Ibid.
134 G.G. Scott, 'Recollections', MS, II, 221–3. For further detail, see Toplis, 118–19.
135 Brownlee, 'Scott's Design', 175, implies stronger support from Gladstone than the evidence bears; see BL, Add. MS 44531, ff. 15, Gladstone to Cowper, 14 June ('On a question of this nature I had no intention of placing myself in opposition to the judgments especially to the combined judgments expressed by yourself and on behalf of the FO . . . in any other way than by bringing into notice statements which had reached me . . .'); 17ᵛ, to Scott, 21 June ('I do not hold . . . that your appointment is absolute and is to hold even though your designs should (rightly or wrongly it matters not) be disapproved;'); f. 19, 22 June 1860, to Cowper ('I think you will find it necessary to exhibit to Parliament any design prepared by your appointed architect . . . under the circumstances of this present case in which the judgment of the H of C is to be called in aid.' – described by Brownlee as a positive order).
136 G.G. Scott, *Explanatory Remarks on the Designs for the New Foreign Office now laid before the House of Commons* (n.d.), 16. Toplis suggests that this design is RIBA *Drawings Coll. Cat., The Scott Family*, [84] 12; see Brownlee, pl.10a.
137 SRO, Wemyss MS RH4/40/3, 30 July 1860.
138 *Times*, 7 Aug. 1860, p. 5; SRO, Wemyss MS 4/40/3, Manners to Elcho, 1 Aug. 1860.
139 E.A. Freeman, 'The Foreign Office – Gothic or Classic', *Nat. Rev.*, X (Jan. 1860), 48, cited by Brooks, *John Ruskin*, 155.
140 Toplis, 116, refers to *Remarks on a National Style, in reference to the proposed Foreign Office, Shall Gothic Architecture be denied fair play? Thoughts suggested by reading a pamphlet entitled 'Remarks on a national Style, in reference to the proposed Foreign Office'*; *Classic or Pseudo-Gothic. A reply to a pamphlet entitled 'Shall Gothic Architecture be denied fair play?'*; and Sir Francis Scott, *Shall the New Foreign Office be Gothic or Classic? A plea for the former: Addressed to the Members of the House of Commons* (7 May 1860). See also 'A Practical Man', *Remarks on the Designs proposed for the New Government Offices* (1857); and A.J.B. Beresford Hope's *Public Offices, and Metropolitan Improvements* (1857).
141 *PP* 1859, sess. 2 (122) (153) XV, pp. 367, 371, *Official letters by which Mr Scott was appointed Architect of the proposed new Foreign and India Offices*.
142 G.G. Scott, 'Recollections'. MS II, 226.
143 Ibid., 227.
144 Ibid, 231–2.
145 *Sat. Rev.* X (1860, II), 111.
146 Toplis, 125.
147 G.G. Scott, *Remarks on Secular and Domestic Architec-*

148 G.G. Scott, 'Recollections', MS II, 234, cited Toplis 126.

149 RIBA *Drawings, Cat. Scott Family*, [84] 24–32. Toplis's ascription seems more likely than Hersey's suggestion that Scott 'worked methodically through *Stones of Venice* from Venetian Gothic to Quattrocento and into High Renaissance' (G.L. Hersey, *High Victorian Gothic: a study in associationism* (1972), 208), though Toplis has misunderstood Scott's comment about the Ionic order, and his argument that its use indicates that Scott was not the author thereby falls (p. 126).

150 24 & 25 Vict., c. 33. It was subsequently found necessary to acquire a fragment of the Park by 25 & 26 Vict., c. 74.

151 PRO, Work 6/307, 19; RIBA Lib. MS SC. GGS. 4/2 1–18, Cockerell to Scott, 12 Apr. 1861.

152 *3PD* CLXII, 1374 (2 May), CLXIV, 45 (28 June), 293–4 (4 July 1861).

153 'Elcho led in his usual easy, fluent, conversational, & self-satisfied manner', T.A. Jackson, ed., *Parliamentary Diaries of Sir John Trelawny*, 187.

154 *3PD* CLXIV, 507–15 (8 July 1861).

155 Of the banking and brewing family; MP (Lib) 1857–71.

156 *3PD* CLXIV, 515–17.

157 *Letters of Queen Victoria 1837–1861* (1908), III, 443 (8 July 1861).

158 *3PD* CLXIV, 521–4.

159 Ibid., 527–32.

160 3rd s. of 2nd Earl Fortescue; MP (Lib.) 1857–74.

161 *3PD* CLXIV, 532–4. Palmerston told the queen that 'Fortescue confided in a low voice . . . some weak arguments in favour of Gothic', *Letters of Queen Victoria 1837–1861*, III, 443.

162 *3PD* CLXIV, 524–6. For Ruskin's argument, see *Stones of Venice*, III (1853), ch. ii.

163 *3PD* CLXIV, 517–22.

164 Palmerston to the Queen, 8 July 1861, *Letters of Queen Victoria 1837–1861*, III, 443.

165 *3PD* CLXIV, 535–40.

166 See *King's Works*, VI, 460.

167 *3PD* CLXIV, 545–6.

168 Eastlake, *Gothic Revival*, 312.

169 Henry James, 'London' (1888), *English Hours* (1981 edn, Oxford), 14. (I owe this reference to Professor Ken Young.)

14. A Gothic Triumph

1 *Builder*, 3 Sept. 1859, p. 589.

2 *Survey*, XXXVIII, ch. v.

3 Ibid., 85.

4 Ibid., 86, 101; *3PD* CLXXI, 908–9 (15 June 1863).

5 J. Physick, *The Victoria and Albert Museum* (1982), 33.

6 Ibid., 34–7.

7 *Survey*, XXXVIII, 89, quoting *BN*, 24 Feb. 1865, pp. 130–1.

8 Ibid., 90.

9 See Mark Girouard, *Alfred Waterhouse and the Natural History Museum* (1981, New Haven & London).

10 *Survey*, XXXVIII, 90.

11 Ibid., 104.

12 The story is told in ibid., ch. ix.

13 *BN*, 22 Apr. 1864, pp. 297–8; *Quarterly Rev.*, CXII (July 1862), 186–7; quoted *Survey*, XXXVIII, 141.

14 Feb. 1862, pp. 46–7, quoted, *Survey*, XXXVIII, 146.

15 *3PD* CLXXI, 909–12 (15 June 1863).

16 Ibid., 924.

17 *Survey*, XXXVIII, 147.

18 *3PD* CLXII, 75–91, 2 July 1863.

19 Ibid., 92–102.

20 Ibid., 110. But Palmerston, 12 June 1863, had told Lord R. Cecil that the front would be completed with stucco, and the glass domes converted to brick, with skylights, *3PD* CLXXI, 806.

21 *3PD* CLXXII, 113–14. Sir Charles Wentworth Dilke, Bt (1810–69) was one of the commissioners for the 1862 Exhibition.

22 MP (Lib.) 1862–8.

23 *3PD* CLXXII, 116–20.

24 MP (Cons.) Oxfordshire 1841–78; pres. BoT 1852, 1858–9.

25 *3PD* CLXXII, 133. The designs by Fowke, and by the contractors' architect, John Johnson, although exhibited in Feb. 1863, seem to have made no impact on the public. Fowke's *François premier* treatment is illustrated, *Survey*, XXXVIII, Pl. 38c.

26 The same demand for a contemporary style was being made in France, E. Viollet-le-Duc, *Lectures on Architecture*, transl. B. Bucknell (1881), II, 167. But le-Duc warned architects that if they did not play their proper part, the public, 'already weary of an unmeaning extravagance and lavish profusion, will ultimately insist on the erection of four plain walls in rubble and stucco, which will give repose to the eye and not empty the purse'. Ibid., II, 100.

27 SRO, Elcho to Fowke, Wemyss MSS, RH4/40/7, 4 May [1864].

28 See Physick, *Victoria and Albert Museum*, pll. v, xvii; Girouard, *Waterhouse*, p. 14.

29 SRO, Wemyss MSS, RH4/40/7, Elcho to Cole, 6 Nov. [1864].

30 Cp *Survey*, XXXVIII, p. 137.

31 *Macmillan's Mag.*, XXV (1871–2), 250–6.

32 Physick, 114–17, 146–51.

33 *Companion to the Almanac*, 1861, p. 221; 1863, p. 270; 1864, p. 123.

34 See p. *Survey*, XXXII, 413–19.

35 *3PD* CLXXXIII, 192 (30 Apr. 1866).

36 'Greek in character, dignified but somewhat plain', according to Arthur Cates, Pennethorne's obituarist. *Survey*, XXXII, 436, quoting *Sessional Papers of the RIBA*, 1871–2 (1872), 59.

37 *Survey*, XXXII, 436, quoting *Minutes of the Senate of the University of London*, 1870, pp. 91–3.

38 *3PD* CLXXXVI, 1237–41 (5 April 1867). *BN* gave a brief description 'of the objectionable façade', 7 June 1867: 'The central portion has an arcade of five arches, a small clock tower in the centre and a very large buttress at either end, surmounted by a canopy containing a statue. The wings are divided into three bays by means of buttresses, with statues in the place of pinnacles, and have at the angles a canopied buttress of less ambitious character than those of the central portion. The parapet is pierced in a very ordinary manner, and the roof is much ornamented by slates of different colours.' Earlier, 17 May, it had noted (p. 347): 'Gothical not Gothic. The arches to the entrance are segmental – of the music-hall type. . . . the roof . . . is not deficient in . . . ornamental iron cresting . . . When all is indifferent it is difficult to select portions for special condemnation.'

39 *3PD* CLXXXVI, 1232–4. In a subsequent debate, Layard compared Old Burlington House to the Irishman's knife, 'which was fit for nothing till it got a new handle and a new blade', *3PD* CXCII, 398 (15 May 1868).

40 See p. 204.

41 *3PD* CLXXXVI, 1234, 1245.

42 Ibid., 1245–7.

43 Ibid., 1323.

44 Lowe was also MP for the university 1868–80.

45 *3PD* CLXXXVII, 1463–8.

46 *3PD* CLXXXVII, 1463–9 (31 May 1867).

47 *Survey*, XXXII, 438.

48 Ibid., 438–41.

49 *Builder*, 14 May, pp. 377–8; *Times*, 9 May 1870.

50 See pp. 177–9.

51 Garling offered an alternative round-arched design.

52 J.H.G. Archer (ed.) *Art and architecture in Victorian Manchester* (Manchester, 1985), 129. Waterhouse

53 visited the principal Gothic town halls of Belgium before beginning work, S.A. Smith, 'Alfred Waterhouse', in J. Fawcett (ed.), *Seven Victorian Architects* (1976), 108, 146. Summerson, *Victorian Architecture* (cited ch. 1), 91, considers that his design 'owed much to the Whitehall efforts [New Government Offices competition of 1857] of Scott and perhaps of [Prichard and] Seddon'.

53 Robert Kerr remarked that 'all the real vigour was now Gothic', *Builder*, 17 May 1884, p. 729, cited D.B. Brownlee, *Law Courts* (1984), 103.

54 Summerson, *Victorian Architecture*, 95–7.

55 Though his brother Alfred stated that his training under his father taught him to 'refuse exclusive adherence to any one school, or exclusive devotion to any one style'. Edward M. Barry, *Lectures on Architecture*, ed. with introductory memoir by Alfred Barry (1881).

56 *Builder*, 16 Feb. 1867, p. 109.

57 *3PD* CLXXXV, 817, 820 (22 Feb. 1867). Of the original six, the 'Italians' P.C. Hardwick and T.H. Wyatt declined, E.M. Barry accepted. In the complex re-shuffling and additions, Lockwood, Garling and Gibson would have counted as 'Italians'. See M.H. Port, 'The New Law Courts Competition', *Arch. Hist.*, XI (1968), 75–93.

58 *Athenaeum*, 2 Feb. 1867, p. 162.

59 H.F. Lockwood, *Report on a design for the Concentration of the Law Courts* [1867], 14.

60 See his *Remarks on Secular and Domestic Architecture* (1857), 200–8, 261–74.

61 G.G. Scott, *Remarks on the Designs for the New Law Courts* [1867], 35.

62 W. Burges, *Report to the Courts of Justice Commission* (1867).

63 A. Waterhouse, *Report on New Law Courts design* [1867], 20.

64 *Ecclesiologist*, XXVIII, 115. Summerson, *Victorian Architecture*, 112, remarks that it is even more reminiscent of the Galleria Vittorio Emmanuele at Milan, just then begun, and (p. 126) 'built by an English firm, and Matthew Digby Wyatt was on the English board'.

65 And this, in turn, a source for design today, as R. MacCormac PPRIBA informs me in relation to his (unbuilt) Spitalfields Market site design. See also C. St John Wilson, 'The Law Courts project by Alfred Waterhouse', *Architectural Reflections* (1992), 206–26.

66 H.-R. Hitchcock, *Architecture: Nineteenth and Twentieth Centuries* (Harmondsworth, pb edn, 1971), 267.

67 These have been given detailed consideration in M.H. Port, 'The New Law Courts Competition, 1866–67', *Arch. Hist.*, 11 (1968), 75–93; Summerson, *Victorian Architecture* (1970), ch. iv; G. Hersey, *High Victorian Gothic* (1972), 142–52; S. Muthesius, *The High Victorian Movement in Architecture 1850–1870* (1972), 183–8; and Brownlee, *Law Courts* (1984). The difficulties of classifying Gothic Revival architecture of the time were indicated by C.L. Eastlake, *History of the Gothic Revival* (1872), 359–60; he attaches no examples to the 'schools' he identifies.

68 Hersey, 135, 153.

69 Led by Waterhouse, the competitors produced printed reports, illustrated by photographs, on their designs. Copies of most of these are in RIBA Library, and the DoE Conservation Unit Historical Library.

70 *Companion to the Almanac*, 1868, p. 135.

71 Hersey, 142.

72 See Brownlee, *Law Courts*, 109–11.

73 Summerson, *Victorian Architecture*, 103–8; Brownlee, 128. *BN*, 1 Mar. 1867, p. 163.

74 Garling's Law Courts design has strong reminiscences of his War Office, but more strongly recalls Fuller & Jones's Gothic Canadian Parliament building, Ottawa, 1859 (which in turn shows the

influence of Scott's entry in the Government Offices competition).

75 *Athenaeum*, 1867, p. 391; *Builder*, xxv (1867), 69–70. Summerson thinks it 'the one that appeals most immediately to the modern eye', 111.

76 See J.M. Crook, *William Burgess and the High Victorian Dream* (1981), 246–52.

77 See Brownlee, *Law Courts*, 106–11. He illustrates the specific resemblance between Louis Duc's Conciergerie façade of the Palais de Justice, Paris (1852–69) and Burges's Strand front.

78 Brownlee, 106, 386.

79 *Sat. Rev.*, 4 May 1867, p. 563.

80 As Burges himself wryly noticed, pasting into his own copy of his *Report* photographs of the Glasgow Stock Exchange and Bradford Town Hall (info. courtesy of Mr Ben Weinreb).

81 *Athenaeum*, 1867, p. 327. Scott called Burges's design 'eccentric and wild', *Recollections*, 275.

82 Yet Summerson remarks on the 'astonishing insularity' of Victorian architecture, *Victorian Architecture*, 115.

83 Scott, *Remarks on Secular and Domestic Architecture*, 203; *Remarks on the Designs for the New Law Courts* (1867), 34.

84 Brownlee cites a number of comments, 137.

85 *BN*, 1 Mar., pp. 153–4; *Builder*, 23 Mar. 1867, p. 208.

86 Summerson, 108.

87 R. Brandon, *Report submitted with Raphael Brandon's Design* (1867), 7.

88 H.-R. Hitchcock, 'High Victorian Gothic', *Vic. Studies*, I (1957), 47–71.

89 Hersey, *High Victorian Gothic*, 40–2, 135, 139–42.

90 Ibid., 144–5.

91 S. Muthesius, *High Victorian Movement in Architecture 1850–1870* (1972), 118. To add to the confusion, Pevsner identifies 'the all-over covering of a façade with motifs borrowed from anywhere ... the display of these motifs without any tension, and thirdly, the complete lack of decided accents' as 'eminently High Victorian' characteristics. 'The First Cambridge Slade Professor', *Listener*, 10 Nov. 1949, p. 808.

92 Muthesius, 188.

93 G.E. Street, *Explanation and Illustrations of His Design for the Proposed New Courts of Justice* (1867), 31–2.

94 For Street, see also J. Kinnard, 'G.E. Street, the Law Courts and the 'Seventies', in P. Ferriday (ed.), *Victorian Architecture* (1963), and A.E. Street, *Memoir of George Edmund Street, R.A.* (1888), ch. viii.

95 *BN* (1867), 57, 58, 95, 117, 186, 202.

96 *Spectator*, 23 Feb. 1867, p. 212.

97 Pevsner's 'the all-over covering of a façade with motifs borrowed from anywhere ...' (see n. 91 above).

98 Though to one critic it suggested rather the Napoleonic Rue de Rivoli.

99 *Spectator*, 23 Feb. 1867, pp. 212–13.

100 *Athenaeum*, 1867, p. 327.

101 J.P. Seddon, *New Law Courts Description of Design* (1867); *Athenaeum*, 23 Mar. 1867, p. 391.

102 *Athenaeum*, 23 Mar. 1867, p. 391.

103 *Quarterly Rev.*, cxxiii (July, 1867), 107–8.

104 *Builder*, 6 Apr. 1867, pp. 236–9.

105 Brownlee, *Law Courts*, 104.

106 For the Lille Cathedral competition – as mishandled as any of the English – see J.M. Crook, *William Burges and the High Victorian Dream*, 170–5.

107 G.G. Scott, *Personal and Professional Recollections*, 208–11.

108 Scott, *Remarks on Domestic and Secular Architecture*, 203. 'The first [characteristic of a palatial style] may be said to be *stateliness*, – which may result from actual extent and elevation, from a noble simplicity of general form, and the avoiding of needless break and subdivisions ... and, lastly,

from a commanding outline, and well-studied proportions.' Cp. SRO, Wemyss MSS, RH4/40/7, John Prichard to Lord Elcho, 26 Nov. 1863: 'My idea is that it [street architecture] should be a happy combination of *stately uniformity* coupled with a *picturesque variety*, not the result of whim or caprice, but of an honest adaptation of the means to the end, – the *result of good planning*.' In a subsequent letter (ibid., 25 May 1864), he described Gothic as 'the most *ductile* and practical and certainly the most beautiful style yet conceived'.

109 G.G. Scott, *Remarks on Domestic ... Architecture*, 269–70.

110 E.M. Barry, *Lectures on Architecture*, 134.

111 G.E. Street, *Some Remarks in Explanation of his Designs for ... the National Gallery* (1867), 24.

112 A.E. Street, *Memoir of G.E. Street*, 51.

113 PRO, Work 17/13/15, Minutes of the judges, 18 Feb. 1868.

114 *Athenaeum*, 12 Jan. 1867, p. 55; *Builder*, 12, 19, 26 Jan., 2, 9 Feb. 1867, pp. 33–4, 40–2, 56–8, 70–2, 92–3. *BN*, however, having ten years earlier vainly urged the government to treat the National Gallery question in connexion with the architectural embellishment of the metropolis, and link it with the proposed palaces of administration in Whitehall (6 Feb. 1857, p. 131), now confined itself to hostile criticism, 1867 (1), 17, 72, 107, 132.

115 *3PD* CLXXXV, 817 (22 Feb. 1867).

116 See pp. 106–8.

117 See p. 146.

118 Brownlee, *Law Courts*, 143–5, 236–7.

119 Ibid., 219.

120 PRO, Work 12/34/4, ff. 80–5 (Galton, 28 Mar.), 87–9 (Treasury to FCW, 6 Apr.), 96 (Street to FCW, 2 May 1871).

121 PRO, Work 12/34/4, ff. 106–8 (Treasury to FCW, 26 May), 111–12 (Street to OW, 26 May 1871). For details of Street's revisions, see Brownlee, *Law Courts*, 209–43.

122 PRO, Work 12/34/4, ff. 136, 120–1.

123 *3PD* CCX, 582 (25 Mar. 1872).

124 *Times*, 7 Sept., p. 8, 'XZ'; 11 Sept., p. 5, G. Cavendish Bentinck; 13 Sept. 1871, p. 10, A. Seymour.

125 Cp his *cri de coeur* in *Athenaeum*, 20 Jan. 1872, p. 85, that until the principles he advocated were acknowledged, 'the architecture of this country must be hollow and false, and truth in architecture is perfectly impossible'.

126 *BN*, 14 July, p. 28; *Architect*, 15 July, p. 26; *Athenaeum*, 29 July 1871, p. 151.

127 *Times*, 19 Aug. 1871, p. 11.

128 See Brownlee, 244–6, for details.

129 *Builder*, 2 Dec. 1871, p. 949.

130 Summerson, *Victorian Architecture*, 115. Pevsner, *BoE, London 1*, (3rd edn, 1973), 321, gives a much more sympathetic analysis.

131 'The architectural treatment ... is masterly, though uncongenial to those who require monumental unification in the design of every public building, even when ... so placed that it never can be seen as a whole.' H.S. Goodhart-Rendel, *English Architecture since the Regency* (1953), 144.

132 The Strand front is also analysed by Kinnard, 'G.E. Street', 232.

133 *Times*, 19 Aug., p. 11; 21 Aug., p. 9 ('W.H. L[eeds]'); 22 Aug., p. 8 (E. Cust).

134 Ibid., 11 Sept. 1871, p. 9. Letters, 21, 22 Aug., 1, 5, 7, 9, 11 Sept. 1871.

135 *BN*, 28 July 1871, p. 73; *Architect*, 30 Sept. 1871, pp. 164–6; see Brownlee, *Law Courts*, 247–8. Godwin was a friend of J.P. Seddon, who also defended Street's designs in letters to *The Times* in Dec. 1871 Both men were friends of Burges, and doubtless saw Burgesian qualities in Street's work.

136 *BN*, 17 Nov., 1, 8 Dec.; *Architect*, 25 Nov., 9 Dec. 1871.

137 See Brownlee, *Law Courts*, 246–8.

138 *Builder*, 2 Dec. 1871, p. 949.

139 *Times*, 6 Dec. 1871.

140 *Sat. Rev.*, 23 Dec. 1871, p. 204.

141 *Athenaeum*, 29 July 1871, pp. 150–1, discerned 'the distinct pronunciation of the interior by the exterior'; and cited the river front of the Houses of Parliament as a warning against giving 'perfect regularity to such a façade as that of the Courts of Justice'.

142 Quoted A.E. Street, *Memoir of George Edmund Street* (1888), 167.

143 J. Fergusson, 'The New Law Courts', *Macmillan's Mag.*, Jan. 1872, 253–4; *Times*, 27 Dec., p. 8; *BN*, 29 Dec. 1871, pp. 500–1, but followed this up with a leader attacking Fergusson's article as 'hardly worthy of its author', 5 Jan. 1872, pp. 1–2. Fergusson had begun very cuttingly: 'Few things can be more encouraging to those anxious to promote the arts of their country than the interest generally felt in Mr Street's designs for the new Law Courts, and nothing more hopeful than the disapprobation with which they have been received.'

144 As shown in a cartoon by E.J. Tarver for an Architectural Association soirée programme, 9 Feb. 1972, illustrated Brownlee, 243.

145 J. Fergusson, 'The New Law Courts'.

146 *Sat. Rev.* 13 Jan. 1872, pp. 42–5.

147 *3PD* CCX, 581 (22 Mar. 1872).

148 Ibid., 585.

149 Ibid., 587, 589.

150 *Athenaeum*, 6 Jan., p. 21; 13 Jan. 1872, p. 54. The notorious E.B. Denison (later Lord Grimthorpe) commented that 'it is evident ... that that body [the RIBA] is making it a kind of Trade Union affair to stand by Mr Street against the public', *Times*, 8 Jan. 1872, p. 9.

151 *3PD* CCXII, 699 (5 July 1872).

152 *3PD* CCXIII, 415–16 (3 Aug. 1872).

153 PRO, Work 2/40, pp. 151–5, 3 Apr. 1873.

154 PRO, Work 12/40/3, ff. 60–70, 9 May 1873.

155 See Brownlee, pp. 252–9; below, pp. 261–4.

156 The influence of German medieval models on Waterhouse's design is pointed out in a RCHME report (particularly the W. front of Andernach abbey with its rows of blind arches; the north door of the Jakobskirche at Regensberg, with animals on either side; and the *Gnadenpforte* at Bamberg). (Ex info. Dr A. Saint.)

157 *Macmillan's Mag.*, xxv, Jan. 1872, pp. 250ff.

158 VAM, Cole Corr., box 8, 17 May, 1 Aug. 1871, Bentinck to Cole; Cole Diary, 14, 15, 20 Feb. 1872.

15. Classicism Revivified

1 Large town halls or municipal buildings in some form of Italianate in the 'seventies include Wolverhampton (1869–71), Birmingham (1874–9), Huddersfield (1875–81), Hampstead (1876), Holborn (1878–80), Kensington (1878), Limehouse (1879), Glasgow (1881), Preston (Library & Museum, 1882), Eastbourne (1884), Burnley (1885) and Dewsbury (1888). See C. Cunningham, *Victorian and Edwardian Town Halls* (1981); and N. Pevsner's *BoE* volumes.

2 Witness Brydon's Chelsea Vestry Hall, 1885.

3 P. Greenhalgh, 'Art, Politics and Society at the Franco-British Exhibition of 1908', *Art Hist.*, 8 (1985), 444–5.

4 *Architect*, 2 Aug. 1884, p. 63.

5 *Times*, 31 July 1884, p. 6.

6 *Architect*, 2 Aug. 1884, p. 63.

7 *Brit. Arch.*, 1, 8 Aug. 1884 (49, 63); 2 Jan. (8, quoting hostile comment in *The Year's Art*), 3 Apr. (163), 21, 28 Aug. (82, 91), 4 Sept. (106), 2 Oct. 1885 (146).

8 *PP* 1887 (184) VII, *S.C. on the Admiralty and War Office (Sites)*, q. 1967.

9 *Builder*, 6 Sept. (p. 320), 4 Oct. (p. 454); 13 Sept. 1884 (pp. 424–5). Leemings' design is illustrated at pp. 326–7 and 460. Reviews of the second-stage men appeared in *Builder*, 1884, XLVII, 346 (Webb & Bell), 388 (Glover & Salter), 424 (Verity & Hunt), 488 (Hall & Powell), 539 (Maxwell & Tuke), 556 (Stark & Lindsay), 588 (Spalding & Auld), 622 (Porter). Other entries reviewed were Robson, 224; I'Anson & Baggalley, 298; Jackson, 388; and Waterhouse, 724.

10 *Architect*, 4 Sept. 1885, pp. 140–2.

11 *BN*, 17 Oct. 1884, p. 624.

12 *Sat. Rev.*, 9 Aug. 1884, p. 173 – respectively Hall & Powell, Spalding & Auld, Tuke & Maxwell, Porter, Glover & Salter, and Stark & Lindsay.

13 *Builder*, 13 Sept. 1884, pp. 356–7.

14 *Sat. Rev.*, 9 Aug. 1884, p. 173.

15 *3PD* CCXCVI, 1170–1 (9 Apr. 1886).

16 Ibid., 1172–6, 1177.

17 See *PP* 1888 (191) LXXX, 1; *Times*, 2 Mar. 1886; PRO, Work 30/989.

18 *PP* 1887 (184) VII, *S.C. on Admiralty and War Office Sites*, pp. iii, iv.

19 Ibid., qq. 1864–6.

20 Perhaps influenced by Brydon's revival in the Chelsea Vestry Hall (1885) of Wren's use of these materials.

21 It was not until May 1888 that public reaction becomes observable. A letter in *The Times* from J. MacVicar Anderson on behalf of the RIBA (22 May 1888) putting forward the Institute's scheme, and explaining the nature of that of the select committee, started a correspondence that was taken up in the professional press. Cavendish Bentinck proclaimed that he was 'one of the few' to approve the committee's scheme, though another MP welcomed its freedom from over-ornamentation and excessive height. See *Architect*, 25 May, 1 June 1888, pp. 296–9, 316–17.

22 *Architect*, 1 June 1888, p. 319.

23 BL, Add. MS 41227, ff. 195–8, 15 Nov. 1892, 'The War Office and Admiralty Sites and Buildings' confidential print.

24 *4PD* LV, 1146 (H. Gladstone, 28 Mar. 1898).

25 *Architect*, supplements, 28 Sept., pp. 26–8; 4 Jan. 1895, p. 31.

26 *4PD* LXXI, 447 (12 May 1899).

27 *4PD* LV, 1296, William Allan (29 Mar. 1898).

28 G. Shaw Lefevre, 'Public Works in London', *Nineteenth Century*, Nov. 1882, p. 680.

29 *PP* 1884–5 (166) XIII, *S.C. on Westminster Hall Restoration*, q. 2611.

30 Ibid., q. 259.

31 A. Quiney, *John Loughborough Pearson* (1979), 186.

32 *PP* 1884 (264) LXI, *Report on Westminster Hall by Mr J.L. Pearson, R.A.*, 4–6, 12.

33 For Pearson's views on, and works of restoration, see Quiney, *John Loughborough Pearson*, ch. 20. See also *Builder*, LXVIII (1885), 57–8.

34 *PP* 1884–5 (166) XIII, *S.C. on Westminster Hall Restoration*.

35 Ibid., qq. 1414–20, 2109–20.

36 Ibid., qq. 409 ff.; draft report by Dick Peddie. *Builder*, 26 July (p. 115), 29 Nov. 1884 (pp. 715–17), 10 Jan. (p. 62), 14 Mar. (p. 366), 21 Mar. (pp. 405–6), 4, 11 Apr. (pp. 473, 505), 9 May (p. 648), 16 May (p. 683), 4 July 1885 (pp. 2–4).

37 *PP* 1884–5 (166) XIII, *Report from S.C. on Westminster Hall Restoration*.

38 Times, 17 July 1884, 16 July 1885 – but the correspondence columns gave more scope to critics (10, 24, 27, 28 Nov., 13 Dec. 1884) than to supporters (1, 26 Dec. 1884). *Builder*, 1884, XLVII, 715–17; 1885, XLVIII, 648, 683. *Brit. Arch.* was also critical, 1884, XXXII, 65, 268. *BN*, however, was mildly supportive: 'We think much of the criticism which has been bestowed on Mr Pearson's scheme has been

wide of the mark, and that in the long run it will probably be carried out very much, if not entirely, as here indicated', 19 Sept. 1884, p. 464.

39 *PP* 1884–85 (166) XIII, v; *Builder*, 29 Nov. 1884, p. 715; 9, 16 May 1885, pp. 648, 683; *3PD* CCXCIX, 799–879 (14 July 1885).

40 Sir G. Campbell, *3PD* CCXLIII, 793 (17 Apr. 1890).

41 Lord Wemyss, 'Memories', I, 335–6 (SRO, Wemyss MSS RH4/40/19).

42 Lodged for a decade in the Horticultural Society's western gallery at South Kensington; transferred to the Bethnal Green Museum in 1885. For Christian's drawings, see PRO, Work 33/1567–81.

43 *3PD* CCCXXXV, 1225 (6 May 1889).

44 See pp. 185–6 above.

45 J. Physick, *Victoria and Albert Museum*, 184.

46 Ibid., 189. The following consideration of the designs is largely based on ibid., 189–200.

47 J.M. Brydon (not invited to compete for South Kensington) had delivered a long paper at the A.A., 15 Feb. 1889, on 'The English Classic Revival of the Seventeenth and Eighteenth Centuries', bringing together an exceptional collection of illustrations of the style. It was extensively reported. See *Architect*, 100–02, 121–3 for a full account; also *Builder*, LVI, 147, 149, 168. *Brit. Arch.*, XXXI, 151–2, 169 published lengthy excerpts on 'Wren and his works'; and *BN* summarised it, LVI, 263. The A.A.'s own organ, however, dismissively remarked that 'though interesting' [it] could hardly have contained much that was new' (although men up for the March examination at the Institute 'looked upon it, coming at this particular time, as manna sent from Heaven': quoted, A. Service, *Edwardian Architecture* (1977), p. 62). *A.A. Notes*, III, 92.

48 Described as beginning 'the modern expression of the cavalier spirit in architecture' (J. Bone, quoted by A.S. Gray, *Edwardian Architecture* (1988), 104).

49 *Brit. Arch.*, 14 Aug. 1891.

50 *Builder*, 8 Aug., pp. 97ff.; *BN*, 7 Aug., pp. 171ff.; *Architect*, 21 Aug. 1891, pp. 106–7.

51 In the view of *A.A. Notes* (VI, 56–7), unduly so; whereas he should have given more consideration to the museum's existing buildings, and the adjoining Science Schools (now the Henry Cole Wing).

52 *Builder*, *BN*, loc. cit.; *Brit. Arch.*, 14 Aug. 1891.

53 *BN*, loc. cit. *Brit. Arch.*, 21 Aug. 1891, p. 131 described it as 'a Michael Angelo Renaissance, which is quite refreshing', found its skyline picturesque, but thought its tower would 'only compete with that of the Imperial Institute'.

54 H. Goodhart-Rendel, 'Brompton, London's Art Quarter', *RIBA Jnl.* Jan. 1956, quoted by Physick, 200.

55 *A.A. Notes*, VI, Sept. 1891, pp. 56–7.

56 *Brit. Arch.*, 21 Aug. 1891, p. 131.

57 Bodleian, Harcourt MS dep. 192, ff. 74–9 (25 Oct. 1892), 139–40 (22 Feb.), 149 (16 June), 147 (1 July 1893).

58 *Architect*, 16 July 1897, p. 33.

59 *BN*, 4 May 1900, p. 603, with fold-out perspective drawing. Also illustrated in *Builder*, 5 May 1900, after p. 443; *Arch. Rev.* XXI (1907), 195–9. Original design, *BN*, 7 Apr. 1899, after p. 473. Cp also W. Crane's praise for Webb's handling of the R. Coll. of Science, *RIBA Jnl.*, 3 ser., XII, 367 (8 May 1905).

60 *4PD* LIV, 679 (4 Mar. 1898).

61 *4PD* LV, 111, 115 (17 Mar. 1898). Harcourt's view was shared by the Bishop of Worcester: 'Our public buildings especially those of modern date are with few exceptions a disgrace to the nation', SRO, Wemyss MSS, RH 40/13, 21 Aug. 1899.

62 *4PD* LV, 1143, 1152 (28 Mar.); 1295 (29 Mar. 1898).

63 *Architect*, 25 Mar., p. 185; 22 July 1898, p. 50.

64 Ibid., 24 Mar. 1899, p. 185. Of the extraneous features only the Charles Street arch was executed.

65 For Gosford, see C. McWilliam, *Lothian* (Harmondsworth, 1978), 222–3; *Country Life*, XXX (1911), 342ff.

66 SRO, Wemyss MSS, RH4/40/13, 40/14 passim; Lord Wemyss, *The New War Office: What it is to Be: What Still Might Be* (1899); *Brit. Arch.*, 28 July 1899.

67 *4PD* LXXV, 1431–3, 1436 (4 Aug. 1899).

68 Ibid., 1441.

69 *Builder*, 29 July 1899, leading article.

70 SRO, Wemyss MSS, RH4/40/13, Buckle to Wemyss, 15 Aug. 1899.

71 Ibid., Wemyss to Buckle, 'Thursday morning' [Aug. 1899].

72 I am grateful to Mr Colin Sorensen of the Museum of London for this information.

73 SRO, Wemyss MSS, RH4/40/13, 10 and 18 Aug. 1899.

74 *BN*, 24 Mar. 1899, pp. 397–8; H.S. Goodhart-Rendel, *English Architecture since the Regency* (1953), 202. These lectures were delivered in 1934.

75 See pp. 74–5 above.

76 Goodhart-Rendel, 207.

77 *Architect*, 3 July 1908, pp. 3–4.

78 *BN*, 6 July 1907, p. 19. Cp. 24 Mar. 1899. For Rickards, see A. Stuart Gray, *Edwardian Architecture* (1988 edn), 308–11.

79 PRO, Work 30/1007–8, 1019.

80 *4PD* CLIV, 1074 (24 Mar. 1906); CLV, 177–8, 740–1 (2, 5 Apr. 1906); SRO, HH 45/47. That the alteration in the towers and archway across Charles Street was by Brydon is unlikely: it occurs on a flier attached to his 1898 signed elevation, ibid., 30/1007. The allegorical sculpture on the arch was the work of W.S. Frith (spandrels symbolising work of the L.G.B., the Bd of Education, and the H.O.) and P.R. Montford (top sculpture: Local Government supporting the aged; Commerce and Industry; and H.O. (Factory Inspectorate) encouraging the young worker).

81 *Arch. Rev.*, XXVIII (1910), 55.

82 Goodhart-Rendel, *English Architecture*, 200–1.

83 Judging from his published lectures on the English Renaissance, his chief admiration was for Jones and Wren. See *Architect*, 1889, pp. 100–2, 121–3.

84 Quoted, *5PD*, LI, 696–7.

85 *5PD* LIII, 2007–8 (Whitehouse), 2009–10 (Cecil), 13 June 1913.

86 See P. Abercrombie, 'Leopold II and Brussels', *Arch. Rev.* XXXII (July–Dec. 1912), 114.

87 They had hoped to secure an additional four rooms in a central attic, but decided that the additional superstructure had too bad an effect. Webb, however, retained a smaller central superstructure both to hide the chimneys at the back and for architectural effect. RA, Geo. V, o. 109, Queen Victoria Memorial papers, ff. 20–47. See ch. 2, n. 251.

88 *4PD* CXXVI, 807–12 (29 July); CXXVII, 772–5 (10 Aug. 1903). PRO, Work 17/5/1; 17/6/4.

89 N. Pevsner, *BoE: London except the Cities of London and Westminster* (Harmondsworth, 1952), 210. See also Gray, *Edwardian Architecture*, 128–9. For Burnet's drawings, see PRO, Work, 33/1199–1221.

90 J.M. Crook, *The British Museum* (1972), 211–16.

91 *Arch. Rev.*, Aug. 1910, p. 59.

92 *Builder*, 17 Apr. 1914, p. 473; Gray, *Edwardian Architecture*, 361.

93 See P. Collins, *Concrete: the Vision of a New Architecture* (1959), 76–86; H. Tanner, 'The New G.P.O. London', *RIBA Jnl.*, 3 ser., XVIII, 149–77 (2 Jan. 1911).

94 *BN*, 29 Aug. 1913, p. 311, details of instructions to competitors.

95 *Builder*, 10 Apr. 1914, p. 442.

96 *PP* 1896 (310) XI, q. 588.
97 *BN*, 12 Feb. 1915, p. 137. A modern critic, looking at the building as erected in the 1950s, only somewhat modified (seven floors grouped between 'qua-basement' and colonnade), remarks: 'The design is strangely undecided ... [it] starts with the well-worn traditional motif of Gibbs surrounds ... and then suddenly turns bleakly utilitarian with seven storeys of absolutely plain windows (of Georgian not of C20 shape). After that the giant colonnade motif appears high up.' There is particular irony about the comment that 'There is hardly any Western country that would have still been ready at that time [i.e., 1950s] to let itself be represented by giant colonnades', in view of the 1913 ban on columnar treatment 'except in isolated features'. N. Pevsner, *BoE: London I, The Cities of London and Westminster* (3rd edn revised by B. Cherry, Harmondsworth, 1973).
98 *Architect*, XCIII (1915), 137–8.

16. Hazards of the Building Process

1 I. Toplis, *The Foreign Office* (1987), 76, 89.
2 Ibid., 97. In 1862, Kelk offered to undertake the Albert Memorial at cost; he subsequently declined a knighthood, holding out for the baronetcy he obtained in 1874. He was MP for Harwich (Cons.) 1865–8.
3 PRO, T. 1/6739A/18527, Scott to FCW, 17 Feb. 1864.
4 Toplis, 139–40.
5 Toplis, 136–9; M.H. Port (ed.), *The Houses of Parliament* (1976), 197–8.
6 See PRO, Work 30/914–71.
7 See M.H. Port, 'The Office of Works and Building Contracts in Early Nineteenth-Century England', *Econ. Hist. Rev.*, 2 ser., XX (1967), 94–110.
8 Toplis, 148–50. For working drawings for India Office see PRO, Work 30/1128–1265, 5229–78. Scott's contract drawings for the F.O. are PRO, Work 30/914–71; but many drawings have found their way to RIBA Drawings Coll., see *Catalogue ... The Scott Family* (Amersham, 1981), 54–5.
9 *PP* 1867 [3873] XXXI, *Royal Commission on Trades Unions, etc.*, q. 2893.
10 Ibid., qq. 2854, 2895, 2827, 2908.
11 Ibid., qq. 2768–75, 2787–9, 2808–13, 1521–41.
12 Ibid., qq. 396–400.
13 Ibid., 2814, 2765.
14 See Toplis, *Foreign Office*, 153 for details. Alterations called for by Hammond of the F.O. were submitted on 13 May 1867, ibid., 161.
15 See F. Harcourt, 'The Queen, the Sultan and the Viceroy: A Victorian State Occasion', *London Jnl*, 5 (1979), 35ff. Digby Wyatt described the ball as 'an essentially national experiment', *Times*, 23 July 1867, p. 9.
16 The Foreign Office was completed at a cost of £285,473, PRO, T. 1/7009B/20313, FCW to T., 26 Feb. 1870.
17 *PP* 1867–8 (281 and 281-I) LVIII, 257ff.
18 PRO, Work 12/96/2, ff. 3–4, 6; 6/307, f. 129.
19 PRO, Work 12/96/2, ff. 13, 17, 18; *PP* 1877 (312) XV, q. 676.
20 See p. 124 above.
21 Scott provided for implementing the Manners' commission plan for building on the north side of Downing Street by including an arcade across the street from the F.O., PRO, Work 30/665.
22 PRO, Work 12/96/2, ff. 22, 27. The foundations contract did not include the Parliament Street front, ibid., ff. 42–3, 22 Jan. 1869.
23 Ibid., f. 34.
24 Ibid., ff. 35 (Scott to OW, 22 Dec. 1868); 55 (Treasury to OW, 18 Feb. 1869). 'This is the first opportunity afforded to their Lordships of expressing any opinion with regard to the total estimated

cost', commented the Treasury secretary reproachfully.
25 Ibid. no. 59 (printed), 27 Feb. 1869. Toplis, *Foreign Office*, p. 179, comments 'Unfortunately the report no longer exists.' Contrary to his further suggestion, there is no reason to suppose that 'relations between Scott and the Office [of Works] were hardly cordial'.
26 PRO, Work 12/96/2, no. 59 and ff. 224–7; Work 30/666–75.
27 PRO, Work 12/96/2, f. 79.
28 Ibid., ff. 82–3, 100. See PRO, Work 30/665–80; RIBA Drawings Coll., *Catalogue ... The Scott Family*, 56–7.
29 PRO, Work 12/96/2, f. 88.
30 Ibid., ff. 103–5 (T. to FCW, 7 Feb.), 108–12 (FCW to T., 26 Feb.), 115 (Scott to FCW, 15 Mar., and FCW's endorsement, 16 Mar.), 123–4 (Scott to FCW, 18 Mar. 1870).
31 Ibid., 145–7 (T. to FCW, 30 Apr.), 153–6 (FCW to T., 16 May), 161 (Treasury to FCW, 14 June), 164–8 (report of Director of Works, 4 July 1870). See p. 66 above.
32 Ibid., ff. 170–1, 22 July 1870.
33 Ibid., ff. 178ff, 6 Aug. 1870; 267–72, 22 July 1871.
34 Ibid., ff. 180v., 183, 185, 187 (list of tenders), 190–1 (Scott to FCW, 16 Sept. 1870). Scott's amanuensis raised the question whether the tenderers should be present when their tenders were opened. Hunt reported that it was the custom 'for Works of magnitude'; so no objection was made, f. 185. Jackson & Shaw were also contractors for St John's College chapel, Cambridge (Scott), and Grimsdyke, Harrow Weald (R. Norman Shaw) – Toplis, *Foreign Office*, 181; A. Saint, *Richard Norman Shaw* (1976), 408.
35 PRO, Work 13/1.
36 PRO, Work 12/96/2, f. 216v.
37 Toplis, *Foreign Office*, 189–90.
38 PRO, Work 12/96/2, ff. 288, 291 (H.O. to OW, 9 May and 19 June), 291v., 292 (OW memo. and draft, 18, 20 July), 293–4 (HO to OW, 27 Nov. 1872, specifying alterations required – new doors from west quadrangle into basement, and from office keeper's to secretary of state's private stair, etc.).
39 Ibid., ff. 301–2 (Scott to FCW, 7 Feb., endorsed by Galton), 303, 305 (Jackson & Shaw to Scott, 4 Feb.), 304 (Galton to FCW, 6 Mar.), 311 (Scott to Galton, 1 May 1873).
40 Ibid., ff. 314–15, 316 (Jackson & Shaw to Scott, 29 Jan., 16 Apr.), 323–4 (OW solicitor's report, 9 May, annotated by FCW, 10 May 1873).
41 Ibid., ff. 319, 325, 326. The estimate was £1680.
42 Ibid., ff. 347 (14 Nov.), 354 (10 Dec. 1874).
43 *PP* 1877 (312) XV, qq. 641–6, 670–3. Scott had still not given his completion certificate in June 1877.
44 D.B. Brownlee discusses this in detail, *Law Courts* (1984), chap. 4.
45 See p. 106.
46 PRO, Work 6/123, block plans approved by CJC, 23 July 1868; details added Oct. 1868 (illustrated, Brownlee, pll. 73, 74).
47 See p. 110 above.
48 *PP* 1868–69 (274) XLVII, App.
49 *PP* 1868–69 (274) XLVII, 129; *3PD* CXCVII, 458–63; *PP* 1868–69 (381) X, *S.C. on site of New Law Courts*. See p. 113 above.
50 *3PD* CXCIX, 168 (11 Feb. 1870).
51 PRO, Work 12/33/1, ff. 178–92 (Street to FCW, 25 Mar.), 194 (Ayrton to Galton, 28 Mar.), 198–9 (Street to Galton, 19 Apr.); 12/34/1, ff. 17–23 (Hunt and Galton, 27 June 1870).
52 PRO, Work 12/34/1, ff. 1–6 (Street to Ayrton, 17 June 1870).
53 Ibid., ff. 24–7 (Ayrton to Treasury, 2 July 1870).
54 PRO, MP 1/9.

55 PRO, T. 1/7004B/19487, 7 July; Work 12/34/1, ff. 30–3 (Treasury minute, 7 July), 51 (Street to Treasury, 20 July), 37–51 (Street's report, 14 July 1870).
56 *PP* 1871 [C. 290] XX, 130–1.
57 *Builder*, 7 May, p. 358; *BN*, 20 May 1870, p. 370. Plans dated Nov. 1870 are PRO, Work 30/1279–83, a section, Dec. 1870, 30/1278.
58 PRO, Work 12/40/2, ff. 1 (Street to Galton, 4 Aug. and minutes thereon by Galton, 8 Aug., and FCW, 5 Oct.), 2 (Hunt's report, 7 Aug.), 9–10 (12 Dec., OW to Street), 13 (contractors' resolutions, 15 Dec. 1870).
59 PRO, Work 12/40/2, ff. 19–20 (OW to contractors, 13 Jan.), 23–4 (tenders), 26 (Street to OW, 21 Jan. 1871). Doves completed their contract on 18 May, instead of the due date of 2 Feb. 1872, partly because of bad weather, Work 12/40/2, ff. 60, 67. Street opposed fining them, as the contract permitted: 'They appear to have done their work well and carefully but perhaps have not quite realized from the first how much time the work would take', he wrote from Florence, 16 Mar. 1872, ibid., f. 45. But the Office exacted the £100 per week due, although there was a saving of £3541 on the excavation work, ibid., ff. 52, (29 May), 67 (14 Dec. 1872).
60 PRO, Work 12/34/4, ff. 60–1 (n.d.), 70–1 (14 Jan. 1871); 30/1280–1 (plans).
61 See pp. ●●.
62 PRO, Work 12/34/4, ff. 74–5 (Ayrton to Treasury, 13 Feb.), 80–6 (Ayrton to Treasury, 30 Mar., with Galton's report, 28 Mar.), 87–9 (Treasury to FCW, 6 Apr. 1871).
63 Ibid., ff. 91–3 (Street to OW, 22 Apr.), 106–8 (Treasury to FCW, 26 May), 111–12 (Street to OW, 26 May 1871); 30/1330 (elevation).
64 PRO, Work 12/34/4, ff. 120–1. See Brownlee, *Law Courts*, 228.
65 See pp. 228–30.
66 PRO, Work 12/40/3, f. 4 (Treasury to FCW, 5 Feb. 1872).
67 PRO, Work 12/34/2, ff. 13–16 (Street to OW, 15 Jan. 1872).
68 PRO, Work 12/40/2, ff. 60 (Street, 14 June 1872). Street had drawn almost all parts at a scale of half-inch to the foot, instead of the usual eighth-inch, Work 12/34/2, ff. 13–14.
69 PRO, Work 12/40/3, f. 10, 2 Dec. 1872.
70 PRO, Work 12/40/2, 64–5 (Hunt, 6 Dec.); 12/40/3, ff. 15 (11 Dec. 1872), 18–19 (14 Jan.), 25 (27 Feb.), 26 (invitees – only 22, with three provincial), 29 (25 Mar. 1873), 117 (list of tenders: prices for whole job, using Portland stone: Bull & Sons, Southampton, £744,344; Baker & Son, Stangate, Lambeth, £816,675; Jackson & Shaw, Earl St, Westminster, £835,132; Perry & Co., Tredegar Works, Bow, £838,700; Lucas Bros, Great George St, Westminster, £849,356; Kirk, Warren Lane Wharf, Woolwich, £861,937; Cockburn & Sons, Dublin, £888,700; Higgs, S. Lambeth, £900,000; Brass, Old St, £906,965; Dove Bros, Studd St, Islington, £924,100; Myers & Son, Belvedere Rd, Lambeth, £934,700; Brown & Robinson, Worship St, Finsbury, £939,400; Holland & Hannen, Duke St, Bloomsbury, £949,473; Trollope & Sons, Parliament St, Westminster, £968,028; Lee & Sons, Westminster Chambers, Victoria St, £976,717; Briggs & Son, Bradford St, Birmingham, £987,200; Peto Bros, Gillingham St, Pimlico, £994,422).
71 Employed as principal contractor for the British Museum from the 1820s.
72 Brownlee, *Law Courts*, 294ff. Primarily railway contractors, the firm had also executed the Winchester Guildhall and the National Provincial Bank in Southampton. Nonetheless, it must be pointed out that Street insisted that Bull's tender

was close to his 1870 estimate, if 15 per cent were allowed for increased prices of materials and labour.

73 PRO, Work 12/40/3, f. 27–8 (OW to Street, 26 Mar.). The figures are initially somewhat confusing, as Street made calculations on the basis of Bull's tender for Chilmark stone and fittings of deal, £719,787, and the fittings of 18 courts, £9450. Allowing £28,000 for warming and lighting, the total, together with foundations at £31,600, was £788,737 (PRO, Work 2/40, p. 157, 27 Mar. 1873). The Works insisted on the more expensive Portland stone with oak fittings, which brought the total to £818,416 (ibid., 167; Work 12/40/3, ff. 36–40).

74 Ibid., ff. 36–40 (29 Mar.); 2/40, pp. 227–9 (17 Apr. 1873).

75 PRO, Work 12/40/3, ff. 50–6, 1 May 1873.

76 Ibid., ff. 88–9 OW to Street, 17 May), 91–2 (minute by FCW), 102–4 (Street to FCW, 22 May), 105–9 (OW to Street, 26 May), 122 (Street to OW, 6 June), 124, 125 (OW to Street, 9, 14 June); 90 (Treasury to FCW, 20 May 1873).

77 Gladstone to Queen, 16 Mar. 1873, Morley, *Gladstone*, II, 454.

78 PRO, Work 12/40/3, ff. 105–9 (OW to Street, 26 May); BL, Add MS 44438, f. 325 (Street to Gladstone, 27 May 1873).

79 PRO, Work 12/40/3, ff. 122, 134–8 (Street to OW, 6, 16 June), 124, 125 (OW to Street, 9, 14 June), 126–9 (Treasury to FCW, 14 June), 155 (OW to Street, 2 July 1873).

80 Brownlee, *Law Courts*, 295, 298–9.

81 The tender required a price 'for the Fittings of one Court' in oak and alternatively in deal, without mention of the number of courts required to be fitted up at that price. Having put £804 instead of £1104, Bulls were unwilling to multiply their potential loss by 18. PRO, Work 12/40/3, ff. 19–201, Hunt's memo., 15 Sept. 1873. Bulls were less unreasonable than one might assume, however, in demanding that there should be drawings for each court before they gave a price, as Street made every court different: 'Each court varies in detail, and all the roofs and fittings are of different design', *BN*, XLIII (1882), 134.

82 PRO, Work 12/40/3, f. 163.

83 Ibid., f. 173 (Street to OW, 13 Aug. 1873), with Office endorsements.

84 Ibid., ff. 174 (Bull & Sons to OW, 15 Aug.), 182–4, 187–9 (Street to Galton, 5 and 6 Sept.), 190–201 (Hunt's memo. 15 Sept. 1873).

85 PRO, Work 12/40/3, ff. 190–240.

86 As is to be seen on the working drawings, e.g. PRO, Work 30/1419 and 1646.

87 Brownlee, 297–305.

88 PRO, Work 2/29, p. 109, 9 May 1865; R. Owen, *On the extent and aims of a national museum of natural history* (1862), pl. II.

89 PRO, Work 2/29, p. 109.

90 Ibid.

91 Ibid., p. 376, 14 Feb. 1866.

92 Ibid., 2/30, pp. 445 (31 Jan.); 2/31, pp. 17 (14 Feb.), 353 (27 Dec. 1867).

93 See p. 271 below.

94 See pp. 100, 151.

95 PRO, Work 2/34, pp. 79–81 (FCW to T., 4 Mar.), 206 (T. to FCW, 14 May 1870).

96 PRO, Work 2/34, pp. 250–1 (FCW to T., 10 June); 17/16/2, ff. 128 (July), 137 (Waterhouse to OW, 1 Aug. 1870).

97 PRO, Work 2/35, p. 343 (FCW to T., 29 Nov. 1870).

98 What Owen had actually proposed was a system of 40-ft-wide galleries on two floors, separated by 'interspaces' of 20ft; 'it would, also, be practicable to utilise the intespaces . . . by arching them over with a roof of glass, spanning from below the side-windows of the ground floor', which were to be 20ft above floor level. Owen, *National Museum*, pp. 80, 86–7; see also *PP* 1863 (390) XXIX, 703, *Estimates, Plans and Sections of Museum of Natural History prepared . . . in accord with the suggestions of Professor Owen*. Thomas Huxley had suggested a system of alternating public and reserve galleries, which could have utilised Owen's plan, placing display cases 'like one long shop window' on the public side, but accessible from the reserve gallery. Waterhouse's arrangement followed this principle, but the keepers complained that they could not arrange the specimens from the back. His namesake, the keeper of fossils, also objected to the two rows of columns in the 50ft-wide front galleries, alleging that if cases were placed between them and the walls, a series of bays would be created 'in which people would congregate and hang about and prevent Students proceeding with their work while the Evil disposed would be able to lurk about unnoticed until they had the opportunity of stealing Specimens'. But after discussions with the architect, the keepers waived these objections. PRO, Work 17/16/2, ff. 157–9, 161 (Waterhouse to FCW, 1 and 9 Feb. 1871); *Survey*, XXXVIII, 208, citing BL, Add. MS 38995, ff. 400–4, T.H. Huxley to Layard.

99 Galton justifiably pointed out that the demand for different layouts arose from keepers who 'may not be alive when the building is finished and the successors may each be dissatisfied'. It was the trustees' function to determine the plan. PRO, Work 17/16/2, ff. 177–8, 25 Feb. 1871.

100 PRO, Work 2/36, pp. 310–14 (Galton's report, 4 Apr. 1871).

101 PRO, Work 17/16/2, ff. 177–8 (FCW to Treasury, 24 Feb.), 196 (Treasury to FCW, 2 May 1871).

102 Ibid., f. 207.

103 Particularly a transverse gallery parallel to the front galleries, and closing openings between the public and reserve galleries. Cp. ibid., f. 161.

104 See p. 232.

105 VAM, Cole Diary, 14, 15, 20 Feb. 1872.

106 The earliest date on the contract drawings, PRO, Work 33/1582–1648, appears to be 21 Jan. 1872 (33/1589).

107 PRO, Work 17/16/2, f. 70, 12 Aug. 1872.

108 PRO, Work 17/16/3, ff. 49, 54, 56, 62, 64, 81. Alterations included omitting hoop-iron bond courses below second floor level, substituting Portland stone for Craigleith and granite, reducing wainscot flooring to 7/8-inch thickness, and reducing the cost of tile paving for the central hall, ibid., f. 70.

109 PRO, Work 17/16/3, ff. 1, 9 (27 Nov., 27 Dec. 1871).

110 The English terracotta manufacturers were Gibbs & Canning (Tamworth), Blashfield (Stamford), Blanchard (Blackfriars), Doulton (Lambeth), and Pulham (Broxbourne). Two German firms were also considered, Villeroy & Boch (Mitloch on Soar), and March (Charlottenburg), PRO, Work 17/16/3, f. 9.

111 Ibid., ff. 89–90.

112 PRO, Work 33/1636.

113 PRO, Work 17/16/3, ff. 89–90 (18 Sept.), 111 (5 Dec.), 111v–12 (6 Dec. 1872).

114 Ibid., ff. 99–100 (14 Oct.), 103 (28 Oct.), 106–7 (28 Nov.), 109–10 (5 Dec., Bakers' revised tender), 117 (6 Dec.), 122 (13 Dec. 1872).

115 Ibid., ff. 129, 17 Dec. 1872; 162v, 16 May 1873; 17/17/1, ff. 304–36, 20 July 1881; Work 2/36, pp. 458, 489 (2, 5 May 1871).

116 Ibid., 17/16/3, ff. 181, 196 (22 Oct. 1873, 15 Jan. 1874).

117 PRO, Work 17/17/1, f. 80.

118 Ibid., ff. 58–60 (Bakers to OW, 28 Aug. 1876).

119 Ibid., f. 56, 28 Aug. 1876.

120 R. Owen, *Life of Richard Owen* (2 vols, 1894), II, 52;

121 PRO, Work 17/17/1, ff. 304 ff. (20 July 1881).

122 Ibid., ff. 250, 253.

123 Ibid., ff. 98–9 (27 Oct. 1876, Waterhouse to Hunt, and Hunt's memo.).

124 PRO, Work 2/36, p. 458, 2 May 1871.

125 PRO, Work 30/1589, 1636, 1640, 2131.

126 PRO, Work 17/17/1, ff. 37, 39 (Waterhouse to OW, 3, 11 Aug.), 46 (16 Aug.), 46–8 (Bakers to Waterhouse, 22 Aug. 1876).

127 Ibid., ff. 112–13 (Waterhouse to OW, 13 Feb. 1879).

128 Ibid., ff. 115 (Bakers to OW, 18 Feb.), 123–4 (Waterhouse to Bakers, 6 Mar.), 125–6 (Waterhouse to OW, 6 Mar.), 127–8 (Waterhouse's clerk to OW, 7 Mar.), 134, (OW memo. 14 Mar.), 140 (Hunt's minute, 10 Mar. 1879).

129 Ibid., ff. 146 (Waterhouse to Bakers), 148 (Bakers to OW, 9 May), 172 (OW to Bakers, 27 May), 174–89 (indenture, 25 July 1879).

130 *Survey*, XXXVIII, ch. v; E.A. Bowring, 'South Kensington', *Nineteenth Century* (June 1877), 576–7.

131 *Survey*, XXXVIII, 79–81, 98–100.

132 Ibid., 100, citing PRO, Ed. 28/6, no. 80.

133 Ibid., 100.

134 J. Physick, *The Victoria and Albert Museum* (1982), 108. Building work by Smith on the range totalled about £8800, ibid.

135 Ibid., 111.

136 Ibid., 161–6; *Survey*, XXXVIII, 108.

137 BL, Add. MS 44617, ff. 41–4.

138 *Survey*, XXXVIII, 116.

139 Physick, 172–5.

140 *Survey*, XXXVIII, 116–17; Physick, 177–83.

141 See p. 185.

142 *Survey*, XXXVIII, 119. The Treasury's obduracy over the South Kensington Museum is evidenced in Chilston Papers, C5/65.

143 *PP* 1897 (223) XII, *1st Report of S.C. on Museums of the Science and Art Department*, p. iii.

144 *PP* 1897 (341) XII, *2nd Report.*

145 *PP* 1898 (175) XI, 1st report S.C. on Museums of the Science and Art Department.

146 See p. 154 above.

147 *PP* 1887 (184) VII, qq. 1027–8.

148 This paragraph is based on PRO, Work 12/88/3.

149 *PP* 1887 (184) VII, q. 1795, 1805–6, 1840–1, 1887, 1912–18.

150 PRO, Work 12/88/3, ff. 1–40. R. Postgate, *Builders' History* (1923), 358–9.

151 PRO, Work 12/88/3, ff. 43–127. The contractor claimed more than £7000 extra, and the final account for Block I was put at £176,662 in 1897.

152 PRO, Work 30/4171, 4187.

153 PRO, T. 1/9057B/12524, T. 1/9185A/15177; Work 12/88/3, ff. 143–56; *PP* 1898 (2) LVIII; 1899 (44) LVII; 1900 (19) LIII. *Appropriation accounts.* The hydrographer, to meet whose views 'much expense was incurred to no purpose in alterations to Block I', then in May 1897 demanded structural alterations in Block II, T. 1/9185A/15177, OW to T., 22 May 1897; Work 30/4186.

154 R.C.K. Ensor, *England 1870–1914*, p. 289.

155 PRO, Work 12/89/1, ff. 1–9; T. 1/9425B/15440, Aug.–Nov. 1899; Chilston Papers, C 6, ff. 170 (FCW to Goschen, Admiralty, 2 Nov. 1899); 195, 298, (FCW to ch. of Exchequer, 24 Jan. 1900, 10 Jan. 1901); C 238/11, Goschen to FCW, 5 Nov. [1899].

156 PRO, T. 1/9185A/15177, no. 8579, 22 May 1897; T. 1/9617A/20505, 14 Dec. 1900; Work 12/89/1, ff. 1–33, memoranda and correspondence July 1899-Jan. 1901; Work 30/4188–91.

157 I.e., *Builder, Building News, Contract Jnl, Times, Standard, D. Chronicle, D. Telegraph.* PRO, Work 12/89/1, f. 41.

158 Ibid., f. 42. Mowlems, contractors for Block II

superstructure bid £20,878, and Holloway Bros, who were to secure the superstructure contract for Block III, £17,880.

159 Lord Selborne, the first lord of the Admiralty, complained to Esher, 'The work on the new building goes on all night . . . It has happened over and over again that I have not been able to get to sleep till nearly 3 owing to the hammering and the noise the men make', Esher Papers, 5/14, no. 95.

160 PRO, Work 12/89/1, 62–7, correspondence between Leemings and Chessums, Jan. 1902.

161 Ibid., 74ff., including 125 pp of printed notes of arbitration proceedings.

162 PRO, Work 12/89/2, ff. 1–21. The highest tender was Nicholas & Co.'s at £118,553.

163 *4PD* XCVII, 551 (H.L. 16 July 1901, Lord Wemyss).

164 PRO, Work 30/3266–86, 4153, 4156–70, 4180–5, 4192–208, 4221–4, 5825–9; *4PD* CLVII, 735–7 (17 May 1906); *4PD* CLXXII, 52–66 (8 Apr. 1907).

165 *PP* 1911 (65, 110, 157) VI, *1st–3rd Reports, Committee of Public Accounts*, q. 879. Large sewers were a perennial cause of delay: the LCC's reconstruction of one under the Western extension of the Royal Courts of Justice seriously delayed work in 1908; and another under the new Board of Agriculture offices (9–11 Whitehall Place) necessitated making changes in the plans, PP, *Appropriation accounts*, 1908/09, 1909/10.

166 Ibid., 1908/9; *4PD* CLVII, 654 (17 May), CLX, 38 (4 July), CLXIII, 427 (25 Oct. 1906); CLXXII, 59, 62 (1 Apr. 1907); CLXXXVII, 735, 761, 768 (2 Apr. 1908).

167 See p. 159. See also *4PD* CLIV, 1256 (NPO); CLXI, 1467, and CLXII, 218 (W.O.).

168 *4PD* CLXVI, 1572 (10 Dec. 1906). See also *Builder*, 25 Apr. 1913, pp. 481–3.

169 *5PD* LVI, 1776. For Taylor's Public Record Office, see PRO, Work 30/2641–754; for Tanner's Land Registry, ibid., 5279–304 and *BN*, 29 Dec. 1905, 9 Feb. 1906, and 13 Dec. 1912; Tanner's Royal Courts of Justice West, PRO, Work 30/4489–94, and *Builder*, 11 July 1908, p. 43; Taylor's Patent Office extensions, PRO, Work 30/2524–77 and *Builder*, 14 Sept. 1895, p. 185, and 9 Apr. 1898, pp. 343–4 (continued after 1903 by Hawkes); Pitcher's Public Trustee Office, PRO, Work 30/4683–700, and *BN*, 2 Aug. 1914, 149ff., and 7 Jan. 1916, pp. 16, 40ff.

170 Although anticipated and exceeded by the Manchester dock warehouses, *Builder*, XCVI (1909), 394 (I owe this reference to Dr Andrew Saint). Plans, PRO, Work 30/4749–67. For Tanner's own account, see *RIBA Jnl*, 3 ser., XVIII, 149–77. A different use of concrete was in a complete fireproofing of the N.G. ceilings by Moss & Son. *PP* 1912–13, VI, q. 454; PRO, Work 17/79.

171 PRO, Work 30/5440–60, 5480–5649. R.J. Allison, the Office architect, had assisted Tanner on the new GPO buildings.

172 *Builder*, 17 April 1914, p. 473.

173 R. Postgate, *Builders' History*, 358–9.

174 *Brit. Arch.*, 28 May (p. 409), 27 Nov. 1891 (p. 397).

175 *PP, Appropriation accounts*; *Brit. Arch.*, 29 May (p. 409), 27 Nov. 1891 (p. 397); P.W. Kingsford, *Builders and Building Workers* (1973), 163–5.

176 *PP, Appropriation accounts*, 1914/15; Kingsford, 171–4. Non-expenditure of £7000 on the Admiralty extension in 1908/09 was ascribed to want of steel, which 'could not be delivered. . . . It is a difficulty that very often occurs', *PP* 1909 (58, 125, 126, 156, 284) VI, *1st–5th Reports, Committee on Public Accounts*, qq. 841, 846.

Envoi

1 *BN*, 16 Aug. 1872, p. 119, citing the *Graphic*.

2 G. Shaw Lefevre, 'Public Works in London', *Nineteenth Century*, XII (1882), 667–86.

3 *3PD* CLXIV, 535 (8 July 1861).

4 E.g. welcoming the Government Offices competition, 7 Oct. 1856, a leading article, noting that the site contemplated covered an immense area and would be costly, declared: 'For our part, however, we should have been disposed to go further. Why not take the whole area comprehended in the magnificent design of Inigo Jones?' After the Commons turned against the competition designs, another leader protested 'most energetically against the adoption of any of those stupendous plans which were exhibited the other day. . . . What do we want with the Hôtel de Ville from Paris on the edge of St James's Park in order that a few hundred clerks may execute their daily tasks?' (12 Aug. 1857).

5 *Builder*, XCVI (1909), 394. (I am grateful to Dr Andrew Saint for this reference.) It was not until 1 Jan. 1916 that LCC regulations on the use of reinforced concrete came into effect, R.H. Harper, *Victorian Building Regulations* (1985), 123.

6 The national product of Great Britain has been calculated (at constant prices) at £494,000,000 in 1851 and £1,948,000,000 in 1901; or £23.7 and £52.5 per head respectively. P. Deane & W.A. Cole, *British Economic Growth* (Cambridge, 1969), 282.

7 P. Greenhalgh, 'Art, Politics and Society at the Franco-British Exhibition of 1908', *Art Hist.*, 8 (1985), 440. Dr Greenhalgh's argument is concerned with the Liberal government and the 1908 exhibition, but it is more widely applicable.

8 Ministry of Public Building and Works, *New Government Office Building in Whitehall* (n.d.), leaflet to accompany an exhibition of a proposed re-development of the Richmond Terrace-Bridge Street site.

9 *Victorian Architecture*, 115.

Bibliography

Manuscript Sources

Belvoir Castle, Leicestershire:
Lord John Manners Papers.

Bodleian Library, Oxford:
Harcourt Papers.
Hughenden [Disraeli] Papers.

British Library, London:
Balfour Papers.
Campbell-Bannerman Papers.
Gladstone Papers.
Iddesleigh [Northcote] Papers.
Layard Papers.
Oriental & India Office Collections, I.O. Surveyor's Reports.

Churchill College, Cambridge:
Esher [Brett] Papers.

Haddo House, Aberdeenshire:
Gordon of Haddo [Shaw Lefevre] Papers.

Hatfield House, Hertfordshire:
Salisbury Papers.

Imperial College London: Archives of the Royal Commission for the Exhibition of 1851.

Kent Record Office, Maidstone. Centre for Kentish Studies:
Chilston [Akers-Douglas] Papers.

Public Record Office, Kew:
Papers of Office of Works, Treasury, and other government departments.

Royal Archives, Windsor Castle.

Royal Institute of British Architects, London:
George Gilbert Scott Papers.

Scottish Record Office, Edinburgh:
Blair Adam [W.P. Adam] Papers.
Wemyss [Elcho] Papers.

Southampton University Archives:
Broadlands [Palmerston and Cowper] Papers.

Victoria and Albert Museum:
Cole Diaries and Correspondence.

Contemporary Newspapers and Periodicals

A.A. Notes (from 1887; as *Architectural Association Journal* from 1905)
Architect (from 1869; as *Architect and Contract Reporter*, 1893–1918)
Architectural Review (from 1896)
Athenaeum
Blackwood's Magazine (from 1824)
British Architect (from 1874)

Builder (from 1842)
Building News (from 1856; as *Land and Building News* 1855)
Building World (1876–94)
Civil Engineer and Architect's Journal, 1837–68
Civil Service Gazette (from 1853)
Civil Service Times 1886–92
Civilian (from 1869)
Companion to the Almanac
Contemporary Review (from 1866)
Cornhill Magazine (from 1860)
Country Life (from 1897)
Ecclesiologist (1841, new series from 1845)
Edinburgh Review (from 1802)
Fortnightly Review (from 1865)
Fraser's Magazine
Gentleman's Magazine
Graphic (from 1869)
Illustrated London News (from 1842)
L'Illustration (from 1843)
Law Journal
Macmillan's Magazine (from 1859)
National Review 1855–64
National Review (from 1883)
Nineteenth Century (from 1877)
Observer
Pall Mall Gazette
Quarterly Review (from 1824)
Royal Institute of British Architects, Journal (from 1894)
Royal Institute of British Architects, Sessional Papers
Royal Institute of British Architects, Transactions, 1842–84. *New series*, 1885–92. (From 1894, combined with *Proceedings* as *Journal*).
Saturday Review (from 1855)
Solicitors' Journal
Spectator (from 1828)
The Times
Westminster Review (from 1824)

Books and Pamphlets

The place of publication is London, unless otherwise indicated.

Amery, C., *A Celebration of Art and Architecture* (1992).
Ames, W., *Prince Albert and Victorian Taste* (1967).
Amory, M., (ed.) *Letters of Evelyn Waugh* (1980).
Anderson, Olive, *A Liberal State at War* (1967).
Anon. ('A Practical Man'), *Remarks on the Designs proposed for the New Government Offices* (1857).
Anon., *The National Gallery difficulties solved at a Cost of Eighty Thousand instead of a Million Pounds* (1857).
Anon., *Arguments for the removal of the Courts of Law and Equity from Westminster . . .* (1841).

Anon., [?H. Gem], *Arguments for the removal of the Courts of Law and Equity from Westminster to Lincoln's Inn Fields being a response of a pamphlet entitled Facts for the consideration of Parliament, before the final adoption of a plan perpetuating the Courts of Law on a site injurious and costly to the suitor* (1841).
Anon., *Classic or Pseudo-Gothic: a reply to a pamphlet entitled 'Shall Gothic Architecture be denied fair play?'*.
Anon., *Designs for the Public Offices* (H.G. Clarke & Co., 1857).
Anon., *L'Hotel de Ville de Paris* (Paris, n.d.).
Anon., *Observations in favour of the Concentration of the Courts of Justice and all the requisite offices in the Vicinity of the Inns of Court and on the means of defraying the expense* (1858).
Anon., *Shall Gothic Architecture be denied fair play? Thoughts suggested by reading a pamphlet entitled 'Remarks on a national Style, in reference to the proposed Foreign Office'*.
Archer, J.H.G, ed., *Art and architecture in Victorian Manchester* (Manchester, 1985).
Ashley, E., *Life of . . . Palmerston* (1876).
Baedeker, K., *London and its Environs* (1905).
Baedeker, K., *Munich and its Environs* (1956).
Barker, F., & Hyde, R., *London As it might have been* (1982).
Barrington, E.I., *Servant of All: Pages from the . . . life of my father James Wilson*, 1 (1927).
Barry, E.M., *Lectures on Architecture*, Ed. with introductory memoir by Alfred Barry (1881).
Bassin, Joan, *Architectural Competitions in Nineteenth-Century England* (Ann Arbor, Mich., 1984).
Beier, A.L., & Finlay, R., eds, *London 1500–1700* (1986).
Belcher, J., *Late Renaissance Architecture in England* (1901).
Bell, Q., *Schools of Design* (1963).
Benson, A.C., & Esher, Viscount, eds, *Letters of Queen Victoria, 1837–1861* (3 vols., 1908).
[Beresford Hope, A.J.B.], *The New Palaces of Administration: An Earnest Appeal to the Competitors, the Public, and the Committee*, by a Cambridge Man (Cambridge, [1857]).
Beresford Hope, A.J.B., *The Expense of the Government and of Mr Beresford Hope's Plan of Public Offices Compared* (1857).
Beresford Hope, A.J.B., *Public Offices and Metropolitan Improvements* (1857).
Beresford Hope, A.J.B., *The English Cathedral of the Nineteenth Century* (1861).
Beresford Hope, A.J.B., *The Condition and Prospects of Architectural Art* (1863).
Biver, M.-L., *Le Paris de Napoléon* (Paris, 1963).

Blake, R., *Disraeli* (1966).

Blau, Eve, *Ruskinian Gothic: the architecture of Deane and Woodward 1845–1861* (Princeton, N.J., 1982).

Boase, F., *Modern English Biography* (6 vols., Truro, 1892–1921).

Booker, J., *Temples of Mammon: the Architecture of Banking* (Edinburgh, 1990).

Brandon, R., *Report submitted with Raphael Brandon's Design* (1867).

Brett, M.V., ed., *Journals and Letters of Reginald, Viscount Esher* (3 vols., 1934).

Briggs, Sir J.H. (ed. Lady Briggs), *Naval Administrations 1827 to 1892: the experience of 65 years* (1897).

Briggs, A., *Victorian Cities* (1963).

Brooks, M.W., *John Ruskin and Victorian Architecture* (1989).

Brown, Lucy, *Victorian News and Newspapers* (Oxford, 1985).

Brownlee, D.B., *The Law Courts: the Architecture of George Edmund Street* (Cambridge, Mass., & London, 1984).

Bruce, Hon. W.N., ed., *Sir A. Henry Layard . . . Autobiography and letters* (2 vols., 1903).

Buckle, G.E., ed., *The Letters of Queen Victoria, 2nd ser., 1862–1878* (1926).

Buffévent, Beatrice de, ed., *Centenaire de la Réconstruction de l'Hotel de Ville de Paris 1882–1982* (Paris, 1982).

Burges, W., *Report to the Courts of Justice Commission* (1867).

Burgess, J., *John Burns: the Rise and Progress of a Right Honourable* (Glasgow, 1911).

Burn, W.L., *The Age of Equipoise* (1964).

Butler, D. & G., *British Political Facts 1900–1985* (6th edn, 1986).

Butler, E.M., ed., *A Regency Visitor: the English Tour of Prince Pückler-Muskau . . . 1826–1828* (1957).

Carswell, J., *The Civil Servant and His World* (1966).

Cawston, A., *Comprehensive Scheme for Street Improvements in London* (1893).

Challis, C.E., ed., *New History of the Royal Mint* (Cambridge, 1992).

Chester, Sir N., *The English Administrative System 1780–1870* (1981).

Childers, S., *Life and Correspondence of H.C.E. Childers* (2 vols., 1901).

Chilston, Viscount, *Chief Whip: the Political Life and Times of Aretas Akers-Douglas* (1961).

Chilston, Viscount, *W.H. Smith* (1965).

Clark, K., *The Gothic Revival* (2nd edn 1950).

Clarke, Sir E., *The Story of My Life* (1918).

Clunn, H.P., *The Face of London: the Record of a Capital's Changes and Developments* (1932).

Cohen, Emmeline W., *Growth of the British Civil Service 1780–1939* (1941).

Collins, P., *Architectural Judgement* (1971).

Collins, P., *Changing Ideals in Modern Architecture 1750–1950* (1965).

Collins, P., *Concrete: The Vision of a New Architecture* (1959).

Colvin, H.M., *Biographical Dictionary of British Architects 1600–1840* (1978).

Cook, C., & Keith, B., *British Historical Facts 1830–1900* (1975).

Crook, J.M., & Port, M.H., *History of the King's Works*, VI (1973).

Crook, J.M., *The British Museum: a case-study in architectural politics* (Harmondsworth, 1972).

Crook, J.M., *William Burges and the High Victorian Dream* (1981).

Cunningham, C., *Victorian and Edwardian Town Halls* (1981).

Daunton, M.J., *Royal Mail: the Post Office since 1840* (1985).

Darby, M., *John Pollard Seddon* (1983).

David, E., ed., *Inside Asquith's Cabinet: from the Diaries of Charles Hobhouse* (1977).

Davis, J., *Reforming London: the London Government Problem 1855–1900* (Oxford, 1988).

Defoe, D., *A Tour through England and Wales* (3 vols., 1724–6; Everyman edn, 1928).

Degrégny, J., *Londres: Croquis réalistes* (Paris, 1888).

Dicey, A.V., *Law and Opinion in England* (1905).

Dickens, C., *Bleak House* (1852–3).

Dixon, R., & Muthesius, S., *Victorian Architecture* (1978).

Dod's Parliamentary Companion, 1861.

Earle, P., *Making of the English Middle Class* (1989).

Earle, Sir L., *Turn over the Page* (1935).

Eastlake, C.L., *History of the Gothic Revival* (1872).

Edwards, P.J., *History of London Street Improvements 1855–1897* (1898).

Ellis, S.M., ed., *Letters of Sir William Hardman* (1925).

Emmerson, Sir H., *Ministry of Works* (1956).

Ensor, R.C.K., *England 1870–1914* (Oxford, 1936).

Farr, D., *English Art 1870–1940* (Oxford, 1978).

Fawcett, Jane, ed., *Seven Victorian Architects* (1976).

Fergusson, J., *Observations on the British Museum, National Gallery, and National Record Office, with suggestions for their improvement* (1849).

Fergusson, J., *A History of the Modern Styles of Architecture* (1862).

Fergusson, J., *Handbook of Architecture* (1855).

Fergusson, J., *History of the Modern Styles of Architecture* (1862, revised 1873).

Ferriday, P. (ed.), *Victorian Architecture* (1963).

Fiddes, Sir G.V., *The Dominions and Colonial Offices* (1926).

Firth, J.F.B., *Municipal London* (1876).

Firth, J.F.B., *Reform of London Government and of City Guilds* (1888).

Firth, J.L.B., *The Coal and Wine Dues: the History of the London Coal Tax and Arguments for and against Its Renewal* (1886).

Fellows, R.A., *Sir Reginald Blomfield: an Edwardian Architect* (1985).

Fletcher, H.R., *The Story of the Royal Horticultural Society 1804–1968* (1969).

Floud, Sir F., *Ministry of Agriculture and Fisheries* (1927).

Foot, M.R.D., ed., *Gladstone Diaries* I & II (1968, Oxford).

Foot, M.R.D., & Matthew, H.C.G., eds, *Gladstone Diaries*, III & IV (1978, Oxford).

Fox, Celina, ed., *London World City 1800–1840* (New Haven & London, 1992).

Freeman, E.A., *History of Architecture* (1849).

Freeman-Mitford, A.B., Lord Redesdale, *Memories* (1915).

Fulford, R., ed., *Dearest Mama* (1968).

Fulton, Lord, *The Civil Service. Vol. 4: Factual Statistical and Explanatory Papers. Evidence submitted to a Committee under the Chairmanship of Lord Fulton 1966–68* (1968).

Gabriel, A., *Guide de l'Architecture des Monuments de Paris/Guide to the Architecture of Monuments in Paris* (Paris, 1991).

Gardiner, A.G., *Life of Sir William Harcourt* (2 vols., 1923).

Garling, H.B., *Suggestions for a Site for the proposed New War Office and Admiralty Buildings* (?1884).

Garrigan, K.O., *Ruskin on Architecture: his Thought and Influence* (1973).

Gibbs, V., *et al.*, eds., G.E. C[ockayne]., *The Complete Peerage* (new edn, 13 vols., 1910–59).

Gilbert, W.S., *The Happy Land* (1873).

Girouard, M., *Alfred Waterhouse and the Natural History Museum* (New Haven & London, 1981).

Gladstone Diaries, see Foot, M.R.D, and Matthew, H.C.G.

Gomme, A., & Walker, D., *Architecture of Glasgow* (rev. edn, 1987).

Gooch, G.P., ed., *Later Correspondence of Lord John Russell* (1925).

Goodhart-Rendel, H.S., *English Architecture since the Regency* (1953).

Gordon, H., *The War Office* (1935).

Gotch, J.A., ed., *Growth and Work of the RIBA* (1934).

Gray, A.S., *Edwardian Architecture* (1988 edn).

Greenhalgh, P., *Ephemeral Vistas: the 'Expositions Universelles', Great Exhibitions and World's Fairs 1851–1939* (Manchester, 1988).

Gregory, Lady, ed., *Sir William Gregory KCMG, . . . An Autobiography* (1894).

Guedalla, P., ed., *Gladstone and Palmerston* (1928).

Guillemard, Sir L., *Trivial Fond Records* (1937).

Hall, H.H., *The Colonial Office* (1937).

Hamer, W.S., *The British Army: civil-military relations, 1885–1905* (Oxford, 1970).

Hamilton, Lord George, *Parliamentary Reminiscences and Reflections, 1868–1906* (2 vols., 1917, 1922).

Hamon-Jugnet, M., & Oudin-Doglioni, C., *Le Quai d'Orsay* (Paris, 1991).

Harcourt Williams, R., ed., *Salisbury-Balfour Correspondence 1869–1892* (Herts Rec. Soc., 1988).

Harding, H., *The Patent Office Centenary* (1953).

Harper, R.H., *Victorian Architectural Competitions* (1983).

Hautecoeur, L., *Histoire du Louvre: le Château, le Palais, le Musée, des origines à nos jours (1200–1928)* (Paris, 1928).

Heath, Sir T.L., *The Treasury* (1927).

Hersey, G.L., *High Victorian Gothic: a study in associationism* (Baltimore, Md, 1972).

Hertslet, Sir E., *Recollections of the Old Foreign Office* (1901).

Hitchcock, H.-R., *Architecture: Nineteenth and Twentieth Centuries* (Harmondsworth, 1958; pb edn, 1971).

Hobhouse, Hermione, *Lost London: a century of Demolition and Decay* (1971).

Hobhouse, Hermione, *History of Regent Street* (1975).

Holmes, Sir C., & Collins Baker, C.H., *Making of the National Gallery 1824–1924* (1924).

Hutchinson, H.G., ed., *Private Diaries of Rt Hon. Sir Algernon West* (1922).

Hutchinson, S.C., *History of the Royal Academy* (2nd edn, 1968).

Imray, Jean, *The Mercers' Hall* (1991).

Inc. Law Soc., *Observations on the Proposed Concen-*

tration of the Courts of Justice . . . (1859).

Institute of Civil Engineers, *Brief History of the Institute of Civil Engineers* (1928).

Jackson, B.H., ed., *Recollections of Thomas Graham Jackson* (1950).

James, Henry, *English Hours* (1905; pb edn, 1981, Oxford).

Jenkins, B., *Sir William Gregory of Coole: the Biography of an Anglo-Irishman* (Gerrards Cross, 1986).

Jenkins, T.A., ed., *Parliamentary Diaries of Sir John Trelawney, 1858–1865* (Camden 4th ser., 40, 1990).

Johnson, Nancy E., ed., *Diary of Gathorne Hardy, later Lord Cranbrook, 1866–1892: Political Selections* (1981).

Jones, R., *The Nineteenth Century Foreign Office: an Administrative History* (1971).

Kaye, B., *Development of the Architectural Profession* (1960).

Kent, W.R.G., *John Burns: Labour's Lost Leader* (1950).

Kenyon, Sir F., *The Buildings of the British Museum* (1914).

Kerr, R., ed., J. Fergusson, *History of the Modern Styles of Architecture* (3rd edn, 1891).

Kilbracken, Lord, *Reminiscences of Lord Kilbracken* (1931).

King, A.D., ed., *Buildings and Society* (1980).

Kingsford, P.W., *Builders and Building Workers* (1973).

Koss, S.E., *Rise and Fall of the Political Press in Britain. I: The Nineteenth Century* (1981).

Krey, G.S. De, *A Fractured Society* (Oxford, 1985).

Law, H.W., & I., *The Book of the Beresford Hopes* (1925).

Layard, Sir A.H., see Bruce, W.N.

LCC [L. Gomme], *Opening of Kingsway and Aldwych* (1905).

Leeds, W.H., *Public Buildings of London* (2 vols., 1838).

Lees-Milne, J., *The Enigmatic Edwardian* (1986).

Linstrum, D., *West Yorkshire: Architects and Architecture* (1978).

Llewellyn Smith, Sir H., *The Board of Trade* (1928).

Lockwood, H.F., *Report on a design for the Concentration of the Law Courts* (1867).

London Topographical Society, *A to Z of Regency London* (1985).

London Topographical Society, *A to Z of Victorian London* (1987).

MacDonagh, O., *Pattern of Government Growth* (1961).

Mace, Angela, *Royal Institute of British Architects: a Guide to its Archive and History* (1986).

MacLeod, R., *Style and Society: Architectural Ideology in Britain 1835–1914* (1971).

Mackenzie, J.M., ed., *Imperialism and Popular Culture* (1986).

Mallet, B., *British Budgets 1887–88 to 1912–13* (1913).

Mallet, Sir C., *Herbert Gladstone: a Memoir* (1932).

Mallock, W.H., *The New Republic* (1877; new edn 1879, reprinted Leicester, 1975).

Malmesbury, Lord, *Memoirs of an ex-Minister* (1884).

Marek, G.R., *The Eagles Die* (1975).

Matthew, H.C.G., ed., *Gladstone Diaries*, v–xi (1978–1990, Oxford); see also Foot, M.R.D.

McWilliam, C., *Lothian* (Harmondsworth, 1978).

Megarry, Sir R., *Inns Ancient and Modern* (1972).

Metcalf, Priscilla, *Victorian London* (1972).

Miller, E., *Prince of Librarians: the Life and Times of Antonio Panizzi of the British Museum* (1967).

Miller, E., *That Noble Cabinet: a History of the British Museum* (1973).

Monypenny, W.F., & Buckle, G.E., *Life of Benjamin Disraeli, Earl of Beaconsfield* (2 vols., rev. edn, 1929).

Morley, J., *Life of William Ewart Gladstone* (1903).

Murray, Lady, *Making of a Civil Servant: Sir Oswyn Murray . . . Secretary of the Admiralty 1917–36* (1940).

Muthesius, S., *The High Victorian Movement in Architecture 1850–1870* (1972).

Nash, T.A., *Life of Richard Lord Westbury*, 2 vols (1888).

Nevill, Lady Dorothy, *My Own Times* (1912).

Nevill, R., ed., *Reminiscences of Lady Dorothy Nevill* (1906).

Offer, A., *Property and Politics 1870–1914: Landownership, Law, Ideology and Urban Development in England* (Cambridge, 1981).

Olsen, D.J., *Growth of Victorian London* (1976).

Olsen, D.J., *The City as a Work of Art* (New Haven & London, 1986).

Olsen, D.J., *Town Planning in London* (New Haven & London, 1964).

Oman, Carola, *An Oxford Childhood* (1976).

Owen, D., *Government of Victorian London 1855–1889* (Cambridge, Mass., & London, 1982).

Owen, *Life of Richard Owen* (2 vols., 1894).

Owen, R., *On the extent and aims of a national museum of natural history* (1862).

Oxford and Asquith, Earl of, *Memories and Reflections 1852–1927* (1928).

Papworth, W., ed., *Gwilt's Encyclopaedia of Architecture* (1899 edn).

Parkinson, Sir C., *The Colonial Office from within 1909–1945* (1947).

Parris, H., *Constitutional Bureaucracy* (1969).

Peacock, A.T., & Wiseman, J., *Growth of Public Expenditure in the United Kingdom* (1961).

Pellew, Jill, *The Home Office 1848–1914* (1982).

Pevsner, N., *Buildings of England, London except the Cities of London and Westminster* (Harmondsworth, 1952).

Pevsner, N., *Buildings of England, London I, The Cities of London and Westminster* (3rd edn revised by B. Cherry, Harmondsworth, 1973).

Pevsner, N., *Buildings of England, Worcestershire* (1968).

Physick, J., & Darby, M., *'Marble Halls'* (1973).

Physick, J., *The Victoria and Albert Museum: the history of its building* (1982).

Physick, J., *The Wellington Monument* (1970).

Port, M.H., ed., *The Houses of Parliament* (1976).

Post Office London Directory for 1897.

Postgate, R., *Builders' History* (1923).

Powell, C.G., *Economic History of the British Building Industry 1815–1979* (1980).

[Pückler-Muskau, H.L.H. von], *Tour in Germany, Holland, and England, in the Years 1826, 1827, & 1828 . . . by A German Prince* (4 vols., 1832).

Pugin, A.W.N., *Contrasts* (1836, 1841).

Pugin, A.W.N., *True Principles of Pointed, or Christian Architecture* (1841).

Quiney, A., *John Loughborough Pearson* (New Haven & London, 1979).

Ramm, Agatha, *Political Correspondence of Mr Gladstone and Lord Granville* (4 vols., London, 1952, & Oxford, 1962).

Reader, W.J., *Professional Men: the Rise of the Professional Classes in Nineteenth-Century England* (1966).

Redesdale, Lord, (ed. E. Gosse) *Further Memories* (1917).

Redesdale, Lord, *Memories* (1915).

Reports of the Royal Commission for the 1851 Exhibition.

Rhodes James, R., *Rosebery* (1963).

RIBA *Drawings Coll. Catalogue: the Scott Family*, ed. J. Heseltine (Amersham, 1981).

Robins, E.C., *Site of the New Admiralty and War Offices, Whitehall: a Letter to the Earl of Morley, First Commissioner of Works* (1886).

Robinson, J.M., *The Wyatts: an Architectural Dynasty* (Oxford, 1979).

Robinson, *The Parks, Promenades, and Gardens of Paris* (1869).

Roseveare, H., *The Treasury: the Evolution of a British Institution* (1969).

Royal Mint, 12th Annual Report.

Ruffhead, A.G., 'Office of Metropolitan Buildings, London, 1840–1855', M. Phil. thesis, Univ. of London, 1973.

Ruskin, J., *The Seven Lamps of Architecture* (1849).

Sadler, *Edward Wilkins Field: a Memorial Sketch* (1872).

Saint, A., *Richard Norman Shaw* (New Haven & London, 1976).

Saint, A., *The Image of the Architect* (New Haven & London, 1982).

Sainty, J., *Office-holders in modern Britain. I: Treasury officials* (1972).

Saunders, Ann, *Regent's Park* (1969).

Scott, G.G., *Explanatory Remarks on the Designs for the New Foreign Office now laid before the House of Commons* (n.d.).

Scott, G.G., *Personal and Professional Recollections* (1878).

Scott, G.G., *Remarks on Secular and Domestic Architecture, Present and Future* (1857).

Scott, G.G., *Remarks on the Designs for the New Law Courts* (1867).

Scott, Sir Francis, *Shall the New Foreign Office be Gothic or Classic? A plea for the former: Addressed to the Members of the House of Commons* (7 May 1860).

Scott, Geoffrey, *The Architecture of Humanism* (1914, pb edn 1961).

Seddon, J.P., *New Law Courts Description of Design* (1867).

Selborne, Lord, *Memorials Pt II: Personal and Political 1865–1895*.

Semmel, B., *Imperialism and Social Reform* (1968 edn, Garden City, N.Y.).

Service, A., *Edwardian Architecture and its Origins* (1975).

Service, A., *Edwardian Architecture: a Handbook to Building Design in Britain 1890–1914* (1977).

Service, A., *London 1900* (1979).

Seton, Sir M.C.C., *The India Office* (1926).

Seymour, C., *Electoral Reform in England and Wales* (1915).

Shannon, R., *Crisis of Imperialism* (St Albans, 1976).

Shannon, R., *Gladstone*, I (1982).

Shepherd, T.H., & J. Elmes, *Metropolitan Improve-*

ments; or London, in the nineteenth century (1827).

Sheppard, F., *London 1808–1870: the Infernal Wen* (1971).

Sheppard, F., *Treasury of London's Past* (1991).

Smirke, Sydney, *Suggestions for the Architectural Improvement of the Western Part of London* (1834).

Smith, Adam, *The Wealth of Nations* (1950 edn).

Soane, J., *Designs for Public and Private Buildings* (1828).

Speaight, F.W., *The Marble Arch: a Suggestion by a Citizen of London* (1905).

Speaight, F.W., *Horse Guards' Parade: a Suggested Improvement* (1909).

Stamp, G., *London 1900 (Architectural Design Profiles 13)* (1978).

Stamp, G., & Amery, C. *Victorian Buildings of London 1837–1887.*

Steegman, J., *Consort of Taste 1830–1870* (1950).

Stenton, M., ed., *Who's Who of British Members of Parliament* (4 vols., 1976).

Stow, J., *Survey of London* (1603; ed. C.L. Kingsford, Oxford, 1971).

Street, A.E., *Memoir of George Edmund Street, R.A.*

Street, G.E., *Explanation and Illustrations of His Design for the Proposed New Courts of Justice* (1867).

Street, G.E., *Some Remarks in Explanation of his Designs for . . . the National Gallery* (1867).

Summerson, J., *Georgian London* (new edn, 1988).

Summerson, J., *The London Building World of the 1860s* (1973).

Summerson, J., *Life and Works of John Nash Architect* (1980).

Summerson, J., *Victorian Architecture: Four Studies in Evaluation* (New York & London, 1970).

Survey of London (various general editors):

   XIII, St Margaret Westminster. Part II: Neighbourhood of Whitehall, I (1930).

   XIV, St Margaret Westminster. Part III: Neighbourhood of Whitehall, II (1931).

   XXIX, XXX, St James Westminster. Part I: South of Piccadilly (1960).

   XXXI, XXXII, St James Westminster. Part II: North of Piccadilly (1963).

   XXXVIII, The Museums Area of South Kensington and Westminster (1975).

Survey of London, Monograph 17, *County Hall* (1991).

Sutcliffe, A., *Autumn of Central Paris* (1970).

Sutherland, Gillian, *Studies in the Growth of Nineteenth Century Government* (1970).

Sykes, C., *Evelyn Waugh* (1975).

Incorporated Law Society, *The New Law Courts. Statement by the Council . . . on the subject of the suggested change of site* (Feb. 1869).

Thornbury, W., & Walford, E., *Old and New London* [6 vols., 2nd edn, 1897].

Thorne, R.G., ed., *The House of Commons 1790–1820* (1986).

Thornton, A.P., *The Imperial Idea and its Enemies* (1959).

Tilley, J., & Gaselee, S., *The Foreign Office* (1933).

Toplis, I., *The Foreign Office: an architectural history* (1987).

Trench, F.W., *Collection of Papers relating to the Thames Quay* (1827).

Trench, F.W., *Letter from Sir Frederick Trench to Viscount Duncannon, First Commissioner of Woods and Forests* (1841).

Triggs, H.I., *Town Planning Past, Present and Possi-* *ble* (1909).

Trollope, A., *The Small House at Allington* (1864).

Trollope, A., *The Three Clerks* (1858).

Troup, Sir E., *The Home Office* (1925).

Tyack, G., *Sir James Pennethorne and the making of Victorian London* (Cambridge, 1992).

Veith, R.H., *Life of Lt-General The Hon. Sir Andrew Clarke* (1905).

Verner, W., assisted by Parker, E.D., *Military Life of H.R.H. George, Duke of Cambridge* (2 vols., 1905).

Vincent, J., ed., *Crawford Papers* (Manchester, 1984).

Vincent, J., ed., *Disraeli, Derby and the Conservative Party: Journals and Memorials of Edward Henry, Lord Stanley 1849–1869* (Hassocks, 1978).

Viollet-le-Duc, E.-E., *Lectures on Architecture*, transl. B. Bucknall (1881).

Waller, P.J., *Town, City, and Nation* (1983).

Walpole, S., *History of 25 Years, I* (1904).

Waterfield, Giles, ed., *Palaces of Art* (1991).

Waterfield, Gordon, *Layard of Nineveh* (1963).

Waterhouse, A., *Report on New Law Courts design* (1867).

Weinreb, B., & Hibbert, C., *London Encyclopaedia* (1983).

Wemyss, Earl of, *The New War Office: What it is to Be: What Still Might Be* (1899).

West, Sir A., *Contemporary Portraits* (1920).

Whibley, C., *Lord John Manners and His Friends* (2 vols., 1925).

Whitaker's Almanac, 1908.

White, W.H., *Architecture and Public Buildings* (1884).

White, W.H., *A Protest against the Amended Design for the Proposed Admiralty and War Offices* (1885).

Wilson, C. St John, *Architectural Reflections* (1992).

Wohl, A., *The Eternal Slum: Housing and Social Policy in Victorian London* (1977).

Woodward, E.L., *The Age of Reform, 1815–1870* (Oxford, 1938).

Working conditions in the Civil Service: Report by a study group appointed by H.M. Treasury (1947).

Wormell, Deborah, *Sir John Seeley and the Uses of History* (1980).

Wright, M., *Treasury Control of the Civil Service* (Oxford, 1969).

Young, K., and Garside, Patricia L., *Metropolitan London. Politics and Urban Change 1837–1981* (1982).

Zanten, D. Van, *Designing Paris* (Cambridge, Mass., & London, 1987).

Zetland, Marquis of, ed., *Letters of Disraeli to Lady Bradford and Lady Chesterfield* (1929).

Articles

Anderson, Sir R., 'The Lighter Side of my Official Life'. *Blackwood's Mag.*, Nov. 1909, p. 606ff.

Anon., 'The National Gallery Difficulty Solved', *Cornhill Magazine*, I (1860).

Anon. 'The Foreign Office: Classic or Gothic', *National Review* X (1860), 24–52.

Archer, J.H.G., 'A Classic of its Age', in J.H.G. Archer (ed.) *Art and Architecture in Victorian Manchester* (Manchester, 1985), 126–61.

[Atkinson, J.B.], 'Classic or Gothic. The Battle of the Styles', *Blackwood's Magazine*, XCI (1862), 283–301.

Briggs, A., 'London: the World City', in Briggs, A., *Victorian Cities* (1963).

Brown, K.D., 'London and the Historical Reputation of John Burns', *London Journal*, 2 (1976), 226–38.

Brownlee, D.B., 'That "regular mongrel affair": G.G. Scott's design for government offices', *Arch. Hist.*, 28 (1985).

Cannadine, D., 'Context, Performance and Meaning of Ritual', in Hobsbawm, E., & Ranger, T., eds., *The Invention of Tradition* (Cambridge, 1983).

[Cole, H.], 'Public Galleries and irresponsible boards', *Edinburgh Review*, CXXIII (1866), 57–82.

Conybeare, H., 'The Future of London's Architecture', *Fortnightly Review*, VIII (1867), 501–17.

Cooney, E.W., 'Origins of the Victorian Master Builders', *Economic History Review*, 2 ser., VIII (1955), 167–176.

Cooney, E.W., 'Organisation of building in England in the 19th century', *Architectural Research and Teaching*, I (1970), 46–52.

Darby, E. and M., 'The Nation's Memorial to Victoria', *Country Life*, CLXIV (1978), 1647–50.

Duffy, F., 'Office buildings and organisational change', in A.D. King (ed.) *Buildings and Society* (1980), 255–80.

Dyos, H.J., & Reeder, D.A., 'Slums and Suburbs', *Victorian City* (1973), ed. H.J. Dyos & M. Wolff.

[Emmett, J.T.], 'The State of English Architecture', *Quarterly Review*, CXXXII (1872), 295–335.

[Emmett, J.T.], 'The Hope of English Architecture', *Quarterly Review*, CXXXVII (1874), 354–88.

[Emmett, J.T.], 'Architecture: a business, a profession or an art?', *Quarterly Review*, CLXXVI (1893), 40–72.

Escott, T.H.S., 'Bernal Osborne', *Fortnightly Review*, XLII (1884), 535–43.

Fergusson, J., 'The New Law Courts', *Macmillan's Magazine*, XXV (1872), 250–6.

Fraser, Maxwell, 'Sir Benjamin Hall in Parliament in the 1850's', *Nat. Library of Wales Jnl*, XV (1967–8), 310–24, 389–404.

Freeman, E.A. 'The Foreign Office – Gothic or Classic', *National Review*, X (Jan. 1860), 48.

Garside, Patricia, 'Representing the Metropolis – The Changing Relationship between London and the Press, 1870–1939', *London Jnl*, 16 (1991).

Garside, Patricia, 'The Development of London: A Classified List of Theses, 1908–1977', *Guildhall Studies in London History*, 3 (1978), 175–94.

Goodhart-Rendel, H.S., 'Brompton, London's Art Quarter', *RIBA Jnl*, Jan. 1956.

Greenhalgh, P., 'Art, politics and society at the Franco-British Exhibition of 1908', *Art History* 8 (1985), 434–52.

Griffin, 'An Imperial City', *Pall Mall Mag.*, I (1893), 668.

Griffiths, 'The War Office Past Present and to Come', *Fortnightly Rev.*, LXXIX (1903), 665–78.

Hamerton, P.G., 'The Housing of the National Art Treasures', *Fortnightly Review*, II (1865), 90–102.

Handley-Read, L., 'Legacy of a Vanished Empire: The Design of the India Office', *Country Life*, CXLVIII (1970), 110–12.

Harcourt, Freda, 'The Queen, the Sultan and the

Viceroy: A Victorian State Occasion', *London Jnl*, 5 (1979), 35ff.

Hardie, 'Hist. of the Rolls House and Chapel', *Middlesex & Herts. Notes & Queries*, II (1896), 49–68.

Harper, C.G., 'The Government and London Architecture', *Fortnightly Review*, LXXII (1899), 523–32.

Harrison, F., 'London Improvements', *New Review* 7 (1892), 414–21.

Hitchcock, H.-R., 'High Victorian Gothic', *Victorian Studies*, I (1957), 47–71.

Hobhouse, Hermione, 'Philip and Philip Charles Hardwick', in J. Fawcett (ed.), *Seven Victorian Architects* (1976).

[Hope, A.J.B.], 'The South Kensington Museum', *Quarterly Review*, CXIII (1863), 176–207.

Howitt, 'Holidays for the People. Michaelmas', *People's Jnl*, II (1846), 171.

Hussey, C., 'The Admiralty', *Country Life*, LIV (1924), 684–92, 718–26.

Hussey, C., 'The Foreign Office's Threatened Glory', *Country Life*, CXXXV (1964), 272–5.

Hussey, C., 'Treasure of the Old War Office', *Country Life*, CXXXV (1964), 1186–9.

Kinnard, J., 'G.E. Street, the Law Courts and the 'Seventies', in P. Ferriday (ed.), *Victorian Architecture* (1963).

Lambert, R., 'Central and Local Relations in Mid-Victorian England', *Victorian Studies*, 6 (1962–63), 121–50.

Lanchester, H.V., and Thomas, P.E., 'Competitions Past and Present', *RIBA Jnl*, 3 ser. XL (1933), 525–42.

Layard, A.H., 'Architecture', *Quarterly Review*, CVI (1859), 285–330.

Lefevre, G. Shaw, 'Public Works in London', *Nineteenth Century*, XII (1882), 667–86.

Lefevre, G. Shaw, 'Public Buildings in London', *Nineteenth Century*, XVII (1888), 703–18.

Lefevre, G. Shaw, 'London Street Improvements', *Contemporary Review*, 75 (1899), 203–17.

Maiwald, K., 'Index of Building Costs in the United Kingdom, 1845–1938', *Economic History Review*, 2nd ser. VIII (1954), 187–203.

Malchow, H., 'Public Gardens and Social Action in late Victorian London', *Victorian Studies* 29 (1985), 103.

Martin, G., '*Wilkins and the National Gallery*', *Burlington Mag.*, CXII (1971), 318–28.

Martin, G., 'The founding of the National Gallery in London', etc., *Connoisseur*, CLXXXV, 280–7; CLXXXVI, 24–31, 124–8, 200–7, 272–9; CLXXXVII, 48–53.

Minty, E.A., 'London's New Public Buildings', *Burlington Magazine*, X (1906), 210–18.

Morris, E.K., 'Symbols of Empire: Architectural Style and the Government Offices Competition', *Jnl of Architectural Education*, XXXII, no. 2, Nov. 1978. pp. 8–13.

Morus, I., Schaffer, S., & Secord, J., 'Scientific London', in C. Fox, ed., *London – World City 1800–1840* (1992).

Pevsner, N., 'The First Cambridge Slade Professor', *Listener*, 10 Nov. 1949, p. 808.

Port, M.H., 'The Office of Works and building contracts in early nineteenth-century England', *Economic History Review*, 2 ser., XX (1967), 94–110.

Port, M.H., 'The new Law Courts competition,

1866–67', *Architectural History*, 11 (1968), 75–93.

Port, M.H., 'From Carey Street to the Embankment – and back again!', *London Topographical Record*, XXIV (1980), 167–90.

Port, M.H., 'A Contrast in Styles at the Office of Works', *Historical Journal*, 27 (1984), 151–176.

Port, M.H., 'A Regime for Public Buildings. Experiments in the Office of Works, 1869–75', in J. Newman, ed., *Design and Practice in British Architecture (Architectural History*, 27, 1984), 74–85.

Port, M.H., 'Public Building in a Parliamentary State', *London Journal*, 11 (1985), 3–27.

Port, M.H., 'An Ædile for London?', *London Journal*, 12 (1986), 57–64.

Port, M.H., 'The Life of an Architectural Sinner: Thomas Wayland Fletcher, 1833–1901', *London Journal*, 15 (1990), 57–71.

Quarterly Rev., CXII (July 1862), 186–7.

Quarterly Rev., CXXIII (July 1867), 107–8.

Quinault, R., 'Westminster and the Victorian Constitution', *Transactions of the Royal Historical Society*, 6th ser. II (1992), 79–104.

Riemann, G., 'Schinkel's Buildings and Plans for Berlin', in M. Snodin (ed.), *Karl Friedrich Schinkel: A Universal Man* (New Haven & London, 1991).

[Robinson, J.C.], 'Fergusson's *History of Architecture*', *Quarterly Review*, CXX (1866), 425–61.

Ruble, B.A., 'From Palace Square to Moscow Square', in W.C. Brumfield, ed., *Reshaping Russian Architecture* (Cambridge, 1990).

Scott, G.G., 'On the Present Position and Future Prospects of the Revival of Gothic Architecture' (23 Sept. 1857), *Associated Architectural Societies Reports and Papers*, IV (1857–8), 75.

Shaw Lefevre, G., see Lefevre, G. Shaw.

Sheppard, F., Belcher, V., & Cottrell, P., 'The Middlesex and Yorkshire Deeds Registries', *London Jnl*, 5 (1979), 176–217.

Sheppard, F., 'London and the Nation in the Nineteenth Century', *Trans. R. Hist. Soc.*, 5 ser., XXXV.

Smith, P., Emmett, J.T., 'The New Courts of Law', *Quarterly Review*, CXXIII (1867), 93–118.

Smith, S.A., 'Alfred Waterhouse', in J. Fawcett (ed.), *Seven Victorian Architects* (1976).

Stamp, G., 'Sir Gilbert Scott's Recollection', *Architectural History*, 19 (1976), 54–73.

Statham, H.H., 'Modern English architecture', *Fortnightly Review*, XXVI (1876).

Statham, H.H., 'How our public improvements are carried out', *Fortnightly Review*, XXXVIII (1882).

Statham, H.H., 'Mr Shaw-Lefevre as an Ædile', *Murray's Magazine*, V (1889), 68–84.

Statham, H.H., 'The Proposed New Government Offices', *Fortnightly Review*, LXVI (1896), 879–93.

Statham, H.H., 'London as a Jubilee City', *National Review*, XXIX (1897), 594–603.

Stratton, M., 'Science and Art Closely Combined: the organisation of training in the terracotta industry, 1850–1939', *Construction History*, 4 (1988), 35–52.

Summerson, J., 'The Victorian Rebuilding of the City of London', *London Jnl*, 3 (1977), 163–85.

Sutcliffe, A., 'Environmental Control and Planning in European Capitals 1850–1914: Lon-

don, Paris and Berlin', in I. Hammarstrom & T. Hall, eds., *Growth and Transformation of the Modern City* (Stockholm, 1979).

Tanner, Sir H., 'The New G.P.O., London', *Jnl of the RIBA*, XVIII (1910–11), 149–77.

Tyack, G., '"A gallery worthy of the British people": James Pennethorne's designs for the National Gallery, 1845–1867', *Architectural History* 33 (1990), 121–31.

Wallace, A.R., 'Museums for the People', *Macmillan's Magazine*, XIX (1869), 244–50.

Whinney, Margaret, 'John Webb's Drawings for Whitehall Palace', *Walpole Society*, XXXI (1946), 45–107, pl. IX–XXVI.

Whitmore, C.A., 'Beautifying London', *National Review* XXVII (1896), 92–102.

Parliamentary Papers

1831–32 (614) V, *S.C. on improving approaches to the Houses of Parliament and Buckingham Palace.*

1835 (598) V; 1836 (569) IX, *S.C. on Arts and Manufactures.*

1836 (517) XX, *S.C. on Metropolis Improvements.*

1837–8 (418) XVI, *First Report of S.C. on Metropolitan Improvements.*

1839 (136) XIII, *First Report of S.C. to consider the several Plans for the Improvement of the Metropolis.*

1839 (466) XIII, 233, *S.C. on Plans for Public Offices in Downing Street.*

1840 (354) XII, 159, *S.C. [HL] on supply of water to the Metropolis.*

1840 (554) XII, 271, *S.C. on the Thames Embankment.*

1840 (410) XII, *First Report of S.C. on Metropolitan Improvements.*

1840 (485) XII, *Second Report of S.C. on Metropolitan Improvements.*

1841 (398) IX, *S.C. on Metropolitan Improvement.*

1842 (476) X, *S.C. appointed to consider the Expediency of erecting a Building in the Neighbourhood of the Inns of Court, for the sittings of the Courts of Law and Equity, in lieu of the present Courts . . .*

1844 [15] XV, *First Report of Royal Commission on Metropolitan Improvements.*

1845 (608) XII, *S.C. on Courts of Law and Equity.*

1845 [348, 619, 627] XVII, *Second, Third, and Fourth Reports of R.C. on Metropolitan Improvements.*

1846 [682] XXIV, *Fifth Report of R.C. on Metropolitan Improvements.*

1850 (612) XV, *S.C. on National Gallery*; App. A, *Report of Commn on state of pictures in National Gallery.*

1851 (642) XXII, *Report of Commissioners appointed to consider the Question of a Site for a New National Gallery.*

1852 (557) XXVIII, 201, *Copy of all Communications made by the Architect and Officers of the British Museum to the Trustees, respecting the Enlargement of the Building . . . .*

1852–53 (42) LVII, 317ff, *Copy of all Communications made by the Architect and Officers of the British Museum . . . respecting the Enlargement of the Building. . . .*

1852–53 (867) XXXV, *S.C. on management of the National Gallery, &c.*

1852–53 (916) XXII, 125ff. *S.C. on Coal Duties.*

1854 [1713] XXVII, *Report of Committees of Inquiry*

into Public Offices (reprinted in 1856 (368) XIV, 13–14).

1854–55 (333) LIII, *Copies of . . . Plans of the Architect of the New Palace at Westminster . . . to extend the Buildings from the Clock Tower Westwards . . .*

1854–55 (382) VII, *S.C. on Downing Street Public Offices Extension Bill.*

1856 (85) VII, 387, *S.C. on St James's Park.*

1856 (193) LII, *Reports by Mr Page and Mr Pennethorne on Thames Embankment and Battersea Park.*

1856 (304) VII, 65, *S.C. on Civil Service Estimates, Class 7.*

1856 (368) XIV, *S.C. on Public Offices.*

1856 (389) XIV, *S.C. on New Westminster Bridge.*

1856 [2106] XXXVIII, 507, *Treasury Minute, 25 Apr. 1856, embodying the government's decision to build at Kensington Gore.*

1857 sess. 2 (50) (111) IV, 295, 335.

1857 sess. 2 (152) XLI, 205, *Award of judges upon designs for new Government Offices.*

1857 sess. 2 [2261] XXIV, *R.C. on National Gallery Site.*

1857–58 (28) XXXIII, 499–503, *Copy of a Memorial addressed to Her Majesty's Government by the Promoters and Cultivators of Science. . . .*

1857–58 (83) XLVIII, 331, *Correspondence between FCW and Treasury, in relation to Erection of Public Offices. . . .*

1857–58 (112) XLVIII, 301, *Sums expended in Purchase of [Kensington Gore] Estate . . . in Building Museum. . . .*

1857–58 (232) XXXVII, 161, *Memorial from RIBA in reference to recent competitions for model Barracks and for Public Offices.*

1857–58 (330) XXXIV, 47, *Corr. between R.C. for Exhibition of 1851 and Treasury in relation to [Kensington Gore] Estate.*

1857–58 (369) XXXVII, 591, *Correspondence . . . in relation to the purchase of nos. 80, 81, and 82 Pall Mall. . . .*

1857–58 (379, 434) XXXIII, 373ff., 491ff., *Copies of all Communications made by the Officers and Architect of the British Museum respecting the want of Space for exhibiting the Collections . . . , &c.*

1857–58 (417) XI, *S.C. on Foreign Office Re-construction.*

1859 – sess. 1 (136), XIV, 113, *Report by Mr John Phipps on the state of the buildings now occupied as the Foreign Office.*

1859 – sess. 2 (120) XIV, *Report of Commissioners of Patents for Inventions, 1858.*

1859, sess. 2 (122) (153) XV, 367, 371, 373, 375, 377, *Official Letters by which Mr Scott was appointed Architect of the proposed new Foreign and India Offices; Expenses; &c.*

1860 (87) XXXIX, 265ff. *Copy of all Communications . . . respecting the want of Space . . . at the British Museum.*

1860 (181) XVI, *S.C. on Public Institutions* (Fowke's plan and elevation for National Gallery in App. 2).

1860 (419) XXXIX, 295, *Returns of Total Amount Expended on the New Buildings and Fittings of the British Museum. . . .*

1860 (441) VII, *S.C. on Military Organisation.*

1860 (483) IX, *S.C. on Miscellaneous Expenditure.*

1860 (494) XX, *S.C. on the best means for providing for the increasing traffic of the Metropolis by the Embankment of the Thames.*

1860 (504) XVI, 527, *S.C. on South Kensington Museum.*

1860 (540) XVI, 173, *S.C. on the British Museum* (App. 8, Oldfield's plan for westward extension).

1860 (577) XL, 123, *Correspondence between FCW and Capt Fowke relating to his plan for alteration of National Gallery.*

1860 [2710] XXXI, 89ff. *R.C. on concentration of Courts of Law and Equity, &c.*

1861 (HL) (201) V, App., Turner's will.

1861 (103) XXXV, 227, *Letters in 1857 and 1858, with plans, from Sir Richard Bromley, relative to concentration of Public Offices.*

1861 (150) (137) III, 869, 875: *Public Offices Extension Bill.*

1861 (211) (372) (476) VIII, *1st, 2nd and 3rd Reports of S.C. on Metropolis Local Taxation.*

1861 (441) XIV, *S.C. on the Courts of Justice Building (Money) Bill.*

1862 (97) XXIX, 169ff. *Copy of the Correspondence between the Treasury and the British Museum, on the subject of providing Additional Accommodation . . .*

1862 (189) IV, 697, *Public Offices Extension Bill.*

1862 (382) LIII, 503, *Copy of plan referred to in Public Offices Extension Bill.*

1863 (182) XXX, 535, *Report . . . of Commissioners of Audit.*

1863 (323) XXIX, 371, *Corr. on purchase by Government of Land and Buildings used for . . . International Exhibition of 1862.*

1863 (326) XXIX, 375, *Statement by Surveyor of Office of Works [on Int. Exhibition site, &c].*

1863 (375) XXIX, 377, *Report from Surveyor of Office of Works explanatory of estimate of Cost of completing Exhibition Buildings.*

1863 (382) XXIX, 381, *Estimate by Capt Fowke, for completing Exhibition Building according to his published design.*

1863 (396) XXIX, 391, 395, *Reports by Mr Fowler on International Exhibition Buildings.*

1863 (353) XXIX, 699, *Amounts contributed by Exchequer and by Commissioners of Exhibition of 1851 . . . [&c].*

1863 [3205] XXVII, *Commissioners appointed to inquire into the present position of the Royal Academy in relation to the Fine Arts.*

1864 (117) XXXII, 167ff. *Copies of Correspondence between the Treasury and the British Museum on the subject of providing Additional Accommodation for the several Collections . . . (1862–4).*

1864 (504) XII, *S.C. on the Patent Office Library and Museum.*

1864 [3280] XXIX, *R.C. on Constitution of Accountant-General's Department of the Court of Chancery, &c.*

1865 (124) XII, *S.C. on Courts of Justice Site bill.*

1865 (132) XLVII, *Correspondence, 1856–65, on proposed thoroughfare between Park Lane and Piccadilly.*

1865 (192) XLVII, *S.C. on Public Offices (Site and Approaches) Bill.*

1865 (192) XLVII, 169, *Copy of plan relative to Public Offices . . . submitted to Committee on Public Offices (Site and Approaches) Bill.*

1866 (186) (452) XIII, *1st and 2nd Reports of S.C. on Metropolis Local Taxation and Government.*

1867 (135) (268) (301), *1st–3rd Reports of S.C. on Metropolitan Local Government and Taxation.*

1867 (196) LV, 211, *New National Gallery, Letter from Mr Digby Wyatt on behalf of Competing Architects.*

1867 [3873] [3952] XXXII, *1st–4th Reports R.C. on Trades Unions.*

1867–68 (281) LVIII, *[Treasury] Commission to inquire into . . . the Accommodation of Public Departments.*

1867–68 (389) LVIII, *Copy of Report and Plan . . . for Opening a Street between the Thames Embankment and the Horse Guards. . . .*

1867–68 (451) VIII, *House of Commons arrangements.*

1868–69 (68) XLVII, 651, *Report by Mr Sheilds, C.E., on . . . Site for New Courts of Justice and their approaches.*

1868–69 (200) (387) X, *1st and 2nd Reports of the S.C. . . . on Hungerford Bridge and Wellington Street viaduct.*

1868–69 (296) X, 871, *S.C. on Public Offices Concentration Bill.*

1868–69 (274) XLVII, *Report of Committee appointed by Courts of Justice Commission to examine all plans submitted to the Commission, with a view to ascertain the Dimensions and measurements.*

1868–69 (336) XXXIV, *Papers relating to the recent changes in the Establishment of the Office of Works.*

1868–69 (381) X, *S.C. on site and charge of the new Law Courts.*

1868–69 [4136] XIII, *16th Report of Science & Art Department.*

1870 [C. 54] XII, *R.C. [Northbrook] on the Constitution of the War Office.*

1870 (455) LIV, *. . . Sums Voted . . . for the Erection of Buildings belonging to the University of London. . . .*

1871 (295) XXXVII, 311, *Letter from Treasury to FCW about removal of Royal Mint to Thames Embankment.*

1871 (334) XI, *S.C. on New Mint Building Site Bill.*

1871 [C. 290] XX, *Report of the Commissioners appointed to advise and report as to the buildings proper to be erected . . . for the New Courts of Justice.*

1871 (176) (223) IV, 351, 359, *S.C. on Mint Building Site Bill.*

1873 (110) VII, *1st Report of Public Accounts Committee.*

1873 (131) VII, *1st Report of S.C. on Civil Services Expenditure.*

1874 (162) IV, 1 *Mint Removal Bill.*

1875 [C. 1113] XXIII, *R.C. [Playfair] on the Civil Service.*

1877 (312) XV, *S.C. on Annual Expenditure on Public Offices and Buildings (Metropolis).*

1877 (55) XXVII, 687, *Report of Committee to inquire into Sanitary State of War Office.*

1881 (304) IX, 537, *S.C. [HL] on London City Lands (Thames Embankment) Bill.*

1882 (235) VII, *S.C. on Artizans' and Labourers' Dwellings Improvement Acts 1875 and 1879.*

1882 (253) XII, 581, *S.C. on Public Offices Site Bill.*

1884 (264) LXI, *Report on Westminster Hall by Mr J.L. Pearson, R.A.*

1884–85 (166) XIII, *S.C. on Westminster Hall Restoration.*

1884–85 [C. 4267] XXII, 561, *Report of committee appointed by the Treasury to examine the subject of central Post Office buildings and establishments.*

1887 (184) VII, *S.C. on Admiralty and War Office (Sites).*

1887 [C. 5226] XIX, *1st Report R.C. on Civil Establishments.*

1888 [C. 5545] XXVII, *2nd Report R.C. on Civil Establishments.*

1889 (228) IX, 473ff. *S.C. on Coal Duties Abolition Bill.*

1889 (323) XI, *S.C. on Post Office Sites Bill.*

1889 [C. 326] LXVI, *Annual Report of the Metropolitan Board of Works for 1888.*

1890 [C. 6172] XXVII, *4th Report R.C. on Civil Establishments.*

1892 [C. 6795-VI] XXXVI (2), *R.C. on Labour, Group C.*

1895 (3 – sess. II) VI, 59, *Bill to provide for Acquisition of Sites . . . in Westminster. . . .*

1896 (310) X, *S.C. on Government Offices (Appropriation of Sites).*

1897 (335) X, *S.C. on Government Offices (Appropriation of Sites).*

1897 (341) XII, 13ff. *First and Second Reports, S.C. on Museums of the Science and Art Department.*

1898 (175) XI, *First and Second Reports, S.C. on Museums of Science and Art Department.*

1903 (74, 140, 212, 304, 305) V, *Public Accounts Committee, 1903.*

1904 (75) LIV, *Estimates etc. for Civil Services for year ending 31 March 1905.*

1904 (207) V, *2nd Report, Public Accounts Committee.*

1908 (108) IV, 927, *S.C. on Public Offices Sites (Extension) Bill.*

1911 [Cd. 5625] XVIII, *Report of Departmental Committee on Science Museum and Geological Museum.*

1911 [Cd. 5650] LX, 475, *Copy of Corr. between FCW and Trusteels of British Museum on . . . Provision of a site for a new Science Museum at South Kensington.*

1912–13 (204) IX, 175, *S.C. on Public Offices (Sites) Bill.*

1912–13 (277) VII, 454, *S.C. on Estimates.*

1913 [Cd. 6740] XVIII, *App. to Third Report, R.C. on the Civil Service.*

1914 [Cd. 7416] XLIX, *Report of Committee of Inquiry into the Architects and Surveyors' and Engineering Divisions of H.M. Office of Works, London.*

Parliamentary Papers: Appropriation accounts

These returns give details of annual expenditure building by building, but it is not always possible to distinguish new works from repairs, maintenance, alterations, provision of furniture, &c.

PP	Sess. no.	vol.	Year of account	PP	Sess. no.	vol.	Year of account
1863	(182)	XXXI	1861/2	1899	(44)	LVII	1897/8
1864	(172)	XXXIV	1862/3	1899	(13)	LI, 489	1896/8*
1865	(137)	XXXI	1863/4	1900	(19)	LIII	1898/9
1866	(137)	XL	1864/5	1900	(53)	XLVII, 487	1898/9*
1867	(27)	XL	1865/6	1901	(20)	XLIV	1899/1900
1867–68	(82)	XLI	1866/7	1901	(49)	XXXVII, 471	1899/1900*
1868–69	(80)	XLII	1867/8	1902	(35)	LXIII	1900/01
1870	(47)	XLVIII	1868/9	1902	(37)	LV, 457	1900/01*
1871	(16)	XLVI	1869/70	1903	(24)	XLII	1901/02
1872	(24)	XLI	1870/1	1903	(67)	XXXVI, 517	1901/02*
1873	(26)	XLVII, pt ii	1871/2	1904	(29)	LV	1902/03
1874	(29)	XLIII	1872/3	1904	(80, 99)	XLIX, 237, 419	1902/03*
1875	(53)	L	1873/4	1905	(37)	L	1903/04
1876	(45)	L	1874/5	1905	(13, 71)	XLIV, 477, 751	1903/04*
1877	(18)	LVIII	1875/6	1906	(10)	LXXII	1904/05
1878	(24)	LIV	1876/7	1906	(4, 5)	LXV, 489, 279	1904/05*
1878–79	(38)	XLIX	1877/8	1907	(9)	LII	1905/06
1880	(22)	XLVII	1878/9	1907	(27, 61)	XLVII, 231, 455	1905/06*
1881	(76)	LXIII	1879/80	1908	(37)	LXVII	1906/07
1882	(38)	XLIII	1880/1	1908	(42, 43)	LXII, 279, 509	1906/07*
1883	(14)	XLIV	1881/2	1909	(13)	LVI	1907/08
1884	(22)	LIII	1882/3	1909	(32, 33)	L, 363, 561	1907/08*
1884–85	(71)	LI	1883/4	1910	(14)	LXIII	1908/09
1886	(36–sess. I)	XLIV	1884/5	1910	(45, 46)	LIX, 427, 557	1908/09*
1887	(8)	LV	1885/6	1911	(7)	L	1909/10
1888	(30)	LXXI	1886/7	1911	(8, 9)	XLV, 393, 231	1909/10*
1889	(18)	LIII	1887/8	1912–13	(14)	LV	1910/11
1890	(21)	XLVII	1888/9	1912–13	(10, 24)	XLIX, 587, 401	1910/11*
1890–91	(68)	LIV	1889/90	1912–13	(475)	LV	1911/12
1892	(50–sess. I)	LIV	1890/1	1912–13	(481, 492)	XLIX, 593, 405	1911/12*
1893–94	(66)	LVII	1891/2	1914	(55)	LVI	1912/13
1893–94	(510)	LVIII	1892/3	1914	(2, 91)	L, 419, 272	1912/13*
1895	(38)	LXVII	1893/4	1914–16	(98)	XLII	1913/14
1896	(17)	LVI	1894/5	1914–16	(95, 101)	XXXVIII, 339, 549	1913/14*
1897	(37)	LVIII	1895/6	1914–16	(423)	XLII	1914/15
1898	(2)	LVIII	1896/7	1914–16	(410, 412)	XXXVIII, 343, 555	1914/15*

* Accounts under the Public Offices (Sites) and Public Buildings Expenses Acts.

Acknowledgements for Illustrations

The following holders of copyright are gratefully acknowledged in respect of the following illustrations.

Austrian National Tourist Office London: 14a. B.T. Batsford Ltd:38b. Canadian Centre for Architecture: 119, 166. Messrs Cecil, Denny, Highton (Adam Woolfit): frontispiece, 56, 59, 60, 65, 69, 260, 278. Conservation Unit Library, DoE: 93, 190, 222c, 223d, 225–6, 229, 235–6. Controller, H.M.S.O.: 1, 49, 65, 78, 99, 129, 139, 141, 165, 198a, 192, 201c, 220b, 238, 243, 251a, 255, 257–8, 263a, 264–6, 268, 270, 272–3, 280–4, 287, 288, 290–2. Mr Ralph Hyde: 103, 105b, 162–3, 177, 221. Mr Peter Jackson: 7, 90–1, 101, 124, 219. GLRO, Photographic Collection: 25, 29a, 33, 34a, 36b, 53c, 67, 128, 125, 142, 150, 286. GLRO, Prints & Maps: 1, 31, 36a-b, 37, 38a, 42, 46, 48, 109, 160, 239a, 241a. House of Lords Record Office: 246b. Paul Mellon Centre for Studies in British Art: 49, 65, 78, 99, 129, 139, 141, 165, 192, 198a, 201c, 220b, 238, 243, 251a, 255, 257–8, 263a, 264–6, 268, 270, 272, 273, 280–4, 287–8, 290–2. Mr Fowke Mangeot, 218; Ministry of Defence Library: 58, 61–4. Musée Carnavalet, Paris: 12a. Museum of London: 86, 89b, 189. National Portrait Gallery: 110. Private collection: 156. Property Services Agency: 55, 279. Professor P. Smith: 82. Royal Academy: 28, 214. RCHME (National Monuments Record): 10, 29b, 54, 55, 83, 138, 146, 159, 200, 240, 250, 276, 279. RIBA Drawings Coll: 105b, 121, 164, 176, 179, 206a, 207a, 210, 212, 252. Sir John Soane's Museum, Trustees of: 106. Society of Antiquaries: 188a. Victoria and Albert Museum, Board of Trustees of: 75, 104a, 145, 152, 175, 218b. Mr Ben Weinreb: 5, 8, 9, 11, 23, 26–27, 44a, 52, 94, 123, 148–9, 190, 205, 215, 223abc, 224, 227–8, 230–2, 233b. Worcester College, Oxford, Provost and Fellows of: 41, 217.

Illustration Sources

Those not listed are from contemporary prints or photographs.

Arch. Rev.: 15, 16, 34b, 41 (XXXI, 341–2), 100 (XXXV, 151), 140 (XXXVIII), 182 (XXXIV–V), 194, 195 (XVIII), 203 (XXVIII), 216 (XXXI), 251b (XXVI), 254, 261–2 (XXIV), 263b (XXIV), 259 (XX), 289, 293 (XXIX). Barry, A., *Life of Sir Charles Barry*, 157. Bruce, W.N., Ed., *Sir Henry Layard*, 72. *Builder*: 17 (XI, 691), 18 (XXVI, 319), 14b (XXXVII, 204), 96a (XIV, 263), 97 (XXIX, 227), 104b (XXII, 475), 135, 151 (XXXVII, 628), 154 (XLVII, 456), 158 (XXVII, 666), 170 (XV, 495), 173 (XV, 551), 178 (XXV, 371), 184–6 (XLVII, 730, 398, 624, 562, 356, 424, 322; XLVIII, 482), 188b (XLVIII, 414), 191 (LXI, 124, 148), 197 (LXXVI, 300), 198b (LXXVI, 300), 201a,b (CVIII, 156ff.), 204 (CVI, 473), 208 (XV, 479, 563), 209a (XVII, 537), 220a (XXV, 855), 222 (XXV, 208–9), 234 (XXV, 293), 242 (XXXI, 10), 244–8 (XLVII, 432, 360, 464, 461, 460, 428, 326, 490, 528, 390, 594), 253 (LXI, 148, 227), 267 (XCV, 166), 271 (CVIII, 178ff.). *BN*: 113b, 213, 237. *Cornhill Mag.*: 98. Eastlake, *Gothic Revival*, 209b. Gladstone, Viscount, *After Twenty-Five Years*: 85. [Gomme], *Kingsway*: 19, Gregory, Sir W., *Autobiography*: 102. *ILN*: 37, 38a, 51; 57, 70, 71, 73, 74, 77, 79, 81, 87–9a, 90, 95, 101–2, 108, 111, 112, 116, 120, 130, 134, 147, 167a, 168–9, 171–2, 174, 181a. Law, H.W. & I, *Book of the Beresford Hopes*, 47. Lewis, Sir G.C., *Letters*: 43. *L'Illustration*: 12b, 21. Original drawings by architects, &c.: 75, 105b, 106, 119, 121, 145, 156, 159, 164, 166, 170, 175–6, 179, 180, 189, 206a, 210, 212, 214, 217, 222c, 223–33, 235–6, 239, 252. *London Illustrated*: 50, 91. New Law Courts, *Reports* by the several competitors: 149, 180, 181b, 222c, 223–6, 228–33, 236. Owen, R., *A National Museum of Natural History*: 285. O.S. map, 25 in., 1st edn, 1. PRO, Work: 49 (30/1278), 65 (30/4492), 78 (30/5891), 99 (30/543, 545), 129 (30/668), 139 (30/1009), 141 (30/6334), 165 (30/2596), 192 (30/1578), 198 (30/1008), 201c (30/6334), 220b (33/1783), 238 (30/1391–2), 243 (30/5886), 251a (33/2265), 255, 266 (30/1007, 1004), 264 (30/1007, 3758), 257–8 (30/3520, 3525), 263a (30/3808), 265 (30/1044, 1046), 268 (30/4198), 270 (33/1212–13), 272 (30/975, 971), 273 (30/5218), 280–2 (30/1281, 1414, 1286), 283 (30/1418–19), 284 (30/1436, 1546), 287 (33/1648), 288 (33/1648), 290 (30/4217), 291–2 (30/3545, 5779). *Parliamentary Papers*: 26, 93 (1851, XXII), 96 (1860, XVI), 107 (1842, X), 113a (1868–69, XLVII), 114 (1868–69, XLVII), 117 (1839, XIII), 118 (1854–55, VII), 122a (1854–55, VII), 122b (1857–58, XI), 122c (1862, LIII), 122d (1865, XLVII), 123 (1864, XXXII), 126–7 (1867–68, LVIII), 131 (1877, XV), 132 (1882, XII), 133 (1887, VII), 136–7 (1896, X), 144 (1897, X), 155 (1887, VII), 188b (1884–85, XIII), 190 (1889, C. 5831). *RIBA Trans.*: 183, 206b. Satow, *The Old Foreign Office*: 32, 143. Scott, G. G., *Personal and Professional Recollections*, 161. Soane, *Designs for Public and Private Buildings* (1828): 3, 115, 153. Trevelyan, G.M., *Sir George Otto Trevelyan*: 39. *Vanity Fair*: 76, 82.

Index